Liberalizing the Mind

Liberalizing the Mind

TWO CENTURIES OF LIBERAL EDUCATION
AT FRANKLIN & MARSHALL COLLEGE

Sally F. Griffith

The Pennsylvania State University Press
University Park, Pennsylvania

Library of Congress Cataloging-in-Publication Data

Griffith, Sally Foreman.
Liberalizing the mind : two centuries of liberal education at Franklin & Marshall College /
Sally F. Griffith.
       p. cm.
Includes bibliographical references and index.
Summary: "A narrative history of Franklin & Marshall College. Combines analysis of
historical context and institutional development with accounts of the college during crucial
periods such as the Civil War and the 1960s"—Provided by publisher.
    ISBN 978-0-271-03723-3 (cloth : alk. paper)
1. Franklin & Marshall College—History. 2. Education, Humanistic—Pennsylvania—
Lancaster—History. 3. Education, Higher—Pennsylvania—Lancaster—History. I. Title.
    LD1871.F22G75 2010
      378.748'15—dc22   2010017179

Contents

Foreword

—⟨⟩⟨⟩—

Collegiate anniversaries provide occasions for remembrance, celebration, and future planning, as well as for generating a college history. The first history of the college appeared for the fiftieth anniversary of the merger of Franklin College and Marshall College in 1903,[1] and the second for its centennial in 1953.[2] In 1987, when the college celebrated the founding of Franklin College, its leaders started planning a more comprehensive work. It was to include the histories of both forebears — Franklin College and Marshall College — and chronicle the momentous changes transforming the college from the post–World War II years to the beginning of the twenty-first century. Historian Sally F. Griffith took on this huge assignment. Her weighty book definitively establishes the significance of the college in national and local history. It demonstrates continuity in the educational vision of the college throughout two centuries and makes the history of the college current to the inauguration of John A. Fry as Franklin & Marshall College's fourteenth president in 2002.

When college president A. Richard Kneedler commissioned this project in 1999, he predicted that it would document how dramatically the college had grown and changed since 1949. Indeed, it does this and more. While the architectural styles of classroom and administration buildings between Buchanan Avenue and Harrisburg Pike recall the heritage of the college from the eighteenth century through the first third of the twentieth century, the teaching, research, administration, and social lives that these buildings currently house are creations of the contemporary period. Since World War II, all divisions of the curriculum have expanded as scholarly fields have deepened and narrowed. Accompanying disciplinary specialization, the curriculum became increasingly interconnected as interdisciplinary programs gave institutional embodiment to the shared issues revealed by advanced research. These linkages appeared initially in the social sciences and humanities. In the natural sciences, they first surfaced with the advent of the program in the Scientific and Philosophical Studies of Mind, and they soon will inform a projected major in Bioinformatics.

College life witnessed similar dramatic transformations. The college responded to the civil rights movement of the fifties and sixties by instituting minority recruit-

ment and scholarship programs. The sixties also brought coeducation, which catalyzed what Griffith considers "the greatest single change" in college history. The arrival
of women in 1969 eventually affected not only the composition of the student body
and student social life, but also the composition of the faculty and administration, the
curriculum, the extra-curriculum, college facilities, and college athletics. Today, the
student body draws from forty-three states as well as forty-four foreign countries,
with 12 to 15 percent of these students having multicultural backgrounds.

In 2010, Franklin & Marshall College is poised to become a vibrant educational
institution for the twenty-first century. As its current president, John A. Fry, looks
forward, he sees the college committing itself to several major initiatives. To address
the rising cost of higher education, Franklin & Marshall is increasing its ability to attract students from diverse backgrounds by admitting talented students without regard to their ability to pay. The college is extending the educating process from the
classroom into student life through College Houses. By offering students more than a
place to sleep and study, they expand the residential experience to include leadership
training in self-government and regular opportunities for informal interchange with
peers and professors. Additionally, the college is enlarging the boundaries of the campus and its classrooms by drawing local institutions into partnerships that enrich the
curriculum and extra-curriculum, increase the audience for college programs, and
reciprocally benefit the Lancaster community.

The college history also shows continuity. Since its beginnings, all Franklin &
Marshall College presidents have declaimed the centrality of the liberal arts to college
education. In 1787, the college founders intended a liberal education to produce leaders for the Lancaster community and the new American republic. Today, advocates of
liberal education are enlarging the content of liberal education so that graduates can
participate in an increasingly technological age of global dimensions. The college will
prepare them for citizenship in their communities, countries, and the world. Sally F.
Griffith's narrative of this evolution resides at the heart of her history of the college,
appropriately named *Liberalizing the Mind*.

Liberalizing the Mind also sheds new light on the history of higher education in
the nineteenth and twentieth centuries. The initial chapters give valuable data to revi-
sionist historians of American higher education who have expanded the history of
the nineteenth-century college beyond New England by emphasizing religious and
regional influences. Griffith locates the founding of Franklin College and Marshall
College in the history of their geographical and religious communities. For both colleges, their situation in the Pennsylvania German American churched community
and the German Reformed Church played determining roles for college enrollment,
fundraising, and curriculum. Until the 1920s, Franklin & Marshall College gave institutional embodiment to one form of German American identity. Its professors prepared students for entrance into the larger American society while preserving the
Mercersburg Theology's emphasis on idealism and historicism.

In discussing the role of the federal government in funding twentieth-century higher education generally and specifically Franklin & Marshall, historians often think first of the various programs located on the educational front of World War II or the Cold War. This history locates the beginnings of federal influence in the twentieth century with World War I. The manpower demands of both world wars threatened the viability of the college by calling on its students and younger professors for government service. In both instances, federal educational programs for military personnel saved the college while drawing it into a national agenda.

Finally, Griffith reveals the role that foundations and corporations have played and play in subordinating local and particular distinctiveness to their larger purposes. For example, to enable funding from the Carnegie Foundation at the beginning of the twentieth century, the college had to reconsider its historic denominational ties, which it retained, in diminished form, until the 1980s. In the postwar period, grants pushed the college to develop a sophisticated disciplinary curriculum informed by advanced research, most notably in the natural sciences. In the present day, educators talk of Franklin & Marshall (and peer colleges) as a university college or research college.

I hope that you will sample various episodes in this lengthy history and find one that especially piques the imagination. Griffith's story about how the college recovered its prosperity in the 1890s made me smile. In the preceding years, Franklin & Marshall students and the Lancaster community thought the college socially and academically out of touch with an industrializing nation. Enrollments and fund-raising fell until the initiative and scholarship of a chemistry professor combined with a winning 1889 football team to reverse the declines. By the early nineties, the college had built its first gymnasium (now the current bookstore and coffee bar), inaugurated a new president, attracted new donors, and enlarged the student body by one-third. From that beginning, Franklin & Marshall developed its reputation as an excellent institution for future medical professionals and natural scientists. By 1937, thirty-two of fifty-two graduates in the physical sciences pursued medical careers and ten entered graduate study in the natural sciences. Such episodes illustrate the continuously changing content of the liberal arts at Franklin & Marshall, which has prepared generations of students for life and not merely a career.

Louise L. Stevenson
Professor of History and American Studies
January 2010

Acknowledgments

—◡◠◡—

The life of a college is a communal enterprise, and writing its history has likewise drawn on the inspiration, the support, and the work of many of us. Provost P. Bruce Pipes first imagined the project and set its course. Provost Ann R. Steiner has seen this volume through to its publication. College archivists Ms. Ann W. Upton and Mr. Christopher M. Raab, along with Mr. Michael R. Lear, enabled our historian, Dr. Sally F. Griffith, to write the narrative. Professor David P. Schuyler, together with Mr. Raab, selected the historical pictures and campus maps of Franklin & Marshall College. College Registrar Ms. Christine A. Yerkes and her staff provided the roster of College presidents and compiled the enrollment figures. Dr. David M. Stameshkin initiated the publication process, while Associate Dean Tamara A. Goeglein finished up the task. Through it all, Presidents A. Richard Kneedler and John A. Fry have lent their enthusiasm and generous financial support to bring our history to life.

Mind Awakening Mind
A College and Its Mission

—⁓—

For over two centuries Franklin & Marshall College has striven to awaken the minds and shape the characters of the young. While specific methods and the social context of education have changed over that time, the fundamental mission has remained the same: to foster "an intensive encounter between talented students of high potential with gifted teachers who have the time, the freedom and the knowledge to lead those young people to their fullest possible development." A. Richard Kneedler offered this formulation during his inauguration as the college's thirteenth president in 1988. The college had marked its bicentennial the previous year, and Kneedler celebrated it as "a piece of living history, the result of the faith, determination, courage and love of thousands" committed to the liberal arts college as "the single most effective means of educating young people for lives of service and leadership and continued learning."[1] This book records and honors that commitment.

More than 150 years before Kneedler's address, Frederick A. Rauch expressed a strikingly similar educational vision in his own inaugural speech as the first president of Marshall College. "Fire only can kindle fire; mind only can awaken mind," he proclaimed. "This mutual influence . . . is what we call education in its widest sense." He too stressed that education must take place on many levels — spiritual, intellectual, and civic: "The fortune of our lives and our government depends not exclusively on useful knowledge but on our character as citizens, and to form this character by cultivating the whole man is the aim of education in the proper sense."[2]

Throughout its history, Franklin & Marshall College has sought to educate "the whole man"—although as the datedness of that phrase suggests, definitions of the appropriate constituencies have changed. As Kneedler pointed out, "those before us cared enough about this tradition to examine its premises, expand its programs, open its doors to new publics and build out from the foundations which they had inherited.

Thanks to them, our faculty, staff, student body, programs and traditions are far broader, more inclusive than they ever were before."[3]

Over its two centuries and more, Franklin & Marshall has pursued its mission of educating the whole person, even as the meaning and methods of liberal education have repeatedly been redefined. For centuries, collegiate education aimed to prepare young men for leadership through intensive study of classical languages and texts, philosophy, literature, and natural sciences. Founded separately, both Franklin College and Marshall College focused on educating members of Pennsylvania's large German American community. As major institutions of the German Reformed Church, Marshall College and later Franklin & Marshall College were known for the predominance of German idealism and a theological movement known as Mercersburg Theology.[4]

Despite its modern reputation, for much of its history Franklin & Marshall was small and financially insecure, like most colleges. In the later nineteenth century many predicted the imminent demise of the classical college in the face of competition from new universities offering specialized instruction in practical areas like engineering and agriculture and emphasizing cutting-edge research instead of passing on eternal verities. Nevertheless, small colleges proved remarkably resilient. For many years Franklin & Marshall resisted pressures to modify its classical curriculum, but in the 1890s it began gradually to change. It developed excellent science programs to complement its traditional strengths in the humanities. The college's greatest growth came in the 1920s after it added education and business programs.

Through the twentieth century, as the college grew, it also lost some of its original distinctiveness. New regional accrediting bodies and the lure of support from philanthropic foundations prompted curricular changes. The ecumenism of the Reformed Church gradually blurred its differences from mainstream Protestantism. The Reformed Church transformed itself through successive mergers, becoming part of the Evangelical and Reformed Church in the 1920s and the United Church of Christ in the 1950s. Moreover, pride in a distinct German American identity was undermined by the crisis of the First World War. By the 1920s, Franklin & Marshall emphasized its colonial American origins and all but erased memory of its German roots. Later in the century it quietly moved away from its denominational ties.

Student life at Franklin & Marshall reflected the emergence of a youth culture that emulated customs originating in elite educational institutions. Students celebrated a "campus life" that was distinct from adulthood and focused on athleticism and social life rather than academics. Although college leaders were uneasy about the growing prominence of competitive athletics, sports contributed substantially to the increased popularity of higher education. Local citizens began to follow college teams avidly, while their sons eagerly anticipated joining the student body to cheer college athletes from the sidelines.[5]

As public higher education expanded throughout the twentieth century, private colleges and universities enrolled smaller proportions of the total number of students. Some schools were able to become more selective, enrolling only those deemed capable of high levels of academic work. Much of the impetus toward selectivity came from faculty oriented toward specialized disciplines and original research. Describing the "academic revolution" after World War II, sociologists David Riesman and Christopher Jencks pointed to the rise of a new type of institution, the academically rigorous "university college": "a college whose primary purpose is to prepare students for graduate work of some kind — primarily in the arts and sciences but also in professional subjects ranging from law and medicine to business and social work."[6]

In the postwar period Franklin & Marshall strove to transform itself from a local college to a rigorous, nationally recognized, selective liberal arts college. After generations of struggling to get by, it was finally able to tap into growing sources of support to become financially comfortable. Increasingly, it aspired to compete with top-ranked colleges. Research-oriented faculty pressed for a more diverse student body whose academic interests more closely resembled those of the faculty itself. Building upon its strength in the sciences, the college developed an enviable reputation for preparing, in the manner of the new university college, a large proportion of students for graduate or professional education.

In the latter decades of the century, as higher education became ever more competitive and market-driven, the college worked tirelessly to enrich its facilities and curriculum. Its long-term vision has remained consistent, however, in offering a broad, humane vision of liberal education within the intimate scale of a small college. In the dawning years of the twenty-first century, growing awareness of the need for lifelong learning and intellectual flexibility has brought renewed appreciation of the value of liberal education. Despite persistent gloomy predictions of their imminent demise, liberal arts colleges have continued to pursue their mission; among them, Franklin & Marshall College has flourished while remaining true to its goal of "educating young people for lives of service and leadership and continued learning."

CHAPTER ONE

Franklin College
"To Make Good Men and Useful Citizens"

—⁓—

An Enlightenment Enterprise

On the morning of June 6, 1787, a number of gentlemen gathered in the courthouse on the square where King and Queen streets crossed at the very center of Lancaster, Pennsylvania. They marched in pairs to Trinity Lutheran Church on South Duke Street. Heading up the procession were the sheriff and coroner, principal officials of Lancaster County. Then came a group of men and boys who embodied the institution that was to be consecrated: a few pupils, the newly appointed faculty, and the Board of Trustees. After them marched Lancaster borough officials and justices of the peace and then, in a body, the regional governing organizations of the German Reformed and Lutheran churches. They were followed by officers of the local Lutheran, Presbyterian, Catholic, Episcopal, Moravian, and Reformed congregations and the Evangelical Lutheran ministers. The Lancaster County lieutenant and officers of the militia drew up the rear.

In a largely Protestant culture not much given to religious ceremony, this weekday gathering must have been arresting. In some ways it followed the pattern of religious processions that were common in Europe, but this event manifested a different, more modern Enlightenment vision of a society of carefully balanced and equal constituencies under the eye of a neutral, benevolent state. Instead of one established church, religion was represented by no fewer than six different Christian denominations. Among the sixty-some men from Philadelphia and Lancaster who had agreed to serve as trustees were prominent lay community leaders, lawyers, physicians, merchants, and manufacturers. They included four signers of the Declaration of Independence; three past, present, and future governors of Pennsylvania; and two men soon to become U.S. senators.[1]

Ceremonies in the Lutheran church, an impressive Georgian brick building, were similarly ecumenical. A Reformed minister from Philadelphia offered a prayer in German, and then a combined choir of Lancastrians and Philadelphians sang an ode in English and a hymn in German. Local Lutheran and Episcopal ministers delivered sermons in German and English, respectively, interspersed with choral music in both languages. After a closing prayer by the Moravian minister, the procession retraced its steps to the courthouse. Relaxing from their roles as representatives of various corporate bodies, participants joined other local citizens for dinner at a nearby tavern. The dinner's purpose, according to Benjamin Rush, a Philadelphia physician and trustee, was "to make [participants] better acquainted with each other." He accordingly conversed with "a Lutheran, a Calvinist, a Roman Catholic and a Moravian minister — all of whom [he] found to be sensible agreeable men." His Philadelphia colleagues did likewise: William Hamilton, a gentleman whose family owned much of the land upon which Lancaster stood, "charmed everybody with his easy behaviour"; wealthy merchant William Bingham "interested the gravest of [the] German company in national politics"; and eminent attorney William Rawle "found his way into their hearts at once by conversing with them upon the subject of their College in *their own language*."[2]

Rush's depiction of cosmopolitan gentlemen in genial and improving conversation with small-town clerics also manifested Enlightenment ideals of tolerance and rationality in the service of public improvement. To Rush, it boded well for his dream of an institution to help integrate Pennsylvania's large German-speaking population into civic life. As trustees met for the first time the night before, he made an impromptu speech congratulating his colleagues upon their presence at this important moment. "We are met here," he began, "to lay the foundation of a seminary of learning the objects of which are of the utmost importance to Pennsylvania." The seminary promised to break down "the partition wall which has long separated the English and German inhabitants of the State." Even board members would form useful connections through their periodic meetings: "Our children will be bound together by the ties of marriage, as we shall be by the ties of friendship, and in the course of a few years by means of this College the names of German, Irishman and Englishman will be lost in the general name of Pennsylvanian."[3]

An anonymous account of the ceremonies published in the *Pennsylvania Gazette* underscored the Enlightenment sensibility behind the new college: "It was a spectacle beautiful in itself, and which we may with certainty pronounce no age or country, nor any set of people, ever beheld before. On the same day, in the same church, and to the *same* set of Christians, the ministers of different religious persuasions successively joined in the worship and adoration of the Supreme Being! A type, however small, of the glorious reign of the Messiah which we are promised will one day come."[4] In the manner of its birth, Franklin College seemed truly fortunate. As its inaugural ceremonies reflected, the college hoped to embody Enlightenment ideals of rationality and tolerance while channeling the power of religion in service of civic virtue.

The founders of the college hoped to meet a number of educational needs within a collegiate structure that had developed in colonial America, but post-Revolutionary

Pennsylvania posed demographic and political conditions very different from those in other regions. The earliest colonial colleges had been founded in areas like New England and Virginia, which had homogenous populations and established churches, to prepare young men to assume leadership positions as ministers or gentlemen. In Pennsylvania, the tolerant policies of its Quaker founder, William Penn, attracted the most diverse population of any of the British colonies. With the exception of a small number of Jews and Catholics, most immigrants adhered to some form of Protestant Christianity, but each group brought its own particular style of religious worship and doctrine. Quakers and other egalitarian Protestant sects rejected clerical authority, and this attitude weakened demand for institutions to prepare an educated ministry. In the absence of an established church to sponsor education, schooling in Pennsylvania was left to private initiative, often through local congregations.[5]

Higher education in Pennsylvania had begun in Philadelphia with a secular academy and charity school promoted by Benjamin Franklin and a group of prominent merchants, physicians, and gentlemen. A new charter in 1755 added a college. It was not government supported and relied upon private subscriptions, lotteries, and fund-raising trips abroad. During the Revolution, the college ran afoul of Pennsylvania's intense political conflict. In 1779, radicals in the state assembly engineered a takeover and transformed the college into a university under a board of trustees dominated by state officials but including representatives of many of the city's religious denominations. At the prompting of its Lutheran representative, the Reverend J. H. Christian Helmuth, a separate preparatory department was added for German-speaking youths; he evidently hoped that it would develop into an important institution for Lutheran theological education.[6]

A College for German Americans

Like the University of Pennsylvania, the college founded in Lancaster in 1787 was envisioned as a collaborative project among religious denominations and secular civic leaders rather than as an institution dominated by a single denomination. But it was the first institution of higher education in America to focus on educating a non-English-speaking population.

Early in the eighteenth century, the first of several waves of migrants from Switzerland and the many small German-speaking states along the Rhine reached America. Most entered through the port of Philadelphia, and large numbers settled on the rich farmlands in southeastern Pennsylvania, while others moved on to the west and south. The numbers of new arrivals peaked in midcentury and then declined, but by 1790 Germans represented about one-third of Pennsylvania's population and two-fifths of the southeastern region's. In Lancaster County, 72 percent of the European population was ethnic German.[7]

These newcomers not only spoke a language different from that of the British majority but were divided among themselves. Until the nineteenth century, central Europe was divided into many small principalities speaking different German dialects and observing different forms of Protestant and Catholic Christianity. Lutheran and German Reformed denominations emphasized leadership by learned clergy as much as English Calvinists did, but pietistic Anabaptist and Mennonite sects were more egalitarian and communal. Among many differences separating these "Church" and "Sect" Germans was the latter's belief that too much book learning encouraged self-conceit and undermined piety.[8]

Leaders of the Lutheran and German Reformed churches worried about a shortage of qualified ministers to lead their growing numbers as well as the lack of higher education for laymen. Without a German-language college in America, ministerial candidates had to go abroad for study. For example, the Reverend Henry Melchior Muhlenberg, who came to America in 1742 as a Lutheran missionary, sent his three sons back to the University of Halle for their education. German Reformed congregations in North America were overseen by the Synod of the Netherlands, which was less than energetic in attending to their needs.[9]

English-speaking Pennsylvanians were also interested in encouraging the education of German speakers in their midst, but for different reasons. In a pattern that would be often repeated, English Pennsylvanians felt alarm at the presence of a substantial "foreign" population maintaining its own language and customs. Some, including Franklin, complained that Germans lacked public spirit. In fact, the political goals of German immigrants and their descendants did differ from those of their English-speaking neighbors. Many of these immigrants had left Germany to escape local rulers' burdensome demands, and above all else they prized freedom from government interference. They were less interested in holding political office than in protecting their rights and especially their property. Their political efforts focused on resisting taxation and any other measures that seemed to threaten property or personal freedom.[10]

The different priorities of German Pennsylvanians contributed to the failure of a mid-eighteenth-century effort to establish charity schools for German children. German Reformed ministers sought to raise funds in Europe, but Anglicans in England and Scotland co-opted the campaign, depicting German children as "woodborn savages" and warning darkly of a potential German-French alliance. In Pennsylvania, the new schools focused on instructing German children in English language and customs. Resenting the emphasis on assimilation, German parents refused to send their children and the program soon collapsed.[11]

American independence increased the sense of urgency to forge a unified national culture out of the country's diverse population. Some observers concluded that the new republic would survive only if its citizens mastered the virtues and self-discipline necessary for democratic government. Disillusioned by factional and ideological struggles during and after the war, Benjamin Rush had written in 1786, "We have changed our forms of government, but it remains yet to effect a revolution in our principles, opinions, and manners so as to accommodate them to the forms of government we have adopted." Many, like Rush, believed that religion was the most effective way to foster such virtues. Recognizing that an established church was out of the question, they turned to education, traditionally performed under the aegis of religious institutions, as a surrogate means to "prepare the principles, morals, and manners of our citizens" for republican government.[12]

Rush also believed that education would help integrate the German-speaking population into the nation. In an anonymous 1785 essay in the *Pennsylvania Gazette*, he advocated creating a college specifically for Germans. Education would dispel the ignorance and prejudice that divided the groups and prepare Germans "to unite more intimately with their British and Irish fellow citizens and thus to form with them one homogeneous mass of people." "Happy State of Pennsylvania!" he concluded. "When the shores of the Ohio and Tioga, and all thy numerous and extensive rivers shall be adorned with churches, courts of justice, and seminaries of learning, filled with men who have been educated in the principles of religion and liberty in our American colleges!"[13]

Rush and his Philadelphia colleagues also probably hoped to advance political goals by collaborating with German leaders. In a private letter written in 1785, Rush expressed the hope that education would wean Germans from the "violent and mistaken zeal in government" that he blamed for their support for his political opponents. Many Franklin College trustees, including German leaders Peter and Frederick Muhlenberg and Daniel and Joseph Hiester, supported a movement to replace the state constitution written during the Revolution with one with more checks and balances. Even as the college was dedicated, participants were keenly aware of the meeting then going on in Philadelphia aimed at producing a stronger governmental structure.[14]

Philadelphia merchants hoped to strengthen business ties with Lancaster, then the largest inland town in the young nation and the center of a productive agricultural region. Lancaster had been laid out in 1730 on land owned by Andrew Hamilton, a powerful Philadelphia lawyer and political leader with close ties to the Penn family. The Hamilton family remained one of the most prominent in Philadelphia's Anglican elite, their wealth swelled by quitrents to be paid on their Lancaster properties until 1815. (Franklin College trustee William Hamilton was Andrew's grandson.)[15] Lancaster's merchants were busy supplying emigrants to the west and south and transporting the region's agricultural surpluses to the port of Philadelphia and on to the West Indies and Europe. In the later eighteenth century, the rise of the city of Baltimore on the Chesapeake Bay raised fears in Philadelphia that this lucrative trade might be diverted down the Susquehanna River. From the 1770s onward, Philadelphia boosters sought ways to improve transportation ties to Lancaster.[16]

Finally, English-speaking Lancastrians wanted a college because it was generally assumed to be an essential feature of a flourishing community. Local elites wanted educational institutions to prepare new generations of statesmen well versed in the common language of classical learning, which had been central in the debates of the Revolutionary generation. As historian Daniel Calhoun has put it, "liberal education linked the motives of individual prestige to the functions of community prestige and defense." Before serving as Franklin College trustees, Lancaster lawyers Jasper Yeates and John Hubley participated in a 1780 effort to establish a classical academy for boys. Yeates, a Philadelphia native and College of Philadelphia graduate, had a long career in local affairs that ranged from membership on the county's Committee of Correspondence in 1776 to the Pennsylvania convention that ratified the federal Constitution later in 1787. But the academy was short lived, and Yeates probably hoped that the new college would provide a classical education for his son John, one of the first students.[17]

Ultimately, Franklin College was born out of the convergence of these different groups and goals. It is not clear exactly who originated the proposal, but members of each constituency contributed to the process of bringing it to maturity. German Reformed and Lutheran leaders began to seek the approval of governing bodies in 1784, and plans were well under way by the end of 1786 to establish a multipurpose educational institution. In mid-December the venerable Lutheran patriarch Henry Melchior Muhlenberg recorded in his journal that his sons Peter, a Revolutionary War general and currently vice president of the Executive Council of Pennsylvania, and Henry, pastor of Trinity Lutheran Church in Lancaster, had "set in motion a proposal to establish a German high school." Earlier that month, a group of prominent Philadelphians had petitioned the state legislature for a charter for a "German College and Charity School to be established in Lancaster." Signers of the petition included Rush, Bingham, Rawle, Peter Muhlenberg, and Thomas McKean, chief justice and subsequently governor of Pennsylvania. J. H. C. Helmuth and Casper Weiberg, pastor of the Race Street Reformed Church and also a University of Pennsylvania trustee, represented German religious interests among the petitioners. As a leader in creating religiously supported organizations to educate the poor, Helmuth was probably responsible for the charter's pledge to include an elementary-level charity school.[18]

The petition painted the institution's goals in broad social terms: diffusing "knowledge through every part of the State" in order "to preserve our present republican system of government" and "to promote those improvements in the arts and sciences which alone render nations respectable, great and happy." Petitioners requested from the legislature a charter "conferring such powers and privileges as are usually given to colleges" and a share in state lands typically set aside to support public schools, "in order that [legislators] may lay a more solid foundation for their extensive and charitable views in establishing this seminary." Appended to the petition was an outline of plans for the college, stressing its goal of "diffusing literature among [the petitioners'] German fellow-citizens." Although it promised to offer a traditional core of the liberal arts — "the learned languages, . . . mathematics, morals, and natural philosophy, divinity" — the prospectus also included modern languages, German and English, and "all such other branches of literature as will tend to make good men and useful citizens." By reserving twenty-eight of forty places on the Board of Trustees, evenly divided, for Lutheran and Reformed representatives, the plan officially committed the college to denominational control — making Franklin the first American college with such an explicit commitment. The other trustees were to be "chosen indiscriminately from any other society of Christians." To further ensure parity between Reformed and Lutheran denominations, the prospectus promised to choose the principal, or president, alternately from each denomination, unless a unanimous vote decreed otherwise. Playing the petitioners' trump card last, the proposal explained that the institution was to be named Franklin College, out of "a profound respect for the character of His Excellency the President of the State." Although there is no evidence that Benjamin Franklin played an active role in the founding of the college that would bear his name, he did, as will be seen, make the largest financial contribution to its fledgling endowment.[19]

The careful balancing of interests and constituencies was reflected in the selection of trustees, already chosen before the petition was submitted to the Pennsylvania General Assembly. They included Bingham's mercantile colleagues Robert Morris and George Clymer, who along with Rush and McKean had been signers of the Declaration of Independence. In addition to seven ministers each from the Lutheran and German Reformed churches, a Moravian minister, and a Catholic priest, many Lancaster residents active in civic causes were also selected. Among them, Casper Shaffner had been a trustee in the short-lived classical academy. Some local trustees had close business ties with those from Philadelphia; Jasper Yeates was Hamilton's agent in Lancaster, for example. Some Lancastrians on the board were busy promoting other improvements: attorney John Hubley and merchant Paul Zantzinger served as Lancaster commissioners, along with William Bingham as president, of the turnpike chartered in 1792 to connect Philadelphia and Lancaster, the first major project of its kind in America.[20]

In late December, Rush wrote his friend John Montgomery about the project. "They have made me a trustee, together with some more of your republican friends," he reported. "I am delighted with the zeal with which the Germans push on this undertaking."[21] Rush and Montgomery had recently instigated the founding of Dickinson College in Carlisle, Pennsylvania. By early 1787, already disillusioned by infighting among Dickinson's leaders, Rush was impressed by the unanimity shown by Franklin College's trustees: "We have no *hum's* and *ha's* among us nor no doubts — or fears of our final success in the glorious undertaking." He reported that Morris and Bingham each pledged £150 in certificates to Franklin College and was particularly delighted that Franklin himself pledged £200 in specie. "The Germans are much pleased with it," Rush wrote Richard Price in February, "and from the zeal and liberality with which they promote every thing, which is connected with the advancement of their religion, I have no doubt but it will, in a few years, rival in funds and reputation, the oldest colleges in America."[22]

With such rosy expectations, Franklin College received its charter on March 10, 1787, together with an appropriation of ten thousand acres of land. The charter reflected the faith that education could meet the needs of the college's different constituencies: it promised a charity school for elementary training of children of both sexes and a college for the advanced education of a more exclusive group, young men destined to lead the new republic. The founders' fusion of religion and public life is reflected in the belief that "training up a succession of youth" to understand "the principles of the Christian religion and of our Republican form of Government in their purity" would preserve both religion and government. By fully understanding these principles, the young would be led "the more zealously to practice the one and the more strenuously to defend the other." The new institution's purpose was to pass on time-honored truths, a function closely allied with religion, rather than to serve as a center for discovering new knowledge. Noting the importance in education of "the zealous and industrious exertions of the members of the Clergy," the charter pledged that the board would maintain the present two-to-three ratio of ministers to laymen.[23]

In advance of the formal dedication, many hands worked to raise interest among the college's constituencies. German-language newspapers published addresses explaining the project. Leaders of the German community throughout the region were invited to the ceremonies and asked to solicit contributions in their neighborhoods. Pointing to the prosperity with which Germans had been blessed since their arrival "in this western land," the letter of invitation predicted that education would enable them to assume greater responsibility for public service.[24]

Helmuth took charge of planning the dedication ceremonies, carefully offering equal roles to all constituents. A difficult choice had to be made, however, when it came to choosing the new college's leadership. As early as January, Lutheran ministers Helmuth and Weiberg wrote to the Reverend Henry Muhlenberg that it was their "plan" that he should be the "Principal" and the German Reformed cleric William Hendel become the "Vice-Principal." The selection of a man whose botanical researches had already earned him an international reputation and who was the youngest son of the leading Lutheran minister in the New World might seem unexceptionable. Yet it appears to have been motivated at least in part by political considerations and to have aroused some interdenominational rivalry. Hendel confessed to Rush that he felt some "uneasiness" at the choice because it represented a "deviation" from the usual practice of deferring to seniority, a deviation that "hardly ever fails to produce disadvantageous Reflections." Having served in Pennsylvania pulpits since 1764, Hendel was clearly Muhlenberg's senior. "It hath been hinted to me very early," he noted, "that the institution would fail if the first principal was not chosen from the Lutherans; this induced me to think, that something more was intended by it, than to give a proof of Regard for a venerable Minister, who had zealously devoted his talents & his time to the service of the Church." Hendel nonetheless assured Rush that he would accept whatever position was offered him. He welcomed Rush's "solemn assurance" that the charter's provision that leadership would alternate between Lutherans and German Reformed would be honored.[25]

At the first meeting of the trustees on June 5, elections had gone as planned. To round out the faculty, the Reverend Frederick Valentine Melsheimer, a Lutheran, was appointed professor of Latin, Greek, and German, and William Reichenbach as professor of mathematics. The fifth position, professor of English and belles lettres, was awarded to the Reverend Joseph Hutchins, rector of St. James Episcopal Church in Lancaster. Melsheimer had come to America as chaplain to a regiment of Brunswick mercenaries; Reichenbach had recently arrived from Germany. "It has given me great pleasure to find," Rush reported in a letter to to his mother-in-law, "that our conduct at Lancaster has given universal satisfaction. Disputes were happily prevented — ancient jealousies were composed, & a foundation was laid for a lasting Union between men of nations & Sects formerly opposed to each other."[26]

Despite appearances of amity and commitment, the fledgling college did not prosper. Twenty-first-century sensibilities might approve the cosmopolitan character of its founders' vision, but the new institution failed to inspire strong attachment on the part of any of its constituencies. With the exception of Benjamin Rush, Philadelphia's trustees quickly lost interest in the project, particularly as they became absorbed in the fight to ratify the new Constitution. Resentment of the Muhlenberg family's prominence in state politics also reduced enthusiasm for the college.[27]

The Enlightenment cosmopolitanism reflected in the college's founding was not the path that most German Americans would take to assimilation into American society. Instead of dissolving into Anglo-American culture, they gradually fashioned an ethnic identity that was both German and American. As a central part of cultural identity, religion was crucial in the formation of an independent German ethnicity during the early years of the new republic. Except for Henry Muhlenberg, neither Reformed nor Lutheran church leaders seemed to feel a strong sense of ownership toward Franklin College. In following years, both denominations found it necessary to establish separate colleges and seminaries.[28]

Moreover, the German American population that Franklin College was founded to serve regarded it with indifference, if not mistrust. As in the case of the charity schools created in the 1750s, many suspected that the college's goal was to anglicize their children. This situation was not helped by Hutchins's patronizing attitude, revealed in his dedication sermon. He assured his largely German-speaking audience that education would inevitably lead to the universal adoption of English, for "the limited capacity of man can very seldom attain excellence in more than one language."[29]

Moreover, the German community wanted elementary education for their children but had little interest in higher learning. Few of the region's farmers destined their sons for the professions, and like many Americans these farmers saw little use otherwise for the liberal arts. Sharing lexicographer Noah Webster's opinion, they asked, "Why should a merchant trouble himself with the rules of Greek and Roman syntax or a planter puzzle his head with conic sections?"[30]

The sketchy evidence of the college's records indicates that few students were actually engaged in higher education. Separate departments were established for German and English students, and a list of students in the English department for the first year showed seventy-eight boys and thirty-six girls, many seemingly children of local trustees. (Significantly, several were from Lancaster's small Jewish community.) Only twelve of these, all boys, were recorded as studying Latin, a crucial sign of engagement in "higher learning." The German department, though smaller than the English, contained more advanced students.[31]

Instruction began on July 18, 1787, in the Brew House, located on Mifflin Street near Trinity Lutheran Church. The building was too small, and trustees asked the state legislature for the Store House, a two-story brick building on North Queen Street put up during the Revolution. In February 1788 the legislature approved the request and included the two lots of land on which the building stood.[32]

With tuition set low, at £4 for the complete course and at smaller sums for partial courses, revenues for the first year were only £200, while another £26 remained uncollected. This was less than half of expenses, which included £450 in salaries for Hutchins, Melsheimer, and Reichenbach — Muhlenberg and Hendel received no salary for their service as principal and vice-principal. To make up the gap, the trustees' first resolution in September 1787 was to begin collecting pledges to the college. Board vice president John Hubley wrote all trustees, asking them to collect subscriptions in their districts and to obtain further pledges and forward the proceeds to the treasurer "with all convinient Speed."[33]

The timing was unfortunate, for three days before Hubley's request, the Philadelphia convention unveiled its finished work, setting off a massive struggle over ratification. Few found it convenient to fulfill their subscriptions — notable exceptions being Benjamin Franklin, who paid the full £200 at once, and Robert Morris, who sent a non-interest-bearing certificate for $600. In February 1788, Rush tried and failed to organize a meeting of Philadelphia trustees. "I lament the languor that has infected our trustees in this city," Rush apologized to Muhlenberg. "The present turbulent era is unfavorable to all peaceable enterprises. Nothing now fills the mind but subjects that agitate the passions."[34]

The coalition of interests that had produced Franklin College dissolved in the new political environment. German voters rejected the Federalist Party in 1788 and subsequently divided deeply in their reaction to the French Revolution. Although Helmuth remained an ardent Federalist, many ethnic German leaders moved to the new Republican Party. Philadelphia's Federalist trustees lost interest in the college.[35]

Nor were Lancaster subscribers more forthcoming. Paul Zantzinger reported that only two on his list, including himself, paid the requested one-third of their subscription; the rest claimed they could not spare the money or otherwise avoided his calls. Failing to receive their full salaries, faculty began to take private pupils on the side. "How could it be possible that our people should sink to such a depth of degradation?" Melsheimer admonished his countrymen in a local German newspaper. He urged them to show the world that they had heads for learning as well as "hands to labor."[36]

The second annual meeting of the trustees in June 1788 was much less sanguine than the inaugural gathering. Only a few trustees attended, primarily local members. Claiming ill health, Hutchins had just announced his resignation, with £90 of his salary still unpaid. New committees were appointed to try again to collect subscriptions. "Our great dependence is in a few, among which we always reckon you one of the foremost," Hubley wrote Rush, "and as no time can be lost the calls on us here being so very pressing, we make no doubt but you will put the business into imidiate forwardness."[37]

But matters did not improve in the college's second year. Only fourteen students enrolled in the German department in the fall term, and the faculty's pay backlog continued to mount. Hopes that the state land grant would offer immediate financial support disappeared early in 1789, when the state refused to pay surveying costs. Failing to persuade the Philadelphia trustees to contribute toward surveying some of the lands, local trustees accepted William Bingham's offer of a loan of £60. In the summer of 1789 Frederick Melsheimer resigned to become pastor of a church, and word went out that the school had closed. "What is to be the fate of our college?" Muhlenberg asked his diary in August. The following year a Reformed minister explained to synod authorities in Holland that the college had failed "because the professors no longer received their salaries in consequence of the prevailing scarcity of money." Writing Rush on botanical matters in 1792, Muhlenberg lamented that the college was "much like the Daughter of Jairus," in need of "a commiserating Hand that could raise it!" He observed that other schools with "fewer Managers" seemed to get on better.[38]

In its attempt to embody an Enlightenment ideal of religious tolerance and interethnic cooperation, Franklin College was the product of a specific moment, on the cusp of the creation a new American nation. The founding enthusiasm did not survive in the intensely partisan world that followed.

Keeping the Institution Alive

Although Franklin College no longer existed as an institution for higher learning, it survived as a duly incorporated body owning land and a building, and its trustees were determined to keep it alive. In this period the term "college" embraced a wide range of institutions, and elementary instruction seems to have been offered to the community in the Franklin College building more or less continuously by teachers acting as independent entrepreneurs. James Ross, author of a widely used Latin textbook, ran a classical school there between 1801 and 1809. In that year, Benedict J. Schipper opened a classical academy "in Franklin College"—using the term in the connotation of a building. When Schipper published a German-English dictionary co-authored with Henry Muhlenberg, several years later, he identified himself as professor of languages in "Franklin Academy." In 1810 two separate schools used the building rent free. In later decades, at a time of active experimentation in educational methods, the college offered space to an infant school and a school employing new educational methods developed by Joseph Lancaster.[39]

For some sixty years, Franklin College trustees kept the corporation alive by meeting periodically, appointing successors for departed members, and attempting to exert good stewardship over its few resources. There are gaps in the records, as meetings were not called for years or failed to secure a quorum. From time to time, funds were appropriated to maintain the building.[40]

The trustees devoted their greatest efforts to converting the ten thousand acres of land granted by the legislature in western and north central Pennsylvania into usable assets. As many would-be land speculators in the early national period learned to their ruin, dreams of finding wealth through ownership of large tracts of mountainous Pennsylvania land were destined for disappointment. Located far from population and transportation centers and largely unsuitable for farming, these acres were hard to dispose of profitably. The only prospective tenants were rough backwoodsmen, who were more likely to squat on lands than purchase them. And even when buyers could be found, the undeveloped frontier economy made it hard for them to obtain cash to make payments. In the early years, the state grant to Franklin College actually drained the institution's resources, because in addition to the expenses of gaining title, it had to pay county taxes. No land was sold until the 1820s, and even then purchasers frequently defaulted and payments were eaten up by agents' fees.[41]

By 1840 the endowment had risen to some $13,000 in securities, with land and mortgages estimated at a value of $25,000, although little of this earned interest. In a day when there were few secure investment options, many of the funds were kept in certificates of the Lancaster Savings Institution — perhaps not coincidentally, its president, Samuel Dale, was secretary of the college — and the rest in personal notes to local men, including trustees. In that year trustees obtained a more convenient location for the institution by selling the original building and land and purchasing and enlarging a schoolhouse at the corner of Orange and Lime.[42]

In its new location, Franklin College served Lancaster as a multipurpose community center. Trustees revived a classical academy in the fall of 1840; one of its instructors, Frederick A. Muhlenberg Jr., was grandson of the college's first president. Trustees also provided space to a Baptist congregation, the Lancaster Lyceum, and the reading room of a literary society. Promoters of this literary society, which included local leaders John L. Atlee and George N. Steinman, pledged to turn over their collections to the college in exchange for provision of room, light, and heat.[43]

As Franklin College's resources grew, trustees began to debate how best to carry out their educational mission. In 1844 they considered fulfilling the promise made in the original charter to devote one-sixth of the endowment to support a charity school. But the idea was rejected, most likely because by this time charity schools were being replaced by tax-supported schools for all students, not just the poor. Known as "common schools," they were the fruit of a nationwide movement to establish uniform school systems run by publicly elected boards of directors. The Pennsylvania state legislature had enabled creation of local public systems in 1836, but because of widespread opposition, especially in German communities, they were not made mandatory until 1849. No explicit provision was made for advanced instruction at what is now known as high-school level. Lancaster established a common school system in 1838 and two years later set up a "secondary department" in two grades, which offered instruction in subjects like grammar, history, geography, arithmetic, algebra, and bookkeeping.[44]

In 1846 the Franklin College Executive Committee conferred with directors of the common schools about combining their efforts on behalf of education. As a result, the college offered free classical instruction to all qualified students; the college paid the salary of the classics professor, while the mathematics professor was paid out of public funds. This relationship continued until 1849, when the school board objected to allowing free tuition to out-of-town students. It may also have taken exception to the trustees' imposition of a requirement that students memorize the Apostles'

Creed, the Lord's Prayer, and the Ten Commandments, that "some brief & popular Treatise on the Evidences of Christianity" be introduced at each level, and that teachers begin each day with prayer. In any case, the school board had already begun to plan for a separate high school under its sole direction.[45]

At this point, college leaders seem to have realized that the institution had reached a turning point. The advent of a publicly funded school system undermined the role that Franklin College had played in secondary education for half a century, but its resources were not sufficient to support a collegiate program. F. A. Muhlenberg, the classics instructor, proposed constructing a house to board out-of-town students, and in September the trustees resolved to raise funds for this purpose. But they dropped the project at the annual meeting in December, when the largest gathering of trustees in many years debated instead fundamental issues of the institution's future. A general agreement seems to have been reached that the college could not flourish in its present form as an awkward hybrid of the interests of two religious denominations and local community.[46]

The first resolution proposed dissolving Franklin College and dividing the endowment between Marshall College and Pennsylvania College, institutions associated with German Reformed and Lutheran denominations, respectively. But local trustees, who had struggled for generations to build up a college for their community, protested, and the motion was withdrawn. Discussion shifted to the prospect of merging with another college — as long as it could be persuaded to move to Lancaster. The following day, speaking for what was now the Eastern Synod of the German Reformed Church, the Reverend John C. Bucher proposed what was in effect a denominational divorce: one-third of the college's assets would be paid to the trustees of a Lutheran college, in return for leaving Lancaster and the German Reformed Church in sole possession of what had been Franklin College. This cleared the way for Marshall College to separate itself from its community, Mercersburg, Pennsylvania, and move to Lancaster.[47]

CHAPTER TWO

Marshall College
Christian *Bildung* on the Frontier

——⌇⌇——

Despite its use of the eminent jurist John Marshall's name, Marshall College's roots were more religious than civic. Unlike Franklin College, it was created to serve the needs of a single denomination, the German Reformed Church in the United States of America. Its founding generation of Reformed ministers shaped a distinctive institutional vision aimed at redeeming a denomination that had gone astray. By serendipity, this reform spirit was infused with German idealism brought to America by a young émigré, Frederick Augustus Rauch, and developed by his successors into an important theological movement, the Mercersburg Theology.[1]

Search for Religious Authority

The German Reformed Church in the United States was founded in 1793, when its governing body declared independence from the Synod of Amsterdam, in part to gain the right to examine and ordain ministers. Yet its new governing body, a synod that met once a year, did not move immediately to found an institution for their education. Formal academic training or degrees were not required to become a minister, and most young men who aspired to the clergy apprenticed themselves to senior pastors. Some inspiring mentors attracted so many disciples that their parsonages became boardinghouse schools, popularly called "Schools of the Prophets." The German Reformed Synod examined candidates for the ministry at its yearly meetings and ordained ministers when they received a call to a particular congregation.[2]

Informal personal instruction followed by examination by a professional body was a common educational path in early nineteenth-century America. None of the traditional learned professions — law, medicine, divinity, even education — required academic credentials for entry, although college training was desirable. Even in college-rich New England, an apprenticeship system dominated preparation of Congregational clergy. In Pennsylvania, the practice reflected a lack of wealth in the German American community and, even more, a patriarchal culture emphasizing local autonomy and deference to authority figures rather than formal organizations. In the Reformed community, seniority was given priority—for example, ministers and lay delegates sat and spoke at the annual synod meetings according to age. This attitude, characterized by one scholar as "peasant republicanism," gave little impetus within the synod to create an educational institution that would centralize authority in a handful of theological teachers.[3]

Nonetheless, an apprenticeship system did not meet the needs of a growing German American population that was expanding geographically. By 1824 only sixty-four German Reformed ministers served some fourteen thousand members in Pennsylvania, Maryland, Virginia, Ohio, and North Carolina. Without strong leadership, many German-speaking backcountry residents were drawn to "Methodistic" separatist groups. Emanuel V. Gerhart, the first president of Franklin & Marshall College, later attributed the German community's "isolation and great spiritual destitution" to the shortage of educated clergy. Decentralized theological training and low standards in ministerial education permitted what he called "discordant elements," such as a more evangelical style of worship. Gerhart charged that some in the community even rejected tenets of the Heidelberg Catechism, the central document of the German Reformed tradition.[4]

Because clergymen played an important role in education in general, even elementary schooling suffered, isolating the German-speaking population intellectually. "The people as a body were not in the main current of American progress," Gerhart recalled, "but pursuing their peaceful avocations in the rural districts, were content to circulate in the eddies of life under the banks." The everyday German dialect was so distinct from the High German used by clergy and teachers that people had difficulty understanding them and reading German texts. Thus, Gerhart insisted, the church "retrograded intellectually, theologically, and morally; and many abuses pertaining to order, discipline, and customs, came to prevail, notwithstanding all the efforts of devoted and godly men to prevent them." Gerhart and others attached to Marshall College considered their institution crucial in bringing German Americans into the mainstream while preserving their distinctive culture.[5]

Doctrinal disputes spurred the founding of many Protestant theological seminaries in the early nineteenth century. After Harvard appointed a theological liberal as its professor of divinity, conservative Congregationalists founded their first seminary at Andover in 1808. Beginning in 1817, German Reformed annual synods discussed the question of a seminary, but it was controversial. Some wanted to ally with Pennsylvania Lutherans, some with Dutch Reformed brethren in New York and New Jersey. In 1819, the synod concluded only that candidates for ordination must be at least twenty-one years of age, have prepared in "the learned languages, theology, and other necessary courses of study," and provide "evidence of good character."[6]

The next year it took up a proposal to found a seminary in Frederick, Maryland. The same session also decided that increased numbers of churches made it necessary to divide the synod into districts, each known as a "classis," and change the annual synod meeting from a general convention with delegates from each congregation to a representative assembly. Some Reformed members interpreted the coincidence of this reorganization and the seminary proposal as proof of a plot to limit the freedom of individual congregations. In broader terms, the proposals triggered an ingrained suspicion of centralized authority that was strong in the early American republic. Critics warned that a legally incorporated seminary would empower the synod to compel congregations to pay for the seminary's support. Several congregations seceded and formed the "Free Synod," denouncing the seminary as "extravagant," "aristocratic," and threatening to "freedom." Over the next decade, more than one hundred congregations joined the schismatic organization; most rejoined the synod in 1837.[7]

Retreating in the face of this opposition, the synod dropped the Frederick proposal. In 1824 the synod accepted Dickinson College's offer to provide space for a seminary professor if he would also teach history and German. Even in this limited form, the idea of a seminary met strong opposition, and the proposal passed only with a tie-breaking vote by the synod's president. The synod did not adopt a charter for the seminary until 1829. The Reverend Lewis Mayer accepted the call to become the first professor and president of the Theological Seminary of the German Reformed Church.[8]

With this less-than-enthusiastic support from the wider church, the seminary opened in March 1825 with five students. Mayer soon complained to the synod that they were inadequately prepared, noting that one student from rural Maryland knew no Latin and was "too far advanced in years, now to make a beginning." Mayer had to improvise what he termed a "peculiar mode of proceeding" to accomplish the intellectual development generally done by classical education: to "unfold the powers of their minds, and to infuse into them a correct mode of thinking, and a readiness in proving, dissecting and joining." Mayer repeatedly insisted that students should know Latin and Greek and "be well grounded in the essential sciences" before beginning theological study. Finding Carlisle uncongenial, he moved the seminary to York in 1829.[9]

Three years later, the synod established a separate "Classical Institute" to prepare students for the seminary. Because none of the available clergy had a sufficient background in classical studies, the synod searched outside its ranks for the institute's first teacher. By chance, the trustees hired a young German immigrant, Frederick Augustus Rauch, and asked the 1832 synod to approve his parallel appointment to the seminary faculty as professor of biblical literature.[10]

Rauch must have seemed an exotic figure when he arrived to be examined by the synod. The only record of his appearance, a pencil sketch in profile made in 1841, shows a slight man with a hairline already receding from a prominent forehead, of precisely the kind then believed to denote high intelligence. To a long-established ethnic community that had seen few newcomers in half a century, he represented a new, Romantic Germany. In addition to his scholarly accomplishments, Rauch was an accomplished musician and had supported himself upon his arrival in Pennsylvania by teaching piano.[11]

At twenty-six, Rauch already had more academic credentials than most faculty at established American colleges. The son of a Reformed minister, he had studied at the universities of Giessen and Heidelberg and received a doctorate in philology from the University of Marburg. Afterward, he offered lectures at Giessen on history, logic, psychology, natural law, and Goethe. But a quarrel with a powerful professor seems to have stymied Rauch's career, and in the summer of 1831 he decided to seek his fortune in America.[12]

John W. Nevin, who became Rauch's colleague several years later, recalled that Rauch rarely spoke about his reasons for leaving Germany: "He always charged himself," Nevin explained, "with some imprudence [in public statements]." At a time when German authorities were repressing democratic expression, Rauch's reticence inspired romantic rumors that he had been forced to flee after defending banned student societies. Whatever the cause, Rauch's arrival in Pennsylvania seemed literally a godsend for the synod's fledgling institutions. The synod approved his ordination as a minister in addition to his joint teaching appointments. Under his direction, the classical institute mushroomed in its first year from 32 students to 74.[13]

Meanwhile, the synod decided, in effect, to put their educational institutions up for auction, inviting interested communities to make their best offers. Lancaster, Chambersburg, and Mercersburg responded. Mercersburg's boosters, inspired by its local Reformed minister, promised $10,000, a stone academy building and lot, and temporary use of two houses for faculty. Lancaster had the advantage of Franklin College's endowment but was encumbered by the original charter, with the college's awkward combination of denominational and local interests. Mercersburg had fewer than a thousand people, but the relocation committee was impressed by its setting: "The situation of the village is healthy; and on every side nature presents the most impressive and charming prospects." Moreover, residents were virtuous and industrious and "board is cheap." In October 1835, the synod accepted Mercersburg's offer.[14]

The village of Mercersburg had been laid out in 1786, but it was still in many ways a frontier community, composed mainly of log structures with a scattering of stone and frame buildings. With a breathtaking view of surrounding mountains, Mercersburg was located at a trading crossroads in Franklin County, just north of the Mason-Dixon Line. A turnpike road provided connections to Baltimore and Pittsburgh. Residents were predominantly Scotch-Irish, including an Ulster-born merchant named James Buchanan. His son and namesake, the future U.S. president, had studied Latin and Greek in the academy building now promised to the new school. Mercersburg also had a sizable free black population and sufficient German Americans to sustain Reformed and Lutheran congregations, though they shared a single church building.[15]

The seminary did not move to Mercersburg until 1837, but the classical institute transferred within a month. Most of the town turned out to welcome two stagecoaches filled with students, representing most of the eighteen who followed the school to its new location.[16]

The synod appointed a separate board of trustees for the institute, and they resolved to seek a collegiate charter to enable the school to grant degrees. At the suggestion of the Reverend Bernard C. Wolff, a Virginian, they named the college in honor of

John Marshall, who had served as chief justice of the United States from 1801 until his death in 1835. The eminent jurist had championed the principle of judicial review, and he might have seemed a model for an institution seeking to bring order to a fractious denomination. The charter, granted on March 31, 1836, expressed founders' "respect for [Marshall's] exalted character, great worth and high mental attainments." Also reflecting the rising social prestige of law in nineteenth-century America, trustees decreed that the college's seal would be composed of Marshall's likeness and the motto *Lux et Lex* — Light and Law. Unfortunately, the engraver reversed the two words; the original order was restored in the seal of its successor institution.[17]

German Idealism and a Unique Educational Vision

In many ways the classical institute-turned-college was typical of the many small denominational colleges founded in this period. Its curriculum included ancient languages, including Latin, Greek, and Hebrew; "Mathematical and natural Sciences," including chemistry, geology, botany, and mineralogy; and "Intellectual and Moral Sciences," belles lettres and history. Inclusion of German language and literature was unusual at the time but followed Marshall College's mission to prepare Reformed ministers, who typically preached in German.[18] Most instruction was in English, however. The charter took pains to declare that "persons of every religious denomination" could be trustees, faculty, or students. At its first meeting the trustees decreed that working regulations would be based upon those at Princeton College, "so far as applicable."[19]

Despite its surface typicality, under Frederick Rauch's leadership Marshall College offered an educational atmosphere unlike anything else in America. Rauch's German education coincided with the birth of the modern university. When Wilhelm von Humboldt founded the University of Berlin in 1810, he proclaimed a new vision of the university as a "learned republic," promising to appoint and promote faculty on the basis of evidence of intellectual inquiry rather than doctrinal purity, family ties, or loyalty to the state. His innovations have been seen as the beginning of the idea of universities as centers of research within specialized disciplines, although this kind of institution did not emerge fully until later in the nineteenth century.[20]

Instead, the early part of the century was a transitional time, when German students and faculty were invigorated by the idea of the university as a place of continuous inquiry. "Knowledge must be considered as something not yet wholly discovered and never entirely discoverable," Humboldt asserted, "[and] must incessantly be sought as such." Natural and moral philosophy had not yet been carved up into distinct academic disciplines, and the ideal of inquiry was, as historian Charles E. McClelland puts it, "the active pursuit of *integrated, meaningful,* and *pure* knowledge." This pursuit was commonly known as *Wissenschaft,* connoting a dedicated search not merely for knowledge but also for self-fulfillment through pursuit of ultimate meanings. (The common translation of this term into English as "science" has obscured its idealist roots.) The teacher's role in inspiring curiosity, passing on habits and tools of thought, and providing a "living example of a *wissenschaftlich* approach to life" was "at least as important as the results of his own personal research or the content of his lectures." To communicate their insights, professors used literary forms ranging from textbooks and essays in the popular press to the more specialized scholarly periodicals that were only then being founded.[21]

This ideal of inquiry fit with the ethos of German Romanticism, as expressed by philosopher Friedrich von Schiller as *immer wird, nie ist* — "always becomes, never is." Inquiry also reflected new ideas about the relationship between education and human development. Goethe had popularized an ideal of cultivation (*Bildung* in German) in which education enabled the organic unfolding of the human personality to its full potential. Self-cultivation was an end in itself, not a pragmatic means to a career, and *Wissenschaft* was the best way to achieve it.[22]

Ideas of *Wissenschaft* and *Bildung* were closely bound up with "neo-humanism," a revival of interest in the art and texts of ancient Greece and Rome. Studying classic texts was seen as a particularly effective means of cultivation. But unlike previous classical education, neo-humanism focused attention on meaning rather than grammatical form. A few young American classicists shared the hope that study of the classics would cultivate a higher, purer personality able to withstand the materialism and selfishness of contemporary society.[23]

The dominant curriculum in American colleges at this time was based on Common Sense philosophy, which had emerged in the eighteenth century as the medieval classical curriculum adapted to the scientific revolution. The many Scottish scholars who found employment in American colleges brought curricular innovations that had made Scottish universities the most advanced in Britain. These included the study of belles lettres, or literary aesthetics, and an expansive approach to moral philosophy stressing not only religion and ethics but economic and political life as well. Moral philosophy thus served as the starting point for investigations that later in the nineteenth century spun off into the new "social" sciences of psychology, sociology, political science, and economics.[24]

Common Sense philosophy maintained that the world and truth were unchanging realities created by God and revealed both in scripture and in the immutable laws of nature. The human mind was a passive reflection of external reality. Human beings were composed of a number of distinct and often conflicting powers, or "faculties," ranging from the purely "animal" and instinctive to the emotional, rational, and moral. In this view, education's goal was to strengthen the higher faculties and instill discipline to enable one to control the more powerful lower faculties. In most institutions, teaching consisted of requiring students to answer questions about or recite information memorized from textbooks. The process of memorizing the contents of approved books was supposed to discipline young minds and furnish them with accepted truths.[25]

At a time when only a few American scholars had been exposed to recent German educational ideas, Rauch was applying them in his Mercersburg classroom. His approach was further shaped by his immersion in German philosophy, particularly the teachings of G. W. F. Hegel. When he emigrated to America, Rauch discovered that Hegel's ideas were virtually unknown in the New World. As historian Bruce Kuklick has noted, the New England congregational theologians who dominated American philosophy had become isolated from intellectual trends in Europe. Amazingly, Rauch's appointment at Marshall College, located geographically and socially on the frontier, placed the small school at the cutting edge of philosophy in America.[26]

Despite his heavy teaching and administrative responsibilities, Rauch resolved to introduce to American audiences the recent advances in German philosophy "in all that relates to the phenomenology of the soul." He planned a trilogy of works dealing in turn with psychology, aesthetics, and ethics. The first volume, *Psychology, or a View of the Human Soul*, appeared in 1840. It was the first book published in the United States to use the term "psychology" in its title. More important, it stimulated American interest in German idealism and Hegel. Following closely the ideas and structure of Hegel's *Philosophy of Mind*, Rauch first composed the book as lectures to his junior class at Marshall College. In the preface he explained that his goal was to "render this noble and delightful science accessible to all classes of readers" by using ordinary language and "taking all his illustrations from nature." The first edition sold out in weeks; a second appeared in 1841 and was reprinted four times by 1850. Noting that the book "abounds with views new to the American reader, if not original with the author," the *New Englander* praised the second edition in 1843. *Psychology* was used as a textbook at colleges such as Dartmouth and the University of Vermont and read by many adults seeking insight into the workings of the mind — including, it is thought, Edgar Allan Poe.[27]

In *Psychology*, Rauch challenged Common Sense philosophy's passive view of the mind. Along with many German thinkers, he insisted that consciousness was active in organizing its own experience. Instead of a radical separation between mind and body, he emphasized their intimate connection. Mind was made up of different aspects that were organically linked through a dialectical process of development. Subjective mind was the first rudimentary consciousness of one's body in the form of sensations, feelings, and impressions; conscious mind developed when one was able to reflect upon sensations as objects. Finally, self-consciousness, or reason, emerged when the mind became aware of its own thinking as such and achieved self-determination, or will. Rauch emphasized that these different aspects represent a single thinking power rather than different faculties.[28]

Unlike the mechanical connections between faculties posited by Common Sense philosophy, Rauch's Hegelian vision emphasized organic relationships between mental stages, using the image of a tree in which all the different components were "produced by the plastic power contained in the seed." The ultimate goal of development was the achievement of human personality, a concept that for Rauch encompassed self-consciousness and awareness of God. His organic vision influenced Horace Bushnell's understanding of human development, expressed in his influential *Christian Nurture* (1847). *Psychology* also introduced the Romantic historicist concept that human cultures themselves were organic entities that developed over time. Change did not abandon the past but included it in more complex forms. This historicism proved to be a fertile seed from which grew the Mercersburg Theology.[29]

Rauch outlined the educational implications of his philosophy in his 1837 presidential inaugural address. Speaking to the Mercersburg community, he avoided *Psychology*'s complex philosophical structure while drawing upon themes and images from German Romanticism. His abundant use of organic metaphors not only flowed from his philosophy but also resonated with his rural audience. He began with the premise that human consciousness developed only through interaction with other persons: "Fire only can kindle fire; mind only can awaken mind. We must be among men to become men; we must be acted upon." Yet learning required a child's own activity. "The mind does not receive impressions like wax," he cautioned. "In receiving it is active; and unless what is committed to memory, is understood, nothing is learned." Education could not cause development, but it provided an environment essential for the growth of the child's potential.[30]

Rauch also addressed questions at the center of recent debates about college curricula. In 1828 leaders of Yale College responded to criticisms of its classical curriculum with a report that became the most widely read antebellum statement on higher education. Its arguments were based on faculty psychology. "The two great points to be gained in intellectual culture," it began, "are the *discipline* and the *furniture* of the mind; expanding its powers, and storing it with knowledge." While Rauch compared the mind to an unfolding organism, the metaphors of the Yale report were static and architectural. It envisioned "laying the foundation of a thorough education," a foundation that "must be broad, and deep, and solid." It argued that a liberal arts education focused on the classics was best suited "both to strengthen and enlarge the faculties of the mind, and to familiarize it with the leading principles of the great objects of human investigation and knowledge." Although the report referred in passing to the importance of character, it focused exclusively on cognitive functions and paid no attention to emotions. Not until Theodore Dwight Woolsey became president of Yale in 1846 was a broader ideal of culture introduced there.[31]

Rauch wholeheartedly supported a broad liberal arts education, but he began from quite different premises, rooted in German neo-humanism. In his inaugural address he argued that "the principal design of education" was "the harmonious cultivation of the latent faculties of the mind": "Only when the reason is fully developed and not merely a few of its parts, only when we are conscious of every power and energy in us, are we entirely *men*; whilst without this full development, we are like plants trimmed down to dwarfs by the knife of the gardener." If, in the interest of practicality, "the mind is cultivated in one direction more than in another, the memory more than judgment, prudence more than feeling, cool speculation more than imagination," he warned, "an unhealthy state of the mind is produced, which must result more or less to our own disadvantage and to that of our fellow-men." The college must develop more than students' intellects: "The fortune of our lives and our government depends not exclusively on useful knowledge but on our character as citizens, and to form this character by cultivating the whole man is the aim of education in the proper sense."[32]

For Rauch, the "symmetrical cultivation of the whole inner man" also involved students' motivation to learn. Attempts to use fear of punishment or even ambition to spur effort stimulated selfishness. Love was the ideal motivator: "love to the subjects taught, . . . love to knowledge, to truth, to goodness, independently of any selfish calculation as to the use and advantage we may derive from them." Love was in turn sparked by the student's interaction with the teacher and his entire approach to learning.[33]

Later in the nineteenth century, the idea of education as the cultivation of the whole man became the basis of the defense of classical liberal arts education throughout the country. But as Rauch expressed it in 1837, it was a new way of talking about education in the United States.

Moreover, Rauch practiced what he preached. Even before the institution was raised to collegiate level, he reported, "Care has been constantly taken to exercise the understanding rather than the memory of the pupils." As a newcomer, he tried at first to follow customary educational practices, but he gradually changed his methods to fit his principles. Joseph Dubbs, the earliest historian of the college, related that "Dr. Rauch was not fond of text-books. . . . Once, we have been told, he undertook to teach logic in the usual way; but after several unsatisfactory lessons he suddenly hurled the book across the room, and exclaimed: 'I don't want it! I can teach you all that is in Aristotle without a book.'"[34]

Although he could be a contentious colleague, Rauch was an energetic and sympathetic teacher. "There was in his nature a joyous element which endeared him to his students," Dubbs reported. "His numerous illustrations were always happily adapted to make his teachings agreeable — to simplify and explain the truth in hand," said former student William Welker. "The business of teaching with him, was any thing but mechanical or formal," recalled John Nevin. "His nature was ardent, generous, enthusiastic; and towards the young especially, standing to him in the relation of pupils, it uttered itself with the most affectionate earnestness and vivacity. His whole intercourse with his students besides, was adapted to win their confidence and engage their love."[35]

The college's disciplinary policies mirrored its educational philosophy. New students officially entered into the Marshall College community through a public ritual of signing a pledge to observe its rules and regulations: "Sensible that all true freedom and manly independence can stand only in an intelligent regard to established law," the student acknowledged, "I have no right to continue in a family or community whose organization in this form I am not prepared to respect." These regulations included requirements for students to attend all classes and morning and evening prayers and spend much of the rest of their time studying in their rooms. Students were expected to attend Sunday services at either the local Reformed church or another of their parents' choosing. They were forbidden to visit local taverns or carry firearms. Punishments rose from private or public admonitions, to confinement in one's room for a period of time, the lowering of academic standing, suspension, "rustication"—being sent home for a period of time — and finally expulsion.[36]

Most of the weekly faculty meetings dealt with infractions. Under Rauch's leadership, faculty members emphasized personal relationships in their response. The most common transgression was skipping classes or examinations, which was treated leniently if the student seemed genuinely remorseful. In June 1837, for example, an older student was called to appear to explain his absence from examinations at the end of the winter session. "The circumstances were aggravating," wrote faculty secretary Samuel W. Budd, professor of mathematics, "but on Mr. Wolfensberger's making acknowledgements to the faculty of his sorrow & his ignorance of the kind of respect due them he was dismissed with admonition."[37]

The strict formal regulations were tempered by Rauch's sensitivity to the psychological needs of developing personalities. Despite one student's repeated infractions, Rauch wrote to his father that the young man was in no danger of moral "ruin." "I have watched him closely (of course in my own way without giving any offence to him)," Rauch reported. He wrote that he was "perfectly convinced" that recent "wild" behavior of the student was a reaction to the unwanted and imprudent attempts of other students, less intelligent than he, "to *bring about a revival*" in him.[38]

In contrast, students considered a threat to their peers' morality were treated more severely. On one occasion, after hearing statements from dependable sources that suggested a student had "become a dangerous inmate of the college," the faculty ordered his immediate withdrawal.[39]

Most early students came to Marshall College to prepare for the ministry, making it an unusually serious-minded group of youths and young men. Even so, young Emanuel V. Gerhart was probably more serious than most when he composed a set of rules in his diary soon after moving with his schoolmates to Mercersburg. Like young Benjamin Franklin, he resolved to rise early, focus on one subject at a time, and "observe system in everything." But he went on to warn himself "above all [to] beware — yes, beware of the ladies," lest he become distracted or, even worse, be drawn into "matrimonial engagement."[40]

Some students were inspired by Rauch's example to find more pleasure in intellectual speculation than in forbidden activities. "Out of recitations, in his room or under the portico of a summer evening," one student was later remembered amusing himself with others "in discussing profound philosophical questions." Although this particular youth had been "somewhat skeptical" about religion when he arrived, his studies in Christian philosophy made him "a firm believer in divine revelation."[41]

Like many educators in the early nineteenth century, Rauch believed that natural environments were safer and more uplifting for students than urban ones, and his Romantic sensibility responded joyously to the mountains surrounding Mercersburg. In an early catalogue he extolled the college's location. Though close to major turnpikes, Mercersburg offered few occasions "for distraction or dissipation of mind" and was extremely healthy. Best of all, the scenery "may be described as more than beautiful;

it is absolutely splendid": "At the distance of from two or five miles, the mountains are thrown around it in a sort of half circle, gracefully irregular and imposingly pictur-esque; forming a vast amphitheatre, from whose towering sides, in every direction, Nature looks forth upon the beholder, through sunshine or storm, in her most mag-nificent apparel."[42] The college consequently offered advantages for all aspects of a student's development: "Spiritually as well as physically, the air that breathes upon it is pure and salubrious, and the skies that look down upon it benignant and free." Rauch gave the location part of the credit for the remarkable "order and good behav-ior" shown by the students.[43]

One aspect of the location was not ideal: Mercersburg's proximity to the Mason-Dixon Line made the issue of slavery a particularly sensitive one. The town's free black population was reputed to harbor escaped slaves on their way north, but most whites feared that open criticism of slavery endangered relations with the South. A substan-tial minority of Marshall College's students were from Maryland and Virginia. To prevent controversy, the faculty expressly forbade students from "taking a decided & public part in this exciting question" of slavery.[44]

Conflict came, nonetheless, in the summer of 1837, when a young New England antislavery lecturer named Jonathan Blanchard came to town. He took a room with Daniel Kroh, a married college student who ran a boardinghouse. Trustee James Carson heard of plans to attack Kroh's house. Warning Kroh to defend his home, Carson loaned him a gun and suggested Kroh carry it through the street to publicize his intentions. No attack came, but when Blanchard set out for the Methodist church the following morning, he was pelted with rocks and eggs. A group of students came to his defense and escorted him back to Kroh's house, where he delivered an antislavery lecture.[45]

The faculty were forced to deal with the issue when another local trustee charged Kroh with "having disturbed the peace of the Town" by sheltering Blanchard and allowing him to lecture and with having violated the college's rule forbidding students to carry firearms. The faculty conducted its own investigation and after much delib-eration cleared Kroh of most charges. But it reprimanded him for allowing himself to become embroiled in a controversial issue.[46]

Struggles of a Pioneer College

Despite its thriving intellectual life, Marshall College was slow to develop physically. In 1836 the German Reformed Eastern Synod authorized construction of "suitable buildings" for both the seminary and college. In light of the low total enrollment for both, the committee decided to put up one substantial building for both seminary and college. The seminary building was located on a high point to the north of the village and was solidly built in the Greek Revival style ubiquitous among American colleges. A large central portico was supported by four Doric columns and topped by an hexagonal cupola–bell tower. With wide halls running the length of each of the three stories, and a raised basement, the building contained forty-four rooms, including thirty-four dormitory rooms, a chapel–lecture hall, a library, four recitation rooms, a refectory, and rooms for a steward. The refectory, or dining room, in the basement was "large enough for a first-class hotel." Though the building technically belonged to the seminary, most of its space was leased to the college. Two large houses for professors were constructed, flanking the building, in 1838 and 1839. Mathematics professor Samuel Budd laid out the grounds, with broad lawns and formal English-style boxwood gardens.[47]

Nearly all of the college's life took place within these buildings. Once the seminary building was completed in 1837, all but local students were required to live there and eat in the refectory. Rauch and Budd formed the core of the early faculty, while other teachers, of science, ancient languages, and belles lettres, came and went with regularity. The faculty was assisted in beginning languages and mathematics by tutors, most of whom were recent college graduates attending the seminary. Trustees decided in 1837 to resume precollegiate training, hoping that a preparatory department would serve as a feeder to increase college enrollments. This soon became the largest arm of the institution, with sixty-two students in 1837–1838, compared with forty-seven undergraduates and nine seminarians. The college had recently established a "law school" boasting eight students, but this was little more than a means of offering degrees to young men who were already reading law in the Chambersburg office of trustee Alexander Thomson. The law students lived in Chambersburg, paid their fees to Thomson, and appeared in Mercersburg only to pick up their bachelor of laws diplomas.[48]

Auxiliary enterprises like the preparatory and law schools were typical among nineteenth-century colleges, which were chronically short of funds. As with any new college, trustees struggled to obtain financial resources to sustain the labor-intensive business of education. They attracted state aid in real money, receiving more than $13,000 in grants by 1839. In return, the college postponed tuition payments for up to twenty-five "beneficiary" students, who were allowed to give an interest-free note payable in four years.[49]

To increase the endowment, trustees adopted the common practice of appointing agents — usually clergymen associated with the synod — to solicit contributions from congregations. The first, the Reverend Henry L. Rice of Chambersburg, was also president of the Board of Trustees. Within a few months in 1837, he inspired nearly $6,000 in subscriptions before his sudden death, caused, it was said, by exhaustion and exposure on his travels. As a sign of the college's "almost irreparable loss," trustees, faculty, and students wore crepe on their left arms for thirty days. The Reverend Bernard C. Wolff took his place.[50]

Subscriptions were slow to come in, and payments on pledges even slower. This doubtless reflected the hard times of the late 1830s but also suggests lack of support for the college. To spur contributions, the board offered donors of $500 perpetual scholarships, entitling them to name one student at a time to receive free tuition. When one beneficiary graduated, another could be selected to replace him. Reformed congregations purchased perpetual scholarships to support the education of young men destined for the ministry. Common among struggling colleges at the time, they increased "contributions" to the endowment but at the cost of reducing tuition income. Some donors were slow to pay on their pledges, prompting the board to limit credit toward a beneficiary's tuition to the interest earned on actual payments.[51]

Meanwhile, Mercersburg residents failed to fulfill the pledges they had made to attract the school. By 1838 they had paid less than $4,000 of the promised $10,000 subscription. Trustees considered legal action to collect the rest but concluded that many simply could not pay and forgave them. Nonetheless, they suspected in 1844 that some of those demanding that the college pay its debts had not fulfilled their subscriptions; trustees began deducting the amount of subscriptions from payments. Such deductions were not unusual; forcing scofflaws to pay on pledges was one of the greatest difficulties institution builders faced in the early nineteenth century. But it may also have reflected growing alienation between community and college. Trustee William McKinstry proposed in 1838 that the college create a "manual labor department," which suggests that local leaders were not wholly in agreement with Rauch's ideas about liberal education. Although McKinstry, a wealthy local merchant, manufacturer, and sometime congressman, was one of the leading local members of the board, his proposal was quietly tabled.[52]

Divisions among the trustees made it difficult to reach crucial decisions. Over the next decade, rising enrollments created a need for more space for the college and the preparatory department. Deciding first in favor of one, then the other, the board was unable to raise funds for even one building. It was finally forced to act in 1841, when a fire destroyed the building used for preparatory classes. Trustees constructed a new building in which preparatory students were not only taught but also boarded, as the catalogue described it, "under the immediate eye of the Rector . . . as a father at the head of his family."[53]

Trustees also seem to have been at odds over whether Marshall College was more a denominational or a local institution. An 1839 resolution to invite the German Reformed Synod to appoint a board of visitors to attend annual college examinations sparked "considerable debate." McKinstry's proposal to include representatives of all the town's denominations was voted down. The belief that the college was more what was called "sectarian" in character may have undermined local financial support.[54]

The performance of the treasurer, local innkeeper Daniel Shaffer, also aroused contention. In 1839 the board asked him to pay interest on $2,000 of college funds that he had neglected to invest. After he stepped down the following year, the board instituted elaborate directions about procedures, especially the need to distinguish between monies designated for endowment and those available for operating expenses. Trustees also discovered that Shaffer owed the college more than $5,000. To retrieve it, they were forced to take possession of his tavern, the Old Mansion House — in effect purchasing it for an appraised worth of $3,510. Giving credit for his expenses as treasurer, they took a note for the rest, which he was unable to pay. The building was rented for several years until a purchaser was finally found. Given that students were forbidden to even enter a tavern, the college's ownership of one reportedly "aroused much amusement" in the community.[55]

Seedbed of Mercersburg Theology

Meanwhile, theological divisions had arisen among college faculty, especially over the issue of revivalism. A much-publicized wave of revivals, known as the Second Great Awakening, spread to the region in the 1830s. In Pennsylvania and the Ohio Valley, the Reformed Church faced competition from German-speaking evangelical offshoots, and many Reformed clergy, including Lewis Mayer, advocated emulating revival techniques to retain their members. The German Reformed Eastern synod even called them the Church's "only hope" and congregations in Reading and Lancaster brought in a leading evangelist, Charles G. Finney.[56]

Rauch openly attacked Mayer's teachings, largely orthodox Common Sense doctrines, as "supernatural rationalism," a term common in theological debates in Germany. Inspired by his comments, several seminary students charged Mayer with heresy. Mayer resigned in 1839, and under the circumstances none of the synod's ministers nominated to replace him were willing to accept the position. A special synod meeting in 1840 elected John Williamson Nevin on the basis of his reputation as a scholar of German history.[57]

Born in 1803 on a farm in the Cumberland Valley of Pennsylvania, Nevin was Scotch-Irish and Presbyterian in background. At the age of fourteen, he had been sent to Union College in faraway Schenectady, New York. In later years, he blamed this school's educational philosophy for psychological and physical ailments that plagued him the rest of his life. Most damning to him was the chasm between students' intellectual training — aimed only at "apprenticing its pupils in the different departments of common academical knowledge" — and their spiritual life. Except for perfunctory required prayers and Sunday services, little attention was paid to nurturing students' religious development. Religious life instead consisted of artificial, "more or less sporadic and irregular appliances" calculated to engineer conversion. In 1820 Union College experienced an awakening, the "mechanical" result, in Nevin's view, of the efforts of the mathematics teacher and "certain 'pious students'" deputized as "obstetricians" of the "new birth." Nevin was among the last of the students to struggle into "a feeble trembling sense of comfort — which my spiritual advisers, then, had no difficulty in accepting as all that the case required." Looking back, he blamed the evangelical method for encouraging an unhealthy "introverted self-inspection" and denying him the supportive environment of an ongoing sacramental religious community. Graduating in 1821, he returned home "a complete bankrupt" in health, "dyspeptic both in body and mind."[58]

After struggling for several years to discern his vocation, Nevin bowed to the expectations of family and friends and entered Princeton Theological Seminary, "the theological Athens of the Presbyterian Church." He excelled there and at the end of the three-year course was appointed to substitute for Professor Charles Hodge when he took a leave to study in Europe. In 1830 Nevin joined the faculty of Western Theological Seminary, recently established near Pittsburgh.[59]

There Nevin became widely known through teaching, preaching, and writing for religious periodicals. For several years he edited a weekly, the *Friend*, whose temperance and antislavery sentiments provoked controversy. Inwardly, however, he was increasingly disenchanted by developments within the Presbyterian Church, particularly the dominance of "the revival system" and growing contentiousness that culminated in schism in 1837. Although initially in sympathy with the reform agenda inspired by the Second Great Awakening, he eventually concluded that New England "puritanism" was trying to impose its ways on the rest of the country. Antipathy to the aggressiveness of New England reformers drove many defenders of local autonomy into the arms of the Democratic Party, and by the 1840s Nevin was one of them. Rejecting the fusion of evangelical reforms and the fulfillment of national destiny, Nevin put himself on the side of liberty and localism.[60]

Nevin's self-described personal awakening began when he discovered the German historian Johann Augustus Neander, a disciple of Schleiermacher. Neander's idealism and historicism raised intriguing new possibilities for Nevin, particularly Neander's interpretation of the history of Christianity as the ongoing embodiment of the divine principle in the world.[61]

Knowing of his interests, the Reformed synod dispatched the Reverend Samuel R. Fisher to persuade Nevin that it was his duty to accept the synod's call to the seminary. Agreeing that he had a divinely given mission, Nevin responded, "I give myself wholly to the German Reformed Church, and find no difficulty in making her interests my own." He found that German idealism meshed with his own sensibility, long uncomfortable with Presbyterian orthodoxy. In good dialectical fashion, Nevin's conversion would transform both himself and the Reformed Church.[62]

When Nevin and Rauch met, they immediately recognized their close philosophical and spiritual affinity. Nevin was impressed by Rauch's "learning and intellectual power" but nonetheless reported himself astonished the following year by the achievement represented in Rauch's *Psychology*. "I could not but look upon it as a strange and interesting fact," he recalled, "that the infant College of the German Reformed Church should have had placed at its head, there in Mercersburg — without care, or calculation, or consciousness even on the part of its friends generally — one of the very first minds of Germany, which under other circumstances might well have been counted an ornament and honor to the oldest institution in the land."[63]

Rauch's death in 1841 was a tremendous blow to the young institution. The immediate cause is unclear, but accounts commonly state that his health had been damaged by overwork. Rauch certainly pushed himself to the point of exhaustion, for in addition to teaching and to directing the college and at times the seminary, he published a number of articles and *Psychology*, prepared extensive revisions for a second edition, and nearly completed his book on ethics. Falling ill in 1840, he traveled to Saratoga Springs in an attempt to regain his strength but refused to put aside work on his book. After his return, he was often too weak to come to his classroom. Theodore Appel recalled, "He called us to his study, where he taught us as he reclined on his cot-bed." When Rauch developed a fever, death came suddenly on March 2, 1841.[64]

Two days later, trustees met in an extraordinary session, resolved to wear crepe to show their sorrow and respect for the learning and piety of their departed president, and adjourned to attend his funeral. At its end, a number of students assisted the faculty in carrying Rauch's body to a grove of trees on the college grounds, a grove that had been set aside for a cemetery.[65]

Even in death, Rauch continued to shape the character of the young institution. "His name became a precious legacy for the College," Nevin later observed, "more highly appreciated after his death than it had been during his life — inspiring those who had the care of it with large and generous views, and at the same time drawing respect to it from abroad." Rauch's example inspired students to greater scholarly ambition. Even his grave, "in its lonely retirement," became "a spot for musing meditation, the close of many a summer evening's walk — breathing as it were an atmosphere around it, that made its memory blessed."[66]

On April 7, trustees asked Nevin to assume the presidency of the college, "for the time being or until permanently filled." They acknowledged not only "the importance of immediate action" but the fact that in "the public mind" Nevin was already recognized as the appropriate successor. Nevin's selection to head both religious institutions of the German Reformed Church was, if anything, even more unlikely than Rauch's had been. Yet, in less than a year in Mercersburg, he had clearly become Rauch's obvious successor.[67]

Nevin agreed to take temporary charge of both institutions, refusing to accept additional salary for his enlarged responsibilities. He assumed that his new position would continue only until the German Reformed Church raised an endowment sufficient to pay a full-time president, but it began to seem that this arrangement might be necessary for some time to come. The following year, trustees asked him to continue "so long as it may be convenient for him" and granted him a scholarship — which he never used — in appreciation for his unpaid service. The funds thus freed up made it possible to attract Dr. Traill Green, a physician from Easton, Pennsylvania, to the long-vacant natural science position. In 1840 the college's search for a suitable professor of English and belles lettres had concluded with the appointment of Nevin's younger brother, William Marvell Nevin. (It was said that the previous teacher, a Middlebury College graduate and a Congregational minister, "could never become quite reconciled to the 'Anglo-German' character" of the college.) A Dickinson College graduate, William Nevin had tried medicine and law before settling on education. He taught at schools in Ohio and Pennsylvania before coming to Mercersburg. Many generations of students at Marshall and at Franklin & Marshall later recalled the younger Nevin's gentle, amiable manner as well as his high principles and crystal-clear mastery of the English language.[68]

John Nevin brought to Marshall College the prestige of his widening theological reputation but also drew it into controversies that swirled around the seminary. After completing revisions for a second edition of Rauch's *Psychology*, Nevin moved on to apply Rauch's ideas to religious questions such as revivalism and the role of the Church in spiritual development. Rauch's conception of the organic link between the ideal and the actual freed Nevin from the dualism of Common Sense philosophy. Combining Rauch's psychology with Neander's Christian historicism, he saw the incarnation of Christ as the historical actualization of the ideal. This Christological approach, in which Christ was the Hegelian synthesis, "the Word made Flesh" uniting spiritual and physical, formed the core of all of Nevin's subsequent writing. He insisted upon the importance of the institutional Church, its sacraments and scriptures, as embodiments of Christ in the life of the world.[69]

From his new perspective, Nevin challenged the legitimacy of revivals. In 1842 a minister preaching in Mercersburg concluded by calling those desiring to be converted to come forward. This was a popular revival technique, but Nevin was alarmed at its use in a Reformed service and refused to support the congregation's decision to call the minister as its pastor. The following year he attacked this practice and the entire New Measure "system" as "quackery" in a pamphlet, *The Anxious Bench*. He charged that revivals treated religion as "a transient excitement" that privileged personal experience and the efficacy of the individual will. In contrast, "the system of the Catechism" nurtured organic growth of "the life of God in the soul" through participation in a common life centered on the Church and the power of the Holy Spirit.[70]

The Anxious Bench anticipated Congregationalist Horace Bushnell's famous attack on revivalism in *Discourses on Christian Nurture*, published in 1847. Both Bushnell and Nevin provoked strong rebuttals from religious leaders, but Nevin's arguments had great influence within the German Reformed Church. Its journal, the *Weekly Messenger*, supported him, as did many ministers who had been uneasy about the growing popularity of New Measures. Nevin's writings inspired greater attention to the Heidelberg Catechism and the sacraments.[71]

In 1844 a young Swiss-born scholar named Phillip Schaff joined Nevin on the faculties of the seminary and college. Educated at the universities of Tübingen, Halle, and Berlin, Schaff had studied under Neander, among other prominent German theologians. His acceptance of the synod's call was the final step in the development of what came to be widely known as Mercersburg Theology, part of a Romantic, high-church movement that was also stirring in the Anglican and Episcopal churches. Sidney Ahlstrom, a historian of American religion, characterized the Mercersburg movement as "the most creative manifestation of the Catholic tendency in American Protestantism" and its leaders as "one of the most impressive constellations of religious thinkers in American history." In recent decades the movement has regained attention from a widening circle of theological scholars.[72]

Nevertheless, Mercersburg pronouncements met heated resistance. Schaff's inaugural address, "The Principle of Protestantism," emphasized the continuity of Christianity across the dividing line of the Reformation. Unaware of virulent anti-Catholicism in America, Schaff praised aspects of Roman Catholic tradition and concluded, "The Reformation is the legitimate offspring, the greatest act of the Catholic Church." He criticized the rationalism and "unhistorical and unchurchly character" of contemporary Protestantism. Nativists within the Reformed Church immediately attacked the work for its "Romanizing" tendencies and brought heresy charges against both Schaff and Nevin. After deliberating for four days in 1845, the synod found both men to be orthodox Protestants.[73]

Through extensive publications, Nevin and Schaff elaborated the implications of their incarnational and historical theology. Much of their work appeared in the *Mercersburg Review*, a quarterly founded in 1849 by the Marshall College Alumni Association expressly to publicize the two scholars' ideas. Denominational journals were preeminent channels of intellectual debate in the early nineteenth century, and the *Review* was widely read in religious and philosophical circles. More than a century later, one intellectual historian termed it "as sophisticated a work as America could then boast," and another gave it primary responsibility for giving "learned credibility to Hegelian theology."[74]

In keeping with his emphasis upon the Church's educational and sacramental function, Nevin saw one of his most immediate tasks to be building up its particular institutions, the college and seminary of the Reformed Church. He warned the synod in 1846, "It will not do to boast of our faith in God, if we put no trust in his institutions [for they exist only] for the accomplishment of its high and holy ends."[75]

The synod planned to celebrate 1841 as the centenary of the establishment of the Reformed Church in America and to raise at least $100,000 to build up its educational arms. At first, Nevin was confident that the goal could easily be met. "We have in the German Reformed body," he pointed out, "a hundred men who easily might give a thousand dollars each without being made perceptibly poorer by the offering, men, too, whose hearts are already sufficiently large and liberal for so generous a gift, if only they were brought to see fully the vastness of the interest which such a movement may be expected to secure." Despite vigorous efforts, however, more than a decade of effort brought the college less than $28,000, primarily from the sale of scholarships. The movement's failure shook Nevin's faith in his new Church home. "The great sin of the German Church is covetousness," he wrote several years later. "The duty of giving is little understood."[76]

Hoping to raise funds for a separate college building, trustees appointed a special agent. Without the board's authorization, the standing Building Committee over-optimistically purchased a supply of bricks, twice, it was said, what was needed for an appropriate structure. In any case, there was no money to erect a building, and Nevin called a halt to the project. The Building Committee was ordered to place a covering over the mountain of bricks on campus.[77]

The rift between Mercersburg citizens and Marshall College begun under Rauch seems to have widened under Nevin. The catalogue of 1844–1845 continued to emphasize that the college's location protected students by providing few "occasions for intellectual or moral dissipation," but the following year a statement was added warning parents and guardians to discourage "a free use of money" on the part of their dependents, and "especially not to authorize their contracting debts." Moreover, it emphasized that parents should "*refuse to pay debts contracted without their authority*." This would restrain those, presumably local merchants, "who [might have been] disposed to take advantage of students by alluring them to form such bills."[78]

In 1847, in the wake of increased incidents of student drunkenness, the faculty sent a strongly worded letter to two merchants, expressing "great pain and grief" at learning that they were furnishing students with "intoxicating drink of various kinds." "We had trusted that you would be more ready to cooperate with us in protecting the morals of the youth under our care," they wrote, "than to place temptation of this sort in their way." This practice not only promoted disorder but also threatened the school's reputation — and future enrollments. The faculty vowed to take legal action if these actions continued. One of those addressed was trustee William McKinstry, who did not respond to the letter.[79]

Meanwhile, students venturing into the village were often harassed by local youths trying to rouse them to fight. In September 1847, one student's response to provocation escalated into pitched battle when he was attacked by a group of local "mechanics," and other students came to his defense. The faculty only "slightly censured" the first student for having risen to the bait but suspended several others who joined the general melee. Such conflicts between college students and artisans were common in antebellum America but nonetheless suggest a particularly uneasy "town and gown" relationship.[80]

Student Life in the Early College

Despite its difficulties, Marshall College continued to develop as a cohesive community under Nevin's presidency. Many of its students planned to become ministers and closely followed their professors' theological debates. Yet they also carried on an independent intellectual life focused around the college's literary societies. Like the adult debate and discussion societies that were ubiquitous in antebellum America, the Goethean and the Diagnothian societies were officially dedicated to "the mutual improvement of . . . members in the exercises of Debating and Composition, in the graces of Oratory, the encouragement of Friendship, and the cultivation of Morality." Nearly all American colleges had such groups, with varying degrees of official support. It was widely believed that experience gained in literary societies complemented the formal curriculum in preparing young men to take their place in public life. At Marshall College these societies also played an important role in training its largely German American students to be leaders and spokesmen for their ethnic community. The faculty recognized the societies' significance in students' personal development and described them as "a department of education, to say the least, fully as important as any other belonging to the system."[81]

The formal curriculum required students to deliver public orations, but most of the students' experience in persuasive writing and public speaking was gained in the societies' regular Saturday morning meetings, when members presented their work and received criticism from their peers. Students also learned basic skills of civic activism by taking responsibility for running the organizations within the structure of written constitutions; offices rotated each month to give everyone experience. Meetings were supposed to be secret, though this often proved difficult because both groups met in the seminary's prayer hall. Each society was also responsible for building a library collection; both were far larger and more varied than that owned by the college itself. In 1844 the Goethean Society's collection of more than two thousand volumes included works of philosophy, natural science, art, religion, history, biography, geography, poetry, and "romance," which included novels by Cooper and Dickens.[82]

Both societies organized a full calendar of public events, including oratorical exhibitions and anniversary celebrations — for the Goetheans, held on Goethe's birthday, August 28, and for the Diagnothians, the Fourth of July — and in alternate years each hosted an address by a distinguished adult. Students dealt with subjects both topical and timeless. The Goetheans' New Year's Day exhibition in 1848, for example, included the orations "True Greatness," "The Crisis of American Youth," and "Plea for the Immigrant" and a debate: "Is the Monarchical or Republican the more stable form of Government?" Societies alternated in selecting commencement speakers until 1845, when the faculty claimed the right to choose the valedictorian. For a time in the 1840s, both societies had German auxiliaries that provided practice in writing and speaking in that language.[83]

Nearly all students joined one of the societies, if only because they dominated extracurricular life. In the interests of recruitment, upperclassmen made a great display of solicitude toward new students. As soon as the stagecoach stopped at the Mansion House in the center of Mercersburg, society members rushed forward to claim newcomers and carry their trunks to campus. This practice was called "electioneering," and an alumnus recalled that no national presidential campaign "exceeded in bitterness those waged in the college in behalf of the societies." The desire to win members minimized freshman hazing, and one of the rare cases of fighting among students in this period occurred when a member of one society impugned the quality of men in the other.[84]

Undoubtedly hoping to channel student energies in the service of the college, Nevin proposed in 1843 that the societies be encouraged to build their own halls as students had recently done at Princeton. His idea was that the buildings be identical in design and located so that they could serve as wings of a college building to be constructed when funds became available. Trustees agreed, promising $500 each if members raised at least $3,500 on their own. Subsequently, the match was changed to one thousand dollars' worth of the stockpiled bricks. To ensure uniformity, Professor Budd designed chaste Greek Revival temples with library and museum rooms in the lower story and a large meeting hall in the upper.[85]

Both societies took up the challenge with enthusiasm, not only contributing from their own funds but soliciting money in Mercersburg and in their home communities as well. They laid cornerstones in solemn ceremonies on their anniversary celebrations in 1844 and 1845. "Never before has the country beheld such an example of daring zeal for the interests of learning, in the same circumstances," Nevin commented. He predicted that having their own halls would encourage students to "feel still more than before their true weight and dignity" and would promote "among the Students that manly sense of self-respect and personal responsibility, which the government of the College is so much concerned to cultivate, as well as in the way of literary improvement generally." James Moore, of the class of 1843, devoted his last vacation before graduation to fund-raising throughout the region for the Diagnothian Society, and in 1847 it sent a member as an agent to raise funds in Washington, D.C. Inevitably, construction costs exceeded initial estimates, and despite the use of several scholarships granted by the trustees, debts persisted into the next decade.[86]

Other student activities included the preparation of occasional newsletters, copied manually with hand-colored illustrations. In the winter session of 1840–1841, rival newsletters, the *Ranala* and the *Rupjonjim,* published student attempts at standard literary genres. "Scene from an unpublished Tragedy" in the *Rupjonjim* ridiculed editors of the competing newsletter as so eager to become "popular Authors" that they neglected their studies. Another issue described the desperate fight against the preparatory building fire: "All ranks of individuals, Professors, Students, male and female, white and black, all lent their aid to stop the raging element, which sent forth its insupportable heat, defying any to face it." In the 1840s it also became traditional at commencement to publish anonymous satires known as "slubberdegullious." A parody Order for Commencement in 1846 commented upon the continued failure to construct a college building: the procession is directed to "proceed to the new College Building," where the orators would "mount the slab and discourse on 'The Sublimity of Vegetation.'"[87]

The college's relatively simple conditions lessened distance between teacher and student. One summer's day, for example, seminary and college students were offered a holiday from classes in exchange for helping to bring trees to plant on the grounds. Led by Nevin, the group hiked far into the mountains, collected appropriate trees, and carried them home on their backs. However tired and hungry, recalled an alumnus, they were spurred "in the midst of it all to see Dr. Nevin — '*venerabl* [sic] *nomen*' — bending under his load, 'faint yet pursuing,' pushing along as an inspiration & example to us all." They planted the trees the next day, and "a goodly number" survived; the author recalled that he visited his own for decades afterwards.[88]

Nevin continued the distinctive approach to collegiate education begun under Rauch, though he did make some changes. The 1847 catalogue explained that instruction methods combined "the advantages of a free oral communication with the use of a text book." Reliance on lectures alone did not work as well in America as in Europe, where students were generally better prepared. However, "mere slavish recitation," in which "both pupil and teacher remain bound perpetually to the leading strings of a text book," was "equally inefficient." Marshall College combined use of a text, "where one can be had," and "free conversational remarks more or less full, sustaining, or mod-ifying, or controverting the author's views, as the case may require."[89]

If anything, Marshall College became more self-consciously German under Nevin. He envisioned the college as a bulwark against the cultural hegemony of "Puritan" New England, fostering a distinct but equally American "Anglo-German" culture. He repeatedly asserted that the entire curriculum was influenced by German literature and philosophy, reflecting its "peculiar *genius*" as an "Anglo-German institution." He thought that the "marriage" of "the German order of thought" with the English was particularly appropriate to "the German spirit of Pennsylvania." Hence, lower classes studied German, and some lectures in the higher classes were delivered in German, as was chapel on alternate Sundays — "the language, under its finest form, serving its proper purpose as a vehicle of rich instruction for the soul."[90]

The college's distinctive philosophical approach did not escape Nevin's critics. The 1847 catalogue noted that attempts had "been made to awaken prejudice against the College" because it did not teach "the commonly received *Philosophy*, as it is termed" — in other words, the Common Sense school. Nevin explained that Marshall College did not teach "the metaphysics of *Locke* and Ethics of *Paley*" because they focused exclusively on "the world of mere matter and sense." Used consistently, this philoso-phy bred "skepticism and materialism." He found it especially perplexing that William Paley, so "rationalistic and unsound, in morals," should be "extensively honoured and trusted, in christian seminaries of learning."[91]

In keeping with Nevin's and Schaff's overriding interest in history, the teaching of history in the college expanded into all four years, divided into ancient, "biblical," Greek, and modern periods. Such extensive historical study was well in advance of most American colleges. Yale, for example, introduced history as a separate subject in 1847 but did not establish a professorship of history until 1865.[92]

Despite the accomplishments of Marshall College, its leaders felt a nagging sense of frustration at its failure to grow. Undergraduate enrollments increased from 74 in 1841–1842 to 109 in 1845–1846, but thereafter declined, reaching 79 in 1848–1849. Fall-ing tuition revenues left the college unable to meet current operating costs, let alone make improvements. Since 1836 the faculty had repeatedly pointed out the need for "philosophical apparatus," equipment for natural science teaching, but trustees were not able to raise the several thousand dollars required. In February 1848, the faculty resolved to petition the state legislature for $20,000 to aid in constructing a college building and purchasing scientific equipment. Two professors went to Harrisburg to present the petition. There "they found the members of the Legislature with whom they conversed, friendly to Marshall College, and willing to admit her claims on pub-lic bounty." But finding that the commonwealth's treasury was empty, the professors resolved to try again later.[93]

Soon thereafter, Traill Green, the natural science professor, announced that he was leaving to take up a position at Lafayette College. His letter of resignation ex-pressed regret that the decision had been necessitated by the continued "want of suit-able apartments and apparatus" for teaching science.[94] It took more than a year to find a suitable replacement. The mathematics professorship had also been difficult to fill after Budd's sudden death in 1846. Thomas Baird was hired in 1847, but he left in the fall of 1849 when trustees cut his salary. Nevin was forced to take on most of the mathematics classes himself.[95]

Nevin's health had begun to deteriorate, and he worried that the college would collapse if he could not continue as president. Always of a melancholy temperament, he was also deeply distressed by the incessant sectarian squabbling within Protestantism. In the words of a biographer, who knew him personally in this period, "At times it appeared to him that the whole enterprise upon which he had bestowed so much labor and thought might collapse at any moment."[96]

Nevin seems to have concluded that no college, however excellent, could thrive in such a remote location. A new railroad being built across the state bypassed Mercersburg, and as he explained in the *Messenger*, new modes of transportation and communication "make the whole world far more impatient than it was only ten years ago even, of all sorts of impediment and limitation in its movements." He became convinced that it was "in such circumstances a clear absurdity, to bury a College in some out of the way valley or village, where it can be reached only through hours of delay and miles of wearisome sand or mud."[97]

Lancaster, on the other hand, had a central location and excellent transportation connections. The Reverend John C. Bucher proposed a merger in 1849 between Franklin College and Marshall College to trustees of the Lancaster institution, but the idea had been under discussion for some time. Bucher lived in Mercersburg and had entertained its faculty in his home. The possibility of merger was raised during a conversation about Marshall College's financial predicament, and it was agreed that an overture should be made to Franklin College. But before Bucher had an opportunity to do so, he received a personal letter proposing a combination from the Reverend Samuel W. Bowman, rector of St. James Episcopal Church and secretary of the Franklin College board. The idea might also have been introduced through Nevin's connections in the Lancaster area, for his wife, Martha Jenkins, was the daughter of Robert J. Jenkins, an ironmaster and political leader from the area. To prepare the synod for this step, Bucher spoke at the annual meeting in October about the need to protect the Church's interests in Franklin College. That body responded by instructing its representatives to be alert in their custodianship.[98]

The Marshall College Board of Trustees met in special session on December 26, 27, and 28 to consider the proposal. Undoubtedly seeking to avoid the influence of local sentiment, they gathered in Chambersburg. Bucher and the Reverend J. F. Messick outlined proposed terms of a merger and presented a statement of Franklin College's finances. In return, Marshall's Financial Committee presented its own statement. Nevin himself spoke on behalf of a merger, emphasizing the precarious state of the college's finances. He expressed, according to Appel, "a clear intimation of Providence that it was a duty devolving on those present."[99]

Parties on all sides spoke. Diffidently but unanimously, the students expressed their hope "for a removal of the College from the village of Mercersburg to the flourishing

City of Lancaster." Even though it would mean abandoning the society halls that they had worked so hard to build, they were convinced that Mercersburg's inaccessibility prevented the college's growth. Should the move take place, they "pledged to devote [their] time and talents to the upbuilding of an institution, which [would] occupy a conspicuous position in the history of [the] country, and exert a widespread influence in the cause of education."[100]

Unsurprisingly, a town meeting in Mercersburg denounced the move as "a great violation of plighted faith" because of the "large sums of money" contributed to the college and seminary "with the most solemn assurance given that the said institutions were to be permanently located at Mercersburg." They also noted that the plan of union between Franklin & Marshall would create a college "completely sectarian in its character." David Krause, a Norristown lawyer, asserted that there was no legal impediment to moving, perhaps because most of the subscribed funds were never paid. One trustee wrote that, though the college had "warm and substantial friends" in Mercersburg, these were exceptions to "the growing indifference, if not opposition, shown towards [the college and seminary] by many in whose very midst these Institutions [were] located."[101]

Trustees voted, 16 to 10, predictably along town versus denomination lines, to investigate "the Expediencey of [the college's] Removal." In deliberations over the next two days, they examined terms of agreement proposed by Franklin trustees, making changes such as inserting the word "and" in the proposed title of "Franklin Marshall College." Most significantly, they added a requirement that the citizens of Lancaster raise at least $25,000 to pay for land and new buildings before the merger could be consummated. Finally, they asked that no decision be made until the synod gave its approval.[102]

The complicated merger process dragged on for more than three years. Protracted negotiations between committees of both colleges and the synod finally produced an agreement in which the synod would buy out the Lutheran interest by paying one-third of the value of Franklin College's assets to Pennsylvania College at Gettysburg. The first announcement of the merger in the *Lancaster Examiner and Herald* predicted speedy completion of the drive to raise the $25,000. "This sum is so small, in comparison with the vast benefits to follow its expenditure," the newspaper wrote, "that there be no doubt of its being promptly raised." James Buchanan, recently returned to his home in Lancaster after serving as secretary of state, was one of those who "took an active and liberal part" in the movement to attract Marshall College. He had purchased a scholarship when the school was in Mercersburg and now subscribed $1,000 to the fund. But most of the actual organizational work was performed by perennial local boosters such as Judge A. L. Hayes and Dr. John L. Atlee.[103]

Nonetheless, sentiment in Lancaster was by no means united behind the project. A public meeting to discuss the merger revealed strong opposition. Some thought classical education a luxury; some disliked the "sectarian" nature of the proposed institution; others wanted to use the Franklin College endowment to support the common school system directly or by establishing a school to train teachers. Still others warned darkly of disruptions by rowdy students. In the face of these protests, promoters of the merger decided to put the question to a public referendum. Active campaigning was necessary to win a narrow victory for the merger. Subsequently, Nevin found that he had to lobby actively in Harrisburg to defeat opponents' attempts to block a new charter for the combined institution.[104]

Slowed by community reservations, the fund-raising campaign dragged on for several years. In December 1850, a letter from "A Friend to Education" called for contributions, noting, "It would be to the last degree mortifying, if a project, so auspiciously begun, so excellent in itself, and promising so many advantages to our town and neighborhood should be suffered to miscarry." The author emphasized that, as a business enterprise, the college would "probably bring and spend as much money [in the community] as one of [its] Factories," that the college would bring to town "a body of educated men," and that it would form the capstone of the local school system. But not until the end of December 1852, and only with threats of legal action against subscribers, could the Collection Committee certify that the sum had been deposited in Lancaster banks. At the same meeting, Reformed trustees attested that the synod had paid the requisite one-third, or slightly more than $17,000, to buy out the Lutheran interest in Franklin College. (Ominously, despite "strenuous efforts," the synod had not been able to raise all the money, incurring a debt for the rest that it took another decade to pay off.) Finally, on March 1, 1853, the Franklin trustees authorized the chairman, James Buchanan, to execute a deed transferring all of the college's assets to the new institution known as Franklin & Marshall College.[105]

CHAPTER THREE

Early Franklin & Marshall
Upholding Tradition and Classical Education

—◦◦◦—

The preamble to the act of incorporation creating Franklin & Marshall College predicted that merging the institutions would confer "a more extensive benefit . . . upon the citizens of this State in the promotion of liberal & scientific learning." It touted Lancaster in classic booster terms as "central, healthy, moral & enlightened, so easy of access from most quarters, so able to assist in advancing the great objects in view & so liberal in offers of substantial aid." For the Lancastrians who made these liberal offers, bringing Marshall College to town was part of an ambitious revitalization program that included a gasworks, a new county jail and courthouse, and Fulton Hall, a grand fifteen-hundred-seat auditorium.[1]

Speaking at the hall's dedication in October 1852, Judge Alexander L. Hayes surveyed Lancaster's recent progress. The early years of the century had been hard, as improved transportation had weakened Lancaster's role as a commercial link between Philadelphia and the West. A new day dawned in 1845 when a group of citizens launched Conestoga Steam Mill, a steam-powered cotton factory. Two others soon followed; together the new mills employed eight hundred men and women.[2]

The college was the next phase in what Hayes depicted as "the intellectual and moral, no less than material improvement of our community." But he warned that the college's Lancaster promoters were still $2,000 short of the $25,000 needed to close the deal. He pointed out that this sum would immediately return to the local economy for construction of new buildings and that the school's annual budget of around $60,000 would be "money principally brought from a distance." From any point of view, it seemed a good investment.

The marriage of convenience between the colleges, or more properly between Marshall College and the Lancaster community, did not go smoothly. Local boosters did not understand the college's distinctive philosophical tradition and educational program nor anticipate how the Mercersburg spirit would dominate the merged institution. Tensions soon emerged within the board and between local citizens and college leaders. Franklin & Marshall's leaders steadfastly upheld the view of classical education developed at Mercersberg. For Reformed trustees, the college was crucial in preserving a German American ethnic identity rooted in the Church — even though the Reformed constituency was never lavish with financial support. Conflicting views of the institution's fundamental purposes ensured that its first decades were insecure.[3]

A Difficult Beginning

At the first meeting of the Franklin & Marshall Board of Trustees early in 1853, there seemed little eagerness to accept leadership responsibilities. James Buchanan, correctly anticipating an appointment from the new Pierce administration in Washington, tried to beg off the honor of election to the presidency of the board. He was overruled. The first three nominees for the office of treasurer refused the job, pleading lack of time. A nonboard member, Jacob M. Long, finally took it.[4]

Most alarmingly, John Nevin announced that he did not want to continue as president of the college. In the throes of a spiritual, physical, and professional crisis, he planned to retire. His research into the early Christian Church brought him to question fundamental Protestant tenets and to consider converting to the Roman Catholic Church. His theological works were under attack as pro-Catholic, and he may have felt that the new college would be hurt by his connection with it. Depressed by recent deaths among friends and family, he had a premonition that he would soon follow. He was also disappointed by Lancaster's slowness in raising the money needed to ensure the merger. Finally, he was demoralized by violent political conflict nationwide that seemed bent on destruction of the Union itself.[5]

Even so, Nevin was loath to see control of the college pass into the hands of his opponents. Theodore Appel, professor of mathematics at Marshall College, recalled that a minority at the board's organizational meeting hoped to take advantage of Nevin's refusal of the presidency "to reconstruct the faculty and to give it a new character and animus." They nominated the Reverend John F. Messick, a leading Mercersburg critic. Knowing this, Nevin allowed his name to be put in nomination, hoping that delay would allow trustees to find another candidate. After his election he took his time before formally declining. "It would be impossible for me to throw myself into it with that sort of confidence and animation," he explained, "that buoyancy of spirit and determination of zeal, which the success of the enterprise demands." At the next meeting, the board elected Philip Schaff. An attempt to "reconstruct" the faculty by removing several members was also defeated.[6]

Nevin also chaired a committee delegated to set up the new college's curriculum, system of discipline, and buildings. The board readily approved the first two items but was divided over plans for the college building. Some wanted to use the old Franklin college building near the center of town, while others extolled locations where they happened to own land. After seeking Buchanan's opinion, the board chose a ten-acre tract on the western outskirts of Lancaster, not far from Wheatland, his estate, because this tract occupied the highest ground in the area and was removed from the noise and distraction of the central business district. The site was commanding but barren of trees and reputed to have once served as the town's gallows hill. Moreover, it stood a mile from the center of town and half a mile from the nearest houses, connected only by a dirt road, which in wet weather became a mass of mud.[7]

The board was also divided on the building's design. The issue was more than a matter of taste, for architecture involved important cultural issues. The growing popularity of Gothic styles in antebellum America reflected a new romantic spirit that rejected Enlightenment rationalism and challenged the perceived materialism and instability of modern life. By the 1830s Gothic had begun to supplant Greek Revival in domestic architecture, and its appeal to tradition inspired several schools to construct Gothic buildings, among them, New York University, Yale, Harvard, and the Princeton Theological Seminary. In the 1840s, the high-church movement in the Anglican Church in England and the Episcopal Church in the United States embraced a Gothic style for church buildings because it offered more spiritual settings for worship. Like the Mercersburg theologians, Anglo-Catholics revived worship practices tied to historical Christianity and its sacraments, which had fallen into disuse because of association with Roman Catholicism. In fact, Nevin and Schaff were writing a new liturgy for the Reformed Church, restoring what they considered its true historical character, before "Puritans" stripped away ancient creeds and sacraments. Hence, it is likely that Nevin chose Gothic for the new college building because it embodied his larger vision for the Church. By literally setting a commitment to the historical Church in stone — or rather, brick — he might have hoped to ensure the college's fidelity to his vision even in his absence.[8]

The committee initially presented two proposals, one from the Baltimore firm of Dixon, Balbirnie, and Dixon. It had recently designed a Gothic Revival building for a Presbyterian church in Baltimore, and it is likely that the firm was invited to submit a proposal because Nevin wanted a similar design for the new college building. As constructed, College Building (see fig. 1) was only partially Gothic, for its main body, constructed in red brick, was a simple three-story rectangle with regular windows. The central entrance was decidedly Gothic, marked by a large square tower with tall pinnacles crowned by finials at each corner. The tower also featured a latticelike array of Gothic windows and two smaller turrets flanking the front door. A two-story wing at the back included a chapel with Gothic windows on the second floor. The building contained six classrooms, dormitory and dining rooms, and a kitchen in the basement; plans for a laboratory were dropped to cut costs.[9]

The plans were simple in comparison to many contemporary Gothic Revival churches, but board members seemed uneasy about the projected expense. By the board's next meeting, someone obtained another proposal, from the young Philadelphia architect Samuel Sloan, then in town to oversee construction of the county courthouse. Sloan's local commissions used more familiar styles: Fulton Hall was Italianate

FIGURE 1 *Goethean Hall, the College Building (Old Main), and Diagnothian Hall were designed by Baltimore architects Dixon, Balbirnie, and Dixon. The cornerstone of the College Building was laid on July 24, 1854, and the building was dedicated on May 16, 1856. The cornerstones of the literary society buildings were laid on July 20, 1856, and the buildings were dedicated a year later. This photograph was taken in 1858. Franklin & Marshall College, Archives and Special Collections. College Archives Photograph Collection.*

and the courthouse was to be a massive Greek temple. The board also asked the Balbirnie firm to prepare plans without "pinnacles, turrets, & other decorations." Local trustee David Longenecker pressed for Sloan's plan, but the board finally adopted the original Dixon, Balbirnie, and Dixon design, at a cost of $18,020. Plans to build houses for faculty had to be shelved.[10]

College finances also shaped the curriculum by setting the size of the faculty. Early on, the board authorized six professorships and two tutorships, to be filled in order "as the income of the institution shall warrant." The list shows the primary place of classical liberal education. First came the president, also serving as professor of moral and mental philosophy; then instructors of disciplines in this order: ancient languages and belles lettres; mathematics and "mechanical philosophy"; natural sciences; German literature, aesthetics, and history; and finally, "agricultural chemistry." Initial appointments, in addition to the offer of the presidency to Nevin, went respectively to William M. Nevin, the Reverend Theodore Appel, the Reverend Thomas C. Porter, and Adolph L. Koeppen. An eccentric and irreverent Dane, Koeppen had lived in Greece before coming to America and making his living as a public lecturer. After he appeared at the local lyceum, the Reverend Samuel W. Bowman persuaded the board to hire Koeppen for the college. The chemistry position was not filled, but the board created an unsalaried "chair of Anatomy & Physiology" for Dr. John L. Atlee, a prominent local physician and trustee. The appointments show that, unlike institutions like Princeton, where the Church connection was less official, Franklin & Marshall did not restrict faculty to members of its denomination. Later, the board ignored a local petition for a professorship "on the theory & practice of teaching." Thus rebuffed, area leaders organized the Lancaster County Normal School in 1855. When the Pennsylvania legislature established a state-regulated but privately funded system of teacher training soon thereafter, its leaders reorganized the institution as Millersville State Normal School in 1859.[11]

Franklin & Marshall formally opened on June 7, 1853. Trustees, faculty, and students proceeded from the old Franklin College building to Fulton Hall, where they were joined by the city's clergy, elected officials, and directors of the public schools. Citizens were said to have "filled the spacious Hall to its utmost capacity." With board president Buchanan presiding during a brief break from Washington, addresses were delivered by Judge Hayes and the Right Reverend Alonzo Potter, Episcopal bishop of Pennsylvania. Representing a county of over one hundred thousand and city of fifteen thousand, Hayes welcomed students and faculty. Lancastrians were a hard-working and prosperous people, he intimated, ready to be led to higher levels of improvement: "We trust [the college] will diffuse a taste for learning throughout this community; that it will give us a more exalted appreciation of the value of those large attainments in science, . . . that it will also imbue us with a taste for that higher literature, whose lofty mission is to infuse into the soul the admiration and love of the beautiful and the true."[12]

Responding on behalf of faculty and students, Nevin eschewed the typical celebratory rhetoric. He described Pennsylvania as a sleeping giant waiting to be awakened by higher education, which would tap the state's "latent spiritual capabilities" as well as its physical resources. But he warned against blind emulation of practices in other regions, especially New England. An "Anglo-German State," Pennsylvania should lead the way in forging an appropriate educational style. The "general course of studies," though in English, should be "of such reigning spirit that both the German language and habit of thought shall feel themselves to be easily at home within its bosom." If Franklin & Marshall College remained true to its mission, "if the city and county of Lancaster see proper," and if the "ambition and zeal of this old German community, now rolling . . . in wealth," united behind the college, Nevin envisioned it as "the ornament and glory, not only of this city and county, but of the entire Commonwealth of Pennsylvania." After much disappointment in institution building, he prayed that the college not be allowed to languish. Making a remarkably caustic allusion to the city's booster agenda, Nevin urged Lancaster not "to perpetrate the *bathos*, of surmounting for all time to come the most magnificent site in her neighborhood with a mere twenty-five-thousand dollar scheme of public improvement."[13]

The college held its first commencement exercises in Fulton Hall at the close of the summer session in August. As customary, each of the seventeen graduates delivered orations in an all-day program capped by Nevin's baccalaureate address. The day before, Marshall College alumni reorganized as the Alumni Association of Franklin

& Marshall College. Despite some residual unhappiness at the decision to uproot their beloved college, alumni vowed allegiance to the new institution. To help preserve their alma mater's special mission, they voted to continue publishing the *Mercersburg Review*, the influential journal of the Mercersburg movement.[14]

In October, among the students who gathered at the beginning of the new college year was fourteen-year-old Joseph Henry Dubbs. The youngest son of a Reformed minister in Allentown, he felt too young for college, but his teachers had decreed him ready to enter as a sophomore. His father had worked hard to raise funds for the merger and during a two-day journey to Lancaster was dismayed to find that no one they met had heard of the new college. Upon his arrival young Dubbs called on the faculty at their homes, to be examined for entrance. In a day of decentralized and unregulated secondary education, college leaders interviewed each prospective student personally before making admission and placement decisions. Dubbs's recollection of his experience offers a vivid institutional portrait:

> Prof. Wm. M. Nevin received me in his study, with all the courtesy and gentleness for which he was distinguished. He opened Virgil's Aeneid at random, somewhere in the fourth book, and said, "Read." I read the passage without difficulty, and he asked me a few questions. Then he gave me a rather involved passage from one of the orations of Cicero against Verres, over which I stumbled a little; but I caught up again in the Satires of Horace. After a little Xenophon and Homer the interview ended, and the professor bowed me out of the room.

For the mathematics examination, Professor Appel took Dubbs to the College Building to work a few problems on the blackboard. Dubbs presented a letter of introduction to Professor Porter and found that his scientific training was ahead of his class. His introduction to Professor Koeppen was characteristically eccentric. After hearing Dubbs read a few pages in German and asking a few questions, Koeppen inquired,

> "What is your name?"
> I told him.
> "Dubs, dubius," he exclaimed, "that means *doubtful* in Latin, but there is no doubt that you understand the German language. Pass!"[15]

Until completion of the new building, college activities were conducted in the old Franklin College building. Compulsory chapel began at 8:30 each weekday morning in Professor Nevin's recitation room on the first floor. After prayers, students took turns making oral performances: underclassmen recited standard literary pieces, and seniors delivered their own orations. A central part of the classical liberal arts curriculum, these exercises embodied its fundamental goal of fostering the orator, the man who combined virtuous character, eloquence, and civic responsibility.[16]

Students then separated into their respective classes — freshman, sophomore, junior, and senior — and moved as a group to recitations in the building's other three rooms. Outside of class hours, students were expected to spend their time preparing for their next recitations or working on literary society business. Those from out of town boarded with "respectable private families" selected by the trustees.[17]

Fewer students appeared than had been hoped — only fifty-three at the opening of school in June. Most had previously attended Marshall College, but many former students had left for other schools, frustrated at the long delay in moving to Lancaster. "Indeed," Dubbs observed, "it must be confessed that there was considerable disappointment. Lancaster was dissatisfied because the college had not brought more money; and the college was disappointed because Lancaster had not contributed a larger number of students."[18]

Disappointment deepened as it became clear just how meager was the dowry that Marshall College had brought to the marriage. During negotiations, trustees reported assets of more than $46,000, including notes, cash, and various forms of accounts payable, and an additional $28,000 in buildings, land, and library and museum collections. This was offset by about fifty perpetual scholarships. When trustees of the new institution tried to collect upon the assets, however, they seemed to dissolve before their eyes. The board offered to sell the college's buildings in Mercersburg to members of the Eastern Synod of the German Reformed Church for only $4,000, if they would establish a high school "of the first order which shall be considered a nursery or preparatory seminary for Franklin & Marshall College." But the board found no takers. A private academy purchased the buildings in 1857 for $8,000 in bonds and mortgages, though only $6,000 was ever collected. In 1853 an audit showed that Franklin College had contributed more than $40,000 in securities, and Marshall College less than $11,000. Moreover, "on examination," the auditors found that most of Marshall's investments were "of doubtful security & that the claims as presented appear of such a vague & doubtful character" that the auditors did not feel able to include them. At the same meeting came disappointing news of the synod's refusal to grant Schaff permission to leave his post as head of the seminary to become Franklin & Marshall president. It seems that his opponents feared that the position would provide too wide a scope for Mercersburg Theology.[19]

The faculty tapped Professor William Nevin to serve as president pro tem and went on with the college's day-to-day business. As secretary-treasurer, Professor Thomas Porter enrolled students and collected tuition and fees. But faculty energies seemed at a low ebb and the professors met infrequently during the winter term. Enrollments declined, with only three students from Lancaster.[20]

During this interregnum, the board splintered, each faction pushing different candidates for president. After his appointment as minister to the Court of St. James, Buchanan offered his letter of resignation to the college but was refused. In his absence the vice presidents presided over meetings, but there was no strong leadership on the board. The board failed to achieve a quorum at the next scheduled meeting in

December 1853 and did not meet again until the annual meeting at commencement in July 1854. There were only nine in the graduating class, but the occasion was somewhat redeemed by the laying of the cornerstone for the College Building. The following day, the board decided to refer selection of a president to a committee of seven, who were directed to identify "some eminent individual" upon whom all parties could unite. A day later the group recommended the Reverend Emanuel Vogel Gerhart.[21]

Although only thirty-seven, Gerhart had earned a reputation as a strenuous worker on behalf of his Church. One of Marshall College's first graduates in 1838, Gerhart had been the earnest young man described in the previous chapter who vowed to foreswear entangling alliances with the ladies. He was also one of the seminary students so taken with Rauch's theological positions that they brought heresy charges against Lewis Mayer. After teaching for a year in the preparatory school, Gerhart was sent to Ohio, where he worked tirelessly to build congregations and fend off the attractions of revivalism. As ethnic German populations expanded in the West, regional synods spun off from the parent Eastern Synod; in 1850 the Ohio synod founded Heidelberg College and Western Theological Seminary. Gerhart was called to be Heidelberg's president and professor of theology the following year and set about with characteristic vigor to build up the new institution.[22]

Attracted by Gerhart's successes and his distance from current theological battles, a weary Franklin & Marshall board elected him unanimously and wrote to inform him of his alma mater's call. "I was taken greatly by surprise," Gerhart responded. He was flattered but would have to decide between his present duty and the "call of a Mother to her son." After traveling to Lancaster to assess the strength of the board's support, he accepted the appointment in September. He was impressed by the college's potential to shape the future direction of the German Reformed Church and asserted that, next to his parents, "whatever [he was] intellectually, morally, or spiritually," he owed "to this Institution." He would not be able to take up his duties, however, until April 1855.[23]

Coming into Order

"I can well remember the day when [Gerhart] arrived in Lancaster," Dubbs wrote many years later, "a young man, with hair as black as the raven's wing." "Dignified and courteous," Gerhart "soon brought order out of what was almost chaos." The pace of activity quickened. The board directed the faculty to report annually on "the state of scholarship, morals, order, deportment & discipline, in the College" and to present its minutes and a record of students' "literary standing" for trustees' inspection. With arrival of a shipment of donated books from Europe, the faculty was directed to organize the college library and locate Marshall College's scientific equipment. Theodore Appel was tapped to serve as librarian.[24]

Gerhart moved vigorously to strengthen academic standards. Perhaps inspired by recent educational reforms at Oxford and Cambridge, he introduced a system of comprehensive written "test examinations" at the end of sophomore and senior years, with promotion or graduation riding on the outcome. "Tests" immediately became the students' most dreaded rite of passage and prompted intensive cramming during the spring of both years. Gerhart asked the board to appoint a visiting committee to observe oral examinations at the end of each term. He also hoped to strengthen admission requirements. Many prospective students tried to enter at the sophomore level or higher, but Gerhart insisted that they be required to enroll as freshmen unless they could meet all requirements for the advanced classes. "This involves the danger of losing students," he admitted. "I know of two whom we have lost during the year in this way." He was sure that "in the end the college will gain both in reputation and in the number of students."[25]

The College Building was completed in 1856, its position on the highest ground in the area affording an extensive view of open countryside for miles around. At its dedication ceremonies Gerhart employed the organic language for which Marshall College had been known, noting that the college, like a young tree, had survived despite the shock of transplantation: "It budded, blossomed and bore fruit in its season, and though the crop may not have been as large as on some former years, still the fruit was ripe and good." Looking forward, he envisioned generations of graduates shaped by the college's "internal vivifying spirit" and "all-embracing atmosphere." They would emerge "from these halls, with habits of thought and feeling, with principles of action, whose influence will be traceable through the whole course of their future life, whether they move the plane, or follow the plough, or minister at the bedside, or plead at the bar, or officiate at the altar."[26]

Marshall College's student literary societies followed the school to Lancaster. They began to raise funds for new buildings to replace those left behind; as in Mercersburg, these new structures would flank the main college building to create a typical college row. The board formally forgave the societies' debts and promised each $1,000 outright and a further $1,000 as an interest-free loan to aid in rebuilding.[27]

Both societies held cornerstone-laying ceremonies at the 1856 commencement. Students began fund-raising in earnest the following year, and seniors petitioned for a reduction in the number of recitations to allow time for the work. They also made personal pledges. "I made a subscription too large for my means," Dubbs recalled, "and as I did not like to ask my father to help me I stinted myself in many ways and actually seemed stingy, though I longed to be liberal." Some gave up smoking in order to pay their pledges.[28]

Society members were responsible for all details of the buildings' financing, construction, and furnishing and took great pride in the results. Designed by the firm that had done the College Building, the society buildings featured more elaborate Gothic detail outside and were decorated inside with frescoes and stained glass windows. "There is no part of the week which I look forward with such interest and pleasure as Saturday morning," one student wrote in 1857, "when our chosen Diagnothian band assemble in our own beautiful Hall to cultivate the garden of Literature."[29]

Societies continued to dominate student life. As Dubbs pointed out, "there were, of course, neither dances nor athletics to attract [students'] attention." Vigorous membership campaigns continued, with liberal amounts of free ice cream offered to lure new students. Dubbs joined the Diagnothians, his brother's society, immediately upon his arrival and read his first essay —"which I remember was fiercely criticised"— three weeks later. Weekly meetings at which students read essays, delivered orations, and debated were "spirited and energetic."[30]

"All the students in those days were philosophers, and could talk learnedly of the systems of Plato, and Kant, and Hegel," recalled William Rupp of the class of 1862, "and the society halls would often ring with debates and essays on the most abstruse philosophical subjects." Nearly everyone considered participation in literary societies essential for their "cultivation of the graces of oratory, the facility of composition, and skill in debate." The experience prepared graduates for leadership in public life, and many were renowned as orators.[31]

Most students lived with families in the community, paying around a hundred dollars a year for board and washing. For several years, the local Reformed minister, the Reverend Henry Harbaugh, unsuccessfully lobbied the Eastern Synod to build a dormitory where scholarship students could live together. Beyond the literary societies, a few informal clubs focused around boardinghouses. Inspired by other colleges in the region, several of these clubs organized themselves into fraternities. The first, a chapter of Phi Kappa Sigma, was founded in 1854. Soon thereafter, Dubbs was among a group of students initiated into the mysteries of Chi Phi by a visiting Princeton student. Later he recalled, "We had an excursion to Safe Harbor in the season of planked shad, and our supper there may perhaps be regarded as the first Chi Phi banquet." A third fraternity, Phi Kappa Psi, was founded in 1860.[32]

At a time when most students missed the supportive environment of home and family, fraternities offered a surrogate sense of brotherhood. Dubbs stressed that he joined a fraternity because Franklin & Marshall lacked the cohesive residential life that had existed at Marshall College. He always defended fraternities, arguing that "when properly conducted they are an undoubted means of social culture." But the faculty opposed them fiercely, fearing that they would weaken the literary societies. William Nevin deplored that fraternities based admission on "good fellowship" rather than "high literary or scientific attainments" and argued that they constituted "secret cliques" that injected divisiveness into the college community. In 1873 faculty began to require students to sign a pledge not to join unauthorized or secret organizations. This only drove the groups underground. "It is wonderful with how much mental reservation the boys sign this pledge," an alumnus later observed, "and how they fortify themselves with numerous *cautela* of their own secret implying."[33]

In their spare time many students read works of fiction, poetry, and history from the society libraries. Those contemplating legal careers attended local court sessions to observe trials. There were plays, concerts, and lectures at Fulton Hall, with celebrities of the day ranging from Henry Ward Beecher and Horace Greeley to Madame Lola

Montez. Living in town, students mingled freely with other young men and women of their own age through evening calls, dancing classes, and formal "sociables." One fine evening in June 1857, for example, junior Henry Douglas and a classmate escorted several young ladies to the College Building. They climbed the tower to view a splendid sunset and the surrounding countryside. Afterward the men treated the ladies to ice cream. Inevitably, students also found more illicit entertainment in local saloons and billiard halls.[34]

There were no organized athletics, but students played croquet, baseball, and lawn tennis on campus, walked and bicycled long distances, swam in the Conestoga River, and skated on local ponds. In 1862 Gerhart expressed hope that more consistent exercise would improve student health and discipline. A few colleges and academies had introduced gymnasiums to improve students' physical fitness, but if the college could not afford a building, Gerhart hoped that at least it could provide exercise equipment. Trustees instead authorized students to raise a subscription to buy equipment, but there is no record that they took up the opportunity.[35]

One favorite pastime was staging elaborate pranks. Breaking into the College Building, students at various times removed classroom furniture, stole the clapper of the college bell, blockaded recitation rooms with railroad ties, and left behind a calf borrowed from a neighboring farm. After participating in one such exploit, Henry Douglas crowed in his diary, "Such was the practical work of the first great piece of mischief that has been perpetrated in the new College building." He anticipated "a great fuss by the Faculty" and the possibility of being expelled if they were detected, but concluded, "We await the result, and rejoice in our Joke." (They were never discovered.)[36]

Hearing a rumor that a member of the senior class had been secretly married, a group of his friends staged a charivari, a venerable Euro-American folk custom. Gathering outside his boardinghouse at midnight, they serenaded the newlyweds for three hours "with flutes, bells, tin-pans & other noisy instruments." Douglas participated, recording in his diary his delight in the "calythumpian serenade" that "'made the night hideous' to the great annoyance of the peaceful citizens of the vicinity." Faculty investigated the matter and found the group, except one who had been "only an accidental spectator," guilty of "disturb[ing] the peace by a mock-serenade . . . in violation of the laws of the city & of the college" and also of entering a nearby tavern, though no alcohol seems to have been consumed. As punishment, students were required to admit "the impropriety of their conduct" and to face public "disapprobation" from the faculty at chapel.[37]

It is not surprising that students participated in traditional folk practices like the charivari, for most came to Lancaster straight from their families' farms. Not all were affiliated with the Reformed Church, but most bore German surnames, and for many English was a second language. Their background was dramatically highlighted in a sermon that Gerhart preached upon the death of Daniel Wommer, a sophomore who drowned in 1856 while swimming in the Conestoga River. Friends carried his body to his boardinghouse and laid it out on his bed, where the rest of the student body and indeed much of the community came to view it. "Men and women, from the neighborhood and from all directions, drew nigh," Gerhart recalled, "and looked on him in deep sympathy and sorrow. It was true: God had said, return thou child of man." The entire college accompanied the casket to the train station for the first stage of the trip home. Gerhart described the sad homecoming:

> In the dusk of the evening, the slowly-moving hearse and several carriages approached the large stone farm house standing on a little eminence to the right of the public road. The feeble mother came forward quietly through the green front yard, and enquired in German, *have you brought my child?* The aged father stood upon the door-sill, his white locks falling upon his shoulders, and looked, and sighed, but he did not speak. The hearse stopped; the gate was opened; the chairs were arranged in the room; his classmates carried him in through the yard, up the steps, over the porch, through the hall, and laid him down under the roof of his father and mother. . . . The neighbors began to crowd in, old and young, men and women. The coffin was opened; we stood around it in solemn silence; and when we saw the old man bend in inexpressible sorrow over the cold body of his son, and heard the feeble mother exclaim: "*Mein liebes Kind, o mein liebes Kind,*" we wept with those that wept.

Gerhart's sermon dwelled upon the suddenness of the tragedy, hoping to impress upon students the fragility of life. He stated, "Think of eternity, of God and of Christ, your faithful Savior, as you never thought before." He might be an administrator and a teacher, but above all else Gerhart considered himself pastor of his students' souls. The tragedy did not shock every student into propriety; a few days later, faculty called one to answer for being drunk and conducting "light & trifling conversation with ladies" even as the funeral procession left the railroad station.[38]

Under Gerhart, the curriculum continued to focus on classical languages and texts and mental and moral philosophy. He increased the study of logic, publishing in 1857 a translation of a German textbook for use by sophomores. As Frederick Rauch's disciple, he sought to keep alive the spirit of German idealism embodied in Rauch's *Psychology*, which long continued as a standard text at the college. But in Gerhart, Rauch's ideas assumed greater religious intensity. His inaugural address stressed that every college must have a "vital principle," which sets its structure, government, and curriculum, provides "the general spirit in which all subjects are investigated and taught," and defines the college's sense of an "ultimate end." He believed that the vital principle of the new college must be the person of Jesus Christ, "who sustains an internal relation to all departments of science as really as He does to the structure of the Bible." Gerhart increased the religious content of the curriculum by adding weekly recitations in biblical antiquities for freshmen and biblical history for sophomores.[39]

As professor of mental and moral philosophy, Gerhart lectured to seniors on philosophy, logic, ethics, and the traditional "evidences of Christianity." "We recognized him as a splendid teacher," Dubbs recalled. He noted, however, that Gerhart was often away from the college on fund-raising expeditions. The literary societies' new halls cost much more than expected, and when unpaid contractors threatened legal action, Gerhart traveled throughout the region, even going door to door, to solicit contributions.[40]

Except for German language and literature, the required curriculum was typical antebellum collegiate fare, though the faculty's frequent use of lectures was unusual. Famed for his elegant and witty lectures on English literature, William Nevin used traditional recitation to teach Latin and Greek. But he encouraged or at least tolerated cooperative forms of informal learning. At examination time, he let it be known in advance that passages to be translated would be written out on his classroom blackboard. The room was located on the second floor but could easily be reached via the roof of a small shed used to store Professor Porter's chemistry equipment. Students regularly organized expeditions to copy the passages, make translations, and distribute them to class members. As Nevin could hardly have remained ignorant of these endeavors, it is likely that he felt that the charade served an educational purpose.[41]

Like most antebellum colleges, Franklin & Marshall had few resources for laboratory teaching, but in Thomas Porter it had a botanist who had connections to a wider scientific community and whose encyclopedic *Flora of Pennsylvania* was recognized for its contribution to the development of systematic botany. He had been pastor of a Reformed church before joining the Marshall College faculty. According to Dubbs, Porter's reputation was such that "it was recognized as his duty to accept the call" to teach for his denomination's college. To build a teaching collection, he solicited contributions from colleagues and took students on expeditions throughout the region to gather botanical specimens. He led a group of aspiring local naturalists in organizing the Linnaean Society to promote study of the area's flora and fauna. On Arbor Day in 1857 he persuaded students to purchase and plant trees on college grounds to form its first arboretum. At a time when learned gentlemen often had wide interests, Porter also published literary translations of works ranging from Goethe's *Hermann und Dorothea* to Schaff's *The Life and Labors of Saint Augustine*.[42]

In 1856 the college basked in the reflected glory of its board president, James Buchanan, returned from England as a favorite for the Democratic Party's presidential nomination. When word of his nomination reached Lancaster, students raced to Wheatland with the news, and many others cheered outside his house. His prominence also brought political turmoil to campus. One graduate used his commencement address to denounce Preston Brooks's attack upon Charles Sumner on the floor of the Senate. Buchanan, prominently seated on the platform, seemed unperturbed but afterward retorted that Brooks had been strongly provoked. In the fall, Buchanan delivered an address at the college, outlining his hope to find common ground between the South and North. As he left for Washington to assume the presidency, college students joined the crowds accompanying him to the train. A ten-man "Student Escort" traveled with him all the way to Washington.[43]

Students debated the looming national crisis at literary society meetings, where the presence of a substantial minority of southern students sometimes made for heated exchanges. In 1856, 15 percent of the student body (eleven of seventy-three) were from Maryland and Virginia. Dubbs recalled that southerners "were apparently 'spoiling for a fight,' and took offense at the slightest allusion" to slavery. This inevitably led to "personal conflicts" that occasionally needed faculty intervention. Even so, in March 1858, Diagnothians debated Kansas's admission under the controversial Lecompton Constitution, without resorting to open conflict. Faculty did not discuss politics in class but were rumored to be politically divided.[44]

Gerhart hated any sort of controversy and disorder, especially student rowdiness or drunkenness. He lamented when faculty failed to attend daily prayers and confided to his diary his disappointment that the new examinations seemed "to be a bore to the professors." "Would resign if I could do it with a good conscience," he confessed in 1857.[45] He became ever more frustrated at the college's chronic state of financial uncertainty. Despite board assurances and his repeated admonitions that the endowment needed their assistance, little progress was made in fund-raising. A plan to sell temporary scholarships raised only $5,150 in three years, while costing $1,000 in expenses.[46]

The financial panic of 1857 brought down several Lancaster banks, taking part of the college's endowment with it. Trustee David Longenecker, president of the Lancaster Bank, fled from town after his bank failed. The Executive Committee could borrow only $1,500 of the cost of finishing the College Building and was forced to take nearly $7,000 out of the endowment. The board had little choice but to approve the move but amended the charter to expressly forbid such actions in the future.[47]

By ruining a number of promising local businesses, the panic's long-term financial effects also influenced the college's future prospects. For the rest of the century Lancaster had few substantial corporations. By 1860 ownership of the cotton mills, its largest industry, passed into the control of Philadelphians. Lancaster attracted a number of small-scale manufacturing firms, but their proprietors showed little interest in higher education. Lack of concentrated local capital hampered development of the kind of elite that supported expansion of other colleges in the region.[48]

In 1859 Gerhart completed a project that he and other Marshall College alumni had contemplated for years — bringing to Lancaster the remains of Marshall's revered first president, Frederick Rauch. John Nevin's eulogy capped a service at the German Reformed Church. Describing the "great and good" man's life and ideas, Nevin hoped to instill in the new community the same reverence that had sparked the old college's unique spirit. "In some sense," he mused, "[Rauch's life] may be regarded as continuing itself in the history of Marshall College, and in the successive classes of students who have gone forth from it year after year, bearing along with them more or less of its spirit into the world." Now, Nevin seemed to be saying, Rauch's remains constituted the old college's greatest contribution to the assets of the new institution: "one of its chief historical treasures indeed, more valuable than any other portion of its literary apparatus."[49]

Years of Civil Turmoil

As war threatened, the college was surviving but not thriving. Enrollments had risen gradually. Gerhart reported to the board that while other institutions had "been entirely suspended by our national troubles," and others "seriously crippled," Franklin & Marshall "has gone forward as usual." Faculty were determined to continue despite national unrest, but it was impossible to remain entirely oblivious to events. Returning from the 1860 Democratic National Convention in Charleston, South Carolina, trustee John Cessna predicted war if the Republicans won the election. Students joined the crowds welcoming President-elect Lincoln in February 1861, and a few days later the student body marched en masse to Centre Square in the heart of Lancaster to welcome President Buchanan home from Washington. "What an experience to a country lad to be in the procession!" a member of the class of 1863 recalled. Once war began, a military camp was established near campus and students took up drill on their own. At one point during the war, Diagnothian Hall was commandeered for use as an infirmary for the Fourteenth Regiment of Pennsylvania Volunteers. Some in the community considered the presence of the former president at the head of the board to be an embarrassment, but Buchanan's repeated offers to resign were staunchly refused.[50]

In the first years of the Civil War, increased patronage by local students offset a decrease in the number of southerners. Even so, a handful of Virginians and Marylanders remained throughout the war, giving an uncommon degree of intensity to debates. "I believe that there were better speeches and recitations made at the time by the students than ever before or since," recalled a wartime student. "We were floating on the outward crest of the wave of nervous excitement." In 1861–1862, college attendance topped one hundred for the first time since the merger. Yet because most students attended on scholarships, the slight growth produced little additional income, and the college repeatedly ran deficits. Faculty salaries represented the greatest expense, and deficits generally meant that they went unpaid. By 1860 the faculty was due more than $1,600 in back pay.[51]

The board decided to cut costs by cutting Adolph Koeppen's position. Trustees had considered the action for several years, for in addition to his irreverent attitudes on religion, Koeppen was poor at maintaining order in his classes. In the spring of 1861, they were so rowdy that a group of the more studious juniors petitioned to be excused from history lectures. The petitioners had tried to quell disruptions by passing a resolution among themselves "in favor of order." But "disorder . . . [grew] to such an extent that it [was] impossible to derive any benefit" from the class. When Koeppen's freshman class also began to run riot, Gerhart decided to let him go. Porter and Gerhart took over his classes in German and Greek, and John Nevin was hired part-time to teach history. The decision was controversial, for Koeppen's erudition was widely admired. In his commencement address, valedictorian Adam C. Reinoehl criticized the board's action. When Reinoehl continued to speak after Gerhart ordered him to stop, the board withheld his diploma and expelled him from the college.[52]

John Nevin had moved to Lancaster in 1855 and built a home, Caernarvon Place, on a small farm near Buchanan's. Continuing to write on religious questions, he substituted for Gerhart at the college during his fund-raising absences. After Buchanan retired to Wheatland in 1861, he and Nevin became close friends. Nevin led a movement to organize a new congregation, St. Stephen's, which worshipped in the college chapel and was jointly served by faculty who were ordained ministers. As the only Reformed church in the neighborhood, it attracted a small congregation of neighbors that included Buchanan.[53]

The year 1863 marked a watershed in the Reformed Church, as Eastern and Western synods united under the general synod and were rechristened as the "Reformed Church in the United States." Nevin's preeminent position in the denomination was highlighted when he presided over the convention marking the tercentenary of the adoption of the Heidelberg Catechism, a founding document of the Reformed Church. Nevin's selection was a fitting recognition of his role in restoring the catechism to a prominent place in the denomination's awareness.[54]

In anticipation of the tercentenary, college supporters lobbied to make Franklin & Marshall one of the primary beneficiaries. They were unusually successful: of more than $100,000 raised, the college received $30,000. The windfall significantly improved the financial affairs of the college, enabling the treasurer to announce in 1865 that it was out of debt.[55]

The 1863 Tercentenary Convention was a high point in Franklin & Marshall's young history, but the spring and summer of 1863 saw a change of fortune. After the Union instituted a draft, enrollments plummeted, as many students preferred to enlist rather than wait to be drafted. In mid-June, Confederate General Jeb Stuart's cavalry raided Pennsylvania, and students responded to the governor's call up of the state militia. Then came word of Robert E. Lee's invasion of Pennsylvania. As Gerhart explained to the board, "the excitement and confusion that prevailed" in Lancaster and in other portions of the state "rendered it impracticable to maintain the discipline of the Institution." The faculty closed the college, "after mature deliberation," on June 26. Several anxious days followed, filled with rumors of nearby fighting and then news of a great battle being waged at Gettysburg. After the battle, Gerhart carried medical supplies to Gettysburg and worked in hospitals there. Commencement nonetheless went on as scheduled on July 29, though seniors were not required to deliver the usual orations.[56]

The following July, in 1864, students again petitioned the faculty to suspend classes because they wished to join the fight to repel the Rebel invasion of Maryland, and because "the agitation & anxiety of the public mind were so great as to render study impossible." After due deliberation, the faculty agreed. When news of Lee's surrender reached Lancaster early on the morning of April 11, 1865, "so great was the excitement" that classes were again canceled in favor of a meeting in the chapel "for the purpose of giving expression to the common joy." The celebration consisted of impromptu patriotic addresses from the faculty and collective renditions of "several national airs."[57]

Debating the Future of the Institution

It is not surprising that enrollments fell in the last years of the Civil War. Yet at its meeting in July 1865 the Alumni Association expressed alarm at the decline and urged the board to find out why "our beloved Alma Mater" was failing to thrive. At its annual meeting at the same time, the board finally accepted Buchanan's resignation and elected in his place John Cessna, a Marshall College alumnus, class of 1842. A poor farm boy, Cessna had routinely walked the thirty miles between his home and Mercersburg. After graduation he served as a tutor for a year while studying law, then launched a career that brought wealth and a prominent role in state politics. He was twice elected Speaker of the Pennsylvania House of Representatives and served several terms in the U.S. House. He played a prominent role in his region, founding several local railroads and attracting a long-distance line, the Harrisburg and Western, through Bedford and Somerset counties.[58]

The board asked Cessna to head a committee "to investigate the general condition of the college." The committee concluded that at a time of rising expectations and competition from other Reformed schools, substantial improvements in facilities and curriculum were needed to attract students. Lack of dormitories left students isolated and weakened the faculty's influence: "There is no bond of union established between Professors and students," committee members argued, "and there is not that opportunity afforded for mutual intercourse which formed a leading feature in the success of Marshall College." The committee therefore recommended building student residences and houses for faculty on campus. (In the short run, faculty agreed to visit students in their rooms at least once every two weeks.) The committee also advocated making the preparatory program an official part of the institution with its own building on campus.[59]

The committee estimated that these improvements would cost $200,000, including $50,000 for new buildings. To raise that kind of money in Lancaster and within the Reformed Church, the college needed to be more responsive to public demands. Noting "the want of interest and sympathy" in the local community, reflected in a lack of financial support, the committee urged changing the curriculum to appeal to a broader audience. "The wants of our age are in a great degree practical," it asserted, "and if we would secure the patronage of the general public, we must pay more regard to studies of that description." The entire curriculum should be "reconstructed," study of mathematics reduced and English literature and "practical Science" increased.[60]

Such criticisms of the classical curriculum were increasingly common in the mid-nineteenth century. They prompted experimentation with new approaches among educational institutions of many kinds. Formerly classical colleges tried adding preparatory programs, electives, new degree courses (such as the bachelor of science, literature, or philosophy), partial courses (in which students studied only one or two subjects), coeducation, and vocational programs in education, engineering, and agriculture. Many Lancastrians resented Franklin & Marshall's refusal to offer vocational programs, and a minority on the board still opposed the dominance of Mercersburg Theology. The current crisis seemed to offer both groups an opportunity to change the college's direction.[61]

At special meetings in January and May 1866, the board moved to take greater control. Trustees prohibited faculty from serving on the board, advocated setting up a visiting committee to observe examinations, and initiated a general reorganization by vacating all faculty positions. The board resolved to add studies in political and constitutional theory and called for introducing, "at an early day," a three-year "scientific course of instruction" leading to a bachelor of philosophy degree, "similar to that provided in other colleges."[62]

Yet this attempt to alter Franklin & Marshall's direction failed just as it had in 1853. Reformers seemed unable to put forward attractive candidates to lead the institution. In fact, many on the board believed that a major fund-raising campaign would succeed only if John Nevin himself could be persuaded to resume a prominent role in the college. When the dust finally settled after several rounds of nominations and negotiations, Nevin agreed to become president and professor of the philosophy of history and aesthetics — an unusual combination for a classical college but one that highlighted history's central role in the curriculum. Gerhart continued as vice president of the faculty and professor of mental and moral science. All faculty were restored to their places, except for Thomas Porter, who in the midst of the turmoil took a position at Lafayette College, his alma mater. As usual, the natural science position proved the most difficult to fill at the low salary offered.[63]

Now a vigorous sixty-four and much improved in health, Nevin explained that he accepted the call only as part of a general movement promising to give the college the resources it so desperately needed. He warned that he accepted "provisionally and conditionally," dependent upon others' readiness to participate in the effort. He asserted, "Too much account is made of my name." Without general support, it would not be enough "to rescue the Institution from comparative insignificance."[64]

After electing Gerhart as vice president, the board passed a resolution praising his service to the institution. It is not clear what he made of his demotion, but he may have felt relief, for he had repeatedly confided to his diary his unhappiness with the burdens and vexations of the presidency. In 1868 the General Synod tapped him for a professorship in the seminary, and he departed for Mercersburg.[65]

To improve its own governance, the board cut the number of trustees from sixty to thirty, maintaining a requirement that two-thirds be members of the Reformed Church. Seeking to strengthen the synod's sense of ownership, the board offered to give it power of appointment, retaining authority to fill interim vacancies and dismiss members for nonattendance. The Eastern Synod accepted and resolved to raise at least $100,000 toward the college's endowment, to better enable Franklin & Marshall "to compete with the leading literary institutions of the State, and to make every way worthy of its past history and character, and adequate to the growing wants of the German Reformed Church in this country." In practice, however, these changes were largely cosmetic. The board continued to be, in effect, self-perpetuating: each year the synod simply approved its slate of nominees.[66]

Despite assurances from the synod, strenuous intradenominational conflict limited its ability to increase financial support. In 1866 the General Synod approved for optional use a new liturgy developed by Nevin's committee. A minority passionately opposed even this limited acceptance, charging that the liturgy made "unsafe" changes in worship and doctrine. Intradenominational contention not only hampered fundraising but inspired the founding of competing institutions. Objecting to use of the liturgy at the college and seminary, dissenters founded Ursinus College in 1869 to represent their low-church principles. The Reverend John H. A. Bomberger resigned from Franklin & Marshall's board to become the first president of Ursinus, and sympathetic congregations transferred their pledged support to the new institution.[67]

At the end of his first year as president, Nevin announced that he had seen enough "vigorous movement" toward financial security to stay in the job. Even so, he declined to be formally inaugurated, feeling that promises had been incompletely fulfilled. He also made it clear that he would not carry out the board's mandate for curricular change. This was not the time for "the establishment of new professorships," he insisted, "but the proper strengthening of the Faculty as it now stands." The college had vacancies in science and German because of its low salaries. "And it is perfectly vain to expect that competent men with families can be got now to fill our vacancies for $1200," he chided. "It is not a living salary; & it is a shame for us to think of exacting such service on such terms."[68]

Trustees responded by raising faculty salaries generally to $1,500 and Nevin's to $1,800, pledging to make up any deficits among themselves. To hold costs down, Nevin advocated hiring "unmarried" adjuncts at low salaries. Meanwhile, the board learned that hopes for new dormitories would have to be deferred in favor of expensive repairs to the College Building. After only sixteen years, gaping holes had appeared in the roof, bricks were missing from the walls, and some of the capstones on the tower had fallen off. Hoping that more polished landscaping would appeal to prospective students, the committee gathered a group of "friends of the Institution" to contribute to a special fund for that purpose.[69]

Upholding the Liberal Education Tradition

In the absence of an inaugural address, Nevin presented his vision for Franklin & Marshall in a series of lectures and speeches delivered at ceremonial occasions. The college opened each term with a formal assembly at which a faculty member addressed students on a topic chosen to set a proper intellectual tone. In September 1866, Nevin's "Master and Disciple" explained education in terms nearly identical to those Frederick Rauch had used three decades before — as the result of a relationship of minds. "It must be mind working upon mind; intelligence meeting intelligence; will infusing itself into will," Nevin stressed. Education could not be imposed from above without the student's active participation. "Indeed, their training is a failure," he warned, "if it do not bring them continually more and more to be a law to themselves, to do their own thinking, and to will their own working." Hoping to reduce rowdy outbursts, he emphasized that "self-government" was far more desirable than "hard-fisted discipline, laid on heavily from without": "We wish to have as little as possible to do with the espionage, the surveillance, the inquisitorial trials, or the penal visitations of a college system of police. Spare us, we beseech you, the misery and pain of all this."[70]

The following summer, Nevin took the occasion of the first commencement of his presidency to stress his determination that there would be no educational experimentation at Franklin & Marshall. He acknowledged, even celebrated, that the recent war had ushered in a new era in world history. But he saw this as reason to reaffirm rather than alter the college's mission to uphold the time-honored place of liberal education.[71]

According to Nevin, the end of the war had opened "a new era of education" in which "new zeal, new liberty, new activity" were being enlisted in its support. Even in Pennsylvania, "proverbially slow and niggardly heretofore in the cause of letters," money was flowing into educational institutions as never before. Yet Nevin regretted that this interest focused only on the utilitarian, material ends of education. He declined to prescribe for other institutions: "It is no business of ours, to denounce or oppose the changes by which other colleges are seeking to adapt themselves to the educational demands of this spirit." But the way of innovation was not to be his college's. He was certain that "our vocation" was "altogether different": to remain "unswervingly true" to the college's original "reigning purpose and character."[72]

In a statement that was reprinted in the college catalogue for many years and frequently quoted elsewhere, Nevin laid out his fundamental rationale for liberal education:

> Let it be our ambition, then, and our care, to maintain in vigorous force here, an institution that shall be devoted supremely to liberal education, in the old and proper sense of the term; *liberal*, as being free from all bondage to merely outside references and ends, and as having to do, first of all, with the enlargement of the mind in its own sphere. This, after all, must remain the true conception of education forever.

No purely "utilitarian, practical, and professional" education could be sufficient "to complete the organization of a true human culture." If everyone else focused on "the outward," it was "all the more necessary" that some few "make all in all of the inward." Nevin continued,

> Never was there a time, when there was more room or more need for education, regarded simply as a discipline of the soul for its own sake. Agriculture, mining, and civil engineering, are of vast account; but not of so much

account, by any means, as the development of a strong and free spirit in men themselves.

In declining to follow popular trends, Nevin claimed a special niche within a changing educational market. Like small manufacturers who survived the rise of mass production by focusing on specialized needs, the small college would continue to observe the labor-intensive craft of cultivating minds, one at a time.[73]

Nevin continued his defense of liberal education in a series of articles for local newspapers in 1869. He explained differences between the college and newer educational institutions — high schools, normal schools, and professional schools — all of which had their own purposes and proper spheres. A college education must be independent of and precede professional training in order to provide "a common liberal culture" upon which all professions depended for "their full dignity and strength." Classical subjects were best suited to the cultivation of a mind capable of taking the broadest possible view of knowledge, of transcending narrow and selfish interests, of "*estimating aright the comparative values of the different kinds of truth.*"[74]

According to Nevin, educational distinctions had become blurred as a host of occupations claimed the status of "learned professions"— producing "our Agricultural Colleges, our Commercial Colleges, and our Polytechnic College of every grade and type." Nevin feared that if all were housed in the same institution, the professional interest would, like "a Jonah's whale," inevitably swallow up the liberal. The "Providential mission and duty" of Franklin & Marshall required it "to keep to our old character and to sail in our old course." He hoped that the specialized role of Franklin & Marshall formed its claim "to the favor and patronage of the community."[75]

After becoming president, Nevin introduced lectures on the philosophy of history in the junior year, in addition to instruction in ancient, medieval, and modern history. Sometimes referred to as "the Science of History"— using science in its older meaning of a system of knowledge — the course was moved to the sophomore year in 1871. It was customary for college presidents to deliver capstone lectures to seniors in philosophy and ethics to show the connections between all the forms of knowledge that they had studied. Rather than waiting until the senior year, Nevin's sophomore history course offered students an overarching philosophical framework with which to integrate all instruction to come.[76]

Nevin's lectures showed the close ties between his idealist philosophy and his commitment to liberal education. For Nevin, history was the "*Progression or Onward Movement of Human Life*" that revealed "the universal relation of the system of nature to the system of living mind in the economy of the world." Liberal education in turn shaped a mind, or whole personality, into one capable of perceiving this true "economy." History was not a mere "accumulation of facts," he pointed out. "The main thing always is the life which is thus breathed into the facts, from what we must call the ideal side of their science." This ideal side came only from the mind "by which they are apprehended and converted into knowledge."[77]

For Nevin, the study of history was the most important subject in "the liberaliza-
tion of mind." Liberal culture and historical science were closely connected: "The grand
utility of history is the science itself introduced into the mind." It produced the "historical spirit," which he defined as "a sympathy with the organic movement of human
life, in which the old and new are continually joined as one and the same existence."
He believed that the hope of the future rested upon expanding this spirit, "the main
power of modern culture and the main hope of the world" in the growing struggle
"between mechanical tradition on the one hand, and blind or reckless radicalism on
the other."[78]

Fund-Raising Frustrations

Repeatedly, however, attempts to build up Franklin & Marshall College were launched
in hope but fell far short of expectations. College leaders tried many approaches to
raising money. An 1869 campaign launched with Eastern Synod approval asked each
baptized member of the denomination to contribute at least one dollar for the college's endowment. But agents found that so many institutions and projects sought
churches' support that they could not get "a proper hearing." The Fund-Raising Committee chairman concluded that energy spent on the Dollar Plan would have been
more productively spent in pursuing large donations.[79]

To give local citizens "some definite object or special inducement" to contribute,
one agent offered free tuition to students from Lancaster city and township once
$15,000 had been contributed to the college. With $50,000, the entire county would
receive free instruction. Some $7,800 was quickly pledged and a special fund-raising
committee considered making the same offer to towns and counties throughout the
region.[80]

But Reformed authorities opposed such appeals to nonchurch constituencies.
Many at the synod feared that the local free tuition plan would create "the feeling among
a large part of our people that the College was no longer an Institution of the Church,
but belonged to the world." Synod leaders suggested instead offering free tuition for
young men preparing for the ministry if $100,000 were raised for the endowment.
They felt that Church members would be ready to support the college if they fully understood that its "*chief object* . . . is to provide the Church with an educated ministry
and membership, as it has been doing." Moreover, the synod warned not to set fund-
raising goals too high, pointing out, "Our people are mostly engaged in agricultural
and not in commercial pursuits." Asking for too much "will discourage them, and
thinking that the amount cannot be raised and will fail, they may not give at all." In
any event, the endowment project was abandoned when Lancaster school directors
also rejected it.[81]

Changes in secondary education presented challenges to classical colleges. The
emerging public school system often did not prepare students for classical higher
education, even while driving private academies that did so out of business. To ensure

a supply of students, many colleges established their own preparatory schools or satellite institutions. At Franklin & Marshall, an enthusiastic young minister hired to raise endowment funds told the board in 1872 that ordinary church members were most interested in a secondary school. But it needed to be a separate institution with its own faculty and building where "students from abroad [could] be provided with a *home* under the immediate care and supervision of their teachers." The Building Committee urged acting immediately "to meet the aroused feeling of the Church," noting, "Unless earnest efforts are put forth on our part to meet and satisfy its demands, it will seek for what it wants in other and accessible places." Under the committee's prodding, the board formally established Franklin & Marshall Academy and borrowed up to $15,000 from the endowment for a new building to be repaid with interest from future fund-raising. Nevin and the faculty urged waiting until money was in hand, but, as Appel recalled, "there was a considerable degree of undue enthusiasm enlisted in the movement," and they were overruled. The new Academy Building opened for the fall term in September 1872. Designed by Samuel Sloan, it contained assembly and classrooms for up to 150 and boarding for 70. Within a few years, nearly half of students enrolling in the college had graduated from the academy.[82]

In 1872 the Alumni Association pledged to raise $30,000 to endow a professorship of English belles lettres and literature, to be held by William Nevin. His lectures on English literature were hugely popular among students, and alumni hoped to free him from having to spend most of his time teaching Latin and Greek. Until the full amount was raised, they promised to contribute $1,500 each year to pay Nevin's salary. In part to deepen the sense of connection between alumni and college, recent graduates William U. Hensel and W. M. Franklin launched a monthly newspaper, *College Days*, in early 1873. It contained assorted news about Franklin & Marshall and college life in general, but at first its most popular feature was President Nevin's outline notes for his Philosophy of History course, running to fifteen installments. "For many years the alumni of our college have been desirous of having these lectures presented to them in some permanent, substantial form," the editors announced. "It is believed that this single feature will make College Days worth the price of subscription to each of the alumni, and recommend it to the literary public who have anxiously waited for their appearance."[83]

Seeking to perpetuate Frederick Rauch's spirit at the college, the Alumni Association teamed with the Eastern Synod to erect a monument on campus. Sculptor Davoust Kern portrayed Rauch in bas-relief as the "Christian philosopher," a medieval scholar in his study, correlating a large "Sacred Scripture" in his lap with a volume of Plato on a desk before him. Scattered around him are books bearing the names of giants of Western philosophy and literature. His sandaled foot rests upon a volume of Bacon, whose materialism Rauch had attacked. Beside it is an overturned hourglass denoting the end of his brief time on earth. Carved on the opposite side of the monument's central block was a bas-relief of North America, western Europe, and Africa, in recognition of the trans-Atlantic sweep of Rauch's vision.[84]

The monument was placed in front of the hall of the Goethean Society, which was named after Rauch's hero. Its unveiling at commencement in 1871 was followed by a cornerstone laying for a dormitory, named in honor of the much-loved Reformed pastor and poet Henry Harbaugh. Located northeast of the existing row of college buildings, the dormitory was also designed by Samuel Sloan in plain neoclassical style and contained rooms for forty students and dining facilities for one hundred.[85]

Once again, hopes dimmed. The Endowment Committee admitted in 1873 that so far the campaign had "not resulted in the pecuniary success hoped for." Moreover, the Finance Committee noted that more than $19,000 of notes given for scholarships in years past remained unpaid and could probably not be collected "without resort to legal measures." To pay for the new buildings, some $26,000 was taken out of the endowment, which had reached a high of $111,000 in 1872. The resulting decline in endowment income brought a deficit in 1873 of $2,600, plus more than $3,700 in unpaid faculty salaries.[86]

The campaign's failure can be attributed to the financial panic of 1873 and to doctrinal controversy. The Reformed seminary had moved to Lancaster in 1871. The board donated four and one-half acres on the southern end of the campus, where two brick houses were constructed for faculty, and seminary classes met in the College Building. This proximity added to intellectual life but opened the college to criticism from theological opponents. Persistent suspicions of Mercersburg Theology's "popish" tendencies seemed confirmed when several men connected with Franklin & Marshall, including a faculty member, converted to Catholicism in the early 1870s. Moreover, redecoration of the college chapel, including intricate Gothic detail in the stucco and an ornately carved communion altar in the chancel, drew fire from low-church ministers. Attacks upon seminary faculty became so extreme that the Board of Visitors was compelled to reassure the synod in 1874 that Franklin & Marshall's teachings were perfectly "Protestant, Evangelical and Reformed." Nonetheless some congregations and individuals refused to pay their pledges, and the college realized little more than $6,000 of the $11,500 originally pledged for the alumni professorship. *College Days'* editors complained of damage done to the college by "continual warfare" within the Church. "Let the doctrinal questions of the Reformed Church be settled by proper tribunals," they pleaded, "but let Franklin and Marshall College be judged by her teachings and held to her own true and peculiar mission."[87]

Enrollments also suffered. After reaching eighty-four in the college and sixty-four in the academy in 1873, numbers fell the following two years. Moreover, Harbaugh Hall proved a bad investment. Its rooms were uncomfortable and difficult to heat. In fact, during extremely cold weather in early December 1872, faculty ended the term early because dormitory rooms were so cold. In addition, the building lacked many amenities — such as central heating, running water, and bathrooms — that would soon be considered essential for comfortable living. Stewards hired to run the dining hall also seem to have been inept or unethical. Students resented the requirement that freshmen live in Harbaugh and left for boarding rooms elsewhere as soon as possible. The college rarely realized anticipated profits from the enterprise.[88]

The board's hopes for fund-raising had been raised by news reports of munificent gifts to other colleges. Referring to such cases, an agent reported that he "sought out men of means and liberality." But the college's leaders were learning that it was not easy to win substantial benefactions. With its largely rural constituency, the Reformed Church had few of the connections with centers of wealth that fueled the growth of other institutions in the region. Moreover, cultivating men of means demanded much time and was unpredictable in its results.[89]

In fact, Franklin & Marshall's first large benefaction came as something of a surprise. During its endowment campaign in the late 1860s, trustees "ventured to present the claims of the college" to wealthy Philadelphia merchant Lewis Audenried, knowing of his Reformed background. Only after his death in 1873 did they learn that he had left $35,000 to Franklin & Marshall to endow a professorship of history and archaeology. A friendship that formed in his last years with the Reverend Joseph Henry Dubbs, pastor of Christ Reformed Church in Philadelphia, prompted Audenried to add a codicil stipulating that Dubbs be the professorship's first incumbent.[90]

Dubbs was an appropriate choice for the position. After graduation from Franklin & Marshall and the Theological Seminary of the Reformed Church, he made a successful ministerial career that took him to ever-larger congregations in Allentown, Pottstown, and Philadelphia. He steered a middle course through the theological controversies of the day. While he was still a student, an interest in history inspired him to take up the popular pastime of collecting historical autographs. Eventually his massive collection of letters and documents included signers of the Declaration of Independence and the Constitution, members of the Continental Congress, and leading politicians, artists, scientists, and religious men up to the Civil War. He wrote for many Reformed publications and was widely known as a lively public speaker and lecturer. A recent address to the Alumni Association emphasized the importance of liberal education in laying an intellectual foundation for adult development. Announcing his appointment, *College Days* praised Dubbs as "a gentleman of broad and liberal culture," with "rare qualifications for the office which he has been invited to fill."[91]

After inheritance taxes, the legacy of $33,250 was invested in railroad bonds and mortgages from several faculty members. The interest was more than enough to pay Dubbs's salary of $1,500, but little was left over to cut into the thousands in back pay owed the rest of the faculty. With Dubbs's arrival, John Nevin asked for a reduction in teaching responsibilities at a corresponding decrease in salary — which in any case had not been regularly paid. The board agreed but asked him to continue delivering his popular Philosophy of History lectures.[92]

As revivalism once again took center stage in mainstream Protestantism, the college risked unpopularity by remaining resolutely opposed. When Dwight L. Moody concluded a sensational nine-week revival in Philadelphia early in 1876, Princeton's president, James McCosh, invited him to hold a service on campus and even canceled classes to accommodate a follow-up meeting. Franklin & Marshall's faculty, in contrast, lamented that "the whipping and lashing of the feelings" associated with Moody's revivals would "drive men farther away from God instead of bringing them closer to Him." When another revivalist held forth at Lancaster's opera house, they declined his invitation to attend. A local newspaper published excerpts attacking revivalism from Nevin's *Anxious Bench,* and although many students went to the meeting, *College Days* reported that "none of them so far forgot the teachings of the Mercersburg theology as to allow themselves to be converted by his method."[93]

Discouraged by the failure of the latest fund-raising campaign, John Nevin resigned in 1876. At a reception in July marking the nation's centennial, the board presented him with "a magnificently-bound" quarto Bible. George F. Baer, a Reading, Pennsylvania, attorney new to the board, lauded Nevin as the institution's spiritual guide: "For thirty-five years the students and friends of this college have looked to you as their pillar of cloud by day and fire by night to guide them aright, nor have they looked in vain." While acknowledging that there might seem little concrete to show for his labors, Baer insisted, "There are no scales large enough to weigh the worth of the systems of truth you have created, developed and nurtured into the full vigor of self-sustaining life."[94]

The board was unprepared to elect a replacement at its annual meeting in June. Even if there had been a clear candidate, the college could not pay a presidential salary. Appointing a committee to raise an endowment for the presidency, the board postponed a decision to a midwinter meeting, in the meantime asking William Nevin to serve once again as president pro tem.[95]

The demoralized condition of the institution's leadership was reflected by the board's failure to meet midyear as promised. When it gathered the following June, the Fund-Raising Committee admitted that nothing had been done. A strong fund-raising effort was "inexpedient," trustees explained, given "the stringency of the times, the unsettled state of the country."[96]

Meanwhile, Nathan Schaeffer resigned as head of Franklin & Marshall Academy to become principal of a new state normal school aimed specifically at ethnic Germans. His final report acknowledged the outside opinion that "what Franklin & Marshall College [needed] at this time more than anything else . . . [was] *young blood.*" He urged the board to hire recent graduates as tutors for the college and academy. Those who showed promise could be encouraged "to go abroad and devote themselves as specialists to some particular line of study with the prospect of a professorship at some future time." Such a practice would combine on the faculty "the wisdom and experience of age with the energy and vivacity of youth" and silence "the voices of dissatisfied croakers."[97]

Some questioned whether the college would survive. Editors of the low-church *Reformed Missionary* attributed Franklin & Marshall's failure to thrive to the "invincible *Dumm heit* of the people of Lancaster" and the indifference and ingratitude of its "secularized graduates." Taking a different view, alumnus William U. Hensel, one of the editors of *College Days*, charged that lay alumni were put off by the increasingly religious tone of the college's curriculum and the tendency to identify its interests with those of the seminary. He published a rare signed editorial, urging that the next president be a layman: "What is wanted is some vigorous intellect, some practical ability, some enlarged ideas at its head, . . . [regardless of whether these be found] in a politician or a preacher." The college was in "a state of general disorder, if not demoralization, [in] its financial management, its scholastic discipline, and all of the appliances for securing its avowed purposes." Claiming a "press of private business" and the failure of subscribers to pay up, Hensel suspended publication of *College Days* at the end of 1876.[98]

Concluding that the college lacked the resources to hire a president of any sort, the board asked the Reverend Thomas Gilmore Apple, professor of church history at the seminary, to fill the position temporarily. Apple was descended on his father's side from German immigrants, who had successively anglicized their surname from Apfil to Appel to Apple. But his first names came from a Scotch-Irish ancestor of his mother's who had been an aide to George Washington during the Revolution. An 1850 Marshall College graduate, Apple had served as pastor of several Pennsylvania churches and joined the seminary's faculty at the time of its move to Lancaster in 1871.[99]

Board president John Cessna reported to a special board meeting in August 1877, "The financial condition of the College renders it imperative to retrench in some direction." He asked the seminary and synod to allow Apple to continue teaching at the college and to serve as acting president at no additional salary "until such time as the board [might] find itself able to pay him a salary commensurate with the dignity and duties of the position."[100]

Quiet Growth During the Apple Administration

Gradually, enrollments began to recover. The vast majority came from areas of Pennsylvania where the Reformed Church was prominent, with a handful from Maryland and Virginia, and one from a predominantly German community in Iowa. Lancaster itself sent only a few students, reflecting continued weakness in the school's relations with the community.[101]

An end to denominational conflict helped the college. The Eastern Synod, battle-weary, nearly bankrupt, and fearing permanent schism, acceded in 1878 to the call of the national General Synod for a "peace commission" modeled after the famous body that settled the Hayes-Tilden presidential election the year before. The synod's final report sought to smooth out doctrinal tensions between high and low factions. A newly established student magazine, *College Student*, expressed hope that the "new era of good feelings" would benefit the college. Success of the rapprochement was symbolized by Ursinus College's award of a doctor of divinity degree to Dubbs.[102]

At the end of his first year, Apple agreed to continue in his capacity as acting president. As the years went on with little growth in the endowment, the temporary arrangement came to seem permanent, although he was never formally inaugurated. In the Church's publications and his statements as head of Franklin & Marshall, he continued to champion the philosophical and theological principles set out by his predecessors. His lectures in philosophy, aesthetics, and especially the philosophy of history were known for being faithful to but more accessible than Nevin's originals. Despite Mercersburg's emphasis on change over time, ideas that had been new in the days of Rauch and still controversial in the days of Gerhart had now become orthodoxy.[103]

But unlike many other institutions, Franklin & Marshall had a philosophical tradition that provided a coherent intellectual underpinning for the entire curriculum. In an overview, Apple explained that the emphasis on philosophy throughout Franklin & Marshall's history was intended not "merely to discipline the minds of its students in the study of Metaphysics, as a sort of mental exercise" but to unify the curriculum and "give it direction, by the principles of a sound Christian philosophy."[104]

Apple emphasized the role of language study in mental cultivation. He joined other academics in seeing liberal education as a counterweight to the excessive materialism of Gilded Age America. "To value education for its own sake," he told the organizers of the College Association of Pennsylvania in 1887, "is to set an ideal before the individual and the nation which is in itself elevating, and which must act as a breakwater against the greatest danger that threatens this nation."[105]

America's classical colleges faced renewed public attack in the 1870s and 1880s. In addition to the perennial populist critics, founders of a postwar generation of educational institutions made classical colleges their rhetorical whipping boys. Whether in the form of new private universities like Johns Hopkins, land-grant state universities like Michigan, or transformed older colleges like Harvard, these institutions embodied the age's romance with size, specialization, and progress. Their ambitious founders hoped to emulate European universities — especially in the freedom and high social status of German professors. Academic promoters proposed a variety of innovations, such as adding electives or eliminating the prescribed classical curriculum, offering an encyclopedic array of subjects, and freeing professors to do original research. To justify departing from the classical curriculum, many ridiculed the ideas of mental discipline and the faculty psychology that was traditionally used as its theoretical underpinning. And just as American industry emphasized division of labor, these critics dismissed the ideal of fostering persons of general cultivation and the possibility of a common civic culture. University promoters did not immediately abandon the ideal of moral development but argued that training in scientific method would do it more effectively than the reputedly "narrow" religious indoctrination provided in "sectarian" denominational colleges.[106]

In the face of this offensive, American colleges either staunchly defended the traditional curriculum or modified it. Employing an argument that Rauch had used back in the 1830s, many college leaders emphasized their mission to educate the "whole man." They defended the classical course as the best means of developing character and spirit as well as intellect. Other schools compromised by adding parallel degree courses, such as a bachelor of philosophy that required no Greek and less mathematics, and a bachelor of science that replaced classics with more science and modern languages. Some allowed students to choose elective courses in the last two years. But Apple resisted all calls for change at Franklin & Marshall. He asserted that enrollments would have been higher if the college were willing to allow a certain number of "irregular" students, who did not take the full classical curriculum or took only scientific subjects. But he was proud that the college had survived without abandoning its principles.[107]

In the breathing space afforded by the denominational truce, Franklin & Marshall College experienced greater stability than it had ever known and quiet if not dramatic growth. It received several large gifts from Reformed Church members on behalf of their denominational college. One had long been promised by the Wilhelm family of rural Somerset County. When the surviving Wilhelm brother died suddenly in 1878, however, he had written his will effecting the promised gift to the college and seminary less than a month before, making it invalid under Pennsylvania law. After extended litigation, trustees succeeded in gaining control of the bulk of the estate, but only after Cessna obtained releases from more than ninety widely scattered descendants. Over $26,000 was withdrawn from the endowment to pay settlements to some thirty heirs. The estate consisted mainly of nineteen thousand acres of farmland and undeveloped land variously valued at $60,000 to $100,000. Dreams of vast coal, ore, and other mineral treasure awaiting discovery were never fulfilled. By 1903 most of the land had been sold, for a total profit of about $18,000. Rental of farmland through the years also provided some income, although managing the estate demanded considerable work on the part of several board members.[108]

Gradually, the college acquired some of the amenities expected of collegiate institutions. In 1881 the literary societies jointly founded and edited a monthly newspaper, the *College Student*, and two years later the senior class prepared the first edition of a yearbook named the *Oriflamme*. (Later editions were published by the junior class.) Literary societies continued to play a prominent role in both college and community intellectual life. A member of the class of 1885 recalled that at the time of the Diagnothian Society's anniversary program "the entire student body paraded downtown and joined with a large representation of Lancaster people in filling Fulton Opera House."[109]

The most encouraging sign that Franklin & Marshall was emerging from its long period of insecurity came in 1884 with the announcement that Margaret Scholl Hood of Frederick, Maryland, would underwrite construction of an astronomical observatory. The gift was the fruit of a campaign by Jefferson E. Kershner, the new professor of mathematics and astronomy. An 1877 alumnus, he had been doing graduate work at Yale when he was called back to teach in 1880. He continued his research during summer vacations and returned to assist at the Yale Observatory during the transit of Venus in 1882. His thesis based on this research earned him a Ph.D. in 1885, the first modern doctorate on the faculty. It was undoubtedly at Kershner's prompting that Apple put an observatory at the head of a list of college needs. Trustees appointed the usual committee, and an article was inserted in Reformed publications stating that an observatory could be built for around $10,000. (Kershner offered this figure when asked for a reasonable but low estimate.) This appeal and the encouragement of her Reformed pastor prompted Hood to offer to establish an observatory in memory of her father, Daniel Scholl.[110]

Trustees put Kershner in charge of designing and building the observatory. He intended it to be capable of advanced astronomical work, which would "bring the college into notice." After visiting sites throughout the Northeast, he assembled the most advanced equipment available at the time, from components ordered from Germany, Ireland, Connecticut, Massachusetts, and Washington, D.C. After failing in an attempt to purchase land on higher ground, a site north of existing buildings on campus was selected. The college community closely followed the process of construction and assembly, for the observatory represented the first step in a campaign that would, as the *College Student* put it, allow Franklin & Marshall "to cope with the best institutions of learning in the land." When the telescope arrived, the newspaper proudly announced that there were only four larger in the United States, including one in the nation's capital. By spring 1885, construction had progressed as far as the dome and then stopped because an additional $3,500 was needed to complete it. The trustees pledged $1,200, and some $700 was raised from the community, but the remaining money had to be borrowed from the endowment. Finally completed in 1886, the observatory was used for instruction and research and as the county's official weather station. Through a telegraph connection to the Lancaster Watch Company, it also served as official timekeeper. Recognizing the observatory's contributions to the college's life and reputation, trustees later canceled the note.[111]

The observatory's dedication was the highlight of the 1886 commencement exercises, though the event was overshadowed by the recent death of John Williamson Nevin. In a funeral sermon delivered in the chapel, crowded with trustees, alumni, and most of the region's Reformed clergy, President Apple affirmed, "It is given to few to impress and mould the thinking and the lives of his pupils as he has done." Nevin had towered above all the rest as the "presiding spirit" of first Marshall and then Franklin & Marshall College.[112]

Evidence of Nevin's continuing influence could be found in the sons of former students who bore his name, many of whom were destined to return to their fathers' alma mater. One of these was Nevin A. Swander, son of the Reverend J. J. Swander of Fremont, Ohio. Young Swander would have graduated in 1884 but died of tuberculosis shortly before commencement. Following his last request, his father sent the college the boy's entire savings, $200, with a brief letter and a request that it be read from his son's vacant chair at the graduation exercises. Apple agreed, noting to the board, "This was an only son and an only child." He stated, "Though small [the gift] yet expresses a great deal of affection and devotion on the part of both the son and the parents for the college." The money went to pay for the observatory's clock, which thereafter bore his name.[113]

As early as 1882, the college and synod had hoped to use the 1887 centennial of the founding of Franklin College and the fiftieth anniversary of Marshall College as a fund-raising opportunity. But beyond appointing a Centennial Committee and authorizing Professor John Stahr as agent, trustees had done little to promote the event. In the aftermath of Nevin's death, the Alumni Association proposed an ambitious fund-raising agenda, including $25,000 for a science building and $30,000 to endow the presidency as a memorial to Nevin, as well as to complete the endowment of the Alumni Professorship of English Literature. The Alumni Association also promised to plan a grand celebration at the 1887 commencement.[114]

Combined efforts of students, faculty, alumni, and trustees produced a memorable centennial celebration, which publicized the college as never before. For five days in mid-June, Franklin & Marshall was the center of an impressive array of speeches, processions, reunions, banquets, and receptions, culminating in a gala "promenade concert and reception" for the entire community. A large arch of greenery bearing the school's motto, *Lux et Lex*, crowned the main entrance to campus, and students draped the buildings with flags and bunting in blue and white, the literary societies' colors. The College Building also sported evergreen garlands and the figure "1787," and a giant U.S. flag was suspended from the tower. At graduation exercises, students donned "Oxford caps and gowns" for the first time. On the evening of the public reception, the grounds were brilliantly illuminated by hundreds of Chinese lanterns. A crowd, variously estimated from three to five thousand, streamed through the arch. Local papers noted that visitors included everyone from the city's social elite in evening attire to respectably dressed workmen and farmers and their families. "Wandering in the leafy shades, under the light of the fantastic lanterns, listening to the buzz of conversation, viewing the faces of the fair," enthused the *Lancaster Intelligencer*, "one might easily imagine himself transferred back two thousand years to the hanging gardens of Babylon." Visitors strolling through campus listened to music from an orchestra in Diagnothian Hall, where faculty held a receiving line. Ice cream and cake were served from the first floor of the College Building. At the Scholl Observatory, hundreds stood in line for hours to catch a glimpse of Jupiter. The evening's success survived even a "stray spark" that prematurely ignited the planned fireworks display atop Harbaugh Hall and a more serious threat of fire later in the evening, when oil from a lamp set greenery on the College Building alight. Students immediately pulled down the decorations and stamped out the fire. The last visitors did not leave until after midnight, closing what the *Daily New Era* deemed "the greatest jubilee ever known in the history of Lancaster."[115]

Despite the amiability, wound like a ribbon through the five days' festivities was a debate on education — in particular the future of liberal arts at Franklin & Marshall College. Not surprisingly, most of the college's supporters emphasized the value of its classical curriculum, but there were voices calling for change. Most prominent was that of William Pepper, provost of the University of Pennsylvania, who was invited to deliver an address on Benjamin Franklin. While praising the great man's many virtues and contributions, Pepper argued that Franklin had anticipated recent innovations in higher education by serving as a model for "the splendid development of the scientific spirit and of scientific education in America." Moreover, Franklin thought that language training should vary according to the student's intended vocation, which Pepper interpreted as a vindication of "the fundamental principle of elective studies." Without referring specifically to Franklin & Marshall, Pepper noted that only now, "after the lapse of a century," were Franklin's ideas being implemented at the University of Pennsylvania and "other prominent colleges." Turning to the present occasion, Pepper challenged his audience to match, out of the present day's great wealth, the generosity of Franklin and the founding generation (and used classical rhetoric in doing so): "Men and women of Lancaster, you have here institutions which stand as faithful witnesses of noble lives consecrated to the public weal, and as silent but convincing appeals to us to bear in mind what they did in the day of small things, that we may be worthy stewards of the larger bounty entrusted to us for a time."[116]

As if in response, Lewis H. Steiner delivered the next day the centennial oration, "The College and the Old College Curriculum." Perhaps no one better epitomized the ideal of broad liberal culture than Steiner, a physician who had graduated from Marshall College in 1846. Member of the Medico-Chirurgical Faculty of Maryland, he had during the Civil War served as chief inspector of the U.S. Sanitary Commission for the Army of the Potomac. In addition to participating in a large number of medical, scientific, and historical societies, Steiner was an active lay leader in the Reformed Church, helping to plan the tricentennial of the Heidelberg Catechism, editing its hymnal, and serving as a longtime college trustee at Franklin & Marshall. He was twice elected to the Maryland state senate as a Republican, and in 1886 he had become the founding librarian of Baltimore's Enoch Pratt Free Library. Now, Steiner extolled his college's unwavering loyalty to "the ideal of a liberal Christian education." Many of their founders and early supporters had been men with German blood, possessing "but little sympathy with the superficial in the material, intellectual or spiritual world." In their footsteps, the college had "grown up to maturity, abhoring a superficial curriculum, and detesting the shams and makeshifts which are not unusual in the enterprises of the age." He lauded Franklin & Marshall's leaders for having the strength of character to withstand pressures to conform to new fashions and forego "the glamour of popularity" with its short-term financial rewards. He derided the "spirit of utilitarianism" that had abandoned the wisdom of centuries of educational experience.[117]

Addressing alumni with a speech titled "The Claims of the College upon the Community," W. U. Hensel agreed that the college's goal was "the proper direction of mind and the true cultivation of the heart." In contrast, local congressman Mariott Brosius responded to a toast to "Lancaster county" at the alumni dinner by vowing that the community would support the college generously only when it acknowledged that education must change to meet modern conditions. "The people of Lancaster county who possess largely its wealth," he argued, "would feel a great interest and pride in the college if they were persuaded that it. . . . was not wasting too much time in pulling out the threads of the fabric of antiquity and looking into the ancient looms, instead of laying hold of the character, studying the mechanism and learning the safe modes of controlling and managing the modern agencies — the social forces which are weaving the mighty webs of our modern life." His remarks were applauded by the *Lancaster Examiner*, whose coverage of the centennial was larded with attacks on the college's "educational dudeism." Professing to stand for the common man, the editorial writer asserted, "It is all well enough to talk about 'culture,' the 'higher life' &c., but the every day fact is that the first thing a man looks for in this world is something to eat." He urged graduating students to press Franklin & Marshall to change. "Boys, after you have tried the world for a dozen of years and measured the requirements of the age by the equipment your college gave you to satisfy public and private requirements, please inform us if you were not compelled to throw aside Homer to study something about the distribution of railroad ties."[118]

Centennial celebrations saw the debate over classical education fully joined. Over three decades since its merger, Franklin & Marshall College had helped to fashion a distinctive German American ethnic culture that asserted its Americanness while resisting absorption into the dominant culture of Anglo-American evangelical Protestantism. What remained to be seen as the college entered the second century of its institutional life was how it would respond to new demands. In coming decades, it would seek to negotiate an equally problematic path between defending liberal education and embracing change.

CHAPTER FOUR

A Modern Awakening
Negotiating Change in the 1890s

—◁∾◽▷—

Franklin & Marshall College saw more change in the decade after John S. Stahr assumed its presidency than in all its previous history. This followed a national pattern, as higher education, with its dual aims of fostering character and developing intellect, was central to changes in American culture in the late nineteenth century. University graduate programs and professional schools became nurseries for new ways of organizing skilled work, while the classical college curriculum gradually evolved into the "liberal arts." Slowly but inexorably the baccalaureate degree become a necessary path to middle-class status.

The break between old and new forms of higher education was not absolute, as claimed by both promoters and detractors. Founders of new universities blended utility, specialization, and professionalism with traditional goals of personal cultivation and moral development. Even university promoters who cast themselves as agents of progress sought to ground innovation in tradition, hence the popularity of collegiate Gothic architecture and Oxford caps and gowns for academic ceremonies. At colleges and universities alike, students themselves embraced a panoply of newly invented campus "traditions," extracurricular activities, and competitive athletics, which increasingly assumed responsibility for character development.[1]

Because of its location, ethnic constituency, and unique philosophical and theological traditions, educational change at Franklin & Marshall followed its own path. Most of its peer institutions expanded their curricula and added vocational programs, though many later returned to the liberal arts as redefined in the twentieth century. Though Franklin & Marshall remained almost uniquely consistent in its commitment to classical education, it gradually embraced a wider range of educational experiences, especially in science. Faculty were ambivalent about student emulation of Anglo-American college customs but hoped to channel their enthusiasm for sports and extracurricular activities into a broader definition of cultivating the "whole man." As always in the chaotic and uncertain process of cultural change, pressure came from the often conflicting goals of several groups, including students, faculty, alumni, and the Reformed Church. Inevitably, response to new demands was hampered by inadequate funding.[2]

Bridges Between Mercersburg Theology and Modern Science

John Summers Stahr epitomized the best of the Franklin & Marshall College's ethnic and theological traditions and the strengths that allowed it to negotiate change on its own terms. Raised in a German-speaking family in rural Bucks County, Stahr entered the college in 1865 as a twenty-four-year-old junior after many years as a school teacher. He intended to go on to the Theological Seminary of the Reformed Church, but Nevin offered to personally direct his theological studies if Stahr stayed on as tutor. With the flexibility of a classically trained generalist, Stahr subsequently assumed responsibility for teaching natural science, German, and political economy. Later, he admitted that he had "felt the burden of responsibility" in accepting such a heavy load but had believed he "was rendering the College a service by doing double duty" in its time of financial need, even if it meant "sacrificing the strength of his early manhood." At various times he also served as treasurer, librarian, and rector of Franklin & Marshall Academy.[3]

Although Stahr was ordained in 1872, his true vocation lay in education, which had come to be seen as an alternative to the ministry for serious-minded men of his generation. Despite formidable teaching and administrative duties, he published essays on many of the subjects under his purview, usually in the *Reformed Church Review*, successor to the *Mercersburg Review*. "Pennsylvania German," his first publication in 1870, was an early attempt to treat the dialect as a legitimate linguistic form.[4]

Intellectual historian Paul K. Conkin has noted Mercersburg Theology's influence on American religious life, especially through its ecumenical vision. Stahr manifested this ecumenism in actions as well as words, working closely with leaders of other colleges in the region and participating in a widening circle of interdenominational endeavors. As the Reformed Church's first representative on the International Sunday School Committee, which prepared standardized lessons used in Protestant churches throughout the world, he persuaded it to add celebrations of major festivals of the Church calendar such as Christmas, Easter, and Pentecost — previously shunned as "popish" corruptions.[5]

In Stahr, the Mercersburg tradition did not ossify into orthodoxy, because he stressed its emphasis on change over time. Richard C. Schiedt, his successor on the science faculty, characterized him as "pre-eminently [a] philosopher, the last and the most widely informed exponent of the Mercersburg Philosophy," whose understanding of science went beyond his predecessors' to incorporate new findings. Like contemporaries elsewhere, Stahr sought to mediate between more traditional religious beliefs and an increasingly cosmopolitan world of academic scholarship.[6]

Unlike more evangelically based institutions, such as Yale and Princeton, Franklin & Marshall did not need to break from its theological roots to embrace new scientific ideas. The Mercersburg tradition had long before rejected the evangelical idea that all forms of knowledge were equally accessible to the same kind of rational, empirical analysis. "There are truths," Stahr told his students in 1886, "which cannot be discovered by a process of induction." This included "the nature of the Deity" and the truth of Creation, neither of which could be comprehended using scientific methods. "Now what reason cannot solve," he told students, "that we clearly discern by the higher power of faith.[7]

Stahr was acutely aware that the college's instruction in the sciences had not kept up with the times. Generations of botany and geology students had taken field trips to collect specimens. Based on the space devoted to these trips in class histories, the excursions were invariably a highlight of the students' year. But in recent years emphasis in scientific education had shifted to laboratory experimentation, which required special laboratory spaces and an ever-expanding array of experimental technology.[8]

Through the 1870s and 1880s, Stahr advocated for the importance of science within liberal education and worked to improve the college's facilities. Franklin & Marshall had a herbarium of about thirty thousand specimens, some dating back to the time of President Muhlenberg, and a large geological collection that the college had no room to display. Stahr repeatedly lobbied trustees to consider the needs of the natural sciences in fund-raising plans. Finally, in 1885, the board asked him to prepare a report outlining what it would cost to "enlarge and strengthen" his department. His response, also published in the student newspaper, presented a sophisticated argument for scientific education that subtly recast the very rationale for liberal education.[9]

Stahr assured the board that he did not advocate a "departure from the well-settled policy and educational position" of the college, only improvement in its fulfillment. He agreed that a college course "is for culture and discipline rather than for specifically practical ends." Nonetheless, he redefined this process by expanding the set of intellectual skills that a cultivated mind should possess "to observe accurately, reason correctly, express [itself] clearly and act rightly." The natural sciences were well suited to developing these abilities. Later, he expanded upon this argument by pointing out, in keeping with the college's idealistic traditions, that true science was not the mere accumulation of facts but the ability to theorize upon them, reflecting a "broad, comprehensive grasp of things." Stahr's emphasis on scientific method as a "marriage of hypothesis and experiment" flowed naturally from the Mercersburg tradition but was only then being embraced by university advocates of science.[10]

Fostering such intellectual skills required more than giving a "smattering" of chemistry, botany, zoology, and geology. "The study of nature, the investigation of natural phenomena, actual work in the field of the different sciences by the student under the direction of a competent teacher whose enthusiasm kindles that of the student, will yield larger and better results," Stahr argued. To ensure competence and enthusiasm on the instructor's part, the college should require that he be able to conduct original research. "A botanist without a herbarium, a biologist or chemist without a laboratory, a minerologist or geologist without a cabinet of specimens or a museum, is no more likely to thrive than an astronomer without an observatory, or a fish without water." The *Wissenschaft* tradition expected teachers to engage in research not as an end in itself but as a means to be more effective teachers.[11]

The college's facilities had fallen far behind those of other institutions, Stahr reported, its equipment so "antequated or worn out" that he felt like "a farmer condemned to mow and rake by hand while everybody around him uses improved machinery." He estimated that rooms for lectures, experiments, and storage of equipment could be provided by constructing a separate building or enlarging one of the wings of the College Building, at a cost between $6,000 and $10,000. For $25,000 or more, a separate hall might be built, with a museum of natural history, attached study rooms, and perhaps a library and an auditorium.[12]

Expansion of knowledge also required a larger, more specialized faculty. Stahr presently taught physical geography, geology, botany, zoology, chemistry, anatomy, physiology, German, and political economy. Although students should learn something about each of these fields, he contended, one person could not "be a *master*" of them all. He urged the board to hire three more faculty, one to teach physics and chemistry and another to teach botany, zoology, and geology, with German to be taught by a professor of modern languages.[13]

In response, the Board of Trustees and Alumni Association added science buildings to its list of centennial projects. As usual, fund-raising was ineffectual and the board extended the campaign for another year. "As no other way seemed to offer [itself]," Stahr later recalled, he volunteered to serve as the college's full-time agent. After a year of traveling throughout the region and preaching many sermons "on the subject of College Education," he reported that the times were "not propitious," because of competition from other Church projects. He predicted that fund-raising prospects would improve once the college had a full-time president.[14]

At the same meeting, President Thomas G. Apple reminded the board that his "temporary" appointment as head of both seminary and college had gone on for a decade. In poor health, he was ready to resign whenever the board saw fit. At the very least, he asked to be relieved of responsibility for the college's "government and discipline." Unwilling to accept his resignation, the board asked Stahr as the "oldest resident professor" to preside over faculty meetings while continuing as agent for another year.[15]

In the meantime, informal curricular change had already begun in response to student demand. In 1887 a specialist in the new "science" of elocution was engaged part-time, and in the fall formal French instruction began under Richard C. Schiedt, who had taken Stahr's courses while he worked as agent. These optional classes were popular even though students received no additional credit. Soon other faculty offered instruction in their specialties. J. E. Kershner taught practical astronomy and surveying to a few seniors, and a group of seniors petitioned J. B. Kieffer to lecture on Greek literature, particularly his specialty of Greek drama. The following year, Schiedt arranged for local physician D. B. Weaver to teach histology and use of the microscope. "Such accuracy and skill I had seldom seen," Schiedt commented, "not even in the best laboratories of German universities."[16]

French was only the first of many innovations at Franklin & Marshall for which Richard C. Schiedt was responsible. Recently arrived from Germany, he followed in Frederick Rauch's steps as a bearer of new German ideas who impressed his strong personality upon the institution. Born in Prussia, Schiedt had received a rigorous gymnasium education, and like many German undergraduates, he attended lectures at a number of universities, including Jena, Erlangen, and Berlin. He participated in scientific expeditions to Italy, Egypt, and the Sahara and came to the United States in 1881 to join an expedition to the Galápagos. Learning that it had been canceled, he found work teaching in Reformed schools. He enrolled at the Franklin & Marshall Seminary, hoping, as he later put it, "to become acquainted with the widely heralded Mercersburg Philosophy." Upon his graduation in 1887, Stahr asked him to take over his courses for a year. As Schiedt later commented, "I never got away."[17]

Schiedt shared Stahr's commitment to transforming the college's science instruction while preserving its classical values. "We both were ardent advocates of the educational value of Greek and Roman literature," Schiedt recalled, "from the linguistic as well as from their ethical, aesthetic, philosophical and sociological point of view." Yet they both believed that a modern college must have a curriculum that recognized changes wrought by "the new scientific methods and views of life."[18]

Schiedt was well acquainted with new scientific methods, through his ongoing research career. During summers he conducted research at newly established marine laboratories at Woods Hole, Massachusetts, and Sea Isle City, New Jersey. His work resulted in numerous academic publications and earned him doctorates from the University of Pennsylvania and Harvard. In 1893 he published a widely used zoology textbook.[19]

Schiedt's emphatic and occasionally explosive temperament fascinated some students and repelled others, for he expected hard and painstaking work. In the spring of his first year, someone set off a homemade firework bomb in front of his desk during junior science class. He indignantly dismissed the class, announcing that no one would be readmitted until the culprit confessed and apologized. A stalemate ensued until President Apple threatened to expel the entire class. The guilty party finally came forward — his son Henry Harbaugh Apple.[20]

Nationally, a small but vocal minority of scientists attacked religion and denigrated the ministry's cultural authority, but many others saw science and religion as allies. "Science is the handmaid of Religion," Daniel Coit Gilman, first president of Johns Hopkins University, assured the Evangelical Alliance in 1887. Similarly, Schiedt and physical science professor Jefferson Kershner embraced research science but also had strong ties to Mercersburg idealism. Before beginning graduate training at Yale, Kershner too had studied at the seminary — Schiedt later quipped that it was in deference to his mother's wishes, but Kershner told a reporter in 1886 that he wanted "to embrace the better opportunities thus afforded for the study of metaphysics."[21]

Schiedt and Kershner insisted that science was compatible with the moral and even spiritual dimensions of college education. In his 1892 opening-of-term address, "The Different Forms of Energy and Their Transformation," Kershner noted that the concept of energy was important for both philosophy and science but its ultimate analysis belonged to the realm of metaphysics. As Schiedt put it, "the unknowable belongs to metaphysics and to religion, the unknown to science."[22]

Birth of an Independent Student Culture

With little progress made in fund-raising, the Franklin & Marshall Board of Trustees continued its tradition of inaction. But the German American community's traditional deference to seniority was waning, and trustees faced increasing criticism from faculty and students. Compared with campus leaders at elite schools like Harvard and Yale, Franklin & Marshall's students were still a serious lot. The vast majority came from a Reformed background, and the ministry was typically the most popular career choice. But eastern Pennsylvania's economic development had spurred the growth of small and medium-sized cities with substantial German American communities. Increasingly students came from middle-class families, a generation or more removed from the farm, who had adopted many aspects of Anglo-American culture. They came to Lancaster with visions of college life shaped by popular fiction and the press. Exchanging newspapers with other schools kept students informed about the latest trends, and many were anxious that Franklin & Marshall should keep up. Through their newspaper, the *College Student*, and the *Oriflamme* yearbook, Franklin & Marshall students expressed new ambitions and agitated for improvements. *Oriflamme*'s first editors explained that they founded the annual to boost their college; it was "too important a college in comparison with other sister colleges to be minus a medium of this kind." In addition to recording the school's expanding extracurricular life, *Oriflamme* made increasingly pointed comments about things that were lacking — especially a gymnasium and laboratories.[23]

Gymnasiums had become prominent features on the collegiate scene since the 1870s, symbols of a growing emphasis on athletic prowess. In the region, Lafayette, Lehigh, and Dickinson built gyms in the 1880s. From of its first issue in 1881, the *College Student* lobbied for a gymnasium, arguing the need "for cultivation of physical as well as mental powers." The college's only exercise equipment was a horizontal bar erected in front of Harbaugh Hall in 1875. The first *Oriflamme* whimsically expressed hopes for a gymnasium in a charming drawing of an infant circling the bar, above the title "Our Jim-Nasium in Embryo."[24]

Expectations rose in 1884 when Apple included a gymnasium on the list of improvements to be made with centennial funds. When nothing had been done by the spring of 1888, students held a "mass meeting" to petition the board for action. A few members of the board strongly opposed a gymnasium, but it did appoint a committee to consider the matter.[25]

As reflected in their publications, Franklin & Marshall students were beginning to see themselves as part of a distinctive collegiate subculture but as yet felt little of the generational distance common at elite schools. Editors of the first *Oriflamme* disparagingly described the "good fellow" who "under all circumstances insists on having a good time," who drinks and smokes incessantly, "has a great fondness of dogs, blood horses, and pool, pooh-poohs at study, and delights in getting the Professors 'off.'" The editors suggested as a better model, the "slow fellow," who enjoys learning for its own sake, cultivates moderate habits and avoids tobacco in the interests of health, and "does not regard the Faculty of his College his mortal enemies."[26]

Oriflamme nevertheless made frequent humorous references to "ponies"— illicit translations smuggled into classes in Latin and Greek — and other techniques for avoiding hard study. Students considered as legitimate any means of getting through the universally detested sophomore test. "It is not the aim of these test examinations to find out how much the student knows," the class of 1885 explained, "but to test the skill, on the one hand, of the students to prompt each other; to discover difficult formulae in their hats and cuffs; to use Latin-English texts, and to devise many other little tricks to get around a professor; and, on the other hand, of the professors to discover and prevent these trickeries."[27]

Enrollment growth in the 1880s brought the size of the typical class year to around twenty-five, large enough to form a cohesive group identity. Each class adopted its own colors and banners, and many assumed badges of status, such as caps for underclassmen, canes for juniors, and high silk hats for seniors. The perennial conflict between freshmen and sophomores intensified, as the latter considered it their right and duty to initiate newcomers — according to the class of 1885, to "teach them proper behaviour towards the faculty and higher classmen" by "stretching" them. In this procedure, sophomores descended upon a hapless freshman, seized him by the arms and legs and pulled him high in the air, giving a painful wrench that often ripped his clothes. Refusing to submit, freshmen banded together in self-defense. Resistance sometimes escalated from wrestling and fisticuffs to open warfare. Most notorious was the occasion in the fall of 1878 when pistol shots were fired and one sophomore was seriously injured. The faculty suspended fifteen freshmen for several weeks, and three juniors were suspended indefinitely for "aiding and abetting" them.[28]

Class conflicts took collective form in the "hall rush." The class of 1886 described a typical engagement in the College Building on the first day of classes in the fall of 1883: "When, in going from one recitation room to another, we passed through the hall, of a sudden, an ear-piercing yell rent the air, and the Sophomores rushed out to 'stretch' us. . . . However, we soon recovered from the panic, and resisted with the strength of desperation. The Sophomores, to their great surprise, discovered that the Freshman class 'was made of sterner stuff,' and was not there for their amusement." Unless faculty intervened, the struggle was likely to go on until both sides were exhausted, each claiming victory. Another opportunity for battle occurred at the end of the fall term, when freshmen tried to hang their class banner from the top of the college tower and invariably encountered sophomores just as determined to prevent them. The battle nearly ended in tragedy in 1889 when a portion of the tower wall collapsed, sending bricks and one of the capstones to the pavement below. One freshman nearly followed but was saved when friends grasped his clothing. Subsequently, the *College Student* pleaded, "Let the tower fight — like hazing and stretching — be things of the past. We are becoming more civilized every day. Let us show it." The contest shifted to attempts to cover the campus and surrounding community with posters proclaiming the superiority of each respective class, with counter efforts to rip them down.[29]

Another popular pastime, rooted in traditional folk protest customs but also common on other campuses, were "cremation" ceremonies marking completion of particularly onerous academic subjects with a bonfire and symbolic execution. One year, juniors attempting to break up a sophomore celebration of the passing of "the monster, Analytical Geometry" provoked a free-for-all water fight. Another time, sophomores tore down part of the fence enclosing the campus for a celebratory bonfire. When they hanged Mr. Test in effigy from a nearby electric light pole, alarmed local citizens reported a suicide. In later years Schiedt's zoology course became the most popular subject for cremation.[30]

Many students now looked forward to participating in athletics at college. Such activities depended entirely on student initiative, inspired by news from other campuses. In 1876 a group called the Alpha Club promoted formation of baseball teams to compete intramurally. The college's first intercollegiate competition was a baseball game in 1877 against Millersville State Normal School. Inspired by their victory, Franklin & Marshall students issued challenges to Lafayette and Gettysburg. A pattern of sporadic activity continued into the 1880s, with seasons waxing and waning according to student interest. In off years, a few students played in interclass contests. In 1881 students successfully petitioned the trustees to reserve an area on campus for a playing field. This meant simply that the land would no longer be rented to local farmers, and the vexing issue of the janitor's use of the campus to graze his own cattle remained for some time. For their part, students undertook to improve the baseball field. "If the students all lend a hand," the *College Student* promised, "the college may be put in the possession of one of the finest ball grounds in the state." A year later, the paper lamented flagging enthusiasm, blaming a belief that showing an interest in athletics betrayed a lack of seriousness.[31]

Football Sparks a Secular Awakening

Through the 1880s, combined pressure from students, faculty, and the broader community brought Franklin & Marshall College to the brink of a break from decades of institutional inertia. By 1889 even President Apple delicately suggested that the board make more concerted effort to raise funds, noting that trustees could help matters by giving more generously themselves. As agent, Stahr advised that the college show some "forward movement," particularly by appointing a president to represent the institution throughout the Church community. The board was not ready to appoint a permanent president but did name Stahr as president pro tem and financial agent for a third year. The final catalyst needed to create a period of exciting change finally came in the fall of 1889 — football. The college's stunning season marked its first steps into the mainstream of American college life.[32]

Football first arose on campuses of elite northeastern universities in the 1870s through a blending of interclass rushes, soccer, and rugby. It quickly spread to other schools. Franklin & Marshall students read about football in the *College Student* and experimented with the game informally. Organized competition began in 1887, when Miles Noll, who had played football at Bucknell, enrolled in the seminary and organized a team. One of its members, junior Henry Apple, recalled that the group's "chief quality" was enthusiasm, for the players had no real knowledge of the game. They practiced in an area north of Harbaugh Hall, where two small peach trees served as goalposts. For their only extramural game, against York's YMCA, they wore baseball uniforms. The following year, students were distracted by the fiercely contested 1888 presidential campaign, and none of the scheduled intramural games came off. Instead, divided almost evenly between Republicans and Democrats, students formed "well drilled campaign club[s]," which marched in the numerous local parades, rending the air with the school yell: "Nevonia! Nevonia!! F. and M." The few who turned out for football practices bided their time and worked to improve the grounds.[33]

Hopes were bolstered by word that William Mann Irvine was coming to the seminary in the fall of 1889. During his five years at Princeton, "Buck" Irvine had become known as a dynamic student leader and athlete. Upon arriving at Franklin & Marshall, he immediately assumed leadership of the student athletics movement. A missionary for a new collegiate way of life, he also devoted his considerable energies during his time at the college to founding an array of extracurricular activities deemed essential to a fully formed campus life — football, glee club, weekly newspaper, and more.[34]

A student athletic association that had grown out of the 1888 gymnasium campaign took charge of the fledgling sports program. At a "mass meeting" in the chapel early in September, Irvine was elected president, and Edgar Campbell, a Lehigh alumnus also at the seminary, became treasurer-manager. They persuaded students to raise a subscription to supplement funds budgeted for athletics. Irvine took charge of a football team strengthened — in the days before eligibility regulations — by veterans in the seminary. He taught them the "Princeton wedge," a new mass-momentum play that enabled the college to overwhelm nearly all its opponents that year.[35]

By November, the *College Student* reported the college to be in the throes of "a complete awakening": "An irrepressible power, in the shape of an athletic bomb, has invaded the sanctity of the institution, and a great stir is being created among the inhabitants thereof." Almost the entire student body followed the team to Millersville for the first game, which Franklin & Marshall won in a rout, 60 to 0. The second, against Bucknell in Lancaster, was tied at the last minute by Irvine's extra-point kick.

Because of Bucknell's strong reputation, a tie was greeted as a moral triumph. "I have seen college crowds go wild over a national championship," Irvine later recalled, "but I never saw a more joy-crazed set of boys than the F. & M. students as they swept out of McGrann's Park on that October afternoon." The team went on to defeat Bucknell at Lewisburg, 16 to 0, and Swarthmore at home, 22 to 4. A 10 to 0 loss to Dickinson at Carlisle was offset by a Thanksgiving Day victory at home, 22 to 0. After the game both teams attended a reception hosted by a local trustee. Later students politely escorted their guests to the train and took up drums and horns for an exuberant victory parade through town, stopping along the way to serenade professors and local boosters. At one stop, Civil War veteran A. C. Reinoehl proclaimed it "the greatest victory since the battle of Gettysburg." The college won a final match against St. John's College of Fordham, 56 to 0.[36]

Aware of the boost football brought to student morale, faculty attended games to show their support, even if Apple invariably left at halftime because of the strain to his heart. Venerable former president Gerhart, now a seminary professor, assured players that "the day would come when ethical and theological writers would use foot ball parlance to teach truth in the same spirit in which St. Paul employed the language of the Greek games." Nevertheless, faculty hoped to contain the "excitement and commotion" inspired by the games. When students celebrated their Thanksgiving Day victory by cutting Friday classes, the faculty spent much time deliberating a response but finally decided to let it go. "The problem before the Faculty was, not to suppress these evidences of vigorous life, but to keep them in the right channel," Stahr explained to the board, "and in proper relation to the more serious and distinctive work of the college in the forming of intellectual and moral discipline and religious nurture."[37]

There was no such ambivalence among Lancastrians, who turned out for home games in growing numbers. "For once town and gown agree," the *College Student* rejoiced, "and this happy state is due to foot-ball." Franklin & Marshall's sensational entry into the world of college football allowed the community to participate in a craze that was sweeping the urban Northeast. Almost overnight in the 1880s, fomented by extensive coverage in mass-circulation newspapers, football was transformed from student pastime to popular entertainment. The yellow press was filled with dramatic narratives about games and lively illustrated accounts of students' pre- and postgame antics. Football's popular triumph was crowned by New York City's invention of the instant "tradition" of Thanksgiving Day championship games, which by 1889 drew tens of thousands of spectators. In Lancaster, local developer B. J. McGrann opened his baseball grounds and stands on New Holland Avenue to the team free of charge, and newspapers emulated the dramatic coverage of their big-city peers. After one thousand people turned out for the first Thanksgiving Day game, one paper commented, "Lancaster has rubbed her eyes, looked about and at last realized that she has the best of the lesser colleges in the State." The *Lancaster New Era* noted that the school's success over "more pretentious teams" brought it greater public prominence than ever before. Picking up the point, students argued that the presence of athletics offered "more inducements to a young man, desiring a college education, . . . and let the world know that we are still alive and ready for business at the old stand."[38]

At the close of the season, students and local boosters held a high-spirited banquet in the team's honor. Over 150 from the college and community attended a dinner at a local banqueting hall festooned with blue and white bunting. As a participant later wrote, the general feeling that evening was that the college had "taken a long step forward in the short space of that first foot ball season." A long series of toasts included Stahr's to "Hercules, the Latest Addition to the Faculty" and Irvine's to "the Manly Game." Seizing the moment, banquet organizers advocated for a gymnasium, widely considered a necessity for athletic success. Enthusiastic Lancaster businessmen pledged $1,100 on the spot.[39]

Whether through fiscal or educational conservatism, senior board members still dragged their feet. But the gymnasium had come to symbolize student-alumni-community dreams for the college, dreams that seemed to be perpetually thwarted by board inertia. Proponents tried to call a special board meeting in December, to push the project forward, but they were blocked by a few leaders, and no further action was taken until the annual meeting in June. Students expressed growing impatience with their elders. The *Oriflamme* published in the spring of 1890 commented that other, younger schools with less money had gymnasiums: "Why? Because they have a board of trustees who are progressive and awake to the best interests of their college." Those trustees understood the need to "keep abreast with the times," lest their institutions "moulder and decay for want of patronage." In the *College Student* writer "Drex" was uncommonly strident in asserting students' "right to demand action on the part of our officers."[40]

By June 1890 momentum generated by the year's successes — reflected in a substantial rise in enrollments — was irresistible. Trustees confirmed Stahr as permanent president and authorized the beginning of work on the gymnasium as soon as the money had been raised. They also approved construction of a laboratory wing at the back of the College Building. Finally, as endowment topped $160,000, the board announced free tuition for all students. This action fulfilled a longtime ambition but was not as altruistic as it might appear. Over the years so many scholarships had been sold that few students actually paid tuition — typically, annual revenues from tuition totaled less than $40. The board's idea was that because college education now included facilities — like library, reading room, gymnasium, and laboratories — that had not been envisioned when scholarships were first sold, they would charge an additional "contingent fee" of $10 per term, or $30 a year.[41]

After the board meeting, trustees joined alumni for their annual dinner, now one of the most popular commencement events, with a meal prepared by "lady friends of the college" and decorations overseen by "Mrs. Dr. J. B. Kieffer." In the nineteenth-century custom of elaborate, all-male banquets, these dinners provided an opportunity for the college to cultivate alumni loyalty and present its plans for the future while alumni revived old friendships. Responding to a toast to the board, its president, John

Cessna, acknowledged the board's reputation as "a slow body" but vowed "that it would not be slow to follow any movement the people of Lancaster would inaugurate for the progress of the college."[42]

Afterward, a public meeting promoted the gymnasium. William U. Hensel, newly elected as the board's "young blood," spoke about the need to cultivate "sound bodies" among students. A. C. Reinoehl acknowledged that "the fine work" of the football team and the Glee Club had sparked his interest in the college and had undoubtedly "done more to give the college a name than anything done in a quarter of a century." He concluded that "the time had come when a gymnasium was as necessary for the success of the college as the college building and the society buildings on either side of it." In response, alumni and citizens pledged $2,450, mostly from local residents.[43]

Hensel, an 1870 graduate, expressed the views of a younger generation of alumni, who supported the college's stand on classical education but wanted Franklin & Marshall to embrace new trends. A Presbyterian, he pressed leaders to underline the "nonsectarian" character of collegiate education. "Its special mission is not to make lawyers, physicians nor ministers," he pointed out, "much less ministers of one particular denomination — but *men*." He supported fraternities, having joined Phi Kappa Sigma in spite of an official ban and served in the national organization's highest office. He argued that student rowdiness could be avoided by "the thorough cultivation of the social life of the college." This required "facilities and opportunities for the growth of those gentler graces and of the refinement which are the outer marks of the gentleman," which fraternities could provide. A prominent Lancaster attorney, Hensel headed the National Democratic Committee during Grover Cleveland's first campaign for president and became state attorney general in 1891.[44]

Stahr's modest inaugural ceremony at the beginning of the 1890 fall term was the college's first since 1855. The address Stahr gave recognized that Franklin & Marshall stood at a turning point that would determine its future relationship with its unique "life and genius," which were tied to German science and philosophy. He noted that the college's ability to inaugurate its own president was "the result of vigorous life within the institution, and new interest manifested by the friends of the college without." In the midst of change, however, he urged the college to retain sight of its "true idea," that education was "such a training of a man's powers as will enable him to use every talent to the best advantage, and make everything tributary . . . to the perfection of his own being and the advancement of the race."[45]

Yet the college must strive to balance competing goods, Stahr warned. It "must have a theory of education and maintain its principles, if need be, in the face of opposition from any quarter." In addition, "it must be in living, loving sympathy with all that is best and most progressive in the theory and method of educational thought, . . . open to every legitimate influence that comes back to it from its surroundings." Stahr believed that there was room for change in the precise methods of imparting "liberal culture," particularly in the later years of the program, when differences in taste and ability had emerged. He thought it possible to address expansion in knowledge and allow some students to prepare for postgraduate work. Moreover, he proposed that the college serve as "a dispenser of knowledge and a patron of science" to the community at large.[46]

Stahr considered athletics, "the training of the body," an essential component of liberal culture, but as a means, not an end in itself. Fittingly, the inaugural ceremonies concluded with the breaking of ground for the new gymnasium, located directly north of the Diagnothian Society's hall. Local architect James H. Warner designed it in English Tudor style, complete with half-timbering, dormer windows, and slate roof, as a "somewhat less severe" complement to the older buildings' Gothic architecture. The main floor consisted of one large room, with dressing rooms, a bowling alley, and a pitching court in the basement. Despite enthusiasm for the building, only about $2,500 of its $6,000 cost had been collected by June 1891, forcing Hensel to take out a loan for the remainder. The board created a new position of physical instructor and director of the gymnasium and hired Irvine, in his third year at the seminary, to conduct exercise sessions for each class. But trustees made no provision for gymnastic equipment, and Hensel and Irvine borrowed nearly $1,000 to purchase apparatus from the Spalding Company. Local businessman H. S. Williamson paid for the bowling alley.[47]

In the meantime, faculty members worked to modernize the college. Classics professor John B. Kieffer became college librarian in 1888. With an annual library budget of only $150, the collection of some five thousand books had languished in a dusty room on the third floor of the College Building. Raising money from "friends of the college," Kieffer expanded the library into two rooms in 1890, installed new bookcases, and fitted out a reading room. As its sole staff, Kieffer opened the library for only two hours on Tuesdays and Thursdays. He urged trustees to appropriate contingent fund money for student assistants and additional subscriptions.[48]

When the board did appropriate funds, the *College Student* exulted, "The conservative element that has held our library in a vice-like grip for fifty years has at last been overpowered, to a certain extent." During the winter, the reading room became site of a senior "reading circle," led by adjunct English professor George Mull, in response to student requests to read more literature. Kieffer moved on to advocate construction of a new library building. Like leaders of the movement to establish public libraries, he argued, in an article in the *Reformed Messenger*, that properly managed libraries prepared students to deal with the proliferation of printed materials. In the present "materialistic and plutocratic" society, libraries taught young men "an internal development" and "a habit of swift and discriminating reading" to enable them to detect and resist "the most insidious and dangerous forms of unbelief."[49]

Schiedt and Stahr also honed their fund-raising skills in hopes of completing laboratories and a natural history museum, respectively. Stahr obtained use of several empty rooms in an upper story of the Academy Building for his natural history collections. He purchased new cases and with the help of volunteer students transferred and reorganized the herbarium and the mineral specimens. Schiedt oversaw construction of a small wing at the back of the College Building with a large laboratory for general chemistry and a smaller one for use by the professor and advanced students. Afterward, he revised chemistry instruction to focus on experimentation, noting proudly that the new plan "so far has only been tried in the classical department of the University of Pennsylvania." The chemistry course included three hours of lab work per week for juniors and optional training in qualitative and quantitative analysis for seniors. Then Schiedt moved on to the biological laboratory, raising some $1,000 for zoology and botany equipment by soliciting "a few friends."[50]

The college's new laboratory-based science instruction offered the kind of training needed by students seeking to attend new graduate programs in science or medical school. Medical schools had begun to outpace apprenticeship as the most popular method for training doctors. These medical schools did not require a bachelor's degree for admission and directly competed with colleges for students. In response, many colleges offered courses and bachelor of science degree programs that in some cases were accepted for advanced standing in medical school. Schiedt's reputation made it possible for his students to skip the first year at the University of Pennsylvania's medical department, which advertised in the *Oriflamme*.[51]

A New Collegiate Education for a New Middle Class

In combination, the improvements of the early 1890s inspired a heady sense of progress and energy in Franklin & Marshall. The most obvious manifestation was a steady rise in college enrollments, which grew by one-third over the decade, while attendance at the academy doubled and that at the seminary grew by nearly half. This followed a national trend in which college enrollments as a whole doubled over the decade, and many more young people entered graduate and professional programs. Collectively, this growth in higher education reflected an effort by a new urban middle class to ensure opportunities for its young. To attract this group's disposable income, colleges had to offer more than the assurance of gentility afforded by the traditional classical curriculum. Without necessarily intending it, Franklin & Marshall's innovations offered keys to the mysteries of preparing for a changing world.[52]

College education had long suffered from negative images in the popular imagination. One was that of the sickly scholar, grown pale and weak from too much study and too little physical exercise. Another was that of the wastrel, tempted into vice and dissipation by too much leisure. New features of college life in the later nineteenth century — athletics, extracurricular activities, and experimental forms of learning — changed public perception of college life by promising to build "manly" young men prepared to face the demands of the future. Historians have noted an increased focus on masculinity, or manliness, in the latter decades of the nineteenth century; physical attributes of individual self-assertion and strength came increasingly to be seen as essential for success in a competitive economy.[53]

At Franklin & Marshall, arrival of football and a gymnasium helped make college education attractive to a new generation of young men. "The parent does not desire his sons to disregard their bodily strength," noted the editors of the first edition of the *College Student* in 1881. The parent would not want to "send them where lack of exercise is encouraged and where physical culture receives no attention at all." Scientific proof of the need for exercise came in 1892 when Lancaster physician Martin L. Herr examined students before they began physical education instruction. Using "anthropometric instruments" included in the new gym equipment, Herr found marked physical "degeneration" from freshman to senior year, and even more during seminary years. This he attributed to students' "lazy, dilatory style" of college life. In contrast, he immediately identified "the foot ball men," whose "carriage was erect, and each muscle performed its function." After reading his article, the mother of one student agreed that her husband had been right to allow their son to play football.[54]

Football promised to build up more than the body. Rightly played, it developed strength of character. As one historian has noted, "manliness" was a quality frequently attached to football in its early days, but it could denote a wide range of qualities, from stoicism and self-control to outright aggressiveness. At Franklin & Marshall, emphasis was on the gentlemanly virtues entailed in good sportsmanship, which should prevail whether one's team won or lost. Hence, students complained about the rough treatment received in Lewisburg when they played Bucknell. "All the manly spirit of college courtesy that is to be expected by a visiting team was entirely wanting," the school newspaper reported. Football also demanded personal discipline. After a resounding loss in 1894, the writer "Observer" blamed the team's lack of commitment to training. "To be of any consequence in a game," he noted, "one must possess first, physical health; which does not only mean being well, but doing well; secondly, must develop pluck and endurance and above all self-control, and these coming in a young man's student life, we cannot, nor will we wish for a better or a manlier method of their development."[55]

Beyond its influence on players, football was believed to have a beneficial effect on the student body. Looking back to 1889, a student essayist noted that "best of all was the quickening of the College spirit — the *esprit de corps*, the influence of which has ever since been felt as a constant challenge to closer fellowship and more effective cooperation in all that is fine and worthy to enter into the body of College tradition, and in promoting all that is wholesome and essential to the larger growth of College life."[56]

Football was the capstone of an array of activities and attributes that made up new ideals of campus life — ironically, most often envisioned in terms of college "traditions." Noting that teams were "to-day making tradition," one student suggested hanging their pictures on the walls of the gymnasium. "Tradition invariably gives additional charm to college life," he explained. "It is to the student what a proud national history is to the patriot." College leaders agreed that these activities benefited students, if only by distracting them from more dangerous pastimes. At an alumni banquet in 1891, Stahr praised the Glee Club and other organizations as the college's "jewels": "I am thoroughly convinced that both athletics and music, as innocent recreation, lift up and develop a true, manly character in young men." A few might "go to excess in these matters," but without these organizations, "such young men would be led astray by some agency far worse."[57]

The growing prominence of another organization, the campus Young Men's Christian Association, marked the college's movement into the mainstream of American Protestantism. A small campus YMCA first appeared at Franklin & Marshall in 1884 and allied itself with an intercollegiate missionary movement based in Princeton. With faculty support, the group organized weekly discussions and lectures on general topics. Emulating chapters at other schools, it published a small college handbook and held a reception for new students. After reorganizing in 1890, the chapter focused on more strictly devotional activities, such as weekly prayer meetings and Bible classes. The college included YMCA activities in its catalogue description of Christian instruction on campus. Explaining that Franklin & Marshall's goal was to confront students "with the claims of Christianity in its most concrete and living form," the catalogue listed a variety of religious activities but emphasized that all its instruction was imbued with "a Christian spirit and by Christian principles."[58]

After attending one of D. L. Moody's popular summer conferences at Northfield, Massachusetts, the Franklin & Marshall YMCA was inspired in 1894 to compile and publish an expanded handbook for new students, with a map of the city, listings of essential services and faculty residences, and floor plans of college buildings. The F&M Weekly commended the widening focus and attempt to be "a prominent factor for good in the college." The following year the YMCA revived receptions for new students and this time succeeded in making them a major landmark of the freshman year, perhaps because of the presence of a large number of young ladies from the local community.[59]

Campus YMCAs blended piety and sociability with an ethos known then and since as "muscular Christianity"—an emphasis on manliness in many Protestant churches. YMCAs helped to allay puritan suspicions of athletic "play" by emphasizing its importance for physical development. As a college student argued, athletic men were better prepared in body and spirit to become "active Christian workers." In the later 1890s the college hired physical education directors from the local Y to teach its classes.[60]

The Reformed Church as a whole had moved into missionary work in the later decades of the century. Reformed schools in Japan brought a number of Japanese students to the academy and college. The first, Masataka Yamanaka, graduated in 1885 and became the Japanese consul in New York. Another, G. Kinzo Kaneko, came initially to study English but, after converting to Christianity, went on to the seminary and was preparing to take up a professorship at the Theological Seminary in Sendai when he died of tuberculosis in 1895.[61]

Of all the new organizations at Franklin & Marshall, the Glee Club best epitomized the new cultural ideal of masculine college life. Such clubs had existed before 1889, generally within the classes, but like other activities they waxed and waned according to student enthusiasm. A new group was organized in the spring of 1889; swelled in the fall with the arrival of Irvine and other seminarians, sixteen men began practicing five nights a week. The *College Student* cheered the club's resurgence as another evidence of "a general awakening" at the college. Joined by the Mandolin Club and outfitted in full-dress suits from Hager and Bros., the musicians soon regaled the community with "the better class of college songs."[62]

Many singers also played football, thus manifesting the ideal blend of virile strength and romantic sensibility, a prominent feature of many of the songs. Emulating the efforts of other schools, the group's business manager organized ambitious concert tours throughout the region. The Glee Club proved an especially potent method of fostering nostalgic affection for the college at alumni gatherings. Recognizing this, the student paper called for a school song to use at concerts. Such a song would "always inspire [the alumnus] with renewed love for his Alma mater," because it "carries him back to the sunniest, gladdest days of his life."[63]

Multiplication of extracurricular organizations and intercollegiate connections created a dense social world separate from that of adults. The class of 1891 reported in the yearbook, "College life has a remarkable effect on the nature, habits and deportment of him who shares its trials and pleasures." At the very least, the auxiliary paraphernalia of this social life introduced many young men to the new world of consumer goods. Beyond displaying one's maturity and cultivation, clothing and accessories were presented as means of expressing group loyalty. Most campus organizations adopted special articles of clothing or insignia to mark their members and demonstrate school spirit. In 1891 the student newspaper praised several campus groups for choosing special sweaters, noting that "caps, blazers, sweaters, buttons, and pins [had] come to be looked upon as exclusively the property of student life." College days were no longer merely a time of preparation for adulthood, but one that "we are told by our predecessors are the gladdest of life," and it seemed "no more than right" that they should have symbolic recognition: "These badges, in a sense, make college more distinct, more real. They are strictly in keeping with the jollity, the brightness and the happy fellowship of academic life." Later, the paper noted that a local clothier had received a large shipment of blue and white flannel hats. "They are the latest thing out," it noted, "and will doubtless prove very popular during the football season." Although the cost of such accessories was deemed "insignificant," it was clear that a student who joined several groups could spend considerable money. For example, as sophomores, the class of 1895 adopted a class cane (made by Zahm, a local jeweler) of English oak with the class year engraved in a monogram on the silver handle.[64]

Resistance to Innovation

Not everyone was enthusiastic about the changes that came in the wake of this modern awakening. Criticisms of the Glee Club's incessant activities prompted the *College Student* to lament "wet blankets" who failed to support the club's efforts "to promote the zeal and enthusiasm which glorifies any institution": "Without enterprise and originality, they are content to stand by and let college life and spirit turn into the very essence of mugwumpism."[65]

For its part, the faculty feared that student activities cut into class attendance, which was mandatory. Early in 1890 faculty summoned a number of Glee Club members to answer for unexcused absences. Henceforth, students were required to apply in advance for permission to be absent for concert tours, and student athletes were required to obtain parents' permission before leaving campus to play games elsewhere. In 1891 the faculty allowed Glee Club tours in December, January, and March but decreed that in future it would permit only one trip a year during college sessions. The faculty were also eventually forced to limit teams' travel for athletic events at other schools. Managers were required to submit lists of team and club members for advance approval and students with unsatisfactory records were not allowed to participate.[66]

In 1891 resentment of the new campus leadership went public when the same group that had brought football and the Glee Club to the college decided to publish a weekly newspaper. As a monthly, the *College Student* could not carry much fresh news. It was actually more a literary magazine, filled with lengthy and sometimes abstruse pieces by faculty and alumni as well as undergraduates. William Irvine, who had worked on the staff of the *Princetonian,* joined with Bruce Griffith, '90, L. C. Harnish, '91, and Luther D. Reed, '92, to propose an independently operated four-page weekly paper modeled on Ivy League papers. *F&M Weekly* debuted in March, proclaiming its intention to promote college interests by championing improvements, strengthening ties with alumni, and advertising its virtues abroad.[67]

In response, the literary societies, which published the *College Student*, called a public meeting that adopted a resolution opposing the new paper's claims to represent students and vowing not to support it morally or financially. The *College Student* itself sniffed that the first issue of the "Weakly" was disappointing and that its inaugural editorial, "by the 'Great I Am,'" (undoubtedly a reference to Irvine) merely repeated what the *College Student* had been saying for years. It denounced the new paper as a "private adventure and a private speculation" that would drain financial support from existing college publications. When the first edition arrived from the press, "a large crowd" of students met in front of the College Building, summoned by the posting of a copy of the offending paper draped in black. The group processed to the baseball field, where they kindled a bonfire with every available copy. Their victory dance around the fire was cut short, however, by arrival of the paper's supporters, who "had laid in a supply of unmarketable eggs at low rates" and unleashed them in "in a broadside."[68]

In retrospect, the *Weekly*'s staff noted that the uproar "extensively advertised" the new paper and increased subscriptions. Its editorial board was enlarged in the fall, and at the end of the first year a dividend of eight dollars apiece was declared. In time, each periodical focused on the strengths of its format, with the *College Student* dropping detailed coverage of athletic events and expanding literary writing.[69]

The *Weekly* fully embraced its role as cheerleader and sometimes nagger on behalf of the new campus culture. Like publishers of community newspapers in this period, editors promoted activities that they had had a major part in organizing. For example, the Glee and Mandolin clubs planned a concert in Fulton Hall to raise money for the gymnasium equipment. Then, in the *Weekly*, their leaders declared it the "duty" of all students to attend, noting the "noble work" the clubs did for the college: "By giving first-class concerts before large and fashionable audiences, they have drawn to us many additional friends, carried our name into new territory, aroused great enthusiasm in the ranks of the alumni, and generally covered Franklin and Marshall with glory." The *Weekly* devoted extensive space to events at other campuses, particularly at Harvard, Yale, and Princeton, and emphasized the importance of constantly advertising the college's virtues — and its own role in so doing. "A college, to grow and prosper, must be known," they editorialized. "There must emanate from it an influence for good and for right. It must be, as was said of Franklin and Marshall by a prominent Philadelphian, last year: 'A place where they make men!' "[70]

Some students balked at the cost of demonstrating proper college spirit. The *Weekly* responded that the time was gone when the ideal student eked a bare existence while living on bread and water: "The student who legitimately spends $300 a year gets more benefit from his college course than the man who spends $200 a year." College education involved more than "a mere study of books." The *Weekly* wrote, "[It]is a world in itself, and it is the associations of college life that do as much to develop a student as the mere class room work." Students who lacked proper college spirit were "almost sure to lack public spirit and progressiveness in the world at large." Students should be willing to deny themselves "other selfish pleasures" in order to support their teams and other worthy campus causes.[71]

The *F&M Weekly* defended a lecture series to raise money for gym equipment by explaining that the school had no money to pay for it and arguing that students had a duty to assist their institution: "Shall we then, when it is in our power by unity of action and by the display of a little public spirit to raise money sufficient for the equipment, be content to see the gymnasium stand empty of apparatus for a year at least?" Many students balked at paying fifty cents for a minstrel show to raise money for the gym, but the paper asserted that "selfishness rather than poverty was the cause of non-attendance." It concluded that if typical students of the past were like those today, it was little wonder that alumni were so "stingy" in their support the college: "A man who refuses to support his Alma Mater both by moral and material influence according to his ability does not deserve the name of graduate."[72]

Recent alumnus "Noss" struck back in the *College Student* at those who used "college spirit" to "whip others into line" behind their schemes. He disliked seeing students aping elite schools: "It is painful to see [the college] giving her strength to the latest crazes and promenading before the country with feathers borrowed from her elder sister across the Delaware." Franklin & Marshall had always prized "principle" over "popularity" and as a result had produced "true scholarship." For his part, the author dismissed the minstrel show as "a downright waste of time for all concerned, as well as an unwise expenditure of money" and the Glee Club as principally of interest to "unthinking minds." He wondered that "earnest students can find time for so much nonsense."[73]

Even at elite schools where the new vision of extracurricular campus life was most dominant, there were always "outsiders" more interested in learning for its own sake or as a stepping-stone to professional careers. Franklin & Marshall students also varied in degrees of academic seriousness. Moreover, student backgrounds ranged widely in affluence and exposure to urban culture. In 1891 the *Weekly* deplored the lack of "polish and refinement" among the "large percentage of our men [who] come from the farms, the shops and small country towns," where little attention was paid to social graces. There may have been tension between students from rural ethnic communities where Pennsylvania German was still spoken at home and those from more thoroughly Anglicized areas. As late as 1903, an English professor noted that, "to a surprising degree," Pennsylvania German was the first language of many students. In contrast, *Oriflamme*'s editors were sufficiently assimilated to mainstream culture to find humor in Richard Schiedt's strong German accent. Parodies of his irregular pronunciations, such as "frock" for frog, and his colorful tirades at student stupidity were yearbook staples.[74]

Attitudes toward campus life also involved competing notions of masculinity. Research-oriented faculty thought sports a childish waste of time. Schiedt, for one, had a Prussian sensitivity to ideals of manliness and honor — a duel fought as a gymnasium student had cost him the sight of his left eye. But for him true manliness was revealed in the tough-minded sensibility of research science. A notice in the *College Student* about a monograph by one of Schiedt's prize students illustrates his perspective. John K. Small, '92, won the first fellowship in botany offered by Columbia's new University Faculty of Pure Science, and Schiedt congratulated Franklin & Marshall for being able "to count so brilliant and promising a young man among her sons." Small was an exemplar not only because he had strong intellectual qualities but because he possessed "the moral courage" demanded by rigorous field research. Schiedt's portrait of Small offers a truly heroic model of the scientist:

> The botanist never has a vacation; while others are enjoying the restful *dolce far neinte* he is struggling day after day, with the intensest eagerness for the supremacy over nature, against the heat of the sun and the icy winds blowing on high mountain peaks, against the poison fangs awaiting him in the thicket of the forest and against the stings of murderous insects. . . . Thus, when we look over the twenty-two titles enumerating Dr. Small's publications in connection with his monograph we feel the force of the moral as well as the intellectual energy stored up in these writings and we rejoice that we may call such a manly man ours.[75]

Negotiating Change in the Curriculum

An atmosphere of innovation at Franklin & Marshall in the 1890s was heightened by continued changes in the curriculum. First came abolition in 1891 of the much-detested biennial test examinations. An early issue of *F&M Weekly* pointed out that such examinations had fallen out of favor with "the leading educators of America" because having to prepare so many subjects at once forced students to "cramm" and encouraged cheating. Although the change followed current educational trends, it eliminated an academic experience that had served as a rite of passage for generations of college students, particularly in admitting sophomores to upperclassmen status. Noting that many other regulations were obsolete, Stahr recommended a general overhaul of the college's rules and regulations. After devoting much time to the revision process, the faculty had the result printed so that for the first time every student could possess a copy.[76]

In 1895 the assessment system was again revised to provide for examinations at the completion of each particular "branch of study" instead of at the end of the academic year. In the unitary classical curriculum, there was no system of separate courses and credits, and varying amounts of time were devoted to different subjects. Professors were directed to give final grades based on a two-to-one average of daily recitations and examinations.[77]

Stahr won board assent to changes that gradually eroded the prescribed curriculum. In 1890, noting frequent requests to study one or two subjects only rather than to pursue a degree, Stahr asked the board to reconsider its ban on "irregular" students. Since then, growing numbers of young men from Lancaster had enrolled, primarily to study chemistry or biology with Schiedt or electrical measurement with Kershner. These young men were officially placed under the category of special students, and the 1894–1895 catalogue reflected the college's modest expansion with a list of 164 regular students, 2 graduate students, and 5 special students.[78]

The same catalogue also formally recognized the limited appearance of electives by dividing senior studies into required and elective subjects. A joint meeting of the faculty and the Committee on Instruction approved Stahr's plan for "optional studies." Under it, all seniors still studied philosophy, ethics, political economy, and English but were allowed to choose among classical and modern languages, lectures and seminars in archaeology and American history, calculus, and advanced sciences such as embryology, astronomy, and electrical measurement. The first class of seniors given this limited choice voted with their feet against mathematics: only nine of twenty-seven elected it, while twenty-three continued with Greek and thirteen with Latin, sixteen chose German, and only three French. Because the size of the faculty did not grow, it became harder to find time for the additional courses. The literary societies were compelled to move their weekly meetings to Friday evenings so that classes could be held on Saturday mornings.[79]

Stahr welcomed one opportunity to add a member to the faculty at little cost to the college, even if the subject hardly seemed to fit most definitions of liberal arts. He persuaded the faculty and the Committee on Instruction to apply to a Department of War program that assigned army officers to college and university campuses to teach military science and drill students in martial maneuvers. Lt. Edgar W. Howe arrived

in the fall of 1894 and organized a company of about sixty students. At first, enthusiastic students wore their uniforms everywhere, prompting the *Weekly* to predict, "The
day when military dress will be the sole costume of the student at F. & M. is near at
hand." But many students soon wearied of the extra work and tried to drop the program. The board eventually made participation compulsory for two years. As the Committee on Instruction noted, "The effect of the drill will be to improve the carriage
and appearance of students, and forms a healthful exercise." For a time, companies of
cadets were a part of student life, giving exhibitions at gymnastic meets and participating in theater productions at the Fulton Opera House. The program broke down during the Spanish-American War, and in 1901 the faculty finally eliminated it entirely.[80]

In one area, the college remained traditional. Rumors began to circulate in 1894
that it would admit young ladies. The academy, in fact, had enrolled a few girls as day
students since the 1870s, and from time to time local educational leaders urged the
college to go coed. Encouraged by the creation of a special physical education course
for women, a delegation of young women visited Stahr and asked to be admitted to the
regular degree course. Acknowledging that the question of coeducation was difficult
but important, he discussed it informally with faculty but decided that the decision
had to be made by the board. The *Weekly* noted that reports in local papers that Stahr
planned to ask the board to admit women had "created a stir among the students" and
revealed a "growing sentiment in favor" of the idea. The college had adjusted easily to
the presence that winter of one young woman, Mary L. Morgan, as instructor of elocution. She had prepared for the aspiring profession of elocution at the Emerson College of Oratory in Boston and was popular with students. Seminary faculty objected
to a woman, however, and withdrew from a joint appointment until a male teacher
could be found willing to take on the ten-week course. (Morgan's connection with the
college resumed when she married one of the instructors, Anselm V. Hiester.)[81]

In fact, Stahr favored limited coeducation. The college lacked resources to "provide the comforts and surroundings and safeguards desirable for the education of
young women in the widest sense," but he thought it possible to allow them to attend
as day scholars. He noted that "experienced educators" unanimously praised the beneficial effects of "the presence and influence of women." The faculty was willing to
make the experiment, and he personally thought that it would bring the college "in
closer touch with the community and insure better work in the class-room," while
offering "higher culture to many who are now debarred from it."[82]

The board tabled the request, however. At least one influential member, W. U.
Hensel, adamantly opposed coeducation. In a public address later that year, he proclaimed himself "unshaken in [his] confidence that no advancement of science, no
permanent development of our education, and no lasting stride of our religion, [would]
so far change the social system as to make the spheres of man and woman identical
instead of coordinate." He made the underlying connections between education and
gender roles explicit in a later statement of his vision of "ideal college life." It involved
"thorough drill in" traditional liberal arts subjects, "with incidental cultivation of baseball, football, general athletics, music, dancing, French, and other manly accomplish-

ments." He advocated "rigid uniformity" in the course of study and "no collegiate co-education of the sexes."[83]

Innovation was further limited by the Franklin & Marshall's anemic endowment. Even with contingent fees, increased enrollments in the early 1890s increased demands on the faculty without bringing substantially greater revenues. The college could not even be sure of paying the salaries of its six full-time professors and four part-time instructors. Often Stahr avoided going further into arrears only by special last-minute appeals to friends of the college. Moreover, enrollments reached the point at which it was necessary to divide many classes into sections, adding to the faculty's classroom hours. Stahr wanted at least three new professorships, to divide the present chairs of English, Latin, and Greek and of physics and chemistry, allowing the faculty to focus on their specialties. In the early 1890s, Stahr's annual reports to the board invariably concluded by urging them to begin planning for a new campaign to increase the endowment, but every year the Committee on Endowment found reasons to wait.[84]

The college still relied principally upon support from the Reformed Church. In an effort to increase funding for college and seminary, the Eastern Synod agreed to share ownership and management of its institutions with the Pittsburgh Synod and the Synod of the Potomac, which included Maryland and areas to the south. The Pittsburgh Synod and the Synod of the Potomac were to appoint three and six trustees, respectively, with nine chosen by the college's board and the remaining twelve by the Eastern Synod. The change increased the board's geographic diversity but was largely symbolic because in nearly all cases synods automatically approved the board's nominations.[85]

For a number of years, the seminary's fund-raising campaigns had absorbed much of the synods' resources. The seminary finally moved into a grand neo-Romanesque building across College Avenue from the college campus in 1894. This relieved overcrowded conditions in the College Building and marked the beginning of a gradual divergence of interests between the two institutions. Meanwhile, the college had not even been able to complete its campaigns to endow the presidency and the alumni professorship or to raise the last $3,000 owed on the gymnasium. These efforts were no doubt hampered by the financial crisis of the 1890s, but board president John Cessna's growing infirmity and crises in his personal life probably also played a role. For several years before his death in 1893, Cessna tried to retire from the position he had held since 1865 but was repeatedly overruled by his colleagues.[86]

A New Generation in Control

George F. Baer's unanimous election in 1894 as only the third president of the board in Franklin & Marshall's history augured a period of more energetic board leadership. Baer's career demonstrated that some in the German American community had moved close to national centers of power and wealth in the later nineteenth century. Baer attended the college for a year in 1860–1861 and subsequently led his local militia company in engagements from the Second Battle of Bull Run to Chancellorsville.

After the Civil War he established in the growing city of Reading, Pennsylvania, a lucrative legal practice that included the Philadelphia and Reading Railroad (PRR). When J. P. Morgan reorganized the PRR in the 1880s after it went into receivership, Baer was drawn into the financier's orbit. The PRR again declared bankruptcy in 1893, setting off the great stock market panic, and by the time Baer was elected president of the board, he was engaged in another round of restructuring that would in 1901 make him president of the entire Reading system. He also headed a complex web of coal and iron companies created to circumvent Pennsylvania laws against railroad control of its anthracite coal industry. Baer helped found a wide range of institutions in Reading and was a leader of his Reformed congregation. Along with a number of college men, including J. H. Dubbs, Baer was a founder and early president of the Pennsylvania German Society.[87]

Baer brought powerful contacts and substantial personal wealth to the presidency of the board. Generally much occupied with business, he left decisions about day-to-day matters in the hands of local trustees, particularly W. U. Hensel. Also a conservative Democrat, Hensel was similarly a pillar of Lancaster's business community. He was founder and president of the elite Hamilton Club, for example, as well as an officer of the Lancaster Board of Trade.[88]

In his 1894 annual report, Stahr attempted to take advantage of the moment to spur the board to action. With continuing increases in enrollment, the college's overall prospects had "never been brighter," he asserted. But as he had repeatedly pointed out, demands were also continuing to mount. He recommended a campaign to build a library, a new chemistry laboratory, and a chapel and possibly enlarge the College Building. At least $250,000 was needed for construction and for the endowment for three new professorships.[89]

The Committee on Instruction supported Stahr's proposals in principle but urged that no new buildings be undertaken until the present endowment of around $172,000 was increased by another $250,000. Committee members hoped that someone could be found to donate one of the buildings "in honor of some deceased friend or in their own names." The board appointed a seven-man committee, chaired by Baer, to plan a fund-raising campaign. It also agreed to pay off the $3,000 still owed for the gymnasium, which Hensel had been carrying and paying interest on as a personal note.[90]

As before, one of the largest material advances of the period came neither through the beneficence of the Reformed Church nor through alumni but from an unexpected quarter. Early in 1897, John Watts de Peyster of Tivoli, New York, announced that he was presenting the college with a library building worth an estimated $30,000. He meant this literally, for he had already had an architect draw plans and awarded the construction contract to a local builder at the time of his formal offer to the board.[91]

De Peyster was not a stranger to Franklin & Marshall. A wealthy descendant of old New York families, he had largely devoted his life to writing on a wide range of historical subjects and to an eccentric assortment of benefactions in memory of family members. The college had first come to his attention in the 1860s when the Diagnothian Society made him an honorary member. A correspondence in the mid-1880s with Diagnothian's secretary Abraham H. Rothermel,'87, resulted in a close friendship and publication of many of de Peyster's literary productions in the *College Student*. He also became a correspondent of history professor J. H. Dubbs. Then began a process of mutual wooing. In 1892, de Peyster gave the college a collection of books on Mary, Queen of Scotts, and the college gave him an honorary D. Litt. He made several other substantial gifts of valuable books and received an honorary LL.D. in 1896. By that time, Rothermel, now a Reading attorney, and Professor J. B. Kieffer ventured to press the college's need for a library building. Many years later, Rothermel recalled that de Peyster replied that if he gave the library, it would be with money he had planned to leave to Rothermel. Moreover, de Peyster vowed to make the donation only if Republican William McKinley won the presidential election that year. He did, and the plans and specifications were on their way to Kieffer in early December. De Peyster directed that the building be named Watts–de Peyster in memory of his father, Frederick de Peyster, and his maternal grandfather, John Watts.[92]

The two-story building was in the fashionable Romanesque style with "a handsome tower" and a large, arched entranceway. The board decided to locate it southeast of Goethean Hall, facing outward to College Avenue. A cornerstone-laying ceremony was held in May, and transfer of books began in November. The finished library finally opened in February 1898, to the delight of students, who had been denied access to books since September. The herbarium and museum of the Linnaean Society moved into former library rooms in the College Building, making it easier to use the collections in science work and providing space for the growing academy. Throughout, serving as librarian as well as professor, Kieffer oversaw construction and the transfer and reorganization of the library.[93]

De Peyster also presented the college with a large, seated bronze statue of his ancestor, Abraham de Peyster, an eighteenth-century mayor of New York City. It had originally been donated to Bowling Green Park in New York City but was relocated because of development in the area. The board agreed to install it in a prominent location in front of the new library. Unwittingly, the decision marked an important transition in the college's history. The library itself had been built on the spot once occupied by the memorial of Frederick Rauch. Over the years, its marble had become pitted and worn, and in 1892 it had been removed to his gravesite in Lancaster Cemetery. Coincidentally, Rauch's psychology textbook, in use throughout the century, was replaced in 1890 by two more-current authors. Although the result of a series of unrelated decisions, installation of the statue of a complete stranger to the college in the place of a monument to one of the founders of Mercersburg Theology vividly symbolized the institution's gradual departure from its founding traditions, into a world shaped by the desires of benefactors.[94]

Shaping a Modern Campus

Moving the Rauch monument was part of a campaign by the Grounds and Buildings Committee to improve the campus's appearance. Over the decades since trees were first planted on the barren hillside, a dense forest had grown up that permitted little but moss to grow beneath. By thinning and trimming trees in the 1890s, the committee achieved the beginnings of grass lawns and eventually was able to induce the janitor to maintain them with a mower instead of letting his livestock range freely. Even after the thinning, Schiedt's census in June 1896 found 486 trees, representing thirty-eight species. As Lancaster's development westward brought new urban amenities, such as water systems and paved streets, college grounds gradually assumed the look of a modern campus, to students' great satisfaction. For years, many had complained about the rustic effect of the "unsightly" board fence enclosing the grounds. The committee removed one thousand feet of the fence along College Avenue, graded and sodded the sloping ground, and paved and guttered the street. Brick walkways were laid out in front of the College Building and a decorative brick and terra-cotta gateway built at the main entrance. Buildings were gradually wired for electric lights, and in 1896 an electric bell was installed to relieve the janitor of the task of ringing the change of classes each hour.[95]

Lack of modern sanitary facilities had long been a problem, particularly in Harbaugh Hall, where students had to draw water from an outside pump. City water and sewer connections were slow in reaching College Hill, and the intention had long been to build a reservoir on city-owned land just west of the College Building. In anticipation of its construction, the gymnasium was designed with space for showers, and hopes soared when work on the reservoir began in 1892. Soon after its completion in 1894, however, its western bank collapsed, unleashing a wall of water — fortunately, in the opposite direction from college buildings — and it was abandoned. City water lines finally reached the college two years later. and local trustee H. S. Williamson underwrote laying pipes to Harbaugh and the Academy Building. Meanwhile, after years of urging from Stahr, the committee installed steam heat in the College Building, Harbaugh Hall, and the gymnasium in 1893.[96]

An alliance of students and local businessmen took on comparable improvements to the college's athletics facilities. Early in 1894, Williamson called a public meeting to formally organize the Franklin & Marshall Athletic and Field Association, composed of students and associate members. Its first project was building a modern athletic complex at the northeastern corner of campus. Principally funded by local businessmen, facilities included a combined football field and baseball diamond, encircled by an oval quarter-mile cinder track, all overlooked by a grandstand. To the north were three tennis courts. The entire area was enclosed by a fence so that admission could be charged. The new track inspired formation of a team, which placed second in its class in its first attempt at the Penn Relays in 1896. The athletic field was renamed Williamson Field in 1899 in recognition of this trustee's support of college athletics.[97]

After the rousing success of its first seasons, the football team found it increasingly difficult to hold the field against the larger schools on its schedule. Editorialists often blamed weak school spirit and lax training, but it was becoming clear that students needed better coaching. When William Irvine left in 1893 to take charge of Mercersburg Academy players were left to their own resources. Teams depended on local contributions and gate receipts to pay for the already substantial expenses of equipment and travel, and there was little money to pay for coaching. Cancellation of the lucrative Thanksgiving Day football game in 1893 brought the Athletic and Field Association to the verge of insolvency.[98]

The seminary's decision to forbid its students to participate in out-of-town events was a further blow. The *F&M Weekly* protested that this barred organizations' "most valuable material," whose contribution had become particularly important as undergraduate commitment waned. Despite its deficits, the Athletic and Field Association decided to hire a coach for the baseball team in 1895. "Other colleges in our class have not been slow to take this step," the *Weekly* pointed out, "and it is becoming more and more evident every year, that, if athletics is to keep pace with the progress made in other departments of the Institution, the work must be of a more systematic character." To provide instruction, athletic teams in effect substituted professionalism on the part of coaches for that of students. In 1896 the association hired A. E. Bull, a former All-American player from the University of Pennsylvania, to coach the team for three weeks. With his help the college team put in a creditable showing against Penn, holding it to twenty-four points and nearly scoring several times. "In the presence of a crowd of nearly 2,000 spectators, among them some of the most famous of Pennsylvania's athletic managers, together with representatives of the leading Philadelphia daily papers," the *Weekly* exulted, "F. and M. put up a game against the University which has seldom been equalled by any of the smaller colleges." The team's performance faltered after Bull's departure, and the association brought in another coach to help the team prepare for the big Thanksgiving Day game against "traditional" rival Bucknell. Importing outside coaches for short periods proved expensive, and in 1898 Stahr recommended expanding the physical education instructor's responsibilities to include coaching athletic teams.[99]

By this time the faculty had divided over the proper role of athletics in collegiate education. Although faculty minutes were circumspect, the 1896 *Oriflamme* offered a satirical account of a meeting in which J. B. Kieffer denounced athletics as "an evil" and football, "an abomination." Latin professor George Mull defended them, in his meandering, multisyllabic way, for promoting exercise and physical training, and the new professor of English defended sports "in a mild, but earnest manner" because they advertised the college and increased local interest, both important to the success of the endowment campaign. Student humorists portrayed Stahr as vacillating according to the most recently expressed statements. At the end, Schiedt denounced the discussion for its lack of decisiveness.[100]

New Dynamics Within the Faculty

The Franklin & Marshall faculty had never been monolithic, but newcomers in the 1890s brought a wider range of perspectives and opinions about college policies. Stahr considered each teacher's understanding of his role to be fundamental to the college's overall influence on students and tried to ensure that new hires fit in with the school's philosophy. Most new faculty either had or were planning to work toward Ph.D's and had attended Franklin & Marshall or similar institutions. George Mull, hired to teach English and classical languages when William Nevin retired, studied classical philology at the University of Leipzig after graduating from Mercersburg College and the Theological Seminary of the Reformed Church. To replace William Nevin, Stahr hired C. Earnest Wagner, who had studied at Oxford after several years as an assistant Reformed pastor, and whose father was a board member. Wagner quickly became an advocate for the more gentlemanly approach to collegiate education favored in Britain, and served as the faculty member on the Athletic Association board.[101]

Anselm V. Hiester became assistant professor in 1894, with responsibility for German, mathematics, and political science. Chosen Marshall Orator at his graduation from Franklin & Marshall in 1889, he taught several years at Palatinate College and studied at Union Theological Seminary, New York University, and the Reformed Seminary. Two years after his arrival, he received a fellowship to study political and social science at Columbia, and Stahr persuaded the board to give him a leave of absence. Upon his return, Hiester's position was renamed as the professorship of social and political science to acknowledge his expertise, though he continued to teach a wide range of subjects.[102]

Hiester's work at Columbia exposed him to leading figures in the development of political science and economics as independent social science disciplines. By the mid-1890s Columbia's Faculty of Political Science had begun to move away from its initial vision of training up a cadre of young men for public service, but under its activist president Seth Low, the university fused "the ideal of the German university" with "the tradition of civic learning and responsibility." Strongly influenced by Hegelianism and historicism, the new social sciences were close to Franklin & Marshall's own philosophical traditions. "Society is no longer regarded as a mechanical compound of independent elements," Hiester explained, "but as an organic unity composed of parts vitally related to one another and undergoing a continuous process of development."[103]

Similarly, in 1895 the college brought back C. Nevin Heller, Marshall Orator of the class of 1890, to teach ancient languages, after he had served as a high school principal. After two years he obtained leave to study at Cornell University. His year's graduate work did not earn a degree, but in a setting of increased demand for college instructors, he bargained for a substantial increase in salary upon his return.[104]

This younger generation of teachers accepted heavy teaching loads approaching eighteen or nineteen classroom hours a week but were less patient with some nonacademic aspects of their jobs. The 1896 *Oriflamme* published a chart of faculty attendance at chapel, for example, revealing that younger members rarely attended. They also absented themselves from weekly faculty meetings, which were heavily dominated by student discipline, particularly the hearing of excuses from students who had exceeded the number of allowed absences. To deal with these complaints the faculty decided to meet every other week on Friday evening and to delegate routine matters of attendance to "the proper officers." In 1902 the faculty office of registrar was created and charged with maintaining records of absences from chapel and recitations. The next year, after the board created the first nonacademic position of secretary to the president, the faculty revised its rules to make the president and secretary responsible for dealing with student absences.[105]

Admissions were another faculty responsibility that had become increasingly burdensome. The catalogue specified subjects or "branches," and even particular authors, to be covered in examinations for prospective students, examinations that were held during several days around commencement and before the beginning of the new year in September. Students failing to meet standards in one or two subjects might be admitted "with qualifications" and the expectation that they work to make up the deficiencies during the year. Such qualifications mounted as fewer public high schools provided adequate training in classical languages and mathematics. For example, Stahr reported that in the fall of 1890, several applicants were told they would have to enter the academy to prepare for college work, and another who should have gone there was admitted provisionally "in consideration of his age." In 1893 seven of sixty applicants were turned down. "There is still some difficulty experienced in securing the standard of attainments which applicants for admission ought to have," Stahr explained to the board, "and for this reason the work necessarily drags in some of the classes." The faculty tried to be "reasonable in its demands" while enforcing standards of scholarship, attendance, and conduct.[106]

The first move toward formalizing admission practices had come in 1887, when the faculty announced that preparatory schools meeting the college's standards would be allowed simply to certify that a student had covered the expected branches of knowledge and attest his "industry and good moral character." Over the years, the numbers of approved schools grew to include both private academies and public high schools. The faculty also acceded to requests from groups of local alumni to hold examinations in their communities.[107]

The College Association of Pennsylvania was formed in 1887 in response to a call from presidents Thomas Apple of Franklin & Marshall and Edward Magill of Swarthmore to fight an effort by the state legislature to tax college and university property. The association took up the question of standardizing admission requirements and soon expanded membership to include secondary schools and institutions throughout the region. In the early 1890s, as the Association of Colleges and Preparatory Schools of the Middle States and Maryland, it began to collaborate with a parallel organization in New England to set uniform college entrance requirements in English. Franklin & Marshall professors J. H. Dubbs and John B. Kieffer were also active in the Middle States Association, Kieffer serving as its treasurer from its founding. Stahr was elected head of the group of Pennsylvania college presidents in 1896.[108]

The Middle States' initiative led to formation of the College Entrance Examination Board (CEEB) in 1900. Franklin & Marshall's faculty decided not to join, preferring to conduct their own examinations, but they agreed to accept CEEB's certificates "to the extent in which they [covered Franklin & Marshall] requirements," and to administer CEEB examinations in Lancaster.[109]

Accommodating senior electives within the structure of a partially prescribed curriculum became ever more difficult. There were simply not enough teachers, classrooms, or hours in the day to allow seniors to fit in all the courses they wanted to take. Although generally advocates of electives, *F&M Weekly* editors noted that their proliferation in the senior year had some negative effects, including weakening of class ties because seniors no longer held recitations as a body. To give time for planning, the faculty began in 1897 to require students in the spring of their junior year to select subjects they intended to study as seniors.[110]

Limited Acceptance of Elective System

Franklin & Marshall students rarely questioned their college's commitment to classical education, but many were eager for more electives. For its prize debate in 1898, the Glee Club set as its topic the question of whether Franklin & Marshall "should have electives in all departments, except that of Philosophy, after the Sophomore year." Many liked the idea of balancing a liberal education with the opportunity to begin preparation for professional training. "There is a great advantage in being able, especially during the last year of your course, to arrange your work so that it will fit in with the work you expect to do after leaving college," the *F&M Weekly* pointed out.[111]

Fittingly, the next step in the college's transformation was catalyzed by a student petition in response to changing demands in professional training. In the fall of 1898, a group of juniors asked to be excused from Greek in order to devote more time to preparation for medical school. "Realizing the important bearing of the question" upon the college's fundamental policies, the faculty referred the petition to Stahr and the board's Committee on Instruction.[112]

"The reasonable request of so many students must be given due weight," Baer commented to Hensel. Personally, Baer thought that Greek could be made optional after the sophomore year, though he strongly opposed cutting back on Latin. "The old argument that the classics were essential as a drill and a scholastic discipline has lost its force," he admitted. He thought that it was possible that comparable training could be achieved "by the study of the new practical things which progressive civilization have forced upon us." He doubted that Franklin & Marshall could "withstand the example of other colleges," but worried that by beginning to change its curriculum, it would lose its character as a liberal arts institution. "It would be very unfortunate," he mused, "if, by any change of curriculum, we should get into the position of Lafayette or Lehigh." (At these schools, generous funding from the region's industrial fortunes brought technical departments into prominence.) But he left the decision to the faculty and Committee on Instruction.[113]

The students' request came at a particularly opportune moment, when the college's forward momentum had seemed to stall. In June, Stahr admitted that fund-raising campaigns had not been "even remotely successful," and deficits threatened to erode small gains made in the endowment. His comments about the Reformed Church's lack of support betrayed uncharacteristic bitterness: despite their "abundant" promises, the synods had come up with little real money, and he compared them to the New Testament character that offered charity only in the empty phrase, "Go in peace, be ye warmed and filled." He concluded, "We must either prepare to contract our operations and give up the hope of making Franklin & Marshall all that parents can reasonably expect for the general education of their sons; or else we must go to work in earnest and secure funds, whether in large or small amounts, so as to meet the increasing needs of the college."[114]

As Stahr acknowledged to Baer, the college's Greek requirements cost it many students. This was made evident in field reports Stahr received from Edwin M. Hartman, the new co-headmaster of the academy. During the summers of 1897 and 1898, he energetically canvassed Reformed communities throughout Pennsylvania, in search of students for the academy and college. He described a number of factors that cut into enrollments. First, Franklin & Marshall faced strong competition from a wide variety of educational institutions, ranging from Mercersburg Academy to Pierce Business College in Philadelphia. Within the Reformed Church, Franklin & Marshall competed with Ursinus College. In one case, Hartman made great efforts to "secure" a particular young man because his father was an elder of his church: "If the son goes to Ursinus I fear for the influence of the whole congregation which seems to be on the fence now."[115]

The college lost many potential students because of its curriculum. In one case, Hartman reported that a "promising" young normal school graduate with whom he had spoken had planned to go to Franklin & Marshall "until the Principal of Pottsville High School told him that he would get far more out of a Latin Scientific course." Other prospective students chose other schools in the region because they offered more electives.[116]

Hartman, a leader of the campus YMCA while a student at Franklin & Marshall in the early 1890s, was an energetic evangelist for liberal education. For example, he set out to change the minds of an Amityville couple who wanted their son to go to a local normal school. They contended that "the college course costs too much, takes too much time, . . . and the mother feared that it would take the boy, their only child, away from them entirely." For two hours Hartman "urged them in every way [he] could," and finally the father vowed he would "give him a college course." Later, the son decided to begin at the normal school and possibly transfer to Franklin & Marshall as a sophomore. "The Normal diploma seems quite an attraction for many a young man," Hartman noted. He had more success in persuading another young man to take a college course at Franklin & Marshall instead of going straight to medical school at the University of Pennsylvania.[117]

Stahr also knew from direct experience that many students left college early to begin work or go into other education programs. Class histories in *Oriflamme* typically reported on students' departures. Eight of forty-four members of the class of 1901 did not return after their freshman year, for example. One was admitted to West Point, three went to other colleges in the area, several took jobs clerking and teaching, and several simply stayed home. Four newcomers took their places.[118]

Stahr probably concluded that some modification of the traditional classical curriculum was necessary if the college was to continue to advance. He told the board that students who did advanced work in biology and chemistry were able to complete medical school in three instead of four years and acknowledged persistent difficulties caused by poor secondary education in Greek. Broadening the curriculum was not an attempt "to make the college course professional or technical" but to address the needs "in the way of liberal culture" of those who intended to take up professional studies after college. In so doing, he subtly shifted the emphasis in his definition of "liberal culture" from specific contents to developmental function. Finally, he pointed out that the Synod of the Potomac had recently asked the college to provide an additional program in science.[119]

"We are thus brought face to face with a question of profound significance," he told the board, "a critical question upon the decision of which the future of the college, its life and prosperity, the fulfillment of the expectations cherished by its friends, and the accomplishment of its mission in the community will largely depend." Commissioned in such terms, the board authorized changes "as will meet the demands of the present time."[120]

The faculty created a new degree course that required no Greek and led to a bachelor of philosophy degree. It required study of French or German and additional sciences. In addition, it reduced the Greek requirement for the bachelor of arts degree to two years, either at the college level or at the beginning level for those with no previous background. In the latter case, applicants should have studied German or French and elementary science and mathematics. Both programs added a few electives in the junior year and advanced courses in biology, chemistry, mathematics, political science, and philosophy, "including pedagogy," to help students prepare for graduate and professional programs. Under the new system it became clear that increasing electives required reorganization of schedules, and the faculty divided the year into two semesters and began to use the term "courses" to refer to units of study rather than to entire degree programs.[121]

Despite the changes, and previous decisions to admit special students, Franklin & Marshall's catalogue continued to present the college's primary goal as "a thorough, liberal education." The catalogue argued that "the full college curriculum" was "best adapted to the attainment of a thorough training for culture and discipline" because it offered a combination of "thorough instruction, harmonious development, and the formation of sound character." The catalogue stressed the importance of close contact with teachers—"men of ability, experience and enthusiasm in their respective departments"—which provided not only personal attention but "the inspiration which the genuine scholar and teacher . . . always communicates."[122]

By revising the curriculum to meet the demands of their constituency, the college's leaders hoped for increased support in return, particularly for construction of the long-desired science building. Chemistry laboratories added at the beginning of the decade could not accommodate additional courses and students, biology classes continued to meet in a regular recitation room, and students studying anatomy under the guidance of a local physician met in the damp cellar of the College Building. In 1898 the Committee on Laboratory and Museum reported pledges of around $11,000 of an estimated cost of $40,000 and once more urgently implored the board to make "all honorable and immediate efforts" to meet this "serious necessity." Another year saw no concrete progress, although the Potomac and Pittsburg synods did begin to discuss raising a portion of the cost. At the 1899 meeting, Baer spurred the board to action by pledging to give or raise $9,000. This was considered sufficient to begin the planning process and to award contracts. Moreover, he promised to pay the salary of a professor of modern languages, relieving science faculty from responsibility for the subjects and enabling them to divide classes into smaller sections and expand the number of electives.[123]

The combined Committees on Grounds and Buildings and Laboratory and Museum, dominated by local trustees Hensel, Williamson, and William H. Hager, set to work immediately. They decided to locate the new building on the site of Harbaugh Hall. In a pamphlet outlining the building's development, they explained that they made the decision with "the greatest reluctance and unfeigned regret" because of the old building's connection with the "memory of a sainted Church Father." Yet the dormitory was a financial liability, in need of much repair and lacking basic modern amenities, such as indoor plumbing and electricity. Moreover, it occupied one of the high points of ground on the campus, and putting the new science building anywhere else would prevent "a harmonious relation" with the rest of the college buildings. Aware that this decision might cause resentment in the Reformed community, the committees promised to make every effort to reuse materials from the old building in constructing the new.[124]

To ensure that the building accommodated the latest methods in teaching science, Stahr, Kershner, and Schiedt were involved from the beginning. They drew up a preliminary design upon which eight architects based their proposed plans. The committee selected C. Emlen Urban of Lancaster, who also examined science buildings at other colleges. Development stopped abruptly in the beginning of 1900, when contractors' bids came in much higher than expected, the result of recent inflation in building materials. Rather than delaying until more money could be raised, a special board meeting decided to use available funds to begin constructing a shell. Trustees concluded that little was likely to gained from waiting, and Stahr commented that seeing construction underway was likely to spur fund-raising. Cornerstone-laying ceremonies were held at commencement in June.[125]

Once more, fund-raising was the college's Achilles' heel. As work on the first stage ended in 1901, only $2,000 in pledges was available toward the $30,000 needed to complete the building. Stahr advocated new approaches to fund-raising, as agents' "more or less minute canvass of pastoral charges" met too much competition from other "church interests." Stahr suggested using Church sources and board members to

FIGURE 2 *Richard Rummell's 1910 lithograph of the college depicts the campus at the beginning of Henry Harbaugh Apple's presidency. Franklin & Marshall College, Archives and Special Collections. College Archives Photograph Collection.*

identify potential large donors and solicit them personally. He hoped that the college's obvious needs, the progress already made on the building, and present good financial conditions would "inspire enthusiasm in the work." The board pledged $17,500, which enabled finishing work to begin.[126]

At the Science Building's completion in 1902, Stahr modestly commented, "It is entirely within the bounds of moderation to say that it is equal if not superior to the best in the country." But the college had had to borrow about $25,000 from its endowment to finish it. Fund-raising had been undermined by the synods' decision to give priority to a grand national church in Washington, D.C., and tardiness in meeting previous pledges. "It is hoped that with earnest and united effort the amount still due will be secured during the coming year," Stahr stated.[127]

The college found it easier to raise significant amounts from individual donors to equip the various departments. Schiedt persuaded Milton S. Hershey, a local candy maker who had recently entered the chocolate business, to contribute $5,000 for chemistry. The family of the late trustee B. Wolff Jr. furnished biology, and others paid for geology, anatomy, and photography equipment. Later, George Baer underwrote the cost of the physics lab, and S. B. Hartman, a patent medicine manufacturer, underwrote the science museum. Unlike most donors, Baer refused to allow his name to be given to the laboratory, telling Kershner, "I have a great dislike to having my name appear in anything."[128]

However much the college benefited from ties with men of wealth like Baer, they could bring unwelcome publicity. Through the spring, summer, and autumn of 1902, Pennsylvania and the nation watched while much of its anthracite coal was held hostage by a labor dispute between the United Mine Workers of America and a group of

Pennsylvania mine owners led by Baer. His refusal to acknowledge the legitimacy of the union had been foretold in a lecture he gave at Franklin & Marshall earlier in the year, when he emphasized the absolute rights of property. "Labor may organize," he admitted, "but it may not tyrannize." By "tyrannize," he meant any effort to limit a man's "right to work by law, by force, by threats, by social ostracism, by boycott, or by insult." The *F&M Weekly*'s editorialist, unawed by Baer's considerable authority, had gently chided Baer for his lack of attention to ethical questions and defended the good that labor organizations were doing.[129]

As the stalemate dragged on through the summer of 1902, Baer supposedly wrote a letter to a minister who had urged him to negotiate with the union. "I beg of you not to be discouraged," Baer allegedly replied. "The rights and interests of the laboring man will be protected and cared for — not by the labor agitators, but by the Christian men to whom God in his infinite wisdom has given the control of the property interests of the country, and upon the successful Management of which so much depends." An uproar ensued when the popular press published the letter, which Baer later denied having written. William Randolph Hearst dubbed him "Divine Right Baer," and his continuing intransigence helped shift public sympathy toward the unions. With impending coal shortages, President Theodore Roosevelt vowed to send federal troops to run the mines, and the owners finally agreed to arbitration.[130]

Fiftieth Anniversary Jubilee Showcases Progress

As the fiftieth anniversary of the merger of Franklin & Marshall Colleges neared, leaders hoped to use the occasion to enlarge the endowment, in part to pay the Science Building's increased operating costs. Held during commencement in June 1903, the jubilee celebration offered a familiar array of orations, sermons and speeches, receptions and banquets. On "Lancaster Day," townspeople were invited to tour campus. A program of speeches highlighting the civic and educational life of the city and county featured an appearance by Pennsylvania Governor Samuel W. Pennypacker, a prominent German American. Alumni, especially the younger generation, played a more prominent role than in 1887. In 1887 an attempt to publish a volume of memorial biographies had failed for lack of subscribers. Now, under the leadership of Samuel H. Ranck, '92, the Alumni Association had begun putting out an obituary record profiling deceased graduates. In 1903 the association published a directory of officers and students from 1787 to 1903 and a substantial history of the college by J. H. Dubbs.[131]

To ensure broad participation, the Alumni Association and a board committee hired the Reverend Miles O. Noll to "work up an interest" and help with planning. The success of his efforts was demonstrated by the turnout on Alumni Day, which featured a succession of meetings and reunions and culminated in a massive torchlight parade. As a seminarian, Noll had helped introduce football to the college, and in some ways the procession resembled a grand pep rally. An alumnus recalled that a record number of Lancastrians lined the streets to watch as hundreds of alumni marched from the Fulton Opera House, proceeded through the old city to the original Franklin College site, and concluded at the present campus. Horse-drawn carriages carrying board president Baer, the few surviving Marshall College alumni, and Lancaster officials led off the parade. Trustees followed on foot. "Then came class after class in order of seniority," Klein notes, bearing color transparencies with their emblems as well as those of other college organizations. Older alumni waved blue-and-white flags while younger ones held aloft lanterns on poles. Interspersed among the marchers were floats depicting "the great events" in the institution's life; some, such as Benjamin Franklin's laying of Franklin College's cornerstone, were apocryphal, while others, such as John Marshall's "baptizing" his eponymous college and the "wedding" of the two institutions, were symbolic. When they came to Williamson Field, marchers gathered around a huge bonfire, joined hands, and sang college songs. Accompanied by a crowd of some twelve thousand, "the celebration continued till midnight, punctuated with college songs, class yells, and an excellent display of fireworks." Klein proudly recalled that visitors from other institutions "said they never had seen such enthusiastic loyalty on the part of any alumni for their Alma Mater as the Franklin and Marshall boys showed that Wednesday night."[132]

Increased alumni participation came at a price. Although most Franklin & Marshall graduates belonged to the Reformed Church, younger alumni leaders were less likely to be ministers. As students, they had been active in the new college organizations and now wanted a greater voice in the college's affairs, to promote their vision of campus life. At first, a committee appointed by the Alumni Association "to devise ways and means for bringing the Alumni into closer touch with the college" contemplated asking for representation on the board. But the committee decided to select an advisory body to work with the board and "secure their active cooperation in promoting the general welfare of the college." The board recognized the committee, but it was unclear how much cooperation it would welcome.[133]

Although generally celebratory, a special jubilee issue of the *Reformed Church Review* also revealed sources of concern. John Stahr's article surveyed the college's often difficult financial history, concluding with the lesson "that it is unwise and unsafe to rely upon pledges and notes which have a long time to run." Stahr also noted that the college still owed "a considerable portion"— more than $21,000 in fact — on the Science Building, adding that it would be "covered without difficulty" if pledges were paid promptly. However, he also found "reason for profound gratitude" in the growth of the college's assets, which resulted in an endowment of nearly $207,000. This was only "the foundation of an adequate endowment, upon which it is necessary to build a much larger superstructure." Looking forward to an enrollment of more than two hundred, he warned that the faculty would have to be enlarged and that there should be greater "division of labor" between the functions of business, management, and teaching.[134]

Other articles pointed to fissures within the faculty, as commitment to particular disciplines weakened a shared vision of classical education. Professor John B. Kieffer, displaying Olympian qualities that had earned him the student nickname of "Zeus," departed from the celebratory tenor of the issue with a ringing denunciation of recent changes in the curriculum. He saw them as "directly opposed to the underlying spirit and purpose of the American college as such" because by abandoning the senior year of the traditional college curriculum, college leaders deferred to students' professionalism. Kieffer stressed that since the Renaissance liberal education had aimed not at "instructing the student, but at developing his nature," in the process imparting such qualities as "ideality, unselfish devotion, many-sidedness in the power of thinking, breadth of sympathy, and loftiness of aim." In large part, the college accomplished this by serving as a precious moment when a young man could withdraw from the world to devote himself to becoming acquainted with "the great heritage which has been bequeathed him" and to exploring how he could best serve himself and others. Premature specialization undermined this transitional quality of the college years and distracted students' attention "from a general preparation for life to the specific duties of life." Too often, Kieffer argued, liberal education was "thrust aside" by professional studies because "the average American boy" is typically "filled with a great and feverish impatience to be, as he imagines, dealing with facts and amassing wealth."[135]

Kieffer placed responsibility for this state of affairs on the current "vogue" for "the university conception of education," caused by "the prodigious prestige and influence of German universities," in the minds of the country's "educated men" as well as "our imported teachers." In a stunning attack upon not only "the German system" but the German national character, Kieffer hinted that "the rapacious brutality and the swashbuckling conceit" recently shown in German foreign policy were attributable to the lack of a proper transition between boyhood and manhood. The very "salvation of the American college, and of the higher and more liberalizing education," he concluded, depended upon preserving the traditional classical curriculum.[136]

Unsurprisingly, the college's science professors praised advances made possible by electives. Jefferson Kershner noted the benefits of being able to devote more time to subjects like calculus and asserted that "no college can now be classed among the higher institutions of learning" without electives. The science faculty also lobbied for ever more advanced equipment. Offering his own theory of development, Kershner asserted that the use of scientific technology "broadens and heightens [the student's] conceptions of the magnitude of the objects studied" and his appreciation of the scientists who built the equipment and discovered the laws of nature. "Reading alone cannot produce great men in any time," he insisted. "Men must come into contact, or even into conflict, with something from without, whether this be material, energy or social forces." For his part, Schiedt faulted conservative "counsellors" at the college for reluctance to change and the lack of aggressive fund-raising needed to keep pace with other institutions.[137]

Other faculty articles also welcomed electives, but for distinct, largely pragmatic reasons. English professor C. Ernest Wagner spoke of the "relief" found in being able to work "along certain congenial lines" with a smaller group that had chosen the subject "of their own free will." This was particularly true because of the great "unevenness" of student preparation and diversity of ability and interest. Pointing to the often "disastrous" consequences of post–Civil War America's ignorance of economic principles, A. V. Hiester urged study of political and social sciences. "The great body of public questions now confronting the American people are economic questions," he pointed out. The jubilee issue displayed no common understanding of the college's educational mission. Significantly, only seminary faculty mentioned Mercersburg Theology.[138]

Samuel H. Ranck's essay on the literary societies was the only nonfaculty contribution. He traced the proud history of literary and debating societies in American colleges in general and Franklin & Marshall in particular but admitted that their days as the center of extracurricular activity were long past. Interclass and intercollegiate competition had long since absorbed much of the energy that had animated the societies' fierce bipolar rivalries. Now, many different organizations catered to a wide range of student interests, and formal instruction in composition and elocution had superseded informal peer collaboration. Society libraries and natural science collections were overshadowed by the college's growing resources. Finally, the old arts of oratory had fallen out of favor, replaced by a widening range of specialized rhetorical forms.[139]

Like the unitary classical curriculum itself, literary societies could not resist pressures of changing student demands and the disappearance of the nineteenth-century vision of a shared civic culture. At first, faculty and trustees had responded to declining membership in the societies by requiring nonmembers to do additional writing assignments. But faculty resented the extra work, and the societies found themselves dragged down by unwilling members. Arguing that "work of this kind, to be successful, requires a certain degree of good will," Stahr persuaded the board to drop the requirement. Despite repeated calls to abolish senior orations, the college continued to require every student to deliver one during the spring term. "Formerly, when there were fewer students in the College and almost all of them looked forward to public speaking as their chief occupation in life," the F&W Weekly admitted, this requirement might have served a purpose. But it seemed antiquated in an age of specialization, "when many of [the] graduates [expected] to become physicians, chemists, teachers, etc." What had vanished from this perspective was the sense that a college education had some connection with shaping citizens capable of participating in public deliberations apart from their occupations, one of the fundamental goals of the classical curriculum.[140]

After many decades of defending its classical curriculum and unique German American environment, Franklin & Marshall College had moved significantly in the 1890s to accommodate, if not fully embrace, the emerging national collegiate culture. Changes in curriculum and extracurricular life came incrementally, but taken together, they marked a striking divergence from the past. In coming decades the college would find that further growth compelled it to move even farther from its distinctive roots.

CHAPTER FIVE

Liberal Culture in the Service of Efficiency, 1900–1918

—⁓—

While Franklin & Marshall's celebration of its fiftieth anniversary highlighted ties to alumni and city, its installation of a new president in 1910 revealed a longing for recognition within the nation's higher education community. For the first time in its history, Henry Harbaugh Apple's induction ceremonies were elaborate and largely secular. Though Apple had assumed office the previous summer, he put off the formal inauguration until the following January to plan a more substantial event. In the meantime he attended A. Lawrence Lowell's inauguration as president of Harvard University and found the occasion "impressive and inspiring"—so much so that he adopted features of Harvard's ceremonies for his own. Gathering at Trinity Reformed Church in downtown Lancaster, a procession of Franklin & Marshall students, faculty, trustees, and nearly sixty representatives from sister institutions formed a rainbow of brilliantly colored robes and hoods as it moved to Fulton Opera House. The sheriff of Lancaster County called the ceremonies to order, "according to an ancient custom," as the *F&M Weekly* put it, little realizing that the custom was a recent import from Massachusetts.[1]

Much of the ceremony in which board president George Baer entrusted the college's seal, keys, and charter into Apple's keeping was also based on Harvard's. At first, as attorneys, Baer and board vice president W. U. Hensel balked at Apple's desire to receive the college seal, because the president of Franklin & Marshall was not a corporate officer and technically therefore not authorized to use the seal. Both men thought the rites something of a "sham" but finally gave in to Apple's wishes.[2]

Princeton University president Woodrow Wilson delivered the principal address, with remarks given by retiring Franklin & Marshall president John S. Stahr; the Pennsylvania governor, Edwin S. Stuart; state superintendent of public instruction and college trustee Nathan C. Schaeffer; and the mayor of Lancaster, J. P. McCaskey. The invocation by the president of the General Synod of the Reformed Church and the benediction by the head of the Theological Seminary of the Reformed Church were the program's only direct acknowledgements of the college's denominational ties.[3]

The *Reformed Church Messenger* was nevertheless delighted by the proceedings. "At no time in the history of the college has an occasion been so magnified," it exulted. "Never before were so many distinguished educators present to help usher in what the friends of the college fondly hope is the beginning of a new era in her history." The *Lancaster New Era* agreed that the event was "epochal in the history of the beloved old institution."[4]

The ceremonies did in fact mark a new era in Franklin & Marshall's history. Apple's twenty-five-year presidency oversaw substantial growth — construction of nine new buildings, a threefold increase in enrollments, and a fivefold increase in endowment — and completion of the college's transition into the mainstream of American higher education. In fundamental ways, the college moved away from the Mercersburg tradition that had distinguished it in the nineteenth century. Maintaining an Anglo-German ethos had become problematic even before World War I intensified pressures to submerge ethnic identifications. In educational philosophy, the Romantic German conception of *Bildung* had long since been overshadowed by Germany's modern reputation for specialized, university-based research. Even at Franklin & Marshall, discussions of liberal education assumed the guise of gentlemanly Oxford rather than that of the College's own nineteenth-century traditions.[5]

Under H. H. Apple the college embraced the Progressive ethos of efficiency and public service and the parallel movement within liberal Christianity toward ethics and social problems. These changes came at the expense of the college's living connection to Mercersburg Theology, in which spiritual authority had been grounded in rigorous philosophy and closely linked to a distinctive German American identity.[6]

Change nonetheless stimulated increased financial support from alumni, other men of wealth, and foundations. The college's impressive physical growth was made possible in part through contributions from older sources in the Reformed Church and from the local community but principally through closer ties to wealthy benefactors. Reflecting national economic changes, contributions came not only from German American businessmen like George Baer and Benjamin Franklin Fackenthal Jr. but from philanthropic foundations of industrial giants such as Andrew Carnegie and John D. Rockefeller. Such resources enabled the college to grow and solidify its financial position, but they came with caveats regarding its educational mission. Hence, even as Apple publicly extolled the virtues of liberal education throughout his administration, Franklin & Marshall College's actual educational experience had changed significantly. Increased attention to vocational and professional preparation set up a tension with the school's traditional focus on personal development, a focus that had persisted for generations.

In part, the college's progress reflected the improved status of the nation's small liberal arts colleges as a whole. Far from disappearing, as had once been predicted, by the early twentieth century they had achieved a stable niche, enrolling as a whole two-thirds of all students in higher education. They benefited from growing dissatisfaction with the university system of free electives, specialization, and large scale. In 1904 Nicholas Murray Butler of Columbia charged that the elective system had produced a "noticeable laxity" in students' "control and discipline." Instead of instilling "habits of industry and application" and "promoting mental and moral growth," the modern university experience seemed to encourage laziness and dissipation. Similarly, at his inauguration Lowell signaled a major shift away from the elective system that Harvard had pioneered. At Princeton, Woodrow Wilson promoted "liberal culture" as a means of restoring unity to a chaotic curriculum.[7]

Elite colleges and universities seized the ideal of liberal culture as an alternative to the utilitarianism of state universities and the specialization of research universities. Like nineteenth-century college leaders, leaders at elite schools saw liberal culture as the best way to prepare young men for leadership roles. But the process was no longer rooted in a unified classical curriculum or religious tradition. Instead, by World War I liberal education had been redefined to mean simply a broad, general background combined with specialization in a single field.[8]

Nonetheless, higher education continued to grow not just because of its training for leadership but also because of the popular appeal of extracurricular campus life. In large universities and small colleges alike, students themselves wove ever denser webs of campus "traditions," actually more often newly invented customs. Closely connected with intercollegiate athletics, especially football, and designed to foster college "spirit," new activities at Franklin & Marshall continued to push aside genuine traditions, such as the literary societies.

Closing Years of the Stahr Administration

Franklin & Marshall had gained widening recognition for the caliber of its education. Reviewing J. H. Dubbs's *History of Franklin and Marshall College*, the *Nation* commented that the college was "something more than the chief school of the (German) Reformed Church." Rather, it was known for its preservation of "the traditions of culture and for conservatism in college life" and its "highly logical course in metaphysics." In the first two years after Rhodes scholarships were established in 1903, two alumni, Paul Kieffer and John Nevin Schaeffer, received the prestigious awards. The college's debate and oratory teams regularly took home top prizes in meets with such neighboring schools as Swarthmore and Pennsylvania State College.[9]

A crowning touch came in 1907, when the national honor fraternity Phi Beta Kappa authorized formation of a chapter at Franklin & Marshall. Classics professor John B. Kieffer had worked for years to this end and attended the annual convention as a delegate of the University of Pennsylvania's chapter, to speak on behalf of Franklin & Marshall. When its candidacy was considered, he disputed "misconceptions," such as that the college's life was too "indiscriminately" mingled with that of the academy and the seminary. The Theta chapter of Phi Beta Kappa was formally organized the following February.[10]

The college's strong academic reputation ensured employment opportunities for graduates in the growing field of secondary education. As a leader of the Pennsylvania Education Association, Stahr worked closely with Nathan C. Schaeffer, state superintendent of public instruction since 1893, to lower barriers between private colleges and the public school system. Stahr had written the first draft of an 1893 law empowering the superintendent to grant teaching certificates to college graduates, which had done much to bring "college-bred teachers" into high schools. After 1898 Stahr taught a course on pedagogy and the history of education for students seeking to enter teaching. As a result, education joined the ministry, law, medicine, journalism, and business as popular career paths for college graduates. Nearly one quarter of the class of 1895, for example, immediately landed teaching jobs. By 1901, the number of men going into teaching exceeded that entering the ministry, and in 1912, 40 percent of students reporting in after graduation had become secondary principals or teachers.[11]

Nonetheless, the college's financial woes continued. Goodwill engendered during the 1903 jubilee celebrations was squandered when the board failed to follow up with a vigorous fund-raising campaign. Noting that the time was "propitious," Stahr urged a campaign in partnership with alumni class organizations. The Alumni Advisory Council and the Committee on Endowment endorsed the idea, but nothing was done, even as rising annual deficits demonstrated the need for enlarging the endowment.[12]

The board was also slow to plan for an impending transition in the college's leadership. Now in his sixties, Stahr continued to carry a full teaching schedule, despite his growing administrative responsibilities. The stress involved in overseeing construction and fund-raising for the Science Building had undermined his health. He had hoped to resign at the time of the jubilee, but close friends on the board persuaded him that the moment was "inopportune." To ease his administrative burdens the board hired E. M. Hartman, co-headmaster of Franklin & Marshall Academy, to assist with fund-raising and offered Professors Hiester and Mull a "small additional salary" to take on Stahr's duties as treasurer and registrar, respectively. They also provided Stahr with "the services of a type-writer" — a term then used to refer to the person, not the machine.[13]

Hartman immediately began soliciting funds and haranguing prospective students in western Pennsylvania. He found it tough going. The well-to-do businessmen with whom he spoke "all gave [him] a respectful hearing," he wrote Stahr from Pittsburgh, but Hartman concluded, "I might as well have talked to stone." Franklin & Marshall, he learned, was "of less interest to them than some things in the moon might be." He preached at Reformed churches and met with boys in the congregations deemed to be college material. Many of these were "tempted to go to business or to medical school" directly from high school; several sought to enroll as sophomores.[14]

Hartman quickly learned that men of means must be patiently cultivated if they were to yield substantial rewards. In Reading, one of the senior Reformed pastors explained the importance of developing relationships with prospective donors: "Dr. Bausman feels sure that I should not expect much from men the first time I met them but that I should 'put them in soak awhile.'" Hartman concluded that the pastor was right: "This isn't what Hensel expected, nor I, but I believe it's the only way this work can be done in most places."[15]

Hartman's influence seemed to wax as Stahr's energies waned. Their relationship soon took on an added dimension after Hartman's marriage to Stahr's daughter Helen. An educator in her own right, she had founded Miss Stahr's School for Girls, a forerunner of Lancaster Country Day School, and later participated actively in the life of the academy.[16]

Early in 1905 Hartman discovered a promising new funding source — Andrew Carnegie, who, after selling his steel empire in 1901, had stepped up his efforts to disperse his fortune in worthy projects such as libraries and church organs for small communities. Hartman advised Stahr that Carnegie was more likely to give money for "some definite tangible object" than for endowment. Based on what Hartman had learned, he asserted that Carnegie was likely to "give us a new Academy building sooner than anything else." Enrollment in the academy now nearly equal to the college's, and its old building was bursting at the seams with students. Carnegie offered to contribute either $30,000 to the endowment or $37,500 for an academy building, to be matched by an equal amount from other sources. Stahr, the Finance Committee, and local trustees concluded that a new academy building would be most "advantageous" and accepted Carnegie's offer without waiting for full board approval.[17]

Meanwhile, Stahr and Hartman also urged the board to enlarge the campus, to provide more spacious grounds for the academy and forestall the danger of being hemmed in by growing residential developments to the south and west of campus. The City of Lancaster owned the area west of the College Building — rechristened Old Main after completion of the Science Building. But open land to the north still belonged to the heirs of the Hamilton estate. When thirty-one acres came up for sale in the spring of 1905 for $32,000, Hartman urged Stahr that it might be their last chance to acquire the land. With the agreement of local trustees on the Finance Committee, Hartman and Stahr took preliminary steps to make the purchase. The full board later approved both actions, though there was substantial criticism of taking funds from the endowment. The board's only move toward raising the necessary money was to extend Hartman's appointment as fund-raiser. The following year, after deliberating "at length" on the academy's future, the board approved proceeding with a new building as soon as the entire cost of $75,000 was "secured in reliable pledges." Nonetheless, a year later the board allowed work to begin even though less than $17,000 had been raised.[18]

As the academy building neared completion in 1908, Stahr described it as "all that can be desired," in terms of "completeness, convenience and thoroughness of construction." Under Hartman's oversight, these virtues came at a high cost, eventually reaching $109,000. Fund-raising was hampered by a national financial crisis and ensuing business depression. Many Reformed congregations simply asked Hartman not to visit, and alumni were not much more forthcoming. Withdrawal of endowment funds for construction and the purchase of new land raised the 1908 deficit to nearly $6,000, though the academy pledged to pay interest on endowment tied up in its building.[19]

Stahr announced his retirement at the 1908 board meeting, arguing that the college needed leadership of "a young, capable, and enthusiastic head" who could appeal to younger alumni and friends. He asked to be allowed to remain as a member of the faculty, to teach the college's well-known courses in philosophy, ethics, and the philosophy of history. Although the board had known that this day was coming, it had done nothing to identify a suitable successor. Many hoped Nathan Schaeffer would take the presidency, but he refused, agreeing to head the Search Committee.[20]

No clear favorite had emerged when the committee made its first report in September. Most favored candidates were Reformed ministers, though some alumni and local board members, led by Hensel, pressed for a "live practical business man." Asked for his criteria, Baer commented, "It is easy to formulate ideals, but not so easy to find a man to size up to your ideals, especially in this extravagant age." He considered executive ability more essential than scholarship, along with the "general culture" to enable him to represent the college "with dignity and force, and awaken enthusiasm in its behalf." Current students, for their part, submitted an enthusiastic petition on behalf of the new modern language professor G. W. Thompson, a highly popular teacher, chapel organist, and sponsor of the Glee Club. Soon after his arrival on campus, Thompson had composed a new rendition of the alma mater, destined to become the official version.[21]

As the deadline neared, friends and colleagues of the Reverend Henry Harbaugh Apple pressed his name with increasing urgency. He had been quietly lobbying supporters within the Reformed ministry for over a year. "Your name is being quietly & favorably used by men who know the genius, spirit & needs of the Church," one of his friends advised him, and promised the support of "the younger men in the Church." Although Apple had the backing of several clergymen on the board, the Search Committee remained divided between him and an unnamed "stranger from the outside" up to the time of the June board meeting. At Hensel's suggestion, the entire board met in executive session on the evening of June 8 to "fully consider and thresh out the whole question." The following day, it announced Apple's unanimous election. Acknowledging the dissension, the *Reformed Church Messenger* urged the Church to unite behind the successful candidate.[22]

A Modern, Efficiency-Minded Leader

Although a clergyman, Henry Harbaugh Apple had already displayed the kind of modern executive skills that many at the college desired. Member of the class of 1888, he had played on the college's renowned football team of 1889 as a seminarian. After ordination he served as pastor of Reformed churches in Philadelphia and York, where he proved adept at increasing congregational membership and fund-raising. The *Messenger* noted that during his eleven years in York his church had contributed $120,000 to the larger Church and had recently spent $20,000 on extensive remodeling. Apple's candidacy had undoubtedly been helped by family connections: He was the son of former college president Thomas G. Apple, and his brother William, a prominent Lancaster attorney, was married to George Baer's daughter.[23]

Following Mercersburg traditions carried forward by his father, Apple signaled his high-church leanings by wearing an Anglican collar for his formal portrait. Nonetheless, as a minister he tended toward moderate social activism rather than theological sophistication. One of his few publications in the *Reformed Church Review*, titled "The Pastor in Relation to the Civic Life of the Community," emphasized the gospel's social meaning. Following Social Gospel ideas, he insisted that sin was not only lodged in individual hearts but "embodied in evil customs, perverted relations, harmful conditions and unjust laws for which the community is responsible." Despite the radical potential of these words, Apple was closer to the conservative side of the movement. A 1901 sermon on labor unrest insisted that class conflict could be resolved only through "brotherly love according to the teachings of Jesus Christ." Pointing to signs of a growing spirit of cooperation in all aspects of life, he told the Manufacturers' Association of York in 1907 that disunity and class antagonism were caused by selfishness. His role as a minister was to foster "a higher and better character" in the community, which coincidentally promised to increase "productive efficiency." As president of Franklin & Marshall College, Apple showed a similarly moderate Progressive spirit that combined pursuit of harmony through shared community participation with a search for efficiency.[24]

One possible drawback to Apple's candidacy was his lack of scholarly credentials. Consequently, immediately after his election, trustee B. F. Fackenthal Jr. tactfully solicited an offer of an honorary doctorate from a friend who was a trustee of Lafayette College. On June 18 Fackenthal informed Apple that he would be receiving an honorary LL.D. five days later. Fackenthal said that he and Baer approved of the idea and that Lafayette's president was "quite agreeable" to the action.[25]

When Apple assumed the presidency in July 1909, his skills as a leader, manager, and fund-raiser seemed particularly crucial. The deficit had continued to grow, and when the board granted Stahr's request to continue teaching, it in effect expanded the faculty without providing additional endowment to pay his salary. Morale had also suffered during the long transitional period. Apple's cousin A. Thomas G. Apple, the new professor of mathematics and astronomy, acknowledged an atmosphere of pessimism and crisis among his colleagues. But he vowed, "[We are] all very ready to fall in line and, shoulder to shoulder, give you their cordial support." Students were also restive, resenting lack of opportunity to participate in decisions affecting them. Referring to "the rumblings of dissolution and change" in the air, the junior class dedicated its edition of the *Oriflamme* in the spring of 1910 to the new president as the bearer of their "brightest hopes and aspirations for a greater Franklin and Marshall."[26]

During his first months in office, Apple set a reform agenda stressing standards and efficiency. "I have had several occasions to address the student body as a whole," he informed Baer in October, "and have impressed upon them the necessity of hard and persistent work." He reported that the faculty was cooperating with his efforts "to organize all the departments of [their] College work" to "do the most efficient service." He introduced curricular changes such as adding a few admission requirements and raising the grade average necessary for graduation. Though seemingly minor, one change marked a significant departure from tradition: it dropped the college's signature Philosophy of History course as a sophomore requirement.[27]

Growing Influence of Private Foundations

In part, Apple's actions responded to new influences in higher education. Powerful new philanthropic foundations offered substantial financial aid in exchange for evidence of greater standardization and organizational efficiency. This coupling was best illustrated in the Carnegie Foundation for the Advancement of Teaching (CFAT), founded in 1905, soon after Carnegie's personal grant for the Franklin & Marshall Academy Building. In his prior personal philanthropy, Carnegie sought to make educational opportunities more widely available and favored small, local institutions like Franklin & Marshall. He intended his new foundation to support higher education by awarding pensions to college and university teachers. But under its director, Henry Smith Pritchett, and a board dominated by presidents of the largest universities, CFAT followed a different agenda. Pritchett deplored the decentralization and lack of uniformity in American higher education and envisioned CFAT as "one of the Great Agencies not only in dignifying the teacher's calling but also in standardizing American education." The foundation's leaders believed that national progress was being thwarted by the presence of many small, poorly endowed colleges, many connected to religious denominations. Hence, they set requirements that they hoped would weed out unfit institutions: to participate in its pension program, institutions had to be nonsectarian and free of state control, employ at least six full-time professors, offer a four-year course of study in the liberal arts and sciences, and admit only students with four years of academic or high school preparation.[28]

Of these criteria, denominational control was the most vexed. Despite its ties to the Reformed Church, Franklin & Marshall had long prided itself on a lack of "sectarianism." Most trustees were nominally elected by one of the three Reformed synods, but in virtually all cases they merely ratified the board's own nominations. In 1908, Baer pointed out that the college could become eligible for the Carnegie pension plan by amending its charter to recognize this reality. Noting that alumni were sharply divided on the issue, Stahr asked whether he should raise it at synod. "I am at a loss to know how to advise you," Baer replied. He suspected that separation from denominational control was "the natural evolution" and would certainly bring "much needed financial support." But he expressed some fear about the transition: "Our people are not fully educated up to the modern conception of a college." Given increased competition for students, cutting the college's connection with the synods might alienate an important constituency. "The vast majority of our students are sent to Lancaster because of family devotion to our church institution," he concluded, and he was unsure whether improvements that might be made possible by greater financial support would attract more students than they would lose. He advised letting the matter rest for the time being.[29]

Apple first encountered the discriminatory policies of the Carnegie Foundation in 1909, when he sought a pension for ailing Professor Dubbs and was informed that the college was ineligible. In 1911 Apple proposed amending the charter to allow the board to elect fifteen members, the synods nine, and the Alumni Association six. His principal goal was to represent alumni who were not members of the Reformed Church, "to hold their permanent interest, strengthen their devotion and increase their support of their Alma Mater." But a secondary advantage was that it would allow the college to receive Carnegie Foundation benefits "without relinquishing [its] denominational relationship." The board did not act on his proposal, however.[30]

By participating in the Association of Colleges and Preparatory Schools of the Middle States and Maryland, Franklin & Marshall had already moved toward greater standardization in entrance requirements. In its definition of a college, CFAT ratified a preexisting movement to standardize admissions by defining requirements in terms of "units" representing a year of high school study of a subject, instead of simply demonstrating mastery of material. Early in 1910, Apple reported to the faculty that if the college added a couple of requirements in Latin and history, Franklin & Marshall could "claim recognition" according to the Carnegie standard of 14.5 units of high school work. Even so, nearly half of new students continued to be admitted with "conditions" in subjects in which they had inadequate preparation.[31]

Apple told Baer that the entire curriculum needed "to be stiffened up," but he considered English instruction weakest. In the spring of 1910 he revived the custom of classroom visits by the board's Committee on Instruction. Accompanied by Apple, it found "serious defects" that led to the dismissal of several instructors. The following year, perhaps under pressure from Apple, the college's somewhat indolent professor of English resigned, explaining that he wished to devote his time to travel and writing. Seeing the opening as "an opportunity to strengthen that important department of the institution," Apple told Baer that he was searching "for a strong man," preferably one with experience in New England institutions.[32]

The faculty had already revised its graduate programs in keeping with standards of "the leading colleges and universities of the country." "Considering that we have neither sufficient teaching force nor facilities for resident work," the faculty told the board in 1905, "we owe it to ourselves as well as to the aspirants for such a degree [to stop awarding doctorates]." It also abandoned the traditional practice of granting master's degrees "in course." Instead, a master's degree could be earned through graduate work in one major and one minor field, culminating in an original thesis. The work could be accomplished through one year in residence or two years as a nonresident.[33]

First Successful Major Capital Campaign

Determined to end the school's long tradition of failed or incomplete fund-raising campaigns, H. H. Apple sought support from several foundations recently created to promote higher education. As in the case of the Carnegie Foundation, the promise of new sources of funding came with conditions. John D. Rockefeller funded the General Education Board (GEB) in 1902 at first primarily to aid education of African Americans in the South. Under the influence of its professional directors, GEB expanded to embrace "the promotion of education within the United States without distinction of race, sex or creed," and in 1905 higher education was added to its purview. Because of Rockefeller's strong ties to the Baptist Church, it was particularly interested in helping smaller denominational colleges. Franklin & Marshall's first attempt to gain its help had been unsuccessful, and soon after he took office, Apple proposed trying again. Perhaps the college had failed to meet GEB's administrative requirements, for GEB's underlying mission was promotion of modern practices. As his adviser Frederick T. Gates promised Rockefeller, GEB aimed to make colleges more efficient by directing resources to deserving institutions. Moreover, to spur increased support by local communities, GEB grants came with a substantial matching requirements and deadlines.[34]

Apple expected GEB to ask the college to raise $100,000 to win a $50,000 grant, plus $40,000 to eliminate deficits being carried on the treasurer's books. He told Baer that he hoped to find "some one in our own constituency" to make a substantial pledge to stimulate others to give. Taking the hint, Baer promised $50,000. But when Apple approached the foundation directly, they told him that the college would have to raise a total of $200,000 to obtain a $50,000 grant. Moreover, they "objected very seriously" to the college's "method of book-keeping."[35]

Apple announced the endowment drive at his inauguration in January 1910, reporting that the "larger part" of the $200,000 had been secured, including more than $100,000 in pledges and a "guarantee" of $50,000 from the City of Lancaster. When formal application was made to GEB, however, it raised the required amount to $225,000, in addition to the amount of the college's current indebtedness and the more than $30,000 taken out of the endowment to purchase land. The total came to $308,000, more than the college's entire existing endowment. Given the immensity of the task, Apple recommended that they postpone the formal campaign to coincide with celebrations of the 125th anniversary of the founding of Franklin College in 1912. This would make the deadline January 1, 1913.[36]

The board approved the campaign, but it was clear that Apple would have to surmount substantial difficulties to succeed. First, there was the continued reluctance of denominational supporters. The Eastern Synod, for example, pledged $25,000 at its 1911 meeting, but "only after a long discussion" of whether they should "make a pledge they were not absolutely certain they could fulfill." The Synod of the Potomac eventually pledged $15,000, and the Pittsburgh Synod, $10,000.[37]

Moreover, the board resisted Apple's efforts to reorganize college management. At the time, much administrative work remained in the hands of the board, particularly local members. The treasurer, an officer of the board, handled financial accounts independently, and standing committees were practically autonomous. For example, in the spring of 1910 the Grounds and Buildings Committee began expensive renovations to Old Main despite a growing deficit and Apple's expressed opposition. In 1910 and again in 1911, Apple called for the "entire centralization in the management of the college by bringing all departments under one head." He felt it to be especially crucial that he be given control over finances through appointment of an assistant treasurer under his direction to manage the college's books. He wanted to introduce a book-keeping system adapted to "the peculiar nature of college administration," to maintain better information. After years of discussion and dragging its feet, the board gradually acceded to Apple's requests. In 1912 it made him an ex officio member of all standing committees, and in 1913 it resolved that "inasmuch as the Board of Trustees [held] the President of the College responsible for the welfare and advancement of all the work of both members of the Faculty and Students," he was authorized "to put into execution such orders and regulations as he [might deem] advisable for the best efficiency of administration, irrespective of former custom and rule or present practice."[38]

Apple also tangled with academy leaders, whose influence had increased during Stahr's administration. In his first report to the board, Apple stated ominously that, "in view of a wide difference of opinion," the precise relationship between the college and the academy and the relationship of each to the board should be defined. It was perhaps inevitable that Apple and Hartman, both ambitious, enterprising young men, would clash. But the academy's very presence on the college campus was also problematic in a time of increasing differentiation in education. Many undergraduates thought that having younger boys on campus undermined the dignity of a modern college environment, and outsiders considered it a relic of outmoded institutional practices.[39]

Consequently, the board discussed the question of "the organic relation" between the two institutions, with E. M. Hartman participating. The board made no decision and referred the question to the standing Committee on the Academy in conference with Apple, Hartman, and co-headmaster Thaddeus G. Helm. Thereafter the matter remained as a source of controversy.[40]

After a promising beginning, the endowment campaign faltered, growing little in the two years after Apple's inauguration. Apple devoted most of his time to fund-raising, meeting with Church leaders and laymen to identify prospective donors and traveling indefatigably to solicit alumni and Church leaders throughout the state and region. The difficult conditions of the Rockefeller grant seems to have made his task harder, for the belief that they were impossible to achieve discouraged participation. Apple planned the 125th celebration to publicize Franklin & Marshall College and interest possible donors. Calling attention to the fact that Franklin College had been founded to educate "the German element of our population," he cultivated ties with prominent scholars of German American history and spoke at the dedication of the Institution of German American Research at the University of Pennsylvania. Hoping to attract the attention of "some influential Germans in Baltimore and Washington," he invited the German ambassador, Count Johann Heinrich von Bernstorff, to deliver the principal commencement address.[41]

When the drive was still $50,000 short of the goal in mid-December, the college secured an extension to July 15, 1913. At the June board meeting, Baer and Hensel raised their pledges by an additional $10,000 and $5,000 respectively in an attempt to spur further giving. Finally, with some $15,000 still to be raised with less than two weeks to go, Baer guaranteed whatever amount was necessary to meet the goal.[42]

Even after the campaign's formal success, college leaders had difficulty collecting on subscriptions. A year later, William Hensel expressed disappointment at the "meagre" payments on subscriptions, particularly from the synods: "While the Eastern Synod seems to be fairly alive to its obligation, I do not like the suggestion that the Pittsburgh Synod or its ministers have an apparent 'grievance' which may delay the payment of their money, nor do I see much definite promise from the Potomac Synod." Later, he took the unusual step of expressing his dissatisfaction openly, charging in a letter to the *Reformed Church Messenger* that the Church was not supporting its college. Of the more than $300,000 raised in the campaign, he noted, the majority, about $170,000 had been given by some thirty members and former members of the board, and another $80,000 came from sources with no connection to the Reformed Church. In fact, $25,000 had come from Hensel's own Presbyterian congregation in Lancaster. And yet, the 650 preachers and 1,055 congregations of the three Reformed Synods claimed to be unable to pay $50,000 toward the endowment of their own college. Hensel threatened to resign if there was "no well-directed and promising movement toward this end" soon. His words seems to have had the desired effect, for the fall meetings of all three synods took action to collect on the pledges. In 1916 total endowment had risen to $550,000.[43]

Increased enrollments and raises in fees in addition to endowment earnings produced a rare surplus of several thousand dollars. Apple insisted that the enlarged endowment income should go first to raise faculty salaries, which had remained static despite the period's inflation. Following "a protracted, frank, and confidential interchange of views" in executive session, the board agreed to boost salaries from 20 to 25 percent, to a high of $2,000 for long-standing faculty members.[44]

Increasing Dissension Within the Faculty

Following the deaths of longtime professors J. H. Dubbs and J. B. Kieffer in 1910, Franklin & Marshall College continued its tradition of hiring men with ties to the Reformed Church. The Reverend H. M. J. Klein, holder of one of the last Ph.D.'s granted by the college, was named Audenreid Professor of History and Archaeology. The classics position went to John Nevin Schaeffer, son of a seminary professor, who was teaching at Princeton after receiving an Oxford B.Litt. under his Rhodes scholarship. The new professor of modern languages, the Reverend Victor W. Dippel, had taken a

Ph.D. from the University of Pennsylvania and taught at Temple before becoming pastor of a church in Lebanon, Pennsylvania.[45]

Even so, growing professional, political, and intellectual differences were evident within the faculty. As foreshadowed by the *Reformed Review*'s jubilee issue, there was a growing sense of distance between scientists, who were largely oriented toward the German research model, and humanists, who were more attracted to an Oxbridge ideal of gentlemanly cultivation. Richard Schiedt was clearly leader of the former camp. He wielded particular influence because of the great esteem he was held in by prominent members of the board. Fackenthal pledged $40,000 toward the endowment drive in 1910 specifically to endow Schiedt's professorship, largely out of respect for Schiedt's scholarly achievements. An ordained Reformed minister, Schiedt also served as supply clergy for many churches in the area, even as he frequently shared his scientific knowledge through popular lectures and occasional stints as an expert witness or ad hoc public health officer. He was consequently one of the best-known members of the faculty.[46]

Schiedt had high standards for teaching and research and did not hesitate to criticize colleagues who failed to measure up. Seeking to cut expenses in 1910, Apple proposed eliminating one faculty position and shifting courses in oratory and English to Klein. "As a friend of yourself and of the institution," Schiedt wrote him, "let me beseech you to protest against such an imposition, for it is utterly impossible to do any kind of decent work under such conditions." Klein had studied in Germany, and Schiedt hoped that Klein would "introduce a worth while method of history study into the college curriculum." Moreover, he said, sociology professor A. V. Hiester wanted to work with Klein in "laying out a plan of historico-sociological studies which would be equal to that of the best college in the land." But with such a workload, Schiedt warned, Klein would "only be able to follow the same old line of kindergarten recitations which is so utterly unworthy the work expected from a modern college." He urged Klein to bring the issue to the Committee on Instruction, by outlining the "actual amount of labor required" in teaching so many hours and students. Schiedt cautioned him, "If you do not protest *now* they will inflict a good many more duties on you in the fall." He continued, "I am very much afraid that our standard of scholarship is gradually descending." He was not able to persuade Klein to resist Apple's plans but kept up a constant stream of criticism.[47]

In contrast, one of Apple's staunchest allies on the faculty was George F. Mull, the meek classics professor who, among his many administrative caps, served as secretary of the faculty and board. Immediately after Apple's appointment, Mull wrote to pledge his unreserved "allegiance and cooperation," in part because of his love for Apple's father. Committed to the ideal of liberal education as instilling character and higher ideals, he told Apple, "The College waits, not to be made larger, but *more fit*." Later, Mull wrote Apple to express appreciation for the way he stood up to the many "obstacles," the "disparagement and depreciation," he frequently encountered. It was likely that some of this disparagement came from within the faculty.[48]

Mull clearly believed that the emphasis on original research had gone too far at Franklin & Marshall, as elsewhere. When informed that he would receive an honorary doctorate at Apple's inauguration, he protested that he had not earned it: "What have I ever done, with all my sweating, to enrich the domain of scholarly achievement? I have never discovered a 'new muscle in the left hind leg of a frog' to adorn it with the 'sesquipedalian pomp of a Latin name.'" He was not, he concluded, "an 'original researcher,' and original research, we have long been told, is the only *really real* thing that Ph.D. spells." But he would accept the honor as one who appreciated scholarship, for without it, "the scholar's vocation would soon be gone."[49]

Political differences within the faculty were on public display during the three-way U.S. presidential campaign of 1912. Schiedt presided over a public meeting to rally support for the Democrat, Woodrow Wilson, while Hiester headed up a rally for Teddy Roosevelt and the new Bull Moose Party, and Mull served as chair for the Republicans. Asked the *F&M Weekly*, "Who said Franklin and Marshall was one-sided in her views?"[50]

Continuing Divergence of Student Culture

A cheating scandal in 1913 also brought to light a wide gap between official and student notions of academic honor. A formal honor code developed jointly by representatives of the faculty and student classes had been in effect since 1903, but it had no means of enforcement. The code did establish the first official student government in the form of a student senate. The system had quickly broken down, and student publications frequently lamented the prevalence of cheating on examinations.[51]

A group of seniors protested conferral of salutatorian honors upon a student whom they charged with "wholesale cheating in recitations and examinations." They complained that the faculty closed their eyes to "obvious facts" about the prevalence of cheating. When faculty investigated further, they discovered that the principal complaint was not that this student had cheated, for everyone admitted that cheating was almost ubiquitous. Rather, they resented this particular person's "selfishness." They charged that he had transferred to Franklin & Marshall in his junior year "with the avowed purpose" of achieving a Phi Beta Kappa key and had employed "unfair means" to do so. These included choosing easy, nonscience courses and refusing to participate in extracurricular activities. All students interviewed admitted that they would not have objected to his cheating if he had not been selected for an honor.[52]

A faculty committee concluded that students generally condoned "a certain amount of cheating, particularly when it [was] resorted to to avoid a failure in recitation, or pass a difficult subject, or when the examination [was] considered unreasonably difficult." Conversely, "cheating to secure an honor" was considered "wrong and reprehensible." The committee concluded that teachers were not showing sufficient vigilance in preventing cheating nor severity in punishing it. Because all the other honor men also admitted cheating, and the fact that in previous years honors had been awarded on "no better grounds" than in the present instance, they decided to take no action but resolved to use "the present agitation" to reduce dishonesty. In response, the board created the separate Committee of Discipline dominated by local trustees and committed to overseeing both faculty and students. Trustees urged the faculty to adopt an honor system such as that "in use at Princeton and other Colleges."[53]

After a semester of deliberation, the faculty and student body approved a new honor system developed by the Student Senate. It required students to sign a statement at the conclusion of examinations, attesting that they had not cheated, and for the first time it explicitly obligated them to report violations to a member of a court of students. The *Weekly* warned that such a system would not work because it encouraged "tattling" and undermined friendship, but the student body approved it overwhelmingly after Professor Stahr argued that the system must have some means of enforcement.[54]

The college also moved gradually toward greater oversight of extracurricular activities, in part because of students' failure to honor their financial obligations. The faculty created a board of governors to direct athletic programs in 1910 and a board of control for all other organizations in 1914. Stressing the importance and delicacy of regulating student activities without infringing on their educational value, Apple urged the Board of Trustees to create an administrative position devoted to overseeing student life, but it did not respond.[55]

Campus life was increasingly seen as crucial to the undergraduate experience, but the college had lost its only dormitory when it demolished Harbaugh Hall. Students lamented the lack of facilities on campus, but their principal concern was for what they perceived as a dearth of "school spirit," that elusive quality about which student publications seemed perpetually to obsess. Beginning in the 1890s, fraternities and eating clubs had established chapter houses and in the absence of on-campus housing played a growing role in student life. By 1916 more than three out of five students were members of one of the four nationally affiliated fraternities (Phi Kappa Psi, Phi Sigma Kappa, Chi Phi, and Phi Kappa Sigma) or one of the four local clubs (Paradise, Franklin, Harbaugh, and Marshall). Fears that these organizations fostered narrow group loyalties at the expense of the common good seemed to be confirmed by the rise of fraternity cliques vying to control access to offices and desirable roles in the dramatic club plays. Echoing the rhetoric of the day, students calling for clean politics passed legislation prohibiting selling or trading votes.[56]

Without the physical proximity of dormitories, students stressed extracurricular activities as a means of fostering a proper spirit. As reflected in their views regarding cheating, many students embraced an autonomous college culture that reflected adult values in the distorted manner of a sideshow mirror. In a day when American political leaders and intellectuals alike were preaching about the need for civic participation, college students translated the ubiquitous demand for "public spiritedness" into a call for school spirit.[57]

Progressive-minded academics like Woodrow Wilson argued that higher education must recognize its civic role "to implant a sense of duty" in the younger generation. At Franklin & Marshall, A. V. Hiester prominently used the prevailing rhetoric of community. In 1903, for example, his opening address, "Citizenship and Higher Education," argued that higher education's goals went beyond practical knowledge or culture for its own sake, to include preparation for the "duty of citizenship." "Bosses rule," he argued, "because of the lack of public spirit." Students translated this civic duty into one of active participation in college life. Editorials routinely denounced the "selfishness" of students who thought only of "getting their money's worth of instruction." One *F&M Weekly* editorial defined the duty of the true college man in these terms: "to give himself, while he is a student, wholly and entirely to the cause of the betterment of his college; to use his talents, if they can be used, to help or to keep up the various college organizations . . . ; to patronize and support college functions; to shun the clique and to vote honorably; to help to cultivate an enthusiastic but nevertheless a refined 'college spirit.'" Students who focused on study and grades were condemned as "polers" or "grinds."[58]

Most faculty accepted extracurricular activities as an integral part of the college experience. In fact, the very conception of "well-roundedness" in higher education had shifted subtly from a curricular issue to one that embraced learning in and out of the classroom. "[Extracurricular activities] are most desirable and may be used as very effective agencies in our educational system," Apple told the board. "The training which men receive in connection with some of the responsible positions which they occupy is far greater than we imagine." Apple also noted, though, such activity must be carefully balanced with course work. The problem was that students often arrived with "an apathetic attitude" toward studies and found activities so much more satisfying that they neglected class work.[59]

Just as the Progressive search for community sometimes degenerated into repression, student calls for participation began to sound ominously like demands for conformity. For example, after pointing to the disappointingly small attendance at the latest mass meeting before the football game, the *Weekly* announced that attendance would be taken at the next gathering "and the names of absentees posted on the bulletin board." This would quickly reveal "who of the students lack the proper college spirit." Later, the *Weekly* threatened to publish names of students who sat comfortably in the stands during football games instead of joining the cheering section on the sidelines. When a freshman who was dragged out of the grandstand left the game, the paper dismissed him as "a good example of what a Franklin and Marshall man is not."[60]

This preoccupation with group cohesion was evident in changing attitudes toward hazing newcomers. In the last decades of the nineteenth century, the supposedly "natural" rivalry between freshmen and sophomores had typically been expressed in more or less spontaneous scuffles and in hall rushes that persisted despite official efforts to repress them. At the turn of the century, hall rushes were replaced by an official cane rush conducted on Williamson Field according to specified rules. Taking a variety of forms, the cane rush involved a battle to push a cane through massed opponents. Although the shift to greater organization of student activities at Franklin & Marshall followed the pattern at other schools, it produced more rather than fewer injuries: in 1901 they included a broken rib; sprained knees, ankles, and wrists; dislocated fingers; black eyes; and bruises. The *Weekly* called for abolishing the event, but the next year the contest drew an even larger audience of students and local citizens. As injuries mounted, the faculty banned the event in 1907. Students called for a replacement, arguing that a contest between freshmen and sophomores "fosters college spirit" by settling the question of "class superiority." In the absence of a sanctioned event, students returned to the customary free-for-all skirmishes. In 1910 a committee of upperclassmen established a "rope rush," or "tie up," that it hoped would serve the function with fewer injuries. In this competition students were given pieces of rope and, at a signal from the president of the senate, rushed onto the field and, working in groups of no more than three, attempted to tie up members of the opposing class. Even so, older practices persisted. An incoming freshman wrote home in 1914 that he had arrived "too late for the class scrap which took place this afternoon."[61]

Over time, college "traditions" became ever more formalized and repressive. Freshmen and sophomores had long vied openly for supremacy, with sophomores asserting a special "duty" to restrain and educate "green" newcomers. In 1902, when four sophomores were arrested for pasting posters around town, their proclamations merely warned freshmen to behave. Occasionally, the conflict flared into open violence. In 1905 some fourteen sophomores seized a freshman and were in the process of forcing him to remove a poster his classmates had plastered on the window of a local grocery story, when another freshman, Oscar Gingrich, rushed up to his defense. Gingrich was seized, blindfolded, and taken out of town. Tried and convicted of being "too fresh," he was ordered to perform several "stunts" as punishment. When he refused, he was hit with a paddle. Gingrich responded by pulling a revolver from his pocket and shooting one of his tormentors in the arm before being disarmed. Faculty concluded that the hazing of Gingrich "merited the severest condemnation" and placed the sophomores on probation for a year, while it reproved Gingrich for carrying a gun. W. U. Hensel, chairman of the board's Committee on Discipline, was asked to speak to the students on the legal penalties for hazing. Student opinion, in contrast, ran strongly against Gingrich. The faculty rejected their petition to force him out of the college, but student ostracism eventually had the same effect.[62]

Over time, freshmen were required to submit to a growing number of ritual humiliations to prove themselves worthy of inclusion in the student body, with sophomores receiving official powers of enforcement. In 1910 sophomores plastered the campus and surrounding community with posters listing freshman regulations. Described by the *F&M Weekly* as "college lore and tradition," these included requirements to wear a prescribed cap and observe an evening curfew, except when attending all-college events. In 1915 the Student Senate itself set freshman rules, which included observing curfews of 8:00 P.M. on weeknights and 10:00 P.M. on weekends, wearing specific caps every day except Sunday, attending all mass meetings, and doing tasks set by athletic leaders. The new regulations came with a pragmatic rationale. "The long tested and tried traditions of the American college demand that the new men be properly initiated into the life of the college," the *Student Weekly* explained. "It has been found that the Freshman must be orientated to his surroundings before he can reap the full benefits of college life."[63]

Students made these changes, emulating practices on other campuses, and enforced them in the face of adult opposition. "Who gave the sophomores supreme authority to run the college, anyway?" an alumnus of the class of 1878 wrote the *F&M Weekly* in 1911. "Have the president and faculty abdicated their authority, and handed it over to the sophomores?" He predicted that the custom was doomed "here in free America," but in coming years freshman restrictions and humiliations continued to increase. Faculty often tried to restrain hazing but found itself powerless to prevent the proliferation of student "traditions." In 1912 Apple argued that concerns about freshmen should not be how to haze them but "how to shape them into the spirit and life of our institution."[64]

The changing climate is illustrated by the evolution of the Pajama Parade, destined to become a particular Franklin & Marshall tradition. In 1909, in spontaneous celebration of a football victory over Swarthmore, students gathered in the late afternoon, adopting "a grotesque appearance" by donning "night-shirts, bathrobes and pajamas." In classic charivari tradition, they armed themselves with horns, whistles, and "other noise-producing instruments" and marched from the college to the train depot in the center of town to meet the returning victors. Students carried team members to a waiting carriage and pulled it to campus for a celebratory bonfire and speeches. Similar demonstrations were held in later years to mark the close of a successful football season or even to prepare for a big game like the annual Thanksgiving contest with Gettysburg. On some occasions, each class assumed different "gaudy costumes"; in 1910 freshmen chose "the night-gown costume" and sophomores sported red hats and ties.[65]

After World War I, the Pajama Parade evolved into an initiation rite in which freshmen were forced to process through the city dressed in pajamas while being paddled by sophomore tormentors. Intensification of hazing rites may have been an unconscious preparation for modern life, where large organizations required subsuming individuality and accepting prescribed roles. Yet this does not explain why hazing grew at Franklin & Marshall at a time when other colleges rejected such practices or forced them underground into fraternities. One reason might have been the eagerness of German American students to embrace mainstream American customs. The waning role of religion in student lives and the weakened authority of the Reformed Church in an increasingly diverse student body might have prompted a search for new ways of fostering community. Certainly, the *Student Weekly* defended the college's hazing "traditions" in 1915 by noting the need to create community among young men whose only formal connection was "the classroom and the books." Campus leaders may have been reacting to the preprofessional focus of many students, particularly those in the sciences. Without the sense of "brotherhood" produced by "the terrors of initiation," the *Student Weekly* warned, the college "could be reduced to a temporary unanimity between grinds!" In 1916, the paper worried that more than one in five students did not participate in extracurricular activities, leaving the three-fifths who belonged to fraternities and residential clubs to assume the burden of sustaining essential campus activities. It may also not be a coincidence that hazing became more prominent as the college moved away from a prescribed classical curriculum, which had served as a rite of passage for generations of students.[66]

Standardizing the Curriculum

In his inaugural address, Apple honored Franklin & Marshall's tradition of liberal education and defended it against proponents of specialization or vocationalism in undergraduate education. He depicted the college experience as one of coming of age, a time for the growth of personality, in which "the student comes to it a boy and goes out a man." He noted that professional schools increasingly required baccalaureate degrees for admission, motivated "not only by the desire for greater dignity" but by recognition that "narrowness in education is accompanied with a narrowness of outlook which prevents a full development of a man's powers in his special line of work." Nevertheless, under Apple's leadership, Franklin & Marshall's formal curriculum became ever more specialized.[67]

Even before his arrival, the faculty had begun to deliberate whether to follow the trend at many American colleges of requiring students to focus much of their elective study within departmental majors and minors. A talk to college and seminary faculty in November 1910 showed that Apple was thinking along the same lines, although he warned that elective studies beginning in the junior year should not be allowed to become so advanced and demanding that they weakened the goal of "well rounded" education. Perhaps referring to Schiedt's notorious courses, he noted that "distinctively technical work" required so much time that it "[robbed] the student of inclination and strength for important drill and training in other lines of development." The purpose of college "is first to train its students to noble manhood, through noble scholarship and noble personal associations," according to Apple, "and second to extend the boundaries of knowledge." The problem was how to organize college work to effect these goals.[68]

Apple moved slowly. In 1912 he proposed a new course of study leading to a bachelor of science degree; unlike the Ph.B., it would require no ancient languages and offered concentrations in chemistry or biology. In presenting the new program to the board, he argued that the B.S. degree was "in accord with the curriculum of all other colleges of Pennsylvania." Although this proposal was a further move away from Franklin & Marshall's emphasis on ancient languages, foreign language study continued to play a major role. Students were required to take a total of fifteen years of several languages at secondary and college levels, more than any other institution and over twice the national average.[69]

Three years later, the faculty adopted an even more far-reaching revision. Early in 1915, the faculty Committee on the Curriculum recommended allowing either Latin or Greek for the A.B. degree, eliminating the need for the Ph.B. degree. Moreover, the committee advocated adopting concentration and distribution requirements,

similar to a system introduced at Harvard University in 1910. After a largely prescribed freshman year, students were given greater freedom to select courses, within
requirements of fourteen semester hours in a major subject and ten hours each in
three minors. Majors and minors were to be distributed among three general areas:
languages and literature; history, social sciences, and philosophy; and mathematics
and the physical and natural sciences. Candidates for the A.B. degree could major in
the first two areas, and candidates for the B.S. in the third. All students were required
to study English, history, mathematics, psychology, economics, the Bible, and ethics.
The implications of this curricular change in terms of the college's view of knowledge
were signaled in the catalogue in 1915. Previous overviews of the curriculum had reflected a belief that all knowledge was unified and logically related, beginning with
philosophy, classical languages, and modern languages and then moving through the
social and physical sciences. Now subjects were simply listed in alphabetical order. The
introduction explained that the curriculum included "such intellectual disciplines as
have been approved by centuries of testing, as well as those modern subjects which
are of equal importance."[70]

Presenting these changes to the board, Apple stressed the need to conform to
general standards in higher education. Dropping the Ph.B. would put the curriculum
"in harmony with the practice of the best colleges today," he explained. The faculty
had concluded that the Greek requirement was driving students away from the classical course and reasoned that the new curriculum served the larger interest "of offering to the largest number of students the benefits of a classical, liberal education."
Similarly, in 1916 Apple described the major/minor system as "in accord with the practice of the best colleges in the country." It ensured "a well balanced course for each
student," while allowing "opportunity for special effort in some one department of his
selection."[71]

Changing Leadership

The years that marked the completion of Franklin & Marshall's first modern endowment drive and the transformation of its curriculum were a watershed in the college's
history. This was dramatized by the departure of a number of men who had played
significant roles in the college's development. First, in 1914, came the death of George F.
Baer, president of the Board of Trustees for two decades. He died three days before a
U.S. Supreme Court decision outlawed the holding company of assorted coal mines
that he ran for J. P. Morgan.[72]

Baer was succeeded by William Hensel, who had served on the board for nearly
a quarter century. A Presbyterian, Hensel was the first board president who was not a
member of the Reformed Church. Although already in failing health, he pledged to
work on behalf of "a bigger and a better Franklin and Marshall College," not in physical terms, though he dreamed of "a great central memorial refectory" to bring students together on campus. He envisioned instead a higher intellectual climate that
included revivified literary societies, wider use of the Library, and

such literary culture that they who will not draw the bow with Ulysses, nor drink of the Bandusian fountain, nor 'sing arms and the man,' must at least linger at and draw from the wells of English undefiled with Shakespeare, Milton, Wordsworth, Macaulay, Carlyle, Matthew Arnold, and other masters of modern style; and incomparable with all others — the translators of the King James Bible; that every alumnus not only shall be tinctured, but saturated, with a sound philosophy and correct ideas of life, and go out into the world a better citizen and patriot for having tarried in the College until his beard was grown.

To Hensel, an institution embodying such a vision was more worthy than "an educational factory of far larger and much meaner output." His presidency was short, however; he died in February 1915. The faculty's memorial tribute, written by his close friend Richard Schiedt, saluted him as "a staunch advocate of classic learning, an ardent lover of the best in literature, unsurpassed as a master of expression and unrivalled in eloquence, . . . easily recognized as the best exponent of the life and learning of our college." Although Baer and Hensel had been practical men of the world, both were essentially products of the nineteenth-century classical college, generalists who excelled at public oratory. It may be more than coincidence that the most sweeping revisions of the curriculum took place after both had departed.[73]

Benjamin Franklin Fackenthal Jr. became the next president of the board. Although he proudly claimed a German American parentage like that of his predecessors, Fackenthal's education represented a clear departure. Born in 1851 in Easton, Pennsylvania, Fackenthal left school at fourteen to help his ailing father manage an ironworks. His father taught him surveying, bookkeeping, and business methods, which Fackenthal later considered "as valuable, and perhaps more so, than the country school education would have been." In the 1870s he took several courses as a nondegree student in Lafayette College's chemistry and metallurgy departments. He subsequently became president of the Thomas Iron Company and was involved in a wide range of manufacturing, mining, and financial interests. Elected a Franklin & Marshall trustee in 1899, he was most interested in its emerging science programs.[74]

A third anchor of the old Franklin & Marshall College was lost with the December 1915 death of John S. Stahr. After retiring as president, he had continued to serve as the J. W. Nevin Professor of Mental and Moral Science, Aesthetics, and the Philosophy of History until his election as emeritus professor earlier in the year. Apple wanted Klein to take over the position, but the board's Committee on Instruction asked Apple himself to teach aesthetics and the philosophy of history. After Stahr's death, Apple also taught the capstone senior course in ethics. This was the role that the college president had traditionally played, but Apple preferred not to teach in order to focus on administration.[75]

For the next eight years, Apple delivered lectures on the basis of notes his father had used when he was president between 1877 and 1889. As these had been, in turn, adaptations of lectures delivered by John W. Nevin himself, they represented a direct connection with the college's Mercersburg traditions. Recognizing the distinctive character of the college's aesthetics course, Edgar Fahs Smith, provost of the University of Pennsylvania, urged Apple to edit his notes for publication. "I am sure that Franklin and Marshall College is unique in that particular field," Smith insisted, pointing to a "general consensus of opinion" that it was "very strong" in aesthetic theory. He continued, "It would be a pity if that sort of teaching would be abandoned." Despite this encouragement, the aesthetics book was never published.[76]

War and Crisis in German American Culture

Even more than normal attrition wrought by the passage of time, events of 1914–1918 played a major role in Franklin & Marshall College's waning distinctiveness as an Anglo-German institution of the Reformed Church. As European nations descended into war in the late summer and fall of 1914, members of the college community were drawn into the debate over America's response. Despite the college's German American character, few openly supported the German cause, while many hoped that the United States could stay out of the conflict. Some eagerly seized the opportunity to differentiate themselves as "Old Stock" German Americans, as opposed to more recent immigrants.[77]

When classes began in September 1914, among the usual opening of school stories was an alumnus's account of his "thrilling adventure" when caught in the war zone during his European travels. Soon, however, nearly all thought of war was swept away by delirium at the football team's first — and only — victory, 10–0, over the University of Pennsylvania. After decades of serving as Penn's season-opening whipping boy, Franklin & Marshall's stunning triumph inspired understandable hyperbole. "The bloody carnage now taking place in Europe could not be compared to the awful havoc wrought by the wearers of the Blue and White upon the sons of Old Penn within the very walls of the City of Brotherly Love on Saturday," the F&M Weekly exulted. "Not since the day when the Liberty Bell made history has such consternation broken loose and pandemonium reigned supreme." During the game, the fifteen-man team was cheered on by about fifty "enthusiastic, yet fearful undergraduates," who managed to rival "the noise made by the 3,000 or more Penn rooters" in the packed stadium. Afterward, the "heavy voiced rooters" prepared a banner proclaiming their victory and paraded down Market Street into the heart of the city, shouting and cheering to all passersby. The group invaded City Hall itself, according to the Philadelphia Evening Bulletin, circling through the first-floor corridors, with "a series of yells that brought the machinery of the various departments to a standstill for several minutes."[78]

Back at home, college and academy students flocked to meet the football team's train. They were hustled into automobiles and paraded throughout town for several hours before arriving at campus. Finding this celebration insufficient, the Student Senate decreed the following Monday a holiday from recitations in order to prepare a giant bonfire. Under the direction of a committee of seniors, freshmen hastened to gather flammable materials. The student body of more than three hundred gathered in the evening, armed "with all kinds of noise-making instruments." A procession led by the cheerleaders paraded to the center of town and returned for the bonfire on Williamson Field. Congratulatory speeches by faculty, coaches, and team leaders gave much of the credit for the stunning upset to Coach Charles W. Mayser. The celebration concluded with a now-traditional rendition of the alma mater. The general sense of goodwill extended into the next day, when the Student Senate censured a group of sophomores who attempted to haze a freshman after the bonfire. The faculty was even moved to excuse student absence from classes, although trustees suggested that Apple "improve the opportunity" of his announcement "to clearly define the powers of the [student] Senate in all matters pertaining to responsibility of the Faculty for the discipline of the institution."[79]

As the European war settled into bloody stalemate during the winter, students continued to focus on the campus world of sports and extracurricular organizations, while adults became increasingly embroiled in debates between advocates of peace and proponents of preparedness. Within the college community, Prussian-born Richard Schiedt was the most strongly affected by the European conflict. He had maintained close ties with family and friends, some of whom were now members of the government. Pride in his native land and culture made him bristle at press reports of German atrocities, which he denounced as "English lies," the work of reporters in the pay of the English government. "Never in the history of the world has there been such a systematic, ruthless onslaught against a belligerent nation on the part of a neutral power as we witness at the present time in this country," he protested in the *Reformed Church Review* in 1915. Confident of his standing in Lancaster, Schiedt frequently appeared in public venues to offer alternative information and interpretations. He was a leader of the Lancaster German-American Alliance and prominent in local efforts to raise money for the German Red Cross.[80]

In the winter of 1914–1915, Schiedt participated in a massive national petition campaign organized by German American leaders seeking an embargo on the sale of war materials. Although presented as a defense of American neutrality, the movement was widely seen as an attempt to manipulate government policy in the interest of a foreign power, triggering what historian John Higham described as "the first passionate outburst of anti-German hysteria." Followed in short order by the onset of German submarine warfare and the discovery of German saboteurs inside America, the petition drive "spread an image of the German-American community riddled with treason and conspiring under orders from Berlin." Hence, well before the United States entered the war, suspicion focused on what Higham called the "hyphenated American," the resident of divided loyalty.[81]

Higham considered this "the most spectacular reversal of judgment in the history of American nativism," for Germans had been widely considered the most desirable of immigrant groups. Certainly, Schiedt was ill suited to navigate the shoals of the new popular mood, and he continued to speak out as openly and obstreperously as before. When German submarines sank the *Lusitania* in May 1915, he was heard on several occasions to comment that the American victims had been warned not to take passage on the ship, which was carrying ammunition. He continued to rail against the "German ophobia" and "clouded vision" of local newspapers, for failing to report or sufficiently condemn Allied atrocities. In response to one of his letters of protest, a *Lancaster Intelligencer* editorial commented, "Dr. Scheidt is a man whose high character and distinguished abilities command the most sincere respect and his letter is, therefore, all the more interesting and remarkable as an exhibit of the effect of the great war and of the German philosophy of militarism."[82]

Others at the college stressed the patriotism of Pennsylvania's German Americans. In February 1916, President Apple used the occasion of an address to New York City alumni to emphasize the "undoubted universal loyalty" of the German Americans of his region. Noting the difference between "Old Stock" Germans and more recent immigrants, he pointed out that Pennsylvania's German Americans were descendants of eighteenth-century settlers who had played a significant role in the American Revolution, and these "were as truly Americans as any of the English speaking people." Apple admitted, "The situation of true-hearted American citizens of German birth or descent has been extremely trying since the European war has stirred up old animosities and friendly neighbors have grown to glance at each other with doubt and distrust." Although acknowledging that Pennsylvania's German Americans felt natural ties of kinship to Germany, he stated, "They have the firm conviction that the best future of the world is somehow bound up with the aims and purposes of the Allies."[83]

Aided by his brother, Joseph H. Apple, '92, publicist for the New York Wanamaker's department store, and Howard C. Hillegas, '94, city editor of the *New York Herald*, Apple's talk attracted widespread positive attention in New York and national publications. The *Herald*'s editorialist hoped that Apple's words would be "read by every one of the legislators in Washington who is trying to make Congress an adjunct of the Berlin War Office." The piece was reprinted in *Collier's Magazine* under the title "No Hyphen in Lancaster County." "Incidentally it gives the college some good advertising," Joseph Apple wrote his brother.[84]

The *Student Weekly* also exulted in the way Apple's address "gave to the college more newspaper publicity than any other single event in recent years." Yet on campus relatively little attention was paid to the mounting war fever, apart from an ongoing debate over whether compulsory military training was appropriate in colleges and universities. Eventually, moved by the example of "an ever increasing number of higher educational institutions of [the] country," the Student Senate asked trustees to establish "some form of military training or drill." The board referred the proposal to the Committee on Instruction, which took no action. *Oriflamme*'s only reference to the changing tenor of public life was a welcoming poem that began with the line "Friends, non-hyphens, countrymen, lend us your ears."[85]

Franklin & Marshall at War

By 1916 Franklin & Marshall had reached an unequaled level of prosperity. With completion of the fund-raising campaign, the endowment exceeded $553,000, and the 1916–1917 academic year saw a surplus in operating funds of almost $7,300. The student body was the largest in the college's history: 289 undergraduates and 30 graduate students. Underclassmen plunged into the usual whirl of poster fights and tie-up contests, with a large freshmen class of 98 emerging victorious. The *Student Weekly* reported about alumni fighting with U. S. forces against Pancho Villa at the Mexican border. The football team capped a previously winless season with a victory over Gettysburg, prompting most students to defy the faculty and skip classes to build another mammoth bonfire on Williamson Field. Early the following morning, a fire believed to be of "incendiary origin" destroyed wooden grandstands on the western side of the field.[86]

Meanwhile, the board paid $20,000 to repurchase the five acres donated to the Theological Seminary of the Reformed Church when it moved to Lancaster, along with two faculty houses. Apple urged the board to begin planning for the college's future growth, pointing to the need for dormitories, fraternity houses, an auditorium, a larger gymnasium and new athletic field, a central heating plant, and a separate church building. A board committee outlined construction projects worth $165,000 and called for another $250,000 for endowment and scholarships. The college joined a fund-raising campaign of all the educational institutions of the Reformed Church in the United States on the occasion of the 400th anniversary of the Protestant Reformation. The goal was to "awaken our people to the vast importance of Christian education" and raise a combined $1 million, with Franklin & Marshall's share at $125,000.[87]

All grand plans were put on hold when the United States declared war in April 1917. Instead of envisioning further growth, college leaders scrambled to ensure its survival in the new world of mass mobilization. Like many other all-male institutions of higher education, Franklin & Marshall faced the threat of having to close down if all prospective students were called for military service. In seeking to show that liberal education could serve national ends, the college established its first direct links with the national government.

Despite strong student support for military drill, the board dragged its feet in establishing a program. *Student Weekly* editors finally took the initiative in March 1917 to gather information that Apple used to set up a program. When war was declared a month later, displays of patriotic fervor were muted because students were busy protesting suspension of a group of seniors who had held a public dance without permission. But forty-five students enlisted within weeks of President Wilson's call for volunteers, and by May another eighty had left to work on farms. Intercollegiate games were canceled and class sessions shortened to make time for drill.[88]

At a meeting of college and university presidents in Washington, Apple was heartened to learn that government leaders agreed that "indiscriminate" enlistment of students was not an efficient use of manpower. As Newton D. Baker, secretary of war, put it, "It takes the best men in the country and places them in positions which easily could be filled by others, while positions which only college and university men could fill to the best advantage of the country would be left vacant or filled by men of less efficiency." In effect outlining a strategic role for higher education, Baker emphasized that "sane and intelligent" patriotism dictated that college and university students should stay in school to develop their special skills for future service in science or leadership positions. In a collegewide address, Apple employed the common rhetoric of the Progressive era by characterizing Baker's policy as "conserving and developing our intellectual resources." Nevertheless, thirty-one students left school early to attend an officers training camp at Fort Niagara; among them was junior Richard C. Schiedt Jr. Bowing to the continuing exodus of students, the faculty canceled final examinations and moved commencement up a week.[89]

With establishment of a conscription system for men between twenty-one and thirty, Apple did not know, as the board met in June, how many students would return in the fall. "It was evident," he later noted, "that the minds of students were greatly confused and there was eager and intense desire for action." In fact, "it was freely prophesied that colleges would soon close their doors and the students scatter till the end of the war." He delayed hiring new faculty and stepped up recruitment. When school resumed, 210 students appeared, 73 of whom were freshmen. Classics professor J. Nevin Schaeffer delivered an opening address, stressing the role of college education in preparing for future service.[90]

As the nation settled into a wartime routine, the college tried to continue as much as usual while responding to demands touching upon all aspects of life. Students organized a band that played at football games and military parades alike. Intercollegiate athletics continued, and when the football coach was drafted in midseason, a high school teacher took over. "The heatless, wheatless, meatless, smokeless (and as one of the Professors added, brainless) Mondays pervaded the Campus," H. M. J. Klein recalled, "in a frenzied effort to save everything for the boys at the front." A coal shortage at the height of the winter closed Old Main, and classes met in the Science Building and the library. Following a plan of the Association of College Presidents of Pennsylvania to free students for farm or industrial work, classes met on Saturdays and holidays, to enable the semester to end a month early.[91]

Campus sentiment as reflected in the student newspaper was moderately patriotic. From time to time the *Student Weekly* expressed pride in students and alumni serving in the military, but it rejected calls to repress German culture. The paper argued that the noble and uplifting thoughts of Goethe, Schiller, and many others had nothing to do with German's present militarism and were best approached in their original language. "Let us consider fairly and justly," the *Weekly* concluded.[92]

To avoid a vast regulatory apparatus, national leaders decided to rely upon citizens' spirit of self-sacrifice to ensure voluntary compliance with wartime measures. Many Americans responded with a multitude of organizations, drives, and pledge signings — "activities," John Higham has noted, "that often acquired a semi-obligatory status."

"Enthusiastic cultivation of obedience and conformity" became a fundamental duty. Even the Reformed Church, which had long resisted moves toward centralized bureaucracy, organized a national service commission to work with the interdenominational Federal Council of Churches. The pressure to conform fell most heavily on German Americans who had opposed American entry into the war. Often, even sincere efforts to contribute were greeted with suspicion. In Richard Schiedt's case, his stubborn refusal to bend to the demands of the times strained bonds of loyalty based on more than three decades of dedication to the college and the Lancaster community.[93]

Wartime Departure of a Beloved Professor

At the declaration of war, Lancastrians were called upon to sign a pledge of loyalty to the president and the nation. Richard Schiedt refused, arguing that he had made a formal pledge of loyalty when he became a naturalized citizen; to ask him to repeat it now was an attack upon his integrity. Apple later reported that he personally asked Schiedt to sign: "As President of the College I urged him on account of his previous Pro-German activities to make a public statement of his position." Schiedt would not back down but repeated his reasons for refusing to a local paper. This aroused much "bitter comment" but no concerted pressure to conform.[94]

According to Apple and other faculty, Schiedt continued openly to criticize the war and ridicule patriotic efforts of those around him. (The comment about "brainless Mondays" quoted above was most likely his.) He charged that students enlisted or went to work on farms mainly to avoid taking examinations, and he tried to dissuade the college's two janitors from subscribing to the Liberty Loan drive.[95]

Schiedt's prominence and his position as a German-born American made him a tempting target for the patriotic press. In the fall of 1917, *Chronicle Magazine* wrote to persons of German birth and descent whose named were listed in *Who's Who* and the *Social Register*, asking them to affirm their allegiance to the United States government and to express their opinions about the country's entrance into the war. "Being assured that the request was prompted by conciliatory motives and was not intended for publication," Schiedt responded to the magazine that he "swore my oath of allegiance on the 8th of October, 1892, without reservation and restriction, and my Prussian training has taught me that the violation of an oath is self-annihilation. However, allegiance does not mean blind submission. I was and will continue to be opposed to the entrance of our country into this war." The *Chronicle* published his statement, which was picked up by the *New York Times* and then found its way to the *Reformed Church Messenger*. Meanwhile, a Lancaster woman told friends that while riding a Pennsylvania Railroad train, she had overheard Schiedt making "disloyal statements." Her story soon spread widely, inevitably with "various embellishments."[96]

The *Lancaster New Era* noted that these reports "created a lively commotion in church and college circles on the question of his loyalty." At the annual meetings of the three synods, Apple encountered "a very grave feeling of bitterness towards Dr.

Schiedt." A special board meeting in November dealt with a number of war issues, including financial implications of declining enrollments. The board rescinded the honorary degree conferred upon Count von Bernstorff, a decision "based upon the moral turpitude of the German Ambassador as proved by the disclosures of the State Department." Afterward, local trustee Charles Baker raised the matter of "certain disquieting rumors concerning the loyalty of a certain member of the Faculty." In light of their action regarding Bernstorff, Baker believed that trustees "should [have been] looking after the matter in [their] own household."[97]

After an "earnest" discussion there was general agreement that the trustees could take no action "based on mere rumor" but that even hints of disloyalty hurt the college. Nor could they tolerate "a divided allegiance in the teaching force of the College in this most critical time of our country's need of, and most just claim upon, the patriotic devotion of all her sons." The board asked Baker to head a committee to meet with Schiedt.[98]

Schiedt explained to the committee how he had come to write the statement to the *Chronicle*, asserting that it represented his position and stating, "I cannot change [it] because I am neither a coward nor a hypocrit." He opposed the war: "I am against all war, ardently desiring peace." But he insisted that he never mentioned the subject in his classroom or in public. He pointed out that he had allowed his only son to enlist and his daughters to work for the Red Cross and was himself conducting war-related research under the auspices of the National Research Council. Finally, he "expressed most forcibly his absolute loyalty to the country of his adoption" and assured the committee "that at no time since the United States had declared war upon Germany had he by word or deed done anything which would indicate disloyalty." Fackenthal strongly supported him, insisting that controversial statements were merely "the Schiedt way of saying things," and threatening to resign if his friend was forced to leave the college. The committee concluded that it would be best to postpone action until the June meeting. "So many things happen in six months," one member wrote, "[that] by June the war may be over or Schiedt may be a colonel in the German Land-Gewehr."[99]

Hope that the problem would simply go away did not reckon with Schiedt's mental and physical deterioration under stress, nor with the resentment of some of his colleagues. In January, chemistry teacher H. H. Beck mounted in a prominent place in the Science Building a poster advertising a lecture at the Lancaster YMCA titled "The Atrocities of the Germans." The speaker was a well-known anti-German agitator, and Beck must have realized that Schiedt would feel compelled to respond. The next day it was discovered that someone had scrawled the words "Champion Liar of the United States" across the poster. Immediately a hue and cry was raised, and word of the unpatriotic "attack" quickly spread through the local and regional press. "It was patent to one and all," screamed the account in the *New Era*, that the "cunning" and "cowardly" offender "was motivated by unscrupulous designs not only to affect the attendance at the lecture at the Y.M.C.A., but to throw a doubt into the minds of the students on all points connecting the brutalities of the war with the Disciples of Frightfulness."[100]

Local trustee William Hager immediately proposed offering a $100 reward to help find the culprit. Baker had his own suspicions and asked Schiedt directly if he had done it. When Schiedt admitted that he had, Baker called a meeting of all local board members. But before it could assemble, Schiedt presented his resignation to Apple, claiming declining health as the reason but offering to teach the rest of the semester. Hager reported that he had seen Schiedt, who was in his words "all in" physically and mentally, and offered to contribute money to allow Schiedt to go away to rest. The local trustees group agreed unanimously that Schiedt's resignation should be accepted and should take effect immediately but that his salary should be paid to the end of the academic year. Their goal, Apple explained to Fackenthal, was to allow Schiedt "to care for his health immediately" and also "to avoid any further possible trouble that might arise out of his nervous condition similar to the one that had recently occurred." Because he had resigned, they agreed that there was no need to deal with the "other question." According to Apple, the group "considered [it] a favor to him to close the matter this way." Because it had no formal authority, the group recommended that the Committee on Instruction be convened to act on the resignation.[101]

With Fackenthal's assent, the committee met a week later and accepted Schiedt's resignation effective immediately "on account of the state of his health." One member, G. D. Robb, noted that he regretted taking the action, because of Schiedt's contributions to the institution, despite having felt for a long time "that [Schiedt's] influence with the boys was not always wholesome." Apple quickly arranged for several young scientists from the University of Pennsylvania to cover Schiedt's courses.[102]

Soon voices were raised in protest at the college's handling of the matter. Alone among the trustees, Hager objected that Schiedt should not have been required to stop teaching immediately and questioned the Committee of Instruction's authority to remove Schiedt. Student response was muted, in part because news of the resignation coincided with the death of A. T. G. Apple, the much-loved teacher of mathematics and astronomy. The student paper simply reported that Schiedt had resigned because of poor health, adding that illness had nearly forced him to step down several times before. A week later, 129 students petitioned the board for Schiedt's reinstatement. The effort seems to have been inspired by Schiedt's claim that without him students would not be able to complete their biology work, because the petition objected not to any injustice in the college's action but its impracticability. Students protested that Schiedt's sudden departure would cause "[their] scholastic work and the College in general [to] suffer, irreparably." Some feared that their admission to medical school would be endangered.[103]

The faculty made no formal statement regarding their colleague's departure, but faculty secretary George Mull inserted a comment into the minutes that left little question about his opinion. He noted that Schiedt's resignation "on ground of ill health" was "a palpable subterfuge to forestall dismissal on the ground of disloyalty, which would surely have happened."[104]

Meanwhile, some younger alumni were more sensitive to what they saw as the board's denial of Schiedt's rights. In the absence of a formal statement from the college, there was considerable confusion about details in the case. Some of those close to Schiedt initiated a letter-writing campaign charging that he had been dismissed without a proper hearing and promising "a lively time during commencement week." J. Andrew Frantz, a recent alumnus and Harvard Law School graduate, challenged the Committee on Instruction's "alleged dismissal" as "apparently invalid and extra-legal." "To our minds," Frantz wrote, "it is not a question of Americanism or un-Americanism. We merely want to know whether justice has been done and whether all the proceedings were carried on in a perfectly legal and ethical manner." Some alumni were particularly suspicious because the board, in an "apparently autocratic manner," had in recent years failed to renew several professors' appointments.[105]

Committee of Instruction members J. W. Wetzel and A. H. Rothermel wrote Frantz that Schiedt had resigned, giving his ill health as the reason. Rothermel, also a lawyer, pointed out that not only did the committee have "general powers to engage and dismiss teachers in the college," but its decision had already been ratified by more than a majority of the entire board. He pointed out that when Schiedt resigned because of ill health, it was eminently fair to allow him to stop teaching while continuing to receive his salary. Rothermel asserted, "When Dr. Schiedt said his health was not good, I believed it; and when he offered to resign I thought he meant it." Any subsequent complaint was unreasonable and, "as [Frantz would] surely admit, without any legal merit." "Of course," Rothermel concluded, "we all know there are other factors in the question." Rothermel commented that he did not want to discuss them. They all had hoped that Schiedt could remain at Franklin & Marshall, but this, according to Rothermel, "became daily more difficult because of his own indiscretions. When he resigned, he himself cut the Gordian knot and made everyone's duty plain."[106]

Thereafter, the movement to reinstate Schiedt dwindled away, even after the Lancaster woman withdrew her charge that Schiedt had made disloyal comments, explaining that her previous statement had been based on mistaken identity. The *Student Weekly* reported that the news was hailed "by Dr. Schiedt's friends, and they are numbered by the hundreds." Because his long service to the college had brought "much honor to the institution," the *Weekly* expressed pleasure "for the institution's sake, as well as for Dr. Schiedt's."[107]

Richard Schiedt's resignation undoubtedly saved college leaders from a painful and divisive action. From President Apple's point of view, Schiedt's departure removed a long-standing source of irritation, even if it also meant losing one of the college's most prominent and productive scholars and teachers. The *New Era* story announcing Schiedt's resignation summed up his qualities this way: "Possessed of a wide circle of intimate friendships, [he was] a man of genial warmth, enthusiasms and personal attraction; a brilliant scholar, logician and orator, and in the realm of biology and kindred sciences standing at the forefront of educators and scientists in this country."

Nonetheless, because of his unflinching loyalty to his native country, he "found himself strangely alone among his colleagues in his attitude on the war."[108]

Enlisting the Colleges

Pressing problems remained, most prominent being a continued decline in enrollments. During the 1917–1918 academic year, fifty-six students left school — sixteen enlisted, six were drafted, and the rest went to work in industry or agriculture. Apple reported to the board that this rate of departure was typical, but he predicted that there would be "few if any students over twenty-one years of age in American colleges at the beginning of next year." He noted that various federal agencies were joining educational leaders in trying to persuade younger students that attending institutions of higher education was the best way "to prepare for service of the highest order to the nation." He urged alumni and Reformed Church members to help with the "patriotic effort" of recruitment: "To give up liberal education for a single year in America would mean later a year of defective leadership, of blind guidance, and of national life on a lower level."[109]

Even more troubling was the prospect that the draft age would be lowered to eighteen. "It was an anxious question as to whether the colleges would have any students left to them," Apple recalled. He had already raised the possibility of admitting women. Other colleges were doing this to maintain enrollments, and a number of Lancaster residents and Church members sought to enroll their daughters. But Apple expected that alumni would oppose the idea.[110]

In the end, the federal government came to the college's rescue by, in effect, enlisting the entire institution. When Congress lowered the draft age to eighteen, the War Department established the Students' Army Training Corps (SATC), to allow men subject to the draft to continue their education while preparing to be soldiers. Under the program, colleges and universities leased their facilities and staff to the government, which in turn paid all expenses to feed, house, and instruct young student-soldiers in a combined military and academic curriculum drawn up by a War Department committee. Along with more than five hundred other institutions nationwide, Franklin & Marshall eagerly applied to participate. In the fall, 248 young men were enrolled under this program, while another 51 not subject to the draft followed the regular curriculum. The campus was transformed according to the needs of military life: the Academy Building and Old Main became barracks, while literary society buildings were used for study and recreation. For a time, nearly all manifestations of student life disappeared. Students wore military uniforms and were subject to military regulations and discipline. The newspaper, clubs, and fraternities were suspended, although some sports teams continued. In contrast, the YMCA, which had struggled for years to attract students, revived with support from the War Camp Community Service program.[111]

"This date marks the beginning of a memorable year for the College," George Mull began his minutes of the first faculty meeting of the year. "From an Institution devoted to the arts of peace it has become a vital part of the organized energy of the country consecrated to the winning of the war as quickly as possible. In other words, the normal functions of the College have been superseded by the needs of the government in the establishment of the Students Army Training Corps." The college's eager participation in the national program along with most other schools in the area, including even Quaker Swarthmore, showed how homogeneous American higher education had become. "The way these colleges embraced the war, sometimes with unseemly haste," argues historian Bruce Leslie, "suggested the extent to which they had converged on a national, Anglo-Protestant culture and had abandoned the identities that separated them half a century earlier." This uniformity was dramatized by mass induction ceremonies conducted simultaneously at schools throughout the country on October 1, 1918. At Franklin & Marshall everyone gathered in front of the new Academy Building. As at other colleges, addresses by leaders of the nation's military and President Wilson were read, followed by a statement by the president of the college. Wilson's message noted that the ceremony marked students' passage from the status of separate individuals to a collective identity with "the entire manhood of the country," while their schools had become "essentially government institutions." Then the commanding officer at each school "administered the oath of fealty to the nation, first to the members of the Faculty and then to the student soldiers." As historian Carol Gruber notes, the program "was the fulfillment of the higher education's service ideal."[112]

After the armistice in November, the college was just as suddenly demobilized, and all programs closed as of December 21. The War Department paid generously for the costs of reconversion, and regular academic work resumed at the beginning of the second term in January. Less than half of SATC students elected to continue, but many former students returned to the college as soon as they were discharged from the service. The college's collaboration with the federal government was particularly satisfactory from a financial point of view, leaving it with a profit of more than $17,000, which helped pay for the purchase of the seminary land and extensive renovations to turn one of the seminary residences into a president's house suitable for entertaining. Acknowledging that public opinion had deemed the SATC program a failure, Apple concluded that it had had not been in existence long enough to judge of the efficacy of combining military drill with college work. Nevertheless, he found an essential tension between liberal education and military training: "The essence of one is liberty, of the other discipline. . . . The college ought to inculcate in every student the spirit of loyalty and service to the nation, but its students must go to suitable separate schools for the technical training to arms as for every other form of technical or special training."[113]

With demobilization, Franklin & Marshall's first experience of government-sponsored education left few clear traces, but it set a precedent for a relationship that grew throughout the century. The college had worked hard in many ways to prove its patriotism and the importance of liberal education in the development of leadership skills needed for modern warfare. It pointed proudly to the 201 alumni and 121 undergraduates who served in the army and navy, more than half as commissioned officers.

"The college stands in the front rank," Apple asserted, "in the list of Colleges in Penn-sylvania in the number of men in service in proportion to the roll of graduates and undergraduates." The college's wartime experience, including but not limited to Schiedt's departure, moved it further toward assimilation into Anglo-American culture. Apple and many other education leaders strove to persuade the nation that higher education was essential to the national interest as well as to the personal development of individ-ual students. Insofar as this was accepted, it proved a mixed blessing, for along with increased government support came a loss of institutional control over curriculum and student life.[114]

CHAPTER SIX

Building a Greater Franklin & Marshall, 1919–1934

—∿∿—

Closing his first postwar report to the board, President Henry Harbaugh Apple observed that the Great War had brought the American college to "a new stage of life." Regarding possible changes at Franklin & Marshall, he promised that they would "come gradually and with due regard to what has thus been tested as well as to the needs for new conditions." He pledged "the best effort of Faculty and students to realize a larger and greater Franklin and Marshall College."[1]

The greater Franklin & Marshall that emerged during the 1920s was both larger in size and dramatically different in character. A comprehensive master plan transformed the campus, while the student body more than doubled and became more diverse. The influence of the Reformed Church waned as the proportion of students from Reformed backgrounds declined and religious worship played a less prominent role in college life. Anxious to emulate other educational institutions and to gain the approval of powerful accrediting organizations, the college joined a general trend of increased uniformity among the nation's colleges and universities.[2]

Changing Curriculum with the Times

Fundamentally, Franklin & Marshall College expanded during the 1920s because it began to offer the kind of curriculum that many Lancastrians had long clamored for. Apple's first step was to establish the Department of Education, the college's first explicitly professional program. It was a defensive measure to hold on to an already important constituency: by the beginning of the war nearly half of each graduating class found employment in secondary education. Franklin & Marshall's one course in pedagogy, established by John Stahr and continued by H. M. J. Klein, was barely sufficient to meet state requirements for a provisional teaching certificate. When

longtime superintendent of public instruction N. C. Schaeffer died in 1919, his successor made it clear that requirements would be expanded.[3]

Apple appointed Peter Harbold, a graduate of Millersville State Normal School and
Franklin & Marshall with a master's degree from Harvard. He had headed Millersville
before the war, and Apple assured the board that Harbold's experience would enable
them to "offer advantages superior to most colleges." As the first professor of education, Harbold introduced a series of courses designed to meet state requirements, although Apple stressed that they also contributed to "the general culture of the student."
The change had little immediate effect on enrollments: during the first two academic
years after the war, numbers merely returned to prewar levels, around three hundred.[4]

This lack of growth must have been disappointing, even disturbing, for elsewhere
higher education was in the midst of an unprecedented postwar boom. Between 1917
and 1920, college and university attendance grew by about 25 percent, at some places
by nearly 50 percent. As student numbers continued to mount through the 1920s, it
became clear that higher education had indeed entered a new era. The war had demonstrated the usefulness of modern knowledge and expertise, from applications of
science in manufacturing to accounting and management in business. Most postwar
enrollment growth came in technical and vocational fields, with nearly two-thirds of
undergraduates choosing occupational majors. In business, 117 new higher education
programs were introduced across the United States between 1919 and 1924. Locally,
Lancaster's economy had become diversified through creation of many small and
medium-sized manufacturing firms. At first their proprietors had little interest in formal higher education, but by the 1920s many sought business management skills.[5]

These considerations undoubtedly influenced Franklin & Marshall's decision to
introduce a new department and degree in business administration. It also responded
to changes in public education that further reduced the pool of students prepared for
traditional liberal arts education. New comprehensive high schools offered commercial and technical training as well as college preparation, and progressive notions of
education for social efficiency put more emphasis on social studies and civics than on
history and foreign languages. Consequently, Franklin & Marshall was forced to admit increasing numbers of students with conditional acceptances. In 1919–1920,
nearly 18 percent were "unclassified," largely, Apple told the board, because curricular
changes in many high schools "prepare boys in a different scale than in former
years."[6]

Early in 1921, Apple made an "extensive" presentation to the faculty about further changes that the state Department of Public Instruction planned in high school
curricula. To respond, he urged creating a department of business administration
that offered its own degree, a bachelor of science in economics. Instead of the extensive
list of courses required for admission to the bachelor of arts and bachelor of science
programs, this new program simply required fifteen units of high school study with
four years of English and two of math. After extended debate the faculty agreed to
recommend the program to the trustees.[7]

Expecting many alumni and board members to resist the innovation, Apple presented a lengthy rationale in his 1921 report. Ignoring Franklin & Marshall's long ad-
herence to a classical curriculum, he portrayed the college's history as one of progressive
expansion to serve its constituency and "realize the ideals" of the original Franklin
College charter, which spoke of "diffusing knowledge" and promoting "improvements
in the arts and sciences which alone render nations respectable, great and happy." His
immediate argument was that a program in business administration would enable the
college better to serve the needs of its community and that the increased complexity
of economic life made it a legitimate field of study for a liberal arts college.[8]

The expansion of higher education business programs was part of a movement
to establish management as a profession. Professionals were believed to have a broad,
cultured vision and facility with abstract theories, qualities that liberal education was
supposed to be particularly good at developing. As Apple explained, "It is recognized
that the profession of business administration requires adequate preparation involving a broad vision and mental grasp of the facts and principles of industrial, commercial and civic development." Modern business had become too complex to rely upon
experience alone. Successful leadership required just "those habits and qualities of
mind which have their foundation in a liberal education" — "a broad outlook in life"
and knowledge of "the principles that underlie business," as well as of "efficient business practice." Hence, the college's program would focus on "fundamental principles"
to provide the desired "mental discipline," while offering "the technical knowledge and
the habits of thought that make for efficiency in business." The program would also
perform a public service by preparing business men for "the obligations of citizenship."
Required courses in English, ethics, economics, history, sociology, education, and foreign language would "secure an appreciation of the physical and social environment
in which business is carried on."[9]

Seemingly with little debate, the board approved the new Department of Economics and Business Administration and a new faculty position to staff it. Its first incumbent, Horace R. Barnes, held a B.A. from the University of Pennsylvania and had
taught business at schools in the region and served as bursar at Penn. Like most faculty in this new field, he did not have graduate degrees.[10]

Response to the new program was immediate: total college enrollment in its first
year jumped more than 20 percent, to an all-time high of 388 undergraduates. More
than half, 200, were new students, 76 of whom chose the new business program. For
the first time, bachelor of arts students were a minority on campus, with 34 percent of
undergraduates; 35 percent were enrolled in the bachelor of science degree program,
20 percent in business, and 11 percent in a premedical program. Enrollments continued to climb throughout the decade, reaching 753 in 1930, more than two and a half
times the 1920 level. Looking back in 1929, Apple told the board that the new program
had been a response to "another opportunity to adapt the curriculum to students'
needs." Whatever the motive, it was the catalyst for wholesale change at the college.[11]

Without explicit board authorization, the college had already offered the option
of a two-year premedical course that, while not leading to a degree, fulfilled most

medical school requirements. In effect, this track formalized a situation that had long existed, in which students simply left for medical school without taking a degree. Franklin & Marshall's reputation for excellence in scientific training already attracted students from outside the college's traditional constituency and region. In 1920–1921, for example, twenty-three freshmen and sophomores were listed in the premedical track. Most were Pennsylvanians, but others came from New York City; Brooklyn; New Rochelle, New York; Puerto Rico; and Mexico.[12]

Similarly, the Committee on Instruction urged the board to consider expanding the physics department into a full-fledged electrical engineering program. Over the years Professor Jefferson Kershner had established a nationally recognized applied physics laboratory that placed graduates in major engineering positions. Kershner was a demanding teacher whom many students dreaded — his nickname was "Tuffy" — but in whom committed researchers found a devoted mentor. He also contributed technical expertise to local and national industry. Larger institutions had tried to lure him away, but his dedication to the Reformed Church kept him at Franklin & Marshall. His sudden death in 1922 seems to have effectively ended the push for an engineering program at the college.[13]

Building a "New" Colonial College

By widening Franklin & Marshall's constituency, curricular changes helped lay the groundwork for the college's impressive physical growth in the 1920s. Even so, its leaders faced perennial difficulties in fund-raising and decision-making. In the early 1920s, fund-raising efforts were scattered among a number of projects, including Forward Movement, an ambitious Reformed Church campaign affiliated with the interdenominational Interchurch World Movement. Another challenge grant from Rockefeller's General Education Board promised $100,000 to endow faculty salaries if the amount was matched by $200,000 from other sources. Moreover, board president B. F. Fackenthal, Jr. insisted that increasing endowment was more important than new construction.[14]

The board also held competing priorities. Fred W. Biesecker, an alumnus and vice president of the board, offered $30,000 for a new gymnasium to bear his name. But other trustees insisted that the need for dormitories was greater, and Biesecker undertook to unite the projects by raising his pledge to $75,000 if others subscribed $150,000 for dormitories. To minimize overlap with the Forward Movement campaign, the board focused fund-raising efforts for buildings on alumni, an increasing number of whom were not Church members. To aid in the effort, the board acted on an issue that had long been deliberated: allowing the Alumni Association to elect two members of the board.[15]

Initially the building campaign made little headway during the postwar recession. In 1922 local supporters set the stage for a new initiative, as some 125 alumni and businessmen attended a banquet at the Brunswick Hotel. Speakers included Henning W. Prentis Jr., sales manager for Lancaster's Armstrong Cork Company, who pressed "the duty of an Alumnus to his College," though not himself an alumnus. During the evening several gifts were announced, including $10,000 from the Williamson family for a new concrete football stand in memory of H. S. Williamson, a longtime trustee. Later in the year, business and civic leaders formed the College Club, "to ally the city and the college more closely than ever." H. M. J. Klein was elected president, with an executive committee dominated by manufacturing and commercial owners.[16]

The campaign was formally launched in 1923, on the anniversary of Benjamin Franklin's birth; a well-orchestrated local effort aimed to raise $50,000 for a dormitory to be named Franklin Hall in recognition of the original college. The campaign opened with a luncheon for team captains at the Hamilton Club and a dinner for some 120 campaign volunteers at the Brunswick Hotel. College officials delivered "spirited speeches" to motivate volunteers, who quickly obtained $35,000 in pledges, using personal solicitation techniques perfected during wartime fund-raising drives. A second dormitory was funded through a bequest of more than $110,000 from Mary E. Santee of Philadelphia, in memory of her father, Charles Santee, and her fiancée, Jacob Y. Dietz, both former board members.[17]

Meanwhile, a number of separate construction projects gradually coalesced into a comprehensive building program. Preliminary gymnasium plans had already been drawn up by Philadelphia architect William C. Prichett. Some board members called for a central heating plant, while others wanted to encourage fraternities to build chapter houses on campus. The Committee on Grounds and Buildings agreed on the need to consider "the general arrangement of the Campus and the places to be reserved for possible buildings that may be erected in the future." Early in 1923, the board approved development of "a general plan" for the campus, with a budget for new buildings set at $300,000. During the spring the Grounds and Buildings Committee visited campuses in the area, including Haverford, Swarthmore, and the University of Pennsylvania, and selected the Philadelphia firm of Day and Klauder.[18]

The choice placed Franklin & Marshall firmly in the mainstream of campus planning. The college's habit of putting up buildings in an eclectic range of styles had gone out of fashion. Educational leaders had been converted to the idea of grand planning by the stunning Chicago World's Columbian Exhibition in 1893. As if hoping through architecture to restore the lost coherence of the prescribed classical curriculum, designers and educators spoke of the need to achieve a "general unity of effect" among the many buildings now expected of a modern institution of higher education. They sought architecturally unified buildings grouped around quadrangles or grand public spaces with clear axial lines and focal points. Day and Klauder was nationally known for its work for college and universities, including Princeton, Yale, Cornell, Pennsylvania State, and the universities of Colorado and Pennsylvania.[19]

Choice of a unifying architectural style was crucial. The head of the firm, Charles Z. Klauder, was best known for his work in the popular collegiate Gothic, which he used even for a forty-two-story tower at the University of Pittsburgh. Even though Old Main, Franklin & Marshall's first and most distinctive building, was an important early example of Gothic Revival, Klauder's plan for the college employed Georgian or Colonial Revival style, which his firm had recently used for the new University of Delaware campus. It is not known who made the decision at Franklin & Marshall, but the choice seems to have met several needs.[20]

Colonial Revival architecture had become increasingly popular in the early twentieth century. For many Americans it evoked a simpler and purer "olden time." Lancaster had few surviving colonial-era structures, but local leaders had recently shown new interest in the city's colonial heritage and were in the process of restoring the old city hall in Penn Square to its colonial form. In higher education, Georgian style was a way to emphasize an institution's antiquity. Franklin & Marshall's adoption of it pointed to its origins in eighteenth-century Franklin College — even though that school had existed only briefly. (college began referring to itself as "the colonial college for men.") Intentionally or not, the style deflected attention from Marshall College and its German American roots. It seems likely that Apple and the board felt the colonial style to be a fitting symbol of the "new" Franklin & Marshall.[21]

Still, debates continued over the precise character of that new college. Expansion revived unresolved issues about the status of Franklin & Marshall Academy, for example. Its head, E. M. Hartman, objected strenuously that Klauder's initial placement of dormitories encroached on the large oval east of the main academy building. He charged that taking part of the academy's grounds "destroys the beauty of the landscape and militates against the efficiency of the school in the matter of discipline," because college students would be living near academy boys. A joint session of the Grounds and Buildings and Finance committees with Fackenthal and Apple as ex officio members worked out a compromise location north of the Science Building, with two more dormitories to be built later further north. Afterward, in a letter to George Mull, Fackenthal reflected that the site selection had been "a tough proposition." He called the compromise "something that best suits us all, but does not exactly suit any of us." Not everyone was satisfied, for the following June, alumni trustees supported Hartman in their report to the Alumni Association. Perhaps because of the controversy, alumni fund-raising for the dormitory project fell short. Plans to name one of the new buildings after former President Stahr were dropped; it became Franklin-Meyran in honor of board member L. A. Meyran, whose $25,000 gift completed the funding.[22]

Apple wanted a new auditorium large enough to accommodate assemblies and church services for the growing student body and for expanded audiences for special occasions. At first the building committee wanted merely to enlarge the chapel in Old Main, but Apple finally won the board to his side in 1924. He argued that a new auditorium could be a memorial to the late William U. Hensel, using income from a portion of a trust fund he had created that eventually would come to the college. Apple insisted that the enlarged project would have a much greater appeal to the college's supporters than "small things done at intervals." Confidence would be stirred by what he called "the evidence of our faith in ourselves to do big things for the College."

Moreover, "the most successful colleges" had undertaken major construction projects "without waiting until they had gathered sufficient funds to pay cash for it, because time is needed to gather funds."[23]

Klauder considered Hensel Hall the "crowning feature" of his plan. Its simple Georgian lines were given a slightly ecclesiastical note by a handsome white lantern spire—"such as may be seen," the *Student Weekly* noted, "on some old New England churches today." He placed it on College Avenue, forming with the Academy Building an east-west axis that crossed a north-south axis running from the front of Old Main to Biesecker Gymnasium. The auditorium's rear entrance opened onto a quadrangle formed by the dormitories and gymnasium, a quadrangle envisioned as a center of extracurricular student life (see fig. 3). But some board members protested that this placement blocked the view of the academy from College Avenue and sought to locate the auditorium near the corner of College and Buchanan avenues, far from the center of campus. As the issue continued to be debated through 1924, Apple conveyed to the board Klauder's conviction that his positioning of the auditorium was "an essential feature of the whole scheme and necessary to its architectural beauty and symmetry." Klauder also felt that his "expert opinion on a matter of this kind ought to have the confidence of the Board which employed him." The board finally agreed.[24]

To foster alumni ties, the board created a new position of secretary of the college, a step that had been deliberated for years. Its first incumbent, the Reverend Robert J. Pilgram, class of 1898 and a prominent Reformed minister, began gathering information about some three thousand living former students and alumni. He edited a new alumni publication, *Franklin and Marshall Alumnus,* launched in November 1924. Student publications had occasionally tried to include alumni news, but there had never been a periodical especially for graduates. Its very first article, illustrated with a photograph showing foundation work under way for the dormitories, hailed "The New Franklin and Marshall" and announced "the greatest building program ever undertaken by Franklin and Marshall College."[25]

The year 1925 saw the largest fund-raising campaign in Franklin & Marshall's history, in terms of both the goal and the size of the organization carrying it out. The goal was originally set for $250,000, but alumni planners enlarged it to $500,000, to include converting the old gymnasium into a student center and establishing an endowment for maintenance. William A. Schnader, '08, deputy attorney general of Pennsylvania and head of the Philadelphia Alumni Association, headed an executive committee of notable alumni. Because of the ambitious goal, the committee hired "expert service" in the form of a professional field organizer and authorized an expensive preparation program, to be paid for out of the proceeds of the campaign. Over coming months, the *Alumnus* was filled with news of campaign plans and inspirational pieces by college officials. Teams of volunteer solicitors were organized "in every place where Franklin and Marshall alumni dwell." Information packets were prepared for distribution to some thirteen thousand prospects. A publicity department set out "to spread the story of Franklin and Marshall over the civilized world."

FIGURE 3 *This September 1925 sketch illustrates the new campus envisioned by Apple and Charles Z. Klauder. The college erected Dietz-Santee and Franklin-Meyran Halls to the south of Hensel Hall, but not the identical two dormitories to the north. Hartman Hall is on axis with Hensel, while Biesecker Gymnasium is to the right. The Franklin & Marshall Alumnus described this complex of buildings as the "heart of campus." Franklin & Marshall College, Archives and Special Collections. College Archives Photograph Collection.*

The department's first major achievement was attracting a motion picture newsreel company to record the process of moving the observatory from its site, now the center of the planned quadrangle. Soon movie audiences around the country saw footage of Franklin & Marshall College students pushing the building along greased skids — the cameraman's angle obscured horses turning a windlass that did most of the work.[26]

The campaign envisioned an intensive canvass of all prospects in September 1925, but many local organizations were not ready then. By November $183,500 had been pledged, far short of the goal. One in five alumni pledged, contributing less than half of the total, with most support coming from Reformed Church members and local residents. The Executive Committee continued the campaign until every alumnus had been reached, but total subscriptions remained under $200,000 at the end of the decade. The alumni, like organizations at other colleges, shifted their energy to creating a college fund, to cultivate "steady and continuous cooperation" and regular annual contributions.[27]

Students themselves eventually took up the task of converting the old gymnasium into a campus center. Commuting students especially needed a place to eat and relax between classes. Former Student Senate president Harold J. Budd raised the idea in late 1926, after attending a national student conference, and the response was so enthusiastic that Campus House opened within a month. Students contributed most of the labor, while administrators donated furniture, and faculty wives made curtains for the windows. At first there were three rooms in the basement for pool, bowling, and cards, with the upper story fitted out as a lounge and meeting place. Later a lunch-room was established in the basement, with profits going to pay operating expenses and the remaining debt on the renovation.[28]

Soon Campus House was filled with students throughout the day. An informal survey at the end of the first semester of operation found that two-thirds of respondents used it. Some came to watch the school's pocket billiard "sharks," others to participate in tournaments in billiards, bowling, chess and checkers. Many of the college's group meetings, banquets, and campuswide dances were held there. Hoping that its function as a meeting ground would encourage school spirit, the *Student Weekly* praised its "socializing influence." Further improvements were made over time. As freshmen, the class of 1932 raised money for a new piano, and the senate sold megaphones to buy a radio. With alumni contributions, the board added a fireplace to the upper room and built a wing on the south side for men's and women's cloak rooms.[29]

In 1927 Apple told the board that overcrowding in science courses had reached the point at which the chemistry department would have to hold some labs in the evening. Moreover, laboratory facilities, once state of the art, were now so outdated that he judged it best to put up an entirely new building for chemistry and renovate the present Science Building for the other sciences and for administration. But further construction was hampered by the fact that the college still carried debt from its previous program.[30]

Board president Benjamin Franklin Fackenthal Jr. announced at the annual meeting in 1928 that he had decided to give Franklin & Marshall up to $150,000 for a new science building. That sum marked the largest single gift in the college's history, but as planning got under way for a building to house the chemistry and biology departments, the cost rose to $240,000 by the time construction began at the end of the year. Charles Klauder designed the building in the now-standard Georgian style, in red brick with limestone trim. He selected a site just west of Biesecker Gymnasium, with a graceful triple arch connecting the two buildings and helping to shape a new quadrangle formed by the Academy Building to the west and Dietz-Santee dormitory to the east.[31]

Not an alumnus, nor even a college graduate, Fackenthal joined the board in 1899 because of his membership in the Reformed Church, but his greatest interest had always been in its science programs. Now seventy-eight, he was winding up his business involvements and turning increased attention to "his" college. At the new building's dedication in November 1929, Fackenthal recalled feeling both pride and envy when his friend James Gayley presented the Gayley Laboratory to Lafayette College in 1902. The two studied together there in the 1870s, and Gayley became the first president of United States Steel Corporation. His gift to Lafayette inspired Fackenthal, he said, "with the hope that I might some day be able to erect a building for Franklin and Marshall College." A new generation of U.S. Steel's leadership was represented at the dedication of Fackenthal Laboratory by his friend Charles M. Schwab, who was the principal speaker. Beyond paying the laboratory's entire cost, which topped $250,000 by completion, Fackenthal gave, Apple reported, "careful personal study and direction to all details, in which he [was] so eminently qualified by scholarship and experience." As Fackenthal was a man accustomed to command, there may have been some friction with architect Klauder, himself determined to exercising professional authority.[32]

Using money from accumulated surpluses, the old science building was renovated in 1929. The work enlarged classroom and laboratory space for the Department of Physics, created ten new classrooms for other departments, improved office space for the dean, and even provided offices for senior faculty, an innovation intended to facilitate individual meetings with students.[33]

An indoor swimming pool had been envisioned in initial plans for the building program but was cut when fund-raising fell short. Fackenthal announced that if the remaining debt of the building fund was paid off by July 15, 1930, he would pay for a pool. A local drive in Lancaster quickly met the challenge, and work began almost immediately on yet another Georgian building, with large windows within recessed arches and a seventy-five-foot pool and viewing stands. It adjoined Biesecker Gymnasium on the east, and Klauder designed it with an entrance porch facing College Avenue, an entrance that was to be symmetrical with the front of Hensel Hall. In the process of construction, the size of the entrance was cut back, and conflicts emerged that soured the relationship between Klauder and college leaders. No evidence has remained of the exact character of the disagreements, although final costs exceeded estimates. Whatever the case, when the board met to dedicate the new building on January 22, 1931, it voted to "rescind all previous resolutions referring to the employment of Mr. Charles Z. Klauder as architect." It was an unfortunate ending to a relationship that had done much to transform the very image of Franklin & Marshall. Ironically, Klauder performed a similar erasure: when he died in 1938, his *New York Times* obituary left Franklin & Marshall off the list of institutions for which he had done significant work.[34]

The college's efforts to create an impressive new campus were countered by local government. Taking advantage of the high ground it owned directly west of Old Main, the city of Lancaster put up large water towers in 1925 and 1932. Generations of students dubbed them "George" and "Martha" in reference to the tall, pointed top of the first and the broad, rounded roof of the second. Despite this allusion to the nation's first president and his wife, the looming metal structures did little to enhance the dignity of the campus.[35]

Fund-raising campaigns throughout the 1920s gathered more money than ever before in the college's history. Nevertheless, none achieved their initial goals. The Forward Movement campaign in the Reformed Church met only half of its goal. Even so, the college's share was nearly $200,000, enough to secure the General Education Board grant. With several substantial bequests from members of the Reformed community, Franklin & Marshall's endowment in 1929 exceeded 1 million dollars. Though the college was better off financially than it had ever been, its position in many ways remained precarious.[36]

Managing Growth

Franklin & Marshall's growth in the 1920s presented many challenges in dealing with increased size and changing educational program. As enrollments climbed, the board authorized several new teaching positions each year, expanding the faculty over the course of the decade from fourteen to forty-four. As it grew, the faculty's makeup, organization, and fundamental understanding of its role as educators was transformed.[37]

Increasing size enabled the college finally to follow the trend in American higher education toward specialization of knowledge within increasingly autonomous academic departments. Although professors spent most of their time teaching required introductory courses, as a group they were able to offer a wider range of different topics, for the first time giving reality to the idea of elective courses. Some academic departments that had previously been a catalogue fiction became real: for many years, for example, three separate departments listed only one faculty member, A. V. Hiester. Changes over the decade heightened the role of the departmental major. Faculty increased the number of courses required for the major and expected work in the major to begin in the sophomore rather than the junior year. Later the faculty dropped requirements for minor fields in each of three areas of study. Instead, each student worked out his course of studies with the chairman of his major department, according to what would "best meet his particular needs and increase his efficiency in his major field."[38]

With more than one instructor in many fields, faculty members were able to find colleagues in their areas of interest. This was appealing because of the loss of the sense of a unifying vision shared across disciplines at the college. By the end of the decade nearly all departments had at least two members, while mathematics, Romance languages, and business administration had more than three each. Significantly, the only exception to this trend was in the classics: where the college had had three men teaching Latin and Greek in 1919, now there were two.[39]

Traditionally, standing within the faculty had followed seniority. Some resisted the idea of organization into graduated ranks, from full professors down to instructors, as presaging a bureaucratic system. Nevertheless, the board established ranks and maximum salary levels in 1925. "This recognizes both ability and effort," explained the Committee on Instruction, "and affords an encouragement and incentive for development and larger service." In practice, the change made little difference at first, for the most senior members were automatically designated as professors and heads of their respective departments.[40]

The question of rank was ticklish because of disparity in academic credentials. In 1919, three of fourteen teachers had an earned a doctorate, while one, J. N. Schaeffer, had an Oxford B.Litt.; seven had master's degrees; and two, Apple and Mull, held honorary doctorates. Fewer had theological degrees than in the past, although many came from a Reformed background and had studied at Franklin & Marshall. By the end of the decade, the proportion of faculty holding doctorates and master's degrees remained about the same: more than one-quarter had Ph.D.'s or the equivalent; more than half, a master's; and the rest, bachelor's degrees. A number of those with a master's had completed all course work toward the Ph.D., and each year several took unpaid leaves to complete their degrees. Fewer of those arriving during the decade had connections to the Reformed Church.[41]

Perhaps most important, a great deal of coming and going during the decade left a diminishing institutional memory of the "old" Franklin & Marshall. In 1926 the board distributed a portion of a substantial surplus to faculty as a bonus based on seniority. The board's list showed that only three of thirty-one faculty members had been at the college before Apple's presidency began in 1909. The median length of service was only five years. In 1927 George Mull's retirement and Anselm Hiester's sudden death further weakened connections with the past. In addition, more teachers stayed only a few years before leaving to take positions at larger universities with lighter teaching and administrative loads.[42]

During the 1920s public opinion changed toward abuses of civil liberties that had occurred in the heat of wartime patriotism. The board might have been responding to this change in sentiment as well as recognizing a need to restore connection with the college's past in 1927, when it elected both George Mull and Richard Schiedt to emeritus professorships with stipends. Introducing the resolution to elect Schiedt, his longtime supporter William Hager emphasized the major role Schiedt had played in establishing the modern sciences and his powerful influence as a teacher, counselor, and friend to his students and as a public writer, speaker, and preacher. Restored to a position of respect, Schiedt again became a familiar figure on campus.[43]

Increased turnover made faculty more aware of how Franklin & Marshall compared with other institutions. In 1924 the faculty moved to bring the college in line with practices at most liberal arts colleges by discontinuing its small graduate program. At first the board resisted the idea, but the faculty eventually was able to persuade it that demand for graduate study was not sufficient to pay for increased requirements that had become the national standard for a master's degree.[44]

Apple took another step to bringing Franklin & Marshall into line with prevailing standards by inviting an inspection by the Association of American Universities (AAU), which he described as "the highest rating body in the country." Established earlier in the century to secure common standards among the nation's universities, the AAU also claimed to regulate colleges because they prepared students for graduate work. In the spring of 1924, an intimidating group of administrators from the universities of Illinois, Missouri, Chicago, Pennsylvania, and Columbia visited Franklin & Marshall "for the purpose of making a rigid examination of the work of professors and students, analysis of scholastic conditions and records, as well as general conditions and activities of the College," and data about graduates' later success. They put the college on AAU's class A list of approved standard American colleges, providing welcome endorsement and enabling automatic transfer of credits to any university.[45]

Deference to external standards was also evident in the college's curriculum, once its most distinctive feature. Throughout the decade, Apple and the faculty worked to, as he put it, "meet the needs of the present age." For example, following the model of the war issues course developed for the SATC, the required course in history abandoned all traces of Nevin's philosophy of history, focusing instead on the roots of contemporary problems.[46]

In 1927 the faculty revised its B.S. program to include social science majors, allowing students to concentrate in economics, politics, education, psychology, or sociology without having to fulfill the A.B. program's more rigorous Latin requirements. Apple explained to the board that the change was especially aimed at students interested in preparing for law schools, an increasing number of which now required bachelor's degrees. He told the board that the new bachelor of science in social science curriculum had been "commended by authorities of Law schools and those interested in thorough preparation for the profession of Law." After Hiester's death, the social sciences were reorganized, with economics moving into the business administration department and separate departments of political science and sociology. A year later, the Latin requirement for admission to the A.B. program was lowered from four years to two. "[Franklin & Marshall] does not wish to let the world see that even here the tendency is for the business courses to be over-crowded — the classical — starved," the *Student Weekly* observed wryly.[47]

Through the Association of College Presidents of Pennsylvania, Franklin & Marshall participated in the "Pennsylvania Study," the Carnegie Foundation for the Advancement of Teaching's long-term investigation into the effects of education. Based on early results, Carnegie examiners in 1929 required the college to improve its student advising in order to stay in the study. Department chairmen at Franklin & Marshall began meeting with their advisees at least once a month, "to stimulate their intellectual interests, to guide their reading, and to do what seems best to make their reading and study effective."[48]

A faculty committee studied innovative educational programs at Swarthmore, Haverford, Dartmouth, Columbia, and Princeton. It concluded that the college lacked the financial resources to implement most features of these programs, especially the emphasis on small class sizes. Swarthmore's pioneering honors program, begun in 1922, relied, after all, upon $4 million from the General Education Board. Nevertheless, convinced that "college education should mean much more than the passing of isolated courses," the committee thought it feasible to establish comprehensive examinations. First introduced at Harvard, the practice of examining students at the end of their senior year to assess mastery in their major field of concentration became widespread in the 1920s as a way to restore a measure of coherence to the curriculum. Apple explained to the board that such an examination tested a student's command of "a wide field of knowledge" rather than a single course and assessed "his ability to use in new combinations the ideas and processes with which [the field] deals." Consistent with the growing curricular autonomy of academic departments, the plan let each department set the material to be examined as well as requirements outside the major.[49]

As a historian of the Carnegie Foundation's programs points out, the Pennsylvania study was part of its agenda of "promoting social stratification based on knowledge." There was also an element of elitism in the establishment of new honors programs, as schools sought to provide a demanding liberal arts experience for a select group of intellectually gifted students. Apple cooperated with the Carnegie project and the new comprehensive program, but by the late 1920s expressed growing concern at trends in higher education. In practical terms, he feared that the pressure to establish small discussion groups disadvantaged poorer schools like Franklin & Marshall. But his principal objection was that the idea of reserving liberal education for "those of the highest mental endowment" created "an intellectual aristocracy." He repeatedly questioned whether a focus on superior or gifted students underestimated the social usefulness of educating average or "mediocre" students. Often, he pointed out, differences in high school achievement were the result of a lack of opportunity or poorly developed study skills. He had seen many young men flourish in a challenging college environment. "Some of the ablest leaders in college have come from this group of least promise," he reminded the board. More fundamentally, he insisted that advocates of liberal education must look beyond questions of "personal success and competition" to address education's highest aim, fostering conditions for democracy in coming generations. "The very structure of democracy" required that leaders be developed for "every grade of life." He also criticized the Carnegie program as too narrowly focused on measuring individual intellectual achievement.[50]

Franklin & Marshall's adaptation to outside influences was most striking in the 1920s in religious instruction. Religious thought and experience had traditionally been the basis of the college's very existence, but there was little classroom instruction in doctrine. Instead, the institution relied upon the more subtle influences of its philosophical and classical courses, liturgies of daily chapel and Sunday services, and the faculty's presence as model "Christian gentlemen." By the 1920s, all of these influences had changed considerably. Philosophy, as taught in the classical curriculum, had splintered into a number of academic specialties. Mercersburg Theology had lost much of its influence within the Reformed Church, and the college's ordained ministers — Apple, Klein and Hiester — were thoroughly imbued with the social reform spirit of liberal Protestantism. As a consequence, where John W. Nevin had once envisioned the college as a prophetic counterbalance to the materialism of post–Civil War America, Apple saw nothing wrong with adapting to changing times.

Franklin & Marshall continued to proclaim its Church connection even as Reformed students represented a dwindling proportion of the total enrollment. In 1916 only half of freshmen were Reformed, while more than 30 percent belonged to other mainline Protestant denominations. Members of other Protestant groups came in smaller numbers, and 5 percent of students were Roman Catholics. (One student described himself as "non-committal.") A decade later, only one-third of the student body came from Reformed backgrounds, while 56 percent were from other Protestant denominations. Moreover, one in ten students were Catholic or Jewish. Still, only two students gave no religious affiliation. Change was even more pronounced in the later part of the decade, as Reformed students declined in actual numbers as well as in percentage. By 1930 only one-quarter had Reformed ties.[51]

Reformed leaders worried about the condition of their denomination. One troubling sign had been the Forward Movement's failure to meet its goals, although this was typical of the ambitious postwar national fund-raising campaigns. German American ethnic identity was eroding, especially in urban areas, and in rural sections of Pennsylvania where the Reformed Church had been most prominent, some membership was being lost to independent fundamentalist congregations.[52]

One response was a reexamination of the denomination's educational practices. In 1922 Howard Omwake, newly appointed as dean of Franklin & Marshall, participated in a special symposium on religious education. "Are the Reformed Church Colleges providing the atmosphere and training for their students which will produce men and women of strong, positive Christian ideals," he asked, "who become later enthusiastic leaders in Christian Work?" According to Omwake, Franklin & Marshall had for many years prepared young men not only for the ministry but for adult lives directed by "high Christian ideals" and "positive Christian principles." He argued that this influence could be enhanced by creating a separate department of religious education. In recent years even former bastions of theological conservatism, such as Yale and Princeton, had joined a general movement to establish departments of religion; the hope was to preserve a religious dimension in higher education while leaving other fields free to focus on secular concerns.[53]

Soon thereafter, the board approved a new professorship of philosophy and religious education, to relieve Apple from his teaching responsibilities. Two men were hired, one focusing on religious education and another on philosophy and psychology. For the first, Apple recruited the Reverend Paul M. Limbert, a Franklin & Marshall College and seminary graduate. Apple presented the opportunities of the position in rather traditional terms: the prospect of training "multitudes of young men who in time would become the leaders of our Church." Limbert replied that he was more concerned about the need to find "better methods of developing the religious life in our modern society." He believed that introducing college men to "the present movements in religious education" was as important as studying the Bible and the history of Christianity. Elijah E. Kresge, a Franklin & Marshall College and seminary graduate who had earned a Ph.D. from the University of Pennsylvania with a dissertation on Kant, became professor of philosophy and psychology. Reflecting the fluid character of the new fields, titles of the departments and the men's positions kept changing. Nevertheless, Kresge taught the Bible course required of all upperclassmen, and, when the faculty was divided into ranks, was named head of both departments.[54]

Under Limbert, the Department of Religion (sometimes Religious Education) focused principally on practice and social context. Its primary goals were "giving a knowledge of the bible not only as religious literature but as a practical guide to life" and preparing men to become leaders in their local churches and communities. In keeping with trends in the Reformed Church as a whole, the courses reflected the general tenor of liberal Protestantism of the day. For example, a 1926 report to the synod on the state of the Church commented on one reason the denomination had avoided controversies besetting other groups: "We have long since shifted the emphasis from doctrine to life and are living true to our heritage of being a very tolerant church."[55]

This focus on more practical manifestations of religion reflected Protestantism's turn away from idealism, but it had particular significance in what had once been Mercersburg Theology's flagship institution. The change was evident in changes in the philosophy curriculum. For a time, Kresge continued to teach the signature courses in ethics, aesthetics, and the philosophy of history, which contained the essence of the Mercersburg tradition. In 1926 he substantially reorganized the curriculum, introducing courses on recent trends in philosophy and on William James, whose pragmatic interpretation of religious experience was widely embraced in liberal circles. Similarly, the ethics course required of seniors surveyed "the different types of Ethical thought" and applied "ethical principles to the problems of the individual and of society."[56]

As the faculty expanded, the splintering of Mercersburg Theology was fully institutionalized through creation of departments of psychology, philosophy, and religion. In 1926 Ray H. Dotterer became the first full-time professor of psychology. Like others who pioneered new departments, his ties to the college and the Reformed Church enabled him to serve as a bridge between old and new. Alumnus of both college and seminary, Dotterer served as pastor at several churches before returning to graduate school at Johns Hopkins and taking his Ph.D. in 1917. He had also worked with John B. Watson, the founder of behaviorism, and in 1928 established a new course in experimental and applied psychology. Similarly, Apple hired John B. Noss in 1928 to teach philosophy and religion. Descended from a family of distinguished Reformed missionaries, he had been raised in Japan before attending Franklin & Marshall, graduating as valedictorian of the class of 1916. After theological study and a period in the ministry, he earned a Ph.D. at the University of Edinburgh. The additional staff made it possible for students to choose between several courses in fulfilling their required religion course. In reporting to the Eastern Synod on the progress in religious education, H. M. J. Klein noted that work was being "conducted according to the highest academic standards," because "each professor [had] received special training in his field and each [held] the degree of Doctor of Philosophy." Significantly, Klein emphasized not the specific content of religious or philosophical instruction but compliance with contemporary academic standards.[57]

Most colleges and universities had long since dropped compulsory attendance at morning chapel, but a few, like Yale and Franklin & Marshall, resolutely continued, reflecting their belief that shared worship strengthened student development. Enforcing the requirement produced contention between administrators and students, but most agreed that without on-campus housing, daily chapel played an important role in bringing members of the institution together. It was often an occasion for nonreligious celebrations and discussions of the entire student body. During national railroad strikes in 1920, for example, Klein and Hiester explained the causes of the labor unrest. Students voted to offer their services to the railroads "to help to stabilize the country in the national crisis," adding that their action was not intended "as an un-friendly act towards labor, but as a patriotic act with a view to serving the public." In 1917 Apple had given control of Friday services to students for pep rallies or discus-sions as they saw fit.[58]

The college did move chapel an hour later, to 9:10 A.M., in response to declining postwar attendance. The appearance of the celebrated evangelist Billy Sunday brought out a rare capacity crowd. But as enrollments grew, the chapel in Old Main could no longer accommodate the entire student body. Faculty made attendance optional for seniors and later dropped the number of required services to three per week for fresh-men and sophomores and two for upperclassmen. The requirement was periodically enforced by threats of suspension.[59]

Even religiously inclined students complained that chapel services were unin-spired. A contributor to the *Student Weekly* noted that few students participated in responses, because they were "devoutly engaged in preparing their nine-thirty classes, or perusing even more questionable literature." He recommended that "the present monotonous ritual" be replaced by a "a simple, living, and flexible service" that left out the Apostle's Creed because many students could not in honesty say the words. He urged eliminating the "abominable and degrading system" of "chapel slips" as "posi-tively murderous to any vestige of genuine religious atmosphere."[60]

After the completion of Hensel Hall in 1926, the college separated religious and secular observances. An hour-long general assembly was held in Hensel each Wednes-day morning, aimed at bringing all faculty and students together for a "worthwhile" meeting, with outside speakers featured in addition to the ubiquitous pep rallies. Short chapel services "of a purely devotional or religious" character were held in the chapel in Old Main three mornings a week, and faculty and students were required to attend at least once a week.[61]

St. Stephen's, the college's Reformed congregation resident in the chapel since 1865, was a casualty of the changing religious environment. Stressing that Franklin & Mar-shall was a "denominational, not sectarian" Christian college, leaders had always al-lowed non-Reformed students to attend Sunday services in their denomination's local congregation. Increasingly, many Reformed students sought to worship in local churches, which had active Sunday schools and more lively services. Students orga-nized a choir in an attempt to invigorate St. Stephen's services, but attendance declined steadily. After examining programs at other Reformed and Lutheran colleges, a fac-ulty committee concluded that students should be encouraged to "become affiliated in voluntary worship and service" in local congregations. As Klein put it, students' religious life and sense of commitment to the Church would be more effectively de-veloped if they were able to "share in the work and worship of a congregation under normal conditions"—including the opportunity to meet young women. An evening service could be held in the chapel one Sunday a month, at which "some minister of scholarly ability and prominence" might preach and meet with students informally.

All but one member of the faculty approved the proposal — the holdout being classics professor John Nevin Schaeffer. Faced with this decision, St. Stephen's congregation decided to suspend services and dissolve its organization.[62]

Franklin & Marshall's formal affiliation with the Reformed Church continued for more than four decades, but the organic connection between daily life and religious worship — where the liturgy itself had been written by college leaders — was lost. The change was probably inevitable, given the growing diversity of both student body and faculty and the general process of secularization in higher education, but it marked one more step in the college's turning away from its heritage.

Administrative Growth

The post–World War I period also saw gradual emergence of a modern administrative structure based upon separation of teaching and management functions. This was long after many institutions of higher education had created administrative bureaucracies, but the process had been delayed at Franklin & Marshall by lack of funds. The first step in this direction was the 1919 hiring of Howard R. Omwake as the first dean of the college. In addition to teaching French, Omwake assumed many day-to-day tasks related to student life, including admissions, student advising and discipline, graduation requirements, oversight of the boards of governors and control, publication of the catalogue, and "the general relationship of students with Professors." A brother of Ursinus College president George. L. Omwake, he also helped help foster more cordial relations with the sister Reformed institution. During their first year, Omwake and education professor P. M. Harbold created the first student services office, a teachers bureau to help graduates and alumni find employment. The following year Omwake inherited additional administrative functions previously performed by George Mull as secretary of the faculty, including registration and keeping records of attendance and grades.[63]

Gradually, tasks performed by the faculty were delegated to others. Myrtle A. Doner, who had become Apple's secretary in 1920, was named treasurer of the faculty, with responsibility for collecting fees and keeping the books, previously faculty duties. In 1929 the board finally agreed to appoint a comptroller to maintain a set of books "according to most modern accounting practice for institutions." The first incumbent, Robert M. Wade, attended board meetings as the only administrative officer besides Apple and board secretary H. R. Barnes.[64]

Before the war, several young women with college degrees had been employed to run the library under faculty direction. In 1924 a faculty committee petitioned the board to upgrade the library by hiring "a male executive." Appointed in 1927, Herbert B. Anstaett held a bachelor's degree from the Columbia School of Library Service, where he returned in 1932 for a master's, through a fellowship from the Carnegie Corporation of New York. His assistants, Marian A. Hiester and Elizabeth Clarke Kieffer, were relatives of former faculty members. After his arrival Anstaett assumed the job of sorting campus mail, previously handled at the president's house by Mrs. Florence Apple.[65]

The college's natural history museum had been housed in the Science Building since its completion in 1902. The museum flourished under the amateur direction of Michael W. Raub, a local physician and noted ornithologist, who contributed an important collection of stuffed birds. After his death in 1915, faculty oversaw the museum until H. Justin Roddy became curator in 1926. Recently retired as head of the natural science department at Millersville State Normal School, Roddy was widely recognized as a ornithologist, botanist, and geologist. Receiving only a small annual salary, he worked energetically to further increase collections. In the 1930s he began creating displays of figures in their natural habitats, emulating practices at major natural history museums.[66]

As student activities expanded throughout the decade, the position of student secretary was created in 1927, with responsibilities for student orientation, supervision of student organizations, and management of Campus House. Reflecting the position's mediating role between student and adult culture, the first incumbent was Harold Budd, the recent graduate who had led the campaign to renovate Campus House. He lived in one of the dormitories and, according to Apple, served "to exert a wholesome influence upon the life of the students on the campus."[67]

Straddling academic and extracurricular worlds, the physical education department was a continuing source of concern. In keeping with its commitment to develop the whole man, the college had provided some form of physical education since the 1890s. But physical education was for ordinary students, while intercollegiate athletics aimed at producing winning teams, and it often proved difficult to reconcile the two functions. As at most colleges, intercollegiate competition was in the midst of a slow and often awkward transition from an initial stage of student and alumni control to administrative management. Various hybrid committees of boosters, alumni, faculty, and students were responsible for hiring coaches, who came and went with striking rapidity. One of the most successful in combining the roles of teacher and coach was Charles W. Mayser, first hired as professor of physical education and coach in 1913. Half of his salary of $2,000 came from the college and half from the athletic program, funded by gate receipts. After Mayser's football team's stunning 1914 upset of Penn, Iowa State College lured him away by offering far more than Franklin & Marshall could pay.[68]

Athletics became increasingly disorganized after Mayser's departure. Appointed to investigate the situation, a committee of the Advisory Council of the Alumni Association issued an alarming report in 1923. "College spirit" was in "a deplorable state," with student athletes openly flouting training rules, playing outside the college for pay, and often choosing money over college loyalty. "Many students look upon athletic ability as a justification for demanding pay for their services," the report commented, and there seemed to be no shortage of boosters willing to give them what they asked. The committee also criticized the "chaotic" system of control, with authority divided among a faculty committee, a board of governors, and a trustee committee.[69]

In response, Mayser was brought back at twice his former salary and now earned more than anyone else at the college except Apple. The board refused to centralize control of athletics, but Mayser was given "absolute responsibility and authority" within the physical education department, in consultation with the board's Committee on Athletics and the Board of Governors. With the addition of J. Shober Barr, '22, as assistant athletic director in 1926, the intramural sports program expanded, hoping to induce every student to participate in some form of physical exercise. Freshmen and sophomores not engaged in organized sports were required to attend twice-a-week classes in the gym. In 1926 the board established a single athletics committee — composed of representatives from the board, faculty, alumni, and Student Senate — responsible for intercollegiate athletics, including the hiring of coaches and scheduling. Mayser himself introduced and coached a highly successful intercollegiate wrestling team, which in its first ten years won sixty-nine of eighty meets and had three undefeated seasons.[70]

The Athletic Committee's dependence upon gate receipts, primarily from football, meant that during losing seasons the entire program was threatened with insolvency. In 1928 the board assumed the entire cost of the football coach's salary, as well as the medical costs of a student who broke his back while playing football. In 1931 Apple finally persuaded the board to put athletics "in the same relation to the college administration as all other departments," that is, under the full authority of the professor of physical education, who reported to the dean of the college. A full-time resident coach was added for football, basketball, and baseball, and two assistants in physical education assumed many of the management responsibilities. Finances came under the oversight of the comptroller.[71]

The board blocked some of Apple's reorganization efforts. It approved Apple's recommendation to put all college funds under the comptroller's jurisdiction but refused to give the comptroller authority over student organizations. More frustratingly, alumni leaders foiled Apple's attempt to create a new position of vice president to take control of fund-raising from the alumni secretary; they argued that the president of the college had no power over alumni affairs.[72]

The board also rejected a proposal to hire a superintendent of grounds and buildings. The expansion of the campus during Apple's tenure from five to sixteen buildings meant that neither the Committee on Grounds and Buildings nor Apple had time or expertise to oversee its increasingly complex operations. Apple eventually delegated management of campus facilities to the comptroller.[73]

Student Culture Reigns Supreme

Extracurricular and social activities, which even before the war had absorbed much attention, came to dominate student life over the next several decades. Franklin & Marshall was typical of American higher education in the early twentieth century, as rising enrollments in high schools, colleges, and universities created the perfect environment for development of an independent youth-peer culture. Sheltered within these institutions yet increasingly autonomous from adult supervision, young men and women cultivated their own styles of dress and values. Full-blown youth culture was late in arriving at Franklin & Marshall, but the 1920s were the tipping point, when academic life became subordinate for most students to social life, and proms and fraternity parties formed the high points of the student calendar.[74]

By the end of the decade, Franklin & Marshall had become a more local institution, with more than one-third of its students, 38 percent, coming from Lancaster City and County. Eighty percent were from Pennsylvania and another 13 percent from New York and New Jersey. It should be remembered, however, that in the interwar period nearly all institutions of higher education drew principally from local or regional constituencies. Even with its national reputation, half of Harvard's undergraduates in 1929 were from Massachusetts, a smaller state than Pennsylvania, and most of the rest came from New England. Like most colleges, Franklin & Marshall paid little formal attention to recruiting. Alumni, particularly the many who had gone into teaching, directed likely students to the college. James Darlington, a native of New Bloomfield, Pennsylvania, who entered Franklin & Marshall in 1926, recalled that his high school principal, "a zealous Franklin and Marshall graduate," had persuaded him to attend there.[75]

Through the Reformed Church's foreign missions, the college attracted a few students from Japan and China. Perhaps because of the Reformed mission in Baghdad, an Assyrian student, Aziz Alexander Koorie, popularly known as Ajax, had attended before World War I. In the 1920s, the Reformed Church established ties with its Hungarian brethren, bringing a small number of Hungarian students to the college. In addition, several came each year from Canada and Central America.[76]

It is unclear whether the increased presence of local students extended to members of Lancaster's African American community. No official records refer to the subject, but Frederic Klein later recalled that there were "a few" black students when he began teaching in 1929. Like many white students, they attended for a year or two and left without graduating.[77]

An increasing number of students were Jewish. Some were from Lancaster, but many came from northeastern cities that had in prior decades seen an influx of Jewish immigrants from eastern Europe. Many of the immigrants' children met discrimination at elite eastern colleges and universities, where upper-class students complained that their Jewish peers were too ambitious, lacked social graces, and paid insufficient attention to extracurricular life. To deal with the so-called Jewish problem, administrators in some schools set admission quotas to limit their numbers. There is no evidence that Franklin & Marshall leaders attempted to discourage or limit Jewish enrollment in this period. In fact, its strong reputation for premedical preparation seems to have attracted Jewish students who may have been denied entry elsewhere. After Princeton limited its student body to two thousand in the early 1920s, it had nearly the same number of Jewish students that Franklin & Marshall had at one-quarter the size of overall enrollment.[78]

Perhaps in response to the growing size of the student body, "traditions" related to introducing newcomers into college life became more dense and complicated — and violent — with each passing year. College leaders' attempts to contain the violence met limited success but resulted in giving a modicum of institutional sanction to freshman regulations.

As the first postwar year opened in 1919, the *Student Weekly* printed a long list of freshmen rules. New students were obliged to wear distinctive and generally demeaning items of clothing, like blue caps with green buttons, and were forbidden actions associated with mature masculinity, like smoking, dating, and staying out at night, while they were required to carry matches for the use of upperclassmen. As long as they obeyed the rules and deferred to their elders, freshmen were not to be subjected to hazing, but sophomores were empowered to take appropriate action to enforce the rules.[79]

Eventually a special Student Senate tribunal was set up to deal with infractions. If convicted, students received their penalties during the next day's chapel service. Punishments were meted out according to the crime: a freshman caught speaking to a girl was forced to wear a skirt, while one who walked on the grass had to wear a sandwich board with the words "Keep Off the Grass," and one who refused to attend mass meetings had a large yellow streak painted down his back. Later in the decade, as violence by sophomore "enforcers" got out of hand, the faculty reluctantly agreed that extreme cases of "delinquency" could be referred to the dean and the Executive Committee.[80]

Sanctioned contests like the "tie up" between freshmen and sophomores were widely viewed as a way to channel adolescents' natural aggressions. Unfortunately, rules could not completely prevent tragedy. At the beginning of the 1923–1924 academic year, two freshmen reported home that they had participated in the annual tie up "and came out of it without a scratch." A sophomore, Ainsworth Brown, was not so lucky. When he fell in the middle of the melee, he received a spinal injury that resulted in paralysis and eventually death. Afterward the college replaced the free-for-all battle with a tug-of-war, part of a series of competitions that included pushball, football, debate, wrestling, and basketball; each freshman victory was supposed to be rewarded by removal of one of the regulations.[81]

Clandestine battles persisted in connection with official events. To improve their odds at the tug-of-war against the larger freshman class, sophomores typically abducted some freshmen, took them for "a little joy-ride," and left them a distance from campus. Despite the potential for stiff penalties, kidnapping was a popular form of hazing, made much easier by increased access to automobiles. In 1924 sophomores used five cars to transport more than fifty freshmen to an old tobacco barn near Mountville, where they were left to make their way back, sans trousers. A "machine-load of Freshmen" rushed to their rescue, and many returned just in time to participate, in their underwear, in the tug-of-war before a large crowd of townspeople and students. When they lost, they were showered by a fire hose, prompting the *Student Weekly*'s coy comment, "It is sometimes not a little embarrassing to be in wet underwear in the presence of ladies."[82]

The most successful new freshman event was the Pajama Parade. Before the war, all students had on a number of occasions marked important football victories by spontaneously parading through the streets of Lancaster dressed in pajamas or night shirts. But beginning in 1921, the parade became a regular fixture of the lead-up to one of the home football games. It also became a central feature in the initiation of freshmen, who alone were now required to wear pajamas, while at first sophomores donned bath robes and upperclassmen wore school sweaters. Led off by the football team riding in automobiles, the bizarre procession made its way to the center of the city, while freshmen handed out programs and displayed "porcelain trophy cups" (chamber pots) to the crowd. On the steps of the courthouse, they sang, danced, and cheered at the commands of upperclassmen. They were forced to surrender their right shoes, which upperclassmen threw into a large box and nailed it shut. As they attempted to retrieve their shoes, freshmen were showered with flour. Crowds of Lancastrians who turned out to witness the proceedings seemed to enjoy the entertainment, and the *Student Weekly* commended Mayor Musser and the police department for their assistance and the freshmen for "the fine spirit shown."[83]

The parade was so popular that it continued for decades, with repeated embellishments. In 1923 it started with a mass meeting that featured a boxing match and a "smoker" in the old gymnasium. Once more led by the football team, the order of march of the previous year was reversed, with seniors in front wearing old straw hats, followed by juniors with their shirt tails hanging out, and sophomores "heavily armed with paddles, which the Frosh were so kind as to donate." (Forewarned, some freshmen put on old suits and sweaters under their pajamas.) In pouring rain, they again performed at the courthouse for a large crowd, this time under the control of the Black Cats, a sophomore honorary society. It had been founded in 1921 as the Skull and Crown Society, ostensibly to fight fraternity politics, but spent most of its energies enforcing freshman regulations. At their direction, freshmen blocked traffic by pulling streetcar trolleys, proposed to pretty girls encountered along the street, and climbed light poles and tried to blow out the lights.[84]

The next year, the Student Senate promised to add "new features in the way of entertainment" in addition to "the old-time fun of other years." In fact, new torments were added each year, as each class of sophomores tried to outdo their predecessors. Beginning in 1925, freshmen were required to carry a lighted candle as they marched, and if it went out, they were paddled until they got it going again. The evening seemed to be considered great fun. "There were socks galore," the *Weekly* reported, "lusty wallops administered by the dutiful sophomores; and one soph said to a freshman as he split his paddle with a single blow, 'This hurts me more than it does you.'" Later in the decade, city leaders wearied of traffic jams and required students to avoid major streets and hold their performances at one of the downtown parks.[85]

Viewing these evolving traditions as part of a separate sphere of student initiative, Franklin & Marshall's faculty tried to remain aloof. In 1920 the new dean presented a set of freshman regulations, but the faculty declined to approve them, concluding that it "should have no official connection with the matter." Perhaps hoping that public occasions like the Pajama Parade forestalled more violent ad hoc attacks on freshmen, the administration did not interfere, although it worked through the Student Senate to restrain paddling. In 1929 an attempt was made to restrict paddling to a gauntlet run between Campus House and the president's and dean's houses, where students customarily stopped to greet the administrators. Afterward, sophomores were urged to throw their paddles away for the rest of the parade.[86]

By the end of the decade, extreme hazing practices came under attack from families of local students and from some who considered them "antiquated remnants" of a bygone day. But many insisted that it was the only way to prevent "cockyness" in the large group of newcomers. For their part, most freshmen seem to have accepted the requirements and harassment, at least up to a point. Such practices were common at men's colleges, and many considered them part of the price of admission to the campus community. Freshmen prepared for the Pajama Parade by padding themselves with cardboard and hoped to get through the ordeal as best they could. Asked much later about how they had felt about their treatment, alumni who attended Franklin & Marshall in the 1930s insisted that the experience played a benign or even beneficial role in integrating them into the college community. Many seemed to think of submitting with good humor to the initiatory rites as a way of showing their maturity as well as their respect for the community they were joining. Edward Shilling, '41, saw following the rules as a way "to 'pay your dues,' 'to learn the ropes' before assuming a role of leadership." Many believed that enduring the experience together also fostered a sense of solidarity within the class. Most did not consider the required hat, or "dink," to be a form of hazing. "It helped me get acquainted," Paul Eyler, '34, recalled. For those like Harry Langford, '33, who were the first in their family to attend college, wearing the "dink" was "really a status symbol." As a Lancaster boy, wearing the cap off campus "sent the message to the locals—here's somebody who's on the way to making it." At any rate, there was always the hope that the requirement would be dropped if the football team won the Thanksgiving Day game with traditional rival Gettysburg.[87]

As the Student Senate debated eliminating freshman rules in the spring of 1930, Sid Friedenberg, a freshman from Philadelphia, passionately defended the institution in a letter to the *Student Weekly*. His youthful reading of popular college novels like *Stover at Yale* had given him "a definite longing to go to college." His fantasies were fulfilled when he arrived at Franklin & Marshall: "I gloried in it. I bathed myself in the romance of wearing a dink and button." Although in time some of his illusions were shattered, "the memory of those first few weeks, of being paddled, of wearing a dress and signs, of being left out in the country by traditional enemies and made to walk back, these things I shall never forget." He urged the senate not to "deprive a future freshman of something he will probably never forget, something that will grow bigger as the years pass, something that he will always associate with youth and carefreeness."[88]

At the center of campus life stood the fraternity system. One by one, local clubs affiliated with national fraternities and became part of an expanding network of students and alumni. Harbaugh Club joined Lambda Chi Alpha in 1917, Franklin Club joined Sigma Pi in 1918, and Marshall Club joined Phi Kappa Tau in 1921. As at colleges and universities throughout the nation, fraternities at Franklin & Marshall became a major point of student interest and anxiety in the 1920s. Their prominence reflected the fact that, for many students and their parents, success in college was defined in social rather than academic terms: membership in a prestigious fraternity or an athletic team, leadership positions in student organizations, and a reputation for congeniality were often deemed more important than high grades and scholarly honors.[89]

The faculty, most of whom had been members as undergraduates, no longer resisted fraternities. Campus fraternities and clubs housed and fed many students and, given the college's difficulty in raising money, seemed likely to continue this role for some time to come. As early as 1910, Apple proposed encouraging these groups to build houses on campus, where they could be more effectively supervised. Between 1910 and 1920, fraternities began organizing an increasing number of purely social occasions. Founded in 1912, Junior Week featured a dizzying round of concerts, athletic events, dances, and parties during the week between winter and spring sessions, most of which were hosted by fraternities. One of the chief advantages of these activities seems to have been the students' ability to invite young ladies from the community, increasingly considered essential to an occasion's success. After the war, when dating came to play a far greater role in relations between the sexes, the fraternities' help in this respect made them even more important.[90]

Fraternities vied for prestige among themselves and, in combination against the ranks of "unorganized" students, for control of all aspects of campus life. Fraternity members competed for major elective positions in student government and extracurricular organizations, as well as for plum parts in the Green Room Club's theatrical productions. Campus politics rose to fever pitch in 1916, when a group of students sought to affiliate with a national fraternity Delta Sigma Phi without the permission of the Student Senate. Led by existing fraternities, the senate refused recognition even when the faculty approved Delta Sigma Phi after a year's probation.[91]

When the senate persisted, the faculty abolished the current system of student government as unrepresentative. Despite the ensuing protests — the *Student Weekly* called the action "one of the most odious coups d'etat that has ever been perpetrated in the annals of Franklin and Marshall College" — the stalemate went on for several years. Fraternities worked together through an Inter-fraternity Council, which made sure that the *Weekly* maintained its news blackout against the outlaw fraternity.[92]

The controversy lay at the roots of one of the college's more notorious hazing cases. In the fall of 1919 a Lancaster freshman named Robert Duttonhofer refused to wear a cap and brandished a gun at sophomores who had attempted to admonish him. His offense was no doubt compounded by the fact that he had joined the ostracized Delta Sigma Phi fraternity. To punish him, a group of sophomores abducted Duttonhofer and bundled him out to Conestoga Park, gathering reinforcements from fraternities and clubs. They beat him with paddles, later claiming that they were careful to avoid "internal injury." To humiliate him, they clipped his hair and one of his eyebrows, dressed him in a striped prison suit, and displayed him at several college organizations and at a local high school prom. He was paddled once more and abandoned in a meadow several miles from campus.[93]

Such violence was common in hazing, where the use of paddles was rationalized as less likely than bare fists to do permanent physical damage. Given that 1919 was a year in which social outsiders such as radicals and labor organizers faced even greater violence, Duttonhofer's treatment might have seemed relatively mild. In fact, the *Student Weekly* commented that if he had not been living at home, "he would have returned to his boarding place and nothing further resulted." Instead, his parents, "unacquainted with the customs on College Hill," reported the outrage to the local press, and stories of the students' "mob rule" spread throughout the region. Claiming that their son had suffered injury to his spine, the Duttenhofers threatened to prosecute fifteen sophomores for aggravated assault and battery.[94]

After an exhaustive investigation, the faculty suspended ten students for varying periods and rejected a motion to condemn Duttonhofer for carrying a revolver. Campus opinion, conversely, was outraged that exaggerated press reports had damaged the college's "good name and reputation." Some accused Delta Sigma Phi of complicity in the suits against the sophomores.[95]

Seeking reconciliation, Delta Sigma Phi leaders helped persuade the Duttenhofers to settle their suit against the sophomores and drop criminal charges. In turn, the fraternity petitioned the faculty to intercede with the other fraternities. Student sentiment began to shift, but it still took a year for Apple and faculty and Inter-fraternity Council committees to end the feud. In early 1921 the council formally recognized the new fraternity, and later that year a new student government was organized. As before, the senate was composed of representatives of fraternities and clubs and "unorganized" students. Among other things, the senate was empowered to oversee the latest attempt at a student-regulated honor system. Within two years, the rapprochement had proceeded so effectively that Delta Sigma Phi was accused of colluding with five other fraternities to control elections to *Oriflamme* leadership positions.[96]

Even with one more fraternity, increased enrollment meant that a smaller proportion of students could be fraternity members. In 1923 around 44 percent were fraternity members. In 1926 another local club, Alpha Pi was created, but the percentage of fraternity members fell to 38 percent. With increased competition, pledging came to dominate freshmen's attention during their first semester, a crucial period of adjustment to college life. In 1923 the Inter-fraternity Council made its first attempt at self-regulation, which was revised almost annually thereafter. Seeking to inspire greater attention to academics, the faculty released monthly standings based on the grade averages for each fraternity.[97]

With a gift in memory of Edmund Sykes, a member who died in World War I, Chi Phi sought permission to build on campus in 1924. The board was in the midst of its building program, and Apple urged setting a general policy regarding fraternity houses. The Committee on Grounds and Buildings worked out an agreement with Chi

Phi representatives, whereby the college granted a building license that could be revoked if "the form of good conduct" was violated.[98]

The committee and fraternity considered "the most desirable location" to be the part of campus adjoining Buchanan Park and Race Street. Opposition came from academy leaders, who envisioned that area as potential room for expansion, and from campus architect Charles Klauder, who wanted to preserve it for later college development. Klauder thought the area around the new gymnasium more appropriate, as, in his experience, "fraternity boys desire above all things to be near the athletic activities and the gymnasium." But Chi Phi had prominent members on the board, including William Schnader and Dr. Theodore B. Appel, '89, state secretary of public health. Klauder finally acceded to Apple's vision of a "fraternity row" along Race Street.[99]

Chi Phi's house was completed in 1928, but Apple's hopes were thwarted by other fraternities' inability to obtain funding. Noting that "it is the policy of many institutions to help Fraternities in the erection of their houses," he urged the board to consider loans to help with the construction, but fiscal conservatives opposed the idea of loaning even unrestricted endowment monies. Meanwhile, several fraternities rendered the issue more or less moot by purchasing and remodeling houses in the neighborhood.[100]

Jewish students were barred from membership in many national fraternities because of religious requirements in the charters. A group of students formed their own club in 1926 and applied for recognition as the first step in becoming a fraternity. Divided over the desirability of Jewish students, the faculty balked, claiming that the group violated the college's prohibition of "sectarian organizations." The students persevered and under the name of the Towers Club petitioned again two years later, pointing out that they had helped to raise "the standard of the Hebrew Students" at the college. A faculty committee concluded that the group had met all requirements, and after a spirited discussion it granted approval in 1930.[101]

Beyond the social world of the fraternities, extracurricular organizations catered to a wide range of student interests and career goals. Emulating organizations at other schools, the most exclusive were honorary societies whose stated aim was to bring together the leaders of each class to serve as a counterbalance to fraternity "politics." Societies were created for the three upper classes in 1921, but the strongest was the sophomore society, the Black Cats, because their mission combined the lofty purpose of supporting "college spirit" and the more entertaining one of enforcing freshmen rules. In 1928 the group won affiliation with the Druids, a national sophomore honorary fraternity. The Black Pyramid Society was originally founded for juniors but eventually became a senior society. Its professed goal was "promotion of better fellowship" within the class, "the abolition of politics in so far as it is possible and the support of everything that tends to the better interests of Franklin and Marshall College and the Junior Class." At the end of the decade the senate instituted Tap Day exercises, at which new Druid and Black Pyramid members were announced.[102]

Some new groups, like the campus chapter of the Pennsylvania State Educational Association, Phi Upsilon Kappa for prospective ministers, and the John Marshall Law

Club, prepared students for specific professions. Others sought more generally to inculcate into students habits associated with different types of professional expertise. The science faculty founded the Thomas C. Porter Society in 1911 to seek "the enlightenment of its members and the furtherment of interest in the Natural Sciences at Franklin and Marshall." It included faculty and students who were elected from among those who had done several years' work in the natural sciences. Meetings began with scientific papers delivered by members or invited guests and concluded with hearty receptions. Parallel organizations for the humanities emerged in the late 1920s, including a history club organized by H. M. J. Klein.[103]

Other groups aimed at fostering skills in public speaking to more popular audiences. The Post-Prandial Club met for dinner every three weeks at the Brunswick Hotel and under Klein's guidance practiced the genial art of after-dinner speaking. Faculty and community members were invited as guest speakers.[104]

The Calumet Club signaled the beginnings of a new self-consciously intellectual and slightly bohemian subculture at the college. The name referred to a peace pipe that new members smoked as an initiation ritual; it symbolized the intention of fostering a sense of congeniality and no doubt also referred to the widespread use of tobacco among the literati. The club's membership was limited to a select group of younger faculty and their most promising students. "It was an élite group at a time when élitism was nothing to be apologized for," recalled Richard Altick, who was invited to join the group in the mid-1930s. Faculty members were relative newcomers, the most senior being S. N. Hagen, who joined the English faculty in 1924. Papers emphasized the arts and contemporary intellectual life, with discussions of Chekhov, Eugene O'Neill and T. S. Eliot. Looking back, Altick counted his Calumet experience as one of the experiences that turned him toward an academic career. The "collegial conversation" among "a lively assortment of professors who shared sympathies and freely talked about them in our presence" provided an attractive vision of a possible life of the mind.[105]

The college theater group, the Green Room Club, had been in existence since 1899. After a period of inactivity in the early 1920s, it grew in prominence and ambition despite the fact that students had to play female roles because the faculty barred the participation of women. Led by Darrell Larsen, a charismatic professor of English and public speaking, the club's schedule expanded to three productions a year. Larsen joined the college in 1927 in a temporary teaching position before an attempt to break into Broadway but somehow never left. Eschewing the light comedies prevalent on most campuses, the club staged increasingly challenging works, many of which had recently opened in New York.[106]

As was the case at many campuses in the 1920s, the first stirrings of student activism came from an unlikely quarter, the YMCA and Student Volunteer movements, as these groups moved beyond a focus on muscular Christianity and mission work to take up issues like pacifism, international disarmament, and social justice and displayed more incipient political radicalism than any other group in higher education. At Franklin & Marshall, the YMCA supplemented its freshman orientation work in the 1920s with lecture and discussion series that brought to campus prominent liberal and even socialist speakers. In 1927 they hosted Norman Thomas, then head of the League for Industrial Democracy, who gave a speech, "Why I am a Socialist," at an assembly and an extended chapel.[107]

A new group founded in 1928, alternately called the Social Problems or Liberal Club, went even further in challenging the status quo. Returning from a year's graduate study at Columbia, the Reverend Paul Limbert organized field trips to New York City; destinations ranged from Chinatown restaurants to NAACP headquarters in Harlem. "We were brought face to face with reality when we saw the Jewish sweatshops and a gentle Jewish gentleman conducted us through the building of the largest Jewish newspaper in the world," one student recalled. Organized to continue exploration of social issues, the new club quickly made a big splash by hosting a debate on the nation's preparedness policy, with invited speakers Rear Admiral Charles P. Plunkett and Norman Thomas, by then the Socialist candidate for president.[108]

To Apple's consternation, Thomas was even invited to dinner at the Phi Sigma Kappa fraternity house during one of his visits to campus. He had been invited by J. Granville Eddy, '30, one of the most radical students on campus. A thorn in the side of the administration as his fraternity's representative to the Student Senate, "Red" Eddy remained in Lancaster after graduating at the top of his class. He was a frequent candidate for local office as a Socialist and later as a Communist.[109]

Through their participation in the Inter-collegiate Newspaper Association and exposure to national student publications, leaders of the *Student Weekly* participated in national debates over individual freedom and tolerance, debates fueled by students' growing resentment of any form of adult interference. Along with many other young people of the day, *Weekly* writers enjoyed the iconoclastic writing of H. L. Mencken and some attempted to emulate him in their columns. They reprinted articles from the *New Student*, a left-liberal publication of the National Student Forum, an association of political clubs at many eastern campuses. By the end of the decade, *Weekly* editorialists had begun to criticize many aspects of student culture. Dismissing freshmen rules as a "great high school institution," they questioned "the value of forced loyalty."[110]

Amid the proliferation of extracurricular activities, interest in the Goethean and Diagnothian literary societies continued to decline; the *Weekly* reported in 1928 that only 16 percent of the student body were members and that even fewer participated actively. The societies did not falter for lack of support from faculty and alumni or publicity from student publications, and they benefited significantly from the fact that membership was a prerequisite for election to Phi Beta Kappa. Both tried to appeal to newer tastes with humorous mock trials and topical debates, but at their core they remained nineteenth-century institutions, rooted in a vision of common civic discourse that no longer seemed relevant in a specialized twentieth-century world. In 1920 both societies deposited their libraries in the college library, where they were eventually assimilated into the main collections. A few years later the college, faced with a severe shortage of classrooms, took over and renovated rooms on the lower levels of the buildings.[111]

Franklin & Marshall had always attracted academically serious students, and its postwar expansion brought new groups who were indifferent to the world of social and extracurricular activities. Some of these "outsiders" saw academic work as a path to a middle-class job, others as the first stage in a professional career, and still others as an opportunity to think deeply and critically about the nature of life and society. Campus leaders denounced students who thought only of preparing for a career as "grinds," but occasionally leaders expressed grudging admiration for the grinds' commitment and hard work. The profile of J. Stanley Cohen of Lancaster in the 1923 *Oriflamme* reflected this ambivalence: "Here we have a man who travels his own path without bothering the rest of the world. Where he hangs out in his spare time has never been discovered, but since he expects to finish his course at F. and M. [in three years] it is very likely that he has no spare time." He planned to attend medical school at Johns Hopkins and seemed assured of success, for "men of his type generally know what they are after and put forth every effort to reach it." Over the years, the yearbook commented more acerbically about students who seemed to spend all their time at the Science Building.[112]

Perhaps more typical of Franklin & Marshall students were Robert and Jay Kneedler, sons of a contractor from Greenville, Pennsylvania, near Pittsburgh; the brothers attended the college's A.B. program together from 1923 to 1925 and recorded their experiences in a series of letters home. They boarded with a Mrs. Frey, who seems to have made heroic efforts to feed them. Their reports home regarding hazing experiences were laconic — they judged the freshman rules to be "not so bad," but later reported simply, "We had a hot time in the pajama parade." They played tennis whenever they could find an open court, often with Andrew Truxall, an instructor from their home town. Like their parents, they were active in the Reformed Church and reported attending chapel and church regularly, although they were often unimpressed by the preaching. They went to YMCA meetings but joined few other organizations. They faithfully attended intercollegiate athletic contests, debates, and class events and, once freshman rules were suspended, ventured downtown to the movies and vaudeville house. Fairly diligent in their studies, they received good grades but like many students had considerable difficulty with the required course in advanced algebra. After two years, both transferred to Cornell University so that Jay could study engineering.[113]

Many students became so involved in extracurricular and social activities that they had little time for studying. Each year a number were dropped from the rolls because of poor academic performance, about 3 percent in 1923–1924, for example. A study of enrollments between 1911 and 1925 reported that only 53.2 percent graduated. More than one-quarter of those who left transferred to other schools or entered military service, but over two-thirds of the rest quit because of "poor scholarship," with only 6 percent dropping out for financial reasons. A freshman advisory program made up of sixteen faculty was established in 1925 in an effort to reduce student failures. Hoping to identify and help students at risk, the college began to administer new intelligence tests to freshmen at the beginning of the fall semester. Over the decade the failure rate gradually declined.[114]

Apple and the faculty attempted to channel student energies in productive directions, but in attempting to regulate student activities, they tried to find a delicate balance between overinvolvement and neglect. "While supervision is necessary," Apple told the board in 1929, "it must not infringe on the rights and privileges of students for the free use of their own powers and talents or restrict the exercise of responsibility." In terms that harked back to the Franklin & Marshall's idealist tradition, he explained that despite a young man's immaturity, the college "must never forget that in this sphere he is to make himself and he must not be denied that freedom in which alone he can develop and strengthen his own personality." Nonetheless, the faculty imposed some restrictions on social functions, such as requiring college dances to be properly chaperoned and to end at 1:00 A.M. Students who were caught drinking at college events or who arrived drunk were suspended. And fraternities that broke the rules risked losing their ability to hold social functions "at which ladies [were] present," obviously a major limitation to social life. Students easily obtained alcohol at roadhouses or speakeasies in town, and even at the height of prohibition "beer was easy to come by" in German American Lancaster.[115]

The faculty fought a never-ending battle to hold down the influence of intercollegiate athletics, especially football. The faculty had long barred students who failed courses from playing on intercollegiate teams and restricted involvement of nondegree students. Before the war, Apple participated in the Inter-collegiate Athletic Association and in debates of the Association of College Presidents of Pennsylvania over "the right and wrong use of intercollegiate athletics." In the 1920s, Franklin & Marshall joined the Middle Atlantic States Collegiate Athletic Conference, which imposed additional rules to prevent players from transferring from school to school in order to continue playing long after their graduation. In 1925 Apple joined leaders from Gettysburg, Dickinson, Muhlenberg, and Ursinus to form the Eastern Collegiate Athletic Conference, which adopted more stringent regulations, including a requirement that students spend one year in residence before being eligible to play.[116]

Apple himself contributed to a rising tide of criticism of college football in the mid-1920s, through a series of articles collectively titled "Wanted — Honest Football," distributed by the North American Newspaper Alliance. Noting that he had himself played football in college and considered it the "king of sports," he denounced a host of abuses — the "furtive professionalism, fake scholarships, barefaced bribery, scouting, kidnapping"— that accompanied zealous football rivalries. But more fundamentally, overemphasis on winning undermined the very purpose of higher education. "In our college," Apple concluded, "we aim constantly at the democratic ideal, and it is my opinion that extreme specialization — which carries a boy to achievement in only a single field — is not compatible with this ideal." Although the series brought him and his college positive publicity, most who responded doubted that much could be done to remedy the situation.[117]

At Franklin & Marshall attempts at reform met resistance from alumni and local boosters, who had for decades provided informal financial aid to some football players. In 1924 they set up a loan program to be administered by the Board of Governors. When explaining the plan to the trustees, the Alumni Advisory Council argued that it would help "to curb an undoubted evil" in the uncontrolled "buying" of unqualified students at the expense of "worthy students who have athletic characteristics." Under the new Eastern Collegiate Athletic Conference, alumni criticized the fact that Franklin & Marshall was using only seven of an allowed twenty-two athletic scholarships. The plan ended in 1928, when the conference banned separate aid programs for athletes and directed that student aid be controlled by school administrations.[118]

It was all the more galling in 1929 when Franklin & Marshall was criticized in a famous report on intercollegiate athletics issued by the Carnegie Foundation for the Advancement of Teaching. The *Student Weekly* complained that the report was based on a short visit to campus several years before, before the college joined the Eastern Conference. Apple acknowledged to the board that even now, "alumni or ardent supporters of athletics" were paying "a small amount of money." He added, "I have no definite knowledge which I could report or upon which I can form a decided opinion." He noted that college authorities had known about general conditions and were trying to correct problems, but he expressed the opinion that the situation was "far more encouraging than at any time in the past."[119]

The Twenties Boom Ends

In his reports and public statements at the end of the decade, President H. H. Apple was fond of recounting the dramatic progress made during his administration. But he was also aware that much more needed to be done merely to keep pace with other colleges. In his annual report to the board in 1928, he compared Franklin & Marshall to characteristics of the "Effective College" outlined by "the expert judgment" of the Association of American Colleges (AAC). Under its criteria, Apple reported, the college's endowment of 1 million should be three times larger; its tuition should be raised to more closely approximate actual costs of education, in tandem with a system of financial aid for "poor but worthy boys"; at least ten additional faculty should be hired and salaries increased.[120]

The college had no formal financial aid program, although some needy students were given jobs in the library or laboratories, and sons of ministers received tuition discounts. At Apple's urging, the contingent fee was raised throughout the decade, reaching $300 in 1928. After studying practices at other colleges, the board approved the principle of granting support based on financial need and scholarly qualifications, but only after a long discussion of whether to consider athletic ability. In practice, the awarding of financial aid remained largely ad hoc, and a certain amount was always found for promising football players and wrestlers. Librarian Herbert Anstaett recalled how local student Richard Altick came to study at the college in 1932: "We were sitting on the porch at the President's House one afternoon, and along came Mrs. Altick with Richard to ask Dr. Apple what he might be able to do for Richard in seeking an education at Franklin & Marshall. Dr. Apple assured them that he would take care of him." Altick worked in the library throughout his college career, eventually serving as Anstaett's assistant. Other students supported themselves through a variety of jobs; in the last days of prohibition, one of James Farmer's classmates "pretty largely paid his way through college by mixing up and selling illegal gin."[121]

In the early 1930s, as the effects of the Great Depression began to be felt throughout the nation, the pace of change at the college slowed. Enrollments remained stable at first, around 750, but in 1932–1933 fell by 5 percent, which Apple reported to be less than the national average of 10 to 20 percent. More than one-quarter of students received financial assistance or held jobs on campus. On the positive side, Apple observed that students showed "an increased seriousness" about their studies.[122]

To preserve the liberal arts at Franklin & Marshall, Apple was finally compelled to eliminate one of the last vestiges of its classical curriculum. Enrollment in the A.B. program fell to 18 percent in 1933, with 43 percent of students enrolled in the B.S., 10 percent in the B.S. in social science and 29 percent in the B.S. in economics programs. In the spring of 1933, Apple went to the faculty with a proposal that in effect eliminated the Latin requirement for a bachelor of arts degree. He argued that the change followed "the more flexible systems" at most other colleges and universities and without lowering standards "would greatly increase and widen the service of the institution for the needs of this modern day." He pointed to the "formidable list" of leading institutions that had dropped the Latin requirement; Franklin & Marshall's requirements were "forcing many students, against their own wishes, into the Bachelor of Science curriculum" because those without preparation in Latin could not major in English or modern languages. After lengthy discussion, the faculty approved the change, with the provision that A.B. students who did not take Latin or Greek be required to take courses in Greek and Roman civilization. Afterward, the proportion of students in the A.B. program rose to 28 percent in 1933–1934, with 36 percent in the sciences and 33 percent in the business program.[123]

Despite his efforts to bring Franklin & Marshall in line with national trends, Apple began to criticize "self-constituted or official standardizing agencies" that seemed to want to make colleges "alike even down to the minutest details." In his opening address in 1930, he stressed that each college in America had its own "unique character and form" while sharing "essentially the same foundation and purpose." Although different, he hoped that each could be "efficient" in training men and women for "good citizenship and successful service" in their "particular sphere." Among the differences, one that was most important to Apple was Franklin & Marshall's identity as a Christian college, animated by the "fine Christian character" and "active Christian influence" of the trustees and faculty. He considered this to be "a vital force in the development of personality."[124]

The ideological turmoil aroused by the Depression changed Apple's political outlook. Through the 1920s he had maintained a rather conservative brand of Progressive Republicanism, emphasizing collective over individual needs but emphasizing moral and spiritual uplift rather than government action. In an opening address in

September 1932, he emphasized the need to prepare students for a new kind of leadership in the coming social "reconstruction": "Those who will lead us out of the wilderness must have more than technical knowledge and skill. They must be capable of managing not only one field of endeavor, but of understanding and managing the gigantic whole of modern civilization." In Apple's view, these new leaders must understand the social as well as the economic demands of the time, "to guide safely in the widest distribution of the comforts, conveniences and wealth which a machine age can and of necessity must produce."[125]

Apple's enthusiasm for "reconstruction" quickly waned after the Democratic Party came to power. In the spring of 1933, at the unveiling of a portrait of himself commissioned by the class of 1932, Apple delivered an address proclaiming, "Not systems, not machines, but personalities will shape the future of civilization." Education must "provide a broader training for personality, well grounded in moral character." And in his last opening address in September 1934, he attacked those "unbalanced reformers" advocating collectivism: "Regulation by government in the field of private enterprise is an encroachment upon the rights of individual liberty."[126]

Even so, the college accepted federal money to provide part-time jobs that enabled students to stay in school. In the spring of 1934, Federal Emergency Relief Administration funds paid more than sixty students to work on campus, and during the fall eighty earned money through work in campus offices and on special projects in the city. At the same time, by practicing "rigid economies," such as canceling spring sports in 1933, the college regularly achieved small budget surpluses.[127]

The pressures of the national economic crisis took their toll on Apple's already fragile health. He had collapsed during commencement week in 1926, making public a heart condition that increasingly restricted his activities. By 1932 it had worsened to the point that he offered to resign if he were guaranteed a specified allowance as president emeritus. After discussing the matter in executive session, the board appointed a special committee to assist Apple during the coming year and to consider the question of his successor. Things continued as before, until Fackenthal wrote Apple in the summer of 1934 to express his "final judgment" that the time had come for him to retire. Apple could be "justly proud" of his significant place in the college's history, but Fackenthal cautioned him: "[Present burdens of administration] are heavy indeed and make demands on nervous and physical reserve that you can ill afford." He advised Apple "most earnestly, simply to request retirement" and leave the details to the board's discretion.[128]

Apple's letter of resignation to Fackenthal was dated August 15, 1934, to take effect at the end of the academic year, to leave time for finding a successor. Characteristically, Apple began by summarizing the advances made at Franklin & Marshall during his administration. But he acknowledged that the institution was entering "another period" with problems with which a new generation must deal. The board paid appropriate tribute to Apple's accomplishments and voted him an annuity of $5,000 for life, to take effect upon his retirement.[129]

"We have just come to the close of a definite and distinct period of development and growth in the history of Franklin and Marshall College," Apple reiterated in his annual report. It was time to make plans for the future: "It would seem suitable for an old president to make it possible for the college to have the guidance of a younger man who has training for the peculiar problems of the future and who could expect to give his life to carry them to completion." Apple was right that the next quarter century would see even more far-reaching changes, but it would be the work of more than one man.[130]

CHAPTER SEVEN

The College in Depression and War, 1935–1946

—◁◌◁◌▷—

The 1930s and 1940s were a time of challenge and crisis for Franklin & Marshall, as for the nation as a whole. But even as the college struggled to maintain enrollments when Depression and world war kept young men out of higher education, seeds were planted for its subsequent transition into a selective liberal arts institution. As a member of the faculty recalled, President John A. Schaeffer "inspired all to feel that F.&M. was an excellent small college and should be sold as such to the public." Seeking to attract more qualified students, it moved into an educational market that had grown in scope and competitiveness as affluent Americans looked beyond their local or denominational schools for their children's education. Participating in this wider market offered possibilities for advancement but also increased competition. Institutions with national reputations stood to benefit the most, while those, like Franklin & Marshall, with more regional and denominational constituencies were more vulnerable. Meanwhile, the expansion of state-funded institutions threatened to draw away local students. To meet these challenges, college leaders hoped to emphasize a growing academic reputation to move into a different educational niche.[1]

The federal government began to play a larger role in higher education in this period. As Republicans, most of the college's board and administration opposed government interference in principle and often criticized New Deal programs. But like most independent schools, Franklin & Marshall welcomed federal aid when it came in the form of National Youth Administration (NYA) work-study funds with no strings attached. As America braced for war at the end of the decade, the college scrambled to win government patronage by recasting its programs for the emergency. As during the First World War, leaders were eager to participate in wartime educational programs. Military demands for technical training heightened the college's existing strength in the sciences.

During the 1930s the influence of wealthy trustees and alumni grew as the Reformed Church's role waned. A revision of the college's governance structure, made necessary by the union of the Reformed and Evangelical denominations, established the board's independence. No longer drawn from the Reformed ministry, Franklin & Marshall's presidency lost a certain degree of its traditional authority, while board leaders expected to run the college just as they did their businesses. The board's president in the 1930s, Benjamin Franklin Fackenthal Jr., exerted particular influence by virtue of his substantial benefactions to the college.

A Businessman at the Helm

Fackenthal's preeminence showed in his control over selection of a new president. At his request, H. H. Apple offered his resignation in August 1934. Apple urged the board to act quickly to name his successor and ensure a smooth transition, but Fackenthal did not present the letter until the midwinter board meeting and, as chair of the search committee, kept the process entirely out of public view. By March even Apple was impatient and at a local alumni banquet urged the board to make its decision soon. In the news vacuum, rumors circulated that the committee was divided over appointing a clergyman. "Our task is hard enough without having people, who perhaps have never helped the college to a dollar, nor helped in any other substantial way, advising us how to proceed," Fackenthal fumed in response to an anonymous letter in the press.[2]

Fackenthal's committee does not seem to have begun work in earnest until mid-May; on the eve of the board's June 4 annual meeting it still had not made a decision. In executive session on June 3, Fackenthal proposed John A. Schaeffer, an alumnus who had been approached about the job only a few weeks earlier. The board invited Schaeffer for an interview, telling local newspapers that he was at the top of a list of ten finalists. Schaeffer met with the committee the following weekend and was offered the job on the spot. After mulling it over for several days, he accepted, and Fackenthal called a special board meeting for June 28 to ratify the selection. Impressed by his credentials and family background, the board did so overwhelmingly, with one dissenting mail vote that was later reversed to make it unanimous.[3]

Selection of John A. Schaeffer, '04, both affirmed and departed from Franklin & Marshall traditions. He was a distinguished alumnus who had earned a doctorate in chemistry at the University of Pennsylvania and taught at the Carnegie Institute of Technology. His achievements in applied chemistry won fellowships from the American Association for the Advancement of Science, London's Royal Society for the Arts, and the American Institute of Chemists. Although not a minister, he had strong ties to the Reformed Church and to Franklin & Marshall. His confirmation certificate had been signed by former president E. V. Gerhart. His father, Nathan C. Schaeffer, Pennsylvania's longtime superintendent of public instruction, was a trustee for many years. His uncle, the Reverend W. C. Schaeffer, had taught at the seminary, and his cousin, John Nevin Schaeffer, was currently the college's professor of Greek.[4]

What made Schaeffer's selection unusual was that he had not been associated with higher education for more than two decades. Schaeffer left teaching in 1911 to become chief chemist for the Picher (later Eagle-Picher) Lead Company of Joplin, Missouri. During the war he developed a method for making optical glass that had previously been a closely held German secret. In 1922 he became vice president for manufacturing and in 1931 assumed control of the research program. After twenty-four years in private industry, Schaeffer was more businessman than scientist. Comparing him to Harvard's President James Conant and other scientist-presidents, the *Alumnus* argued that Schaeffer's long business experience had "prepared him to give wise and capable direction as an executive."[5]

Schaeffer's decision to return to academia to serve his alma mater could not have been easy. At $9,000 a year, his new salary was undoubtedly a pay cut, and he had to fend off an effort by his company's board of directors to dissuade him from leaving. Nevertheless, assured of the full support of the college's board, he concluded that the presidency of Franklin & Marshall offered "an opportunity for far greater service." However strong might have been his sense of obligation to Franklin & Marshall, he was also pleasantly surprised to learn during his interview of its financial stability in spite of the continuing economic crisis. "This must be attributed to the splendid work which you have done," he wrote Apple.[6]

Arriving in Lancaster in August 1935, Schaeffer quickly moved to ensure that that stability continued. There was general disappointment at the low enrollment at the opening of fall term; at 670 it was slightly above the preceding year but still below levels of the early 1930s. It was also substantially less than the 750 to 850 that Schaeffer calculated to be the most efficient use of the college's present equipment and faculty. At current rates of attrition, he estimated that it was necessary to have a freshman class around 300 in order to reach "a proper and balanced enrollment," and he set a goal of increasing it by at least 50 students a year over the next four years.[7]

As Schaeffer told the board, other institutions of higher education had become much more aggressive in recruitment. However one might regret this "prevalent trend," the college had fallen behind because of its failure to adopt modern methods. He immediately initiated vigorous efforts to attract more students for the next year. Calling them "valuable assets of college training," he increased support for the symphony orchestra and Green Room Club, the campus theater group. He enlisted local music teacher Harry A. Sykes to revive the moribund Glee Club. He planned to sponsor performances of these groups in the surrounding area "to bring the cultural side of [the] college to the attention of prospective students."[8]

Schaeffer and the faculty recognized that it was not enough simply to raise the college's profile, because most institutions were offering financial aid to attract and retain students. When he arrived, 43 percent of students received some form of aid through grants or reduction of fees. As Schaeffer told the board, as long as the college was not making full use of its overhead in terms of faculty and facilities, it made sense financially as well as morally to admit students even if they could not pay full price. (Decades later this practice became known as "discounting.") He had learned that some faculty were dissatisfied with the way that financial aid was administered under Apple. Soon after his arrival, Schaeffer was greeted by an unnamed faculty member — most likely his cousin, J. Nevin Schaeffer — who proposed using scholarship money strategically to improve the quality of the student body. The sole professor of Greek and co-author of a well-known Greek textbook, Nevin Schaeffer had taught classics at Franklin & Marshall since 1910. He had consistently criticized changes that weakened the college's traditional liberal arts character and now found allies among younger academically oriented faculty and the new president.[9]

Pointing out that a sizable number of students at the bottom of their classes received financial aid, this faculty member suggested shifting some of this money to merit-based scholarships. President Schaeffer appointed a committee chaired by Professor Schaeffer to plan such a program. At the October faculty meeting, the committee proposed creating a dozen scholarships of $250 toward the contingent fee of $350 and basing them on merit rather than financial need. It pointed out that in recent years a wide range of schools had "entered into keen competition for students of high quality" by offering similar scholarships. Perhaps best known was the National Scholars program created at Harvard in 1934. Merit scholars were expected to improve their institutions by bringing "a better tone" to academic life, ensuring a successful body of alumni, enlarging "their circles of friends and admirers," and in general adding to "their prestige as educational institutions."[10]

Like the new president, committee members stressed the importance of making the college more competitive. This could be done, they argued, by raising the college's "prestige" and "improving the quality of its work." They buttressed their case by citing a recent pronouncement by Frederick P. Keppel, president of the Carnegie Corporation, that the independent college, "if it is to survive as a characteristic feature of American education and American life . . . must become a very different place," in particular improving the nature and quality of its "output." Through the new scholarships, the faculty committee hoped to begin to improve Franklin & Marshall's "output" by raising the quality of its "inputs." Perhaps influenced by Nevin Schaeffer's experience as a Rhodes scholar, the criteria were not purely academic. Recipients had to be in the top fifth of their high school classes, but "qualities of manhood and character, leadership, and physical vigor" would be considered along with scholastic ability. Ten scholarships were to be distributed according to geographical regions within Pennsylvania and Maryland, with two reserved for "at large" candidates.[11]

Until the 1920s, even the most prestigious colleges and universities had admitted nearly all students who met their entrance requirements, and many who did not meet those requirements were allowed to enroll as conditional or special students. As enrollments mushroomed after the war, some institutions began to pay more attention to admissions. Finding that administrative measures had little impact on student culture, college leaders turned to selective admissions to shape the educational environment. A common belief was that, as Schaeffer's committee asserted, "good students beget good students." A few liberal arts colleges, most notably Dartmouth and Swarthmore, won national reputations by instituting selective admissions policies and honors programs.[12]

In contrast, Franklin & Marshall's growth in the 1920s was largely accomplished at the cost of lowering entrance requirements, and some students lacked the preparation, skills, or abilities that many faculty believed necessary for academic achievement. During the Depression, the college maintained enrollments by accepting as transfer students some who had flunked out of other schools, and in 1933–1934 it stopped requiring failing students to leave school. Many faculty resented this relaxation of standards and the damage done to the college's once-proud academic reputation.[13]

Apple had repeatedly insisted that it was the college's mission to develop the capabilities of average or even "mediocre" students, but not all faculty felt the same sense of educational vocation. They longed for brighter students and looked enviously at more selective institutions. At the high point of enrollments in the late 1920s, some students and alumni called for capping the student body. Most of the board opposed the idea, citing economic reasons and fears that Reformed students or children of alumni might be turned away.[14]

The new scholarship program was launched in the spring of 1936 under Nevin Schaeffer's direction. It was an immediate success. The application process publicized Franklin & Marshall, and some unsuccessful applicants enrolled anyway. On the basis of placement tests administered to each incoming class, education professor P. M. Harbold found that the "scholastic average" of the new freshman class increased over the previous year by about 10 percent. He predicted that if trends continued, "the College should continue to attract a larger per cent of high grade students, which is the primary point of beginning in the rather long process of raising still further the standards of scholarship in College." After it was noted that at-large scholars had better records, their numbers were increased to three in 1938 and the amount of the scholarship raised to $300.[15]

During the next five years President Schaeffer's programs raised both the college's total enrollment and the academic quality of its students. This success came by dint of hard work — in the absence of specialized admissions personnel, much of it done by the faculty. The faculty Committee on Enrollment coordinated a wide range of recruiting activities, including campus visits by groups of high school students from Lancaster and five surrounding counties. Later these visits were replaced by a single Franklin & Marshall College Day, during which students were brought to campus to observe classes and activities. Fifteen faculty volunteers spoke at high schools and college fairs in the region, and in late May of each year they traveled widely to interview prospective students.[16]

The college also enlisted alumni aid in recruitment. Copying sales practices, Franklin & Marshall distributed cards to all alumni and asked them to provide names of "prospects" to be visited by faculty interviewers. Schaeffer personally urged each alumnus to set a goal of recruiting at least one new student every three years. He considered alumni "a potent force in college development" and traveled widely to meet with all the alumni associations. He estimated that alumni had directed a hundred students to the college in his first four years in office. A survey of freshmen in 1939 confirmed this impression. Asked why they had chosen Franklin & Marshall, new students pointed first to the course of study offered and second to the influence of family or others who were alumni.[17]

Hoping to reverse the declining presence of Reformed students, college leaders especially sought help from alumni in the Reformed ministry. A 1936 survey of religious preferences of college students found that only one-third of Pennsylvania's Reformed students attended Protestant church–related schools, while 43 percent went to state schools, and 24 percent to independent schools. To improve these figures, religion professor Charles D. Spotts cultivated closer ties with ministerial alumni, and marketing professor Noel P. Laird designed a poster for church bulletin boards highlighting "the advantages of the College." During the school year Spotts and his wife invited groups of Reformed students to their home to "foster fellowship and a spirit of church loyalty among the students who belong to the College in a peculiar sense."[18]

Schaeffer created a publicity department staffed part-time by Wallace L. Robinson, '11, formerly of the *Lancaster News Journal*, to expand coverage of the college in "cosmopolitan papers." With the help of several students paid by the National Youth Administration, Robinson sent local and regional papers news releases about athletic teams and campus events and prepared original stories about students' college achievements for their hometown and high school papers. Robinson's "theory," Schaeffer explained, was that his "chief function is to attract the finest type of boys to F. and M."[19]

The immediate response to the recruitment campaign was gratifying: 97 more new students arrived on campus in 1936, and total enrollment rose to a record 775. It continued to grow over the rest of the decade, reaching 966 in the 1939–1940 academic year. These numbers were made possible by increases not only in numbers of students entering the college but in rate of retention. Schaeffer attributed this to greater care taken in admissions and oversight during students' careers. No admissions records remain for this period, but it is clear that increased interest in Franklin & Marshall made it possible to exercise some selectivity. Admissions were overseen by Richard W. Bomberger , who had become dean in 1931 when Howard Omwake left to become president of Catawba College. In the fall of 1938, Schaeffer told the faculty that Bomberger had selected the entering class "with extreme care," which Schaeffer hoped would decrease the numbers of students who failed or dropped out. Two years later Schaeffer reported to the board that "many more students" had been rejected. As a result, the proportion of students from the top two-fifths of their high school classes rose from 36 percent in 1938 to 54 percent in 1940.[20]

Schaeffer also noted that administrators had made "a determined effort to broaden the geographical distribution of our student body" in order to widen its "sources of interest." The proportion of Pennsylvania residents decreased somewhat, from four-fifths in 1930 to two-thirds in 1940, with slightly more than one-quarter coming from Lancaster City and County. The percentage from the nearby states of New Jersey, New York, and Maryland increased to nearly 30 percent, with a smattering from ten other states in New England, the Midwest, and the South. A few came from Central and South America, generally to prepare for medical school. Throughout the decade there was a small contingent of Iraqi students, graduates of the Reformed Church's American School for Boys in Baghdad, whose principal was an alumnus.[21]

Geographic diversity is now generally believed to be inherently desirable in an educational institution, but it is also most commonly associated with the most selective schools. It was not an ideal that was generally realized in the 1930s. In 1934, when only 12 percent of the nation's young people even entered college, nearly four out of five attended schools in their home state. And as Dartmouth discovered, increasing geographical diversity often meant reducing social and economic diversity, because students who came from farther away tended to be from more affluent backgrounds. Dartmouth's President Ernest M. Hopkins hoped to preserve "the old country boy constituency" that had produced many prominent alumni, but by the end of the 1930s the sons of businessmen and professionals greatly outnumbered farmers' and laborers' children. The growing numbers of Franklin & Marshall students from urban and suburban New York and New Jersey probably came from wealthier homes than those from rural and small-town Pennsylvania.[22]

In some schools, national scholarships and regional quotas were covert means of restricting the numbers of "socially undesirable" Jewish or other ethnic students. As Jewish students from northeastern cities sought educational opportunity throughout the country, some schools limited their numbers by setting quotas on out-of-state students and charging differential tuition rates. This was not true at Franklin & Marshall, where the proportion of Jewish students continued to grow. In 1935–1936, they formed the second-largest denominational group, at 14 percent of the student body, with members of the newly merged Evangelical and Reformed Church at 22 percent. This was the last time that the president's annual report noted church affiliation, suggesting that Schaeffer was not entirely comfortable with the situation. In 1940 he acknowledged the diversity of the student body by exempting Catholic and Jewish students from chapel requirements. Faculty concern was partly responsible for its negative response to a 1936 petition to form a second Jewish fraternity. Some moved immediately to deny the request, while others expressed reluctance to see any new national fraternities. After deliberation, a committee concluded that the college already had enough fraternities.[23]

Modernization with a Conservative Bent

Schaeffer continued rhetorical support for Franklin & Marshall's liberal arts traditions. His inaugural address on December 6, 1935, "The Fundamentals in a Liberal Arts Education," included by now standard elements: exposure to "the entire field of human endeavor," training "to think and analyze properly," and close contact with inspiring faculty. But he paid most attention to liberal education's role in preparing for a vocation. According to Schaeffer, the liberal arts college should continue its traditional role of providing "a broad cultural training to those who are desirous of entering the professions, research or specialized work" and preparing others to "properly fulfill their functions as citizens." Significantly, he also asserted that the college must help the undecided student identify the specialty "most fitted to his talents." At the same time, as one who had attended the college in the days of J. S. Stahr, Schaeffer paid homage to "the philosophy learned in these halls, that all knowledge is one."[24]

In part, Schaeffer stressed time-honored ideals because he considered the liberal arts college a bulwark against radicalism. While it was a time of "seeming experimentation and strife," he celebrated the fact that Franklin & Marshall remained "true to the basic principles of justice and spiritual freedom on which it was founded." Yet for all their political conservatism, Schaeffer and the Board of Trustees continued to press to make the college's curriculum and general atmosphere if anything more modern, as defined by contemporary trends in higher education.[25]

The college drew heavily on faculty expertise in new departments of education, religion, and business administration, to increase oversight of students' educational and extracurricular life. Freshman orientation programs were expanded. The religion department assumed sponsorship of the YMCA, which was renamed the Student Christian Association, and the department's faculty took charge of what had become a three-day program. Seeking to inculcate faculty ideals of campus life before upperclassmen could exert their influence over freshmen, orientation opened with welcoming talks by faculty and student leaders, such as H. M. J. Klein's "The Significance of the Chapel Environment." In the 1920s education faculty began administering an English placement test, and later in the 1930s it added a battery of psychological and aptitude tests for use in student advisement.[26]

Despite efforts to improve student performance, substantial numbers still flunked out. Some twenty-five students left school in the first semester of the 1937–1938 academic year, for example, and midyear grades found more than one-quarter of the student body on probation. Schaeffer exhorted the faculty "to put forth an effort to interest students in the work to a greater extent." The entire college addressed these concerns in the fall of 1940 by focusing a variety of initiatives around the theme "Improvement in Scholarship." Acknowledging that "during recent years we have not succeeded in creating an atmosphere which challenged all students to achieve excellence in their academic work," a faculty committee offered programs aimed at the needs of students at each stage of their careers. President Schaeffer spoke to freshmen on "the importance of scholarship," after which faculty discussed proper methods of studying and organization. Dean Bomberger addressed sophomores on "the dangers of overconfidence," and Professor Noss held a forum for upperclassmen on "discovering a meaning in a college education," emphasizing the value of courses outside the major.[27]

Business professor Harold Fischer established a personnel bureau in 1936 to help students and alumni find employment, particularly with corporations. Fischer employed "sound personnel practices" to ensure a match between individual and job and to develop good relationships with employers. On the basis of interviews he classified seniors "as to the type of work for which they [were] qualified and in which they [were] interested"; then, drawing on faculty reports, he rated them according to a scale of his own devising "on the basis of scholarship and personality." He presented the results to prospective employers, recommending only students whom he judged most qualified. He believed that these practices paid "dividends" in increased numbers of on-campus interviews. Finding too many students "drifting without chart or compass," he also offered career counseling.[28]

Fischer also sought to expand opportunities for part-time work during the school year and directed all student employment on campus. Echoing critics of New Deal work programs, he told the board that "in the administration of student aid funds considerable care must be exercised" to prevent "the undermining of initiative, independence, and responsibility, and the acquisition of undesirable habits of work." He therefore established a system of close supervision that rated students on "punctuality, dependability, industriousness, and cooperativeness."[29]

The bureau formalized ties with area businesses that had been developing for some time. A particularly close relationship with the Armstrong Cork Company had begun when it expanded into linoleum production in 1907. By the 1920s, spurred by a college recruitment program launched by H. W. Prentis Jr., more than twenty college graduates worked for the linoleum division as salesmen, managers, accountants, and chemists. Armstrong managers often came to campus to speak to business classes or organizations, and occasionally their staff attended lectures at the college. Soon after he created the bureau, Fischer arranged a talk by Armstrong's personnel manager on "opportunities for the college man in industry."[30]

President Schaeffer consistently encouraged students in all majors to consider business careers. Like his predecessors, he emphasized the value of liberal arts education in developing "personality," but he connected this quality with "certain traits required by business firms today in addition to scholarship." He emphasized the importance of "well-roundedness," a quality produced by combining academic achievement with extracurricular activities to gain exposure to "other things than pure book knowledge." Yet he also stated flatly in an opening-of-term address that "big industries" required a B average for consideration for employment.[31]

Using alumni organizations, Schaeffer worked to bring more men of wealth and influence onto the board, particularly from beyond the college's traditional base in eastern Pennsylvania. Attending a banquet of the New York City Alumni Association on the eve of a football game with Fordham in 1936, he met Paul Kieffer, '01, a prominent New York attorney. Schaeffer lobbied Fackenthal to bring Kieffer onto the board, and he was elected the following spring as its first member from the New York area. Two years later, two more New Yorkers joined him, Frank D. Fackenthal, provost of Columbia University and nephew of the board's president, and Joseph H. Appel, recently retired as executive head of John Wanamaker, New York, and brother of the former college president. They supplemented the business acumen of such other longtime members as William H. Hager, president of Hager and Brothers, one Lancaster's largest department stores, and Henry A. Reninger, president of Lehigh Portland Cement Company in Allentown.[32]

Still, Schaeffer recognized that science was the principal jewel in Franklin & Marshall's crown. Each year his annual report paid most attention to this side of the college, especially its "preeminent" premedical program, which regularly enrolled about one in five students. He also pointed proudly to students who each year received graduate fellowships at prominent universities. Among the fifty-two science majors in the class of 1937, for example, twenty-one were admitted to medical schools, eight to dental schools, three to schools of osteopathy or veterinary medicine, and ten received fellowships to graduate programs in chemistry, physics, geology, and biology. Another three took jobs in the chemical industry, and one went to teach science at the American School in Iraq.[33]

Even so, science faculty recognized that admission to professional schools was becoming more competitive. Premedical faculty frequently revised course offerings with an eye to changing recommendations by professional associations. After attending meetings of the Association of American Medical Colleges in 1935 and 1936, for example, faculty introduced courses in zoology, embryology, and botany. When medical schools began to recommend a broader education in English, psychology, politics, and sociology, the biology and chemistry departments reduced the number of courses required for their majors. In fact, growing numbers of premed students taking sociology helped fuel substantial growth in that department. Later in the decade, faculty established a committee to screen medical school applications to discourage students with "no chance for admission" and to direct applications to the most "appropriate" schools. As medical school advisor Frederick Foster told the *Student Weekly*, "Only the cream of the crop is skimmed off. If a student doesn't have good grades, he hasn't a chance of entering medical school." By 1940 the education department was enlisted to administer the Strong Vocational Interest test and identify criteria to use in the selection process.[34]

The few changes in the general curriculum in this period were in the direction of greater freedom of choice. Specific courses in psychology and political science were replaced by general social science requirements. At the end of the decade the faculty attempted to remove a last remnant of the classical curriculum by eliminating the single required senior course in ethics. The head of the philosophy department had proposed this, arguing, "Freedom of choice is the foundation of Ethics." The board refused to approve the change, but it was finally achieved during curricular revisions in 1945.[35]

Building an Academic Quadrangle

The ambitious construction program of the Apple years was capped under Schaeffer with addition of a new library and a classroom and office building dedicated to the liberal arts. Significantly, both were products of generous individual gifts rather than fund-raising campaigns. Caroline S. Keiper, widow of former board member Lanious B. Keiper, bequeathed the residue of her estate to the college to erect a building to be known as "The Liberal Arts Building," requiring only that it contain a plaque in memory of her husband. The idea of a special building dedicated to the liberal arts seems to have been Caroline Keiper's, for it had not been on a list of new buildings that Apple envisioned in the early 1930s, and the *Student Weekly* noted that such a building had long been her dream.[36]

At its first meeting after Schaeffer's appointment, the board at Fackenthal's suggestion voted to rename the Science Building as Stahr Hall in honor of the president who had built it. Fackenthal announced that William H. Lee of Philadelphia had been hired as college architect and showed preliminary plans locating the Keiper Liberal Arts Building south of Stahr and forming a quadrangle with the library to the south and Old Main and the literary society buildings to the west. Schaeffer and Fackenthal hoped to be able to begin construction of a new library so that they could be dedicated during a sesquicentennial celebration planned for October 1937.[37]

Apple had called for a new library since at least 1928. Watts–de Peyster had long been inadequate for the college's needs; it had been built for a student body less than one-fourth its present size and at a time when library practice organized books loosely in subject-related alcoves. Over the years, collections grew and were recataloged and the space rearranged to create areas for study and research. Many books were moved to stacks in the basement. Despite vehement protests, the stacks were closed to students in 1930 in an attempt to stem the chronic disappearance of books. In the early 1930s collections were bolstered by a $15,000 grant from the Carnegie Corporation, part of a national program to enlarge college libraries, but by mid-decade acquisitions had to be put on hold for lack of space.[38]

The close physical relationship of the projected library and liberal arts building reflected the increased role of research in teaching in the humanities and social sciences. Apple envisioned rooms in the new building for seminars, conferences, and group study and recommended setting up working collections of books to relieve congestion in the library. As planning for the Keiper Liberal Arts Building began under Schaeffer, another feature was added, a theater designed especially for the Green Room Club. Under the direction of Darrell Larsen, the group's productions drew growing attention and praise but suffered from Hensel Hall's inadequate facilities and poor acoustics. Schaeffer believed the club's performances were an important form of advertising for the college; he was probably responsible for removing the ban on female actors early in 1936. The first coed production, "Accent on Youth," featured Mary Zimmerman, daughter of a local board member, which might explain why the board did not object to the change. The innovation offered senior Richard Altick the opportunity to begin his *Weekly* review, "For the first time in its history last Friday evening, the Green Room club was at home on high heels." He added that "Miss Zimmerman proved once and for all the wisdom of the decision to do away with female impersonators."[39]

Despite energetic efforts, Schaeffer and Fackenthal were unable to locate a bene-factor for the library. Prospective donors complained that New Deal measures under-mined their securities and burdened them with heavy taxes. "If it had not been for adverse legislation and the disturbance that is constantly going on at Washington," Fackenthal told Apple, "I surely would have built that library."[40]

Fackenthal had the architect prepare drawings for both buildings, in the now-standard neo-Georgian style. While Watts–de Peyster had faced outward to College Avenue, with its entrance visible far down James Street, the two new buildings faced each other across the quadrangle. The new library offered only an uninteresting side wall to the street, while Keiper, on its College Avenue side, offered a graceful curving stairway that framed the doorway to the Little Theater. With no donor in sight, the board authorized only the construction of Keiper in the spring of 1936. At its corner-stone laying in November, Schaeffer hailed the building as a symbol of renewed inter-est in the classics. "A classical course is just as essential as it was 100 years ago," he stated, calling it "the hallmark of a cultured man."[41]

The search for a donor finally ended in March 1937. "For six months I have been hunting for a man who would build a library," Fackenthal announced at a special board meeting. "And now I have found him. It is I."[42]

Some on the board objected to tearing down forty-year-old Watts–de Peyster, especially A. H. Rothermel, who had been instrumental in securing the original gift for the college. Schaeffer attempted to deflect these objections by promising that the college would maintain the "identity of the site" through a special alcove covering the same space as the original building and through a special tablet commemorating the first building. Later, Rothermel asserted that Schaeffer and Fackenthal told him that they planned only "an enlargement" of the library and that the front of the build-ing and the name would not be changed. He gave his assent, only to find at the next board meeting that the old library had been "demolished." Librarian Herbert Anstaett recalled that the architect had intended to retain the old building's walls, but it proved too expensive. According to Anstaett, the old foundations and one wall had been "kept for the sake of sentiment." Rothermel was doubly outraged that the statue of de Peyster's ancestor that had stood in front of the library was moved to the southern end of campus.[43]

The new building featured a large, two-story reading room with seating for more than two hundred, a cozier browsing room, study and conference rooms, and carrels and private study space within five stories of book stacks. (Perhaps because of cost over-runs, two tiers of stacks and an elevator were not installed until more than a decade later.) Separate rooms were designated for the college's collections of rare books, man-uscripts, historical papers, and artworks; for use of a record collection recently do-nated by the Carnegie Corporation; for special collections of textbooks and Lincolniana; and for the Historical Society of the Reformed Church in the United States. The music room soon became a center for informal appreciation classes in which local citizens joined faculty and students in listening to the "illuminating interpretations" of sociology professor Jerry Neprash, who had been responsible for the Carnegie gift. Looming over the circulation desk in the main lobby was a large mural by John Charles Wonsetler that allegorically portrayed "research, practical and philosophical."[44]

Marking One Hundred and Fifty Years

The dramatic announcement of Fackenthal's gift of a $250,000 library, reported in the *New York Times*, provided effective copy to launch the Sesqui-Centennial Endowment Fund campaign. Fackenthal's gift fulfilled one of Schaeffer's three goals for the celebration; the other two were to reach an enrollment of 850 and to double the endowment to $2 million. The stock market crash had reduced the college's endowment to $910,000 in 1930, and by 1937 it had rebounded to only $1,078,000. Campaign literature stressed that increasing the endowment was closely linked to Schaeffer's other goals, maintaining the new buildings, supporting the faculty needed to teach an enlarged student body, and reducing the college's dependence on tuition.[45]

To hold down expenses, the board "drafted" business professor and board secretary H. R. Barnes to manage the fund-raising campaign. To publicize the occasion, H. M. J. Klein edited a series of handsomely illustrated pamphlets. Initially projected as a documentary history, the *Franklin and Marshall Papers* contained brief essays on an eclectic range of topics about the college: "facts" of its founding, histories of its campus and chapel, changing "aims and ideals" of education, and the continuing prominence of scientific learning. Later numbers published speeches delivered at the celebrations. Throughout, the essays paid greatest attention to Franklin College and the prominent role played by Benjamin Franklin — and continued the wishful fiction that he had attended its dedication ceremonies. Relatively little attention went to the institution's German American or Reformed roots. The August 1937 number — "The Value of the Church Related College," Schaeffer's address to a Reformed group — portrayed the college's current role simply to be offering a generalized "religious atmosphere" in which students of Christian faith felt comfortable.[46]

Celebration of the sesquicentennial spread over four days in October, each with ceremonies and addresses underlining facets of Franklin & Marshall's tradition. As at the college's 1887 centennial, there was much discussion of educational ideas. On the sesquicentennial Education Day, addresses by Union College president Dixon Ryan Fox, Massachusetts Institute of Technology president Karl T. Compton, and Union Pacific Railroad president William M. Jeffers discussed the relationship of "the College" to, respectively, the liberal arts, science, and business administration. Fox lamented that the expansion of education in recent decades had lost sight of the idea that college education was principally to produce "a competent, cultivated, influential and serviceable man." Vocationalism had been pressed on students not only by the current belief that education "pays," but by "professional dictators" in graduate schools, whose entrance requirements consumed nearly all undergraduate time. Fox called for reclaiming a vision of the liberal arts as study aimed at producing graduates with "inquiring mind[s]," high ethical and aesthetic values, skills for constructive citizen-ship, and capacity for "reflective thinking." The other speakers defined education only in the most general, intellectual terms, focusing instead on the virtues of science and business in modern life.[47]

On Commemoration Day, at the unveiling of a portrait of former Greek profes-sor John Brainerd Kieffer, John Nevin Schaeffer offered a word portrait of his prede-cessor that embodied the virtues of an older vision of liberal arts education: "Here students have the chance to develop and strengthen their character 'by the constant challenge to duty of a system of ethics which still rests on a religious foundation,' . . . [by the study of language and literature that] deals with 'human hopes, and human lives, and human deeds,' . . . [and] the cultivation of a broad and liberal background that will give meaning and purpose to life." Several other speakers, like New York Uni-versity president Harry Woodburn Chase, depicted higher education as an inocula-tion against the ills of the present age, with its demands for instant gratification and easy answers. Speaking at the alumni dinner, trustee Paul Kieffer expressed hope that members of an institution like Franklin & Marshall "can do our bit in molding a pub-lic opinion against enemies within even as we gird against those from without." At the dedication of the Keiper Liberal Arts Building, prominent historian Roy F. Nichols emphasized the crucial power of the liberal arts "to cultivate and extend the imagina-tion" in the midst of "an elaborate mechanized civilization which seems contrived not only to save us labor but also save us thought."[48]

Finally, a service in the college chapel marked Religious Observance Day. Presi-dent of the Theological Seminary of the Reformed Church George W. Richards preached, noting that he had graduated with the class of 1887 in the midst of Franklin & Marshall's centennial celebration. He stressed that the college church played an im-portant role in showing students that there is no conflict between mature religious faith and modern natural and social sciences. "The catholicity of the ideals of Frank-lin and Marshall College" had always been shown in its rejection of divisiveness and "sectarian" exclusiveness, and Richards urged college graduates to be "free from pro-vincialism, partisanship, sectarianism, and to have a world-wide outlook, cosmopoli-tan sympathies."[49]

Ironically, this catholicity, in Richards and in the Reformed Church as a whole, set the stage for a further loosening of the college's religious ties. In the spirit of Mer-cersburg Theology's ecumenism, Richards had long worked to unite the Reformed tradition's many different branches. As head of the Reformed Commission on Closer Union, he engaged in discussions with several Protestant denominations through the 1920s. These bore fruit in a merger between the Reformed Church in the United States and the Evangelical Synod of North America. This latter denomination was descended from nineteenth-century German immigrants who had been members of the Evan-gelical Church of the Prussian Union, produced when King Frederick William III forced a merger of the Lutheran and Reformed traditions into a single state church. Strong-est in the Midwest, the denomination is perhaps best known in the twentieth century for having nurtured two of the most influential American theologians of their age, brothers Reinhold Niebuhr and H. Richard Niebuhr.[50]

The 1934 Plan of Union did not try to negotiate points of doctrinal difference or institutional organization, expressing faith that the spirit uniting them would enable them to find appropriate forms. Richards was selected as president of the first general synod of the Evangelical and Reformed Church. One important question was the fate of its educational institutions, for the old Reformed synods would be dissolved once the merger was completed. As head of the new organization's Association of Schools, Colleges, and Seminaries, President Schaeffer appointed a special committee to consider the schools' legal status. The committee recommended that each institution amend its charter to vest property rights in its respective trustees, to be held "in trust" for the Evangelical and Reformed Church. Boards should become self-perpetuating, with a majority to be ministers or members of the new denomination. Franklin & Marshall's board followed most of these recommendations, but with several significant differences: it vested all property in the trustees for the use of the college, and although a majority of the new thirty-man board were to be Evangelical and Reformed members, the new charter made no reference to clergy. It also permitted the General Alumni Association to nominate four places on the board. After a lengthy legal process, the revised charter went into effect in 1940. The moment marked a changing of the guard in terms of the board's leadership, a change underlined by election of three corporate executives: John K. Evans, '11, a vice president of General Foods; Henning W. Prentis Jr., now president of the Armstrong Cork Company; and Wayne C. Yeager, vice president of the Atlantic Refining Company.[51]

The Sesqui-Centennial Endowment Fund drive raised less than $131,000 toward its goal. The shift in the composition of the board toward men of wealth began to pay off, as more than half of this sum came from the board itself. Despite the large proportion of Lancaster students and Schaeffer's efforts to cultivate strong ties with the local community, only about $25,000 came from local alumni and citizens. Schaeffer vowed to continue to work toward the goal of achieving an endowment of $2 million within five years.[52]

Growing Apart

The emerging dominance of wealthy board members and the waning of religious tradition as a cohesive force produced an environment in which the college's different components — students, faculty, administrators, alumni, and trustees — increasingly saw themselves as competing interests. This had long been true in higher education, particularly at elite colleges and universities patronized by the wealthy, but it was relatively new at small institutions like Franklin & Marshall. The heavily polarized political environment of the 1930s further heightened tensions.

One sign of an emerging professional consciousness within the faculty was the 1933 organization of a campus chapter of the American Association of University Professors

(AAUP). Like all professional groups, the national organization sought to enhance members' ability to control conditions of and access to skilled work; its pursuit of autonomy stressed the ideal of academic freedom. Leading AAUP members at Franklin & Marshall were Paul L. Whitely of the psychology department and Barrows Dunham and Darrell Larsen of the English department. At the chapter's founding, there reportedly were eight members; two years later it had grown to twenty. As Whitely explained to a *Student Weekly* reporter, its meetings allowed faculty "a more open discussion of matters of interest" and worked to "maintain their freedom from the attempted doctrination and propaganda spreading of college administration and influential alumni."[53]

Despite the antagonism implicit in this statement, the chapter showed its good will toward the new Schaeffer administration in 1935 by organizing a series of faculty talks broadcast over local radio station WGAL. Opening with the college's alma mater as its theme song, the twenty-eight-week program featured fifteen-minute addresses in each person's area of interest, ranging from H. M .J. Klein's explanation of the "diplomatic background of the Ethiopian dispute," to Whitely's take on "the psychology of behavior." The venture was so successful, Schaeffer told the board, that other schools copied it, and it was repeated a second year.[54]

The AAUP chapter took no formal action before World War II, perhaps because it was not yet well enough established within a faculty that was divided both politically and professionally. The English department seems to have been a center of professional ambition. Under the chairmanship of S. N. Hagen, who had a Ph.D. from Johns Hopkins, the department had hired a number of promising young men with new-minted Ph.D.s from elite universities and no previous connections to Franklin & Marshall. English major Richard Altick recalled Barrows Dunham, whose Princeton Ph.D. was in philosophy, as "the central figure in a coterie of young faculty . . . whose opinions echoed those of the *New Republic*, the *Nation*, George Jean Nathan's *Smart Set*, and Mencken's *American Mercury*." From Barrows and his friends, Altick "learned most directly the bent of mind that, in my inexperienced judgement, was close to cynicism but actually was no more than rudimentary sophistication." When Dunham left for Temple University in 1937, he was replaced by Lyman Butterfield, Harvard A.B. and M.A. His specialty was eighteenth-century English literature, and Altick recalled that he "took great pains with his lectures, despite his imperfectly suppressed conviction that he was casting pearls before swine." Winthrop Nelson Francis, "a handsome man with a quiet air of assurance that bespoke what would later have been called his WASP background," had a Harvard A.B. and a Ph.D. from the University of Pennsylvania. Altick's "particular mentor" was M. Ray Adams, a Princeton Ph.D., in whose classes Altick "realized that the study of literature, properly so called — expressions of thought, sensibility, and the creative imagination distinguished by formal beauty — was a serious and endlessly engrossing business."[55]

Other teachers saw their calling less in terms of academic disciplines and more as a matter of fostering development in "average" students. Charles E. Meyers's Shakespeare courses were popular with athletes, for he was known as an easy grader. "It was a pretty well understood thing," recalled John Peifer Jr., '36, "that if you wore a coat and tie to his class and if you sat in the front row, you got an 'A.'"[56]

History department chairman H. M. J. Klein had long combined teaching with civic activism. A moderate progressive, he led a movement in the 1920s to unseat Lancaster's powerful Republican "boss" and for a time wrote a daily column for the Democratic *Lancaster Intelligencer* despite opposition from Apple and the Committee on Instruction. Klein was widely known as an entertaining and inspiring speaker and frequently spoke to local organizations. An ordained Reformed minister, he often served as a supply preacher and over the years was invariably called upon to deliver funeral orations. An interest in international affairs sparked by the First World War led him to help found Lancaster's Rotary Club. He was also a leader in the Lancaster County Historical Society and a member of the Lancaster City Planning Commission, and as president of the Lancaster Chamber of Commerce in 1933, he organized the city's participation in the National Recovery Administration. Not surprisingly, he published little in the way of scholarly work, but beginning with the *Franklin and Marshall Papers*, he composed a number of chronicles about the college and other Reformed institutions.[57]

Klein explained his philosophy of education in a 1912 lecture, which in keeping with Mercersburg tradition emphasized "the unconscious influence of personality" over pure intellect. He objected to educational specialization that gave one person the mission "to make men good," leaving by inference all the rest to simply "[make] men wise." The "best moral asset of any educational institution" he considered to be "a number of men in a faculty of real worth of character who go about their own affairs with good heart, and friendly spirit, and allow their normal life and usual nature to have whatever effect it may." In this spirit, Klein taught by eliciting student participation in class discussions. "He would always have the students stand up and read," his son Philip S. Klein recalled. "Then they'd talk about the paragraphs he had read." Many students still bore the accents of their rural Pennsylvania origins, and Klein believed that this practice gave them experience in public performance and improved their diction. His courses emphasized the historical background of current events in the 1930s with particular emphasis on the rise of Fascism.[58]

Another son, Frederic S. Klein, '23, returned to teach at the college in 1928 as a Columbia A.B.D. His interests also ranged widely. An accomplished cellist, he helped students organize the Symphonic Orchestra in 1930 and led the group for many years. It soon grew into one of the college's most prominent cultural organizations, each year offering several major concerts that premiered compositions by local musicians. For several years Frederic Klein led the Franklin & Marshall Ambassadors, a handpicked combo from the orchestra who played on the SS *Normandie*'s Christmas cruises to France. He also organized the Gramophone Society, which presented phonograph concerts, allowing students to hear "the highest types of musical compositions." Fascinated with airplanes, he sponsored the Aero Club, whose members received ground instruction from the manager of the local airport. As the sole American history instructor,

Frederic Klein developed a research seminar that used original sources, but he published little in this period.[59]

Soon after Philip Klein received his Ph.D. in history at the University of Pennsylvania in 1938, President Schaeffer offered him a job. Klein protested that his hiring would appear to be the height of nepotism, but Schaeffer replied that it was *he* who was responsible for hiring faculty — Klein's father had nothing to do with it. With Philip's arrival, wags referred to the history department as the firm of "Klein, Klein & Klein." The 1940 April Fools' issue of the *Weekly* reported that Frederic Klein had resigned to pursue his flying career: "His position on the faculty will be taken by a newcomer to the campus, Professor——— Klein." Finding the situation rather awkward, Philip took a position at Penn State in 1941.[60]

The *Student Weekly* offered occasional glimpses into tensions within the faculty. A satirical play in 1934 depicted an attempt by old-guard faculty in the English department to block curricular reforms. "You can't tell me a group of students assemble for a course because they want to!" one protests in opposing a proposed poetry seminar. A tongue-in-cheek epilogue the next week praised the faculty's successes in holding back "the onslaughts of culture" and in removing "three of the most promising junior members" over the last six years. It praised the business department for producing students who were "towering monuments to our ideal"; the psychology and education departments were ridiculed as purveyors of "delightfully doubtful so-called sciences." "A Letter Home" revealed the lightness of the typical student's workload. Some teachers "are real finnecky and make us study," the writer noted, but he had been "lucky enough" to take two history courses. One English course had made him work, but he'd avoided that this semester by registering early.[61]

Such tensions were rarer in the sciences, where many faculty had arrived with Ph.D.s already in hand. Some, like James M. Darlington, '30, returned to their alma mater after graduate work at major research universities.[62]

Faculty resentment of the administration can be inferred from repeated official pronouncements — against smoking in class, for example, or reminders to enforce rules regarding class attendance and complaints about letting classes run over into chapel period. In 1938 Schaeffer "expressed the feeling and conviction that the College Administration was not given the proper co-operation by the faculty as a group." He pointed to faculty who ignored administrative memos and neglected to go through the personnel department when hiring students. The faculty was also divided over the practice of declaring school holidays after big football victories. Paul Whitely introduced a motion to discontinue the custom; provoking heated debate and a 17–17 deadlock that was broken by President Schaeffer's negative vote.[63]

Some students demonstrated their own disaffection with the conservative establishment. Student journalists championed liberal causes of the day, particularly free speech and pacifism. A characteristic editorial in 1935 condemned attempts to censor student newspapers for "the priggishness, stupidity, and fear of truth and independence that too often lurks beneath the skim of culture that covers an educator's mind."

Following a trend on many college campuses, opinion at mid-decade was strongly antiwar. In 1937 several hundred students attended a peace rally organized by the Franklin Club, the Student Senate, and the Lancaster Emergency Peace Campaign Committee. Students attending a 1939 peace assembly pledged to refuse to fight in a war on foreign soil. Editorials throughout the decade registered growing dismay at the rise of Fascism in Europe, but most strongly rejected any idea of military response.[64]

Many students' religious attitudes reflected the Reformed Church's own cosmopolitanism. More than half of the class of 1941, for example, chose John Noss's World Religions course to fulfill their senior religion requirement. But their tolerance clashed with the rising tide of fundamentalism in the surrounding community, reflected in the 1933 founding of Lancaster Bible College. *Student Weekly* columnist D. B. Bucher regretted that "we on College Hill" were thought of as "'irreligious,' atheistic, or 'agnostic'" merely because they did not accept the literal truth of biblical stories like Jonah and the whale. Bucher defended the college's ecumenism. "The whole world is broken up into denominations and sects," he pointed out. "At least our religion is characterized by a tolerance which permits Jews, Catholics, and Protestants to mingle freely on our campus with little or no friction over religious matters."[65]

Widening political differences within the college community came into vivid relief in the spring of 1940, when it was announced that H. W. Prentis Jr. would be the principal commencement speaker. President of the conservative National Association of Manufacturers, Prentis had gained a national reputation as an outspoken critic of the New Deal. *Weekly* columnist John McCandless called the choice "unfortunate" because of Prentis's reputation as an exponent "of a philosophy of business and government which is rapidly being discarded by many of the leading educators, economists, and philosophers of our day." Prentis's pronouncements might please influential alumni, but they hurt the college's reputation and purpose as a progressive liberal arts college. This purpose included, according to McCandless, training students to "be righteously incensed that men like Mr. Prentis are allowed to dodge [their] responsibilities with a lot of loose talk about 'free enterprise' and the 'American way of life.'"[66]

When the *Student Weekly* issue containing this column appeared, faculty adviser W. E. Weisgerber ordered printers not to mail the usual copies to advertisers, outside subscribers, and other college papers. A faculty committee reprimanded McCandless and censured the *Weekly*'s editor, Robert M. Landis, for allowing the article to appear. Claiming that he did not want to continue writing a column without the freedom "to express [his] personal opinions freely," McCandless had already resigned from the staff. A proposal to establish faculty oversight was quickly dropped when the rest of the staff threatened to resign en masse. Landis vowed to continue the paper's policy "of free expression within the bounds of good taste." The issue of censorship re-emerged later in the year when business professor Harold Fischer confiscated and burned pamphlets being distributed on campus by alumnus J. Granville Eddy, the local Communist candidate for Congress. Landis protested that Fischer seemed to think students lacked the maturity to evaluate the principles of a recognized political party.[67]

In contrast, a group of students led by Floyd Worley, president of the Student Senate, organized the Prentis for President Club and urged him to run in 1940. The *Weekly* reported that one student had left school because he objected to being taught by "Communist propagandists." The range of student opinion was suggested by a straw poll taken on the eve of the 1940 election. Some 61 percent of students supported Republican Wendell Wilkie, with 34 percent for Franklin Delano Roosevelt and 4 percent for Socialist Norman Thomas. Not surprisingly, two-thirds of fraternity men went Republican, while "unorganized" students were somewhat more evenly divided: 55 percent Republican, 35 percent Democrat, and 10 percent Socialist. An exception was the Jewish fraternity Zeta Beta Tau, 85 percent of whose members supported Roosevelt. Similarly, Frederic Klein's history students divided 31 percent in favor of military action against Germany, 44 percent for aid short of war, and 24 percent for complete isolation from the conflict.[68]

Some of the most radical students were associated with religious groups. In 1940 the Student Christian Association organized a series, "The College Man in the Community," which hosted speakers like Joseph Gant, a "Negro ministerial student" who discussed race relations in Lancaster. The association's president, John McCandless, organized an intercollegiate conference in Lancaster featuring Howard Thurman, dean of Howard University. Influenced by the Ashram philosophy, a number of students established a cooperative house off campus.[69]

Revival of Student Life

Under Franklin & Marshall's financial constraints in the early 1930s, students often complained about a lack of outside speakers and social occasions on campus. After mid-decade, there was a resurgence of activity. As part of his program to publicize the college, Schaeffer instituted an annual concert by a noted musician. The first, by violinist Albert Spalding, drew a sellout crowd, which Schaeffer described as "the most colorful audience Hensel Hall has ever seen." Several bequests allowed the college to expand programming of prominent visitors. In 1937 H. M. North Jr. left $25,000 to fund lectures on law or allied subjects. The following year the Mary Kate Snyder Fund was established to support assembly programs. Among visitors to campus, the most popular was a Hampton Institute quartette featuring folk music and spirituals in honor of Negro Education Week.[70]

In 1937 the board instituted an additional arts activities fee of $4, to ensure funding for the Green Room Club, the Symphony Orchestra, and the Glee Club, for which students received tickets to every performance. The proposal argued that the fee secured the financial base of each group and maintained "certain cultural values" that should be part of a liberal arts environment. The system worked so well that it was expanded several years later to fund a series of all-college dances and a subscription to the *Oriflamme*, which had nearly expired for lack of subscriptions. The new program scored a coup in 1938 when it brought the nationally renowned Paul Whiteman

Orchestra to Lancaster during homecoming. The group put on the same full-dress evening concert that they would shortly give at Carnegie Hall, and to everyone's delight Whiteman appeared at halftime of the football game to direct the college band while his vocalist, Joan Edwards, led singing of the alma mater. The good feeling engendered during the visit was capped by Whiteman's letter to Frederic Klein, who had organized the appearance: "The boys and I decided," he wrote, "that if we were going back to school again, we'd all pick F.&M."[71]

Also adding to campus intellectual life and attracting public attention to the college were lectures sponsored by the Lancaster branch of the American Association for the Advancement of Science, which several faculty members had helped found in 1934. For many years the group brought in an impressive list of nationally known scientists to speak at monthly meetings in Hensel Hall. Its membership had to be capped at nine hundred, the seating capacity of the hall. Later in the decade a special relationship with the college's Porter Scientific Society enabled students to join for fifty cents.[72]

After a period of relative quiescence in the early 1930s, enthusiasm for freshman regulations revived in mid-decade. The Druids continued to claim enforcement responsibilities, but soon after Schaeffer's arrival he expressly forbade paddling of wayward freshmen. The now-traditional Pajama Parade was observed each year with growing abandon, as freshmen escalated from proposing to young women at the direction of upperclassmen to grabbing and kissing any young female who happened to be on the street. In 1935 the *Weekly* reported that freshmen "lived up to the numerous stories they had heard about what a good pajama parade really should be like." By the end of the decade, freshmen invaded stores and restaurants in search of prey. After speeches, songs, and cheers on the courthouse steps, freshmen had taken to mobbing downtown theaters to gain free entrance. Eventually theater owners distributed free tickets to prevent the attacks. Then, too, it had become customary to begin the evening by forcing freshmen to run a gauntlet, known as the "bake oven." First running between Hensel Hall and Campus House, it later extended back to Biesecker Gymnasium. In 1940 the *Weekly* complained about the conduct of both freshmen and upperclassmen: the gauntlet's "dangers to freshman limbs" were deemed "not worth the brief delight it brings to a few sadistic upperclassmen," while "the night-gown spectacle" had degenerated into "a wild mass of raiding parties, foraging for squaling [*sic*] young womanhood." Several weeks later, after Druids injured several freshmen, the faculty disbanded the organization and suspended freshman regulations for the year.[73]

Student pranks also became increasingly destructive. After it was first painted on Halloween 1933, the de Peyster statue bore much of the brunt of student attention. Even after its move to the southern end of campus with the completion of the new library, the practice of painting the statue in some imaginative fashion was by 1939 defended by the *Student Weekly* as "a yearly occurrence, pregnant with tradition and meaning to the entire F. and M. Student Body." When A. H. Rothermel deplored their lack of respect, students dismissed him as "puritanical" and claimed that the custom was needed at a college so sorely lacking in traditions. On the eve of big football games students organized "Expeditionary Forces" to paint up their opponents' campuses. The administration generally treated such escapades leniently, but when they extended to cutting down a tree in Buchanan Park, Schaeffer expelled the students responsible.[74]

Aware of campus trends, Franklin & Marshall students quickly joined the goldfish-swallowing fad sweeping America in 1939. It began on March 3, when several Harvard students received national publicity for swallowing goldfish. Franklin & Marshall jumped on the bandwagon on March 20, when junior Frank Pope accepted the bet of Karl Hildebrecht, proprietor of Hildy's Tavern, and swallowed three fish. The feat was probably planned, for it was recorded by an *Intelligencer Journal* photographer. Asked why he'd done it, Pope said, "I did it to show up those Harvard bums and sissies." More students came forward to consign ever-larger numbers of fish to their fates, until the biology department was able to persuade them that eating goldfish alive was not only cruel but could make them sick.[75]

As public opinion grew less tolerant of youthful high jinks, local board members instructed Romance language professor V. W. Dippell to end his customary practice of bailing out students who ran afoul of the police. The *Weekly* noted that he had long served as a go-between with local authorities, helping to recover stolen properties that "often [had found] their way into dormitory rooms and fraternity houses." Declining forbearance in combination with student readiness to assert their "traditional" rights sparked increasingly violent clashes with Lancaster police. In fact, students came to think of these "rowbottoms," or spontaneous riots, as traditional accompaniments of big football weekends. When city leaders banned the Pajama Parade in 1941, students held a bonfire and pep rally on campus. Defying faculty restrictions on hazing, fraternity men smuggled in paddles and tried to shunt freshmen into an impromptu gauntlet. Later rowdy students on College Avenue and Frederick Street protested what they saw as unwarranted interference with their rights; they began by pulling fire alarms to attract the police, and their activity escalated into a full-scale riot as some attacked a police cruiser with paint bombs, broke street lights with rocks, and opened fire hydrants.[76]

The later 1930s were a golden age for Franklin & Marshall athletics, when its football teams excelled, as well as those in basketball, wrestling, cross-country, swimming, soccer, tennis, track, and golf. The 1935–1936 year was so successful that the Lancaster Chamber of Commerce, the Manufacturers' Association, and the Foremen's Club united to give a banquet in honor of all teams, the first such occasion since the heady days of 1889. President Schaeffer was an ardent booster and often accompanied teams to away games. The college won conference championships in most sports during the period, and during 1938–1939 had a combined record of sixty wins, seventeen losses, and three ties. That year athletic director Charles Mayser was elected president of the Wrestling Coaches Association of America; his squad placed fourth in National Intercollegiate Wrestling Association Championships held in Lancaster. The football team capped the decade with an upset victory over Dartmouth College in 1940. The triumph was somewhat marred when a few rowdy "camp followers" left Hanover "badly smeared with yellow paint."[77]

The Green Room Club continued to confer distinction upon the college with four ambitious productions a year, playing to capacity audiences from the city as well as the college. Membership in the club was limited to those who had participated in at least three productions; members selected plays and set policy, while Darrell Larsen directed and designed each production. The group's challenging 1938–1939 program — Edward Wool's *Libel*, Sinclair Lewis's *It Can't Happen Here*, George Bernard Shaw's *Androcles and the Lion*, and Shakespeare's *Twelfth Night* — attracted a full-page story in Philadelphia's *Public Ledger*. *Time* took note the following year of the club's production of John Webster's seldom-seen seventeenth-century drama *The Duchess of Malfi*. Titled "Braver than Broadway," the review commended the troupe's courage in taking on a work that had daunted even Orson Welles. The Theatre Collection of the New York Public Library asked for a set of production photographs for its archive. Larsen directed summer stock in Michigan, taking along some of his best students, including Franklin Schaffner, '41, later to become a prominent Hollywood producer and director.[78]

Facing New Challenges

With Fackenthal Library's completion in 1938, President Schaeffer noted that Franklin & Marshall now possessed "a well-rounded physical plant" sufficient for an enrollment of 850. Despite progress made under his administration, he repeatedly warned the board of future challenges. As enrollments reached "the point of saturation as governed by its physical plant," the college could look for increases in income only through an enlarged endowment.[79]

Moreover, Schaeffer worried that growth of public higher education in the decade threatened ruinous competition for small independent schools like Franklin & Marshall. In 1937 he warned against initiatives to establish junior colleges in the areas from which most of the college's students came. Even worse, from his perspective, was the prospect that Pennsylvania's teachers colleges, descendants of nineteenth-century normal schools, would be empowered to offer general baccalaureate programs. Calling this "a distinct danger to the liberal arts colleges in Pennsylvania," Schaeffer joined with the Association of College Presidents of Pennsylvania to fight legislation authorizing the change. Later, he reported to the board that the Department of Public Instruction was trying to accomplish the same end by other means, by spending millions on a building program at teachers colleges. He feared that if enrollments declined, "these added facilities, built and maintained at State expense," would be used as an excuse to convert the schools into baccalaureate colleges.[80]

As the 1940s began, such concerns paled in comparison with the deepening shadow of world war. Beyond general fears, leaders of all-male colleges and universities worried that the country's slow but inexorable movement toward war would empty their campuses. Faced with what seemed a threat to its very survival, Franklin & Marshall's leaders worked with other colleges and embraced an unprecedented degree of government involvement in the college's affairs.

The first danger signal came in mid-1940 with creation of the first peacetime draft in the nation's history. Franklin & Marshall opened its academic year with an enrollment of 959, an all-time high, and the draft affected only men between twenty-one and thirty, but Schaeffer feared that many students would enlist rather than wait to be drafted. A faculty committee was established to offer advice on selective service issues. Despite growing sentiment in favor of military preparation, the Student Senate rejected a faculty proposal to substitute a patriotic parade for the annual Pajama Parade. The senate insisted that doing so would "break a strong thread in the pattern of F. and M. Tradition."[81]

Seeking government funding, members of the Aero Club had persuaded college authorities to participate in a flight-training program under the Civil Aeronautics Authority (CAA). The campus CAA program, previously available only at engineering schools, offered ground school and flying preparations for licensing examinations under Frederic Klein's direction. During the summer of 1940, the college set up a flight classroom in the unfinished third floor of the Keiper Liberal Arts Building. With aid from the National Youth Administration and the U.S. Navy, the Aero Club obtained a full-size Corsair biplane, dismantled it piece by piece at the airport, and reassembled it inside the classroom. In the fall the faculty agreed to give two credits for an aeronautics course "for the duration of the emergency." After the college was certified as an Advanced Ground School the following spring, a further four credits were approved.[82]

The year 1941 was a time of turmoil everywhere but proved especially trying for Franklin & Marshall. In January, Schaeffer attended a series of conferences of higher education associations at which the future of the academic exemption was a major concern. By the beginning of the second semester, fifty students had dropped out to enter military service. Looking ahead to the graduation of a large senior class and the likelihood that the draft age would be lowered to eighteen, Schaeffer saw financial crisis on the horizon. The college depended heavily on student fees for operating income — they represented some 63 percent of revenues in 1940–1941. Early in April, he confided his fears to Fackenthal. Pennsylvania's governor had just offered Schaeffer an appointment in a war-related program, and he suggested that "retiring from the college for a time" might help save money. But Fackenthal "seriously objected" to the idea, and Schaeffer dropped it.[83]

A few days later, on April 6, 1941, Schaeffer died without warning, victim of a cerebral hemorrhage. After funeral services two days later, an emergency meeting of the board asked H. M. J. Klein, "the senior member of the faculty," to serve as acting president. According to a colleague, Klein was "universally known as a peacemaker," and he announced at his first faculty meeting that he hoped "to continue as usual." But he soon faced several contentious issues. At that meeting the faculty responded to pressure from "certain" board members to revise the curriculum to instill in students greater appreciation for "democracy and liberty." The faculty's Committee on Curriculum defended the present curriculum and unanimously endorsed the principle of academic freedom: "The principle of freedom of teaching would be violated by any attempt to prescribe, through syllabi or in any other way, what a professor shall teach in the courses for whose conduct he alone is responsible." However, the committee offered to schedule assembly lectures "on the origin and growth of liberty."[84]

Klein also had to fill an unusual number of faculty vacancies created by sudden death, resignation, calls to military service, and serious illness on the part of longtime teachers. With a few exceptions, college presidents typically hired new faculty in this period, and Apple and Schaeffer had handled all personnel matters with the board's Committee on Instruction conferring perfunctory approval after the fact. But in this, as in many matters, Fackenthal asserted an increasingly prominent role. As the college's greatest benefactor, he was not an easy man to contradict, nor was Klein eager to do so.[85]

When longtime English professor Charles Meyers died suddenly in July, Fackenthal insisted that the son of an old friend be hired in his place. "I know nothing about the qualifications of this young man," Fackenthal wrote Klein, "but I am sure that his father would not seek the appointment for him if he thought he was not qualified." Noting that hiring him as an instructor at a salary of $1,800 "would save [the college] a lot of money," Fackenthal concluded, "His appointment would be specially pleasing to me."[86]

It would, however, be anathema to the Department of English, which was eager to hire Richard Altick, a star alumnus who had just completed his doctorate at Penn with a number of impressive publications already to his credit. Various faculty members predicted "an open revolt" if the other man was appointed. Klein and English chair S. N. Hagen drove to Fackenthal's estate near Easton, where Hagen presented a petition requesting Altick's appointment signed by all available members of the department. According to Fackenthal, during their interview Hagen "made himself disagreeable" by arguing that "it was in the province of the faculty . . . to fill these vacancies, whereas [Fackenthal believed it was] in the trustees." Ultimately, Klein decided "on [his] own responsibility" as acting president to offer the position to Altick. The new faculty member was "recognized as one of the most brilliant students [the college had] ever had," Klein explained to Fackenthal, and "in every respect" was the "best equipped man for the position."[87]

But more than academic qualification was involved in his decision. As Klein told Fackenthal, he was "trying to avoid a public scandal in the interest of everybody concerned." Fackenthal's candidate not only lacked an advanced degree but was notorious within the community for his "immoral and objectionable" character. Klein attempted to soften his announcement by assuring Fackenthal, "You have been so fine in your whole attitude toward the College, that I do not want to see it marred at this stage by insisting on an appointment which I know would be resented by the college community." Fackenthal acquiesced, but on the basis of the morality question, not the faculty's right to make hiring decisions.[88]

Because of an epidemic of infantile paralysis, Franklin & Marshall opened its 1941–1942 year two weeks late at the request of the state Board of Health. In the summer, as it became clear that enrollments would be down substantially, a special faculty meeting decided to make another round of recruiting visits in the immediate area. Despite these efforts, enrollment was down more than 10 percent. Klein attributed this decline to the draft, enlistments, and increased "opportunities for lucrative positions" in the booming war economy. His opening address stressed that education was just as important a form of service as joining the military or working in industry: "We must train intelligent citizens and the statesmen of years to come."[89]

A Professional Administrator

A search committee headed by board vice president William H. Keller began work by giving "earnest thought" to the kind of person needed in the present "chaotic" times. The group, which included New Yorkers Frank Fackenthal and Paul Kieffer, agreed that despite their own "very happy experience" with Schaeffer, reliance on businessmen might not be best in the long run. They decided to seek a man with experience in educational administration and "sympathy for scholarship."[90]

Theodore A. Distler had been dean at Lafayette College for seven years when he became president of Franklin & Marshall. The first president since John W. Nevin who was not an alumnus, he earned bachelor's and master's degrees in business administration from New York University. He taught public speaking and worked in admissions and student services there until his move to Lafayette. Frank Fackenthal, a golf partner, had suggested he apply for the position at Franklin & Marshall. The search committee commended Distler's "firm" and "sound convictions concerning the education of youth": "He has a very agreeable personality, is reputed to be a good speaker and to know whereof he speaks." At forty-two he was widely reported to be the youngest man to hold the presidency, but that distinction actually belonged to E. V. Gerhart, who had been thirty-seven at his election in 1854.[91]

The college community could derive little pleasure from Distler's selection, coinciding as it did with the loss of its greatest benefactor. On October 10, en route to the special board meeting to ratify the decision, B. F. Fackenthal Jr. was killed in an automobile accident. In shock, the board met briefly to unanimously affirm Distler's appointment.[92]

Distler took office on December 1, 1941. Four days later he appeared at his first board meeting, at which the principal business was election of New York attorney Paul Kieffer as its president. Two days later, the Japanese attack on Pearl Harbor plunged the nation again into world war. The following morning, Richard Altick, then in his first semester of teaching, "felt called upon to make some rather perfunctory remarks" to his students about the need to maintain a sense of perspective. It was important "to maintain, even in times like these, some receptivity to a beauty that transcended and would outlast the terrible stresses of the moment." Most of his colleagues made similar comments, he recalled. He noted, "None of us could have been very persuasive, especially when we saw several vacant chairs in the classroom and knew that their usual occupants must be downtown, waiting in line outside the recruiting station."

Distler recalled that seventeen or eighteen students enlisted that day. The debate team was hit particularly hard when three of its best members left immediately.[93]

The reality of the war was driven home a few days later, when word arrived that one of the first Americans killed in the Pearl Harbor attack was Lee Fox Jr., an early graduate of the college's CAA training program. Fox had visited campus shortly before leaving for the Pacific, Frederic Klein recalled, "dressed in clean and shining Navy 'whites,' with the coveted gold wings of a Navy pilot, the perfect ideal for every flight student."[94]

Distler proved a particularly fortunate choice for president, for his energy, skills in administration and public relations, and wide professional connections matched the needs of the time. Though he had no connection to Franklin & Marshall's traditions, he ensured that the college survived the upheavals of the next decade. Soon after the declaration of war, he sent a telegram to President Roosevelt pledging the college's "whole-hearted support in this crisis": "We stand ready to serve in whatever program you shall decide upon for the colleges and universities of the nation." It would take the federal government and the armed forces many months to settle on higher education's role in the war effort, while enrollments continued to slide. Throughout 1942, Distler threw himself energetically into the business of ensuring that his college was included in whatever programs emerged.[95]

Coming to their new positions with experience at other institutions, both Distler and Kieffer brought governance and administration into line with trends elsewhere. Hosting an informal dinner for the board at Lancaster's Hamilton Club in January 1942, Kieffer outlined his philosophy of governance. In the broadest terms, he believed that college boards should represent "a cross section of the community from which the institutions draw their students and to which their graduates return." The trustees' function was to "to be concerned as to whether the college [was] continuing in the tradition of what [they believed] to be a liberal arts college." He defined liberal education as "the acquisition and the refinement of standards of values — all sorts of values — physical, emotion, aesthetic and spiritual." Such an ideal, he noted "is not different from what Dr. Stahr used to teach us in Ethics — that the proper aim of man in the course of his education, as throughout his whole life, is the perfection of his being." Despite pressures for more practical training, he believed such a goal was all the more essential when freedom was being challenged throughout the world.[96]

Kieffer wanted to reduce the personal authority of the board president. Following current practices in nonprofit management, he argued that the president should function merely as leader of the board and recommended creating an executive committee to act for the board between its semiannual meetings. Moreover, he asserted that the board could not "interfere with details of the teaching even if we were competent to do so." A proponent of free speech, he opposed previous board attempts "to bar certain discussions at the college."[97]

For his part, when Distler first met with faculty on December 10, he asked them to elect five of their own to serve as a war planning committee to help him make inevitable wartime changes. In September 1942 he recommended that faculty elect a committee to evaluate candidates for honorary degrees and, most importantly, to "co-operate" with the president in future decisions about hiring, promotion, and dismissal of faculty above the rank of instructor. Although occurring with little fanfare, creation of this committee represented a significant change in the governance of the college by recognizing the faculty's right to participate in hiring.[98]

Distler also created a new administrative position, director of admissions and dean of freshmen, moving J. Shober Barr from the physical education department. Distler argued that the college had needed for some time "the co-ordination of its enrollment activities as well as a more efficient supervision of freshmen after they enter college." He undoubtedly hoped that Barr's energy and charisma would help in the increasingly difficult process of recruiting and retaining students.[99]

In January 1942 Distler joined a thousand other college and university presidents at a meeting organized by the U.S. Office of Education and the joint National Committee on Education and Defense of the American Council on Education and the National Education Association. A representative from the War Department promised to try to disrupt education as little as possible. Educators in turn pledged their institutions' "total strength" to the war effort. They endorsed a series of measures to ensure the most effective use of individual abilities and institutional resources, which included a system of selective service with deferments for premedical, predental, and pretheological students. Educators also sought to discourage an unseemly scramble for federal programs.[100]

As they had during the First World War, educators emphasized their institutions' dual function to provide training in technical skills increasingly essential for modern warfare and to cultivate humanistic values needed after victory. Although the latter was central to the traditional mission of liberal arts colleges, it was clear that the military was more interested in the former. As a consequence, wartime demands for practical skills placed further emphasis on the college's already strong programs in the sciences.

Following the convention's resolutions, Distler immediately moved to accelerate Franklin & Marshall's academic program by adding two six-week summer sessions, which allowed students to graduate more quickly. For summer sessions only, women were permitted to enroll in the college for the first time. As faculty members began to deal with implications of the accelerated pace, they realized that the comprehensive examination program would be one of the first casualties of war, as it was all but impossible to administer with students entering and leaving at any of four points during the year. The faculty reluctantly agreed to suspend the examinations "during the period of Emergency." The faculty also accepted the assumption that, whenever possible, college courses should contribute "to present national defense." The War Planning Committee asked the Committee on Curriculum , with general faculty input, to identify where "teachable Elements of Defense" could be inserted into regular courses and where special defense-training courses should be added. The committee proposed courses in economics and business, history, astronomy, languages, sociology, and even theater — for which Larsen offered to teach how to make camouflage. New elective courses were introduced in aeronautics, military accounting, communication, photography, and chemistry — including military pyrotechnics, industrial materials, and war gases. Czech-born sociology professor Jerry Neprash offered to teach Russian, and religion professor John Noss, who had grown up in Japan as the child of missionaries, taught Japanese. In addition to regular college courses, the Planning Committee expanded night courses under the U.S. Office of Education's Engineering Science, and Management War Training Program (ESMWT). Working with local business leaders, instructors of these offered training in engineering, science, management, and defense to more than 1,500 employees in the area's industries over the next two years.[101]

At Distler's suggestion, departments not involved in war work offered noncredit liberal arts courses to local citizens "interested in improving their intellectual and cultural status." He explained to the board that the departments hoped to find "a just balance against the emphasis upon scientific and technological knowledge in wartime." During the 1942–1943 academic year, some 143 Lancastrians enrolled in eighteen evening courses; among the most popular were Philip Harry's course in Spanish, Whitely's in psychology, and Larsen's in modern drama.[102]

Many educators called for a comprehensive program through which colleges and universities provided training for the military as well as civilian war work. But both the army and navy seemed in no hurry to go beyond existing reserve programs. The V-1 Naval Reserve program, for example, allowed enlistees to complete at least two years of college; subsequently, if they passed a navy examination, they might enter active duty as aviation students or go on to complete their degrees before entering officers training. College leaders kept a careful eye on planning for reserve programs, and in March Distler called a special faculty meeting to approve curricular changes necessary to offer a V-1 program. Its heavy emphasis on mathematics and physical sciences required shifting some faculty out of their usual fields and hiring several new temporary instructors. Athletics were cut, to free physical education instructors to work with recruits. During 1942 the college participated in several other reserve programs, including the U.S. Army Enlisted Reserve Corps, the U.S. Air Force Enlisted Reserve, the U.S. Navy V-7 programs and the U.S. Marine Corps Reserve. Students who enlisted were placed on inactive duty, subject to call as needed, while they continued their education.[103]

The Aero Club's prewar enterprise proved of inestimable value to the college. In June the navy contracted with the college's CAA flight-training program to provide beginning and advanced training through the War Training Service, in connection with the navy's V-5 program. Over the next two years, the aeronautics department gave three months of ground and flight training to 687 men. At the beginning, the civilian instructors were largely left to their own devices, but finding that cadets preferred a military environment, the instructors "purchased summer khaki uniforms, devised insignia, appointed temporary officers, and provided the first wartime atmosphere on the campus." The college was paid to furnish instruction and room and board for about ninety cadets at a time. They were housed in several dormitories and a former fraternity house on College Avenue and messed in the lunchroom on the lower level of the Campus House, where Mrs. Eura Shipley, known by all as "Ma" Shipley, served "the generous helpings of home-cooked food for which she was famous on the campus." Profits paid to construct a more suitable cafeteria on the upper floor. By employing several faculty members, at a time of declining enrollments, and by providing income, the program helped the college stay in the black.[104]

It soon became clear that Franklin & Marshall's limited dormitory accommodations and lack of a student infirmary put it at a disadvantage in seeking larger programs. The Student Senate had lobbied for on-campus medical care for some time, but the board acted only when compelled by a shortage of local physicians and the need to secure military programs. In the fall, it approved an infirmary plan funded through a new student fee. Alumni in the medical and dental professions helped obtain equipment, and Mrs. Alice Distler organized a woman's auxiliary of faculty, board, and alumni wives. The college's infirmary opened the following spring in the Phi Kappa Tau chapter house.[105]

As spring 1942 turned into summer, Distler and most educational leaders were ever more frustrated by Washington's inaction. Most existing reserve programs applied only to men already in college, which educators feared would arouse popular resentment. Nor could they sustain enrollments indefinitely, as most student deferments were likely to be eliminated. College and university leaders sought to influence federal policies through their associations, but if that failed, many were not above making separate deals for war-related training programs.[106]

Distler assured the board in May that he was "[bending] every effort" to be included in war programs. Repeatedly, he expressed his fear that schools like Franklin & Marshall would be kept from fulfilling their primary mission to prepare leaders for "the world reconstruction which must follow the war." He deplored "the present policy of withdrawing from the colleges a large proportion of the capable youth of the nation" and hoped that the new War Manpower Commission would reassess priorities. If present trends continued, the postwar nation faced a "shortage of skilled and educated young men who are fitted to perform the multifarious duties required by a torn, exhausted world."[107]

He expressed similar sentiments in his inaugural address on May 16, insisting that Franklin & Marshall had a "nobler" purpose beyond that of preparing young men for "the horrible but necessary task of engaging in war": "If we, as a nation, merely achieve great military victories and ultimately bring our foes to their knees, we shall have achieved only the lightest part of our task. Our real work shall then begin. We shall then have to love our enemies, to bind their wounds and heal their sick. . . . We must recognize that our most profound duty is to the world that will follow the peace." Distler's installation was a modest affair, held in conjunction with an early commencement. At his request, planned ceremonies had been scaled back; the college sent formal notices to educational institutions throughout the country with the request that no official delegates be sent. "There was a war-time atmosphere about the whole commencement occasion," H. M. J. Klein recalled, as everyone was aware that nearly all the 150 graduates would soon be in active service; four alumni had already died in action or during flight training.[108]

By September no national plan was yet forthcoming, while the college's enrollment fell to 668. At combined opening exercises and commencement, Distler urged students to work hard as they awaited clarification of colleges' wartime role: "Loafing, wasting time, inefficiency, indifference — these things are out. You are here on special duty, and you have exactly the same obligations as you would were you in uniform and in camp or aboard ship. . . . Our goal must be that of being of the maximum usefulness to a country that is fighting for its existence." During the year, 34 new students enrolled, 62 graduated at midyear, and an additional 235 left, most because they were called up or were drafted, as the draft age was lowered to eighteen and the army closed out its Enlisted Reserve Corps. Students who had joined thinking they would be able to finish college learned that they would be called up in February. Because premedical students were deferred in the first year of the war, their proportion of the total enrollment grew to 27 percent in the summer sessions of 1942 and to 36 percent the following spring.[109]

Distler conducted an increasingly frenetic correspondence with leaders of the educational associations engaged in negotiations with the military. He admonished them not to forget the smaller colleges. "I think we are in somewhat the same position as the so-called small business men of the country," he wrote Hamilton College president W. H. Cowley in October. Distler worried about "the attitude of the government and of the larger universities, both private and state" and thought it essential for small colleges to "take an aggressive position, not necessarily in their defense, but rather as a demonstration of the role which they [could] play." In the meantime he investigated special programs. "I carried my resignation in my pocket," Distler later reported, "because I turned down programs that could have been of some help but that in my estimation and in that of the faculty with whom I consulted were not good programs for us." Early in December he wrote Haverford College president Felix Morley, a member of the principal committee working with the military: "I have still made no effort to get a special program, hoping that the general program might soon be announced. What is your opinion as to the wisdom of waiting?"[110]

Morley replied that he was meeting in a few days with the War Manpower Commission: "[It] may result in getting through certain special programs designed particularly for small colleges which would be as much to your benefit as to ours." Four days later the War Department and the U.S. Navy announced new collegiate training programs. The army program was narrowly focused on technical training, but the navy's College Training Program (V-12), aimed at training officer candidates, included a wider range of liberal arts courses. Distler immediately dispatched Shober Barr to Washington to see Barr's old friend William W. Behrens, a Lancaster native who was involved in the V-12 program. Captain Behrens became the college's chief contact and advocate within the U.S. Navy.[111]

There followed several hectic months of planning and filling out extensive questionnaires, demanding countless hours of work by administrative officers and many faculty. One of the most difficult tasks was finding adequate space to house and feed trainees. In late December, Distler explained to the board's new executive committee that facilities for four hundred to seven hundred could be secured by using dormitories, fraternity houses, and academy buildings. He warned trustees that references to the academy must be "held in the strictest confidence," for word had not yet gotten out about plans to close it at the end of the academic year. After more than forty-five years as its head, E. M. Hartman was in poor health. Most board members agreed that "the academy was built about Dr. Hartman and the question of continuing or discontinuing the Academy would have to be faced eventually," but three local trustees opposed closing it. Hartman stayed on for several years, winding up academy business and organizing its records, and retired officially in 1945. The main academy building was renamed Hartman Hall in his honor.[112]

The college's sense of urgency peaked in late February 1943, when seventy-eight students, mostly members of the U.S. Army Enlisted Reserve, marched in a body to the train station to leave for formal induction ceremonies in Harrisburg. They were accompanied by the college band, Naval Aviation Cadets, faculty, and many other students, nearly all of whom were in other reserve units. Distler assured the inductees that the college's doors "will be wide open to you when you come back," and Darrell Larsen distributed a parting gift purchased out of the Faculty Flower Fund, a gift that contained a New Testament, a book, and cigarettes. "It was a very emotional scene," recalled one student. John Peifer Jr., director of the band, remembered that only about a dozen members were left in the band after the inductees boarded the train: "I don't recall who the bass drummer was, but his brother was leaving. I was standing there and playing the trumpet. I looked at him, and he started to cry, I started to cry, the whole band started. Here were all these guys gone."[113]

Finally, in March the navy announced that Franklin & Marshall had been "approved for inspection and possible negotiation of contract." In April official notice arrived that the college was one of 155 institutions selected for the U.S Navy College Training Program. Franklin & Marshall paid for extensive renovations to secure the contract, such as converting the Chi Phi chapter house to a navy dispensary and sick bay. To oversee the renovations, the board finally agreed to add the position of superintendent of grounds and buildings, first filled by Walter H. Doner. During the spring the campus bustled as the Campus House acquired a new cafeteria on the upper floor and a kitchen, post office, and canteen with soda fountain on the lower level. A campus bookshop that had opened the previous fall on the first floor of Diagnothian Hall expanded into a general store, with a barber shop for trainees. Renovations to the Academy Building provided a mess hall, administrative offices, and dormitories for the V-12 program (see fig. 4). The big eastern room in the library was turned into a classroom for the required engineering drawing course. Civilian students were housed in the seminary dormitory and the co-op house. Even the school calendar was transformed, with three sixteen-week terms beginning in March, July, and November.[114]

FIGURE 4 *Navy cadets in the V-5 and V-12 programs ate meals at one of two mess halls, which were located in both the old (East Hall) and new (Hartman Hall) academy buildings. Franklin & Marshall College, Archives and Special Collections. College Archives Photograph Collection.*

Arrival of the first wave of 552 V-12 trainees in July 1943 made for a dramatic shift in campus atmosphere. They overwhelmed the civilian student body of 156, composed of those under eighteen, those deferred because of premedical and pretheological studies, and those rejected for physical reasons. Only one in five trainees had attended Franklin & Marshall before, and in many ways the scene prefigured the postwar college. Trainees were selected on the basis of nationwide examinations; most had never been to college before. The student body represented in the first year twenty-three states, and in the second thirty-eight states, the District of Columbia, and Puerto Rico. Even so, more than three-quarters came from Pennsylvania, New York, and New Jersey. The greatest element of diversity came from those transferred from active service. Distler noted that the presence of men who had "lived in foxholes on Guadalcanal, who [had] been torpedoed off Brazil or Anzio, who [had] participated in the invasion of Saipan, made us feel very close to the war, and [gave the college] added confidence that [its] work [was] a vital contribution to the cause."[115]

Military routine dominated campus life under direction of a commanding officer, five other officers, and nineteen enlisted men. Beginning with 6:00 A.M. reveille and calisthenics, trainees attended seven hours of classes and physical training each day. They were restricted to campus at all times except for leaves on alternate weekends. Even without military discipline, the newcomers were an exceptionally hardworking group, especially the more than one-quarter who were premedical and predental students hoping to qualify for further professional training. Distler described them as "high calibre students who [tended] to elevate the general scholastic level of the entire student body."[116]

Despite military trappings, classroom work remained largely under faculty control. Uniformed and civilian students attended most classes together, for the V-12 curriculum was much the same as Franklin & Marshall's, requiring English, history, and foreign languages in addition to mathematics, physics, mechanical drawing, and navigation. Although some instructors felt that the accelerated pace of instruction made it difficult for students to do their best work, they tried to uphold academic standards.[117]

Faculty entered into the demands of the new program with enthusiasm, showing a degree of flexibility unseen since the days of the classical curriculum. Before the arrival of the V-12 program, some eighteen professors were already teaching courses outside their specialties because of low enrollments in their fields and the departure of colleagues into the service or other war work. To staff mathematics sections required by the V-12 curriculum, some humanities professors took a refresher course from math professor W. Rue Murray. Richard Altick found Murray to be "a most lucid and patient expositor" and saw "no fault" on the part of the instructor for Altick's difficulties: " I lost touch about the time I was expected to grasp the distinction between the integral and differential calculi as well as the concept of limit." Altick taught advanced algebra instead and also introductory sociology, to free Jerry Neprash to teach physics. Physics professor Howard M. Fry offered engineering drawing, while Lyman Butterfield taught eight sections of American history single-handed, to free H. M. J. Klein for the required naval course The Historical Background of the Present War. Drawing on his summers in Maine, classics professor Samuel L. Mohler taught navigation. Religion professor Charles Spotts, who had majored in biology at Franklin & Marshall before entering the ministry, helped out with that subject. Auditing professor E. L. Lancaster spent much of his time assisting the treasurer with the intricacies of naval accounting.[118]

"Our faculty was working night and day, literally, to get these young men ready," Distler recalled. "[They] had a sense of mission about this. There wasn't anything we could ask the faculty to do that they wouldn't do." In their remaining time, many tutored students who were having difficulties.[119]

In addition to patriotic motives, faculty appreciated the administration's commitment to keep them employed during difficult times. Altick, for one, credited "the non-stop dedication of [the college's] hustling new president" for its ability to emerge from the war in good condition. In addition, to compensate for the shift to year-round instruction, the board raised faculty salaries by one-third; presumably this cost was passed on to the government, which paid the college on a cost basis. H. W. Prentis, chair of the board's Pension Committee, pushed through a retirement plan in conjunction with the nonprofit Teachers Insurance and Annuity Association. All employees were eligible to participate by contributing 5 percent of their monthly pay toward a retirement annuity contract, with the college contributing an equal amount. Retirement age was set at seventy for men and sixty-five for women, although one could continue to serve at the request of the board — and Distler immediately requested that

Professors Hagen and Long, heads of the English and math departments who had long since passed their seventieth birthdays, be allowed to continue. A year later the board approved supplementary pensions for longtime employees who would not be adequately covered under the new program.[120]

Designers of the V-12 program wanted students to get "the best undergraduate education the colleges [could] offer," including extracurricular activities. Competitive athletics and student clubs therefore experienced a limited revival. Swimming, wrestling, and football managed abbreviated seasons. Chief Petty Officers Hugh McCullough and John Rogella, both former professional football players, helped coach. With the addition of war-hardened trainees, only a last-minute loss to Bucknell prevented achievement of the college's first undefeated football season. One permanent wartime casualty was the annual Thanksgiving Day contest with Gettysburg College.[121]

The Green Room Club welcomed trainees as participants and audience. Its first production under the new regime was the war play *Brother Rat*. During off-campus leaves, trainees were often invited into local homes or to parties thrown by the young women of Lancaster's Navy League. The entire campus community was entertained in March 1944 at a concert by Shep Fields and his band, broadcast live from Hensel Hall on the Coca-Cola *Spotlight Band* radio program over the NBC Blue Network.[122]

Throughout the war, Distler and librarian Herbert Anstaett corresponded with former students in the military. With the V-12 program underway, Distler launched a new outreach project, a bimonthly newsletter to the more than nine hundred men who had attended Franklin & Marshall at the beginning of the war or since. He hoped to help sustain morale among young men dispersed throughout the world and, by maintaining "direct personal contact," to encourage them to return after the war. Beginning in August 1943 with a simple four-page mimeographed bulletin, the project mushroomed into a twelve-page printed pamphlet. With editorial help from Anstaett and Altick, each issue contained campus news, excerpts from soldiers' letters, and encouragement, in "Prexy" Distler's informal style, "to the men to carry on and to do their best in spite of the many hardships." He included full military addresses for each man mentioned, to enable former classmates to communicate. Later editions included explanations of postwar educational planning, included the new GI Bill and guidelines for college credit for military studies. Despite cutbacks in the V-12 program at the end of 1944, Distler assured his readers, "[Franklin & Marshall will] weather this storm as we have those in the past, and the doors will be wide open for you to return to finish your education or to come back to have your class reunions."[123]

The only discordant note in this era of good feelings was a 1942 board resolution introduced by H. W. Prentis recommending that the president and faculty take steps "to provide adequate training" for all students "in the fundamental philosophic, economic and religious principles on which the American Republic was founded, and on which its perpetuation depends." A year before, the Curriculum Committee had responded to an unofficial request by upholding the principle of academic freedom. Now it took a more pragmatic tack by arguing that present requirements of a year's study each in history, social science, and religion already provided ample exposure to the principles "on which our Republic was founded and on which it has built through the century and a half of its history and growth." The committee also took issue with the wording of the resolution, stating that "in the teaching of these fundamental principles," students must also be shown "that new conditions compel redefinition of principles" in order "to participate constructively in an evolving civilization." This approach was "in line with what liberal colleges in America are doing" to ensure "the education of leaders and intelligent followers in our American way of life."[124]

Freedom, the committee noted, also had a pedagogical dimension. It contrasted the situation in "some countries" where teachers were "told what to teach" and students were "taught what to think" with the situation in places where teachers believed their function was "to teach youth how to think rather than what to think." The "facts of history" had substantiated the committee's liberal arts conviction "that mastery, by youth, of the thought processes involved in the study of mathematics, the natural sciences, languages, social studies, philosophy, and religion is the best preparation youth can have in order to deal intelligently with religious, social, economic, and political problems that are certain to confront them in facing a changing world." Allowing the student "considerable freedom, under guidance, in the choice of courses" was essential to prepare him "to exercise intelligently all his freedom in full manhood."[125]

A substantial minority on the board, led by Prentis, were not convinced by these arguments. Prentis went on record as stating that "the members of the Board would not be doing their duty as trustees if they did not request the College Administration to institute a course of lectures on the basic principles on which our Government rests." Distler promised a lecture series in harmony with the original motion. The result was "The Origin and Development of American Democracy," delivered during weekly assemblies in spring 1944. Nonetheless, underlying tensions between the board and faculty remained to be dealt with after the war.[126]

With the V-12 program under way, Distler began to worry about the future. In September 1943 he established the faculty Post-War Planning Committee, charging it with ensuring "a thorough liberal education." "One thing, even at this stage, appears perfectly clear," he told the board. "Those institutions with clearly defined purposes and with adequate means for carrying out those purposes, will be the institutions to survive." He thought it likely that the federal government would play a much larger role in higher education after the war, but no one knew what form it would take. "The independent college should seek to place itself in a strong enough financial position to be able to refuse federal aid if it appears to be not for its best interests," he warned. He asked the committee to consider Franklin & Marshall's educational program and physical plant and a financial program to implement both. During its first year the group discussed the ideal enrollment, curriculum, organizational forms, admissions issues like coeducation, and the needs of returning veterans.[127]

As the momentum of the war shifted by early 1944, Distler focused on how to survive the end of military programs. Closure of the flight-training course in the

summer dealt "a severe financial blow," and the navy began to cut back V-12 enrollments in November. Ever hustling, Distler looked for new sources of enrollments. He
contracted with the Veterans Bureau to accept returning veterans "either under present or future legislation." The faculty established the Veterans Advisory Committee to
work with returning servicemen and suggest modifications in curricular requirements
to meet their "particular wants and needs." Only days before, President Roosevelt had
signed into law the Servicemen's Readjustment Act, dubbed the "GI Bill of Rights" by
the American Legion. Included in the act's omnibus package of veterans' entitlements
was the most massive federal support for higher education in American history. Because aid came in the form of subsidies for college tuition, books, and fees and a modest monthly stipend, the program promised to be free of government interference.
Some educators responded to the legislation with jubilation, predicting that the end
of the war in Europe would bring a tidal wave of students back to the men's colleges.
"I cannot share this optimism," Distler told the board. "I feel that some difficult days
are still ahead."[128]

Few involved in the legislation saw the GI Bill as a panacea for the problems of
higher education, for most believed that only a few would take advantage of the educational opportunities. Distler was much more concerned about Roosevelt's proposal to
establish a year of compulsory military training for eighteen-year-olds. He fretted that
the college would be in serious trouble if the armed services were slow to demobilize.[129]

Expecting a postwar world of greatly reduced resources, Distler looked to the immediate community as a backup market. At his urging, the board established the Evening Division to offer college-level work for credit for local men and women, as an
extension of wartime evening courses. By offering higher education to those "who by
necessity must work during the day," the program could "strengthen the industrial and
social fabric of the community" and aid postwar economic adjustment. Pragmatically,
Distler hoped to discourage other institutions from establishing similar programs in
Lancaster and to provide work for full-time faculty if regular enrollments faltered.[130]

There turned out to be less demand for college-credit work than Distler had
hoped. Although several hundred enrolled, many failed to complete the courses. Distler attributed a considerable decline in enrollments for the spring term to "what
must have been an unexpected discovery on the part of some students, namely, that
Evening Division work was real college work." In the second year, only ten of twenty-
three courses made the minimum enrollment of ten students; several noncredit courses
were added, based on suggestions of a group of "representative citizens." Despite this
weak showing, Distler hoped that in the future a full-fledged evening division would
offer "a greatly expanded educational service to the community."[131]

More controversial was the question of admitting women as full-fledged students. The wartime crisis prompted a number of all-male colleges to consider coeducation, and Franklin & Marshall allowed women to attend summer sessions. On the
eve of the war students expressed alarm at rumors that the college was going to admit
women. Although "the national emergency" might make the change necessary, the

Student Weekly asserted, "Coeds would be a nuisance as classmates, are not necessary socially, and would spoil our cherished traditions as a male institution." A columnist later speculated that "girls" might "sublimate" the "row-bottom instinct," but their presence would interfere with classroom discussions of "everything from love poetry to biology." He winced at the thought of "campus organizations swarming with soft, excitable females."[132]

Distler did not want coeducation to be considered as merely a wartime measure. Discussing long-range planning with the board in 1944, he raised as a trial balloon the idea of permanently admitting women while stressing his own neutrality on the issue. He presented it as another means of serving the community at a time when he thought it likely that middle-class families would have less money to send children away to college.[133]

Some faculty agreed with Dean Bomberger that women made better students and would help raise academic standards, but many pointed out that admitting them would force the college to increase its supervision of student life, requiring construction of new dormitories and the addition of new administrators that the college could not afford. The Planning Committee therefore proposed a limited form of coeducation in which women would be admitted only as day students. With only three dissenting votes, the faculty sent the proposal to the board.[134]

Distler's Christmas newsletter included a questionnaire about veterans' postwar educational plans. Warning "Don't get excited about this topic," it included a question about veterans' attitude toward coeducation. The response of recent students and alumni was largely positive, with 60 percent favoring complete coeducation, 17 percent favoring the limited version, and 23 percent opposed to the admission of women. A separate poll of older alumni revealed greater resistance, with only 29 percent of those graduating before 1920 in favor of complete coeducation, 31 percent for limited coeducation, and 40 percent opposed. Post-1920 graduates favored coeducation, with 52 percent for full admission, 24 percent for limited, and 24 percent opposed. Nonetheless, influential alumni were strongly against it, and Evangelical and Reformed leaders feared that coeducation would hurt the denomination's women's colleges. The Reverend Lee Erdman, chair of the Committee on Instruction, commented that in principle "in a democracy where we have organized equal rights of men and women and in a scientific age in which we have come to believe that the female mentality is not inferior to the male, it would seem to be just a bit backward and illiberal not to educate them side by side." Still, he thought that there would probably always be a place for traditional men's and women's colleges. He and Distler did not want to make such a radical change simply for financial conditions and neither thought that limited coeducation was a legitimate long-range policy.[135]

The board's Committee of Instruction asked Distler to appoint a faculty committee "to give full and comprehensive study to the possibility of complete co-education." Professors Harbold, Heller, and Butterfield surveyed twenty-one other liberal arts colleges, some of which had always been coed and some that had admitted women more recently. The professors found that all of the colleges exercised a greater degree of supervision of female than of male students, requiring nonlocal women to live in campus dormitories. They also learned that women earned less of their college expenses, suggesting that they would need more financial aid. In the end, the committee's assessment of the potential impact of coeducation was ambiguous. Committee members agreed that the addition of women would raise standards of scholarship but estimated the cost of new dormitories and dining and athletic facilities at $350,000 to $500,000. Moreover, they admitted that the weight of tradition stood against the change, and something even more "subtle": a suspicion that high-ability male students were less likely to apply to coeducational schools than to men's colleges. In the Northeast, most of the most prestigious colleges and universities continued to be single-sex institutions — a fact that Harvard-educated Butterfield would have been sensitive to. Given this less-than-ringing endorsement, the board shelved the question.[136]

Stretching definitions of liberal arts education nearly to the breaking point, Distler looked far and wide for new programs to sustain the college. He wrote J. Edgar Hoover to inquire about a training program for prospective FBI agents. Distler made repeated efforts to secure an ROTC program. At the request of local hospitals, the college established a temporary program to train medical technologists. In September 1945 it opened the Veterans Administration Guidance Center, with a staff of ten led by two newly hired professors of education. Asserting that "if [the college was] to remain a purely men's college," Franklin & Marshall should "investigate the possibility of giving some technical education," Distler introduced a small pre-engineering program designed for students who planned to transfer to an engineering school after two years or who wanted to include a nucleus of engineering training in their bachelor's program. It was discontinued, however, after one year.[137]

With cuts in V-12, enrollments declined to 485 in the November–February term and to 354 in the March–June 1945 term. Fraternities gradually regained use of their chapter houses, and the infirmary moved to the first floor of East Hall, the original academy building. Distler turned to fund-raising to help balance his budget. "We have come through the third year of war without a penny of indebtedness," he wrote in his newsletter at the end of December. "Now our job is going to be to raise money to keep us going through 1945 and possibly a part of 1946. You may know some wealthy man who might like to help us along the way," he concluded hopefully.[138]

The college benefited from increased contributions during the war. It received more than $20,000 through the Educational Emergency Campaign, organized by the Evangelical and Reformed Church to aid church-affiliated institutions. Attention to the needs of local industries paid off, as Lancaster businessmen gave more than $17,000 in 1944 and nearly $22,000 in 1945. Meanwhile, proceeds of the annual college fund drive rose dramatically, from less than $5,500 in 1941 to $42,000 in 1945, the most successful campaign in the college's history. Although more than two-thirds of this sum came from board members themselves, 970 alumni participated, an increase of nearly 30 percent over any previous year. Distler's attention to servicemen undoubtedly helped bolster the willingness of men to come to the aid of their alma mater, but the most immediate cause was a reinvigorated campaign committee. When the elderly alumni secretary retired, Distler convinced William French to leave a successful insurance business to take the position.[139]

In the end, the V-12 program continued into the fall of 1945. A wave of retirements, a few resignations, and releases of temporary appointees in 1944 and 1945 reduced payrolls by cutting the faculty from a high of forty-five in 1942 to a low of twenty-eight as of July 1945. Retirees included longtime professors S. N. Hagen, William F. Long, V. W. Dippell, H. M. J. Klein, P. M. Harbold, and E. E. Kresge, and their departure heightened a perception of change in postwar years.[140]

As the war drew to a close, the college turned its attention to returning veterans. Distler prepared a pamphlet showcasing Franklin & Marshall's offerings and support available under the GI Bill. Emphasizing the college's liberal arts character, the pamphlet promised "individual, sympathetic attention to the personal problems of every student." Even after Japan's surrender, Distler predicted "a slow, steady growth in [the] student population," as Congress debated the future of compulsory military service. "So long as the government controls the destinies of so many of our potential students," he warned, "so long we shall be sitting on the anxious seat." Nonetheless, he looked forward to a point when the college could return to a normal schedule, with time "for reflection, reading, research, and indeed plain leisure" to restore lagging energies of faculty and administration. Always looking to the future, Distler warned that Franklin & Marshall would face fierce competition in bringing the faculty back up to the size necessary for normal operation in 1946. Already he and the heads of the math and English departments were finding it hard to hire "competent" men. He noted that the college would soon have to face the question of raising salaries, for most local bus drivers earned as much as junior faculty.[141]

In fall 1945 admissions director Shober Barr was inundated with inquiries from thousands of prospective students. When the November–February term began, enrollment had risen to 502, with 249 new students and 87 former students returning from the service. At the beginning of the last accelerated term in March, enrollment reached 797, and three retired faculty were called back to teach part-time. It was clear that the college had survived the challenge of World War II.[142]

As Franklin & Marshall returned to civilian status, many changes were perceptible. Now in possession of the former academy buildings, the college was able to house more of its students. The faculty decreed that all freshmen whose families did not live within commuting distance would be required to live in Hartman Hall. Upper floors of East Hall were renovated to provide small apartments for married veterans. "Even *Hildy*'s had changed somewhat," a veteran wrote in Distler's last newsletter, referring to a favorite student hangout. "The pink elephants are gone from the back room. But the smoky haze and distinctive odor remain." Chapel and assembly attendance was still required, he noted, but veterans were excused from physical education classes.[143]

The college observed the end of war in Europe on May 8, 1945, with a prayer service in the chapel. It marked a fitting end to a long period of upheaval with a memorial service in Hensel Hall on June 2, 1946. Tribute was paid to the 2,552 Franklin &

Marshall men who had served their country during the war, and Professors John Noss and Charles Spotts read the names of the 107 who had lost their lives.[144]

"We, all of us here at the college," Distler commented to the board, "look forward with keen anticipation toward engaging in the work for which the college was founded and for which it has continued to exist." Under his leadership the college had survived and in some ways thrived by adapting to a changed environment, especially the important role of technical and scientific knowledge in modern warfare. As Franklin & Marshall faced a new postwar world, it soon became clear that pressure continued to redefine the meaning of its traditional work as a liberal arts institution.[145]

CHAPTER EIGHT

The Academic Revolution: Setting the Stage, 1946–1956

—◦◦◦—

Looking over higher education in the two decades following World War II, sociologists David Riesman and Christopher Jencks found changes so sweeping that they merited the term "revolution." Everywhere in America, expansion in colleges and universities was accompanied by dramatic changes in form, as institutions used increased resources to pursue what Richard M. Freeland has called "upward academic mobility." Growing demand for trained faculty brought them more material rewards, social respect, support for research, and power in academic governance. As professional prestige was more closely tied to research, even teachers at small schools often felt more identification with their research specialties than with their home institutions. Fewer faculty considered it their responsibility to foster students' social and moral development; increasingly these areas were delegated to administrators. Preferring to teach academically motivated students suited to become apprentice scholars, faculty pressed for ever more selective admission policies. As demand for higher education swelled, some institutions could become much choosier. Riesman and Jencks dubbed these selective, research-oriented schools "university colleges," seeing in them "the fruition of the academic revolution at the undergraduate level."[1]

Among others, Franklin & Marshall College gradually transformed itself into a selective university college after World War II. It used its growing financial resources to raise salaries, improve physical facilities, and create a residential student body. It strengthened academic programs, achieved greater selectivity, and allowed faculty more time for research, even as it continued to emphasize teaching. Yet this version of the academic revolution did not take place without considerable struggle, as faculty, administrators, trustees, and increasingly students vied for a voice in shaping the college's future.

The Great Postwar Boom

In hindsight, Franklin & Marshall stood at war's end on the threshold of its greatest expansion and development. But as the 1946–1947 year opened, what President Theodore A. Distler and other college leaders saw was a short, chaotic period of inflated enrollments as veterans returned, soon to be followed by resumption of the prewar struggle for stability. Few educational leaders foresaw that the 1950s would bring a sharp overall rise in demand for higher education. Nor did they predict that the ballooning postwar birthrate would continue well into the next decade, producing a demographic group soon to be dubbed "the Baby Boom generation," who began to reach college age in the early 1960s.

One of the "fundamental fault lines in American higher education," according to historian Roger Geiger, is the gap between selective schools and "demand-absorbing" schools — those with largely open access, with enrollments that wax and wane according to external conditions. In 1946 Franklin & Marshall and nearly all academic institutions fell into the latter category. The college opened in the fall with 1,275 students, more than 50 percent above the previous spring — exactly matching the average increase nationwide. More than three-quarters of students were veterans. The board waived resolutions capping enrollments at 1,000, to honor Distler's promise to readmit former students who had entered military service. Only about one-quarter of new applicants could be admitted. As president of the Pennsylvania Association of Colleges and Universities, Distler worked with the state's Department of Public Instruction to set up temporary one-year programs to absorb excess demand. The Lancaster Area College Center offered freshman-level evening courses to nearly four hundred during its two-year existence; many students later transferred to Franklin & Marshall.[2]

The college scrambled to provide adequate facilities. The chapel in Hartman Hall was converted into a three-story dormitory wing to house non-commuting freshmen. Administrators made a door-to-door appeal to local homeowners to rent rooms to upperclassmen. Nearly 650 lived in private homes or fraternities that year, while more than 200 commuted. Two Quonset huts from the Federal Works Agency provided additional classroom and laboratory space. Finding housing for new faculty proved even more difficult, and several began their careers at Franklin & Marshall living alone in rented rooms until space became available for their families.[3]

Distler nonetheless moved ahead to fulfill a longtime ambition to establish a geology department, making the college one of only four Pennsylvania schools offering a full program. He asked Richard Foose, '37, a Johns Hopkins Ph.D. and senior geologist for the state's geological survey, to outline a plan for creating a department from scratch. Foose argued that geology was a liberal arts subject as a "fundamental science" that made "a significant educational contribution to the fullness of living." The college was ideal for fieldwork because of its location within driving distance of seven of the nine major physiographic provinces east of the Mississippi. He recommended starting with a two- or three-person department. Distler accepted his plan and asked him to take charge of realizing it. In its first semester, 105 students, twice the expected number, enrolled in three courses. A one-man music department also debuted in 1946, offering courses in appreciation and composition.[4]

With eighty full-time equivalents in 1946, the faculty stood 57 percent above the preceding year. Even so, the teaching load averaged more than eighteen classroom hours per week, with one in four teaching more than twenty-four hours. Wide differences in enrollments across departments were partly the result of returning students' needs to fulfill basic requirements. Dean Daniel Gibson nevertheless assured the board that "morale on the campus was excellent." Most of the faculty accepted the difficulty of hiring more teachers at short notice but also felt that large sections and heavy schedules "were impairing the effectiveness of their work."[5]

There were signs that the faculty's wartime spirit of self-sacrifice was waning. The campus chapter of the American Association of University Professors (AAUP) quickly became a channel for discontent. After discussing teaching loads at its quarterly meeting in December 1946, the group unanimously called for reducing the official teaching load to fifteen hours immediately and eventually to twelve. By large majorities, group members also recommended lowering the student-teacher ratio to fifteen to one, increasing the salary scale, and establishing an effective housing program for new teachers. At an open meeting with AAUP in February, Distler promised to be fully staffed by the beginning of the next academic year, but he also warned that present enrollment levels would not last. The full faculty voted soon afterward to create a budget committee of five tenured faculty and promptly elected leading AAUP members, headed by its president Charles Spotts. He reported at the next AAUP meeting that Distler had "displayed annoyance" when Spotts called a meeting of the committee instead of waiting for Distler to do so.[6]

The college's small endowment of around $1.5 million hampered its ability to recruit and retain faculty. Distler told the board in fall 1945 that Richard Altick, "one of our most brilliant young men," had left for Ohio State University, where he would have more time for research and writing. Distler had trouble finding a suitable replacement and predicted that the situation would only worsen. "Our greatest single need," he told the board, "is free endowment [which represented the] only sure source of income." He made the first of many pleas to the board to increase the endowment.[7]

In 1946 Distler persuaded the board to raise the salary scale by 10 to 14 percent for new faculty, beginning at $2,400 for an instructor but holding the maximum for a full professor at $5,000. He clearly saw himself as an advocate for the faculty, repeatedly stressing that they were "the heart and core of an institution." One of the major functions of a college president, he told the board, was to secure an outstanding faculty and then provide them the resources necessary to do their work. "I have often felt that a college faculty is very much like an Opera Company, or a Symphony Orchestra," he explained at one point, "with the President occupying the role of Conductor, and the alumni, students, and members of the Board providing a sympathetic, understanding and yet critical audience."[8]

Noting the importance of specialized knowledge, Distler extended the analogy: "Each member is a specialist in his own right — a prima donna, who must, on occasion, blow his own horn, or sing his own aria, and upon other occasions must blend in a harmonious whole with the entire ensemble." He saw faculty's increased role in hiring as an inevitable result of specialization: "I just don't think any one man is smart enough to hire a professor of physics, and a professor of chemistry, and a professor of English," he later commented.[9]

Despite Distler's view of himself as "conductor," not all faculty felt inclined to follow his beat. Many came to think of the president and his administration not as their natural leaders but as a separate and likely antagonistic interest. In fact, faculty often complained about proliferation of non-teaching staff, who were playing a greater role in student life outside class. A. G. Breidenstine, who became dean of students in 1947, took charge of most student guidance and discipline and work with student organizations. Several years later he was put in charge of the Committee on Academic Standing, which handled student academic problems that were previously the purview of the faculty's Academic Council. Two years later Breidenstine acquired an assistant to cope with a growing workload that included foreign student counseling and oversight of student activities formally done by a faculty committee. Several new positions were also added in admissions and career guidance.[10]

The board responded to Distler's plea for help with his expanding workload by shifting some responsibilities for internal administration to a new dean of the college, Daniel Z. Gibson, who had been executive officer of the college's V-12 program. He oversaw curriculum, faculty, and all academic matters, while the dean of students handled extracurricular affairs. In the expansive postwar period, most of Gibson's time went to faculty recruitment.[11]

Hiring authority was shared among the dean, the president, and the five-person Committee on Appointments, Promotions, and Dismissals (APD). To fill eighteen new positions in spring 1947, the committee met many times to interview and evaluate candidates and occasionally their wives. Department chairs wielded considerable influence, but so did the other committee members, who sought to ensure that newcomers would be compatible members of the campus community. After meeting with a candidate for a chemistry position, for example, the committee reported, "All those who met him expressed themselves as highly pleased with his manner and personality." Without formal procedures for academic recruitment, news about jobs spread informally within personal networks. Often this process encouraged the hiring of alumni, as faculty kept in touch with top students. Consequently, 45 percent of faculty in 1949 were Franklin & Marshall graduates.[12]

Even so, facing fierce competition for qualified scholars, the college broadened its definition of acceptable candidates. In 1947 Jacob Freedman became the first Jewish faculty member when the APD Committee voted unanimously to hire him as the second member of the geology department. They gave "careful consideration" to his religion, but any concerns about his suitability were allayed by his "entirely acceptable" personality and the fact that he was on the verge of completing a Harvard Ph.D. In contrast, the committee had earlier passed over a Jewish candidate for a position in Spanish, deferring to the department chairman's opinion that his personality "left a somewhat negative impression."[13]

The tight job market finally compelled the college grudgingly to drop its long-standing ban on female teachers, first in emergency situations and then for permanent positions. Luella Frank, a resident of the area with a master's from Columbia, filled a last-minute opening in German in the spring of 1948. Soon thereafter, Nancy Honaman was given a one-year appointment as assistant instructor in economics and business administration. Several members of the board's Committee on Instruction expressed "serious reservation" when asked to approve her appointment; they disliked "breaking a precedent in electing a young woman, . . . especially because of her youth and lack of teaching experience." Distler and Gibson replied that the Lancaster native and Mount Holyoke graduate was "a very able young woman" and moreover that they had found it difficult to fill the temporary appointment. The full board eventually gave unanimous approval. Six months later, Dorothy LeFevre took a permanent position as assistant professor of education. Married to Ivan LeFevre of the sociology and education departments, she had directed a reading study laboratory in the Guidance Center. When political science professor Arthur Kunkle died just before the opening of the fall term in 1949, Vivian Darlington stepped in as visiting lecturer. Also that semester, Ruth Warner Van Horn joined the college as lecturer in chemistry. She had previously taught at Hunter College and worked as a research chemist in industry, moving to Lancaster with her husband, an executive with the Hamilton Watch Company. Despite the arrival of women, teaching staff were still routinely referred to as "men."[14]

Everyone hoped to increase the proportion of faculty with doctorates, but in a competitive market the APD Committee often had to consider applicants who had not yet completed their degrees. Of fifty-five teachers hired between 1946 and 1949, twenty-six or fewer than half had the Ph.D. One-third of the twenty-four with master's degrees had completed all requirements but the dissertation (ABD). As a whole, 43 percent of faculty held doctorates, 49 percent had master's, and the rest — mainly instructors in the physical education department — held only bachelor's degrees.[15]

The emphasis on temporary appointments and frequent departures to more attractive positions produced a high turnover rate. Only eleven of eighteen hired in 1947 were still on campus two years later, for example. In 1949–1950, one-quarter of the faculty were in their first year at the college, while 64 percent had been hired in the preceding four years. Only 15 percent of faculty had served between five and twenty years, while 21 percent had been at the college twenty years or more. Most tellingly, the average number of years of service at Franklin & Marshall fell from sixteen in 1945 to eight in 1949. In this context, presence of alumni among the faculty probably helped provide a needed sense of institutional continuity.[16]

Turnover heightened a sense of confusion that would have in any case been natural in a period of rapid growth. It was evident in the work of the Committee on Appointments, Promotions, and Dismissals (APD). As its name implied, it was also concerned with promotion and dismissal, which before Distler had been the prerogative of the president and the board. Several factors came together in the immediate postwar period to make the committee's work especially difficult and important. First, trustees accepted AAUP tenure guidelines promising that after a period of probation depending on rank, but no more than six years, faculty received permanent tenure and could be fired only for "adequate cause." An influx of new and relatively inexperienced teachers also revealed the inadequacy of departments' informal methods of orienting and supervising new faculty. A long-standing college tradition barred outside observers from classrooms, while there was no procedure for student assessment of faculty.[17]

In 1948 the APD Committee dealt with two cases of faculty whose behavior as teachers had become problematic. A professor of German who had long been considered inadequate and hostile toward students seems to have returned from military service in worsening psychological shape. J. William Frey, the new head of the department, appealed to the APD: "There are many queer individuals and eccentric characters on this earth (our profession, unfortunately, has always had more than its share)," he admitted, "but here is an extreme case that can no longer be regarded as a source for light amusement while the work and the students suffer." Several months later, the committee confronted the case of a chemistry professor who had become belligerent toward younger colleagues. This could not be tolerated in one of the college's most prominent departments, for his behavior was said to have contributed to the departure of a promising young professor. Both teachers had served for many years and thus were clearly tenured. After awkward deliberations including the AAUP chapter president, the APD Committee eventually persuaded both to take medical leaves of absence and subsequently declined to allow them to return.[18]

Thus warned of the perils of inaction, the committee paid closer attention to faculty performance, especially of newcomers. At Dean Gibson's recommendation, committee members discussed methods of evaluation, though agreeing that this was primarily department heads' responsibility. They were stymied about how to assess classroom work, for the faculty had recently refused to institute student evaluations, doubting that a questionnaire "would result in any definite constructive information." The committee feared that direct questioning of students about their teachers might be unethical and would hurt faculty morale. The idea of visiting classes was rejected because of "the difficulties of breaking traditions in that respect on our campus." They finally agreed that Distler would urge department heads to pay more attention to faculty performance. By the end of the decade, the committee met regularly with chairmen to assess all members of their departments, but the committee's authority to respond directly to complaints remained a subject of contention.[19]

A Blurring of Educational Focus

Despite frequent statements about the importance of liberal arts education, Franklin & Marshall College was drifting toward vocationalism. Here, Distler's concern about long-term financial stability dovetailed with his sincere desire to serve educational needs in the wider community. He promoted an eclectic range of programs that some-times had tenuous connections to liberal education. The college's Guidance Center was first established under a government contract to aid veterans in their transition from military to civilian employment. As their numbers declined, the center marketed its services to local schools and industries and took charge of testing freshmen and advising students on academic probation. In 1947 the college added the Division of Graduate Studies as an extension of its wartime science courses. Designed to provide graduate-level instruction in chemistry and physics leading toward a master of sci-ence degree, the program was underwritten by local corporations like Armstrong Cork and RCA and often taught by members of their staffs with advanced degrees. The Evening Division was folded into the new Division of Community Services under a full-time director initially funded by local businesses. It offered instruction in a vari-ety of formats, from "tailor-made" courses for local companies to college-level night classes and popular noncredit programs. "It should be understood that this program will in no way change the day-time program," Distler assured the board, "but it will definitely demonstrate to our community that we want to be of educational service wherever we reasonably can." Some faculty balked, however, when asked to approve college credit for Evening Division courses in child psychology and business English that had no equivalents in the regular curriculum.[20]

Similarly, when local clinics treating cleft palate and hearing problems proposed a cooperative master's program in speech and hearing correction, the faculty approved the program only after extended debate. In 1950 local public school teachers asked the college to offer master's level education courses now required for professional ad-vancement. The Academic Council and a special committee concluded that such a program would require hiring additional faculty and might not be sustainable after immediate local demand was met. Distler instead invited Temple University's educa-tion department to offer courses meeting at Franklin & Marshall. He also entered into cooperative programs with Rensselaer Polytechnic Institute and Carnegie Institute of Technology that allowed students interested in engineering to transfer to either pro-gram after three years. After two year's further work, they would receive a B.S. degree from Franklin & Marshall along with their engineering degree. Within a few years, the college entered into similar "binary" arrangements with programs in engineering, forestry, and journalism at a number of universities.[21]

Distler's desire for a program to bring the college national recognition did give Franklin & Marshall the distinction of establishing the nation's first folklore depart-ment. German professor J. William Frey was already known in the region for his re-search on Pennsylvania Dutch dialect and folklore. In 1946 Distler offered space in Fackenthal Library to the Pennsylvania German Society and invited Harvey Bassler to house his massive collection of Pennsylvania German manuscripts and books there. Soon, Alfred L. Shoemaker, curator of the Historical Society of Berks County, pro-posed establishing a program in American folklore at the college. A leader of the mod-ern folklore studies movement in the United States, Shoemaker envisioned "an archive of American Folklore, patterned after the Scandinavian and Irish Folklore Archives."

Distler responded enthusiastically, telling the APD Committee that as the first such program in the United States it would bring "considerable prestige" to the college. The committee ratified Shoemaker's appointment but suggested that it be made clear that he was responsible for raising the money to endow his position. The college offered to provide a site adjoining the library for the Pennsylvania Dutch Folklore Center and its collections if the Pennsylvania German Society found the money to build it.[22]

Shoemaker and the Bassler collection arrived on campus in the fall of 1948, attracting lively interest among students intrigued by the idea of hosting an interdisciplinary "science of folklore" program. The following spring, Frey and Shoemaker led the organization of the nonprofit Pennsylvania Dutch Folklore Center and launched a weekly newspaper, the *Pennsylvania Dutchman*, dedicated to spreading appreciation of Pennsylvania Dutch culture. The program was swelled by the arrival of its co-editor Don Yoder, an alumnus with a Ph.D. in church history from the University of Chicago, to a position in the religion department.[23]

By the end of 1949, the program's future at Franklin & Marshall was in doubt. Students objected to the fact that college funds were being used to offset deficits of the *Pennsylvania Dutchman*. Hoping to spur fund-raising by the Pennsylvania German Society, the college published a handsome design for a proposed center, but the society focused instead on launching a five-day folk festival at Kutztown. Despite the program's potential "as a source of national recognition for the college," Distler told the APD that he could not long continue Shoemaker's part-time position without a subvention. The program unraveled in the early 1950s when Shoemaker and Yoder left the college. In 1956, the center moved out of Fackenthal, and the board decided to sever ties completely by declining to continue even its current level of symbolic sponsorship. It did, however, retain the Bassler collection and its many outstanding examples of traditional German frakturs.[24]

Distler's eagerness to add a wide range of programs could have put Franklin & Marshall on a trajectory followed in this period by many other institutions, one of gradual evolution from liberal arts college to multifunctional comprehensive university. Under H. H. Apple's administration, the college had added professional programs in education and business, and its majors in chemistry, biology, and now geology were heavily oriented toward industrial or premedical applications that belied the college's liberal arts mission. More subtly, the segmented character of the college's curriculum and the dominance of departmental majors undermined a liberal arts ethos. Several attempts in this period to restore balance between the "broadening" intent of requirements in the first two years and the "specializing" emphasis of the last two were largely failures.

Postwar Educational Debates

"At no time in the history of this country has there been so much ferment and stir about the ends and means of education," the Carnegie Foundation president commented in 1950. One of the most influential of a long line of studies, the President's

Commission on Higher Education concluded that the nation's future depended on providing advanced education to a much larger share of the population than its present narrow intellectual elite. Its most controversial recommendation was to enlarge institutions of higher education sufficiently by 1960 to be able to offer two years of college to half the college-age population and four years to one-third. (In 1940 less than 16 percent of eighteen- to twenty-one-year-olds had received any postsecondary education.) To do this, the commission advocated increasing federal support for higher education, eliminating racial and religious discrimination, and broadening the curriculum beyond a focus on "verbal skills and intellectual interests." To balance more technical training, it recommended "general education" courses — eschewing the aristocratic connotations of the term "liberal education"— designed to prepare young men and women for citizenship in a new postwar world.[25]

Independent colleges and private foundations expressed more traditional views of liberal education. The Commission on Financing Higher Education, sponsored by the Rockefeller Foundation and the Association of American Universities, estimated that only one-quarter of the population had an aptitude for advanced education. It believed that higher education should continue to focus on developing "intellectual promise" and the ability to deal with "abstract ideas" and reason "upon the basis of broad conceptual schemes"; the now-traditional disciplines of the arts and sciences were best suited to accomplish this.[26]

Meanwhile, many institutions did their own planning, but a 1945 report by a Harvard University committee received most attention. *General Education in a Free Society* argued that education should foster values and personal qualities of the "good man" and the "good citizen." It defined these qualities as the ability to "think effectively, to communicate thought, to make relevant judgments, to discriminate among values." More concretely, the report proposed combating overspecialization through a general education curriculum composed of a core of interdisciplinary courses in three divisions: humanities, social sciences, and natural sciences. Ironically, although the report influenced general education programs throughout the nation, Harvard's faculty could not agree on the content of a single course in each division and authorized up to four each as a temporary expedient. With no consensus as to what constituted "core" knowledge, that number only grew.[27]

The idea of divisional organization went back to a program established at the University of Chicago in the 1930s. It sought to reunite common methods of inquiry that had been divided into separate academic disciplines. The undergraduate curriculum at Chicago was based on a core of courses in humanities, social sciences, and natural sciences, courses designed to develop an understanding of the distinctive organizing concepts and methods of thought of each.[28]

At Franklin & Marshall, Distler seemed to hope that the faculty Planning Committee he appointed in 1943 could use a similar divisional system as a counterweight to departmental domination of the curriculum. The result in 1945 was a curriculum divided into four divisions — with business administration accorded separate status — each with its own admission and graduation requirements. The net effect only further diminished what remained of the college's liberal arts core. All students were required to take several "tool subjects": English composition, mathematics (the level varying according to the degree), two years of a foreign language, a laboratory science, and speech. Only two subjects were deemed "essential" to liberal education for all students: religion and American government or history. An honors plan allowed outstanding students in their junior and senior years to conduct independent research culminating in a formal thesis. Senior comprehensive examinations were reinstituted in 1949.[29]

Without a divisional administrative structure, however, departments continued to dominate the curriculum. Specialized courses proliferated, raising questions about their value for nonmajors. In 1948, for example, biology chairman Mitchell Carroll sought to drop the natural science division's requirement of a year of literature. Gibson retorted that every college student should have at least one year of literature to "become familiar with and have some knowledge of a limited number of the great writers of the past." Carroll doubted that present courses did that; he thought a year of philosophy would be more profitable. He was especially concerned by premedical students' disappointing performance on the new Professional Aptitude Test developed by the Graduate Record Office.[30]

Faculty meetings were increasingly taken up in debates over proposals to change requirements, and Distler suggested that a committee "undertake a basic and long range study of the whole curriculum." The faculty authorized a committee of sixteen chaired by Gibson. They also approved Gibson's recommendation that a five-man steering committee be given a reduced teaching load or additional compensation, but this was not implemented. A month later, Distler predicted to the board that when completed in about a year, the study would produce a new curriculum that "will not only retain all the basic essentials of what is found to have been good in the past, but will produce a program which will be much closer to the ideal of a liberal education than our present fairly highly segmented curricula."[31]

The Planning Committee hoped to develop an integrated two-year sequence of interdepartmental courses to provide "a broader as well as a more thorough general education." Gibson reported that the science component seemed to present "the gravest practical difficulties," but the committee hoped to begin in one or more fields in the fall of 1949. There progress stalled. "Major differences of opinion have arisen," Gibson admitted a year later, "not about the ends to be achieved, but about the means to those ends." Social scientists divided sharply between those who wanted an integrated sequence and others who simply wanted to require a series of introductory courses in various disciplines. As trustee Lee Erdman explained to the board, the project was hampered "both in the matter of time and expense, and of the jealous safe-guarding of domains of the various departments." As a third year of deliberation passed without result, the administration asked departments to try to cut back the number of courses offered and hours required for the major.[32]

In the end, the only concrete result was an "experimental" three-semester integrated humanities course, first offered on an optional basis in spring 1951. Developed by John Noss of philosophy, Donald Prakken of classics, Nelson Francis of English, and Richard Jameson of Romance languages, it was organized around broad concepts such as "the effects of pursuit of honor and glory," "the varieties of love," "freedom and bondage," and "justice, divine and human." Like the curriculum at the University of Chicago and the popular adult "Great Books" discussion program, the courses focused on works generally considered classics of Western civilization. Many, like Homer, Virgil, Plato, Aeschylus, and Goethe, had been staples of the college's nineteenth-century curriculum, though they were now read in translation. Others, like *Moby-Dick*, *Huckleberry Finn*, and *Crime and Punishment*, were more recent additions to the literary canon. Leaders hoped that the sequence would eventually be required for all students and would serve as a model for courses in the social and natural sciences. The faculty's Academic Council was put in charge of ongoing oversight of the curriculum.[33]

That Franklin & Marshall's curriculum lacked coherence was the principal criticism of the first postwar assessment of the college by the Middle States Association, which inherited this function from the American Association of Universities. Middle States visitors in 1950 found that the college's curriculum did not fulfill its formal statement of objectives, which "resembles that of other liberal arts colleges which propose to develop Christian gentlemen and cultivated citizens." This was particularly true in the two largest programs in business and premedicine, where students did little work in the humanities and social studies. Moreover, while Distler emphasized to the visitors "the College's church relationship and its resultant interest in the spiritual development of the students," department heads said that they paid little or no attention to religion. "At present, one gets the definite impression that there is more interest in the work of the student in his major department than in the whole development of the individual," the report concluded.[34]

The report noted "the apparent pre-professional emphasis" of much work in biology and chemistry and the entire program in business administration. It was broadly critical of the quality of the business program, noting that the college's Phi Beta Kappa chapter did not even consider candidates for the B.S. in economics degree to be eligible for membership. Among its recommendations was a study of the curriculum "with a view to restoring the College to a truly liberal-arts base" and better integration of the program in business administration into the liberal arts or its transfer "into an admittedly professional school of its own."[35]

The Visitation Committee praised the physical condition of the campus but warned that the college seemed to be "over-capitalized with plant," given its small endowment and "tight operating budget." Writers of the report recommended focusing on raising funds for salaries rather than further expansion. The report also commented on the weak administrative position of the dean of the college, who seemed "more whipping boy than leader of the Faculty." In any case, Gibson announced soon thereafter that he was leaving to become president of Washington College in Maryland.

In his final report, he admitted a certain amount of discord. "With the rapid changes in administrative organization and the sharp increase in the size of the faculty," he explained, "it may take several years yet before various relationships, personal and jurisdictional, have been resolved into a harmonious operation."[36]

Distler disputed many of the report's conclusions and emphatically defended the liberal arts character of his institution. His 1950 annual report argued against what he saw as a false distinction between liberal and vocational learning, between education "for living a life" and "for earning a living." "It is my feeling that in the best sense of a liberal education one does both," he insisted. The crux of his argument was a capacious definition of "a true liberal education," which for him meant being "continually kept intellectually alive and alert with a broad base for his training."[37]

The immediate postwar period saw a reversal of previous patterns of secularization and an emergence of what would be called an American civil religion, which obscured doctrinal differences in a generalized "Judeo-Christian" tradition. Distler himself stressed the importance of religious activity apart from any particular doctrinal content: "Association with religion in some form is an indispensable harmonizing element in life and the mark of a truly educated man." In 1942, for example, he had advised students, "Whatever your religious background may be, . . . associate yourself with the church of your choice in Lancaster, and . . . strengthen your faith."[38]

A faculty-student committee in 1948 reassessed the college's chapel requirement in response to a decline in attendance by Protestant students, some of whom complained about the exemption given to Catholic and Jewish students. The committee recommended reinstituting a requirement of weekly services for all, seeking "to create as worshipful an atmosphere as possible," and providing a budget to bring in outstanding preachers "who could interpret to our college family the vital implications of religion for our day." Meeting strong opposition from some faculty, the proposal was modified to a requirement of four "non-sectarian" religious convocations per semester, thus honoring the goal of bringing the entire institution together for worship. In addition, Protestant students were required to attend six chapels, while Roman Catholic and Jewish students could substitute the same number of periods of religious instruction by local priests and rabbis. During this period religious convocations provided an important setting for collegewide discussions of vital issues of the day, particularly racial and Jewish-Christian relations.[39]

Evangelical and Reformed Church leaders hoped to strengthen ties with Franklin & Marshall. Their annual appropriations to the college begun in wartime rose throughout the 1950s. Reaching nearly $60,000 in 1959, these contributions often provided the margin that kept the college in the black. The board responded to a General Synod request for representation by expanding membership to thirty-five, of which five were selected by the Evangelical and Reformed Church and five by the Alumni Association. Significantly, the revised charter no longer required a majority of the board to be Church members. Meanwhile, fewer than one in five students were now Church members.[40]

Return of Campus Life

The tenor of campus life immediately after World War II was dominated by returning veterans concerned mainly about finishing their degrees and getting on with their lives. Their studiousness helped to produce a combined grade point average in 1946–1947 some 29 percent higher than in 1938–1939. Some faculty complained that grading was too easy, but Gibson credited students' greater maturity and motivation and the college's ability to be more selective in admissions. Many veterans encountered academic, financial, or family difficulties, however, resulting in an attrition rate of nearly 8 percent in the first year after the war.[41]

The men who swelled the student body in the late 1940s were less geographically diverse than the V-12 trainees. Perhaps because many veterans sought to stay closer to home, the proportion of Pennsylvania residents was higher than it had been in the late 1930s, and it rose over the decade, to 77 percent in 1949–1950. The representation of other areas declined reciprocally.[42]

There were more foreign students, however. A Nigerian student, Fanasi Onwuanambe Mgbako, arrived in 1948, supported by a special scholarship offered by the faculty at the behest of a Nigerian journalist who had lectured on campus. Mgbako was active in the college's International Relations Club and attended a number of regional conferences. Other foreign students included Baghdad native J. J. Shamas, who offered to teach Arabic. Three South American students sharing a room in Dietz-Santee attracted attention when they enlivened the drab gray decor by splashing everything with red, yellow, green, and orange paint.[43]

Without formal acknowledgement, the unofficial color barrier at Franklin & Marshall was broken after the war by a small number of African American students. The first to graduate was Sumner Bohee Jr., a Lancaster resident who prepared for medical school and graduated in 1950. He was followed in the class of 1951 by Sydney N. Bridgett and U. Grant Means Jr., both also Lancaster natives. A veteran, Bridgett completed his first year of college courses at the Lancaster Area College Center and was admitted to Franklin & Marshall on the strength of a battery of personality tests suggesting that he had the determination necessary to succeed. Like many students, he lived at home and worked in addition to attending school. The numbers of African American students remained low through the decade, and for many the greatest problem was lack of social opportunities. In 1953 Pi Lambda Phi became the first fraternity at Franklin & Marshall to admit an African American member, Henry W. Wiggins Jr., '55. Even so, Wiggins recalled that his closest friend there was the cook — many fraternities had African American servants — and Wiggins dealt with inhibitions about interracial mixing by inviting friends from the community to dances and parties.[44]

Student leaders were eager to restore normal campus life as soon as possible. As the 1946–1947 year began, the *Student Weekly* acknowledged difficulties caused by overcrowding but urged students, "Take it philosophically and get down to serious work, [as] the best thing we can do is be realists, blow off our excess steam, and then hit the books." Soon, however, the paper returned to its time-honored preoccupation with the state of "tradition" and "spirit" at the college, praising an enthusiastic snake dance that opened a pep rally on Williamson Field. Several weeks later, an editorialist admitted that the war had brought changes: "Such things as freshman dinks, rowbottoms, pajama parades, and the Deitz-Meyran snow battles are but legends.·Overturning police cars on College Avenue is a lost art." No one had even painted the de Peyster statue for several years.[45]

The following September, the student body of 1,368 was so large that the opening assembly had to be held on Williamson Field. Freshman regulations were revived and dinks reappeared. Veterans could refuse to wear them but were asked "to hold their peace and not to incite the Freshmen." An assembly talk by emeritus professor H. M. J. Klein provided the spark that reignited campus traditions. Drawing upon research for a history of the college, he related a number of "humorous anecdotes" about nineteenth-century customs, but what most interested students were his stories of battles between freshmen and sophomores. Soon afterward, freshmen in Hartman Hall attacked sophomores coming to instruct them about regulations. The *Student Weekly* reported, "Obviously inspired by Daddy Klein's assembly talk on former Freshmen-Sophomore rivalry, they marched en masse to Old Main, the battleground of many former struggles." Freshmen hung an effigy on a tree and defended it against assaults by sophomores and allies from nearby fraternity houses. In the struggle, a new twist was added to frosh-soph warfare: both sides tried to seize opponents' trousers as trophies. "Gentlemen, it's back," the *Weekly* exulted. "Spirit is back on the Franklin and Marshall Campus." Frosh-soph battles continued for a number of years, aided by the concentration of freshmen in Hartman Hall and sophomores in the Dietz and Meyran dormitories.[46]

Also making a revival were raucous parades downtown, complete with fireworks, snake dances in Penn Square, and marches through movie theaters. After some initial confrontations, students and police reached a modus vivendi in which students agreed to stay out of the square in exchange for motorcycle escorts as they marched downtown. Relations with local police remained wary but largely peaceful, although some students borrowed union tactics and staged "sit-down strikes" when barred from the square in 1948. Fans also resumed lightning raids on football rivals' campuses. After the Student Council had to use money appropriated for dances to remove paint from Swarthmore buildings, however, raiders were careful to use whitewash when they "decorated" the Lehigh campus in 1948.[47]

After a hiatus of seven years, the Pajama Parade, an event "eagerly anticipated by both the Freshmen and the female citizenry of Lancaster," returned for the 1947 homecoming. Accompanied "by the largest assemblage of police ever seen in the county," over two-thirds of freshmen took part, halting frequently on the way "to kiss the many local beauties who had expectantly gathered along the line of march." In succeeding years the event took on trappings of a typical homecoming parade, with addition of floats in 1948 and selection of a homecoming queen the following year.

During the early 1950s these elements gradually supplanted the specific college tradition, which lapsed despite attempts at mid-decade to revive it. Meanwhile, a new
tradition was inaugurated in 1948, when Alpha Delta Sigma, the professional advertising fraternity, donated an authentic Conestoga wagon. Their idea was to use it to
symbolize the college at public events from pep rallies to civic parades. The next year,
freshmen were tapped to guard it against raids by opposing schools, and in the 1950s
it became a tradition for freshmen to pull it around the field during football games.
Not all traditions made a comeback, however. Distler adamantly refused student calls
and even a formal petition to cancel classes the Monday after a big football game, as
Apple and Schaeffer had done.[48]

To an extent, faculty and administration welcomed revival of extracurricular
activities. But debates over freshman regulations and fraternities revealed differing
expectations about college life. In spring 1948 students and administrators discussed
enforcement of freshman regulations. There was general agreement that some form
of regulations "engender class spirit which eventually leads to school spirit." But faculty and administrators refused to condone use of force against recalcitrant freshmen,
something that many students considered essential to the whole system. Despite faculty disapproval, sophomores regularly added such new torments as forcing freshmen
to wear their pants legs rolled up almost to the knees and to call out "We hail thee
alma mater" when passing in front of Old Main.[49]

Fraternities also revived and flourished; through the 1950s a majority of students
were members. In 1947 the faculty dropped its ban on new fraternities and approved
the petition of a local club, many of whose members were Jewish, to affiliate with the
national Pi Lambda Phi fraternity. For many years it had the most diverse membership of the college's fraternities. Meanwhile, ties between fraternities and adult members of the college community weakened. In the interwar years, many faculty had been
fraternity members and maintained close relations with local chapters, some of which
regularly invited professors to dinner. After the war, fewer faculty had been members
of fraternities as undergraduates.[50]

The faculty regulated fraternity practices, delaying rushing until second semester
freshman year and requiring a C average to pledge. But in the years immediately after
World War II, alcohol became the biggest issue. Since the end of Prohibition, drinking had been technically banned on campus and at fraternities but was generally condoned unless it became public, such as when a student passed out or broke other laws.
Returning veterans, older than typical undergraduates and accustomed to easy access
to alcohol, made no attempt to hide their drinking. Hoping to free itself from a hypo-
critical situation, faculty voted in 1947 to delete explicit statements in the student handbook banning alcohol at social functions. Instead it expressed the expectation that each
student would "conduct himself as a gentleman at all times" and "refrain from any
action which would bring disrepute upon the name of the college"—on pain of suspension. It also authorized a new committee headed by Charles Spotts to develop
"a positive educational approach to matters of student conduct and student morale."[51]

After discussion between members of the committee and leaders of the Inter-fraternity Council (IFC) — and several cases of "excessive drunkenness and ungentle-manly conduct" at the annual IFC Ball — the Morale Committee proposed making student organizations responsible for regulating their members' behavior. The *Student Weekly* reported that fraternity leaders agreed "that the tradition of getting plastered at the ball would have to undergo some modification." Moreover, the present method of enforcement by means of faculty and administration chaperones was awkward for everyone concerned. The faculty therefore decided to experiment with self-regulation, although fraternities were still subject to penalties of the loss of social privileges or the right to pledge new members.[52]

Over the next two years, fraternities repeatedly proclaimed their desire to build a "high reputation for responsible conduct." IFC sponsored good works, such as raising funds to support two "displaced persons," European refugees, to attend Franklin & Marshall, while Phi Kappa Psi offered free housing for a third. Nevertheless, under the new regime, drinking expanded from something done on special occasions to an everyday affair. Seven fraternities set up permanent bars in the basements of their chapter houses, some going so far as to install paneling, elaborate lighting, foot rails, and stools. "It should be said to their credit that the results indicate the exercise of me-chanical, artistic, and inventive skills," Spotts admitted. Though recommending an edu-cational campaign to present "objective facts about alcohol, its use, its effects, and its control," the committee thought the "experiment" should continue for another year.[53]

The new policy ran against public concerns about college drinking and inspired protests from parents, some alumni, leaders of the Evangelical and Reformed Church, and even nonfraternity students who complained that they weren't allowed to keep liquor in the dorms. The faculty revisited the issue in the spring of 1950. After much debate, it voted 40 to 26 to prohibit storage or consumption of alcohol in fraternities or at college functions on or off campus. A committee appointed to draw up regula-tions was strongly divided, with a minority of younger faculty charging that the new rules contradicted the college's general principle of "self-regulation." They also objected, as "onerous," proposed changes to the faculty handbook obligating them as officers of the college to help enforce the rules and chaperone student events. When regulations were finally adopted, Distler "strongly urged" faculty to "assume the responsibility thus placed on them by this action."[54]

Younger faculty were less likely to defend fraternities' rights of self-determination when it came to another aspect of what was coming to be called the "fraternity question"—clauses in fraternities' national charters barring members of certain racial or religious groups. The college addressed this issue in an assembly featuring a debate between Dean Gibson, described as "a non-fraternity man," and P. P. Martin, faculty advisor to the IFC. "It seems to us that every group is, by its nature, discriminatory," asserted a *Student Weekly* editorial. It defended admission requirements as a necessary part of a fraternity's func-tion as "models of democratic government": "It is in a fraternity that many learn to sub-mit to the will of the majority for the first time." But as public opinion began to question anti-Semitism and racial segregation, faculty and administrators were less willing to grant fraternities the freedom to discriminate.[55]

The influence of fraternities at Franklin & Marshall was heightened by a scarcity of social venues on campus. Wartime renovations eliminated spaces in Campus House previously used for group meetings or relaxation after class. Because Pennsylvania's strict blue laws banned parties on Sundays, most college dances were held on Friday nights because they continued into the early morning hours. Fraternities filled the gap on Saturday evenings with private parties, while outsiders were left to their own resources.[56]

A new student union was part of a campus development program put together by the board at the close of the war. At first the board proposed raising $3.5 million for a long list of new buildings, renovations, and equipment and adding $4 million to the endowment, all by the time of the college's 175th anniversary in 1962. A consultant quashed the plan, warning that a campaign with such a large goal and long duration was likely to scare off prospective donors. Moreover, he found little awareness of Franklin & Marshall College among major funders. The board decided instead to begin with a short, intensive campaign in 1947 to raise at least $600,000 to renovate Fackenthal Laboratories and Stahr Hall, to add desperately needed space for seven departments and administrative offices. To strengthen the college's reputation, the board established a public relations department headed by Max Hannum, formerly head of public relations for the Carnegie Institute of Technology.[57]

Distler announced the campaign in conjunction with homecoming festivities in October 1946. A new event, Founders Day, was marked by a formal academic convocation and bestowal of honorary doctorates. Two descendants of John Marshall attended as special guests, and Justin Miller, president of the National Association of Broadcasting Stations, delivered a principal address extolling Benjamin Franklin's wide-ranging accomplishments. At the alumni banquet, Distler outlined plans to remodel Stahr and Fackenthal. Space in Stahr would be doubled by adding wings, and the entire building would be refaced in red brick to bring it into "harmony with the rest of campus." The architect also envisioned creating a new campus gateway by opening archways through the ground floor. These changes, Distler explained, would give the building "features of the Wren Building and the Capitol at Williamsburg, Virginia."[58]

Beginning with a local drive, the campaign reached $800,000 by early 1949. Board president Paul Kieffer congratulated Distler, noting that he could not help feeling that Distler had been "in a very real sense the vital spirit of the whole thing." Indeed, local business enthusiasm for the college manifested the close town-gown relationship that Distler had worked hard to develop. Nonetheless, rampant postwar inflation eroded what could be done with that sum. Costs of enlarging Fackenthal Laboratories, originally estimated at $200,000, nearly doubled by the time the work was completed in the fall of 1949. Meanwhile, estimates for the proposed expansion and renovation of Stahr Hall rose to nearly $700,000. Although Distler urged the board to help keep the campaign going, little more was secured.[59]

Work finally began on Campus House after the Alumni Council dedicated proceeds of its 1949 appeal to the project. The campus post office moved to Old Main and was replaced by a dining hall and snack bar, with a new wing for the kitchen on the western side. A "Student Union" was established on the second floor. Aided by funds raised by a faculty talent show, the Student Council took charge of furnishing the space and planning social events. Complete with leather furniture and tables for card playing and ping pong, the lounge was open each day from 7:00 A.M. to 10:30 P.M. A year later, a television was added, giving most students their first experience of the new medium.[60]

Seasons of Discontent

By 1950 Franklin & Marshall College seemed securely established. Dr. Charles W. Mayo, head of the Mayo Clinic, spoke at the dedication of the enlarged Fackenthal Laboratories. Harold E. Stassen, president of the University of Pennsylvania and sometime candidate for the Republican nomination for the U.S. presidency, spoke at Founders Day exercises. Dwight D. Eisenhower, then president of Columbia University, was unable to attend winter graduation exercises as planned, but he and Mrs. Eisenhower paid a special visit to campus in March. The political orientation of this list of notables was reflected in Mayo's reference to American small colleges as the "bulwarks of our freedom" and Eisenhower's assertion that preserving world peace demanded combining armed might with moral, intellectual, and physical strength to show the world "the American belief that every man is his own master." As ideological contention heated up both at home and abroad after the war, Distler himself had become widely known for his advocacy of the sturdy values of industry, individual responsibility, and community service to ward off the specter of creeping socialism and "statism." In 1949 he helped found Americans for the Competitive Enterprise System, a probusiness and anti-Communist organization, and served as its first Pennsylvania president.[61]

Yet there were signs that all was not well. Enrollments had begun to decline after reaching a peak of 1,423 in the fall of 1948. Of 1,384 students in 1949–1950, fewer than 15 percent were veterans. As their influence waned, the student body was less focused on study. Or, as Distler told the board, "With the return of the so-called more normal undergraduate we shall also have a return of many of the immaturities which were so little present when the college was most largely composed of ex-G.I.'s."[62]

The campus environment was becoming more contentious. Faculty meetings were so heated that peacemakers suggested a special meeting "to iron out some probable mis-understandings between Faculty and administration." Students complained loudly about administration actions, such as stricter parking rules enforced by $25 tickets. One senior satirist suggested supplementing the armbands worn by the new "driveway guards" with uniforms and automatic rifles and adding a "Dean of Gates" to the growing ranks of the administration. Faculty as well as students resented being required to submit daily attendance reports whether or not the faculty member personally required attendance. The student wag recommended installing time clocks and adding a "Dean of Attendance," to be followed by a new "Dean of Expensive and Nonsensical Ideas to Torment Students." "More and more we hear such terms as: junior high school, prep school, navy life," the *Student Weekly* observed. "These terms describe a situation that has no place on a college campus that is dedicated to training men for responsible leadership."[63]

Student leaders demanded greater freedom and responsibility and complained about the childishness of college regulations and fellow students alike. Inspired by a regional conference of the National Student Association, the Student Council sought representation at faculty meetings. Most faculty opposed the idea but agreed that students could have representatives on major committees dealing with student affairs. Many complained about rude behavior at assemblies. A *Weekly* editorial suggested that rowdiness could be avoided by providing programs "of more appeal"—such as offering a "weekly sand-box-and-paper-doll hour" or screening "Howdy Doody."[64]

Students complained more openly about the quality of their education. Several times the Student Council recommended instituting student evaluations of faculty, and several times the faculty refused, although it did prepare a voluntary questionnaire for a teacher's private use. In the spring of 1950, a *Weekly* editorial characterized the advising system as "next to worthless" and complained of the paucity of personal relationships between students and professors. Another writer charged that comprehensive examinations tested memorization rather than intellect.[65]

Students disagreed on a wide range of issues, from freshman regulations to national politics. A debate over regulations drew a spirited crowd to a Diagnothian Society meeting, where freshmen called the regulations un-American, unconstitutional, and un-Christian, and sophomores thought them "necessary to the very existence of any college" because they created school spirit and class unity, were "part of [the] school's tradition," and were simply "more fun." A heated discussion by an evenly divided audience followed. Some, such as a *Student Weekly* correspondent, thought such antics outmoded: "The gay old pastimes of campus painting, gold fish eating, should certainly be left in moth-balls along with the fur coat and the little red car with the attached pennant." In contrast, many students longed for a return of the good old days, when winning a big football game meant a Monday holiday and when Franklin & Marshall was known as a football powerhouse. Students who had long followed college teams complained that Franklin & Marshall's "simon-pure" recruiting policy was causing it to lose to less rigorous schools.[66]

The college divided over issues related to the Cold War. The Student Christian Association opposed universal military training. When its members tried to circulate fliers addressed to "Dear Cannon Fodder" at an assembly, without administration approval, they were denounced as "communistic elements." Dean Gibson charged that their tactics resembled those of Communist organizations, and local papers seized the issue in what the *Weekly* termed "a red-baiting scare." It thought the students involved could not "justly be called Communists," for they were simply "peaceful minded" men who opposed "militaristic tendencies in our country." Later, an assembly heard representatives of the U.S. Army Reserve and the Student Christian Association debate universal military training. Students divided evenly, 49 percent for and 51 percent against.[67]

In early 1950 an event occurred that, tragic in itself, threatened to damage town-gown relations. The disappearance of Marian Louise Baker, a pretty twenty-one-year-old secretary in the treasurer's office, triggered a regionwide search. When her battered body was found several days later, the story became a national media sensation. Distler expressed the college community's shock and sadness at the death and promised every cooperation. He gave police names of some two hundred students who had been off campus at the time of the murder and of one hundred who owned cars. Police interviewed many.[68]

Several days later, twenty-five-year-old senior Edward Gibbs saw police examining his car and then learned that they wanted to speak to him. Instead, he walked into Distler's office and confessed, "I'm your man. I did it." An army veteran, only son of a prominent Pitman, New Jersey, family, Gibbs was married and lived with his wife in East Hall. He told police that he had offered Baker a ride, driven her to a wooded area south of town, and, on sudden "impulse," begun to choke her. After a struggle, he killed her with a lug wrench from his car. Following the arrest, Distler spoke of the college's distress and asked for "a sympathetic understanding of the college's position." Lancaster mayor Kendig Bare affirmed that "no fair-minded person" would see recent "unfortunate events" as bearing any reflection on Franklin & Marshall. Nevertheless, as the case moved swiftly to trial, it did not help that the prosecution rested its case for first-degree murder upon Gibbs's comments at the time of his arrest: "I'm an intelligent man; I've nearly finished college. . . . I never thought you'd catch me." His defense attempted to show that he was mentally unstable and that, a poor student, he had been distressed that he would not graduate. He was convicted and sentenced to the electric chair. His execution a year later left his motive still essentially a mystery.[69]

At the beginning of 1950 Distler told the board that all institutions faced falling enrollments over the next decade because of low Depression-era birthrates. He left several positions open, to reduce the faculty to eighty-one from a high of eighty-three the previous year. With Gibson's departure, Distler combined positions of dean of the college and dean of students and assumed responsibility as head of the faculty himself: "We are a small college and the President must therefore necessarily be leader of the faculty. I have tried delegating this duty to others and it does not work [because faculty want to deal] with the head of the institution." He warned the board that he would have to cut his extensive outside speech-making and committee work. "I felt that this intensive program was necessary in order that Franklin and Marshall would be better known to a wider constituency," he explained. He had concluded it required too frequent absence from campus. He would also have less time to spend on fund-raising, and he called on the board to take more responsibility. More than $300,000 was still needed for renovations to Stahr Hall, and he reminded the board of an "acute" need for a new field house. Biesecker Gymnasium was too small for intercollegiate competitions in basketball and wrestling, which were held off campus.[70]

The board considered plans for a new science museum. The college had long hoped for a separate building to house its natural history collections, now filling the third floor of Stahr Hall and more often visited by school and community groups than college students. Under the direction of emeritus chemistry professor H. H. Beck and an enthusiastic staff of volunteers, the museum opened to the public on Sunday afternoons and by appointment — an attempt to open on weekdays ended when staff found that "visitors on the stairways, particularly children, disturbed classes."[71]

Postwar classroom shortages increased pressure to move the collections. Distler and board leaders had negotiated since the mid-1940s with trustees of the estate of Hugh M. North Jr. with the idea of combining forces to construct a natural history museum on campus. North's will intended the creation of a museum, but the estate's funds were insufficient. Most of his trustees supported transferring to the college the balance of the trust fund, estimated at $200,000, to build and operate a museum consistent with North's will, but securing approval from everyone concerned dragged on for years. Finally, in early 1950 all that remained was to gain assent from the Lancaster County Orphans' Court. As Distler confided to Kieffer, he was eager to get the project moving in order to move collections from Stahr before renovations began — even if the available money would not "build much of a Museum." In June Distler told the board that the latest estimates for construction were nearly $211,000, and he hoped for a substantial gift from "a friend in town" once the trust fund was obtained.[72]

But by the time the Orphans' Court heard the case in July 1950, the situation for the college and the rest of the nation had changed dramatically, as U.S. troops rushed to South Korea to counter an invasion by its northern neighbor. In the eight months that it took to receive an opinion, the college's fortunes took a sharp turn for the worse. When the fall semester opened in late September, ninety students had been lost to the draft, enlistment, and reserve activation, and enrollment declined 14 percent from the previous year. It dropped further, to 1,104, by the beginning of the second semester. Once again, national leaders were maddeningly slow in deciding how to handle the manpower issue. "Too much depends upon what Congress, the President, and Mr. Stalin may do," Distler told the board in October. "If present thinking" were to continue, he worried that the next year's registration might decline by another 40 percent. At any rate, he warned the college to prepare for ten to fifteen years of "either a hot or a cold war." He took a leading role in efforts by the Association of American Colleges and the American Council on Education to press the government to establish universal military training in a way that would "utilize the college to the utmost" and fill military needs while minimizing loss of personal freedom. At home he persuaded a reluctant faculty to approve his efforts to secure some form of reserve officers' training corps. An application to the army failed because the college did not teach engineering. Meanwhile, to forestall an impending deficit, the college revived its annual fund drive among alumni and local industries and began to solicit parents. A separate office of college development was created in 1951.[73]

William Schnader, chair of the board's Committee on Financial Resources, led efforts to find new sources of revenue. He told the board that the president "was a little discouraged" about the failure of the college's finances to keep pace with its educational programs — and the board's failure to shoulder more responsibility for strengthening them. As its vice president, Schnader revived the Executive Committee. The decision presaged a more assertive role for the board — and especially Schnader — in college affairs.[74]

The Executive Committee approved Distler's request for temporary leave to head Pennsylvania's new Civil Defense system. Distler explained that he felt that the governor's appointment to head up the new program was "a call to duty" that he could not refuse. The job was principally to organize and coordinate local groups, and he promised to resign from the appointment as soon as this was done. For several months, he continued to live on campus and meet committees in the evenings while commuting to Harrisburg. Meanwhile, he aided the college's finances by foregoing his usual salary.[75]

The subject of budget cutting was on everyone's minds. Noting his reluctance "to begin a war period with a deficit," Distler told the APD Committee at the end of 1950 that the college would have to cut costs or reduce faculty salaries. "It is necessary that we enter into a period of team play," he stated. But many faculty were not in a team frame of mind. Discussions at AAUP meetings focused on recent growth of spending on student services and administration. An AAUP committee "respectfully" called Distler's and the board's attention to "certain facts," especially that faculty salaries had not kept pace with the rising cost of living. Average wages of manufacturing workers increased 152 percent between 1939 and 1950, while prices rose 73 percent. In contrast, average salaries at Franklin & Marshall had increased only 2 percent between 1932 and 1949. To maintain their standard of living, many faculty members took second jobs and observed economies that hampered their effectiveness as teachers. They called upon the administration to keep salaries at the cost of living and offered to select a committee to work with the administration to identify other places to cut. After meeting with Distler, biology professor James M. Darlington, AAUP vice president, reported that he expressed sympathy with their situation but felt that a faculty committee "might presage unwarranted Faculty participation in administrative affairs." The board authorized a committee of trustees, faculty, and administrators to study possible economies, specifying that Distler, not the AAUP, was to choose committee members.[76]

Franklin & Marshall's AAUP chapter had assumed a central role in faculty life. Four out of five instructors were members, and its four meetings each year provided a rare opportunity for faculty-only discussion and conviviality. Aside from one dinner meeting a year, administrators were not invited. Distler found this unnerving — he sometimes called young faculty after meetings to find out what had happened.[77]

The faculty's growing sense of professionalism and sensitivity about its rights were aroused by challenges to the academic freedom of colleagues elsewhere. AAUP meetings discussed these events and debated issues such as whether membership in the Communist Party constituted grounds for dismissal. (Members were unable to reach agreement in this case.) When faculty members at the University of California resisted imposition of a loyalty oath, Franklin & Marshall's AAUP circulated a petition supporting their struggle "to maintain their historic right of self-determination." Though some were reluctant to proceed without Distler's approval, sixty-seven of seventy-five faculty signed. In spring 1951, the issue hit closer to home when the Pennsylvania legislature considered adding members of state-aided educational institutions to a list of persons required to sign loyalty oaths. A special AAUP meeting approved, 28 to 2, a resolution opposing all loyalty oaths or tests for teachers. Two years later came news that their former colleague Barrows Dunham had been fired from his philosophy position at Temple University for refusing to answer some of the questions put to him by the House Un-American Activities Committee.[78]

Franklin & Marshall was spared its worst fears of a repeat of the disruptions of the early 1940s, although enrollments continued to be a problem through the early 1950s. The Selective Service Act that passed in the spring of 1951 allayed some apprehensions. To ensure adequate numbers of future scientists and other intellectual leaders, Congress created a system of student deferments that tied the nation's institutions of higher education ever more closely to the federal government. Deferments went to college students who ranked in the top half of their classes or who scored seventy or above on a test of "scholastic aptitude" administered by the newly established Educational Testing Service. "It means the lean years will not be as lean as we expected," Dean Breidenstine commented. He predicted a boost in student morale, but the *Student Weekly* noted that "students went after their books with a new zeal and anxiously eyed their averages." Moreover, public opinion immediately attacked the elitism of the new system, and a *Weekly* columnist observed that there was a "barrage of opposition" in Lancaster.[79]

After energetic lobbying, Distler landed a U.S. Air Force ROTC program in air science and tactics. When the 1951–1952 year opened, more than three hundred students, including nearly three-quarters of freshmen, donned the "snappy new sky-blue uniforms" of cadets. Even so, enrollment declined to 1,038, and Breidenstine admitted that the smaller size of the college-age population meant admission of less-qualified candidates than during the GI boom.[80]

If the atmosphere on campus was strained, it was not for want of attempts to improve it. At an AAUP discussion of the "social atmosphere" on campus, mathematics professor Donald Western noted tensions from his vantage point as a newcomer. He commented that the college seemed to be "suffering from growing pains," in that "it [was] hard for the old faculty to absorb the new." To improve communication, Distler and a student-faculty committee revamped the assembly program, cutting back to one meeting a month and featuring members of "the college family" rather than outside performers. The goal, according to the *Student Weekly*, was "to help develop college spirit and to create, on the part of the students, a conscience of belonging to the whole college."[81]

The November assembly, a panel discussion on how to foster better relations among students, faculty, and administration, was disrupted by a "noisy" group of students — members of fraternities recently disciplined for violating the ban on alcohol — who denounced the administration's "dictatorial" policies. Distler was "visibly shaken" at being roundly booed by his own students. He warned faculty that "a spirit of unrest" seemed to be growing on college campuses. He hoped to contain it through cooperation. A series of open meetings in the Student Union aimed at raising "morale" more often dramatized stark divisions on campus. A similar series of meetings of "key students and faculty" at Distler's home the following year produced more expressions of hope for progress, but little real accomplishment. A *Weekly* editor blamed a general "lack of trust" on administrators' failure to explain their actions. Yet when the administration tried to improve communication by publishing a weekly column in the *Weekly*, its editors decided not to run it because the paper represented students, not faculty or administration.[82]

A few days after marking the tenth anniversary of his presidency in early December 1951, Distler suffered a serious heart attack. He did not return to work full-time until the following autumn. During his absence, Dean Breidenstine and other members of the faculty and administration assumed his duties.[83]

During his absence, AAUP held an open question-and-answer session with Breidenstine that focused on relative responsibilities and authority of administration and faculty. John Noss expressed the faculty's "overwhelming sentiment" that it had lost power in recent years. Several complained that the administration burdened faculty members with responsibility to enforce policies they had not made, and many called for a voice in appointing committees, now completely in Distler's hands. Faculty also resented being required to attend faculty meetings — lists of those absent without excuse were regularly preserved in the minutes — as well as formal occasions such as convocations and the annual Reformation Day service in local churches.[84]

Fraternities remained a source of contention. Much of the conflict revolved around the prohibition issue, as faculty dislike for enforcement only made it harder for fraternities to find chaperones for social occasions. Faculty also resented fraternity influence over academic life, such as requests for lighter workloads for events such as the IFC Ball and Construction Week — a period of "voluntary" service that had ostensibly replaced the traditional hazing of Hell Week. AAUP discussions of students often became venues for complaint about fraternities. Paul Martin, faculty representative to the IFC, charged the faculty with "a passive attempt to kill them off by negation and inattention." Too many faculty treated fraternities and their suggestions "as a joke," he asserted, and only gave them responsibility "when the job would be distasteful" for them to perform. He urged deciding what role fraternities should play and then seeking to lead them rather than alternating between permissiveness and repression.[85]

Work finally began on the North Museum and Stahr Hall in mid-1951. Inadequate funds forced "temporary" reduction of the Stahr renovation to the adding of wings on the north and south sides, extending toward College Avenue. During Distler's absence, board members stepped up fund-raising efforts. William French, the new director of development, attempted to interest major donors in long-range projects. He pointed out that although the endowment had grown by a third over the past ten years, it supported a decreasing proportion of total expenses, from 16 to 10 percent.[86]

While the faculty's salary scale remained unchanged, the board offered some new amenities to its compensation package. The College Retirement Equities Fund (CREF) was added to the Teachers Insurance and Annuity Association (TIAA) pension system, allowing faculty and staff to invest a portion of their savings in stocks. The college also joined a number of other colleges and universities in a tuition exchange program for faculty children — a valuable program because faculty had been experiencing a baby boom of their own. Faculty sons could attend Franklin & Marshall free, but this obviously did not help the substantial number of daughters.[87]

More faculty managed to conduct research and writing programs. Some were recent arrivals, but a number had been at the college for many years. John Noss, for example, had written *Man's Religions*, a mammoth survey on world religions, during summer vacations over the course of a decade and a half. The first of many editions was published by Macmillan in 1949 and adopted at dozens of schools in the United States and abroad. M. Ray Adams, chairman of the English department, published *Studies in the Literary Backgrounds of English Radicalism* in 1947. Before the proliferation of university presses in the 1950s and 1960s, publication of such purely academic books was rare. The college put out Adams's book as part of a series initiated in 1938 by H. M. J. Klein, whose other works dealt primarily with aspects of the college's history. College members benefited from new opportunities for international study and research offered by the Fulbright scholarship program. In 1951 senior Richard Druckenbrod won the college's first Fulbright for study in Austria, and Greek professor Donald Prakken received a grant in 1954 to teach in Greece.[88]

But the college's science departments continued to have the strongest reputations. In 1953 Franklin & Marshall's chemistry department was one of only nineteen nationwide to receive a $2,500 grant from DuPont in recognition of "outstanding work in stimulating interest in education in Chemistry." It was a fitting testament to a lifetime of teaching (without benefit of a Ph.D.) by William E. Weisgerber, who had retired the previous year. RCA and Union Carbide, both of which had factories in the area, selected the college for scholarship programs. A fund established by board member John L. Atlee Jr. provided the college's first money specifically earmarked for research. Two events in 1954 gave clear evidence of the college's strength in the sciences: formation of a local chapter of Sigma Xi, the national honorary organization for science research, and receipt of a $10,000 grant from the National Science Foundation (NSF), to Richard Foose of the geology department for summer fieldwork. NSF had been created in 1950, inspired by the success of the wartime Office of Scientific Research and Development in promoting research in basic science. Quickly becoming one of the college's largest benefactors, NSF helped to perpetuate the preeminence of the sciences at the school.[89]

Debating the Role of Athletics

Many students, alumni, and community members continued to deem success in inter-collegiate athletics as most important for Franklin & Marshall's reputation. Some $20,000 a year was allotted for athletic scholarships at this time, about one-fifth of the college's total scholarship money, plus $4,800 in work awards. This was more than many faculty thought appropriate but not enough to compete with resources available at some traditional rivals. Shober Barr had returned to athletics in 1949 as professor of physical education and director of athletics. When he made a number of cuts, boosters blamed him for weakening the college's competitiveness. Some students questioned why the college was building a science museum instead of the much-needed and long-promised field house.[90]

Yet the college's teams often did well. The track team had its first undefeated season in 1947 and took second in the Middle Atlantic Collegiate track meet. In 1950 the football team achieved the first perfect season in college history, and the soccer team took the championship of the Middle Atlantic Soccer League. In 1952 the basketball team set a national scoring record with 1,586 points in nineteen games, and the soccer team had its first undefeated season and was named best in the nation by the National Intercollegiate Soccer Coaches Association. Its star player Carl Yoder was named to the All-American team, the first Franklin & Marshall student to achieve that honor. Even so, many students were upset that administrators kept the 1950 football team from accepting an offer to play in the Cigar Bowl and further frustrated when several feelers to the 1952 team were summarily rejected.[91]

It was a time of widespread change in intercollegiate athletics, as the advent of television seemed destined to draw the attention of local audiences toward teams of the bigger universities. Franklin & Marshall participated in an experimental National Collegiate Athletic Association (NCAA) program to study the effects of television on attendance, when its 1951 game with Washington and Jefferson College was televised locally over station WGAL. In 1952 Barr represented small colleges on a special NCAA television committee meeting, where he spoke out strongly against televising games. "Regional television," Barr stated at the NCAA conference, "would mean electric chair death to our kind of football." His main concern was loss of gate receipts, but in the long run it became clear that television shifted popular attention toward bigger football teams and conferences and heightened the gap between large and small programs.[92]

Upon his return to duty, Distler convened a committee of faculty, coaches, and leaders of all varsity teams to discuss the future of athletics. The NCAA had recently delegated decisions about recruiting rules to individual athletic conferences, and the Middle States Association had also set its own standards. He insisted that Franklin & Marshall complied "not only with the letter but the spirit of the law" as defined by the NCAA and the Eastern Collegiate Athletic Conference but admitted that Franklin & Marshall's limited scholarship program put it in an awkward position, in which it fit with neither "high priced scholarship teams" nor "strictly amateur teams." The time seemed ripe for planning, to meet requirements of governing bodies and "the best educational aims of the institution." The committee and subsequently the faculty debated issues of athletic scholarships and recruitment at length but came to no decision, and the board elected to continue present practices.[93]

Faculty deliberated under a new system for meetings begun in 1953, in which agendas were set jointly by the president and a special faculty committee. To allow for extended discussion of policy questions, the college held some evening meetings and open hearings. In refining procedures for its meetings, the faculty manifested its growing sense of independence. It created its own bylaws, which carefully defined who was (and was not) included in the faculty and hence entitled to voting privileges, and codified the process of setting academic policy. Faculty reconfirmed the requirement to attend meetings, the confidentiality of proceedings, and the binding character of decisions.[94]

A Quiet Centennial Celebration

In keeping with its fragile finances, the college celebrated the centennial of the merger of Franklin & Marshall Colleges modestly. Founders Day in 1952 was extended to a week of appearances by eminent academics and businessmen. Formal observances of the centennial in April 1953 focused on the college's religious ties. These celebrations were an outgrowth of participation in a national discussion of "the nature and function of the Christian College in contemporary America" conducted by the Association of American Colleges' Commission on Christian Higher Education. Franklin & Marshall's committee recommended using the centennial as "an opportunity to *celebrate* our church-relatedness" and to consider how well the college was fulfilling its role as a church-related liberal arts college. The celebration concluded on Sunday afternoon with Church Day, an open house that attracted some five hundred visitors to campus. The many Evangelical and Reformed young people in attendance were feted as prospective students. Although few current students participated, Church Day proved so successful as a recruiting device that it was continued through the rest of the decade.[95]

The college published two scholarly works highlighting its history. Luther J. Binkley, who had recently joined the philosophy department, wrote his Harvard doctoral thesis on Mercersberg Theology; it contributed to renewed scholarly interest in the movement. The Reverend Howard J. B. Ziegler's biography of Marshall College's first president, Frederick Rauch, was based on careful research into his early life in Germany; it dispelled a number of long-standing myths. Both works underlined the importance of German philosophy and theology in the college's development.[96]

Students were more impressed, however, by two less official events that spring. In March, the Diagnothian Society sponsored *A Town Meeting of the Air* at McCaskey High School, which was broadcast over local station WLAN and nationwide over ABC. Congressmen Eugene McCarthy of Minnesota and Carroll Kearns of Pennsylvania debated "who should judge the fitness of our college and university professors to teach?" Afterward, the *Student Weekly* awarded "a T.K.O." to audience members who criticized Kearns's support for HUAC attacks on professors. "This, it seems, aroused the ire of many 'fancy' talking students and faculty," the *Weekly* commented, "and provided the most entertaining portion of the Diag sponsored event."[97]

Another event would go down in college memory as the great "Birdwalk." As North Museum neared completion, curators had to move the "large, fragile and valuable collection of mounted birds" to their new home, a procedure that was too delicate to be entrusted to a moving company. Sociology professor Charles Holzinger came up with the idea of "Operation Birdwalk," in which members of the college community would carry the birds by hand. The *Weekly* urged students who were free at 2:00 P.M. to turn up at Stahr Hall, noting that they would "be doing a great deal to build that intangible thing — morale, which can only arise when students work as an all-college group." More than three hundred students and faculty successfully moved a thousand birds and many other exhibits. Holzinger awarded prizes to those who most resembled the birds they carried or who transported the largest and smallest birds.[98]

Chronic Unrest

Unrest persisted behind the scenes. The AAUP stepped up pressure for salary increases with a report and petition calling on the board to restore the purchasing power of the mid-1930s "if the college is to continue to attract and hold competent teachers." Distler repeatedly stressed the need to increase salaries, but in the tight financial situation the board generally felt little could be done. In June 1953, as the college faced its first substantial deficit in many years and the prospect that enrollments would fall below one thousand, Distler pleaded eloquently that faculty must be retained and strengthened to be ready for "the great influx of students" in the future. The board agreed to a combination of merit increases and across-the-board adjustments. Several foundation grants earmarked for faculty salaries helped — $10,000 for science faculty from the Gustavus and Louise Pfeiffer Research Foundation and $50,000 from the Kresge Foundation, to endow a chair of philosophy and ethics in memory of former professor Elijah E. Kresge.[99]

Several events signaled disquiet within the faculty. Shortly before the beginning of the 1952–1953 academic year, the community was shocked to learn of the suicide of Frederick Foster, longtime biology professor and mainstay of the premedical program. During the year, several faculty members resigned to take positions in private industry, and many expressed frustration at what they saw as an anti-intellectual climate and the poor academic quality of students. The yearly AAUP meeting with administrators focused on these issues. Breidenstine responded that the college attracted many good students, but they were primarily interested in the sciences. "We could fill every Freshman class with pre-medical students alone," he later explained.[100]

In January, psychology professor Paul Whitely unwittingly triggered a crisis when his statement opposing the execution of Ethel and Julius Rosenberg appeared in the Communist *Daily Worker*. Called to discuss the situation with the APD Committee, he expressed regret at causing the college embarrassment. Whitely, a member of the Society of Friends, was widely known for his advocacy of liberal and pacifist causes. "A lawyer from New York City" whom he did not know had asked him to make a statement, and because he responded on college stationery, Franklin & Marshall's name was mentioned in the *Worker's* story. Distler assured Whitely that he was not being asked to remain silent but to be more careful about how and to whom he made statements.[101]

More vexing was the case of Herbert Herington, an associate professor of history. In the years since the war he had made increasingly strident attacks on the administration and a number of his colleagues, in venues spreading from AAUP meetings to his classroom, the campus, and even social gatherings with students. Over several years the APD repeatedly discussed his "acts of noncooperation" with college duties and regulations. Finally concluding that his behavior showed a growing "paranoid pattern," the APD Committee looked into a parent's charges of (unspecified) actions "detrimental to the welfare of the College." After confirming that the student and his father were willing to testify against Herington, the APD Committee informed him that a hearing would be held on the charges. Given his tenure, they were careful to follow due process. The AAUP president was invited to observe; he told Herington that "if the charges were true as presented, he (Herington) would serve the best interests of the college by voluntarily resigning; if innocent, he could prove it in the hearing." Through his attorney, Herington requested a hearing.[102]

Two hearings were held during the summer, attended by attorneys for the college and for Herington, a number of board members, the APD Committee, and the executive secretary of the national AAUP. The five APD members concluded unanimously that "Professor Herington's conduct warranted his dismissal from the faculty," despite tenure. They recommended an equitable financial arrangement "in consideration of the time of the year"; when trustees voted to dismiss him on August 17, they paid $2,500 to his wife. In announcing the action at the first faculty meeting of the year, Distler insisted that the matter had been "conducted in complete accord with good academic practice and due process." The AAUP representative acknowledged that it had been "a good hearing, providing full opportunity for presentation of evidence, conducted in a commendably judicious manner and pursuant to the provisions of the 1940 statement of principles on academic freedom and tenure." He made no comment on the substance of the decision. In the fall, the campus AAUP decided to take no action. Later, it pressed Distler to explain APD's precise authority: did it represent the faculty or the administration and did it have power to dismiss? He emphasized that the committee was advisory only and that it discussed but did not originate dismissals.[103]

There was little open reaction to Herington's dismissal, but it did seem to leave a sour taste in many mouths, particularly as it came at the height of Joseph McCarthy's campaign against "subversives" on many campuses. When radio personality Fred Van Deventer spoke at the Founders Day convocation in October, a number of faculty demonstrated their displeasure at his defense of McCarthy by making loud comments and tapping their mortarboards against their shoes. In a reversal of roles, the *Student Weekly* chastised the faculty's "ungentlemanly" and "childish" behavior. A member of the faculty responded by denouncing Van Deventer's speech as "a stupid, inane and meaningless collection of platitudes and catchwords the like of which I pray I shall never have to listen to again." It is not clear how widespread was the opinion expressed by the *Weekly*'s former managing editor when he denounced the administration as "petty men and their puppets," but his words were some of the harshest in the paper's long history: "As long as they are in control Franklin and Marshall will remain a mediocre place of learning instead of a great one."[104]

Later, Distler recalled that he concluded that fall that he had accomplished about all that he could at Franklin & Marshall. "You need a new challenge and the College needs a new man who has different qualifications in larger proportion than you have," he told himself—particularly skills in developing academic programs and long-range planning. In December he told Kieffer that he was resigning to become executive director of the Association of American Colleges. It was an excellent fit, for the AAC was as committed as Distler to promoting liberal education within independent, church-related institutions. The news was first announced at a special faculty meeting on January 7. He explained that he wanted "to serve in a broader field of education" and that he thought "perhaps F & M needs a new man, a fresh point of view."[105]

The Hall Interregnum

To conduct the search for his successor, Kieffer appointed trustees William Schnader, William Shand, H. W. Prentis Jr., Frank Fackenthal and the Reverend Dr. James E. Wagner, president of the Evangelical and Reformed Church. Kieffer accepted Distler's recommendation that the Search Committee work with a faculty committee, albeit one that was "purely advisory." He remarked that he considered the cooperation between the board and the faculty to be one of the strengths of Distler's administration. Upon hearing of Distler's resignation, AAUP leaders had prepared a petition seeking faculty involvement in the search, only to find that this was already being done. The Academic Council appointed six department heads: Noss of philosophy; Darlington, biology; Neprash, sociology; Spotts, religion; Western, mathematics; and Whitely, psychology.[106]

The impending transition prompted assessments of how far the college had come in recent years and where it should go. Breidenstine stated that weak spots in the curriculum and faculty had been improved. Most recent appointments had doctorates or were close to completing them. As for the students, he acknowledged that "not all" of them could be called "big brains," but "when a Franklin and Marshall student . . . graduated he [was] fairly strong." For his part, Distler urged the board to maintain the college's close ties with the church and the local community.[107]

The faculty too discussed a series of college objectives proposed by a committee. The faculty's response revealed a far different educational vision from that implied in administrators' reports. It accepted "in sense," four statements about the college's educational purposes: "to furnish the means of a full and thorough education . . . and thereby to help the student to discover for himself the great interest, value, and use-fulness of the arts and sciences"; "to enable the student to grow in intellectual vigor and maturity by thoroughness of instruction, challenges to serious study, and insis-tence upon intellectual integrity"; "to increase intellectual curiosity and to develop individual initiative"; and "to prepare the student for advanced education in many professions by teaching him the fundamentals of the pertinent disciplines and by helping him to understand the major problems and to acquire the necessary skills." Apart from these goals—all dealing with cognitive development—the faculty en-dorsed the intent but not the wording of items about developing "some form of" reli-gious faith and appreciation for democratic principles. It declined to endorse items concerning vocational preparation, encouragement of personal self-understanding, promotion of "wholesome recreation," "self-control," gentlemanliness, and a "spirit of neighborliness" and community participation. Although few recognized it, by accept-ing responsibility only for their students' intellectual development, the faculty was turning away from a vision of liberal education as the shaping of the "whole man" that had animated Franklin & Marshall College for a century.[108]

The faculty advisory committee drew up a "brief of specifications" for a new pres-ident, which Kieffer later described as "something in the nature of a chart by which we steered." The committee also participated in interviews of finalists, which did not take place until July. Instead of appointing an acting president from the ranks of the faculty to serve after Distler's departure, as had been done in the past, Kieffer dele-gated responsibility to an administrative committee headed by Henry Marshall and including Treasurer Donald Mylin, Dean Breidenstine, and Professor John Noss.[109]

Despite the faculty committee's involvement in the search, one of its members, James M. "Mac" Darlington, could not say precisely why the board settled on William Webster Hall. In many ways he seemed an excellent match. His academic credentials were outstanding—B.A. from Princeton, B.D. from Union Theological Seminary, Ph.D. from Yale—and he had already served sixteen years as president of two small church-related colleges, the College of Idaho (1938–1948) and Westminster College (1948–1954) in Fulton, Missouri. In announcing Hall's appointment to members of the local community, Kieffer explained that the committee had sought a president who could maintain the college's close ties to Lancaster, who was "a man with deep religious convictions, a man with a progressive outlook, and a man with a pleasing personality which will enable him to fit comfortably into the framework of our com-munity." There seemed to be something for all constituencies in Hall's qualities as an ordained Presbyterian minister, staunch advocate of preserving the distinctiveness of small, liberal arts colleges, supporter of academic standards and residential life, critic of athletic scholarships, and effective fiscal manager who ran his institutions in the black. News stories about his election invariably noted that he had been president at Westminster when Winston Churchill delivered his historic "Iron Curtain" speech there in 1948.[110]

Hall had written a lively memoir, *The Small College Talks Back*, which described frankly and humorously the struggles of running a small college and argued eloquently for the importance of liberal education in terms that appealed to both traditionalists and reformers. Liberal learning gave the student "opportunity to assimilate a knowledge of his background and the world in which he lives and to acquire the critical attitudes of mind which will free him from ignorance, superstition, prejudice, loose thinking and susceptibility to propaganda and demagoguery." As the *Lancaster Sunday News* commented, the "plain-spoken" book "rides herd on a lot of sacred cows." And as the *Lancaster New Era* observed, Hall seemed likely to fit in well in Lancaster: "He is a Kiwanian, a Republican and a member of the Phi Gamma Delta fraternity." Like Distler, he was a leader of Americans for the Competitive Enterprise System. The board ratified his selection on August 2, but he was not able to take office until the beginning of the second semester.[111]

Darlington remembered Hall as "a tall, handsome man, courtly, adept at speaking and writing," and "marvellous" socially. The future of his administration seemed bright when he and Mrs. Hall visited the college briefly in October. Trustees, faculty, staff, and their spouses attended a reception and dinner in the Halls' honor at the Campus House. A group of freshmen serenaded them with college songs; when the Halls left the party to greet them, they responded with cheers and closed by singing the alma mater. The harmonious scene seemed transported from a bygone age. It was mirrored in the formal letter that the secretary of the faculty sent to the board expressing their appreciation at being involved in the presidential search — and offering further help in dealing with problems of mutual concern.[112]

Matters did not stand still during the interval before Hall's arrival. Perhaps most important was the board's decision to apply for federal loans to build two new dormitories and a cafeteria — the first new construction in nearly twenty years and the first new dorms since the 1920s. Although federal support in the form of loan guarantees had been available for some time through the Housing and Home Finance Agency, Distler had refused to use it, doubting that rental income would be sufficient to meet loan payments. Administrators had repeatedly insisted that more and better residential facilities were needed to attract students; Treasurer Mylin estimated that the college lost one hundred upperclassmen each year because their parents did not want them living in private homes.[113]

There was growing agreement that the college's long-standing laissez-faire approach to student life could not continue in the changing climate of higher education — particularly if Franklin & Marshall wanted to compete for more academically able students. Yet there was little consideration of wider changes likely to accompany a shift to a more residential environment. At an AAUP panel discussion of the significance of the new dormitories, some questioned how becoming a residential college would affect relations with fraternities and the surrounding community and how order would be maintained on campus. No one had answers.[114]

The previous financial year had seen an operating loss of slightly less than $10,000, but that number would have been far worse without more than $100,000 raised by development. To balance the next year's budget, the Executive Committee dismissed several administrators during the summer. (They also saved the cost of

Distler's salary, for Marshall and the rest of the committee received no additional pay.) The Administration Committee unanimously recommended raising tuition for the next year, noting that it was below the levels of competing institutions like Gettysburg, Dickinson, Bucknell, and Muhlenberg. The board set tuition at $650.[115]

Faculty meetings revealed strong differences of opinion concerning vocational programs. The guidance and education departments, with organizational support from Henry Marshall, proposed a new Summer School program leading to a master's of education in guidance, specializing in working with children with reading, hearing, speech, and other problems. The proposal provoked "extended discussion" at the December faculty meeting and was tabled for further deliberation at an evening meeting a month later. There, a secret ballot voted, 26 to 17, to return the proposal to the Academic Council for further study. A straw poll showed 26 favoring a program aimed at both certification and a degree, 12 for a certificate program only, and 25 opposing any program. Physics professor F. W. Van Name urged the Academic Council to reexamine the entire program of graduate work and the Evening Division. The faculty did approve several modest changes in terminology, substituting "Government" for "Political Science"— following Sidney Wise's conviction that politics was an art, not a science — and the title of department leaders from "head" to "chairman."[116]

Hall's arrival in February 1955 was characteristically low key. Hall told local reporters that he anticipated no immediate changes and would first work to become acquainted with conditions at the college. Disliking academic pomp, he declined to be formally inaugurated. The appearance of cocker spaniels Dumbo and Thumper, who seemed to accompany Hall everywhere, signaled a more relaxed if not eccentric administrative style. Coincidentally, popular poet Ogden Nash had been engaged to speak at the first assembly of the new semester. Observing the presence of the spaniels at the president's feet, Nash began his talk by greeting his audience, "Ladies, gentlemen and dogs." He spoke about the need for more humor writing.[117]

Unfortunately, the situation that Hall entered was not well suited to his casual, conservative style. Pressure for change had been building for some time, and expectations seemed to have risen on all sides. Plans for a new capital campaign had been put on the back burner during the yearlong transition but could not wait forever. At Hall's first meeting with the board, Marshall read a petition from the Student Council urging prompt action on a new field house. Intramural leagues had been canceled to allow the varsity basketball team to practice in the gym, and few students attended the off-campus games. Noting that the college's athletic facilities "compare less and less favorably" with other schools, students argued that a field house would raise school spirit by encouraging attendance at games and making it possible to hold large social occasions on campus. It would also help make Franklin & Marshall "more of a residential college" by solving "the problem of students going home each weekend." The board took no action, but Marshall assured the Student Council that it would take up the question as soon as the new dormitories were finished.[118]

During the spring, the faculty made a formal request for a sabbatical program.

The AAUP had discussed the issue for many years and presented a proposal soon after Hall's arrival. It envisioned a modest program, allowing only five leaves a year, to be selected by a faculty committee. Faculty could receive a half year's leave at full pay or a full year at half pay after six years' teaching, at least three of which the faculty member was on tenure. AAUP emphasized that such leaves were "widely recognized" to foster "high faculty morale" and promote "outstanding scholarly attainment." With Hall's support, the plan won board approval, though stipulating presidential as well as faculty approval.[119]

Hall did not, however, support a faculty resolution, presented by AAUP president Donald Western, demanding a $500 across-the-board increase, "as a part of the continuing policy of annual increments in faculty salaries." Hall passed it on to the board but told the Executive Committee that he could find no clear statement of policy of "regular and substantial increases." True to his reputation for fiscal conservatism, he argued that under present conditions raises should come as bonuses if there was a surplus at the end of the fiscal year. The AAUP promptly called a special meeting and called this policy "unacceptable," reiterated the previous demand, and initiated a petition for a special faculty meeting. Before this occurred, the Executive Committee approved a budget for the next year that included a 6 percent increase in salaries of $5,000 or more, and $300 across the board to all staff earning less than $5,000.[120]

Hall did try to reorganize the college's administration and finances. Repeated cycles of expansion and retrenchment in Distler's years had created an unwieldy organizational structure, with a large number of positions reporting directly to the president. Hall instituted a more vertical system with four major officers reporting to him: dean of the college, treasurer, dean of athletics, and director of development and public relations. Hall wanted the development director to focus on long-term projects like foundation grants and bequests. For dean of the college, Hall appointed biology chair Mac Darlington. Whether or not Hall realized it, it was a risky but brilliant move, for among younger faculty Darlington was one of those most ambitious to transform Franklin & Marshall into a college of the first rank.[121]

About the same time, board president Kieffer informed Hall that he was stepping down. Kieffer's health was bad, and he thought that "the interests of the College and [the] administration [would] be best served by another President," perhaps one who lived closer to the college and could have "continuous contact with its affairs." The board elected William Schnader, ratifying the dominant position he had already assumed. Schnader and Marshall had often argued with Kieffer that the board should play a more active role in college governance. As if to dramatize the change in regime, Schnader called board meetings to order by blowing a whistle. "I was never quite able to adapt to that disparaging — or so it seemed to me — call to assembly," Darlington commented later. The Executive Committee also scheduled seven meetings each year and increased its role in decision making.[122]

After eight months in office, Hall complained to the board that some of the college's accounting practices remained "incomprehensible." It was not clear what had happened to capital funds raised for the renovation of Stahr Hall, for example, and "other funds [had] been transferred or borrowed or shifted around," while "operating funds [had] been applied to capital purposes," and "more than $50,000 of operating funds [had] been embedded in endowment." Meanwhile, he noted, "commitments seem to have been made for which, so far as I can find out, no provision of funds has been made." Hall also commented that development office expenses were not even recognized in the budget. He called on the Executive Committee or a special board committee to study the matter. He also recommended establishing a reserve for contingencies and hiring a business manager to modernize the college's financial procedures. They were reputed to be so primitive that many daily transactions were handled out of a cigar box in the treasurer's possession. Finally, he wanted the board to hire an outside consultant to conduct a study of the college's operations. The board resisted many of his suggestions, however; pleading lack of funds, it dragged its feet on hiring a business manager and simply appointed a subcommittee to study the college's business operations.[123]

Hall did move the college toward making a decision about the place of intercollegiate athletics. During his first semester, he and Shober Barr met with their counterparts from Muhlenberg, Gettysburg, and Hofstra with the idea of establishing a new athletic conference. Hall and Barr soon realized that they "were in the 'wrong back yard,'" for their colleagues had markedly different standards. The college's situation was becoming untenable: it was having difficulty competing with schools that subsidized sports heavily, while other schools that barred any subsidies were threatening to drop Franklin & Marshall from their schedules. Ursinus, Haverford, and Swarthmore had already done so, and Dickinson and Johns Hopkins warned they would not continue to play the college if its policies did not change. The Athletic Committee recommended discontinuing athletic scholarships beginning with the freshman class to enter in 1957; after putting off a decision for a time, the board finally agreed.[124]

By the summer of 1955 there were clear signs of change. Work on dormitories began, and registration was handled by a newly appointed registrar, Nancy Honaman Rutter, the former economics instructor. Enrollment increased to 1,147 full-time students. The board approved construction of a language laboratory on the third floor of the Liberal Arts Building. Darlington had pushed for the improvement, over Hall's objection that no funds had been appropriated. The board also established a consultative trustee-faculty committee (faculty members to be appointed by the president) to discuss faculty salaries. As a consequence, Franklin & Marshall was one of six colleges recognized at the national AAUP convention for "significant improvement" in faculty representation in governance.[125]

Early in 1956, planning began for a fund-raising campaign. The Faculty Council called for a new study to assess whether the present curriculum assured that students received "a broad and well rounded background consistent with the professed liberal aims of the college." A committee began immediately to meet on a weekly basis. Improvements in the college's finances enabled payment of $30,000 in bank loans and restoration to standing funds of another $30,000 that had been moved to operating accounts three years earlier.[126]

The Executive Committee and board avowed its intention to gradually move toward higher salary levels. This generosity was inspired by the prospect of increased endowment income from a major Ford Foundation grant. Although large foundations like Ford focused greatest effort after World War II on major research universities, they also helped underwrite development of a number of liberal arts colleges into selective university colleges. A Ford-commissioned study published in 1955 warned of an impending shortage of Ph.D.'s to meet the demand for college teachers. To attract able young people to careers in higher education, the foundation announced that it would make "endowment grants" totaling $210 million to support faculty salaries at 615 colleges and universities. The gift was billed as the largest philanthropic grant ever made to American education. Initially, Franklin & Marshall's share was $357,000, but the college was among 126 institutions receiving additional grants, in its case of $89,000, in recognition of efforts to improve faculty salaries.[127]

Still, many things had not changed. Most students enrolling in 1955 sought to enter preprofessional fields, with more than one-quarter in premedicine, nearly that number in business administration, and roughly another quarter in 3/2 engineering programs and the sciences. Only one quarter planned to major in humanities or social sciences. Some 72 percent came from Pennsylvania, with another 18 percent from New Jersey and New York, and only 8 percent from other states and four foreign countries. Despite efforts to recruit more Evangelical and Reformed students, at 12 percent they had fallen to third place among denominations represented in the freshman class, behind Catholics and Presbyterians. The percentage of Jewish students had dropped to 11 percent.[128]

Important constituencies resisted change. Although many board members seemed unaware of it, a few women had been taking classes since the war as nondegree students; during the height of the GI enrollment, many were wives of veterans, but now most were secretaries or daughters of faculty or administrators and planned to transfer elsewhere to complete their degrees. When trustee John D. Meyer noticed a reference to female students in the *Student Weekly*, he wrote Schnader that he was "badly upset." Meyer, vice president of a bank in Tyrone, Pennsylvania, had been invited to join the board in 1944 at Distler's recommendation, based principally on his status as a devoted alumnus, class of 1897, and a bachelor with few relatives. Meyer now worried that someone would try to "sneak" a resolution through the board to admit "girls": "[This] would be untrue to ourselves, our Alumni and the tradition of our beloved college." Schnader reminded Hall that Meyer had recently made a large gift to the college, adding, "He can do much more for us if he has a mind to. I do not want to alienate him if that can be avoided." At the next board meeting, Hall reported to Schnader that in recent years an average of eight women a year had attended as special students. "It might be well to have a stated policy in this regard," he commented, but he cautioned that excluding women entirely would cut a valuable employee benefit. Extended discussion culminated in passage of a motion to bar women from day classes in the next academic year. A year later, Darlington persuaded the board to reverse itself and allow faculty wives and female employees to take day courses.[129]

By early 1956 many in the college community had concluded that Hall was not up to the demands of the presidency. He was widely observed to nod off on a number of public occasions, even during committee meetings. This habit was variously attributed to eccentricity or a case of narcolepsy, but with the hindsight of later medical knowledge it might also be interpreted as a sign of sleep deprivation due to apnea or stress. Whatever the case, Hall's ambitious new dean was particularly frustrated at Hall's reluctance to press forward on new initiatives. "He lacked the discipline and decisiveness required of a college president," Darlington recalled, "particularly the leader of a college with aspirations, and potential, for growth." Darlington recalled his first year as dean as a time "of unrest and frustration."[130]

Hall himself seemed increasingly frustrated by incessant pressure from students and faculty. The *Student Weekly* and the Student Council intensified their lobbying for a field house, while Hall insisted that such major projects should, "for the good of the college, originate on the trustee level." He complained to the board, "This campus seems to me like a kind of Lewis Carroll Wonderland, with everything wrong side around." Faculty were "drawing up plans and passing resolutions without any apparent reference to ways and means," and students demanded a field house without considering how it would be paid for. "People come into my office and ask for this and that in apparent ignorance of the fact that the College operates on an approved budget," he commented.[131]

Underlying tensions finally surfaced at the May Executive Committee meeting. According to Schnader, Hall had been "intermittently talking about resigning" for months. At the meeting, Hall noted that he had "become increasingly conscious of the strains and tensions devolving on the president of a college," particularly in the midst of a major capital drive. He and his wife feared that the demands of the job were shortening his life. Hence, though he professed to be eager to participate in the campaign, he would not promise to remain in office until its completion. The Executive Committee asked Hall to resign, arguing that the college needed "someone as President who could be counted upon for a period of years." He acquiesced in "the best interests of both the college and my family." When Hall's departure was announced early in June, it was attributed to his physician's advice, although he insisted that his health was good. Whatever the precise cause, the college found itself once more in search of a president.[132]

Hall's short presidency seems to have united most of the college in the conviction that change was necessary. Under his successor there would be plenty of change but also mounting controversy about Franklin & Marshall's future.

CHAPTER NINE

Academic Revolution Meets Counter-Revolution, 1956–1962

—⁓—

During the administration of Frederick de Wolfe Bolman Jr., Franklin & Marshall took vigorous steps toward greater selectivity, academic rigor, and a restored focus on liberal education. He challenged the college to think of itself as potentially equal to the nation's best institutions. His ambitions and innovations were welcomed by many but resisted by some faculty, students, and alumni who thought overemphasis on academics endangered traditional college life. Efforts to attract a more geographically diverse student body, for example, undermined community and religious ties. In part, though, college leaders were forced to broaden recruitment, because expansion in the state's public higher education institutions threatened to draw away much of Franklin & Marshall's local constituency. In any case, opposition to change made the period one of the most contentious in the college's long history.

A Dynamic, Cosmopolitan President

For the first time, the board named its president, William Schnader, as acting president, though most administrative work was done by a committee headed once more by Henry Marshall. Also unprecedented was the speed with which the search process proceeded. Schnader quickly appointed a board committee composed of H. W. Prentis, Henry Marshall, Paul A. Mueller, James Wagner, and William Shand, and a parallel faculty committee of John Noss, Paul Whitely, John Moss, Donald Western, and chairman Charles Spotts. The two groups met on June 7, and Schnader, according to Spotts, "made it quite clear" that he expected the faculty committee to play an active role in the process. In early July the joint committee invited a short list of six candidates for interviews. One, Mac Darlington, withdrew his name from consideration.[1]

Frederick de Wolfe Bolman Jr. emerged as the clear favorite, but this time the committees were determined to make no mistake. John Moss traveled to Jamestown,

New York, where Bolman headed Jamestown Community College, which he had helped found in 1951 as the first community college in the State University of New York system. Moss inquired among "persons who were in a position to evaluate Dr. Bolman as a person, his family, and his success in his present position." Finally, Bolman and his wife were invited to Lancaster for a grueling weekend of meetings and informal gatherings with administrators, local board members, faculty, and community representatives. The board confirmed his appointment on August 7, 1956. "It is our sober judgment that the Faculty Committee played a more extensive and decisive role in this process than has ever happened before in the history of the college," Spotts reported to the faculty.[2]

It was evident that the committees sought someone with a dynamic, forward-looking style. Bolman's credentials were similar to Hall's — a B.S. in mathematics from Harvard, a divinity degree from Union Theological Seminary, and a Ph.D. in philosophy from Columbia — but at forty-four Bolman was younger and far more urbane, having spent most of his career in the New York City area. He had taught at Columbia, New York University, and Princeton and had been editor of the Great Books series for Simon and Schuster.[3]

Darlington recalled Bolman as "restless, chain-smoking, scholarly, demanding, precise, a philosopher who understood and enjoyed dialectics but knew when to halt debate and make [a] decision." His favorite saying, which soon became a catchphrase on campus, was "that down-easter's admonition to 'fish or cut bait.'" He quickly endeared himself to that portion of the faculty most committed to change, through his fierce dedication to a vision of liberal education focused on intellectual development and the pursuit of academic excellence. Although he also mentioned the role of residential life in shaping the "whole man," it was clear that he meant this in a much more intellectually rigorous sense than had been the case at Franklin & Marshall for many years. Fraternities and intercollegiate athletics were not high on his list of priorities.[4]

Even before Bolman took office, new energy seemed to pervade the college community. The board approved a $1.5 million capital campaign chaired by Henry Marshall. That sum included $357,000 for endowment to match the Ford grant, $400,000 to complete renovation of Stahr Hall, and an unspecified sum for "expansion of existing gymnasium facilities." The vagueness of the last goal reflected differences within the board about the need for a new field house. The annual Founders Day celebration in October expanded to mark the 250th anniversary of Benjamin Franklin's birth. Festivities included formal dedication of the new dormitories, named after James Buchanan and John Marshall.[5]

The faculty approved Darlington's proposal for a "book-of-the-semester" program. Inspired by a program at Rutgers University, the idea was to select a single work as "focal point" of a series of discussions throughout the semester. English professor Richard Stonesifer chaired a faculty-student committee, which picked British historian Denis W. Brogan's *The American Character*, judging it "an eminently suitable book" because it "involves many different areas of emphasis, . . . cuts across departmental lines, and . . . is a delight to read."[6]

Bolman's arrival on campus late in 1956 opened floodgates of pent-up faculty ambition for heightened professional status, particularly a greater role in governance and more active research careers. Bolman opened his first faculty meeting by stating that these meetings should be a time for deliberating "matters pertaining to the general well being of the college" as well as conducting routine business. A faculty committee that met shortly after Bolman's arrival to discuss research at the college reported that "independent, original research by some, but not necessarily all, faculty" was important both for "growth of the college's academic reputation" and faculty "intellectual development." While nonresearchers might be outstanding teachers if they engaged in wide reading and frequent revision of their course work, the committee asserted that "production of original research" was the most effective way to keep faculty intellectually "alive" and improve their teaching — as long as it was "not too time-consuming and all engrossing." Moreover, faculty who did research often involved their students in research projects, providing "a valuable introduction for students going on to graduate school." The statement contained echoes of John Stahr's 1886 rationale for building science laboratories. But though college leaders had long taken pride in graduates' going on to professional and graduate schools, the committee was now more emphatic that this was one of the institution's principal goals.[7]

The Research Committee noted that Franklin & Marshall already had "a surprising number" of faculty who wanted to do research. These faculty members were held back by a heavy teaching load, low pay that forced many to take additional jobs, lack of financial incentives, poor library facilities in some fields, and "lack of conviction on the part of the former administration that research was of any real value to the college." The committee recommended that the college encourage research by organizing faculty seminars, displaying faculty publications, reducing teaching loads, and finding money to support research. Within a matter of weeks, the college launched a series of evening research seminars.[8]

Bolman first turned his attention to the college's financial operations and administrative organization. Soon after taking office, he asked a New York firm of management consultants to present a proposal for a study of the administration. He immediately began to prepare the next year's budget so that it could be approved at the February board meeting. He reorganized it to show all accounts for which the college was responsible, for the first time divided into categories of educational, auxiliary enterprise, and endowment revenues and expenditures.[9]

At his first board meeting, Bolman won permission for the management study. Stressing the need for a student loan fund, he persuaded trustees to designate funds recently donated in memory of trustee Paul Mueller as the nucleus of such a fund. Bolman noted that applications at that point were 27 percent higher than the previous year's and predicted that admissions would play a growing role in shaping the college's character. More dormitory space and physical education and social facilities were needed to achieve "a truly residential college," and the board agreed to apply for federal loans to build another dormitory and an infirmary. It also approved the Committee on Salaries' recommendation of a further 10 percent increase in the scale for the coming year, though Bolman told both the board and the faculty that he was preparing a system based on merit rather than automatic increments.[10]

Despite modest raises in recent years, Franklin & Marshall was having difficulty competing for new faculty and retaining present members. In 1956 Hall had reported that it was all but impossible to fill vacancies at the instructor level, in large part because of the low salary scale. At the other end, the college lost several of its most productive senior faculty to research-oriented institutions.[11]

Soon after his arrival, representatives from six local industries approached Bolman about establishing associate's degree programs for technicians in electrical and mechanical engineering, chemistry, and physics. The proposal aroused faculty concern because of its vocational character, the problem of maintaining academic standards, and the possibility that they would be forced to teach evening courses. Offering reassurance on these points, Bolman and Darlington won approval from a divided faculty, 35 to 21. One vocational vestige of the college's wartime struggle for existence was left behind when Frederic Klein asked to be relieved of responsibility for the Department of Aviation. The U.S. Air Force ROTC program took over aviation training, and the college allowed its license to expire.[12]

Bolman was undoubtedly aware that local business support was essential for success of the capital drive, which was planned to get one-third of its goal from Lancaster City and County. His April inauguration showcased the college's importance. The usual academic ceremonies in Hensel Hall added a new tradition, in which the board president placed a chain with a silver medallion bearing the college seal around the new president's neck.[13]

Even so, Bolman's inaugural address presented a vision of liberal education more uncompromising than any offered by a Franklin & Marshall president since John W. Nevin. "The Educated Free Mind" stressed that "the prime task of our liberal arts colleges" was in the "training of the intellect." Bolman did not seek to revive the classical curriculum of the previous century but like his forebears argued that training an educated free mind required specific subject matter — a curriculum providing through a "variety of subjects and methodologies" the desired "mental discipline." He insisted that "real intellectual ability" was needed to solve a wide range of national problems. He celebrated America's intellectuals, offering the radical notion that it was "the first job of our liberal arts colleges to make sure of a plentiful supply of good, solid 'eggheads'!" Like Nevin, he admitted that this kind of education was not for everyone and asserted that other kinds of institutions, such as community colleges, should meet increased demand for postsecondary training. But the core task of liberal arts colleges was

> to train, generation after generation, a small coterie of specially qualified men and women who will ask new questions, break barriers of the unknown, solve scientific, social, humanistic and industrial problems — and be capable of formulating new problems. Without such training for an admittedly small but extraordinarily important part of our population the resources of

our civilization will never be exploited, and we shall be dead to the many
real possibilities of human happiness.[14]

Bolman's speech offered a blueprint not only for a more focused and selective
Franklin & Marshall, but for the brave new world to be made by the nation's intellectually best and brightest. It was a prescient statement, coming only a few months before the Soviets launched Sputnik, sparking a national reexamination of education at
all levels. With a report by President Eisenhower's Commission on Education Beyond
the High School, Sputnik dramatized the need for greater educational rigor, particularly in science, if the United States was going to compete with the regimented Soviet
system. A sense of national crisis set the stage for dramatic expansion in federal support for higher education, both directly to institutions and through grants to students.
Franklin & Marshall's Mid-Century Development Program sought to tap into this
sense of urgency by promising that the college would help meet the nation's urgent
need for trained teachers.[15]

Facing New Trends in Governance

Moving Franklin & Marshall into this new world required changes that many within
the community were not ready for. In May, the management study identified numerous points of inefficiency and lack of control. It argued, as Hall had, for the need to
consolidate responsibility for business affairs under a business manager.[16]

More controversially, the report raised fundamental questions about governance.
It recommended cutting the number of board committees and questioned whether
some of their functions were even appropriate to the board level. Noting that the college's bylaws gave several committees "general supervision" over certain areas of college
operations, the report emphasized that under current "generally accepted management principles" board committees reviewed the work of administrative officers and
recommended policies to the board in their areas of assignment. This difference reflected recent changes in governance of nonprofit organizations, changes giving greater
independence to professional administrators. Such changes were at the center of coming debates over the relative power of board and administration.[17]

The board initially resisted Bolman's requests to implement the report's recommendations. Schnader was "disturbed" by the report and concerned about costs of
implementation, and the board referred it to the Executive Committee for further
study. Over time Bolman gradually won assent to its main points. He created four executive officers, appointed by the board at the recommendation of the president and
responsible to him. He invited them to attend board meetings and speak to points in
their areas of supervision. He appointed Richard Stonesifer to a new part-time position
as assistant to the dean of the college with responsibility to ensure academic standards
in the Evening Division and Summer School. To strengthen admissions, Bolman separated admissions from placement and hired a new assistant director; the enlarged staff

traveled more widely to advertise Franklin & Marshall among high school officials. Meanwhile, improved financial record keeping raised efficiency.[18]

Physical education was redefined as an academic department and placed under the dean of the college, "on the theory that if a college supports a physical education program and varsity athletics it rationally does so only because these are educative of the whole man in a college." Bolman argued that this policy was consistent with the board's previous action eliminating athletic scholarships. "This does not mean that we are *de-emphasizing* athletics," he insisted. "It means that we are giving scholarships to those men who can win or deserve scholarships regardless of whether or not they are athletes." He predicted that eventually the college would establish a schedule with schools that followed similar principles.[19]

The board slowly moved to reorganize itself in keeping with contemporary practices. It reduced the number of standing committees to seven and revised its charter to change titles of its officers from president and vice president to chairman and vice-chairmen. The annual meeting moved to October to allow presentation of final fiscal-year reports. In 1960 the board created a second category of membership: current "term trustees" who had served for ten years would become "life trustees" when they passed their seventieth birthday. Anthony Appel, the board's counsel, explained that this was intended to "make room on the Board for younger men without in any way discouraging the older men from continuing their interest and activity." The question of voting rights was left unresolved.[20]

Bolman also had to overcome board reluctance to fund a major study of the curriculum. He explained that it had long been the practice "in a number of other colleges and universities" to release faculty from teaching responsibilities "to make a thorough analysis of all phases of the curriculum and recommendations for changes." The board balked at the estimated cost of about $25,000, but after Darlington took up the campaign, it agreed to fund the analysis out of operating revenues over two years. Darlington noted that foundations no longer subsidized such studies because the material benefits to the institutions were seen to exceed their cost. He stated, "I don't think there is any activity on the campus today which can do more to enhance the prestige of Franklin and Marshall College as an institution of unusual academic merit than a well-planned, well-manned self-study program."[21]

After months of deliberation, the faculty approved a proposal to make attendance at college chapels, assemblies and convocations "expected" rather than "required." Bolman explained that "as [teachers in] a church-related college having the most friendly and warm relations with the Evangelical and Reformed Church," the faculty considered the institution's religious life to be important but realized that at times "some current practices may need change." After "long discussion," however, the board narrowly blocked the change.[22]

Change in the church-college relationship came from outside as well. The merger of Evangelical and Reformed churches had not slaked the movement for unification. After years of discussion and deliberation, leaders of the Congregational Christian Church and the Evangelical and Reformed Church agreed in 1957 to a union, producing the United Church of Christ. This created a large denomination more evenly distributed throughout the United States, but it was unclear whether the Evangelical and Reformed Church's substantial support for the college would continue.[23]

"Fred [Bolman] had great rapport with the faculty, or a great majority of it," Darlington recalled. In many ways, Darlington noted, Bolman was more "one of them" than any president since John S. Stahr. Most faculty applauded Bolman's efforts to improve the college, though some of the old guard, like business professor Noel Laird found him "cocky, arrogant, selfish, and really not interested in the welfare of the faculty as a whole." There was concern, however, that Bolman was not moving fast enough to raise salaries. Salaries were still lower than those at other small liberal arts colleges in the East — despite recent increases, average salaries still provided only about 80 percent of the purchasing power of the late 1930s. Most faculty sought across-the-board raises, but Bolman wanted a merit system; as he told the board, many schools adopted merit increases to enable them to encourage academic talent. A joint faculty-administration-board committee compromised on a 3 percent across-the-board increase, with 5 percent of total salaries distributed according to merit, as determined by the president, dean, and department chairmen. To help fund this, the board raised tuition to $900, putting the total cost in 1958 for tuition, room and board, and fees at $1,667. Comparative data for a number of other colleges and universities in the region showed Franklin & Marshall's total cost to be around the midpoint.[24]

Bolman clearly viewed board meetings as opportunities to whip up enthusiasm for the institution and its potential; his reports grew successively greater in length and rhetorical intensity. The capital campaign showed the need for this cheerleading function, for trustees were slow and not particularly generous in pledging. "It is perfectly evident to all of us that the constituency of Franklin and Marshall could, if they would, give a very substantial sum of money," a fund-raising consultant told the board. "The problem for you and for us is to do what we can to persuade them to take action." Extended through June 1958, the campaign raised $1.1 million, plus a living trust of about $650,000 given by William Schnader, "his family and friends of Philadelphia."[25]

Challenging the College to Think Bigger

Bolman's annual report to the board in June 1958 began by emphasizing the Franklin & Marshall College's academic strengths: "I can report that we rank among the top one hundred colleges and universities in America." He offered in evidence a number of recent yardsticks. Franklin & Marshall ranked ninety-sixth in the number of graduates listed in *Who's Who*. When it came to numbers of graduates earning Ph.D.s, the college ranked in the top 12 percent in humanities and social sciences and in the top 2 percent in the sciences. Over the decade, 93 percent of its graduates applying to medical school had won admission. Its geology graduates had just received five of eight NSF earth science fellowships in Pennsylvania — and 9 percent of the total number nationwide. Though the geology department was only a decade old, Bolman commented, "[It] can well be called our Tiffany department."[26]

Such facts were not trivial. In the face of a "tremendous increase in public higher education," Bolman predicted that in coming years many low-quality and financially poor colleges [might] well go out of existence." Colleges like Franklin & Marshall that had such "Tiffany" departments, would prosper "in the first instance because they [were] worthy of support and, secondly, because their boards of trustees [were] united and strong in the determination to improve their institutions by all available means." Yet, compared with other colleges that were its academic peers — a comparison Bolman made frequently — Franklin & Marshall was "in dire need": "[It] has been performing academically way beyond its means, and this is a condition which cannot continue to exist." It could not continue, in fact, because much of its success rested on the quality of its faculty, which had in effect functioned as its endowment. With growing competition for good faculty — and the weakening pull of ethnic and denominational ties — Bolman asserted, "We shall have to pay for what we want."[27]

The college's endowment provided only 9 percent of costs, down from 35 percent in 1912. Bolman presented charts comparing the endowment, plant value, and alumni giving, in absolute numbers and per student, of twenty-four institutions ranging from elite colleges like Amherst, Williams, Haverford, and Swarthmore to regional schools like Albright, Bucknell, and Dickinson. Franklin & Marshall's endowment had reached a market value of nearly $4.6 million, but in terms of endowment per student, it ranked twenty-first; in alumni giving it was nineteenth.[28]

"This is an extraordinarily critical time in the life of this College," Bolman stressed. An unprecedented expansion in the college-age population was just beginning. Applications and enrollments had already begun to increase. Of freshmen enrolled for next year, the numbers from Lancaster County and the rest of Pennsylvania held steady, but the proportion from outside the state had risen from 36 percent to more than 53 percent in one year, including for the first time students from "distant" states like Arizona, Maine, and Kentucky. (Applications from Lancaster County had begun to decline, dropping 8 percent in 1957.) Bolman hoped that greater selectivity as well as improvements in campus facilities would attract "the highest caliber of students."[29]

Bolman insisted that this moment, when higher education in general had gained national attention, was "the moment for Franklin and Marshall College to drive for money, and drive hard!" Fund-raising advisers told him that the time was coming when the college could expect to raise $250,000 a year for operating expenses, and he hoped that expansion of the bequest program would eventually reap some $1 million a year for the endowment. This could happen — "Others have done these things," he noted — but only if everyone at the college was "determined, vigorous, and resourceful." Bolman stated, "I conclude it is high time we all get into a crusading spirit, if we really believe in this institution and its greater usefulness to American society." Specifically, he asked trustees, alumni, and friends to assume responsibility for securing their "reasonable share" of annual, capital, and endowment funds for the college. The board was so pleased with the report that it ordered it published for use as a fund-raising document.[30]

A New Curriculum for a New Intellectual Community

The Curriculum Planning Committee set to work in February 1958, with Nelson Francis working full-time and Donald Western and Richard Schier half-time on the project. Soon afterward, Francis outlined his view of the project's "mission and opportunity." In his twenty years at Franklin & Marshall, there had been no "complete and successful attempt" to examine the curriculum as a whole. The present curriculum was a "patchwork product of tradition, inertia, and special pleading." In Nelson's view, the committee's task was to plan an entire curriculum "from a disinterested point of view" and then achieve "genuine assent" within the faculty. To assess the effectiveness of the present curriculum, committee members examined courses actually taken by the present senior class and compared them with the results of Graduate Record Examination area tests. They sought the retrospective opinions of the class of 1955 about the value of their education and held several informal Sunday evening discussions with current students. The committee asked colleagues to explain how their subjects contributed to a complete liberal education.[31]

In shaping a new curriculum, the college seems to have paid no attention to its own history and traditions but much attention to practices elsewhere. The committee examined curricula at forty other liberal arts colleges and brought in outside consultants to "subject our own practice and planning to the objective scrutiny of the outsider, who is unaffected by the local situations that may prevent us from following as boldly as we might the course we think best." Committee members were gratified that the outsiders "were on the whole both surprised and pleased with what they found here." The consultants provided valuable suggestions, plus "the kind of boost in morale that comes from being approved by the expert from outside our own circle."[32]

The committee's 1959 final report began by outlining five assumptions about what a liberal arts education should do. It should help "the student to attain as complete an understanding of self as all the knowledge of past and present makes possible"; "provide an appreciation of the complex relationships of the self to others"; "provide for an adequate understanding of the interplay between the self and the physical world"; "help the student to establish for himself a code of values by which to live"; and "provide training in the skills and methods which are needed both to acquire a liberal education and to make it effective." Specifically, the proposed curriculum replaced the semester-hour unit of credit with the course, defined as one subject pursued through a single semester. In contrast with the present system, in which students took at least five and as many as nine courses at once, students would typically take only four, plus one lighter "S," or supplementary, course such as freshman composition or research methods. The committee argued that this new system prevented excessive fragmentation and allowed assignment of more reading and writing. It also reduced the faculty's course load.[33]

Through the spring the faculty deliberated as a committee of the whole in the Marshall-Buchanan dining room, for a total of ten evening sessions. Bolman opened the first meeting by stressing that a college's curriculum was its primary means of shaping student character. He quoted from an American Council on Education report, whose author, Edward D. Eddy Jr., advocated setting high expectations. "The college *can* expect more of its students," Eddy argued. "It rests on the conviction held in common by faculty and students that higher learning demands and deserves the highest possible excellence." Most of the faculty's discussions, however, turned on technical details like scheduling, calculating teaching loads, and the best times and lengths of time to study certain subjects. Many expressed fear that students would find the new curriculum too difficult, prompting Francis to point out that the college's most rigorous programs already attracted the best students. There were substantive debates on the issue of abstract versus vocational learning, particularly in connection with business administration, education, and ROTC.[34]

The faculty then met over three successive days in early June to vote on the new curriculum. The extended sessions were necessary because of intricate maneuvering by some who were seemingly intent on blocking the entire plan. Darlington later recalled that throughout the lengthy process, Bolman "held the faculty" to its task, however "prolonged, and sometimes agonizing." At one point, he was said to have given vent to his frustration by throwing his briefcase across the room. Eventually, the faculty adopted most of the committee's proposals. They voted rather narrowly (45 to 36) to make the course the unit of study and credit. In overwhelming numbers they approved moving to a single program awarding the bachelor of arts for thirty-two regular courses plus three "S" courses. They discontinued the education major, creating instead a faculty committee to supervise teacher training. Economics was established as an independent department, and business administration dropped specialized majors in favor of general concentrations in management and accounting. Faculty rejected discontinuing ROTC, 43 to 33, and tabled the idea of a five-year program for working students.[35]

New distribution requirements included "S" courses in English composition, public speaking, and research; extended study of a foreign language (through the fifth course for modern languages or the fourth for Latin or Greek, with placement examinations for those with previous study); a two-course humanities sequence or one course in English literature and one in philosophy; one course in literature, fine arts, or music; one course in religion; one course in mathematics; a two-course sequence in an abstract science (physics or chemistry) and one in a descriptive science (biology or geology), or vice versa; a two-course sequence in medieval and modern European history; and one each of two social sciences. Two hours per week of physical education were required in the first two years and thereafter until students passed tests in physical fitness, swimming, and several sports (like tennis, golf, handball, and squash) deemed most likely to be continued in later life.[36]

Concentration requirements included at least six courses, an "S" course in independent reading, and a comprehensive examination. Special interdepartmental majors could be arranged with the approval of all departments involved and the Academic Council. Once approved by the board, the entire program would take effect in the fall of 1960. Although by no means a return to the unified classical curriculum of the

nineteenth century, the new curriculum did reverse the trend of weakening core requirements that had prevailed since the 1920s. It also helped shift emphasis away from
preprofessional training.[37]

Bolman's administration pressed forward on other fronts. The new business manager, Paul R. Linfield, revised accounting operations to follow recommendations of
the American Council on Education and introduced the college's first accounting
machines. In preparation for the long-delayed Stahr Hall renovation, administrative
offices moved to East Hall, combining with others previously located in Hartman. This
freed space for physics, geology, and psychology laboratories and classrooms and offices, but Bolman warned the board that these departments needed their own building.
If present "deplorable conditions" in their laboratories were long allowed to continue,
in Bolman's words, "we shall be in a much weakened academic position in the very
areas for which we have been best known."[38]

A third dormitory and a modern infirmary were completed in mid-1959, named
to recognize alumni who had made significant contributions to the college: Schnader
Hall, after the board chairman, and Appel Infirmary, for the Appel family, who had
served as faculty, presidents, and trustees, and most currently, through James Z. Appel,
as college physician since 1934. Nearly three-quarters of the student body now lived
on campus or in fraternity houses. To Bolman, the college's increasingly residential
character provided "an opportunity to develop a full college campus life as was never
before possible." To address the college's increased responsibilities, a full-time residence
hall manager was hired to oversee dormitory life and student activities and to supervise thirty-four student counselors. Bolman wanted to add a "well-trained staff of psy-
chologists and clinicians," but the board agreed only to hire outside experts to screen
students suspected of mental or emotional problems but not to provide therapeutic
treatment. The college contracted with an outside caterer to run the dining halls, which
Bolman predicted would raise food quality and quantity.[39]

The most important missing piece of the residential life puzzle was a new physical education center, now a necessity for the new curriculum. It would also provide
"proper space for many other college and community activities," Bolman told the board,
and would help the college compete for "high quality students." Despite cajoling by
Schnader and Bolman, there was little enthusiasm for the project on the part of older
alumni and board members, who felt that the college had other more pressing needs.
Bolman made strenuous efforts to persuade trustee John Meyer to give the bulk of the
money for a building that would bear his name; Bolman visited him several times in
Tyrone to express this point: "No other project we can undertake will so clearly influence *all the students of this College* for decades and decades to come."[40]

Student Culture Resisting Change

Bolman and most of the student body agreed on the need for a physical education
center. But by this time it had become abundantly clear that, of all components of
Franklin & Marshall College, student culture was most resistant to systematic planning

and change of the kind that Bolman envisioned. As faculty and administrators allied themselves with the project of transforming the college into an academically rigorous, selective liberal arts institution, they came into conflict with students' fierce attachment to "traditions" of campus life, especially those involving drinking, freshman regulations, and fraternities.

After the president's inauguration, *Student Weekly* observed hopefully that Bolman "had all the appearances of a dynamic leader," but there was little immediate improvement in areas of most interest to students. Participation in extracurricular activities seemed to be waning, causing suspension of yet another effort to revive *Hullabaloo*, the college humor magazine. The Diagnothian Society, which after World War II had managed to attract a few members by holding lively debates on contemporary issues, finally gave up independent existence and merged with the Goethean Society. A Student Council survey found that few students listened to the campus radio station, WFM, set up in 1951 with expertise from the physics department. Nearly everyone, though, read at least part of the *Student Weekly*. Almost half the student body frequently left town on weekends, but about three-quarters said that they would attend more athletic events if they were held on campus.[41]

Few students were as enthusiastic as faculty about recent innovations. The Book-of-the-Semester program generated little interest. Though the campus was "blanketed" with posters urging students to read *The American Character*, only one-third did so. Meanwhile, students observed that raises in faculty salaries seemed inevitably to bring higher tuition and fees. The *Weekly* greeted news of an increase philosophically, noting that money for improvements had "to come from somewhere." But the paper commented, "Unless we are to turn into a different type of school, a limit will have to be reached soon." Total costs were already higher than at other local schools.[42]

One of Bolman's first efforts to reach out to students was a "smoker," in which a dozen students were invited to discuss current issues with nine faculty and administrators. It focused on perennial concerns about student drinking and cheating. Students pleaded for relaxation of current "prohibition" policies, referring to a prewar Golden Age when college policies had reputedly been more tolerant. (The growing number of students from other states, where often the drinking age was eighteen, were not prepared for Pennsylvania's strict regulations.) The students placed much of the blame for cheating on overcrowded examination rooms and lax professors, though admitting that student attitudes played a role. Bolman appointed a student-faculty committee to consider alcohol regulations, but hopes for change were dashed when it received a letter from the governor of Pennsylvania stressing that it was illegal for any person to sell or give alcohol to minors. College authorities felt they had no choice but to maintain present rules. In fact, as a result of the discussion of the issue, the faculty adopted a new statement explicitly forbidding storing, serving, or drinking any alcoholic beverages in fraternities or dormitories.[43]

Fraternities were under growing pressure to change. After the war some individual chapters challenged membership restrictions mandated by national organizations.

Pointing to the action of a Dartmouth fraternity, the *Student Weekly* in 1956 urged leaders of the five Franklin & Marshall fraternities that had discriminatory clauses to work toward their elimination. Some did in fact try to enlist the Inter-fraternity Council and Student Council in a movement against discrimination, only to be threatened with loss of their charters by their national officers, in turn under pressure from southern chapters. Subsequently, AAUP agreed that college authorities should cooperate with student fraternity leaders to resist pressure from the national organizations, as had been done at Williams and Amherst. The Delta Sigma Phi chapter successfully defied its national leadership by admitting a Japanese American freshman, Francis O. Kuroda, becoming the first of that fraternity's chapters granted "local autonomy" in selection of members. At the faculty's instigation, the board in 1960 notified all fraternities of its opposition to discrimination on the basis of race or creed.[44]

Although few openly defended fraternities' right to discriminate, objections to freshman hazing continued to inspire appeals to college traditions. In 1954, in keeping with Cold War tensions, sophomores had added a new torment: whenever an upperclassman shouted "air raid," freshmen were supposed to throw themselves to the ground. The following year, the *Student Weekly*'s special freshman edition included an editorial explaining that such customs were necessary to ensure that each succeeding class "prove themselves worthy of the F&M label." A faculty member responded with an impassioned attack on the whole system: "This writer has no knowledge of any other place where actions bordering on sadism are practiced on such a large scale as they are here at this college in the relations between sophomores and freshmen." He questioned sophomores' motives: "The ugly truth is that the situation as it exists here, creates an atmosphere and outlet for the outpouring of sadism by those within whom such tendencies exist." The professor's concerns illustrate a growing consensus among American intellectuals that repressive social phenomena are linked to abnormal psychological states. He continued, "It is bad business for those who partake in it, and disgusting for the rest who have to see it."[45]

In the fall of 1957, the coincidence of particularly "vulgar, obscene, and character-degrading" behavior by sophomore persecutors and the selection of William Whyte's *The Organization Man* as the second Book-of-the-Semester seems to have sparked a shift in campus opinion. The administration swiftly posted notices outlawing "vigorous hazing" beyond regulations outlined in the student handbook. The Student Council passed its own resolution, urging freshmen and sophomores to cooperate in carrying out the "controlled hazing program" that had been "the traditional custom." The faculty approved government professor Sidney Wise's resolution that advocated outlawing all forms of hazing. Wise followed up with a letter to the *Weekly*, characterizing the Student Council's endorsement of "controlled hazing" as "a distilled blend of confused logic, bad taste and poor English." He noted "the absurdity of several hundred freshmen parading about the campus with bared knees and crossed eyes while clutching copies of William Whyte's monumental warning on the perils of conformity." Some students expressed dismay that the "fun" was being taken out of freshman year, but columnist Bob Stern challenged the oft-expressed belief that hazing created a unified freshman class. "Do we want to encourage the type of unity that is fostered by ordeals?" he asked. "The majority of prisoners at Buchenwald were extremely unified." The Student Council deliberated through the year and eventually developed freshman regulations that the faculty considered acceptable. These required freshmen, for only one week in September, to wear dinks and identification badges; to attend every college function as a group; to memorize the alma mater, names and locations of campus buildings and fraternities, and names of the president and deans; and to address upperclassmen as "Sir."[46]

Campus lectures and assemblies had long sought to enrich campus intellectual life; increasingly, they challenged what many faculty considered to be students' conformity and passivity. In the 1957–1958 year the new "Topics" series brought nationally known speakers to campus for evening lectures that were open to the general public for a small fee. Under Richard Stonesifer's direction, these appearances were coordinated with courses or other events on campus. Vance Packard, for example, came to speak at a time when a government seminar was discussing his controversial book, *The Hidden Persuaders*. William Whyte appeared on a panel with trustees Arthur Sinkler, president of Hamilton Watch, and Frederick Foltz, head of the Foltz-Wessinger Advertising Agency. The program brought out a standing-room-only crowd to Hensel Hall, where students and local citizens alike "badgered" Whyte with questions about his book. Discussions were held afterward at the literary society and some fraternities. The following year, anthropologist Margaret Mead appeared in connection with a campuswide discussion of her book *Male and Female*. She presided at an afternoon panel on "modern dating patterns" (a panel that included representatives from all-female Hood and Wilson colleges, where the work was also being read) and lectured in the evening. Later, academic authorities on sex differences in the fields of sociology, biology, and psychology gave talks aimed at majors in those departments but open to everyone. Stonesifer credited the program with increasing enrollments in the college's small anthropology program. When Arthur Miller's play *The Crucible* was assigned in the fall of 1959, many students were excited at the possibility that he might visit campus with his new wife, actress Marilyn Monroe. But he was occupied with a new Broadway production, and instead students heard critic Kimon Friar on Miller's influence on contemporary drama, Senator Eugene McCarthy on the political environment in which the play had been written, and Yale historian Edmund S. Morgan on Puritan society, as well as seeing a Green Room production of the play. The Book-of-the Semester program was featured in an article in *Saturday Review* and in materials from the National Book Company and was emulated by a number of other colleges.[47]

To the extent that these discussions influenced some students, they applied their criticisms to their immediate environment. "Halloween in Lancaster is, to say the least, different from Halloween in our home communities," the *Student Weekly* commented, describing Halloween "rowdyism," in which mobs of young men roamed the streets intent on ripping clothing off any young women they encountered. The city seemed to suffer from "a rather unusual form of a mass neurosis" in which sex seemed to play "an abnormally exaggerated role." Campus leaders had long complained of student apathy, but the Book-of-the-Semester program provided new explanations for malaise. One student reader of *The Organization Man* pointed out that lack of response to the book "validates one of William Whyte's strongest charges, namely, that college students rebel at the thought of thinking." He reported that only about 10 percent of students in one of his classes had found time to read the book, while a majority knew "hundreds of details of Halloween's Operation Lingerie."[48]

Noting a decline in grade averages, many students charged that faculty were raising their standards and that the administration was clamping down on easy "cake" courses. One senior asserted that Bolman pressured professors to "toughen the 'cake' departments" in order "to make another Haverford out of this place." Another student reported that one of his teachers told his class he had been ordered to "tighten up" his grading if he wanted to continue teaching the course. Administrators denied a concerted policy to raise standards, though some admitted that new teachers might have higher expectations.[49]

Behind the scenes, Bolman and Darlington told the board of plans to raise standards for both faculty and students. They considered the two as inseparable and essential to enhancing the college's prestige. Bolman reported that despite an increase in the numbers of applications recently, there was a decline in the class standing of those who actually enrolled. He concluded that part of the problem was that Franklin & Marshall offered relatively little scholarship and work funding and was therefore "losing out in the competition for brains in the classroom." For the first time, he stressed the need to raise the quality of students not only to improve the intellectual environment but to retain a high-quality faculty. "To a faculty member a student body of high IQ is a fringe benefit of first magnitude," Darlington told the board. Even though numbers of college-bound students were growing, the college had to step up recruitment efforts if it wanted to attract top students, for "there [would] never be a surplus of high calibre students." In contrast, Darlington admitted that he had identified only fifty-one among the current faculty of eighty-five that the college wanted to retain.[50]

Inevitably, the tenure process was affected. In recent years, the APD Committee had taken greater care in making promotions, but tenure continued to be principally a matter of time — those who remained on the faculty for a maximum of six years achieved tenure automatically. Bolman told the committee in 1957 that their work would significantly affect the college's future intellectual climate. He wanted to raise salaries, but warned, "A high-priced, second-rate institution will not survive." Under his influence, the committee denied promotion to a member of the history department, in large part because of his casual attitude toward teaching and examinations, especially in his repeated use of the same true and false test. The next year the committee set up more formal procedures for evaluating candidates, such as gathering information about education, degrees, anonymous assessments from senior departmental colleagues and students, reports on classroom visits, samples of syllabi and examination questions, and grade averages. Also included were judgments of faculty research and publication activity, contributions to committees, and personal qualities of "intellectual vigor, considerateness, cooperativeness."[51]

One of the first cases under the new system aroused an unprecedented controversy, when Bolman postponed a tenure decision for an English professor instead of passing on to the board the APD Committee's favorable recommendation. Ironically, the issues in this case were that the teacher was too hard on mediocre students and too openly critical of less demanding colleagues. Bolman later asserted that he simply wanted more information, but a rumor spread that tenure had been denied, prompting several students to organize a petition drive on their teacher's behalf. They asked that the situation be clarified, because, "as students paying for the privilege of education," they had a right to be informed. Bolman insisted that matters of appointment were confidential. In any case, tenure was granted the following year.[52]

As part of the shift to the new curriculum, Darlington recommended cutting the number of faculty committees to free up time for teaching and research; the Academic Council cut thirty-three faculty committees to nine. The two most important were now elected by the full faculty and chaired by the dean: the Academic Council oversaw curriculum, admissions, and scholarships, and the Professional Standards Committee, replacing the APD Committee, exercised authority over tenure, appointments, promotions, dismissals, sabbatical leaves, and research awards. In many other cases, especially those related to student affairs, faculty committee functions were shifted to administrators. Chapel and campus religious activities became the responsibility of the chaplain, for example. The Tree Committee, upon which generations of faculty had lavished attention, was eliminated, although the faculty was encouraged to "bring its esthetic sensitivities and silvicultural lore to bear" on the superintendent of buildings and grounds.[53]

Planning for Future Expansion

Bolman had already moved on to the next major project of his administration, a substantial long-range plan. He laid the groundwork by sending each board member two recently published books on higher education: *College and University Trusteeship* by Morton A. Rauh, supported by the Carnegie Corporation, and *Memo to a College Trustee: A Report on Financial and Structural Problems of the Liberal College* written by Beardsley Ruml and Donald H. Morrison for the Ford Foundation's Fund for the Advancement of Education. The first discussed the changing function of college trustees and the second, serious financial challenges facing liberal arts colleges. He proposed that the entire board meet for an extended period, "not to discuss immediate and pressing problems," but to consider the larger question of "*the role and purposes of this particular Board of Trustees.*" Such retreats were becoming common in many kinds of organizations, he pointed out, and they made it possible to rise above preoccupation with immediate details and take "a long-range point of view." Moreover, as trustees were often individuals from diverse backgrounds and were less often alumni than in the past, retreats provided an opportunity for members to get to know one another better.[54]

The first board retreat was held in Princeton, New Jersey, with expenses underwritten by trustee Elmer H. Bobst, an executive with pharmaceutical firm Warner Company. Meeting for a day and a half in advance of the regular October meeting, the retreat began with a discussion of the responsibilities of boards, led by two visitors, Harold W. Dodds, a former president of Princeton, and Laird Bell, a former chairman of the board of the University of Chicago and member of several other college boards. Both emphasized that present trends in governance saw boards of trustees playing a crucial role in long-term planning for development and excellence. But, according to Dodds and Bell, after trustees decided on overall policy on the advice of the president, they left actual management to professional staff. On the second day, administrators outlined major issues that would define Franklin & Marshall's future, including size, facilities, financial resources, and its relationships with the new United Church of Christ, with the Lancaster community, and with other academic institutions.[55]

The question of the college's optimal size received particular attention. One of the books that Bolman had distributed to the board argued that expansion offered small colleges a way out of the dangerous financial squeeze created by limited resources and the need to raise faculty salaries. Its argument that this was an especially propitious time for expansion helped weaken opposition on the board to the idea of raising enrollment levels to 1,600. Bolman noted that applications continued to climb, and there were many indications that the college was becoming better known "and that increasingly students [sought] admission to Franklin and Marshall College along with the best . . . eastern colleges." Even with higher admission standards, he noted, the college had to turn away "an impressive number of good candidates for lack of space or instructional provisions." What he did not mention was that most of these unsuccessful applicants came from one or two categories: admissions director Bruce Westerdahl later acknowledged that if the college simply admitted the best students, 60 to 70 percent of the student body would be premed and half would be Jewish. To maintain a more balanced student body, the admissions office applied quotas that held the proportion of premeds to around one-quarter, while the proportion of Jewish students remained around 17 percent.[56]

Bolman pressed the board to approve a long-range plan to answer the question, "What should Franklin and Marshall College be ten, twenty, and thirty years from now?" To do so required "careful and competent research" as well as "a dispassionateness that goes beyond Lancaster, the past, our immediate national needs, indeed way out yonder into a space age which none of us here today may experience!" The work would be conducted by a committee of trustees, faculty, and administrators appointed by Schnader, with the assistance of a full-time staff member. With tentative board approval, the Executive Committee later authorized a budget for an office of research to direct the project.[57]

It was not clear that the board had fully absorbed Bolman's effort to educate them about changing practices in governance. He began his comments at the formal meeting by emphasizing that the college had two kinds of leaders: "a lay board of trustees, which is the policy-making group with a great variety of functions; and an executive staff, which is a professional group employed to carry out policies of the board in all their detailed functions." In his concluding remarks, Bolman underlined what he clearly considered to be an essential board function — giving and getting money. To make "a real break-through from its prior history," he asserted, Franklin & Marshall needed to quadruple its endowment, and this was a board responsibility. He noted that in the history of higher education, boards determined the wealth of their respective institutions and reiterated a suggestion that each member take it upon himself to "discover" a million dollars in endowment for the college, in himself or others.[58]

It soon became clear that it was not always easy to distinguish between policy setting and implementation, as a controversy arose regarding the college's response to the National Defense Education Act (NDEA). Passed in 1958 in response to what was perceived as a national "educational emergency," the act represented the most massive federal support for higher education to date; among other things, it offered low-interest loans to students studying education, mathematics, sciences, and foreign languages — all defined as "skills essential to the national defense." The federal government provided 90 percent of loans if individual institutions made up the other 10 percent. But, as former president Distler warned, the money came with strings attached — it required students receiving loans to sign a statement that they did not "believe in," have membership in, or support any organization advocating violent overthrow of the U.S. government and, in addition, to swear an oath of allegiance to the United States. Franklin & Marshall needed to increase financial resources to attract superior students, but its leaders objected strenuously to the requirements as an infringement of students' civil liberties. In fact, Bolman joined a protest by the Association of American Colleges, and the college's AAUP lobbied its congressional representatives in an effort to have the act reversed. But though some (wealthier) institutions declined to participate, Bolman concluded that "not to do so would have deprived students of needed funds for their education." He did not seek board approval, reasoning that "no policy issue was involved," because the college had already accepted federal building loans.[59]

When national and local news stories quoted Bolman regarding his opposition to NDEA requirements, some board members seem to have been made aware for the first time of the college's participation in the program. Schnader immediately criticized Bolman for applying to the program without board authorization. "One of the things that I think we must guard against," he wrote, "is the tendency on the part of an active administrative staff such as the College now has, to barge ahead and take command and to treat the Board of Trustees as somewhat of an unnecessary nuisance that must be put up with." The Executive Committee discussed the issue but gave the administration's action retroactive approval. But the episode demonstrated the potential for conflict.[60]

As the 1960s began, many in the college were engaged in fine-tuning courses and regulations in keeping with the new curriculum. Content in most humanities and social science courses had to be expanded to fit the new four-course load. In the first two months of 1960, the faculty reviewed and approved 321 courses; ultimately the total number of courses offered at the college was reduced by about 19 percent. Their efforts were rewarded when Columbia University's Institute of Higher Education singled out Franklin & Marshall's curriculum for particular praise in a 1961 study of liberal arts colleges. One remaining issue was the ROTC program. Bolman told the board that he had "grave concerns" about how well it would fit with the "more strenuous" new curriculum. He had hoped that ROTC courses could be deferred until after the freshman year, but air force regulations did not permit this, though the air force did approve a plan that cut in half the ROTC courses taken during the first two years. Bolman noted that in any case few students were involved.[61]

To prepare the college community for the change, the Book-of-the-Semester program that spring featured Edward D. Eddy's *The College Influence on Student Character*. A brochure on the program distributed throughout the college and wider community explained that the book had been chosen to challenge the community "to take a long, hard look at all aspects of college life — particularly at how well we do that thing which we, as a liberal arts college, are supposed to do: to make men of character, men able to reason, men sure of the meaning of being men."[62]

Work on the long-range plan began in earnest in the spring semester; Bolman appointed religion professor G. Wayne Glick as director of research for the project. His approach was influenced by the work of Sidney G. Tickton, an economist for the Ford Foundation, who adapted for small colleges techniques commonly used by large industries. Tickton served as a consultant, as did Knox College president Sharvy Umbeck, who had recently completed a similar exercise. (Tickton estimated in 1961 that about sixty liberal arts colleges were undergoing similar exercises; eventually some two hundred used the approach.) Study groups and task forces investigated a wide range of issues, such as assessment of faculty competence and teaching loads and special programs for gifted students. Faculty and administrators were invited to comment at various stages along the way. Demographic and economic data related to higher education was gathered as well as information about the college's operations over the preceding decade.[63]

The result was a document that sought to take a close, realistic look at Franklin & Marshall's prospects and make explicit assumptions upon which quantitative projections could be based. It was a hard-headed process, in keeping with the pragmatism of the day and the belief that values could in most cases be translated into quantitative terms. "Thus," the introduction to the final document explained, "if you assume that good faculty will be increasingly hard to get, you will evaluate as precisely as you can how many dollars each year for the next decade you will need to get and hold good faculty."[64]

In many ways, the plan codified trends already under way, particularly efforts to shape a more selective and geographically diverse student body and a fully professional faculty. "The explicit and controlling assumption of Long Range Planning has been that Franklin and Marshall will continue to commit itself to excellence," the preliminary document began. Its first priority was avoiding the mistake of "insisting upon excellence without the concomitant measures necessary to achieve excellence." Later versions emphasized that improvement was crucial for the college's very survival: "If private colleges cannot produce those intellectually qualified to meet the needs of our society, if they cannot prepare for graduate and professional schools, for business and industry, and if they fail of academic excellence, then death will surely follow." The plan outlined priorities arising from this commitment.[65]

The plan's centerpiece was a series of assumptions about the coming decade, for the nation as a whole as well as for Franklin & Marshall. They were strongly influenced by Tickton's expansionary assumptions. Some — such as that the number of students in higher education would nearly double by 1971 and that the number of students applying to liberal arts colleges would increase and make possible greater selectivity — came to pass. Others, particularly that the United States would "continue to enjoy a high income economy without a war or other national disaster" and that prices would continue to increase at an annual rate of 1.5 percent, were far from the mark, with serious implications for the future.[66]

Assumptions for the college concerned admissions standards, teaching methods, new programs, and heightened scholarly activity among faculty. The bulk of the plan was comprised of economic projections arising from the assumptions. These projections posited a gradual expansion of the size of the student body to 1,600 by the 1967–1968 academic year and a teaching faculty of 112, and a commitment to increase average salaries at the rate of 7.2 percent per year. This last figure was based on the amount necessary, with compounding, to double salaries within ten years. It had been proposed in 1957 by President Eisenhower's Committee on Education Beyond the High School and was frequently cited in AAUP statements. Bolman first endorsed this principle in the 1960–1961 budget, calling the goal necessary "to keep this College in a competitive position with similar institutions." The college's work was subsequently selected as a case study for the Seminar on Long-Range Planning held by the Association of American Colleges in cooperation with the Ford Foundation.[67]

When Glick first began work, Schnader warned him to leave the issue of coeducation out of the deliberations, insisting that it was simply too expensive. (Glick pointed out that if enrollments were going to increase, additional dormitory facilities would have to be built anyway.) Glick and Bolman discussed the issue with administrators at several coed schools, but in the end framed the long-range plan with the expectation that the college would remain all-male for the foreseeable future.[68]

Deliberations that contributed to formulation of the document were nearly as important as the final product. One of the most revealing was a faculty-administration "smoker" in May 1960 that discussed an early draft of the plan. Most comments touched on how to improve the quality of the student body. Many faculty were convinced that admitting women was the single most effective way to do this: as Darlington put it, "Girls are potentially better students than the boys." Another source of acute concern was the college's "image" or lack thereof: admissions officers reported that it was little known even in Philadelphia. There was agreement that for students and their counselors a college's image was shaped by the kind of student it admitted and that Franklin & Marshall had been hurt in the past by its reputation as "a flunker's paradise." That this had changed was reflected in the number of students now who were flunking out. But others noted that as the college tried to expand its geographic reach, many outside its traditional constituencies had simply never heard of it. Some hoped that the faculty's excellent reputation would change this, but admissions people stressed that this had little impact on high school seniors and counselors. The thorny and persistent question seemed to be how a school acquired or changed its reputation. "The main images are images of place," mused Richard Stonesifer. "Swarthmore and such colleges have been extremely successful in selling themselves almost as a way of life."[69]

To polish the college's image, Bolman revived the position of assistant to the president and director of public relations and made it part of his Executive Council. He enlisted Stonesifer, who had already played an important role in advertising the college through his weekly program, *New Books of Significance*, on local television and his work on the Book-of-the-Semester program. With the aid of board members Robert W. Sarnoff, chairman of the board of NBC, and J. Hale Steinman, publisher of the *Intelligencer Journal*, Stonesifer scored a public relations coup the following spring when *Business Week* ran an extensive article on Franklin & Marshall's modernization program.[70]

Despite another increase in tuition, numbers of applications did in fact continue to grow, so much so that in 1960 the freshman class was filled by early May for the first time since 1946. Bolman told the board that competition had "become so hot and heavy" that on separate occasions an admissions officer was offered bribes to admit particular applicants. Quality as measured in average test scores and class standing steadily increased. Nearly three-quarters of the class of 1964 came from the upper two-fifths of their high school classes. Significantly, the proportion of local students dropped to 10 percent, with 33 percent from the rest of Pennsylvania and 37 percent from New York and New Jersey. Bolman discussed the problem of attrition with the board, underlining that it was crucial not to admit boys who were unlikely to succeed at Franklin & Marshall. "To admit an incompetent or even marginal student brings discredit to the boy, to the family, and to the institution," he warned.[71]

With board approval of the long-range plan in October 1960, Bolman's ambitious agenda was completed. He seemed confident that he had achieved leadership of the board. At the beginning of his formal report, he apologized for the large amount of data included but explained, "One of my jobs is to give the College a sense of direction. Just as important is for me to report to you fully and accurately just what is happening at the College, and to pass on my recommendations to you for such policy action as you properly wish to take." He continued,

> Not long ago I heard some sound if brief advice given to boards of trustees of colleges. It was suggested that at each meeting the first consideration of the board should be: Shall we fire the president? If the answer to that question

is yes, then the next problem is for the board to find a better president. But if the answer to the initial question is no, then the next consideration is: How can we implement, supplement, and strengthen the actions and proposals of the president? The fecundity of this advice I leave to you![72]

Bolman's opening convocation speech was similarly confident. He proclaimed the 1960s the "decade of the egghead": "Professors and other intellectuals are now in control as never before, planning the security and well-being of megalopolis . . . and proceeding to plan our national well-being and our international relations in a myriad of respects." At Franklin & Marshall at least, his confidence seemed well justified. A decline in attrition resulted in a student body of 1,341, giving the college a head start on its planned expansion. The long-desired physical education center seemed assured as a low-key campaign raised over $703,000 from trustees and the local community. A large new field house would be added to the north side of Biesecker Gymnasium and Fackenthal Swimming Pool, with much of the former gym converted into offices for athletic programs; at its dedication the physical education center was named after longtime coach and teacher Charles W. Mayser.[73]

In addition to a distinguished roster of speakers on campus that fall, students were electrified when both John Kennedy and Richard Nixon made campaign visits to Lancaster. Formation of political clubs for both candidates reflected an increasing spirit of activism, already manifested the previous spring in strong support for the student sit-in movement then sweeping southern colleges. Although *Student Weekly* editorials and columns had often weighed in on issues of civil rights and race relations, there had hitherto been little in the way of action. Now, the Student Council followed its resolution supporting lunch counter sit-ins by appointing a committee to raise money to help participants. One group of students formed the Committee for Social Action, and another raised $500 to support a desegregation lawsuit in Alabama.[74]

Reaching the Limits of Change

Not everyone was happy with the situation, however. The transition to the demanding new curriculum seems to have caused some institutional fatigue, and some faculty were unhappy with the new merit system. Bolman admitted to the board his belief "that certain members of the faculty [were] not worthy of salary increases and that the precious funds available should be used to hold outstanding talent." He warned trustees that they might be approached by discontented faculty and asked them to remember "that a vital principle [was] at stake for this College and its future in preserving a merit system which [would] preserve funds to hold the best teachers."[75]

Student unease was reflected in *Stupid Weakly*, a special Halloween edition of the student newspaper, which referred to Bolman as "Der Herr President" and showed him in a doctored photograph holding aloft Yale and Andover pennants. "From every quarter of the campus comes the cry that the new curriculum is out for blood," an editorial reported in early November. Student complaints about heavy workloads, overcrowded classes, and poor food quality in the cafeterias joined perennial protests in the pages of the *Student Weekly* about lack of alcohol. In February an open session to discuss campus problems drew 350 to Hensel. Bolman attributed most problems to a "lack of communication" between students and administrators. He outlined changes of the past four years and took questions from a panel of student leaders and from the audience. Concerns ranged from increases in tuition, large classes, and the fate of the new hockey team to more familiar subjects like alcohol and the board's stand against fraternity discrimination.[76]

Several weeks later, frustration on campus erupted in the first substantial student riot since the war. The catalyst seems to have been the Inter-fraternity Council's decision, under pressure from the administration, to fine ten of eleven fraternities for violating construction week regulations. The evening of April 12 began with about two hundred students marching around Hartman Oval shouting, "We want Bolman," and "various other remarks," the *Weekly* reported. Many of the complaints voiced by students during the evening revolved around perennial fraternity beefs, such as bans on alcohol and athletic scholarships. Fueling their shouts, which were liberally laced with obscenities, was resentment at greater academic demands. Protestors charged that the new curriculum was making "everybody" flunk out and that Bolman wanted to turn Franklin & Marshall into "a college of eggheads."[77]

Dragging burning effigies, the swelling crowd marched to the president's house and demanded to speak to Bolman. He appeared on the steps and, joined by Stonesifer, attempted to respond. A cold spring rain was falling, and the group agreed to move the discussion indoors to Hensel Hall. For several more hours, Bolman, Darlington, and other members of the administration attempted to respond rationally to student complaints before a crowd ranging in size from five hundred to eight hundred. While a small number of students at the front of the hall tried to conduct an orderly discussion, a much larger group milled around in the back and spilled out onto College Avenue. They blocked the street with a bonfire of tables and campus signs and pelted police and firemen with mud and rocks. Arrival of a cameraman from the local television station shortly before ten o'clock seemed to excite the crowd, and some pelted Bolman and Darlington with raw eggs handed out by fraternity leaders. At this, the administrators departed.[78]

This explosion prompted self-examination on all sides. The *Student Weekly* was particularly chagrined that few participants seemed to have any idea why they were protesting: "They were just rioting for the hell of rioting and because, for some distorted reason, they feel strongly against Dr. Bolman." The few who attempted to conduct a reasoned discussion seemed "on the surface, to be concerned with the lack of communication between administration and students." On this point, the *Weekly* felt that Bolman bore responsibility for "his past aloofness, for the fact that few students [had] been made to feel free to even greet him on campus." But ultimately, editors felt that the protests were simply symptoms of the fact that "F and M is in the

process of a revolutionary transition" from "a good-time institution" to one dominated by academics.[79]

The faculty unanimously deplored recent events, reaffirmed the college's goal "of
pursuing excellence in all fields of college endeavor," and urged immediate disciplinary measures in response to any future "breaches of gentlemanly conduct." Schnader
called for tighter controls over student organizations, and some board members wanted
the ringleaders to be expelled. But in fact the incident prompted Hadley DePuy, newly
appointed dean of students, to push for greater student self-government. Bolman admitted to the board that a small core of students was extremely disaffected and perhaps one-third of the whole were "students of average or low ability, of a kind that we
will wish to eliminate from the campus in the future." He reported that many students
and alumni had written to express support for the administration. Some students had
even come to him the following day to apologize. Bolman commented, "[This was]
something I never thought of doing to President Abbott Lawrence Lowell when I was
a member of a large ruckus in college."[80]

There also appeared to be more intractable causes. Bolman attributed part of the
unrest to the influence of disaffected faculty "who [did] not support the striving for
excellence that [was] the College's announced goal for the 1960's," some of whom
"simply [were] not up to the pressures of the new curriculum." In many cases, there was
little that could be done because these faculty members were tenured. He also blamed
some of the unrest on the campus's "physical inadequacies." The only common space
on campus had been lost when the upper level of the Campus House was taken to
provide a larger college bookstore. Bolman concluded that higher priority should be
given to a new college union. He also charged that the new dormitories had been
badly designed and constructed. In an implicit slap at the college's long-standing architect, he asserted, "No one in this day and age should build long dormitory corridors,
sound-reverberating walls, doors which when locked can readily be pushed open,
and a host of other details, all of which make students want to live any place else." He
lamented that "about 400 students now must live for some 40 years in residences
improperly designed and improperly equipped."[81]

In the riot's aftermath, Bolman resolved "to forgive, forget, and correct inadequacies in student life and affairs." Yet the event only heightened disaffection of many
alumni and local residents. Bolman reported receiving only one critical letter from an
alumnus, "something of a perennial critic," who protested his program to convert the
college "into an 'egghead' institution in an effort to emulate Ivy League colleges and
universities." Bolman replied with the same comment he had made to the rioters: "And
what's wrong with eggheads?" Yet this correspondent echoed the concerns of many.
At commencement, trustee John Meyer found little enthusiasm for the new regime
among his acquaintances in the faculty and administration. "Are we giving up our old
College with its wonderful traditions," he wondered, "for an Educational Manufacturing plant with a superintendent who rules over his artisans and laborers with methods of the type of a Simon Legree?" He reported complaints that Bolman didn't attend

alumni meetings and never spoke to students whom he passed on campus. Meyer suggested to Schnader, "If you were to put your ear to the ground among the better thinking people of Lancaster you would hear ominous rumblings."[82]

By objective measures the college continued to improve. A new parking lot helped lessen congestion on campus. The area between Campus House and Stahr Hall, long cluttered with parked cars, was turned into a pedestrian mall, and Hensel Hall was redecorated. Scores and class standing of the new freshman class again rose. The National Science Foundation selected the college to hold summer science institutes for high school teachers. Bolman planned new programs designed to enhance the college's prestige and attract "superior students." These included an expanded honors program, a distinguished professor program and new provisions for study abroad, master's degree work, and introduction of Slavic languages and literature.[83]

Mac Darlington had previously announced his desire to return to teaching at the end of the 1960–1961 academic year. In reporting his decision to the board, Bolman described him as "one of the outstanding deans in this country," a "tireless worker, a fearless innovator, and our intellectual leader." He was succeeded by G. Wayne Glick. His work in directing the long-range plan had provided an extensive introduction to the field of academic administration, but nothing could have adequately prepared him for the events of his first year in office. It was destined to be one of the stormiest in the college's history.[84]

In retrospect, it might seem inevitable that men with such strong personalities as Frederick Bolman and William Schnader would clash. The two worked together as president and chairman of the board for more than five years with outward amicability and remarkable success, yet each held strikingly different assumptions about governance — especially the professional autonomy of faculty and administrators. In 1961 and 1962 these differences came to a head. Inevitably, philosophical differences were magnified by issues of personality.

Both men agreed that the biggest threat to Franklin & Marshall's future was its anemic endowment and that bequests were a good way to increase it. Schnader repeatedly urged creating a full-time position devoted solely to bequests and annuities. Bolman agreed, but the position proved difficult to fill because it required someone with the skill and stature to work closely with wealthy and powerful people. Schnader proposed his friend A. Douglas Oliver, an estate planner for the personal trust department of a major Philadelphia bank, who would be retiring soon. Bolman agreed that someone of Oliver's experience and "mature years" would be ideal.[85]

At its 1961 October meeting, the board authorized a committee to negotiate with Oliver to head the college's bequest program "for such period and upon such other terms and conditions as the Committee may deem appropriate." In the negotiation process, however, Schnader and Bolman had a serious falling-out, with Bolman charging that Schnader's handling of the matter contravened current professional standards, especially that the college president should control communication between professional staff and trustees.[86]

Schnader insisted that Oliver should be considered not as part of the regular administrative staff but as a personal friend who could raise a lot of money for the college. Furious at Bolman's opposition, Schnader threatened, "If you repudiate this agreement, I will regard it as a complete repudiation of me." Ultimately the contract was approved, naming Oliver as vice president in charge of the college's fund-raising activities.[87] The board also appointed Glick as another vice president empowered to perform the duties of the president of the board in his absence, as had previously been done with Darlington. It tried to respond to Bolman's concerns by specifically stating that both vice presidents reported to the president of the college.[88]

Schnader was incensed at what he saw as Bolman's betrayal, and this feeling only grew when the *Student Weekly* published an article critical of Oliver's hiring. The story began by referring to rumors around campus "that things [weren't] quite what they ought to be" and cited charges by unnamed "responsible sources" that the appointment "[represented] an illegal act" by Schnader "and a personal insult to President Bolman." According to these sources, Schnader had made the contract "with the knowledge of only a few, if any, of the other trustees" and had foisted it on the board "signed, sealed, and delivered." The *Weekly* reporter had interviewed Oliver, who said that both Schnader and Bolman had been involved in the negotiations, but the story added, "Just which story is correct the *Weekly* could not determine."[89]

Schnader held Bolman responsible for the story. Schnader was further angered when Bolman refused to punish the *Weekly* or even make a public statement contradicting its allegations. In private, Bolman denied to Schnader that he had had anything to do with the article and said that he had told the editors, "I deplore the article, . . . it is in extraordinarily bad taste, . . . it hurts the College, and . . . it is bad journalism." He told Schnader that he had "told everyone that [he] was conversant with all of the facts in connection with this appointment from the beginning." But Bolman refused to take any action against the paper, defending its "freedom of the press."[90]

The personal rift between the two men was deep but might have been smoothed over if other issues had not simultaneously exacerbated their differences. For several years, Schnader had complained to Bolman that political activities of some Franklin & Marshall faculty were hurting community relations. He and Henry Marshall criticized the prominent roles that government professors Sidney Wise, Richard Schier, and John Vanderzell played in local Democratic Party affairs. Both sides in the controversy seemed unaware that Franklin & Marshall faculty had always been active in local politics, but it was true that most new faculty were liberal Democrats in a community that was now resolutely conservative. Bolman tried to mediate between trustees and faculty, defending the latter's civil rights while urging them not to publicize their connection to the college.[91]

Rising student activism also affected the college's image in the community. The Committee for Social Action, part of a nationwide antinuclear movement, held a small peace march on Veterans Day. The sixty students and faculty who marched were far fewer than the two hundred at a peace rally in 1938, and the present group sought to distance themselves from Communist-inspired marches by carrying placards with slogans like "Neither Red nor Dead, but Alive and Free." Yet the event seems to have confirmed local perceptions that the college had moved to the left. After interviewing a few administrators and student leaders, a reporter from the conservative *Lancaster New Era* subsequently concluded that the campus was dominated by liberals.[92]

In mid-February 1962 town-gown relations were further strained when word leaked out of college attempts to acquire Buchanan Park, the city park that occupied the twenty-two acres west of the original college grounds. The college had long been surrounded by residential development on three sides and industrial sites along Harrisburg Pike to the north. Bolman and the board feared that lack of space would block future expansion. Local board leaders, cooperating with John Vanderzell as chairman of the City Planning Commission, had worked for months on an idea of buying a piece of land that could be exchanged for Buchanan Park. Although they tried to work in secrecy, news leaked from a confidential session of the city council. A huge public outcry resulted. Numerous city groups protested, pointing out that the park was one of the city's oldest recreational spaces and served as a playground for thousands of children. Faced by the uproar, city officials backed away from the proposal. Schnader blamed Bolman:

> I have pleaded with you to adopt a policy which would stop our faculty members from taking a hand in local political campaigns in Lancaster. I have pleaded with you to have a policy adopted which would guide the STUDENT WEEKLY and which its staff could not violate without fear of disciplinary action. You have stubbornly refused to take action in either direction. . . . You cannot offend the local people who support the College financially, and expect them to go out of their way to do things for the College.

Bolman denied that politics had anything to do with the opposition, blaming the *New Era* for putting the college "in a position of trying to take a lollipop away from a baby."[93]

Frustrated at Bolman's failure to publicly repudiate the *Weekly* story, Schnader distributed on March 14 an eleven-page history of the negotiations with Oliver and distributed it to every member of the board and faculty. "As one who resents anything reflecting on the good name of our College," he wrote in a cover letter, "I cannot permit the article in the Weekly to remain uncontradicted." Inevitably, the document reached the press and further publicized the dispute between Schnader and Bolman. Six of ten local trustees, Dr. John L. Atlee Jr., Kenneth O. Bates, Frederick S. Foltz, Nathaniel E. Hager, William Shand, and Arthur Sinkler, issued a statement urging an end to discussion of the matter in "the best interests of the college." Nevertheless, faculty and students, through the Student Council, kept the issue alive when they stepped forward to defend Bolman and the principle of freedom of the press.[94]

Attempting to allay local criticism, Bolman spoke to the Lancaster Sertoma Club. He referred to charges that Franklin & Marshall was distancing itself from Lancaster, focusing too much on academics rather than "human values," and turning its back on local students. In response he detailed the many contributions that the college made to the city. He defended the faculty's rights to participate in politics. "When scholars choose to exist in monastic seclusion, they are suspected and denounced with cries that they refuse to be 'regular fellows,'" he noted. "When on the other hand, scholars participate in local activities, particularly in controversial activities, they are denounced as meddlers, or told they ought to teach their classes and retreat into ivory towers." Regarding changes at the college, he admitted that the new curriculum was rigorous but necessary to keep "pace with the demands made on the young men in the 1960s." Moreover, the college had had to decide what kind of institution it was going to be "and what sector of American education" it was going to serve: "[We] devote ourselves to top quality undergraduate education for talented young men, because the American public has decreed that this is precisely what it wants colleges like ours to do."[95]

Since the 1920s, Franklin & Marshall had played a central role in educating the area's business and professional leadership. Bolman offered a different vision of college education, a vision oriented toward forming national networks and meritocratic standards. As Jencks and Riesman noted, in this period university colleges aimed "to help their students transcend whatever subculture they [were] born and raised in, and move them out into a slightly more cosmopolitan world" by exposing them to "heterogeneous classmates"—at least demographically, for they were more uniform in terms of academic aptitudes. Bolman explained that Franklin & Marshall, like "most good colleges," sought a more geographically diverse student body: "There are tremendous advantages to students that come from living on a campus with people from different areas and different social strata." He noted that, in proportion to applications, twice as many students from Lancaster County had been admitted as from elsewhere, yet numbers of applications from local students had fallen markedly in recent years. Only 5 percent of that year's freshman class came from Lancaster County, down from 26 percent in 1955. "We want Lancaster County students," he concluded, "but if a boy has the backing that will allow him to leave home for his undergraduate years, if he can spend these four vital years in an environment different from the one in which he has grown up, he will probably wish to do so."[96]

At the June board meeting, Schnader presented a report—his first as chairman. Continuing for more than thirty pages, it asserted that the board must reclaim direction of college affairs, which had of late been usurped by a "third entity . . . created 'out of the blue' known as 'The Administration.'" He charged that many of Bolman's actions had been "in derogation of the functions of this Board" and of the authority of the chairman of the board as the chief executive officer of the corporation that legally owned the college. Bolman was "trying to run everything himself . . . ignoring, almost totally, the Board of Trustees and its Committees"—during a previous meeting Schnader had used the term "dictator." Bolman's own regular report avoided mention of Schnader's statement and the controversy as a whole, continuing to stress that the college's survival depended on its ability to make big changes. As the meeting began, the board gave him a standing vote of approval for his work.[97]

Nonetheless, Schnader refused to give up. By July he found an issue in which Bolman was vulnerable — spending on physical plant improvements out of surpluses without prior board approval. Schnader requested information about such expenditures over the previous five years from Paul Linfield, business manager and treasurer. Linfield explained that during this period the administration's practice had been to budget only for routine maintenance, holding off on major expenditures until it knew whether there would be a surplus. In fiscal years 1958–1959 and 1959–1960, for example, over $200,000 had been spent on improvements such as installation of air-conditioning in Fackenthal Library, renovations to East, Hartman, and Stahr halls, improvements in Goethean and Diagnothian halls, and the new bookstore. Similar work in the next two years totaled more than $374,000. In none of these years had the board or its relevant committees been consulted.[98]

This information seems to have been enough to sway a majority on the board. A board statement, written by Schnader, later maintained that in the area of the management of property and finances responsibility was by law "almost entirely that of the Board of Trustees." It charged that Bolman "had ceased to function as the agent of the Board to carry out its directions in the management of the College's property and finances."[99]

At the beginning of August, Bolman left Lancaster as he did each year for a month's vacation at his family's retreat on an island off the coast of Maine. On August 23, Schnader called to tell him that "a majority of the Board wished an immediate change in the President's Office" and to request his resignation by noon the next day. Bolman asked to meet with the Executive Committee before any action was taken, but Schnader refused. Bolman then wrote to all members of the board, asking that he be permitted to meet with them, along with his attorney, "to discuss any charges which may be stated against any actions [he had] taken in the past." He asserted that if he were simply to resign with no discussion of the issues involved, "it would be interpreted as a sign of guilt." "I feel no guilt," he insisted. "Moreover, I have always stood ready to conduct the affairs of the College in accordance with procedures prescribed by the Board so long as I remain your President." He protested that "the timing and the substance" of Schnader's demand were "not only unfair to [him], but also [were] not in the best interests of the College."[100]

But Bolman was not permitted to attend the special meeting called for September 5 at Philadelphia's Bellevue Stratford Hotel. Thirty-one of forty members attended. Bolman's supporters, including seven of nine Lancaster trustees, came armed with a statement from former board president Paul Kieffer opposing the contemplated action, but Schnader refused to allow it to be read. They also carried letters of admonition from a number of trustees unable to attend the meeting, from the executive officer of the American Council on Education, from Dean Glick and former Dean Darlington, and from the faculty's Professional Standards Committee. But Bolman's defenders were outvoted by a narrow margin in two test motions, one seeking to give Bolman notice of the charges against him and to allow him to appear with counsel, and another to use a secret ballot. During a break, a supporter telephoned Bolman and informed that a majority were prepared to vote for his removal. He tendered his resignation, which the board accepted "with regret."[101]

In the matter of his successor, a majority defeated a motion to appoint a joint trustee-faculty search committee, as had been done on the two previous occasions. They accepted Schnader's argument that the delay inevitably involved in the work of such committees would cause a loss of momentum at a crucial time. Instead, the board elected one of its own, Anthony R. Appel, as the next president. Appel, forty-seven, was descended from a long line of Franklin & Marshall leaders and alumni and was the grandnephew of Henry Harbaugh Apple. An attorney, he had been a trustee and the board's counsel since 1957. He had assumed leadership roles in fund-raising drives but had no experience of academic administration.[102]

If the board had simply secured Bolman's resignation and appointed a search committee, backlash from the college community might well have died down after the first expressions of shock and protest. After all, the bylaws specified that the president was appointed by and served "at the pleasure of the Board of Trustees," and nearly two years earlier Bolman had advocated a model of governance in which the board's most important action at each meeting was to decide whether to keep or fire the president. But by declining to follow the precedent of faculty involvement in selecting his successor, the board had, perhaps unwittingly, breached crucial professional norms in a way that could not be overlooked. It also brought into high relief the question of who was actually in charge of the college. As trustee Frederick Foltz commented to a *Philadelphia Sunday Bulletin* reporter, Schnader believed that colleges should be run by their boards of trustees, while Foltz believed that the president must be in charge. "A number of the board members don't know the difference between running a business and running an educational institution," he said. "That was very evident."[103]

Response to the news of Bolman's forced resignation was immediate and intense. Lancaster's newspapers lauded all that he had accomplished in the short span of six years. "In guiding F&M through a difficult period of transition and expansion," the *Intelligencer Journal* editorial commented, "it was perhaps inevitable that there would be conflicts between the college president and others who, it might be said, were equally strong willed." "What some of his critics have called aloofness, in actuality was the mark of a man concentrating on large problems, intent on living up to the high standards he had set for himself and his college," it asserted. The editorial predicted that his record of accomplishments, as well as the trustees' "summary action," would produce "wide criticism." The more conservative *Lancaster New Era* was particularly critical of the trustees' manner of action: "Any man — professor, instructor or president of a college is entitled to that much consideration — if not legally, certainly ethically and morally." Both papers commended Appel but questioned whether he was qualified for the presidency.[104]

On September 6, Appel came to campus to meet with administrative staff. Meanwhile, an emergency AAUP meeting considered the faculty's response. Resolutions prepared by the Professional Standards Committee were approved and signed by sixty of ninety-five faculty. The statement challenged the board's actions on the grounds that it violated the principle of "academic due process" and that it ran counter to "the fundamental concept of fair play inherent in judicial procedure." Moreover, Appel's election violated a tradition of faculty participation in the selection of the president. In fact, this action had deprived Franklin & Marshall of its leading position "among enlightened institutions" regarding faculty participation in the selection process. This alone was "a grievous blow to the prestige of [the] College." Pointedly, the statement concluded, "Our only hope for the future of our College lies in the knowledge that a sizable minority of the Board of Trustees strongly opposed the malpractices giving rise to the action of which your telegram advised us."[105]

Appel appeared before the faculty the following day. Clearly seeking to reassure them, he made an opening statement affirming the changes made in recent years, the importance and professional independence of the faculty, and values of academic freedom and freedom of the press. He urged the faculty to understand that the majority of the board had acted out of "deep interest" in the welfare of the college and to accept their decision to elect a new president immediately in spite of "the well accepted policy" of faculty participation. After he concluded, a motion of support was approved by a voice vote. But this action was immediately called into question when AAUP president Luther Binkley read the faculty's statement of the preceding day. He then presented a series of resolutions prepared by the Professional Standards Committee. The first, commending Bolman for his work "in shaping Franklin and Marshall College into a true community of scholars bent upon attaining excellence in liberal arts education" and expressing regret at his departure, was adopted by acclamation.[106]

The second called on the board to establish a joint trustee-faculty committee to select a new president. Speaking on behalf of the resolution, Mac Darlington reiterated the contents of the letter he had sent to the September 5 meeting. "In my thirty-six year association with the College as student, alumnus, teacher and administrator," he asserted, "I have known of no action that was so inept and so unjust." To dismiss "an administrator of this calibre would be a complete abandonment of intelligent stewardship," as well as a denial of due academic process. It would injure the college's morale and reputation and make it much more difficult to find "a knowledgeable, experienced and self-respecting successor." This resolution was also adopted by acclamation. At Sidney Wise's motion, a secret ballot was held on the previous motion of support for the new president. This time the vote was quite different: 23 for, 11 against, and 35 abstaining. The numbers reveal not only a lack of support for Appel but strong divisions with the faculty itself.[107]

Receiving such a ringing lack of endorsement, and hearing warnings from departmental chairmen that the college faced mass resignations by its best faculty if he remained, Appel resigned a week after his election, to take effect at the next board meeting in October. In the meantime, Bolman and Schnader and their supporters continued to argue their respective positions in the press and in correspondence. As *Philadelphia Bulletin* reporter Peter Binzen strolled the campus in the aftermath of

Appel's resignation, he observed widespread discontent. "As new students exchanged pleasantries under the elms this afternoon," he observed, "leaders of the faculty revolt mapped further strategy aimed at deposing the chairman of the board of trustees." Referring to Appel's resignation, one professor told Binzen, "We won the last battle. But the war is Schnader."[108]

Schnader survived the assault, but the moment proved to be a defining one for a generation of Franklin & Marshall faculty. Recalled in almost mythic terms as the day when "the faculty fired the President," the story was invariably passed on to newcomers as the point at which the faculty emerged as an independent force within the college. The conflict leading to Bolman's departure was characterized as "a clash of personalities," and it was certainly that. But also at stake were contesting visions of governance in higher education, particularly the authority of academic administrators and faculty. The position held by Bolman and the leaders of the faculty eventually prevailed even if it met a temporary setback.[109]

Perhaps nothing so well expressed the values of the rising academic profession as Bolman's parting words to the faculty. He enjoined them to serve the interests not of a single institution but of a more transcendent ideal:

> Remember that there is a world of higher learning to serve. Corporate boards have stockholders, lawyers have clients and the right, doctors have patients and health, management has profit and the public interest. You have students and learning. Be beholden to these interests. Your good work at Franklin and Marshall College is one manifestation of a general dedication I am thinking about. You must be loyal to the particular so long as an organization will serve both you and the ideals we share.[110]

Yet, even as the faculty emerged as a significant force in collegiate governance, challenges to their professional authority would soon arise from a different quarter — radicals among the student body and younger faculty.

CHAPTER TEN

Academic Revolution Meets the Sixties Revolt, 1962–1968

The academic revolution went forward at Franklin & Marshall in the 1960s under the leadership of President Keith Spalding. Like institutions of higher education throughout the nation, the college responded expansively to increased government and private funding by putting up more buildings and establishing new curricular and extracurricular programs. Modernizing its fund-raising program, it completed by far the largest campaign in its history to match a major Ford Foundation grant. But demands of planning and fund-raising strained internal relations, especially between administration and a faculty anxious to exert its new-found role in governance. Managing change was further complicated by growing activism on the part of students and younger faculty inspired by the civil rights and antiwar movements. Seeking consensus within the college community, Spalding's leadership style emphasized consultation and deliberation.

The 1962–1963 academic year that had begun with the forced resignation of Frederick Bolman became known within the college community as "the year of four presidents." Following Anthony Appel's resignation, a chastened board followed the previously established procedure, whereby G. Wayne Glick, vice president and dean of the college, served as acting president until a successor was named. A trustee-faculty search committee headed by stalwarts Henry Marshall and Charles Spotts set to work immediately. At the outset committee members defined the ideal candidate as a "competent scholar" with substantial administrative experience and fund-raising ability. But a long list of possible candidates encompassed many fields — rumor had it that the name of former vice president Richard Nixon was included.[1]

An Effective Administrator and Communicator

In late November, Henry Marshall and geology professor John Moss paid a visit to Keith Spalding, assistant to Johns Hopkins University president Milton S. Eisenhower.

Spalding thought they would ask him to suggest names of candidates, but instead they asked him to consider becoming one. Critics of the board's treatment of Frederick Bolman had warned of damage to the college's reputation, and Spalding sensed that the committee was finding it hard to attract suitable candidates. At any rate, he recalled, "I'm relatively sure I was not at the top of the list."[2]

Indeed, Spalding was not a typical candidate for the presidency of a liberal arts college. A psychology major at the University of Kansas, he had become a journalist after serving as a fighter-bomber pilot with the U.S. Marines in the South Pacific. By the mid-1950s he was an editor at the *New York Herald Tribune* but wanted wider scope to "make things happen." He became administrative assistant to Milton Eisenhower, who was then president of Pennsylvania State University, and followed him to Baltimore in 1959. Eisenhower was known to rely on strong administrative assistants, of whom much was expected but who in turn gained valuable experience. "He wanted assistants with ambition, ability, and drive equal to his own who sought to shoulder increased burdens," observed Eisenhower's biographers, "who did what [he] desired before being asked and then did a little bit more." Spalding's close relationship with Eisenhower provided an intensive apprenticeship in academic leadership. When contacted by the Franklin & Marshall Search Committee, Spalding was forty-three years old and ready for a new challenge.[3]

The Search Committee deemed Spalding well suited for the college's present need to "strengthen the understanding between trustees, faculty, and alumni and improve our communications with foundations and other sources of financial assistance." When the full board confirmed the committee's decision at its February 1963 meeting, they telephoned Spalding and asked him to drive up from Baltimore to join them. "I'd like to spend a long time here," Spalding told *Student Weekly* reporter David Harrison soon after taking office in mid-April. Observing that the conflicts of the previous fall were still fresh in many memories, Spalding commented, "The sooner people stop talking about the Bolman-Schnader affair the healthier this place will be."[4]

There were reasons for concern about the college's future. Recent fund-raising efforts had been unsuccessful. In 1961 the Ford Foundation had invited an application for one of its major challenge grants to independent liberal arts colleges. In fact, Ford's Special Program in Education played a significant role in shaping the emergence of a group of select universities and liberal arts colleges into regional "peaks of excellence." To apply, colleges prepared a ten-year projection of plans and needs, known as a Ford Profile; those showing greatest ambition seemed most likely to be selected. But the previous May college officials had learned that their application was rejected, news that presidential assistant Richard Stonesifer acknowledged to be "a serious blow" to their hopes. College leaders had also presented a proposal to the Longwood Foundation in August for a large grant for a science center, but after Bolman's departure Longwood deferred action pending an assessment of the new administration. Shortly before Spalding's election, Stonesifer left for a post at the University of Pennsylvania. His parting statement to the *Weekly* expressed concern that the college was not getting its share of large foundation grants. He warned that continued progress depended on increasing the endowment, presently around $5 million, to $8 million to 10 million.[5]

Many in the college were still smarting from the 1962 Middle States Association evaluation. On the one hand, there was some gratification in its criticisms of Schnader's method of hiring the vice president for development and his creation of "life" trustees with power to vote and hold office indefinitely. On the other hand, the report expressed reservations about the new curriculum and long-range plan, for which everyone had expected only praise. Noting that the college's stated objective was to provide "a liberal education of high quality," evaluators questioned whether this was possible under the high projected student-faculty ratio.[6]

It was no surprise that the report noted a shortage of art and music courses, but it also questioned the dominant role given foreign languages. Even more alarming were numerous criticisms, however implicit, of the college's prized science programs. Scientists on the committee came from research universities — Columbia and Johns Hopkins — and made no distinction between research and liberal arts institutions. As they saw it, the "central questions" for colleges like Franklin & Marshall were how to "keep up with the rapidly growing body of scientific knowledge" and maintain "a stimulating intellectual environment" to ensure competent instruction in new scientific areas. The "one generally recognized" way to maintain "an alert, up-to-date staff" was to participate "in modern creative and original research" independent of teaching or student participation. They recommended that faculty take regular leaves to "join with active university or other institutional research groups" and attend "full-fledged scientific meetings and conferences." They doubted that sufficient exposure to new scientific developments could be achieved by attending regional conferences, taking "refresher" courses, studying teaching methods, or writing anything other than scientific monographs. Evaluators also applied research university norms in their recommendation to cut the number of "service" courses oriented toward nonmajors and to use a large auditorium for introductory course lectures. Noting a shortage of research facilities, they urged immediate steps to build the planned science center. Perhaps most surprisingly, they deemed the biology curriculum outdated and lacking in attention to recent advances in molecular biology, genetics, and evolutionary studies.[7]

Middle States evaluators also failed to ratify the faculty's professional self-image. They observed little faculty interest in ongoing curricular experimentation, now that the new curriculum was in place, and only "a small amount" of research being done, much of it with students at a rudimentary level. "Many of the faculty seem to feel that research would *interfere* with teaching," they noted. "Few of them regard active productive scholarship as necessary to teaching."[8]

The absence of a glowing commendation was a blow to the college's pride in its recent progress. Summarizing the evaluators' report to the board, Bolman acknowledged that both the Middle States Association and Ford Foundation staff "seem to charge us with not 'thinking big,'" particularly about the college's long-run financial situation. "We are accused of lacking boldness and vigor," he concluded. Bolman recommended a "crash program" in development. At an AAUP discussion of the report in the fall, some thought the criticisms unfair. Others responded, "We seem not to be what we think we are or would like to be." The consensus was that the college must work even harder.[9]

Under Glick's interim administration, incremental improvements did continue. After years of discussion, the college launched its College Scholar program for "superior" students, a program aimed at attracting "extraordinarily able students who will leaven the entire student body" and draw "high-quality faculty." Supporters argued that despite improvements in incoming students' academic credentials, some of the best seemed to be "retrograding" perhaps because the large number of required introductory courses did not challenge them sufficiently. The scholar program exempted participants from most requirements to offer "greater independence and an enlarged responsibility for their own learning"; team-taught interdisciplinary seminars united "the best minds among their fellows." Fifteen freshmen and sophomores were selected, and the program began in 1963 with its own seminar space in Diagnothian Hall.[10]

Glick also initiated the program of Faculty Summer Research Fellowships and in the first year raised enough money from the General Foods Fund to support eight grants. Awarded by the faculty's Professional Standards Committee (PSC), many fellowships supported work in the social sciences and humanities for which there was as yet little federal aid. The faculty formed a standing committee to conduct ongoing evaluation of the curriculum and approved the psychology department's petition to be reclassified as a natural science, in keeping with the orientation of its faculty's research interests. A new administration computer made it possible to process grades electronically.[11]

The board approved plans for a large dormitory complex for four hundred students and a central dining facility for one thousand. The board had recently acquired a forty-five-acre tract of land half a mile west of the campus on Harrisburg Pike. Subsequently named the Baker Memorial Campus in recognition of a bequest from Charles G. and Miriam R. Baker, the area replaced athletic fields displaced by new construction.[12]

Formal campus activities stressed intellectual discussion; the lineup of visiting speakers that year included Will Herberg and W. H. Auden. A series of student-faculty forums opened its second year with a discussion of Marxism by Solomon Wank, a new history professor. The forums had begun auspiciously the previous year when a paper on Wallace Stevens by new English professor Gerald Enscoe sparked a lively debate about Christianity. The *Student Weekly* termed the forum a "spectacular success" and welcomed the chance "to hear faculty opinion expressed on matters that are personal and exterior to classroom subject matter." In the program's second year faculty were encouraged to join students in the dining halls afterward for further discussion; on occasion debates continued long afterward in lively correspondence in the *Weekly*.[13]

In the midst of the turmoil at the beginning of the 1962–1963 academic year, one significant change at the college had gone unremarked: Franklin & Marshall's long-resented chapel requirement had been quietly dropped. Without public acknowledgment, the freshman handbook section on campus worship changed, the word "expected" substituted for "required" in connection with morning services. A group of students with the support of Chaplain Robert Taylor had petitioned to have the requirement lifted, and the administration seems to have deemed it unnecessary to seek board permission. The handbook continued to note the college's historical relation to the United Church of Christ (UCC) and Franklin & Marshall's appreciation of "the diversity of religious expression of belief." Two years later, weekday worship was discontinued altogether. For several years, a Sunday morning chapel service was held in its place, but it was also dropped for lack of attendance.[14]

Arrival of the new president in April revived hope for change. But Keith Spalding moved slowly, aware that his authority was circumscribed by lack of academic credentials. Moreover, he followed Milton Eisenhower's first principle of administration — "consult, consult, consult." He declined to discuss plans for the future, saying that he wanted to learn from discussions with all members of the community. At the end of his first day on campus he dined with student leaders at Dean Hadley DePuy's home, where talk ranged from ways to stimulate student participation to the advising system to the American League pennant race. Like his predecessors, Spalding worked to develop community ties by speaking at many group meetings and public occasions. But often his decisions were especially influenced by advice from an informal group of government faculty.[15]

Spalding did make several informal innovations that presaged a more worldly orientation. First, he had no formal ties with the United Church of Christ or indeed any religious organization. Before accepting the presidency, he consulted with UCC's national head, who raised no objection to his appointment. But after his arrival in Lancaster, Charles Spotts invited him to a dinner, where a number of faculty active in the UCC tried to persuade him of the importance of membership in a church community — indeed, this had been a bedrock tenet of Mercersburg Theology. "I was ready to maintain that I could be religious and believe in things spiritual," Spalding recalled, "but I could do that by myself." In another departure from college tradition, Spalding served liquor at receptions at his campus residence. "[At first] I didn't know any better," he explained. Having come from a university where social occasions were invariably well lubricated with alcohol, he had not realized that it was banned on campus. "There were people who loved me for it, but it was an outright breaking of the rules," he admitted. Subsequently, the rules were reinterpreted to permit alcohol at presidential functions.[16]

Spalding knew that the college was impatient for change. "It is clear that the College is on a threshold of improvements in many areas," he told the board, "and its Faculty, its students, and individual Trustees with whom I have talked want some major accomplishments to be realized in the near future." Regularly putting in fifteen-hour days, he favored a hands-on style of administration; he discontinued Bolman's staff council as prone to delay.[17]

His first priority was reviving fund-raising. Even before selection of a new president, an informal meeting of the board's Development Committee concluded that a long-term campaign was needed to raise "a goodly sum of money — much more than it has ever undertaken in the past." At his first board meeting, Spalding agreed: "I think we must do fund-raising of rather massive proportions." This required new approaches: "Our needs are so great that we cannot be put in the position of being told that we can not have a successful capital fund-raising campaign because we have already 'scoured' the Alumni." He thought a goal of $20 million over ten years was not out of line "so long as we have a compelling story to tell and have good staff work behind our plans." By summer, the ten-year goal had risen to $25.25 million.[18]

Spalding was inaugurated at the beginning of the 1963–1964 academic year. His address defended liberal education, in a judicious blend of the rhetoric of academic excellence and of character building. Pointing to technological and scientific advances made since World War II, he asserted that the work of the great research institutions could not continue "unless the young men and women who [came] to them [had] been soundly educated." He rejected prophecies that the private, independent liberal arts college was "doomed to extinction." Rather, it had a "vital mission" to provide "not only the best preparation for a satisfying life and for making a living" but also "the best foundation on which to build specialized knowledge and undertake a creative life." In a classic formulation of liberal arts education, he characterized it as "a liberating experience": "It frees the mind of a young man from the shackles of ignorance, undue pride, intolerance, dogmatism, provincialism, and prejudice." It "opens his mind and lets him discover that learning is a real adventure. It creates the scientist rather than the devotee of scientism. It inspires the humanist and leads him to life's deeper meanings. It serves, in short, to provide the substance which must dominate our educational concern — the free man."[19]

Spalding praised Franklin & Marshall for its "intellectual vigor," "institutional loyalty," and high proportion of graduates going on to graduate and professional study. Above all, he believed that in the process of its recent advancement the college had found an "intangible" identity in its collective commitment to "seek true excellence." For Spalding this ideal was perfectly described as "a community of scholars," a phrase that included faculty and students but also trustees, administrators, and alumni who appreciate the scholarly institution and "protect its integrity, support its efforts and encourage its development."[20]

A New Activist Spirit on Campus

Spalding did not refer directly to great social debates of the moment when he characterized Franklin & Marshall as a place of "intellectual ferment," but from the beginning of the term it was clear that this community was more aware of events outside its walls. In coming years, the college would be shaped and sometimes shaken by outside forces that threatened to disrupt leaders' careful planning. Earlier in 1963 the civil rights movement had returned to the forefront of national attention. Images of brutal treatment of nonviolent demonstrators in Birmingham, Alabama, filled the evening news. President Kennedy finally sent comprehensive civil rights legislation to Congress, and in August two hundred thousand marched on Washington for the largest demonstration in the capital's history.

The movement reached even Lancaster, where the local African American community was confined to the poorest housing in the southeast section of the city and until recently had been barred from all but menial and domestic employment. Over the summer of 1963 college and seminary faculty joined picket lines protesting lack of black salesclerks at local department stores. The businesses eventually hired African American clerks, but attempts to end segregation at swimming pools were less successful.[21]

In the fall Chaplain Robert Taylor organized a tutoring project for "potential dropouts" at the junior high in the predominantly African American Seventh Ward. A committee on race relations headed by Solomon Wank developed proposals for a summer remedial program and exchanges with historically black schools and helped admissions expand recruitment of African American students. The Academic Council and admissions staff considered how to reach out to "more qualified Negro students" and "disadvantaged" students from urban and rural areas. This work had some effect, for twenty-eight black students applied, up from five the previous year, but their ability to enroll was limited by their great financial need.[22]

Inevitably, heightened attention to race relations focused concern on fraternity discrimination. Little seemed to have changed in the three years since the board expressed its opposition to discriminatory clauses in fraternity charters. In September the board's Executive Committee discussed the issue with fraternity presidents and faculty advisors. Ten of eleven organizations assured the board that they had declared local autonomy in selection of members, and the eleventh promised that it would take steps to do so. The fact remained, however, that only one fraternity, Pi Lambda Phi, had black members. At the beginning of the fall 1963 semester, a *Student Weekly* editorial proclaimed that fraternity bias must end, and seventy-nine faculty and administrators signed a petition with a similar demand. Spalding told fraternity presidents that the college was now focused on the question of de jure discrimination, but in future it would have to look at de facto conditions.[23]

Fraternities were not the only local organizations to receive closer scrutiny. The *Weekly* questioned the college's ties to the Hamilton Club, a social center for Lancaster's business elite, which had no Jewish or African American members. The paper noted that all seven local trustees were members, as Bolman had been; Spalding had been proposed for admission. When Eleanor Roosevelt visited Lancaster in 1955, she declined to attend a reception in her honor there because of its discriminatory policies. The faculty approved—by a narrow margin—a resolution calling on the college to withhold patronage from any organization or business that discriminated "on ground of race, religion or national origin." AAUP consequently canceled plans to hold its winter banquet at the local Holiday Inn, because its national organization condoned discrimination by its southern affiliates.[24]

The faculty's actions reflected a generally liberal attitude, but some newcomers to the college were driven by even more intense moral and ideological fervor. In the early 1960s, a younger generation of activist graduate students influenced by the civil rights and nuclear disarmament movements began to challenge their elders' professional norms, especially the priority given to research and values of objectivity. Some, radicalized by experiences in the South, rejected moderation and pragmatism as ploys to preserve the status quo. Charles Haynie, a newly arrived mathematics instructor, was the most visible exemplar of this generation at Franklin & Marshall. As a Cornell graduate student, he participated in civil rights demonstrations at the 1960 Democratic National Convention and in 1961 was arrested in Jackson, Mississippi, while taking part in the Freedom Rides, which were challenging segregation in public transportation. Before coming to Lancaster, he spent the summer of 1963 — including his honeymoon — registering voters in Fayette County, Tennessee. He told the *Student Weekly* that he had chosen Franklin & Marshall because of its well-known struggle for academic freedom and his belief that liberal arts colleges were best suited to show students "what is going on in society and not to produce a technician." He had not yet completed his Ph.D.[25]

The new activist spirit was on display at the first student-faculty forum of the year, Report on Summer '63. Junior government major Peter Hartjens described his experiences at the march on Washington, a seminary professor spoke on the role of Christian faith in public life, and Solomon Wank reported on the civil rights movement. Haynie described conditions in Tennessee: "I did not know this existed today on this continent," he said. He was haunted by the idea that he was able to return to a normal life while there were people "down there in Fayette County and other places like it who [couldn't] vote, or take a bath, or even attempt to remedy peacefully the injustices they face daily." Anxious to convey realities of life for southern blacks, Haynie invited students to his home to hear tapes of civil rights demonstrations. At one of these sessions the group decided to petition the local congressman to sign a discharge petition for civil rights legislation that southern segregationists had bottled up in Congress.[26]

The campus was shocked by John F. Kennedy's assassination on November 23. Several weeks later, Martin Luther King issued an electrifying call to action to a packed Mayser Center: "The wind of change is blowing all over our world today." He criticized not only those who tried to block integration but those who sat by and did nothing. As if on cue, Haynie's group circulated their petition and obtained some 1,200 signatures. College and seminary faculty and students canvassed door to door the following weekend and acquired another 1,600. Haynie told the *Weekly* that he hoped King's speech would change local thinking about civil rights and counter a "defeatist attitude" among students.[27]

The college's connection with the United Church of Christ tied it to the civil rights movement through its sister school, Tougaloo Southern Christian College in Jackson, Mississippi. Although predominantly African American, Tougaloo was one of only two integrated schools in the state and a hotbed of civil rights activity. Its president, A. Daniel Beittle, visited campus in December and urged students to "consider teaching in Southern Negro colleges" after graduation. When the Mississippi legislature threatened to revoke Tougaloo's charter, Franklin & Marshall's AAUP held an emergency meeting to formulate a protest. The next day the entire faculty approved a resolution directed at the governor of Mississippi. A small group of students connected with the Committee for Social Action met separately to express their indignation. Physics instructor David Sagal and freshman Dennis Brookshire traveled to Jackson during spring break to investigate and found the situation "unbelievably tense." Tougaloo's theater director, P. William Hutchinson Jr., '57, told them he feared for the safety of his family.[28]

Meanwhile, college leaders worked to realize their idea for a precollege enrichment program (commonly known as PREP) for African American students. "We cannot do what some larger colleges and universities are doing," Spalding told the board, but "we can provide a program which nobody else appears to be providing." The idea was to offer special summer work in reading, writing, and math — subjects deemed crucial for college achievement — to students soon to be freshmen at historically black universities in the area. But funding still had to be obtained. After they were turned down by the Ford Foundation, planners received word in May 1964 of David Rockefeller's offer of $40,000 to launch the program. Under Glick's direction, Gerald Enscoe and Robert Taylor organized an eight-week session aimed, as the student paper put it, "to overcome the loss of human talent among culturally deprived students." Additional money from other foundations, local churches, and individuals made it possible to pay all expenses as well as a stipend in lieu of summer earnings for fifty-five young men, all African Americans, including several who had been admitted to Franklin & Marshall. PREP's first run was deemed a success and became a prototype for subsequent federal programs.[29]

Even so, the program was too small to attract ongoing outside support, for foundation, philanthropic, and civil rights leaders preferred programs that reached larger numbers of students and extended over longer periods. PREP's second summer went on with support from the National Scholarship Service's Fund for Negro Students and small local gifts. Nineteen Mississippi boys and girls just entering their senior year in high school were selected to participate.[30]

The Academic Revolution Reshapes College Life

For most students, life was still dominated by more traditional concerns of study and extracurricular activities. Big weekends in 1963–1964 included concerts in the new field house by the Dave Brubeck Quartet, the Smothers Brothers, and the Lettermen. On social occasions the decline in numbers of local students — only 5 percent of freshmen were from Lancaster County in 1963 — had the unanticipated consequence of making it harder for students to meet local women. To provide dates for big weekends like homecoming and the winter Snowball, student groups "imported" busloads from women's colleges. Often the process of matching up dates was not handled in the most graceful manner. Spalding observed the arrival of one of these buses soon after he came to campus. "The picture is engraved on my mind," he recalled years later, of a "horde of young men." These students surrounded the bus and picked women as they disembarked. Those who went unclaimed retreated to the bus in dismay.[31]

Such scenes reinforced Spalding's conviction that Franklin & Marshall must eventually become coeducational. "I wasn't the only one who was concerned about that," he acknowledged, "but the only one in a position to do anything about it." Even so, he took no action at first. He later explained that the early years of his administration were not the right time to make such a fundamental change. As a new president, he needed first "to heal the wounds [which] were pretty deep" and then to improve the college's financial condition. But he began quietly to raise the issue with faculty leaders. His approach was typical of his indirect style of administration: "What I did," he recalled, "was to talk with leading members of the faculty, on the walk, and say, 'Wouldn't it be great if we could . . . ?' And then you wait a little while and it comes back and people are pounding on your desk saying 'Why can't we do this?' It was a formula and it worked."[32]

Academic improvements continued. A program of outside evaluation of departments began in 1964 with physics and biology. The college acquired a new Burroughs 205 computer for faculty and student use, under oversight of a faculty committee. Its one thousand vacuum tubes in gray metal cabinets were housed in a room below the swimming pool, and the newspaper reported that the computer was capable of doing two hundred thousand additions per second.[33]

Each year saw reductions in curriculum requirements. In 1963 the English department revised its introductory course to combine literature and composition, thus eliminating the required supplementary course in composition and allowing English faculty "to teach within their area of main interest, literature." A pattern of focusing on academic study of literature rather than skills instruction continued in 1964 with creation of a separate department of public address to teach the required speech course. The faculty also lowered the foreign language requirement from five terms to four.[34]

In keeping with the proliferation of academic knowledge, numbers of courses offered continued to grow: departments added new ones; new departments were created, as anthropology separated from sociology; and committees planned future expansion in humanities and new programs in fine arts and area studies. Conversely, many faculty hoped to reduce or eliminate "service" courses. The chemistry department successfully petitioned to end the master's program in chemistry, citing a lack of faculty interest and the poor quality of students it attracted. The Academic Council cut courses in advertising, sales, insurance, and transportation, and the English department strongly opposed a proposal to establish a joint journalism program with Penn State.[35]

The faculty's growing specialization fueled criticism of the curriculum. Teachers hired in recent years had trained in a wider range of fields — new history faculty, for example, had expertise in medieval, Middle Eastern, and Russian history. They resented required introductory courses that prevented them from teaching in their specialties. In spring 1965, the Committee on Area Studies proposed programs on Russia and Asia and a cooperative program in African studies with Lincoln University, urging that greater attention be paid to non-Western societies and cultures. Similarly, professors in foreign language departments criticized the humanities sequence for teaching texts in translation. The Committee on the Continuing Evaluation of the Curriculum received so many requests for changes in distribution requirements that the Academic Council proposed reconsidering the entire curriculum. This provoked "considerable discussion" in the faculty and passed only when Spalding cast a tie-breaking vote in its favor.[36]

The history department created a new curriculum for its majors, replacing broad surveys with seminars and special topics courses. One of the first of its kind, the curriculum attracted widespread professional attention. Proponents explained that the old courses focused on "a narrow range of political experience and on restricted concepts of human behavior" and that changes reflected less confidence in a "stable corpus" of knowledge in Western civilization.[37]

The college came to an amicable agreement with the U.S. Air Force to phase out the ROTC program. The decision was based on declining enrollments and commissions, but it fortuitously eliminated a source of future conflict. Some attributed reduced interest to growing numbers of students continuing to graduate and professional schools, while many faculty simply felt that the program did not belong at a liberal arts college.[38]

In keeping with ambitions of the age, the student newspaper expanded to twice-weekly publication, to offer more extensive and timely news, with a resulting change in title to *College Reporter*. A co-editorship was instituted to handle the increased workload, the first being juniors David Harrison and Richard Kneedler. They sought to stimulate discussion, particularly about the perennial issue of student apathy. Editorials urged the administration to keep students better informed, while Charles Haynie advocated more student involvement in course design and a curriculum focused on "the hard questions." Another new faculty member, sociologist Jetse Sprey, responded by deploring "the rantings of the small, but noisy, category of self-professed 'non-apathetics' who are aroused about everything, but know practically nothing." He agreed that students who did little but study hurt the college's intellectual climate, but he believed that the faculty's "intellectual snobbism" did more to discourage participation in campus life. His survey of students found less frustration and alienation among those with clear postgraduation plans. The major division on campus, he concluded, was not between premeds and others, as many claimed, but "between those who [were] 'bright' enough to go on for further 'higher' learning and those left to be dumped on the labor market."[39]

A Changing Board-Administration Relationship

Behind the scenes, Spalding worked carefully to establish his authority over the board, preferring quiet persuasion to overt exhortation. He later reflected on his approach in a letter to trustee R. Graeme Smith, who became a friend and ally. "It will be a long time before I achieve the venerability associated with oracles and therefore be able to 'teach' trustees how they should act," he observed. "I can properly persuade and influence them as we face particular issues, and I can properly engage them in discussion of developing problems." But he was reluctant to "preach" or to reinstate the kind of seminars that Bolman had held "for philosophical explorations" of governance.[40]

An example of Spalding's leadership style was the formulation of a policy statement on academic freedom and tenure. Before his arrival, administrators discovered that written procedures regarding tenure and dismissal were unclear. Moreover, the board had never formally adopted AAUP's 1940 statement of principles. The task of preparing a comprehensive statement of the college's philosophy and practices fell to the faculty's Professional Standards Committee, who worked on it throughout 1963–1964. Following recent AAUP recommendations, the committee created an elected standing committee, the Judicial Committee, to hear cases of dismissal for cause. Foreseeing that some on the board might have reservations about the statement, Spalding discussed with the PSC how best to introduce it and consulted with "senior members of the faculty" while writing its preface. He also paved the way by commenting at a prior board meeting that the college attracted top scholars not only because it had achieved favorable salary levels but because of its "climate of academic freedom." Privately he assured a leading trustee that the new dismissal procedures would make it possible to dismiss someone "for example, on the grounds of moral turpitude."[41]

Even so, the board greeted the statement with "considerable discussion" and "a number of questions." Trustees finally approved it in principle with the understanding that Spalding and Schnader would revise and resubmit it for final approval. Much of the revision was done by trustee Graeme Smith, a distinguished Connecticut attorney, and the document was endorsed by the board in October. Spalding later called it "one of the most impressive policy documents this College has ever had" and noted that other institutions used it as a model.[42]

Spalding recognized that the college's tenure and academic freedom policies were the source of "misconceptions or misunderstandings" in the local community. Hence, the preamble placed academic freedom within the context of American traditions. Freedom was "the right of every human being," not a special privilege of academics. Moreover, effectiveness of liberal arts education depended on "a climate of freedom," for it needed "an atmosphere which not only tolerates but encourages searching inquiry, unfettered thought, open discussion and free expression of ideas."[43]

Yet this right was not absolute. Faculty had "sober responsibilities" as scholars and citizens not to abuse their freedom. These responsibilities were couched in terms of professional self-regulation: each "must weigh carefully the validity of his opinions and the manner in which he expresses them. He must always recognize his limitations outside his fields of special competence. He must be aware that not only he but his profession and his institution may be harmed by rash acts or statements." The document linked this responsibility to the tenure system by charging members of the faculty with "broad authority" to maintain standards of scholarship and professional conduct in hiring, promotion, and tenure: "The faculty must therefore not only accept an obligation to foster high standards of professional conduct but must also willingly bear responsibility for the discipline of those who fail to comport themselves in keeping with their academic trust."[44]

Planning and Its Discontents

James Darlington later observed that one of the hallmarks of the Spalding administration was his "penchant for institutional planning, using task forces of diverse composition." This was first displayed when, after more than a year of discussion, the college undertook a large-scale study of student life. AAUP got the ball rolling by inviting representatives from Williams and Amherst to speak about how they had dealt with "the problem of fraternities"— the former by banning them and the latter by taking control of their finances. Later, AAUP asked the faculty to call for a long-range study. Spalding also mentioned the need for such an evaluation, at a dinner for more than one hundred students, faculty, and alumni, noting that fraternities seemed to be "groping for some clear definition of their role and purpose." Fraternities were in fact under increased financial pressure of maintaining aging chapter houses and meeting more rigorous housing regulations. Neighborhood opposition blocked attempts to buy better properties. Dean DePuy floated as a trial balloon the idea that the college might construct new housing for fraternities, financed through federal loans, on the condition that it held the mortgage and received title to the present houses.[45]

In October 1964, Spalding announced creation of a special committee headed by Frederic S. Klein and composed of four other faculty, one administrator, and two students — including the president of the Inter-fraternity Council (IFC) — to study the fraternity system at Franklin & Marshall. Acknowledging that there were strong feelings for and against fraternities, Spalding insisted that as president he had an obligation to honor the college's historical commitment to them. He reflected that "any abrupt or thoughtless change in that situation would cause harm and financial strain for the College, and possible injustice to individuals and groups who have contributed materially and personally to the fraternity chapters." He charged the committee to examine student life as a whole and urged it to take as much time as necessary and keep deliberations private.[46]

The makeup of the student body continued to change as its numbers grew. The class of 1968 had a record-high 509 members, 85 percent of whom had graduated in the top two-fifths of their classes. Northeastern states continued to dominate, with 37 percent from Pennsylvania, 20 percent from New York, 19 percent from New Jersey, 12 percent from New England, 6 percent from Maryland, and 6 percent from other states. Fewer of the students, 45 percent, planned to major in the natural sciences, with 24 percent aiming at social sciences, 6 percent at business, and 6 percent at humanities, with 17 percent undecided. The college no longer reported religious data, but a survey by a sociology student the previous spring identified half the student body as Protestant, 30 percent as Jewish, 10 percent as Catholic, and 10 percent self-described as nonreligious.

Regarding economic status, 30 percent called themselves upper-middle to upper class, 35 percent middle class, 25 percent lower-middle, and 10 percent lower class. Fifty-five percent were fraternity members, and 75 percent planned to go on to graduate or professional schools.[47]

The growing proportion of students from urban and suburban areas outside Pennsylvania testified to the college's widening reputation. But it also carried seeds of dissatisfaction. When the college was more local and homogeneous, it had been easier for students to find entertainment and social connection in the community. Now more cosmopolitan students considered "townies" to be "a figure of fun." In addition, downtown Lancaster, like many American cities, was deteriorating, as middle-class residents moved to the suburbs, leaving students more dependent on limited campus resources for entertainment. Conversely, local residents were less likely to attend campus events. Under new directors Edwin Brubaker and Hugh Evans, Green Room theater productions were often controversial. "There was a lot of theater coming out in the sixties which was pretty heavy stuff for your local Lancaster college supporter," David Shaw, '65, recalled. On-campus entertainment reflected changing student tastes. A fine art films series appealed to artistically adventurous students with Ingmar Bergman's *Wild Strawberries* and to a broader audience with *The Mouse That Roared*. The folk music movement was well represented by appearances by Peter, Paul, and Mary and Oscar Brand. For the latter, the Student Union bused in five hundred "girls" from six women's colleges and student nurses from Harrisburg, Lancaster, and Reading.[48]

The freshman orientation program was extensively revised in 1964 to improve the students' intellectual integration into campus life. As a *College Reporter* editorial noted, previous orientations' focus on dinks, tugs-of-war, talent shows, and talks on school spirit had become "an anachronism." Hoping to introduce freshmen "to the life of the mind at a time when they were most receptive," faculty planners asked freshmen to read three recent novels on the theme "reactions to the American culture" before arriving on campus and to attend a faculty panel discussion of these books.[49]

Even so, that fall saw a resurgence of traditional college spirit, sparked in part by the football team's success. After a string of losing seasons, the team went undefeated in its second year under coach George Storck. Student enthusiasm mounted with each victory, and by the end of the season stands in Williamson Field were once again packed. Larry Graham, '65, a veteran member of the team, was amazed when it returned from a victory over Dickinson College to find that "the whole college came out to meet the team." Celebrating a new spirit of optimism on campus, the *Reporter* gave much of the credit to the football team. "It's difficult to generate enthusiasm on a campus that's almost literally evacuated on weekends," the paper pointed out. Now, if the campus was empty on Saturdays, it was because everyone had gone to an away game.[50]

With victory came new interest in dimly remembered college traditions. At homecoming, students paraded through downtown Lancaster for the first time in fifteen years, with fraternity floats and bands from both Franklin & Marshall and rival Carnegie Tech. Beforehand, five hundred students marched down College Avenue to the dean's and president's houses, chanting "Go, Go, Go!" until Spalding came out to give a pep talk. The event ended with a giant bonfire near Schnader dormitory. Confusion about college traditions sparked a comical chain of events. Freshmen, who had been spared the traditional hazing, smarted under alumni criticism that they had shirked duties to form a line to welcome the team onto the field and pull the Conestoga wagon around the track at halftime. They protested that no one had told them about these traditional expectations. During the game, rumors circulated that it had once been customary to declare Monday holidays after a homecoming win. Afterward a few students decided to test this tradition. Beginning in Hartman Oval with about 75 students, a crowd grew despite efforts of Student Council president Mike Yaggy and dorm counselors to discourage it. By the time the group reached Dean DePuy's home, there were 250, some obviously intoxicated. They moved on to Spalding's house, where about 100 sat down on the lawn and broke into "We Shall Overcome," complete with guitar accompaniment. This half-parodic "demonstration" ended when Coach Storck told students that the team appreciated their enthusiasm but that Monday classes must go on as usual.[51]

As in the case of the 1961 riot, student observers pointed to systemic problems. They saw the event as the result of "a desperate lack of communication at many levels of the College" and the absence of more appropriate ways to express complaints. A *Reporter* editorial also urged more college traditions, not as "a return to the past," but in recognition that they "are frequently a very effective way to involve new students in a school." One junior argued further that traditions helped foster a sense of emotional connection, something lacking in the college's present dry, "purely rational" atmosphere. Later an assistant dean discussed school traditions with freshmen and promised they would be included in future handbooks. A survey of freshmen found large majorities in favor of resurrecting dinks, the frosh-soph tug-of-war, and the required learning of the alma mater, though the same number opposed physical hazing. After the final home game ended in victory, students marched to Penn Square, escorting the football team in the Conestoga wagon and coaches and captains of the soccer and cross-country teams in cars. (The soccer team had won a berth in the NCAA national playoffs.) Freshmen were given the honor of carrying the goalposts. Students' attachment to at least an idea of college tradition showed the resilience of an autonomous student culture, often but not exclusively attached to fraternities and athletics, that resisted assimilation into the faculty's purely academic vision.[52]

Meeting the Ford Challenge

Fall 1964 was an especially crucial moment for the college, for the Ford Foundation had invited it to reapply for a challenge grant. Ford selected schools on the basis of their potential to serve as "models of excellence in their regions," tradition of scholarship, quality of leadership, promise of making "pace-setting improvements," and base of support. One of the grant's goals was to prod colleges to modernize planning and development operations, and the extensive screening process required a detailed pro-file with long-range plans. When questions were raised in AAUP and faculty meetings about growth in the administration — often referred to as "the population explosion in East Hall"— Spalding outlined the work needed for successful fund-raising. Later, faculty drew lines more clearly between itself and the administration by revising its rules of order to withdraw faculty status from the dean of students, the director of college development and the business manager.[53]

In the process of preparing the ten-year plan for the campus's physical development, Spalding incurred the wrath of the AAUP and Academic Council, who feared they were being shut out of genuine deliberations. After discovering that Spaulding had presented a general plan to the board before AAUP had had a chance to discuss it, the association complained about his administrative style. The AAUP resolved that the plan must be regarded as temporary and discussed how to ensure greater faculty involvement. At a faculty meeting the next day, Spalding reiterated that the plan had only been approved in its broad outlines and that there would be many opportunities to discuss it.[54]

Faculty were also concerned that the board had removed the enrollment cap of 1,600, substituting an expectation that the student body would gradually increase to around 1,950, a size allowing better balance among academic fields. The present student-to-faculty ratio would be retained until it was financially possible to reduce it, which would mean an expansion in the faculty from the present 105 to around 140.[55]

Insisting that the proposed campus plan involved "serious academic questions," AAUP appointed three committees to examine it. One committee report questioned the projected arrangement of buildings, especially the loss of open space and implicit "zoning" into residential, academic, and administrative areas. Another charged that the idea of constructing a six-story "high-rise" dormitory along with small units for fraternities seemed to give priority to "primarily social rather than intellectual" values. A third report called a student-to-faculty ratio of ten to one essential to meeting "the College's professed goal of academic excellence." It also argued that if the college was going to expand, it was a propitious time to move toward coeducation, which had not even been considered. AAUP approved these concerns, especially the need to move toward coeducation. After the report, more than two-thirds of faculty signed a petition calling for the college to make a commitment to coeducation. Most of those who did not sign also favored change but thought there should be more study first; only ten to twelve faculty were reported to strongly oppose coeducation. Spalding presented the petition to the board's Executive Committee, which was discussing terms of a possible Ford challenge grant. The petition sparked "an extended discussion of the problems of co-education," with general agreement that Spalding should handle the matter at some time in the future.[56]

When it seemed that the desired changes were not forthcoming, the Academic Council's Executive Committee brought resolutions to the full faculty, criticizing inclusion of fraternity housing in the campus plan and urging "immediate consideration to coeducation" in the planning process. The faculty approved both, and Spalding presented them to the board but asked that action be delayed on coeducation to allow time to study the question.[57]

Spalding might have been reluctant at that particular moment to launch a debate on coeducation, for at the June meeting the board took up the Ford Foundation's offer of an unrestricted grant of $2.2 million dollars — if the college raised another $6.6 million by June 30, 1968. The challenge was an impressive vote of confidence from the foundation, which had offered larger amounts to only eight other colleges. But the three-to-one match was the most rigorous that the program imposed, and the amount was far more than the college had ever raised. Spalding might have thought that reaching the goal would be hard enough without raising an issue likely to antagonize many alumni and trustees.[58]

Avoiding conflict would not be easy, however, as the nation entered one of the most divisive periods in its history. In spring 1965 attention turned to Selma, Alabama, where blacks were brutally assaulted while attempting to register to vote. Franklin & Marshall's faculty passed a resolution calling for federal legislation to ensure voting rights, while a campuswide protest meeting heard calls to go to Selma for a planned march. An interracial group of eleven faculty, students, and administrators responded and on their return described their experiences at a special forum.[59]

Through the Committee on Inter-racial Affairs, the college continued to seek ways to improve educational opportunities for disadvantaged students. Admissions joined a national program encouraging African American students to attend college. Among students, the Committee for Social Action organized the "Fast for Freedom" to raise money for the Council of Federated Organizations in Mississippi and collected books, clothing, and money for Freedom Schools in Tennessee. Inspired by new federal programs, the Student War on Poverty group mentored local schoolchildren. During the summer the project continued as a summer day camp for junior high students from the Seventh Ward.[60]

The campus was more openly divided about the nation's deepening military involvement in Vietnam. A forum in February heard faculty who favored sustaining the nation's commitment to fight communism, as well as those who wanted to get out immediately; afterward, the first student editorial on the issue adopted the former position. The college's first "teach-in" on the war, in May 1965, also aired different faculty points of view. Through a telephone hookup, the campus participated in the first nationwide debate from Washington, D.C. Lancaster conservatives, alert to subversion in their midst, complained that the college was giving a platform to communist sympathizers. As was his pattern, Spalding defended free speech while seeking ways to forestall future crises. Soon after the teach-in, he told the board's Executive Committee that he hoped "to work out, in appropriate consultation," a policy regarding inviting and presenting speakers on campus. Experience had shown that controversial speakers "[could] be accepted on a college campus," he assured them, "if the rules governing their appearance [were] well worked out and thoroughly understood."[61]

At the end of a crowded academic year, Spalding reflected on the rise of student unrest nationally in a talk to a local group. He commended the idealism of the current generation of students, who had grown up in unprecedented affluence, but admitted that they were prone to moral absolutism. "I know from many conversations with young men at Franklin and Marshall that they have deep feelings," he explained. "They are serious to the point of being almost humorless; they have commitment to egalitarian ideals which we have long preached as being central to a democratic society; and their purposes are lofty." He speculated that the college had not seen an "extremist student revolt" like the Free Speech Movement at the University of California at Berkeley because Franklin & Marshall already offered students freedom of expression, opportunities to participate in decision making, and stronger bonds with faculty and administration — but he "hastily knocked on wood" afterward.[62]

The First Crisis Year

The college began its 1965–66 academic year with a revival of the opening convocation, a tradition dating to the nineteenth century. Spalding saw it as a "way of celebrating, with appropriate dignity, the momentous adventure that the opening of college always points to." "It is the kind of adventure that is certain to change every one of us in still unimaginable ways," he said prophetically. Delivering the main address, Dean Glick injected uncommon intensity into the customary function of inspiring new students to take their education seriously. He dismissed the "illusion that 'freedom' is the absence of viewpoint" and insisted that a liberal education should force each student to wrestle with profound issues: "A liberal college is a place where you ought to learn that an 'open mind' means, not an empty one, or a cowardly one, but a sensitive and an inquiring one."[63]

At its first meeting of the year, the faculty voted to express their "earnest appreciation" to the Ford Foundation for its challenge grant and to promise "full support" to trustees and administration in their efforts to meet the ambitious matching requirement. But the outward show of unanimity hid deep fissures within the community. The Academic Council soon criticized Spalding for seeking federal Great Society funds to expand PREP without consulting them. Pauline M. Leet, the new director of special programs, envisioned a number of new enrichment projects, while council members wanted more funding for area studies programs. Spalding responded that he and Leet had merely investigated options; in any event, he had thought that the faculty agreed on the importance of programs "for the culturally deprived." The council replied that it had "no lack of enthusiasm for the culturally deprived," but spoke out of "concern for scholarly research." Council members feared that a "massive" program like the one Leet had in mind "would alter the shape of the College."[64]

Escalation of the Vietnam War over the summer sparked a surge in campus activism. Shortly after the semester began, representatives of the prowar American Friends of Viet Nam and antiwar National Committee for a Sane Nuclear Policy held a public debate. Several weeks later, the college joined thirty other schools in a closed-circuit teach-in originating from the University of Toronto about U.S. actions in Vietnam and the Dominican Republic. The Lancaster Committee for a Negotiated Peace in Viet Nam, composed primarily of faculty and students, organized early morning picketing at the Hamilton Watch Company near campus. Hamilton had recently expanded to make fuses, timers, and safety and arming devices for rockets and bombs, and picketers distributed leaflets urging workers to "stop being a cog in the war machine and end [their] part in the slaughter of innocent people." Picketers did not persuade anyone to leave their jobs but did irritate the company's president, Arthur B. Sinkler, a board member since 1956. He had been one of Bolman's staunchest supporters and was active in the Ford campaign.[65]

Student opinion was probably best represented by the *College Reporter*'s comment that the picketers reflected "the intellectual bankruptcy of traditional pacifist idealism." To ask employees "to give up their well-paying jobs" for a nebulous goal of ending the war was "the most ridiculous Alice-in-Wonderland nonsense." In contrast, when the *Lancaster New Era* depicted the teach-in as an attempt to spread the "Communist Line," the *College Reporter* was outraged, and the Student Council denounced the biased coverage. But the board conducted "an extended discussion of the responsibilities of members of the faculty in the conduct of their teaching" and the responsibilties of the administration "to assure full presentation of all points of view in extracurricular and education programs." After the teach-in, trustees questioned use of college facilities for "controversial affairs involving attendance by the public." They directed Spalding to prepare a plan to regulate meetings on campus.[66]

In mid-October Charles Haynie marked a national weekend of antiwar protests by organizing a march to Penn Square that drew about twenty participants. They were met by a countermarch of more than twice as many veterans, loudly cheered on by onlookers, while plainclothes policemen tried to keep the two groups apart. Spalding was inundated with letters demanding that he dismiss Haynie and other faculty protesters. Meanwhile, in Harrisburg legislators proposed a resolution denouncing "war resistors, conscientious objectors, and believers in non-violent action" as "traitors to the greatest nation on earth." They also sought to revoke state scholarships and grants to students who demonstrated against the war.[67]

The possibility of losing state aid was a real threat, because Franklin & Marshall students received increasing amounts of financial support from the state and federal governments. Spalding promised the faculty that the college would do everything possible to defend academic freedom, but it nonetheless asked the Academic Council to appoint a faculty committee to keep track of the legislation. The Student Direct-Action Committee circulated a petition protesting the resolution's attack on their right of peaceful protest. They gathered an estimated 100 to 125 signatures, while another student petition supporting the government's policies in Vietnam eventually reported more than 1,000.[68]

Into this volatile mix came a new figure, Robert Mezey, a prize-winning poet hired on a one-year contract. Soon after his arrival in Lancaster he was well known as a leader of the Hamilton picketing. A staunch pacifist, his opposition to the Vietnam

War seemed rooted in an anarchic artistic sensibility, which he expressed at a student-faculty forum, The Artist and Social Action. The draft had emerged as a focus of anti-war sentiment, with the burning of draft cards a central feature of demonstrations in Washington, D.C., that summer. Congress reacted by making it a felony to destroy one's draft card, thus uniting issues of free speech and opposition to the war. Speaking as an artist, and not thinking of himself as a representative of the college "or any institution," Mezey stated during the forum that he favored burning draft cards "under certain conditions and for specified reasons." His statements were reported to the *New Era*, whose front page the next day proclaimed that he was teaching students to resist the draft and tear up their draft cards.[69]

In the ensuing uproar, Lancaster veterans demanded Mezey be fired, and several trustees telephoned Spalding to express their concern. Spalding called Mezey, Dean Glick, and English department chairman Robert Russell to his office for a series of meetings. Mezey insisted that the *New Era* story "fictionalized to a great degree" what he had said. But a statement to Spalding hardly resolved the issue. Though Mezey denied that he had ever directly told a student to burn a draft card, he admitted that if a student asked for his advice, he would have to express his opinion that card burning was "the lesser of two evils, the greater one being killing a man in opposition to God's commandments." Mezey viewed his forum statements as an expression of his "rights as a free citizen."[70]

Fearing that trustees would intervene to get rid of Mezey, Spalding announced that, in keeping with provisions of the new college policies, he was suspending Mezey "to assure that the considerations of accusations" against him could "continue in a calm and rational manner." Draft resistance was big news throughout the nation and reporters from major wire services joined local media at Spalding's press conference.[71]

Beginning the following day, November 2, the PSC's "informal inquiry" to determine whether there was adequate cause for formal dismissal proceedings continued almost daily for two weeks. The committee met with Spalding, Russell, and Mezey, who was advised by history professor Norman Zacour. They learned that there were no complaints about Mezey's conduct in the classroom, where he was considered an inspiring teacher. They admitted that it was impossible to know precisely what Mezey had said at the forum, although he "probably was injudicious." On November 12, they concluded that there was no adequate cause for instituting dismissal proceedings against Mezey and recommended his immediate reinstatement.[72]

The PSC's announcement showed that their deliberations had been driven by a desire to preserve an open intellectual environment: committee members expressed fear that Mezey's dismissal would inhibit the teaching of other faculty "more sensitive, more timid, more anxious about security for themselves and their families."[73]

Transmitting the report to the board, Spalding gave both principled and pragmatic reasons for sustaining its decision. "There is no reason to fear the free expression of ideas, even unpopular ones," he insisted. "It is the proper business of a college to provide a place and circumstance where ideas of all sorts can be discussed and explored, and each individual, student or faculty member, can arrive at his own conclusions through the exercise of dispassionate discourse and unfettered thought." He also noted that similar incidents were taking place at colleges and universities around the nation; the college's reputation might be damaged if it took "a position inconsistent with that of other highly reputed institutions with which we like to be compared."[74]

Under William Schnader, the board itself was most concerned about the case's legal issues. It emphasized the college's commitment "to obey the law and to require obedience to law by members of its administrative staff and by members of its faculty." Mezey had denied making the statement attributed to him, and the federal government had "not seen fit" to pursue the case, which would have established the facts in a court of law. Not feeling it appropriate to adjudicate his guilt or innocence, the board canceled his suspension, with an expectation that in future he would "be guided by the principle of responsibility, both as a scholar and a citizen" as outlined in college policies.[75]

Repercussions of the Mezey affair were felt for some time. The faculty was deeply divided between his supporters and his critics. Those who wanted to censure him saw their hand strengthened by Mezey's public response to the board's decision. He disparaged Lancastrians and their newspapers and dismissed the board as a "cabal of absentee bankers" who had no right "to judge [him] in any way, as a teacher or an individual." The *College Reporter*, which had supported Mezey up to that point, chided his irresponsible statements and lack of concern for the college. The PSC counseled Mezey regarding his "professional responsibilities" and warned him "against further injudicious statements." Sixty-five faculty signed a petition commending the PSC, Spalding, and the board "for the judicious and courageous manner in which they . . . upheld the principle of academic freedom" and deploring Mezey's statements to the press.[76]

Some faculty criticized Spalding for suspending Mezey in the first place. They saw the decision as further proof that he was too sensitive to opinions of board members and the Lancaster community and too ready to place public relations above principles. In recent months, Wayne Glick had been increasingly at odds with Spalding, and the Mezey affair finally "crystallized" Glick's sense of their incompatibility. He tendered his resignation while the PSC was in the midst of its deliberations. To his surprise, Spalding promptly accepted it and made it effective December 31 rather at the end of the academic year as was customary. Spalding assured the faculty that Glick's leaving had been voluntary, that he had the option of remaining on the faculty, and that the faculty would participate in selecting his successor. Glick's statement, read in his absence, urged his colleagues to reconcile their divisions: "The emotions of all of us are raw, and that quality we laud — dispassionate intellectual concern — is, I am convinced, in grave peril." A special faculty meeting several days later approved a resolution expressing faculty members' appreciation for Glick's "unrelenting efforts," as dean and acting president, "to build strength out of chaos."[77]

AAUP president Charles Holzinger blamed Spalding's "lack of candor" for the faculty's current dissatisfaction. The group decided to focus on making sure that the new dean represented their interest and perspective. Implicitly criticizing Spalding's qualities in this area, the AAUP called for someone with "the deepest understanding of academic values" and the ability "to reflect faithfully the academic heritage and mission of the College." Holzinger elaborated these concerns in a memo to the AAUP Executive Committee: "There is a wide-spread feeling in the faculty that the President does not understand academic modes of thought, and that the new dean must understand these and be allied with the faculty [if their alienation was not to deepen]."[78]

Yet it could not be said that there was one single perspective shared among the faculty, for it — like faculties at most colleges and universities in the 1960s — was increasingly divided. This fact was brought out in the midst of the Mezey controversy when the *College Reporter* published Richard Schier's scathing attack on Charles Haynie. His antiwar activities had been an issue in the recent mayoral election, and Schier, a government professor long active in Democratic politics, charged that Haynie's "exhibitionism" only played into the hands of Lancaster's Republican establishment and did nothing to further "his professed cause" of peace in Vietnam. "I prefer to elect good people," Schier asserted. "Mr. Haynie apparently enjoys defeating them so that he can picket their successful opponents." Schier insisted that he questioned "the wisdom of [Haynie's] conduct," not his "right to pursue any course he wants." He urged that in exercising their rights, faculty members employ "some modest sense of institutional loyalty."[79]

Haynie's supporters and colleagues in the math department rallied to his defense, and letters for and against Haynie and Schier joined others about the Mezey affair in crowding the pages of the *College Reporter*. Denouncing Schier's attack as unprofessional, Haynie's allies urged Glick to bring the matter before the PSC. Schier's colleagues responded that Schier had not criticized Haynie's professional competence, and the matter was finally resolved when Schier sent a "magnanimous" letter to Haynie. Several months later, Haynie announced that he was returning to graduate school to study the history of science.[80]

On the board, more liberal members breathed a sigh of relief that academic freedom had been upheld, all the while hoping that the controversy had not done too much damage to the college's fund-raising prospects. By chance, much of Lancaster's social elite attended a cocktail party a few days after the board's decision, and Sinkler described the scene in a letter to Schnader: "Truly, it was just like Queen's garden party in Alice in Wonderland. . . . Everybody was mad at somebody, or somebody was mad at everybody, and trustees, who really had nobody to get mad at, simply were mad at themselves." He took comfort "in the fact that — at least as of last Sunday morning — Franklin and Marshall College has been remembered in everybody's will for substantial amounts of money. Of course, if you believe everything that was said, all the wills were changed first thing Monday morning." Sinkler doubted that the college would be hurt in the long run and believed that the institution had actually been strengthened. In coming weeks, Spalding's allies on the Executive Committee fended off Schnader's attempt to strengthen board control over the faculty. Kenneth Bates pointed out that Schnader's proposal contradicted the new Statement of Academic Freedom and Tenure, "which," Bates said, "I think we all agree is an important asset to a top flight liberal arts college." He recommended deferring action until "the emotional excitement" of the Mezey affair "had had a reasonable opportunity to die down."[81]

Hoping to prevent future controversy, the Executive Committee approved a new policy that defined many campus gatherings — classes, colloquia, student-faculty forums, and meetings of student government and departmental clubs — as "internal" events that were closed to the public. Advance notice was to be given the college of all events open to the public, such as films, plays, lectures, and concerts. This approach sought to allow free discussion without offending local sensibilities, but it did little to lessen growing estrangement between town and gown. Meanwhile, Spalding joined several other academic leaders in drafting a statement for the Pennsylvania Association of Colleges and Universities, defending their right to bring controversial speakers to campus. In a talk at a local Presbyterian church, Spalding continued to defend the idealism of college students, recalling that "only a short time ago," educators had complained about student apathy.[82]

Tensions flared again briefly the following spring, when Spalding announced that salaries for the next year would increase 6.6 percent, less than the promised 7 percent. At the request of AAUP leaders, Spalding met with the entire faculty to explain. While assuring the faculty that the board gave highest priority to raising salaries, Spalding noted that the policy of doubling salaries over ten years had never been formally enacted. Officially recognizing a trend begun under Bolman of considering the college as a peer of the nation's top private colleges, the board had adopted a goal of seeking parity in faculty salaries with a comparison list of colleges. Reflecting the college's heightened expectations, the list included the nation's most prestigious liberal arts colleges: Amherst, Antioch, Bowdoin, Carleton, Colby, Colgate, Davidson, Grinnell, Hamilton, Haverford, Kenyon, Knox, Lafayette, Oberlin, Pomona, Reed, Swarthmore, Trinity, and Williams. Spalding also noted that budgeting was complicated by the merit system and demands of hiring new faculty in a competitive market.[83]

This meeting was followed immediately by four long special meetings to deliberate Academic Council recommendations for revising the curriculum. Billed as a "reform" of the 1959 program, the changes represented a retreat from the belief that all students should have the same broad core of experience. As a chemistry professor stated during an open forum, "[Nonmajors] do not want to learn from us and we are not interested in teaching them." In the face of strong antipathy of both students and faculty, all specifically required courses were abandoned. Instead, Academic Council proposed general distribution requirements of any two courses each in humanities, social sciences, and natural sciences and one in fine arts. After much debate and

parliamentary maneuvering, the faculty agreed. To broaden their experience somewhat, advanced students were required to take an interdisciplinary seminar or one course
outside their major. (The intent was thwarted by subsequent failure to create such
seminars.) In foreign languages, specific numbers of courses were dropped in favor of
requirements to demonstrate a fourth-level course competence. Bowing to the desire
of English department members to focus on literature and literary criticism, the Academic Council proposed dropping the writing requirement. After much debate, the
faculty voted narrowly to retain an expectation that students demonstrate "proper command and comprehension of the English language," without establishing a mechanism
to monitor it. In presenting the new curriculum to the board, Spalding emphasized
that it followed "developments in many leading institutions of higher education" in
allowing greater flexibility to meet individual student interests. The net effect further
emphasized departments and individual disciplines over general education and promoted the preparation of students for graduate training.[84]

Soon, tensions between faculty and administration were overshadowed by more
public crises arising from opposition to the war in Vietnam. During Easter weekend
the new campus chapter of Students for a Democratic Society held its first public action, a thirty-six-hour fast and vigil in front of the Lancaster draft board office. Twenty
to thirty students and faculty participated at one time or another. They faced considerable hostility, ranging from name calling to destruction of their signs, repeated attempts at physical intimidation, and assaults — including motorcyclists who drove over
seated protestors. Haynie blamed local police for failing to provide adequate protection, and when his charges of assault against one man were later dropped, Haynie told
reporters, "This place remains like Jackson, Mississippi." The attacks prompted a larger
demonstration the following day, in defense of protestors' freedom of speech. An impromptu student-faculty forum heard reports from students Sam Tuttleman and Neil
Sheneberger and faculty Haynie, Mezey, and Samuel Allen. Spalding and faculty leaders met with local officials, who promised better police presence in future. Police were
in fact much in evidence in the next few weeks, which saw growing numbers of vigils
at the draft board and demonstrations in the streets of Lancaster.[85]

Relatively few students participated in these protests, but generational disaffection was being shown in other ways throughout campus. Hopes for improvement in
the social environment now focused on the need for a student center — and, for some
members of the community, for coeducation. Never very understanding of all that was
necessary to make such things happen, students showed less patience and deference
than ever before. In February a *College Reporter* editorial questioned the veracity of
"East Hall"— now the catchall term for the administration — because Spalding had failed
to act on a science building or a student union. Unaware of the heavy amount of traveling he was doing to raise money for those projects, the *Reporter* also criticized Spalding
for having little contact with students. In a forum on the New Left, sophomore Peter
Goodman pointed to the lack of progress toward coeducation as proof of the futility
of working within "the system":

We might circulate a petition first, to indicate that there was support among the students for co-education; we might take the petition to the Dean, or to the President, who would "consider" the matter.

After awhile, a few of our leaders would be called down to East Hall, where the Dean, or the President, or the Assistant Dean, or the Secretary for development, or the janitor, would tell them how interesting their request was, and how gratifying it was to see students doing something besides partying. The leaders would be put on a special student committee to consider the matter which, they would be solemnly informed, would require long and careful study. . . .

If enough stalling takes place, the interested students will graduate before the matter comes to a head, and the rigamarole can then begin for a whole new batch of students. This is called working within the system.[86]

Less-politicized students gravitated toward that other facet of the 1960s, the drug counterculture. Claiming to have information that students were holding "pot parties" on campus, city police raided several dormitories in May, giving the dean of students only fifteen minutes' notice. They arrested four students for possession of marijuana and unspecified pills; two were later released for lack of evidence, and one subsequently pled guilty to possession of narcotics. The College Mental Health Division's annual report also remarked on growing student alienation. Many were performing below their abilities, and some wanted to transfer, not only because of the lack of women on campus, but because of unhappiness with the college's professionalism.[87]

The sense that all was not well was confirmed by the release in May 1966 of the final report of the Committee to Study Student Life, dubbed the "Klein Report," after its chairman Frederic Klein. Its findings were sharply critical of many aspects of the college's nonacademic environment. It noted that the college had in the previous decade "undertaken fundamental and far-reaching changes regarding . . . curriculum, our faculty, and . . . patterns of student recruitment." Yet its physical facilities had not kept pace: "The result has been a markedly more gifted, sophisticated, heterogeneous and expectant student body on an undeniably frustrating campus."[88]

The committee's members included men whose experience of the college differed greatly: Klein, who had been an undergraduate in the early 1920s and had taught there since in 1927, was the leading representative of the "Old F&M," while Samuel Allen, one of the few African American faculty members, had only just joined the college in 1964. Yet all agreed that a liberal arts education must foster development of the "whole" student. "Intellect is not all even in college life," the introduction asserted, "indeed, negative repercussions from the recreational sphere may on occasion undermine academic enthusiasm." These repercussions were in fact doing so now: "If the College fails to respond to the problem detailed in the report more vigorously — and more quickly — than it has to date, we may anticipate at the very least a significant and melancholy growth of student alienation in the future." The report's findings challenged the college to commit itself to a greater concern for students: "Franklin and Marshall must not become known as that zealous college where preoccupation with faculty prestige and administrative dynamism precluded a decent and prudent attention to the quality of student life."[89]

The committee played admirably to Spalding's long-range goals by giving highest priority to the issue of coeducation: committee members advised that "the College should seriously consider all practical opportunities for the establishment of educational facilities for women in the college community area," either through direct coeducation or creation of a coordinate women's college nearby. Although the committee saw significant practical problems standing in the way of coeducation, it agreed that other arguments for remaining as a men's college — "sentimental tradition" and the belief that an all-male school prevented "undue social distractions" and provided "a better atmosphere for entrance into a professional 'man's world' " — were all outmoded. Perhaps most compelling for members like Klein, who had long defended the college's single-sex status, was the understanding that the shift away from a largely local student body had dramatically changed the social situation on campus. Klein recalled his own experience in the early 1920s: "In a small old college you could find some social life in the community." But the committee's deliberations had changed his mind. The reality now was that, "with people coming in from all over the country and living on campus, there was no social life at all." Moreover, as the final report concluded, providing an opportunity for young men and women to share intellectual and academic and well as social life would create "a more wholesome and natural atmosphere."[90]

The committee's other findings were even more damning. Noting perception of "a certain malaise of atmosphere" and "a suggestion of underlying, but widespread, student discontent," it found problems in much of the college's nonacademic environment. Despite a "commendable calendar of cultural events," facilities were inadequate for informal gatherings. Campus House was the only place on campus where students and faculty could meet "in friendly non-academic relationships," but it was too crowded and hurried for any but the most superficial exchanges. Hence, "highest priority" in construction plans should be given to a campus center that would house a wide range of functions. The committee reserved its strongest criticisms for the dormitories, where poor design and choice of building materials produced uncomfortable noise levels. With few provisions for study and typing, many students were driven to the library — which was also overcrowded — or empty classrooms in search of a quiet space. The committee recommended taking immediate action to provide small-unit accommodations.[91]

The committee's findings regarding fraternities were less clear-cut, perhaps the result of a compromise among its members. Although it found housing conditions to be "far from ideal," it concluded that fraternity houses should remain the responsibility of students themselves, "as one of the obligations associated with the independence and self-government which can be considered as one of their chief advantages." The committee did not think it appropriate for the college to provide campus housing specifically for fraternities. But it did recommend changes to the fraternity system because of its dominant role in social life. While acknowledging that all chapters had eliminated discriminatory clauses from their charters — and five of the eleven had now admitted black students — it noted that each year some students were not admitted to any fraternity. It recommended a new pledging system to ensure that all interested students receive a place in one of the fraternities.[92]

Despite its criticisms of fraternities, the Committee to Study Student Life stressed that they had provided social outlets even for nonmembers at a time when "the College itself has fallen short in its own responsibilities to students in non-academic areas." The committee recommended that the coming five-year period should be seen as "a serious challenge period" in which everyone should seek to improve the quality of student life; a second study should then be conducted to assess whether progress had been made.[93]

In receiving the report, Spalding noted that some recommendations could be handled directly through administrative action, but others would be referred to the board for implementation or further study, and still others would "require long discussions with interested parties if they are to be made effective." The college had already applied for federal housing loans and could quickly move to build a small-unit dormitory for 175 to 200. The board also agreed to give a student center high priority, but there were also important academic needs to be addressed, most notably a science center. In addition, the college needed space for its growing art program. Leonora Owsley Herman expressed interest in underwriting an art building as a memorial to her husband, Leon Herman; Spalding spent much time during the spring and summer traveling to her home in Florida to negotiate the deal.[94]

Various college constituencies discussed the Klein Report during the following year, but there was no action on coeducation. The Inter-fraternity Council took up the report's recommendations for revising the selection system, although some members argued that "the very nature" of the system involved inclusion and exclusion. At the IFC's request, Spalding appointed a committee to devise a new bidding system guaranteeing fraternity membership to freshmen who agreed to join any fraternity. Although the system seemed to work smoothly for a time, it was later abandoned.[95]

During the summer, work on the science center faced a new roadblock when bids came in at more than $4 million, 1 million above previous estimates. The executive committee decided to go ahead at the higher price. "I only hope I was able to convey to the Trustees that when they agreed to do that, they took on an added obligation of considerable proportion," Spalding wrote Graeme Smith. "I tried, but that kind of talk always sounds so preachy that it probably gets taken with a grain or more of salt." Excavation for the building began in August.[96]

A Changing of the Guard on the Board

Spalding also asked for Graeme Smith's help in smoothing the way for an important transition in the college's leadership. William Schnader had been ailing in recent months and had begun to talk to close friends about stepping down as board chairman. Spalding hoped through "some quiet planning" to prevent a situation in which Schnader abruptly announced his resignation and called for an immediate election of a replacement to force selection of his picked candidate. Spalding and his closest allies on the board quietly pressed the name of Robert W. Sarnoff, who had recently been named president of the Radio Corporation of America. Sarnoff was not an alumnus but had been on the board since 1960. The college needed "a chairman who is nationally known and who has the capacity to 'open doors' in centers of wealth throughout this country," Smith told Henry Marshall; it was not necessary that the chairman be an alumnus. Sarnoff agreed to take the job as long as Sinkler would head the Executive Committee and take responsibility for day-to-day matters.[97]

Sometime in the fall Spalding and Arthur Sinkler called on Schnader. They proposed Sarnoff's name and immediately suggested that they call fellow trustee Elmer Bobst — then in Hong Kong — to ask him to formally invite Sarnoff. Bobst had recently announced a major gift to the science center, in return for which the Executive Committee promised to name the building after him. Thus boxed in by Spalding's careful planning, Schnader made no objection to Sarnoff as his successor. In recognition of his long history of generosity to the college in time and money, the board held a special convocation in Schnader's honor in October. In December it ratified Sarnoff's election and conferred upon Schnader the title of chancellor of the college.[98]

Over the course of the year the board made several changes in the charter and bylaws. Subsequent further revisions showed that these alterations were first steps in a gradual process of streamlining and centralizing executive authority. In June the charter was amended to explicitly name the president as the chief executive officer of the college, with "full power to enforce the rules and regulations adopted by the Board of Trustees for the government of the faculty and the students of the College" and responsible only to the board. Schnader and others on the board hoped that this would strengthen Spalding's hand with the faculty. The board was authorized to create visiting committees, which Spalding hoped would increase opportunities for participation in — and financial support of — college affairs. A clause was added specifying that the power of the various types of trustees — term, life, and advisory — would be defined in the bylaws. In December, revisions to the bylaws delegated expanded powers to transact the corporation's business to an executive committee, renamed the overseers.[99]

In the meantime, the new dean of the college, Keith O'Brien, was installed during the opening convocation in the fall of 1966. The first academic dean to come from outside the college in many years, O'Brien had been executive assistant to the president of Colgate University and had a Ph.D. from Stanford University. The first faculty meeting of the year also came with a change: for the first time in the college's history it did not open with a prayer. Asked about this, Spalding explained that he and Chaplain Taylor had decided to omit the prayer after some faculty argued that "prayers were not particularly appropriate or necessary for the business of the faculty." Another faculty tradition passed away in October, when O'Brien announced that attendance was no longer required. At the same time, the faculty took a step toward giving the Academic Council the legislative authority of a faculty senate, by authorizing the council to make decisions about new courses, subject to a veto by the full faculty.[100]

Compared with the previous academic year, 1966–1967 was quiet. Committees of the faculty, administration, and student body busied themselves with planning on many fronts. Dean O'Brien developed procedures for setting faculty salaries that ensured "constant dialogue." With a $50,000 planning grant from the Independence Foundation, Franklin & Marshall proposed organizing a regional computer network under the direction of psychology professor Richard Lehman. The idea was to exploit a new "time-sharing" potential in computer technology that allowed simultaneous use by many people — the foundation of the Internet — by means of connections over telephone lines. An advisory computer facilities committee of faculty agreed that teaching uses should be given priority over administrative data processing and research.[101]

Various steps were taken to improve conditions on campus, including remodeling the Campus House coffee shop. A faculty dining room was established in the Benjamin Franklin Residences, where faculty and guests could eat and converse in more private surroundings. It proved unexpectedly popular. Trustees purchased a large house in a residential area west of campus and contributed funds to remodel it for use as the president's house. Spalding suggested renaming the old house on campus Nevin House for use by guests and possibly as a faculty club or alumni center. The Fine Arts Club launched its fall movie schedule using a new thirty-five-millimeter sound projection system donated in memory of Darrell Larsen by one of his former students, Arthur M. Rosen, '50. Through the Class Council, students themselves took the initiative to create a temporary recreation center in Hartman Hall.[102]

The focus of campus activism began to shift from public protest to criticism of the college itself. For some students one of the most compelling issues was the quality of dining room fare. Students designated a tree in front of the Campus House as a place to express dissatisfaction with the college; the Protest Tree was often festooned with samples of offending rolls, ham, and even entire platters of food. In addition, the grading system came under particular scrutiny because of its use by the Selective Service System. Many students were more concerned about grades' power over their lives — and hence more critical of arbitrary faculty practices. Peter Goodman, designated as a "far left" columnist for the *College Reporter*, generalized dissatisfaction with grades to a wider social critique. Grades symbolized "the subordination of learning to the dictates of the 'system'; to the Selective Service, but also to the demands of Armstrong Cork Company, Schick Safety Razor, and Hokomo Joe Peanut-brittle, Incorporated." Higher education turned "the raw material — students' minds — into finished products," and preprofessional studies were "the kindergarten of the Organization Man, the Cheerful Robot, whose brain will be used as is needed."[103]

The issue of class ranking was an especially delicate one because it was used not only for the draft but in applications for graduate school, fellowships, and many jobs. A committee to study the entire question of class ranking had been at work for several months when some of the younger members of the AAUP chapter pressed the issue of the use of rank in class by the Selective Service System. The group narrowly passed a resolution asking the administration not to release grades and rankings. When word of the action leaked to the local press, O'Brien stated that college policy was to follow the wishes of each student, releasing class standing information only if requested. Discussion of the resolution at the next faculty meeting underlined strong differences within the ranks. Speaking in its favor, history professor Louis Athey denounced the practice of class ranking as "an invasion and misuse of the role of the faculty," an "intrusion into student-faculty relationships," and an affront to "the conscience of individual faculty members." Emphasis on grades fostered attitudes and habits among students "detrimental to the free spirit of inquiry essential to a liberal arts college."[104]

In his response, Mac Darlington stressed due process. The AAUP resolution circumvented proper governance procedures, for the faculty-authorized committee was even now "carrying out its extremely difficult assignment with good judgment and in good faith." Class rank could be discussed when its report was presented. Students also weighted in; fifty signed a resolution supporting the resolution, but student representatives were unanimous in their concern that the proposal might hurt the interests of individual students. The faculty voted by a large majority to table it.[105]

The faculty deliberated many curricular issues in four days of meetings in May. It eliminated calculation of students' rank in class and voted to send a student's grades to his draft board only at his specific request, adding a statement opposing the use of grades and rank in class by the Selective Service System. It also created an opportunity for students to take one course a year on a pass/fail basis. At the close of business, an exhausted faculty approved Kenneth Brookshire's motion instructing the Academic Council "to consider at their earliest convenience an alternative means of faculty government." Many had concluded that the hard-won right of direct participation in governance took too much time and energy.[106]

Down to the Wire with the Ford Challenge

Franklin & Marshall's development program had not gone smoothly. The first year of a large campaign generally saw the largest contributions, yet by the fall of 1966 the college had slightly more than $2 million toward the necessary $6.6 million. Recent controversies were clearly part of the reason; Spalding admitted to Bobst that the program "suffered a rather severe setback because of the problems of the poet." This was not strictly because large donors had been alienated, but because "the very necessary staff work that keeps a fund-raising effort at high momentum had to be postponed during that tense time." Spalding himself was almost constantly on the road to meet with prospective donors.[107]

Most of the following year was absorbed in the struggle to meet the Ford challenge. At the beginning of July 1967, nearly $3 million of the $6.6 million was yet to be raised. Spalding warned trustee leaders that team captains were having trouble getting volunteers. When approached, prospects pleaded lack of time or claimed to be unhappy with the college's handling of the Mezey affair or its treatment of fraternities, but Spalding believed such excuses would disappear if success was assured. He was also concerned that a rumor was spreading among professional fund-raisers and leaders of other colleges that Franklin & Marshall's campaign was failing; if the rumor gained general currency, it would create a "wave of pessimism" that would make it nearly impossible to raise money. The largest gifts so far had been from bequests and institutions, and potential donors looked critically at the absence of large gifts, particularly from board members. They had provided only 12 percent of funds received, below the 15 to 30 percent typical of major campaigns elsewhere. A fund-raising firm brought in to assist assured the board that the Ford challenges had enabled the sixty-five other colleges that had received them to substantially increase their assets. Ironically, their successes heightened pressures on everyone else, for now "any college which intends to be among the best has to run pretty fast just to stand still."[108]

The board conducted another round of solicitation among its own members and the alumni office organized a special program to bring alumni back to see the tremendous changes made on campus. Frederic Klein was commissioned to write a brief history of the college. Spalding timed announcements of gifts to suggest rising momentum. In successive weeks in October came public announcements of Leonora Herman's gift of an arts building, $250,000 for the science lecture hall from Morgan S. Kaufman — a friend of William Schnader's — and a further gift of nearly $250,000 from Schnader himself. In December came news of a gift from board chairman Robert Sarnoff of $200,000 earmarked for a new student center, which was intended to serve as the focus for the final phase of the campaign — its estimated cost of $1.75 million was said to be roughly the amount left to be raised. In January the Charles A. Dana Foundation offered $250,000 to establish four faculty professorships, a gift to be matched by an equal amount. By the end of April, $1.4 million was still needed, and Spalding warned the board of the damage to the college's reputation if the campaign failed.[109]

As the July 1968 deadline drew near, fund-raising activities reached fever pitch. Several hundred local alumni volunteers made personal solicitations. Alumni, faculty, students, and trustees participated in a national alumni telethon. Finally in mid-May came word of a $1 million gift from the Gustavus and Louise Pfeiffer Research Foundation, of which Elmer Bobst was a director. In recognition, the new science facilities were designated the Gustavus A. Pfeiffer Science Complex, Bobst having relinquished the naming honor. The campaign went over the top with a gift of $830,000 from RCA toward purchase of one of its computers.[110]

The hard-won success of the Ford Foundation challenge was a major milestone in Franklin & Marshall's emergence as a top-level liberal arts institution. Spalding could now shift his focus to deal with the many problems in student life that had become increasingly obvious in recent years. But in the last years of the sixties his carefully calculated approach to change encountered repeated disruptions of normal college life, disruptions fueled by local conditions but reflecting rebellions sweeping the nation.

CHAPTER ELEVEN

Reasoning with the Whirlwind, 1968–1970

During the last years of the 1960s, Franklin & Marshall College shared fully in the turmoil of the nation's most divisive period since the Civil War. Unrest and alienation among many students and a significant minority of faculty, emergence of a youth counterculture, a civil rights movement torn between desires for inclusion and autonomous empowerment — all left their mark on the college. Meanwhile, the changing role of women in American society produced what was arguably the greatest single change in the college's history — admission of women in 1969.

Dissidents attacked fundamental features of the postwar academic revolution: specialization, expertise, and success as defined by test scores, grades, research grants, and graduate school admissions. Some younger faculty, particularly in social sciences and humanities, challenged academic professionalism, especially as embodied in the system of peer review. Ideologically, sixties radicals were far different from the fraternity men who had pelted President Bolman with eggs in 1961. But by the end of the decade radicals too challenged the single-minded focus on intellectualism and academic excellence that had been at the center of Bolman's vision. Adopting New Left critiques of education's ties to the "military industrial complex," disaffected students and faculty called for a more humanistic kind of liberal education allowing for greater individual freedom, personal expressiveness, and social engagement. Invoking the popular ideal of participatory democracy, they demanded greater power in college governance. As campus unrest rose throughout the nation, dissent threatened to bring the educational process to a stop.

At Franklin & Marshall 1968 began with changes in the college's system of governance that would shape its response to turmoil in coming years. The faculty created a representative body to replace the time-consuming "town meeting" format. The Academic Council argued that a senate could be more flexible and efficient in making decisions, while the full faculty kept its rights of review and referendum. Deliberative work would be done in standing and ad hoc committees made up of senators and other members of the community.[1]

Coincidentally, students had voted in referendum to dissolve their student senate system of government. Calling it unwieldy, ineffective, and undemocratic, student leaders themselves initiated the movement. Spalding found it "a puzzling and most remarkable display of political action," but students around the country were taking similar steps to protest convoluted systems that hampered student initiative. As the faculty considered its new senate, professor Lee Robbins proposed that students be included. To the surprise of many, the necessary two-thirds agreed. The new College Senate was composed of fifteen faculty — three from each of the three divisions and six at large — the president, dean of the college, and three students, one each from sophomore, junior, and senior classes. Without a separate group to speak for the entire student body, Spalding consulted with members of the Black Pyramid honorary society and formed the ad hoc Committee of Nine to come up with a new format for student government.[2]

Ongoing expansion of the college campus culminated in 1968 with completion of the new science center and a dormitory filling out the east side of the new residential quadrangle. The old observatory had been razed to make way for these buildings and a new one, named the Joseph R. Grundy Observatory in recognition of support from the Grundy Foundation, constructed on Baker Memorial Campus. Work also began on Charlotte Street two blocks east of campus on a simple, functional building for the psychology department. Under the leadership of Kenneth Brookshire, it had doubled in size in recent years and grown in professional reputation. The new building provided state-of-the-art facilities for faculty and student research, part of improvements in psychology, anthropology, and mathematics departments supported by a major grant from NSF's College Science Improvement Program (COSIP). With thirty rhesus monkeys, the new psychology laboratory now possessed the kind of experimental facilities found at only a handful of liberal arts colleges. (NSF support of Franklin & Marshall remained strong; it was tenth among small colleges nationwide in NSF grants in 1966, and the COSIP grant was one of only fifteen made in the program's first round.) The building was named after Paul L. Whitely, a long-time professor who had established the department's research tradition.[3]

In planning the Herman Arts Center, trustees abandoned the practice of imposing a single architectural style on the entire campus and approved a modern design. Located on the old bowling green at the southern end of campus, the center was envisioned as the first building in a fine arts complex eventually to include theater and music buildings. Overseers authorized a new planning council with faculty, administration, and student representation to set guidelines for land use, design, and the future size of the college.[4]

Planning for Coeducation

Franklin & Marshall finally began a deliberate move toward coeducation. Frustrated by the slow pace, many contended that Spalding opposed the change. Later, he argued that it had been necessary to proceed slowly: it was "a profound change" for Franklin & Marshall and "everybody had to have some understanding of what it meant and why we did it. You couldn't do it with a great minority opposed because they could simply drag their feet and make it fail." Moreover, he discouraged discussion of the issue until the Ford challenge had been met. Before he asked the board to consider formal approval, he wanted a thorough study of how to implement coeducation, with "sound cost estimates."[5]

Franklin & Marshall was only one of many all-male institutions considering some form of coeducation, among them Yale, Princeton, Williams, Wesleyan, Trinity, Kenyon, and Hamilton. Proponents offered a wide range of reasons, but those that seemed to carry the most weight with trustees and alumni related to the tremendous changes in gender roles taking place in the wider society. "It is clear to me that women's role is changing," Spalding told an alumni group. Increasingly women exerted influence not only as wives and mothers but also "as a permanent part of the world of affairs." Pragmatically, the popularity of all-male colleges had fallen markedly. Applications dropped in the late 1960s at the most prestigious single-sex schools; at Franklin & Marshall, they declined 17 percent between 1965 and 1967 alone. Single-sex education no longer carried the social prestige that it had once had, and coeducation was considered more modern and "normal."[6]

At the beginning of 1968, Spalding delegated the task of organizing and chairing a special task force on coeducation to Paul Newland, recently named secretary of the college. Participants were Luther J. Binkley, Bradley R. Dewey, W. Roy Phillips (the new director of athletics), Ruth Van Horn, and Sidney Wise, with Dr. John Atlee Jr. as liaison with overseers and Dewey with the Academic Council. Arguing that no change should be made until the committee completed its work, the overseers rejected an Academic Council recommendation to admit women as transfer students, but did approve discussing an exchange program with Wilson College. Spalding told the faculty in March that it was indeed "time to move" but asked that plans be kept confidential for the moment — perhaps to avoid controversy in the crucial last days of the Ford campaign. Students, who necessarily took a more short-term perspective, expressed dismay at the lack of action. Ted Watson, president of the Student Union Board, decried the "abnormality" of the social environment: "We who are leaving the college look back somewhat bitterly at our years of social sterility." In April Spalding finally publicly confirmed that a task force had been charged with outlining steps necessary in a transition to a coeducational institution.[7]

The task force set to work in late spring 1968. Paul Danielson, Robert Isler, and Jessica May were added as student members — May was one of two student wives admitted the previous fall. "Everybody on that committee wanted coeducation and expected it to happen," she recalled. Ostensibly, its charge "was to study the feasibility, but what we actually did was plan it." Her experience taught her that committees could perform multiple functions: "You're drawing in people from different constituencies, you're building a consensus, you're disbursing information at the same time so that opinion begins to coalesce behind it [without the need for formal announcements]."

Another important function was persuading the board, thought to be least in favor of the change.[8]

Task force members visited a number of coeducational schools on the college's comparison list. They read research literature about coeducation and drew upon data gathered by other schools considering the change. They discussed ratios of male to female students, parietal rules, curriculum, and admissions with student affairs administrators at coeducational institutions. They hired a campus planning firm to map out changes in housing and facilities necessary to accommodate women. The task force's interim report was ready in July, but Spalding was not in a hurry to see the final version completed. He explained that there was a "very real and practical need to prepare the matter for discussion with the Trustees." They were not yet ready to make the decision, and pushing the issue prematurely "[would threaten] the possibilities of a constructive solution."[9]

He might have hoped to delay board consideration until completion of a process of reorganization begun in 1966. At its meeting in October the board approved in principle "a refinement" of the charter and bylaws, a refinement presented by Sarnoff and Spalding as a way to manage college affairs "more efficiently and conclusively." One change strengthened the overseers by eliminating the need for the full board to ratify its actions. Another eliminated the multiple types of membership established under Schnader and reduced the board's size to a maximum of twenty-five. Upon reaching the age of seventy, trustees now moved to honorary status, with the right to attend meetings but not to vote. This effectively took the franchise from several elderly life trustees who staunchly opposed coeducation. The president's power was further enlarged by making him a voting member of the board during his term of office; the chairman of the board was described as the corporation's "principal," but not executive, officer.[10]

One other change eliminated reservation of one-seventh of board membership for representatives of the United Church of Christ. Spalding assured the board that he had discussed the move with UCC leaders, who told him that it would not been seen as an unfriendly act. Although no public attention was drawn to this change, it marked the official end of Franklin & Marshall's relationship with the Church that had, in a much different form, founded it and strongly shaped its early character. The gradual separation had been the result of evolution on the part of both institutions; college leaders believed that a secular identity was necessary to continue its rise to national prominence, and the Church was shifting its commitments away from higher education. Ultimately the General Synod concluded that the UCC should focus on the nation's "great moral, social and ethical issues." The only formal acknowledgment came early in 1970 when the overseers approved a general statement of policy: "The church-college relationship is a dynamic, constantly changing one." Both parties now believed the traditional arrangement was no longer appropriate, "and sought to maintain the benefits of their historic relationship while permitting each institution to develop its programs to meet the challenges of a changing society in its own way." The college had dropped mention of its historic connection to Mercersburg Theology in its 1967 catalogue.[11]

During the board's October meeting, Spalding also reported that the Task Force on Coeducation had almost completed its work. Students organized a rally, which was planned to coincide with the board's noon break, to demonstrate their desire for coeducation. More than eight hundred attended, and — with oversight of dorm counselors in white arm bands — their good manners drew approving comments from several trustees. Student leaders presented Sarnoff with a petition seeking coeducation signed by more than half the student body. Several freshmen circulated their own in opposition during the rally but obtained only twenty-five signatures.[12]

The task force released a draft summary of its conclusions and recommendations two weeks later. Although its formal charge had been to focus on the feasibility of adopting coeducation at Franklin & Marshall, members also emphasized the desirability of the change. Their studies showed that, far from having an adverse effect on the caliber of male students, coeducation would increase applications from males as well as attract highly qualified women. In general, task force members concluded that moving to coeducation was feasible if done gradually. Their research suggested that a sixty-to-forty male-to-female ratio would provide "a balanced social life," but costs of providing housing all at once would be prohibitive. They recommended moving toward this ratio over ten years, though the pace could be accelerated if applications increased sufficiently and if funding was available. The report's most important recommendations were to begin immediately to accept applications from women and to publicize the college's new status.[13]

Many faculty had long argued that admitting women would strengthen the social sciences and humanities, and the task force members gave much thought to curriculum and staffing issues. They concluded that there might be "minimal need for additional faculty in some areas" but that curricular changes should be aimed at general improvement regardless of gender. They recommended hiring more female faculty but noted that Franklin & Marshall already had more women on staff than many coeducational institutions of comparable size. A director of physical education for women would be needed, along with a few changes in support services, like counseling and the infirmary. The task force recommended including women in planning campus cultural and social activities and especially in planning the projected college center.[14]

The Task Force on Coeducation hoped that creating a more satisfying campus environment would make sororities unnecessary. Membership in fraternities had dropped precipitously in recent years. Many students found pledging to be "a huge bore," the *College Reporter* observed. "The demand for house loyalty and spirit seem petty to a generation concerned with the larger problems of the fate of mankind." Many thought fraternities would "either disappear from the campus by dint of their own failure to attract members" or by college fiat. Hence, the task force recommended discouraging creation of parallel women's organizations.[15]

The task force noted that parietal rules were a source of unrest on other campuses and that the trend was to eliminate them. Attempts "to legislate particular relationships" between the sexes only invited abuse, and committee members were unanimous in thinking that rules were justified only when they served to protect students' "right and need for privacy and security" consistent with the college's primary "business" of education. They concluded that students should be allowed to set dormitory rules.[16]

With release of the draft report, the task force began an intense round of consultation with all members of the wider college community. The full text was published in the *College Reporter*, and an open meeting was held for students. The faculty reviewed the report in a meeting as a committee of the whole, after which the College Senate endorsed, it with two faculty abstentions. The Alumni Council Executive Committee expressed concern about coeducation's effect on fraternities, on numbers of male applicants, and on the geographic spread of the student body but later endorsed the plan unanimously. A copy of the final report was sent to all alumni with a questionnaire asking for their opinions.[17]

Acknowledging the final report, Spalding asserted that he was now convinced not only that coeducation was desirable and feasible but that it was the only course of action possible to realize Franklin & Marshall's "mission as a college":

> This College exists principally to offer young people the fullest possible opportunity for intellectual development, self-realization, the beginnings of self-fulfillment and a reach toward maturity. To expect that these characteristics can be more firmly established and maintained in an academic program and campus life marked by a monastic context is to expect the impossible. . . . Your recommendations, then, can be viewed not only as being based on a social ideal of considerable grandeur but also as being of benefit mutually to society, this institution, and all students of either sex who might avail themselves of the opportunities offered by this College.[18]

Anticipating the debates to come, Spalding warned task force members that "any latent opposition" would focus on details. "In deliberations on matters of such broad scope as this one," he noted, "it is typical of committees or boards to concentrate on details and specific recommendations [particularly when uncertainty about outcomes makes the decision difficult]." "Personally, I am at this point much less concerned about hammering out every dent in every specific proposal than I am about the over-all decision," he wrote. "I believe the time has come to *decide to go co-ed*, and I will try to bring about that decision." He responded to letters from trustees and alumni on the issue and was surprised to discover that many older alumni agreed that it was time to admit women. Alumni responding to the questionnaire were 80 percent in favor of coeducation, 60 percent strongly so, with only about 13 percent strongly opposed. Of those with daughters near college age, 87 percent said that they would be pleased to have them attend Franklin & Marshall.[19]

Overseers debated the report on December 6. After a "wide ranging" discussion of some five hours, they voted 6 to 1 to recommend that the board authorize admission of women in the fall of 1969. Before the board deliberation, however, they asked Spalding for more detailed implementation plans, including financial projections and a fuller statement regarding the desirability of coeducation.[20]

This request responded to statements by Ed Smoker, the lone opponent among the overseers. He complained that Spalding's charge to the task force had "put the cart before the horse" by asking it to focus on feasibility rather than on whether coeducation would be good for Franklin & Marshall. Although "many groups say they *want* coeducation," he contended, that was "not necessarily a good reason for giving it to them." He maintained that the decline in applications was a passing fashion and argued that the college could not afford the cost of conversion.[21]

The requested reports afforded Spalding an opportunity to make his most ardent appeal on behalf of coeducation. "Everyone who knows testifies to the folly of a man speaking with any certainty about the education of women," he began. "It does in fact require some sense of the ridiculous for an adult, male, college president — even one with daughters — to make pronouncements about the educational needs, motivations, and desires of young women." But he insisted that there was more to the "overwhelming" support for coeducation among students, faculty, and administration "than the attraction of novelty." Coeducation was essential to the institution's continued improvement because it was crucial to fostering a healthy and satisfying environment for true learning. Noting the "common lament" about the present "barren" campus climate, he commented, "It is an observable fact that women in significant numbers set the social tone, the manners and morals of a campus." He also argued that they would bring "new insights and responses" to academic discussions in all subjects. Pragmatically, he stressed that without coeducation it would be difficult to attract able students and faculty. He concluded that the preference for coeducation was not a temporary "fashion" but "a part of a continuing social movement" that was changing the role of women in American society: "It is the wish of many of us who are devoted to Franklin and Marshall that it be a part of this significant progressive movement. We have determined on careful and very cautious reflection that Franklin and Marshall has much to offer women who aspire to full lives. In a quite unsentimental way, we wish to make a contribution to society of increasing importance by making available to young women of all kinds and varieties of backgrounds the opportunities which result from the kind of quality education Franklin and Marshall offers."[22]

Despite his enthusiasm, Spalding warned that the move to coeducation would have to take temporary precedence over other needs, such as salary increases and new construction. Nonetheless, his report showed how task force recommendations could be implemented without undue effort or expense. He argued that start-up costs could be much lower than estimated. In particular, with "imagination," Marshall Hall could be renovated at one-fifth of the cost estimated by the task force. Whenever in the past the issue of coeducation had been raised, one of the most powerful objections had been the projected cost of providing suitable dormitories for women. But recent expansion of

FIGURE 5 *Two of the first female full-time students, Annette Rineer and Linda Geist, hold the seal of the college in 1969. Franklin & Marshall College, Archives and Special Collections. College Archives Photograph Collection.*

campus facilities had already paved the way. "The trustees, all of them men," Spalding recalled, tended to focus on "having to fix all that plumbing." He asked a number of female staff and students to visit Marshall Hall and report on what had to be done to make it acceptable to women. Asked about removing the urinals, Registrar Nancy Rutter responded, "We don't have to do that right away." In the meantime, she suggested planting flowers in them. The group, however, recommended more and larger mirrors, space for ironing boards and laundry facilities, and curtains to enclose group showers. Spalding estimated total costs at $188,600, including establishing a new security force that would be necessary in any event. Much of this could be funded from reserves and Ford Foundation funds.[23]

On January 17, 1969, the full board gathered for a special meeting at the 21 Club in New York City. Debate was "earnest, sometimes vehement," Spalding reported to the faculty, with ample time allowed for expression of all points of view. Several members wanted to postpone decision to allow more deliberation, and others pleaded that there should be a place in American higher education for single-sex institutions. Calling the meeting "a great event in decision making," the Reverend Edward O. Butkofsky was impressed by the openness and honesty of the discussion: "I think the fact that there was some opposition made it necessary for us all to make a reappraisal of our own position." The official vote was 14 to 3 in favor; mail votes put the number at 20 to 8. Spalding was pleased that the three men present who voted against coeducation stated for the record that they would work for its successful implementation — and several of their daughters were among the first to submit applications. Immediately afterward, the Office of Public Relations sent out thousands of formal announcements to applicants, alumni, parents, and individual, corporate and foundation donors:

> *The President and Board of Trustees*
> *take Pleasure in Announcing*
> *that Franklin and Marshall College is*
> *Accepting Applications for Admission*
> *from Qualified Women Students*
> *Who wish to Enter the Freshman Class*
> *in September 1969.*[24]

Encountering the Sixties

As the issue of coeducation moved through the deliberative process, Franklin & Marshall was equally engaged in other issues of the age, often with less affability. In October 1967 the student-faculty Vietnam Peace Committee sent several busloads of students and friends to march on the Pentagon. Students for a Democratic Society (SDS) began to protest the presence of CIA and military recruiters on campus, at times with counterprotests by conservative students who formed a chapter of Young Americans for Freedom. College leaders sought to balance protestors' rights to express their beliefs "in an orderly fashion" with protection of others' rights to be interviewed. Speaking at a Parents' Weekend forum, Spalding insisted that the college must "make it very clear" that "there are some things a college will not tolerate — the limitation of freedom of others, actions of unreason or demagoguery, activities which are not properly part of a learning community."[25]

Beyond politics, a campus counterculture had emerged, marked publicly in April 1967 with a "be-in" in Buchanan Park. College officials tried to play down reports of student drug use, but periodic "busts" by local police testified to its existence. Dr. James Appel, director of college health services, admitted in 1968 that college physicians had observed a drug problem for five or six years. At first, students began experimenting in college, but later in the decade many arrived with habits formed in high school. The college tried to deal with the problem by educating students about dangers of drug use. The Committee on Student Conduct issued the "Statement Regarding Mood-Altering Compounds" in 1967. It acknowledged the inconsistency in society's pervasive use of legal drugs like nicotine and alcohol and balanced disapproval of the use of illegal drugs with "positive concern" for users. Although it set no firm rules about penalties, the statement noted that persistent drug use would be considered a sign that the student was "not constructively engaged in the academic endeavor" and might be subject to suspension.[26]

The college gained unwanted national attention when a 1970 Associated Press article depicted marijuana use as ubiquitous on campus. It estimated that half the college smoked regularly, including athletes and faculty. It quoted an assertion by dean of students O. W. Lacy — in comments he had believed to be off the record — that experimentation was normal in a "highly intellectual student body" accustomed to question authority. Lacy noted that college authorities did not seek to prosecute or arrest students but to educate them. The board responded by restating the college's drug use policy and instructing college personnel to continue efforts to educate students about dangers of drug use. Trustees acknowledged that the college "is not and cannot be a law-enforcing agency," but "neither can it tolerate or condone the violation of law by its members."[27]

Meanwhile, as the civil rights movement shattered into liberal and radical factions in the mid-1960s, the college's efforts to help the disadvantaged planted seeds of opposition to its own academic values. PREP continued, since 1966 largely with funding from the Upward Bound program of the U.S. Office of Economic Opportunity. In 1967 over three-quarters of its graduates were still in college, some at Franklin & Marshall itself. Don Hughes, for example, entered the college in 1965. Already active in the civil rights movement, he became field secretary for the Student Non-violent Coordinating Committee (SNCC). Interviewed in the *College Reporter*, Hughes criticized the NAACP's focus on middle-class goals and expressed his admiration for Malcolm X.[28]

Increasingly, many younger urban blacks were drawn to Malcolm X's black nationalism. After the national SNCC organization expelled white members in 1966, history professor Samuel Allen defended its action in a student-faculty forum as a legitimate response to white hypocrisy. He portrayed the black power movement as an essentially conservative effort at self-determination. In 1967 twenty-two black Franklin & Marshall students formed the Afro-American Society (AAS) "to speak for our collective interests." Benjamin Bowser, '69, noted that members held a variety of views but shared a concern about "misunderstanding" of their situation by both administration and students. Its first president, sophomore Samuel Jordan, had recently launched a *College Reporter* column intended to represent far left opinions. One of his first pieces denounced the college for its part in the "Northern Collegiate Rent-a-Negro Movement," which stripped the black student "of ties to his Negro heritage" and made him a "receptacle for white ambitions and values." He asserted that black students were becoming estranged as they realized that colleges recruited them "simply to assert [their] liberality." He charged college officials with failing to help black students who encountered discrimination in the community and asserted that PREP had only been a ploy to win the Ford grant. In March 1968 the Afro-American Society brought to campus Muhammad Ali, who advocated "total separation" of the races.[29]

The years 1968 through 1970 saw all these movements converge into the social upheaval typically known as "the sixties." Together with much of the nation, the college experienced recurrent periods of unrest. Unlike more sensational events at larger universities, there was little violence or destruction of property at Franklin &

Marshall. As at most small liberal arts institutions, the college's size allowed for better communication between groups and prevented formation of a critical mass of
radical students necessary for concerted action. Administrative flexibility and insistence on deliberation helped keep conflict from escalating into violence. Radical
leadership was also somewhat limited by the absence of graduate students, who
dominated movements at large universities — though to some extent this role was
filled by junior faculty. Even so, a seemingly interminable succession of controversies divided the college community and left psychological and interpersonal scars
that would be long in healing.[30]

In April 1968 Martin Luther King Jr.'s assassination shocked the campus community and brought interracial tensions into high relief. At noon the following day,
some two hundred students and faculty answered an SDS call for a vigil on the steps of
Hartman Hall. Afterward about five hundred attended a memorial service in Hensel
Hall. Hoping to prevent riots like those elsewhere, college officials and members of
the Afro-American Society cooperated with city leaders in busing "wandering bands
of restless young people" to the service. Nevertheless, members of the Afro-American
Society demonstrated their sense of alienation from the college community by staying outside while Chaplain Taylor, President Spalding, and English professor Gerald
Enscoe spoke. The AAS entered as a body only when Samuel Allen rose to talk. To
speak for the AAS, Emanuel Towns came to the stage, escorted by two other students
as bodyguards. His expressions of anger and despair at the failure of peaceful methods of reform and his predictions of future violence drew a standing ovation from
blacks in the audience.[31]

Afterward the Afro-American Society and the Committee to Combat White
Racism, an SDS offshoot, organized a teach-in on racism. Speakers predicted open
conflict in the streets. A more moderate meeting held by the Committee for Human
Rights examined black housing problems in Lancaster. The group's chairman, Jon
Plebani, publicly asked Spalding to cut his ties with the Hamilton Club, which still had
no Jews or African Americans among its membership. The group met with Spalding
personally and "with courtesy, reasonableness and deep earnestness" asked him to resign. He explained that his responsibilities as president required him to "associate with
those of influence and prestige in the community" and represent the college's perspective to them, but the students replied that it was more important to uphold the college's principles of nondiscrimination. Spalding consulted with the overseers and many
members of the college, aware that any decision was bound to upset one constituency
or another. After due deliberation, he announced his resignation from the Hamilton
Club at the end of May 1968.[32]

The college's recruiting efforts had begun to bear fruit: its sixty African American students in a total enrollment of 1,700 represented a ratio second only to Swarthmore among Pennsylvania colleges. But as Spalding and O'Brien assessed the situation
in mid-1968, they admitted that the college must do more than simply increase numbers. They asked the new College Senate to discuss the relative priorities that should
be given to "attracting well prepared, highly motivated, highly talented students" and

to "seeking out students deprived by poverty, race, minority status or for other reasons." Experience had shown "that it is naïve to assume that a college can adopt both courses simultaneously without careful planning and perhaps some special programming." The senate committed the college to "deliberately use its energies and resources in behalf of deprived, disadvantaged, high risk students."[33]

Freshman orientation in the fall of 1968 was planned in cooperation with the Afro-American Society to focus on racial injustice and urban problems. Freshmen were asked to read *The Autobiography of Malcolm X* and the recent report of the Kerner Commission on Civil Disorders. James Farmer, former executive director of the Congress of Racial Equality, spoke, and AAS members led discussion groups afterward. The *Reporter* commended the AAS's insightful "reason and passion," with the exception of its "apparent self-appointed spokesman," Emanuel Towns: "We believe that everyone is getting a little tired of having Manny Towns declare war on them every time they attend an official College function."[34]

The 1968–1969 year saw radicalism increase among a small number of students. It was probably inevitable, given escalating confrontation nationwide — including an SDS-led takeover of a Columbia administration building and riots at the Democratic National Convention in Chicago. The college's chapter of SDS had only about fifteen active members, but a nonmember predicted in September, "[It] will, by God, sit in somewhere before the year is over."[35]

A controversy in October highlighted a widening rift between liberals and radicals. The Afro-American Society, the Committee for Human Rights, and Sidney Wise, faculty sponsor of the Fine Arts Film Series, planned a showing of *Dutchman*, a controversial film about white racism, to be followed by a discussion. After the audience moved to the library's browsing room for the discussion, Benjamin Bowser of the AAS asked whites to leave because blacks were not comfortable talking with them there. "So ended another experiment in dialogue," Wise commented wryly in a letter criticizing Bowser's abrogation of a prior agreement. "In other days, such conduct would have been described as rude, indeed boorish. Nowadays, it is simply regarded as militant and the standards of civility that should obtain at least in an academic community are discarded." Bowser responded that Wise's "obsession with dialogue" and notions of civility were fronts for "paternal condescension": "I am not exhibit 'A' or an entertainer and I refuse to 'dialogue' whenever Sidney Wise decides he want to give me advice." In the ensuing newspaper debate, philosophy professor Leon Galis mused that they might be seeing the limitations of rational debate. "What is, on the one hand, the academic's weightiest obligation can sometimes become his greatest liability," he admitted. "That is, in his zeal to meet his commitment to dispassionate rational inquiry, he may simply come to assume, without adequate grounds, that there are no circumstances under which rational inquiry can fail to be useful and appropriate."[36]

A general sense of unease that fall was heightened by recurrent weekend invasions by bands of local youths who attacked students and their dates and rifled items from dorm rooms. In view of rising vandalism and the pending arrival of women, the administration had already considered creating a campus security force, but increasingly violent episodes prompted the College Senate to call for immediate action. The administration hired security guards for weekends and appointed a committee to work on a long-term solution.[37]

The mood lightened briefly early in 1969 with the board's approval of coeducation. Students posed with a fake gravestone for their classmate "Monas T. Cism" and eagerly observed as young women arrived at the admissions office for interviews. But excitement was short lived. A series of controversies divided the campus, each posing challenges to prevailing norms of academic life.[38]

Radical Challenges to College Authority

The first was sparked by a vigorous local campaign against illegal drug use. In mid-January countywide raids by state and local police resulted in twenty-nine arrests, including four Franklin & Marshall students arrested for selling narcotics and another four for possession. Much of the evidence against them was supplied by a student serving as an undercover agent for the police. Then, in separate cases in February, two other students withdrew from the college to avoid facing the Committee on Student Conduct. Both admitted using marijuana to Dean Lacy, who told them he would recommend suspension if they remained. An ad hoc Committee on Student Rights — mainly SDS members — called a Sunday evening meeting in Hensel to denounce denial of rights of due process in what it termed "forced" resignations. The SDS position paper suggested that it hoped to channel student indignation into a wider social critique: "For the first time in our lives many of us are directly threatened by the police repression. We are now experiencing only a small part of the oppression that blacks, other minority groups, and white working class people have lived with all their lives." The meeting demanded that the Committee on Student Conduct be made up only of students, elected by themselves; at present it was composed of four students, three faculty, and the dean of students. Claiming that the college planted informers on campus, the Committee on Student Rights also condemned the college's "complicity" with law enforcement officials. A separate circular called for an end to Lacy's power to "force anyone out for whatever reason might strike his fancy." Three SDS leaders presented their demands to the administration the following morning. There were rumors of a sit-in at East Hall or a class boycott.[39]

As would be his policy throughout the period of unrest, Spalding responded immediately with a statement circulated to the entire campus. Because the "proposals and demands . . . affect many persons in the several constituencies of the College community," he explained, "it seems appropriate to bring these matters to the attention of all members of the community so that they may be well informed participants in the consideration to be given to them." He repeatedly stressed the college's commitment to liberal values, urging "full and rational discourse," and deferred to the authority of the new collegial deliberative body, the College Senate. Because the Committee on Student Conduct was a committee of the senate, it would have to be consulted, as would "the larger community, which would also be affected by such a change." He promised not to oppose "a searching reconsideration" of the issues as long as it "took into account the legitimate interests of the College and all of the affected constituencies." He flatly denied that the college "promotes or tolerates devious methods," such as planting informers, but acknowledged that it "willingly cooperates with civil and judicial authorities, acting in legitimate manner."[40]

Succeeding rounds of public meetings and administrative flexibility seemed to dissipate the energy that SDS had hoped to generate around the issue. The College Senate held an open hearing a week later that revealed strong student desire to control the Committee on Student Conduct and student life in general. But the issues became enmeshed in ongoing deliberation of a new student government. At Spalding's suggestion, the Committee on Student Conduct allowed those who had withdrawn to petition for reinstatement.[41]

On Tuesday, February 11, one day after presenting their demands in the discipline case, three SDS members returned to Spalding with a new demand — that representatives of the military or "of secretive organizations" not be allowed to recruit on campus "as long as this country's ruling class [used] the military to engage in the illegal and immoral repression of people." Navy recruiters were scheduled to visit campus the following day, and SDS threatened "any and all action necessary to effectively block the presence of the above mentioned personnel on our campus." Using the common parlance of student radicals, the demand was described as "non-negotiable."[42]

Spalding's statement to the entire community again stressed the college's commitment to expression of all views, including peaceful dissent, but asserted that it would "not tolerate violence in any form." This he defined as "activities which restrain or harm persons, deny access to buildings or property, cause damage to facilities, or any illegitimate activities which limit the freedom of movement or the freedom of expression of other members of the College." Several hours later came an announcement that the College Senate would meet on Thursday to consider the college's recruitment policies; the navy visit was postponed pending that consideration. Spalding emphasized that the college sought "to accommodate a sensitive situation and to bring reason to bear in a situation that carried with it the threat of violence by a small group of students." But he reiterated that the college would not tolerate violence or any attempt to restrict the freedom of its members.[43]

At the senate meeting a wide range of opinions about the legitimacy of military recruiters was expressed. Some faculty believed that on-campus recruitment served no educational purpose at a liberal arts college and should be eliminated. While it voted unanimously to appoint a committee to examine "all phases" of the college's recruitment program, a motion to continue present policy pending its report passed by a single vote.[44]

Protesting lack of action, a group of students under the new name of the Student Peace Committee called for a peaceful demonstration against a planned visit of a CIA representative on March 7. Hearing rumors of plans to take over the counseling office, Dean Lacy met with the group to emphasize the college's determination to use "legitimate power" to deal with "illegitimate or violent activities." On the appointed day a small number appeared to protest the presence of "war-makers" on campus, together with a few counterdemonstrators and over one hundred observers. In addition to the usual placards and posters, demonstrators staged a "guerrilla theater" enactment of global "crimes" by the CIA, played by a pig recruited from a local livestock firm. Most of the crowd dispersed once the CIA representative entered the counseling offices without incident. Nor was there resistance when U.S. Navy recruiters visited campus the following month.[45]

In the meantime, few students bothered to attend open meetings to discuss issues before College Senate committees and the Committee of Nine's proposed student government. "Students don't want more power," the *College Reporter*'s new editors commented. "It is 'Student Leaders' who want more power." The editors saw little point in "manufacturing a government, for its own sake, that will be as useless as our last." In contrast, Spalding pointed out that the absence of duly constituted student representatives made it difficult to proceed with important matters like a statement of student rights, responsibilities, and freedoms and a system of faculty evaluation.[46]

Using the Protest Tree as their primary forum, radicals attacked Spalding's use of handpicked committees to develop a system of student government. When the old system had been abolished, some hoped that students would govern themselves through self-constituted ad hoc committees. Many also hoped that student membership on the new College Senate was a first step toward a student voice in tenure decisions, something that most faculty strongly opposed as a threat to their professional autonomy.[47]

Asserting that Franklin & Marshall now served only to train "middle and upper class students for elitist positions in society," the SDS proposed a "Department of Liberated Humanities" that dispensed with "analytical methods and normative models which are no longer useful tools of critical analysis." Controlled only by its own students and faculty, the proposed department would offer courses like Oppressed People, Forces of Oppression, Potentials for Freedom and Liberation, and miscellaneous courses on American radicalism, bureaucratic phenomena, rock music, and revolutionary art. Full scholarships would be offered to ensure participation by minority and working-class students, and everyone would be encouraged to take part-time jobs in local industry and farms to gain contact with working people. Although a *Reporter* editorial found the proposal unrealistic and full of "empty rhetoric," it acknowledged that the courses would deal with topics that were presently ignored.[48]

Using existing petition procedures, students had already added new courses on African American issues. At the request of a group of black and white students, Louis Athey offered that spring The Negro and Reform, and Robert Mickey offered White Racism and Black Churches in America. Lewis Myers, a black alumnus and assistant director of PREP, who was advising the college on urban recruitment, proposed an interdisciplinary course on "what it is like to be Black and live in America." Faculty in history, sociology, anthropology, economics, government, literature, and philosophy volunteered to participate on top of their usual three-course load. Assembled rather hurriedly during the fall of 1968 to meet deadlines, The Black Experience in America received Curriculum Committee approval despite concerns about its loose organization. Adebisi Otudeko, an assistant professor of anthropology, agreed to serve as coordinator. A native of Africa, he was one of only two black faculty members. In the end, forty-nine students enrolled, twelve of whom were black.[49]

In March 1969 the Afro-American Society initiated a meeting with Spalding and other college leaders, to recommend ways to better support black students at Franklin & Marshall. These included more African American courses, preferably in a department of black studies, more black teachers and staff, a house off campus "to serve as the nucleus for black thought and black life," and more financial aid. Spalding promised to refer the proposals to the appropriate committees or administration personnel, warning that responses might "not necessarily conform to the letter of their demands." Subsequently, the Curriculum Committee approved in principle a prospectus for a black studies program similar to one being considered at Harvard. Noting this positive response, a College Reporter editorial commented, "F and M is fortunate that there is no reason to revolt because the faculty and administration listen to and care about student needs." As the semester came to a close, the Reporter pointed to disturbances at other campuses — including occupation of the Cornell Student Union by a group of black students — and expressed relief that there was no disorder at Franklin & Marshall because "essentially there is nothing to revolt about." The hottest controversy on campus concerned changing the academic calendar.[50]

The "Black Experience in America" Crisis

Unfortunately, these statements proved premature. In the midst of final exams the college found itself embroiled in a complex and potentially explosive standoff between faculty and black students in the Black Experience in America course.

On May 21, the day before its scheduled final examination, a group of black students in the course informed Otudeko that they were boycotting the test. They presented a statement of "Initial Demands," written in consultation with a larger group of black students:

> The ridiculous assumption that the black students at F&M shall be tested upon their blackness by whites is another attempt by the whiteman to assert his control over the black mentality. We shall not submit to the mental enslavement that whites have continually attempted to perpetrate; that enslavement in which the "master" now "bodaciously" attempts to tell us "how" blacks are to think. You have stood in front of this class all semester telling us all about "bad white-folk" and still you so very boldly attempt to run the biggest psyche game we have experienced. We shall not take your final examination in blackness.

Instead, the students demanded an apology from the faculty "for the exploitation of our blackness," an exemption from the final examination, and an automatic "A" for every black person in the course.[51]

Six of the seven faculty in the course met later that evening to discuss the statement. They greeted it with a mixture of "surprise, shock, anger, incredulity, dismay, and guilt." None had been aware of any dissatisfaction with the course. Only Otudeko had attended many of the classes; most of the rest had come only to the sessions they taught. Term papers had recently been returned; some of the black students had written highly subjective personal statements and had received low grades. Most faculty members suspected that an underlying motive was fear of receiving a poor grade. But they were of differing minds about the extent to which the faculty might have been responsible for the student's perception of exploitation and about the legitimacy of changing assessment methods. In the end the group rejected the demands but promised to support any petition to withdraw from the course.

When Otudeko conveyed this decision to the students, a group of about twenty black students came to his office and asked the faculty to explain their reasons. The teachers explained that the exam's purpose was to assess students' mastery of a body of knowledge, not their "blackness." They assured the students that they had had not meant to exploit them and expressed regret that anyone had seen it that way. Unmollified, the students left. The faculty agreed to proceed with the exam.

Meanwhile, the Afro-American Society voted to join the protest and to prevent administration of the exam. They composed the "Midnight Document" to explain their demands. It continued at greater length the militant language of the initial statement, adding charges that faculty had misled and exploited black students in the course. Faculty had "proved to be grossly unable to lend anything to the course other than their technological competency in their respective specialties," while black students had been "the ones who gave the white professors and the white students vast insights into the black psyche, the black experience and black thought." Black students had been forced to "get up and serve as resource material, which when translated into action means, 'please be a rat for our study of rat behavior.'" For having been "placed us in the capacity of a professor," they believed they all black students deserved to receive As.

The next morning, some thirty to forty black students blocked the entrance of the assigned examination room in Old Main and posted a sign stating that there would be no examination. When faculty arrived on the scene, they announced that the exam would be a take-home. But when some white students picked up the questions, black students confiscated their papers. A little later, faculty gathered in the anthropology seminar room in Goethean Hall to discuss their next step. As they arrived, a few black students were waiting at Oteduko's office just across the hall; later their numbers were swelled by other AAS members.

Early in the day, Spalding had been alerted that black students were staging some kind of "sit-in" at Old Main. He asked the assistant dean of students, James Gordon, to look into the situation. After obtaining a copy of the initial demands, Gordon went to Goethean and saw what he perceived to be "an orderly 'sit-in,' a peaceful protest with no implications of force or duress." He entering the seminar room, where the faculty were discussing whether to mail exams to students' homes.

Nonetheless, sometime before Gordon's arrival, some students had stated that the faculty would not be allowed to leave until their demands were met. Gradually students assembled a makeshift barricade, and a few lay down in the corridor; others gathered outside the seminar room windows. This step-by-step "blockade" seems to have been impromptu, and there was a certain amount of uncertainty about how rigorously it would be enforced. Students did not interfere with movement of other professors who had offices in the building, but when several of the course's faculty tried to leave to use the restroom, they were told they could leave only one at a time and under escort. "From this point forward," one faculty recalled, "I was convinced that we were acting under duress, although no one physically tested the blockade."

Professors then received a copy of the "Midnight Document," whose additional criticism of the course prompted a sharp change in the tone of the discussion. Gordon later commented that it gave some teachers "a clearer understanding and greater sympathy." One now recalled that he had said early in the course that black students would serve as "resource persons" because only they could speak to the subjective experience of being a black man in America. Some argued more vehemently that the course's experimental character warranted departing from normal procedures. There were heated debates between advocates and opponents of taking a hard line, while members of the group differed considerably in their sense of being under duress.

The discussion became even more "fiery" when one teacher proposed allowing all students to grade themselves if they had completed a term paper. Some opposed the idea strongly, while others pointed out that this kind of self-evaluation had been done in other courses. The proposal was put to a secret ballot and passed 4 to 3. The students in the hallway agreed to the plan, if the faculty also made a written apology and guaranteed amnesty. After doing so, the faculty left Goethean about 1:15 P.M.

A potentially explosive situation had been brought to a peaceful close, but its long-term effects on the college were magnified by the community's subsequent reactions. The seven faculty met soon thereafter with Spalding, who had been preparing for an overseers meeting and had not been told of the precise character of the situation. He called a special faculty meeting to inform everyone of the facts in the case. Having secured their own release, the beleaguered faculty now found themselves under attack — on one side for cowardice and unprofessional conduct and on the other for lack of understanding toward the students. They were also disturbed to learn that some of their colleagues had known of their predicament and treated it with "an air of levity."[52]

At the faculty meeting Sidney Wise recounted events of the preceding two days. Spalding emphasized that the seven faculty had been forced to act without clear guidelines and with little support and argued that their agreement should be honored while a clear policy be set for the future. He advised against any immediate action, but many in the faculty wanted to take a strong stand against the students. A motion condemning their actions was finally tabled by a vote of 45 to 38, to provide time for consideration.

A statement to the college community summarized events and noted the faculty's "deep concern with the manner in which the demands were presented and the way faculty members' efforts to reach a reasonable solution were received." The faculty would meet again the following week.[53]

Spalding distributed a lengthy statement in advance of this meeting. Unaware of the depth of feeling on campus, he urged considering the incident closed and focusing on the issues it revealed. Reflecting on the year's events as a whole, he believed that the college had narrowly averted the "disruption and violence which has infected and damaged some other fine institutions" but needed to avoid extremes of complacency or reaction:

> We must learn all we can from the incidents we have faced. The subtle shadows they cast have demonstrated the natural history of disruptive confrontation. Without ever having matured into full-scale disruption, happily, they have nonetheless revealed the vulnerability of a college to the threat of violence, reaction, polarization and escalation. They have shown how quickly a trigger issue can get lost in other emotion-laden concerns. We have seen how rapidly and surrealistically two or more logically unrelated events or issues can become one morass of confusions and discontents. We have learned that the academic process cannot operate in a climate of crisis. We have learned that in every incident, we are limited by human frailty and the myopia of the moment.

Spalding believed that the college needed to find ways to deal with discontent while preserving values of democracy, reason, and academic integrity.[54]

But when the College Senate met on May 26, strong feelings within the faculty made it impossible to avoid further debate on the incident. The senate approved a series of principles underlining the college's commitment to freedom of thought and expression, including preservation of "the right to think, and talk, and move about freely." The college would publicize how students could bring grievances about faculty professional conduct, but it would refuse to recognize "agreements reached under the threat of intimidation." Finally, the senate resolved to appoint an ad hoc committee to investigate the incident and make appropriate recommendations. The faculty declared decisions made on May 22 "null and void."[55]

The final faculty meeting of the year was more positive. O'Brien was leaving to become president of Bloomfield College, and Spalding noted that during the search process for his successor, many faculty had urged him to appoint "a Dean who was familiar with the special problems of this college, and with its people and processes." He announced that the new dean would be John Vanderzell, longtime member of the government department.[56]

Reflecting on the events of the year in his State of the College address to the Alumni Association, Spalding returned to the need to protect academic freedoms. He noted that "every good college is, in a sense, a microcosmic reflection of the vectors at work in the society at large." Pointing to the violent confrontations at more than thirty campuses that year, he admitted that most educators were "baffled and distraught." He feared that the "hostile reaction of the public and, more directly, of legislators" would escalate conflict further. It was essential to distinguish between peaceful protest and violent disruption, "between non-conformity of youth and the terror tactics of the extremists." He reiterated that the college would "not tolerate violence or disruption" but stressed, "We have at hand the means to meet forcible interference if it should be threatened and we are prepared to make use of those means, swiftly, purposefully and firmly."[57]

Dean Vanderzell appointed a seven-man committee, the Committee to Investigate May 22, later called the Western Committee, composed of mathematics professor Donald W. Western, serving as chairman; history professor and alumnus John Joseph; Ronald D. Potier, director of admissions; T. Roberts Appel II, an alumnus and Lancaster attorney; John S. Schropshire, a Harrisburg high school teacher and member of the PREP staff; Gregory B. Colvin, a sophomore and member of the College Senate; and Leon Glover, a Lancaster native and junior at Gettysburg College, who also tutored for PREP. Schropshire and Glover were African Americans, Joseph a native of Iraq, and the rest white. At its first meeting, the group agreed to give highest priority to obtaining a clear understanding of the events. To ensure that they gain the perspectives of the students involved, they promised that no information given to them would be used as evidence if charges were brought later. The committee met weekly into the fall, gathering information from a broad range of participants. They also consulted outside scholars of black culture, such as historian Eugene Genovese.[58]

The Western Committee's final report, issued the following November, emphasized the event's complexity. It outlined many points of conflict and confusion that had set the stage, some arising from differences in perception between black students and white professors, but many based on contrasting understandings of the nature of higher education itself. Some problems were inherent in the course's inception, for in the rush to put together a proposal, it departed from Lewis Myers's original vision of a course to foster self-understanding among black students. Instead it offered a hodgepodge of approaches to racial issues from the perspective of different academic disciplines. Most of the black students in the class did not appreciate the difference until it was too late. Their confusion was magnified by the faculty's lack of clearly defined objectives.[59]

Faculty had unintentionally encouraged black students' misperceptions about the nature of the course. Leon Galis told them that he would "rely on the black students in the course as 'resource persons'" when it came to "what it *felt* like to be black in America." Several teachers invited some of the black students — and none of the white — to participate in panel presentations during their sections of the course, contributing to black students' impression that the course was primarily subjective. Moreover, it was not made clear that the term paper was supposed to be a typical academic work. Only when papers were returned on the eve of the final exam did "comments and grades on the papers finally drive home the point that the intent of the course was to deal with objective rather than subjective treatment of Black experience."

The committee's investigation also highlighted black students' predicament at Franklin & Marshall. Their small number made them stand out within a much larger body of white students, who were often naive in matters of race relations, if not openly racist. Mostly from Northeastern inner cities, the African American students felt uncomfortable with the affluence of their surroundings and overwhelmed by the highly competitive academic environment. They told the committee that they could relax only among fellow black students, a fact that gave heightened social prominence to the Afro-American Society and to "Afro-Hall," a section of Rauch Hall where black students were clustered. There, values of "brotherhood" and group solidarity were prized above those of individual achievement and expression. Hence, decisions to protest the handling of the course were made collectively and included the demand that all black students receive the same grade. Some students told Spalding that they felt they had no choice but to participate in the AAS action. On top of their sense of loyalty and fears of ostracism, they believed that all black students would be punished no matter what they did. For these reasons the Western Committee recommended against holding individual students responsible for specific actions.

The Western Committee found the students' actions "understandable" within context but did not condone their decision to use "force rather than reason" to resolve their problems. (Leon Glover submitted a minority report arguing that the students' actions were acceptable because the faculty had destroyed their "faith in institutional methods" by resorting to traditional grading practices after leading students to believe it would be a far different kind of course.) It concluded that attempting to prosecute individuals would not aid a "constructive resolution" of the crisis, but that it should be made clear that in future the threat or use of force would not be tolerated. Among the committee's substantive recommendations were that as the college discussed a black studies program, consideration be given to the fact that some goals might be better served "outside the regular course structure."

Coeducation and Continuing Controversy

By the time the report appeared, the college community had moved on to other issues, although tensions engendered within the faculty continued to shape events. The faculty was polarized — between advocates of educational experimentation and defenders of academic standards, between those who hoped to involve the college in the pressing political issues of the day and those who wanted it to remain professionally objective. Yet the complex collegial system of governance that had evolved over the previous two decades could function well only with a certain degree of consensus. As at many other institutions in this period, the extended period of unresolved conflict undermined consensus and depleted crucial reservoirs of trust. In the meantime, continued war in Vietnam and unrest in America predisposed many college students to direct action. Even those who were not particularly interested in politics participated in the spirit of the times by means of countercultural dress, rock music, drugs, and cynicism toward "the establishment."

Joining President Spalding at the center of controversy was the new dean, John Vanderzell. Determined to defend academic standards, he quickly became a lightning rod for attacks from radical students and faculty. Years later, at Spalding's retirement, Vanderzell recalled the difficult years of his first deanship: "When I was very, very young I used to pray for things. . . . Round about — which is the way the system works, I guess — the prayers were answered too. . . . This was back in the days when baseball catcher's mitts were big — about the size of a dishpan. Spalding made a beaut — big, yellow leather, trimmed in black. I sent up a plea for a Spalding catcher's mitt. And forgot about it — until about 1969. Then it occurred to me — I had not made myself clear. I wanted to *have* one, not *be* one!"[60]

Over the summer the administration had focused on preparing for coeducation. Jo Ann Whitsett became a new associate dean of students, and Meredith Lee Dean a physical education instructor. Marshall Hall and the first floor of Atlee Hall were readied for women. The Task Force on Coeducation had expected to enroll up to 50 women at first, but so many highly qualified women applied that the ceiling was raised. In September 120 women appeared on campus: 83 freshwomen in a class of 590, plus 37 upper class transfers and exchange students from Wilson College. With an unexpected decrease in attrition, total enrollment rose to an all-time high of 1,850. Increased numbers of applications translated into higher average SAT scores for all new students, but competition for the limited number of women's spaces assured that their scores were higher yet. Defying expectations, women who applied to Franklin & Marshall were much like men in their interests and career goals; a majority of both sexes planned to be science majors, and equal proportions of men and women wanted to be doctors.[61]

Given the college's long history as an all-male institution, introduction of women to Franklin & Marshall went relatively smoothly. This was partly a result of the administration's careful planning but partly a reflection of changes that had already taken place in campus culture. Unlike Dartmouth and Williams, there were no cases of overt hostility to women. Incoming male freshmen might have had the most negative feelings, because their female classmates received so much attention — and because male freshmen felt little hope in competing with upperclassmen for the women's attention. Integration of women into the classroom and into extracurricular activities went more smoothly than their inclusion in social life, however. Some women were dismayed to find that friendships with male students did not translate into dates on Saturday night. Perhaps discouraged by the sixteen-to-one ratio or intimidated by the women's intellects, many male students continued to turn elsewhere for weekend dates. Admitted as a transfer student, Cathy Voelker recalled that "a lot of fast friendships were built up between males and females and fewer romances." A women's forum made a "lighthearted" request to import men from other schools for mixers, but male students were not amused. Some blamed the college's reliance on fraternities for social life, because few of the new women responded to fraternities' blanket invitations to their parties.[62]

Inevitably, the new year brought fresh controversies. Reactions abounded at the news that the Student Union Board (SUB) had booked a performance of *Tom Paine*, an off-Broadway play featuring acrobatics and nudity. This caught the attention of the local press and the district attorney. Dean Lacy asked to meet with SUB members. Fearing censorship, AAUP members showed up to observe, provoking Lacy to complain of faculty interference in his work with students. In the end, Spalding commented, "We struck the liberal establishment pose," meaning that the college "defended the students, the decision, eschewed censorship, etc." He was bemused to find that the production was "pretty tame at that," the nudes having been "all covered by diaphanous material" and the actors "an earnest young touring company trying to establish itself on the college circuit and not looking forward to being arrested."[63]

Students protested against the college's physical education requirement and lamented the lack of a student government, but in the fall most attention focused on the national moratorium movement, which hoped to develop a groundswell of opposition to the Vietnam war through marches and public education. On October 15 organizers urged fellow students to participate in antiwar outreach instead of attending classes. Predictably, differences emerged over whether the college should allow faculty to suspend instruction and students to miss classes without consequences. Dean Vanderzell announced that the college would not interfere with "lawful expressions of conscience" but "presumed" that professors who canceled classes would inform their department chairmen of plans to make up the work. This sparked an angry memo from five sociology and anthropology professors charging that his statement had insulted their professional authority. They pointed out that the college arbitrarily canceled classes during the opening convocation and speculated that its decision not to support the moratorium was prompted by its "value-laden nature." They protested Vanderzell's intervention "in what we see to be purely a faculty matter, and one which has clear ideological undertones." They also took exception to Vanderzell's request that faculty submit course syllabi to his office.[64]

Thirty professors (out of 155) signed an open letter supporting the moratorium. They agreed to "set aside our commitments to the academic routine on that day to underscore our profound belief in the need to end this war now." Unevenness of faculty opinion across disciplines was shown in the fact that 15 of the signers taught in the social sciences, 12 in the humanities, and only 3 in the sciences. On October 15, about 740 members of the college community handed out leaflets, rang doorbells, and picketed in Lancaster and surrounding areas. The day ended with a torchlight rally in Hartman Oval. Spalding joined 76 other college presidents in signing a statement urging Nixon and Congress to step up the timetable for troop withdrawal. He emphasized that he spoke not for his institution but as an individual, out of "the depth of [his] concern" for the damage that the protracted war was doing to American society. Some trustees criticized him, but he was warmly applauded when he explained his action at a Parents' Day assembly. He thought most of the presidents signing the statement hoped to show their respective communities that "we share their concern" and also to express appreciation that moratorium organizers had not tried "to use the campus as a staging area for the politics of confrontation."[65]

Despite the prominence of controversy and the great changes in recent years, some aspects of campus life had changed surprisingly little. Enthusiastic freshmen of both sexes organized the first pep rally in three years, with women now among the cheerleaders. The band boasted its first majorette, freshman Jeannine Lehmer, winner of a number of state and national awards for baton twirling. During homecoming, thirty-three former players were inducted into the new Football Hall of Fame. The *College Reporter* noted with bemusement recurrent "disturbances" in the dormitory quadrangle that had nothing to do with politics. Unaware that they were re-enacting Franklin & Marshall traditions, male freshmen and upperclassmen waged periodic battles, now armed with shaving cream, water balloons, toilet tissue, fireworks, and occasionally furniture. One modern innovation was background music blaring from stereo speakers set up in dorm windows. On one occasion combatants proposed uniting for "one grand panty raid" on Marshall Hall, but they were dissuaded by a cordon of dorm counselors under Dean Lacy's command.[66]

As the fall wore on, some in the Afro-American Society complained about the college's slowness in responding to their requests of the previous spring. In fact, administrators were working on the issues, but as always the wheels of academe turned slowly. Spalding had at first thought to respond to the request for an off-campus house by offering one of the college's, on a basis similar to the Hillel House recently established on College Avenue to enable students to keep kosher. Ironically, he learned that providing separate space solely for one racial group would be seen as a violation of the 1964 Civil Rights Act. Discussions between the administration and AAS dragged on throughout the academic year, finally resulting in permission to create the Black Culture Center and Museum on campus. In the meantime the AAS, now with a membership of eighty, held its first Black Culture Day in November and expanded the event to a weekend the following April.[67]

Vanderzell surveyed "black-relevant" courses in various departments to see if "an academically legitimate" program could be developed from existing offerings, using a procedure for creating general studies majors. A senate subcommittee finally presented a proposal in March for the Black Studies major based on a core of ten courses. Steps had been taken to hire an African American counselor, but the drawn-out character of the academic hiring process meant that the new member of the counseling staff did not arrive on campus until the following spring. Many of the other AAS proposals required more substantial financial commitments, which were difficult in the college's worsening financial situation. Spalding flatly told the AAS that the college did not have the resources to support a community center. Vanderzell encouraged departments to seek out African American and female candidates, but progress was hampered by tight budgets and suspicions that academic standards might be compromised. The history department's request for an additional instructor in African American history was turned down for financial reasons.[68]

It was becoming common knowledge that the college's finances were increasingly precarious. Cutbacks in government aid and declining foundation and private support coincided with rising inflation and increased costs for new programs and facilities, turning the small surpluses of previous years into widening deficits. Spalding noted that the college was experiencing donor "burnout," which was common after major fund-raising campaigns. Many foundations shifted their focus to pressing social problems, and national and state legislators reacted to campus unrest by threatening to limit student grant and loan funds. This was of particular concern because more than 40 percent of incoming freshmen now received aid, compared to 27 percent five years before.[69]

Yet expectations within the college community continued to rise. Student leaders complained about inadequate funding for the Student Union Board and the student center and asked for a full-time coordinator for social activities. AAUP called for a 10 percent increase in faculty salaries. Calling a special faculty meeting to explain the college's worsening financial situation, Spalding offered a 5 percent increase instead.[70]

Challenging the Academic System

Following a trend at many schools, dissidents at Franklin & Marshall focused on the educational environment. A student-faculty forum on grading provoked extended discussion. Most speakers agreed with new history professor George Hand that grades interfered with real learning and with Gerald Enscoe that the structure of courses and departments prevented study of vital contemporary problems. Later, history department chairman Solomon Wank recommended creating an experimental college to try out new forms of learning.[71]

As in the Mezey affair four years before, one particularly charismatic newcomer became a focus for general discontent. Henry E. Mayer had been hired as a part-time lecturer in history. As a graduate student at the University of California at Berkeley, he had helped lead the 1964 Free Speech Movement, and by the time he came to Franklin & Marshall, he had become a spokesman for a generation of disaffected students. He told a researcher on campus unrest that they were "responding as outraged human beings to all the brutalizing and irrational conditions — racism, poverty, militaristic anticommunism, bureaucratic and technological inhumanity — that disfigure and trouble this country and diminish the quality of human life."[72]

Mayer immediately assumed a prominent role on campus, first in the moratorium movement then as advocate for educational change. He called for restructuring the entire grading process, to give students greater freedom and encourage cooperation and mutual trust. Mayer appealed to a number of students who were hungry for what they perceived to be more intense, authentic experience. One freshman wrote a note to Spalding on a napkin to express her dismay at the college's obsession with grades: "I want the kind of learning that ASSAULTS me," she said. She despaired that teachers whom she admired "because of their ability to ASSAULT [her] with their knowledge and insight" felt they could not teach the way they wanted to at Franklin & Marshall.[73]

Later, a committee asked to mediate in what became known as "the Mayer affair" described it as "a strange tangle brought about by confusions, misunderstandings, and errors" on the part of nearly everyone involved. Magnified by the community's polarization and abetted by the looming financial crisis, the conflict mushroomed into a formidable challenge by advocates of student rights. At the center of the conflict was the Professional Standards Committee, symbol of the faculty's postwar rise to power.[74]

Mayer had been hired for a temporary position but was told that a permanent one would be opening up upon Frederic Klein's retirement. The stage for conflict was set when Wank suggested to Vanderzell, as Professional Standards Committee (PSC) chair, that the department could save the college money by bringing in only one candidate — instead of the usual two or three. The dean agreed, as long as the candidate was "of top quality and came with the support of the department." This departed from the standard procedure, whereby PSC passed on the acceptability of several top candidates while the department made the final selection. The history department took Vanderzell's assent to mean that PSC had effectively waived its right of rejection. Once the history department voted unanimously to hire Mayer, it sent out letters of rejection to the other candidates even before his PSC interview.[75]

But there were doubts in many quarters about Mayer's suitability. He had not completed his doctoral dissertation and seemed more intent on teaching and activism than on doing so. The previous spring, in a panel on graduate education at the Organization of American Historians, he strongly criticized the stultifying effects of "professionalization" in graduate schools and pointed to the wide gulf between the "insular professional role" inculcated there and students' desire for social engagement. At Franklin & Marshall he followed up criticisms of the grading system by proposing an experimental, nongraded course for the spring semester. Arguing that "genuine learning can only begin when the necessity to please others is removed," he also asked to submit satisfactory-unsatisfactory notices in lieu of midterm grades for freshmen. There were rumors that he and other teachers allowed students to grade themselves. When Vanderzell inquired about his grading practices, Mayer refused to respond. Claiming that academic freedom included complete control over grading, he dismissed the dean's request as an "impermissible intrusion into the affairs of my classroom."[76]

Mayer's statements touched a tender nerve among faculty already sensitized by unresolved grading controversies in the Black Experience in America episode. Many agreed with Richard Schier's opinion, expressed in an essay in the *AAUP Bulletin*, that the academic profession was being undermined by young radicals seeking to replace intellectual rigor with "affective education." Noting that many radicals had not finished their doctorates, Schier dismissed their "retreat to radicalism" as a strategy to gain tenure. During the college's expansion, strong demand for teachers had resulted in hiring many without their doctorates. The percentage of faculty holding the doctorate had thus declined to less than 60 percent, and in the social sciences to less than half. (Fifty of fifty-three science faculty had doctorates.) Longtime faculty who had struggled to raise the college's professional standing feared that their efforts were now being sabotaged.[77]

The purpose of the Professional Standards Committee, obviously, was to uphold standards and to represent the interests of the college as a whole as against those of particular departments. On January 19, 1970, PSC interviewed Mayer "at considerable length." He later charged that they grilled him about his educational policies and grading practices. Subsequently, they "discussed his candidacy at greater length," continuing through a second meeting. It was not until nearly two weeks later, on February 2, that they decided not to recommend him to the president for the position.[78]

Despite rules of confidentiality, news of the decision quickly leaked out, and Mayer and his supporters among students and faculty responded with outrage. The Department of History called PSC's decision an unwarranted interference with the department's prerogatives and asked the committee to reconsider. Mayer charged publicly that his rights to a fair hearing had been denied: he had been "accused, tried and judged *in absentia*" for unspecified complaints, although he suspected that they concerned his grading practices. PSC cited its practice of confidentiality in declining to disclose its reasons. Mayer responded that this "tradition of academic civility and collegiality" merely "[masked] the unscrupulousness" of the process. He charged that Vanderzell had "managed, guided, dominated and perhaps intimidated" the rest of the committee. Raising their own issues, students complained that they had no voice in the decision-making process. A group of about thirty met to plan a response; when sociology instructor Anthony Lazroe, also on a one-year contract, announced that he also had not been rehired, a protest movement took shape. George McGoldrick, author of a petition seeking reconsideration of both cases, saw that the movement united "students from different factions of the college community" toward a common goal. Even so, the Afro-American Society rejected an attempt to include its issues on a list of demands.[79]

In anticipation of the coming furor, Spalding issued a five-page memorandum on February 4, restating the college's policies regarding disruptions. When PSC declined to reopen the case, a meeting of about three hundred students voted on February 11 to strike. Their manifesto announced that they would boycott classes and peacefully encourage others to raise issues within their classes. Their goal was "to mobilize the student body to show that students are rightfully concerned" to have a role in their own education. In addition to supporting Mayer and Lazroe, they hoped to widen discussion to issues of students' "academic freedom," "the right to determine the kind of education" they wanted, and the administration's "meaningless channels" for discussion.[80]

The following day Spalding issued a three-page memorandum rebutting the charges. He attributed most to "misinformation, an intricate web of rumors and half-truths, and a limited understanding of the requirements of sound professional practice in faculty personnel considerations." Without providing details, he asserted that "due process is not at issue." He staunchly defended the institution's reputation "for experiment and change" but vowed to protect "the professional processes of the College." Finally, he promised a forum to discuss the "valid educational issues" involved.[81]

Nonetheless, when Spalding met privately with PSC, he stressed the importance of ensuring that candidates for permanent faculty positions be "the very best available." The economic crisis in higher education had changed the market for academics, and there was now "no need to accept candidates whose professional qualifications [were] marginal or those to whom the attainment of full credentials [was] problematical."[82]

About fifty students picketed classroom buildings on February 12 and around one hundred marched to Spalding's house in the afternoon to confront the monthly overseers meeting. Anticipating this, Dean Lacy arranged for a handpicked group of students, including two members of the College Senate, to communicate their concerns with Spalding and three overseers. This meeting was already underway when the marchers arrived. At an evening strike meeting, "the interested students of Franklin and Marshall" rejected Spalding's proposal for dialogue. "We find it contradictory, at the very least, to be told, on the one hand, that we are misinformed, and on the other, that we cannot be informed." They demanded that both teachers be hired, that teaching methods be left "to the discretion of each professor and his students," that the PSC be restructured with equal numbers of faculty and students, and that all administration decisions be subject to student veto. More generally, many students complained that the educational atmosphere at the college was too narrowly professional — as reflected in the stress placed on completion of the doctorate. Their statements frequently echoed rhetoric of national student protests, as when a leader quoted a pamphlet from a strike at San Francisco State.[83]

With the strike threatening to continue into the following week, and the image of red clenched fists sprouting on surfaces throughout campus, Spalding called a special faculty meeting for Monday afternoon at Goethean Hall. To reach it, professors had to negotiate an ice-covered sidewalk lined by an ominous gauntlet of around four hundred students, who conveyed their opinions of particular figures by cheering or hissing as they passed. Continued into a second day, the discussions showed the faculty to be as divided as ever, with many suspicious of the motives of the president, dean, and PSC. There was general agreement that students had some cause for dissatisfaction. The meeting mandated new grievance procedures for faculty and students and debated how to give students a formal role in evaluating teaching effectiveness, increase their representation in governance, and examine the college's "educational objectives" as a whole. On the morning between the two meetings, students and faculty packed Hensel Hall for a forum sponsored by the Black Pyramid honor society. To allow further discussion by the entire community, the faculty meeting was adjourned until February 26, and strike leaders agreed to abandon their picketing. In the meantime, the PSC had announced that it recognized that a vacancy existed in the history department and requested a return to the usual practice of presenting two or more candidates for its consideration.[84]

In response to student requests, Spalding declared February 26 a "day of discussion" when most classes would be canceled to consider issues before the faculty. The administration distributed a thick sheaf of mimeographed proposals submitted by faculty and students; proposals were taken up in small student-moderated groups. Low student attendance suggested that concern was not universal, but when a plenary session pooled the groups' conclusions, it was evident that participants wanted greater representation in the senate and less emphasis on grades.[85]

Many supported a proposal for the "Tom Paine Program," an alternative "learning community" within the college, put forward during the strike by Tom Glenn, George Hand, Henry Mayer, and John Snyder. All were young, relatively new teachers, and none had completed their doctorates. They envisioned an egalitarian communal group of about two hundred students and five faculty members, who would over the course of a year collectively create their own structure, calendar, and curriculum. "The learning community would result in the growth of an order based on relationships among the participants and a thoroughgoing respect for the integrity of their emotional and intellectual needs," the proposal explained.[86]

The program drew upon general interest at the time in fashioning more creative, less hierarchical learning environments. Yet in some ways it unwittingly looked back to the college's earliest days. Its rejection of narrow professional norms and disciplinary boundaries echoed the philosophy of Frederick Rauch, especially his stress upon organic development of the whole person rather than of intellect alone. Here, however, the underlying rationale had little to do with Christian Romanticism but much to do with strong links to New Left critiques of corporate capitalism. Most of the seventeen-page proposal was devoted to a passionate attack on the present system of higher education as an "institutionalized learning experience [that was] in reality a manipulating, digesting, and purveying experience." "[It] not only makes a shambles of the personal lives of the human beings trapped within its structure," proponents wrote, "but also constitutes an integral part of the process by which American society reproduces itself and its anti-human values." The end result was "professionalized" education in the service of the postwar "military-industrial complex" that had gutted the true purpose of liberal arts education.[87]

Its authors also harked back to the nineteenth-century understanding of liberal education as a preparation for participation in public life. They asserted that the primary goal of the liberal arts was to "enable students to become intellectually autonomous, self-respecting people." The stress the authors put on process over structure had been strongly shaped by their personal experience as political activists. In his memoir of the Free Speech Movement, Mayer later noted that it had sparked a "long process of collaborative self-education" that he saw as a model for a kind of education "that broke the boundaries of the classroom and the departments." He quoted from Thomas

Paine's observation in *Rights of Man* that revolutions summon "genius and talents" that otherwise lay dormant—the same passage used as the epigraph for the 1970 proposal.[88]

Reconvening at the close of the Day of Discussion, the faculty voted to transfer much of its decision-making authority to the College Senate. The faculty referred proposals for changes in the composition of the senate to that body, setting the stage for increased student representation, and by a vote of 85 to 36 renounced the faculty's right of veto over senate actions. Sharp disagreements remained, however, over the role students should be given in evaluation of faculty. The faculty retained control over PSC and the Judicial Committee.[89]

As it seemed that a number of issues were on the way to resolution, the tenor of life temporarily returned to normal. Ad hoc committees were appointed to consider the makeup of the PSC and to prepare a general statement on the college's educational goals. Interim grievance procedures were established, based on national AAUP guidelines regarding academic freedom. Deliberations that had gone on since 1963 culminated in approval of a new academic calendar that ended the first semester before winter holidays. The senate doubled, to eight, the total number of pass/no pass courses that students could take and expanded the number of student senators to six and reduced faculty membership to twelve. And it decided to abolish the physical education requirement, bowing to a combination of student boycott, faculty conviction that it was not "sufficiently central" to the goals of liberal education, and the college's mounting deficit. At the end of the year, the Committee on Recruiting appointed the previous year finally reported its conclusion that on-campus recruiting should continue, with privileges offered to all organizations offering lawful career opportunities.[90]

Nevertheless, crucial questions remained unresolved. The Department of History insisted that it was too late to simply restart the interview process, as PSC had directed. Wank argued that no other candidates would agree to come to campus under present conditions and that it would be embarrassing to the department to go through the motions of interviewing. After a long discussion, PSC reaffirmed its position that the department must present two or more candidates. Three outside faculty, Robert Russell, Kenneth Brookshire and Frederick Suydam, acknowledged by both sides as impartial, agreed to try to mediate. Their initial assessment was that there had been a "complete breakdown of the cooperative effort necessary for the making of a departmental appointment." Mistakes on both sides had been inflamed by "irreconcilable positions and personal animosities" and made rigid by public exposure. They recommended that the process begin again with more than one candidate and laid out ground rules to deal with the most contentious issues.[91]

Vanderzell and the PSC were also in the process of conducting a search for a sociology department chairman. It was generally considered to be a weak and troubled department, where high turnover had left few senior faculty. The administration had decided to hire a prominent figure from outside, preferably one with sufficient stature to warrant a Dana Professorship. The task was complicated by the fact that the discipline of sociology itself was seriously divided over fundamental—often ideologically based—questions of methods and content. After meeting with one candidate, PSC members questioned "whether he [was] in the main stream of Sociology although it was recognized that there may [have been] some difficulty in defining the main stream of that discipline." Not surprisingly, the department's faculty attacked PSC for failing to hire a candidate they favored, as well as for controlling the hiring process as a whole.[92]

Negotiations between PSC and the history department dragged on through March and into April with no progress. When the first candidate came to campus, he promptly withdrew after meeting with members of the department and about a dozen student majors. The department argued that this would be the case with any qualified candidate and returned to their position that the PSC must reconsider Mayer as their only candidate. Mayer had already announced at a public meeting that he would refuse to participate in the interview process. The mediation committee continued to support the PSC's demand that more than one candidate be presented.[93]

The Department of History conducted many of its debates publicly, through letters to the *College Reporter* and open meetings, and the absence of public response from PSC encouraged circulation of rumors and personal attacks, particularly against Vanderzell. *Reporter* columnist James Peck depicted the scene as a circus, with "Wank's Trained Tigers" in one ring, "Vandy's Life-Size Puppets" in another, and clowns in the third, exhibiting "fantastic talents for absurdity" and hurling "invectives at everyone." He criticized all sides for seeking their own amusement at the expense of the welfare of the college as a whole. In the meantime the Black Pyramid Society pledged $1,000 to support the Tom Paine learning community, and its authors submitted their proposal to the Committee on Special Programs.[94]

Students gathered periodically outside East Hall to protest lack of action on the Mezey case. On April 17, Spalding and Vanderzell spoke with a group of about 175 students and faculty in an attempt to explain the professional issues underlying the impasse. Adding to a general feeling of unease were escalating incidents of vandalism, theft, minor arson, and bomb threats that forced the college to evacuate offices and classrooms. The cumulative effect, noted the *Reporter*, was an impaired academic process and a general "paranoid mentality." Students were experiencing "the fragile nature of any institution" that tried "to accommodate a great variety of ideologies."[95]

Tensions finally came to a head when Mayer declared at a meeting of history majors that the department and PSC had reached an impasse. Samuel Allen proposed that students themselves raise about $10,000 to pay Mayer's salary. In an attempt to alleviate some of the "animus" that had developed and to lessen "rumor and misinformation," the mediators issued a memorandum to the community outlining their perspective. Given the stands of both parties, they could "see no satisfactory solution at this point."[96]

The following Monday, April 27, a group of students began a sit-in on the second floor of East Hall. They attacked the PSC's handing of the matter and called upon the faculty to "put its petty politics aside and resolve this impasse immediately." Numbering between twenty and forty at any one time, students merely occupied the hallways and did not attempt to interfere with normal functioning of the administration. But their presence was clearly a distraction and a mounting source of tension to the staff.

On Wednesday, Spalding asked them to leave, promising to make an announcement within 24 hours, and they departed.[97]

Spalding had already called a faculty meeting for the following morning to discuss the financial crisis. There he announced his decision that, in light of the irreconcilable positions of the PSC and history department, no appointment would be made to fill the history position. The ensuing discussion revealed deep divisions within the faculty: 103 had already signed a statement supporting the administration, while Professor Wank protested passionately that his department's position "had been widely misunderstood" and warned that the decision would only intensify the problem. A motion to reconvene the faculty later in the day for further discussion was defeated.[98]

A crowd of more than 500 students waited for Spalding outside East Hall. After he announced his decision, over 150 moved immediately to take over the building. Remaining staff left, and officers moved operations next door to the Mayser Center. At the beginning, Spalding noted, "some students were hostile and belligerent but many more were cautious and restrained." They agreed to allow security personnel access to their office and promised not to break into locked files or desks.[99] Intending a long stay, students brought in essentials — food, bedding, books, and stereo equipment — and organized themselves to maintain order. Outside, changing shifts of faculty, administrators, students, and security guards maintained a vigil. Spalding later credited the faculty's tireless efforts to maintain communication with students with lessening hostilities and preventing an escalation of conflict.[100]

At 5:00 P.M., Spalding officially notified demonstrators that they were "in violation of law" and that college officials were preparing to take legal action. In the evening a delegation of those who had "liberated" East Hall met with Spalding and Lacy. They presented a list of "non-negotiable" demands — credit for courses that Mayer might teach if he was paid directly by students, equal student-faculty representation on the PSC, and a promise of general amnesty to those involved. They also voiced support for a black cultural center and for demands by the college's new women's liberation movement. Spalding repeated that the occupation was breaking the law, pointing out that they were now in the second phase of the procedures established to deal with disruptions. As long as they occupied the building, there would be no negotiation and no amnesty. If they did not leave the building by nine o'clock the following morning, they faced immediate suspension, to be followed by a court injunction. When his message was conveyed to East Hall, the students decided to leave immediately. Spalding reported to faculty the next day that apart from accumulated trash and some graffiti, there was minimal damage to property. In the aftermath, a committee of five students and five faculty began to raise money to pay Mayer's salary for the following year.[101]

Cambodian Invasion

But the college's particular controversy had already been overtaken by much larger events. During the evening of April 30, while students still occupied East Hall, President Richard Nixon announced on national television that he had ordered troops into Cambodia. College campuses across the nation mobilized to protest. When news came the following Monday, May 4, that four students had been killed at Kent State University, many campuses erupted. Moderate students who had stayed on the sidelines now felt compelled to express their outrage and frustration. As the faculty gathered that evening to discuss reports of the committee to consider the makeup of the PSC, about five hundred students and faculty met across campus to debate how to close the college down. "Our quarrel is not with the college," they stated, "but with the United States Government." Yet they were striking to "call a complete halt to all regular business until Nixon's reckless and unconstitutional course is reversed." They continued, "We have no choice. We must first create a massive political movement to protest and reverse the policy of imperial escalation. Only then can we resume our daily tasks. To persist in our normal routines now is to give tacit approval to the routine of presidential betrayal and the senseless death of helpless people." There was minor vandalism, as a few students pulled fire alarms, smashed windows, and tried to break into the art studio. Later in the evening the college radio station, WWFM, played a statement from Spalding expressing his "feeling of deep disquiet" at Nixon's actions. Nonetheless, he rejected calls to join a nationwide academic strike. He acknowledged students' individual right to boycott classes but warned that they must not interfere with the college's mission to stand "as a bastion for the defense of the intellectual and personal freedom of all persons."[102]

The following morning, about 125 students blocked entrances to classroom buildings and the library, though a handful of others determined to attend class got through. Many gathered for another of the numerous rallies to be held on Hartman Oval that week, while faculty and staff circulated throughout campus, making themselves available to talk. Spalding announced that he had joined a group of college presidents in sending an urgent request to Nixon to reconsider his action and speed the withdrawal of troops. He also sent a telegram to Pennsylvania's senators, seeking to convey "the depth of dismay and disquiet" of students' reactions to Nixon's announcement. He emphasized that the sentiments went far beyond those of "militant students" to include "strong feelings even among those sober, earnest moderates who are the finest of our youth." By afternoon a certain degree of equanimity had been restored, and a few classes met.[103]

Agreeing with Spalding that it was advisable to find a compromise that would "leave decisions as to action up to the conscience of each individual student" while keeping the college open, the faculty and senate quickly approved a plan allowing students to decide among fulfilling academic requirements as usual, taking an incomplete, or taking a grade or a pass/no pass on the basis of work done up to May 4. When Spalding announced the plan to a mass rally of students that evening, he received a standing ovation of approval. He also reiterated the expectation that no one would block faculty and students wishing to continue "the normal academic activity of the College." On paper at least, the college resumed normal operations the next day.[104]

Ironically, Nixon's Cambodian "incursion" allowed Franklin & Marshall to bring a tumultuous year to a remarkably peaceful end. "Very frankly, from my perspective in the Dean's office," Vanderzell later commented, "it was almost a relief when the protest movement focused on Viet Nam rather than on the kind of internal administration of the college." As a freshman, Sean Flaherty, '73, observed events as they unfolded. He noted that the college's flexible response "pulled the rug out from under the protest" because it kept the school open while allowing those who wished to protest the war. The *Intelligencer Journal* estimated that some 90 percent of students and faculty dropped "business as usual," though most stayed on campus for a while. A full schedule of antiwar seminars was organized, and many students engaged in antiwar work. The Student Arts Festival scheduled for the weekend of May 9 and 10 was transformed into the Peace Festival, and some 260 students traveled to Washington, D.C., the following week to lobby. Eventually, Flaherty recalled, "most people just went home early."[105]

Although Franklin & Marshall had not experienced the violence that occurred elsewhere, the sense that it was a community of scholars had been all but shattered.[106] During the week after the strike, Spalding and Vanderzell were visited by a large group of faculty, who expressed their concern at the "erosion in academic standards and academic integrity" and the administration's lack of firmness in discipline. They insisted on an end to the recurrent disruptions of the academic program. The two men also met with another delegation deploring "what they [perceived] to be an erosion of the College's willingness to be innovative," a "retrenchment" in individual freedom to experiment with new ways of learning. Noting this polarization, Spalding told the faculty that he would work to encourage discussion, but said, "You people had better begin to talk with one another [in search of] rational consensus." In summing up the year to his friend Graeme Smith, he commented on the "distressing rigidity of polar positions on the part of a good number of the faculty."[107]

It was not clear how agreement would be reached. After four days of meetings in May, the faculty could come to no agreement about changing the PSC. There was general consensus that students' assessments of teaching effectiveness should be heeded but no agreement about how to do this. PSC efforts to hire a chairman for the Department of Sociology failed, and Spalding appointed Mac Darlington to administer it while a new search committee was formed. Spalding told the overseers that he was "following precedents," but the action was seen by some as overreaching.[108]

Of greatest concern now was the college's financial crisis. Throughout American higher education, expansion fueled by the great postwar economic boom had come to an abrupt end, exacerbated by a conservative backlash against campus radicalism. A chastened atmosphere prevailed as the administration faced mushrooming deficits. In coming years outward turbulence died down, but the college was left with long-standing residues of distrust, which made achieving stability all the more difficult.

CHAPTER TWELVE

Retrenchment and Reassessment, 1970–1982

—⁓—

After the excitements of the previous year, Franklin & Marshall's 1970–1971 academic year had the feeling of a morning-after hangover. In fact, the coming decade presented all institutions of higher education with a new set of challenges. Instead of expansion, the 1970s brought wrenching retrenchment and reorganization. By the end of the 1960s, it had become clear that costs were rising faster than income. Inflation affected all areas of the economy, but it was particularly troublesome in labor-intensive fields like education.[1] The academic revolution had also brought rising standards that entailed ever-increasing costs for faculty salaries, research support, and lower student-teacher ratios and for student services, campus facilities, and initiatives to redress social inequity. Meanwhile, revenues from government, philanthropic foundations, and individual donors failed to keep pace with rising costs and in some cases declined. This new age of limited resources forced Franklin & Marshall, along with its peer liberal arts colleges, to adapt its management practices. Use of advanced practices in investment, planning, and admissions helped lay the foundation for the college's future financial stability. But they also further linked its fortunes to an increasingly competitive national market among selective liberal arts colleges. Meanwhile, as academic job opportunities constricted, fewer students went on to graduate school, prompting re-examination of the university college model and reappraisal of the college's proper mission in liberal education.[2]

The mood among students had changed too, as a quiet sense of futility replaced confident pronouncements of revolution. The *College Reporter* commented that students had returned to campus that fall with "feelings of powerlessness" and a cynical inability "to accept good faith on any issue." College committees continued their work to resolve issues that had so recently sparked intense passion. But, seeing little immediate change, many students turned away from social action and toward cultivation of small, like-minded groups of friends.[3]

Dissident activity waned, with only a handful of students participating in occasional antiwar picketing. Reaction was mild to a revelation that the college's Afro-American Society had been among black student groups at twelve Pennsylvania schools targeted by the FBI for surveillance and intimidation. The *Reporter* wanted to know whether the privacy of student records had been violated; college officials insisted that they followed American Council on Education guidelines regarding confidentiality of student records.[4]

A Turn Toward Efficiency

Much of the administration's energy during this and coming years was absorbed in meeting the college's financial crisis. In many cases it responded to the changed economic environment by modernizing its management. The board had acted the previous spring to improve stewardship of financial resources by adopting a "total return" policy of endowment management. Prompted by high postwar rates of return in the stock market, economists and investment professionals began recommending calculating capital gains along with interest and dividends in considering a portfolio's earnings and spending a prudent percentage of the whole. In 1969 several influential books published by the Ford Foundation advocated this new approach. Franklin & Marshall was one of the first higher education institutions to adopt it and saw the market value of its endowment increase by 30 percent in the first year, rising in 1971 to more than $12 million.[5]

Over the next two years Spalding and finance vice president Paul Linfield also moved the college to a cash flow budget. This meant basing budgets for the coming fiscal year on real funds received the previous calendar year rather than on estimates. Undesignated gifts were placed in unrestricted endowment that functioned as a bank — Spalding liked the metaphor of a "surge tank" — to absorb deficits and retain surpluses to build up capital. To effect the recycling, the board authorized Spalding to take up to $1.5 million from unrestricted endowment, to be followed by "intensive" fund-raising efforts to restore it.[6]

The college also modernized long-term planning. Toward this end, teams of administrators, faculty, and trustees had recently participated in a two-year program sponsored by the American Foundation for Management Research, and in 1970 Spalding appointed many of them to the Long-Range Planning Council (LRPC). "Those institutions which correctly assess the demands of the future and prepare to meet or accommodate those demands," he predicted, "will be the institutions which provide the intellectual leadership in the years ahead." Appointing Frederic Klein chairman, Spalding asked the council first to determine the college's "optimum size."[7]

But the most crucial immediate issue was the college's spending. Its operating deficit in 1969–1970 had been $423,000. With increased tuition income, cuts in nonsalary budgets, and a general hiring freeze, leaders hoped to hold the current year's to around $250,000, but even this forced the board to dip into endowment. By 1971–1972, Ford

Foundation funds would be used up, and the board instructed Spalding to cut deeper. To prepare the faculty for coming financial hardship, Spalding called a special meeting and provided detailed information regarding the college's "precarious" situation. He called on the entire institution to develop a comprehensive strategy to protect quality, "take some calculated risks, share some burdens and sacrifice all non-essentials."[8]

Dean John Vanderzell spent much of the fall in a process that became known as "rostering"—setting maximum numbers of faculty positions for each department. Using formulas originally developed by math professor Walter Leser for a study of teaching loads, Vanderzell conducted extended negotiations with department chairmen. Inevitably, these conversations entailed wider educational issues. For example, when Vanderzell concluded that the history department could be cut from nine to eight positions, Solomon Wank responded that nine was the bare minimum to staff its curriculum. Developed in the expansive 1960s, it emphasized small, specialized seminars; now it required more faculty than could be supported in light of enrollments. Vanderzell thought the department must accept responsibility for the consequences of its curricular decisions. He agreed to set a roster of nine but not to fill one position in the next academic year.[9]

By spring 1971, resignations, retirements, and nonrenewal of contracts cut permanent full-time academic staff from 142 to 135, with another three reductions taking effect at the end of the following year. Administrative and staff positions were reduced by around 10 percent. But two decisions foreshadowed further cuts. First, the Long-Range Planning Council concluded that a smaller student body, around 1,800, would allow better interaction between students and faculty and fit with existing facilities. At a time when the pool of students was expected to shrink, many colleges turned to smaller size to maintain quality. Second, the faculty voted to eliminated the language requirement. In recommending this move, the Curriculum Committee rejected the argument — once a basic tenet of the college's classical curriculum — that foreign language study played a unique and indispensable role in liberal education. The committee considered it "an extremely valuable pursuit" but no more so than other disciplines not required for graduation.[10]

Meanwhile, old governance and students' rights issues remained. Administrators and trustees worked assiduously to create formal guidelines for unrest-related emergencies and to develop ever more elaborate codes of rights and responsibilities, and evaluation and grievance procedures. The proliferation of formal policies and procedures reflected the general paradox that the sixties' demands for greater freedom spawned ever more bureaucracy instead. College leaders refined processes for dealing with student discipline cases, with an eye toward both students' demands for due process and recent court decisions expanding the rights of minors.[11]

The faculty continued to debate how to involve students in decisions about tenure and promotions. In September it instructed the Professional Standards Committee (PSC) to "continue to regard effective teaching as the primary responsibility of every faculty member." After much deliberation, the faculty asked the senate to appoint a student-faculty committee to work with the PSC to develop a procedure for student evaluation of teaching effectiveness. The resulting Committee on Teaching Effectiveness (COTE) prepared a computer-processable questionnaire to gather information about students' opinions. It was first administered the following spring.[12]

Despite its name, COTE members concluded that teaching effectiveness in and of itself was "seemingly so complex, intangible, and idiosyncratic" that it could not be defined in a quantitatively measurable way. There was general agreement, however, that "certain aspects" of "teaching behavior" could be considered "components" of teaching effectiveness. Thus the committee decided to focus on "the presumably attainable goal of quantifying student opinion about some of the more important of these characteristics." COTE recommended administering the questionnaires in every course each semester, at least for untenured faculty, but making results available only to the dean of the college, PSC, instructors, and department chairmen. Even so, committee members stressed that faculty who used "eccentric" or innovative teaching methods might receive low ratings according to the criteria and still be effective "in their own unique fashion."[13]

The Committee on Educational Goals, formed the previous spring as part of the college's response to student unrest, had been hard at work. Its charge was to prepare a general statement of the college's objectives, an analysis of how well its graduation requirements related to them, and an evaluation of "any apparent contradictory thrusts." It ultimately identified "some broad areas of agreement" about the present state of affairs in higher education but not surprisingly agreed on few specific recommendations. Instead, most of the report was devoted to an insightful and even-handed account of the recent history of liberal arts education. It outlined the rise of a university college ethos at Franklin & Marshall, an ethos that emphasized preparation for graduate school over more traditional notions of broadening and humanizing students and developing their critical faculties. This shift had been caused by the faculty's "increasing professionalism and research orientation" as well as the fact that growing numbers of college graduates went on to graduate schools — more than two-thirds of Franklin & Marshall students in the recent past.[14]

In the 1960s this "preprofessional consensus" had come under attack from junior faculty who rejected its ideals of value-free objectivity and from a new generation of students. The report characterized this generation as possessing "little internal motivation for rigorous academic study" and lacking "habits of perseverance, diligence, and self-reliance which are necessary if motivation is not too well developed." Demanding greater "relevance," the students had allied with disaffected junior faculty. On the one hand, the report charged, "In terms of substance, relevance often means 'self-centeredness.' Students want to study what they want to study at times and in a manner that they choose." On the other, professionally oriented faculty often "emotionally rejected out of hand" such attempts at change as "proposals for ungraded courses, field work, and a de-emphasis of reading and writing"—seeing them only as leading to a "lowering of standards." Now the collapse in demand for Ph.D.s heightened the need to reconsider the college's goals.[15]

As for conclusions, the Committee on Educational Goals asserted that "no committee *selected* to represent disparate educational philosophies could be expected to reach unanimity upon the issue of goals, and then have their conclusions accepted by a faculty representing an even wider array of such philosophies." They identified three options: to continue the present "acrid" debates, to seek to impose a single view "by naked power," or to find some way to achieve "peaceful coexistence." They recommended the third, along with "controlled experimentation" with alternatives to "the modal preprofessional curriculum." Some way to offset the power of departments and preprofessionalism was needed to ensure that the college offered "the liberalizing influence of an undergraduate liberal arts institution."[16]

Meanwhile, the college's financial stringencies removed some of the faculty's most vociferous proponents of experimentation, as the contracts of several were not renewed and others were denied tenure. In addition, Gerald Enscoe resigned to join the faculty of a new experimental college. In the spring, Henry Mayer, who had taught his own courses off campus as student-funded "People's Professor," announced plans to return to California.[17]

Planning Collectively for Retrenchment

Despite previous cuts, the budget for the following year showed a widening deficit, while the board instructed Spalding to present a balanced budget for the year after that. The effort to do so began with the new senate Budget Priorities Committee (BPC), using a procedure developed at Princeton University to ensure that budgets accurately reflected institutional objectives. In response to faculty complaints about lack of involvement in decisions, the senate's Committee on Committees recommended beginning the process of setting budget priorities by convening a broadly based group somewhere off campus at the beginning of the 1971–1972 academic year. The result was the "Poconos Conference" — a phrase that came to stand for a wrenching retrenchment that haunted the memories of a generation of surviving faculty. The Committee on Committees invited thirty-three students, faculty, and administrators to attend a two-and-a-half-day conference. Vanderzell and his new assistant, A. Richard Kneedler, planned the agenda. (Kneedler, an assistant professor of French, was one of several in departments vulnerable to cutbacks who moved into the administration in this period.)[18]

An unexpected shortfall in new enrollments that fall intensified the sense of urgency. Applications had declined slightly from the previous year, leading to an increase in the proportion admitted. Of even more concern, the "yield," or percentage of admitted students who actually enrolled, declined from nearly half in previous years to 29 percent. Admissions officers attributed these changes to increased competition among institutions for a decreasing number of suitable students and to the fact that many were turning to less expensive public schools.[19]

The Poconos Conference opened by discussing the college's goals, missions, and objectives and then took up its present financial predicament; higher education's "big

picture" for the next two decades; and the "PPBS" method of programming, planning, and budgeting. Attendees divided into groups charged with formulating solu-
tions to Franklin & Marshall's current problems. Deliberations were framed by one
overriding imperative: to cut around half a million dollars from the operating base to
achieve a balanced budget. The task was given heightened intensity by the admonition that many private colleges would not survive the present financial crisis and projected decline in college-age population. Of the five "models" produced, Vanderzell
observed a common theme: Franklin & Marshall should maintain and strengthen
"those areas necessary to a liberal education" and preserve distinctive areas. Nevertheless, each model offered different definitions of liberal education's "core disciplines."
For example, some considered physics, religion, or sociology essential; others saw them
as peripheral. And though all the models recommended eliminating one or more
"weak" departments, these differed from group to group.[20]

Excerpts from conference proceedings were distributed to the entire college community; these formed the basis for deliberations that would in turn guide the Committee on Budget Priorities' conclusions. Issues were debated in the *College Reporter* and
in many public meetings. The conference's report was met with much skepticism, even
hostility in some quarters. Some disliked Spalding's insistence that he alone control
the nonacademic budget, not trusting his promise to do there "the same harshly candid
evaluations of service functions and performance." Skepticism about the reality of the
financial crisis prompted Spalding to distribute more detailed budget statements.[21]

The ad hoc AAUP Committee on Alternative Budgetary Models headed by Charles
Holzinger marshaled "a week's intensive effort" by some forty-five faculty members to
develop an alternative model, dubbed "Model F." The committee rejected further reductions in faculty, arguing that priority be given to academic excellence — defined in
terms of both "effective instruction" and the present range of programs. It noted that
Franklin & Marshall's student-faculty ratio was already higher than its comparison
colleges and that its administrative expenses were above the average in a recent study
of forty-eight private colleges. It proposed reducing the deficit by cutting positions in
admissions; public relations; alumni and college development; evening, summer school,
and special studies programs; and academic computing. It argued that some forty faculty could assume these duties on top of their teaching — in effect returning to the way
things had been done before the college's postwar expansion.[22]

Ultimately, the Curriculum and the Budget Priorities committees rejected "wholesale elimination" of departments in favor of cutting positions to even out workload
inequities, particularly where dropping requirements had reduced enrollments. The
Committee on Budget Priorities concluded that "to survive we must be a quality institution, not only academically but in all phases of the College's life." It rejected increasing
revenues by raising tuition or admitting more students, because of potential damage
to student quality. Its "most agonizing decision" was to recommend only a small sum
for salary increases — particularly regrettable given the inroads inflation was making
in purchasing power. It hoped that introduction of a January term in 1973 would provide opportunities to earn additional income and spur curricular experimentation.[23]

Not all faculty were convinced. Many of those who spoke at a faculty meeting on the reports challenged assumptions "that the budget must be balanced and that the enrollment picture was gloomy." Speaking for the board, Arthur Sinkler stressed its belief that continued deficits were "a sure road to ruin." When some faculty complained that the BPC had not taken account of Model F, Leon Galis explained that the committee "was not confident that any random forty faculty members would have the expertise to move effectively into any but the most routine tasks." It saw little sense in cuts in admissions or development "when competition for both students and income [were growing] keener." Pointing to the severe administrative cuts already recommended, Galis commented, "One of the most startling things, in fact, that our Committee has to report is that, contrary to popular belief, administrators are absolutely indistinguishable from faculty members with respect to their capacity for suffering pain." BPC chairman John Moss showed a similar perspective when he thanked Sinkler for attending the faculty meeting: "In my, maybe cynical, point of view, we have on our hands at the College a group of vociferous faculty members who put their concept of the well being of the faculty before the best interests of the College as a whole."[24]

The final version of the budget released in April balanced income and expenses at more than $8.7 million. It marked completion of the transition to a cash basis, with help from a record $451,000 in unrestricted gifts raised in 1971. Total salaries were cut more than 6 percent, 5.7 percent in instructional and 8.5 percent in administration and staff. Because of the unpredictability in admissions, tuition remained unchanged.[25]

It had been a wrenching process, but most of the community seemed to accept the retrenchment. "If the College hadn't already had a rather robust governance system," Richard Kneedler commented later, "it would have been very hard for managers to make the necessary cuts." But "the dominant number [of faculty] . . . understood the stakes" and agreed that it was important to protect the endowment. Having worked for many years to make the college "modern," most agreed about the need for a professional administration. The idea of faculty taking on administrative work was "very romantic," but "most of the faculty didn't think it was a good idea." For Kneedler, who had just joined the administration, "it was a great time to learn. You could see a culture forming around certain values."[26]

The administration's urgency in pursuing a balanced budget was to some extent explained when the board subsequently announced a $6 million fund-raising campaign. "By meticulous planning and stringent recasting of budgets," Spalding stated, "we have overcome the fiscal crisis and have established a stable financial base for forward planning." Efforts could now resume "to maintain Franklin & Marshall in the front rank of liberal arts colleges." The campaign sought gifts not to cover deficits — an approach unlikely to succeed with most donors — but "to invest in a healthy institution to assure a dynamic future." With retirement of its chairman, Robert Sarnoff, the board elected Charles A. Siegfried, '30, former president of the Metropolitan Life Insurance Company and a trustee since 1967.[27]

Aptly titled "The Quality Dimension," the campaign focused on enriching student life. Improvements included $2.8 million for the long-wished-for college center and $1 million for extracurricular programs. Facilities for publications, film, radio, television, and conferences, and workshops for art, music and crafts, would make the center a focal point for activities to encourage student and faculty interactions outside "traditional classroom boundaries." Director of development John Synodinos stressed that the center was necessary to compete with the college's peer liberal arts institutions. Similarly, Charles Siegfried emphasized that Franklin & Marshall "must maintain, and even improve upon, its traditional concern for the individual student and his problems whether intellectual, emotional or social." The college could justify higher tuition costs only on the basis of "superior quality" in all areas.[28]

Even so, the retrenchment hurt student and faculty morale. Returning from a meeting of the American Association of Higher Education, Spalding told the overseers that Franklin & Marshall's innovations in areas such as budgeting, governance, and curriculum were recognized by leaders in the field, but on campus there was a general air of negativity. A sense of malaise persisted, reflected in reluctance to risk innovations that might be too costly or trigger departmental rostering.[29]

In the fall, fearing that the college was reneging on its commitments to minority students, members of the Afro-American Society presented a list of fourteen demands to Vanderzell. When they saw little progress after a month, some forty members of the group protested by staging a five-hour sit-in in Spalding's office. The Student Conduct Committee, made up of four students and three faculty, concluded that their actions violated the college statement barring "disruptions of academic process"; the committee imposed disciplinary probation against the Afro-American Society and admonished Spalding for failing to immediately inform students that they were violating college policy.[30]

Among the most visible radicals remaining on campus, four students who were opposed to faculty cuts attempted to counter the college's "rosy PR image" by presenting their own version to a group of prospective students and parents at an admissions meeting. The group — Jack Sanders, Walter Clebowicz, Barry Eberly, and Dick Heus, inevitably dubbed the "F&M Four"— were called before the Student Conduct Committee. They appeared with attorneys, who raised due process issues. This stymied proceedings because the committee did not follow an adversarial system. After extended negotiation and debate, the committee concluded that the four had not violated rules regarding academic disruptions.[31]

During the initial hearing, a crowd of students — one wearing a clown suit — gathered outside the building to protest. A few climbed onto the roof and attempted to "harass the whole procedure." The rude behavior of some students toward college officials and student committee members prompted criticism of college officials for allowing "bad manners and filthy mouths" to replace "rational discourse and the free exchange of ideas." "It is time to extricate ourselves from the jungle of bureaucratic procedures which confuse rights with license and boorish behavior with moral conscience," demanded English professor Sanford Pinsker.[32]

Noting his responsibility to the board for the orderly conduct of the college's affairs, Spalding called for revisions to the disciplinary system. To avoid a legalistic process, the senate approved a plan that made a pool of faculty available to advise students charged with violations. Even so, Spalding warned, "The simple overarching fact is that without goodwill, civility, the acceptance of the legitimacy of agencies of the College and the credibility of the processes under which they operate, a collegial approach to the governance of the affairs of the College is not possible."[33]

Failing to kindle a campuswide movement against rostering, dissident students and faculty turned to legal measures. Forming the ad hoc Committee to End Discrimination at Franklin & Marshall College, they filed a formal complaint with the U.S. Department of Labor that Franklin & Marshall had failed to comply with federal hiring standards regarding women and blacks. The complaint was ultimately dismissed, but Spalding recognized the college's vulnerability on the issue. Overseers had already approved development of affirmative action policies, and the administration had issued directives encouraging the hiring of women and minorities. But retrenchment cut those most recently hired, which included a disproportionate number in these categories. The senate formed the Committee on Minority and Women's Affairs, and the secretary of the college's office assumed responsibility for personnel administration.[34]

Several years without significant pay increases sparked interest in unionization. The local AAUP chapter invited a spokesman from the Pennsylvania division to discuss collective bargaining and later established a committee to study the subject. The Pennsylvania State Education Association launched a drive to organize non-teaching employees. Lancaster was well known for resistance to unions, but unequal medical benefits offered staff and professional employees and the moratorium on salary increases aided the organization effort, particularly among nonclerical workers. Hoping to forestall unionization, the administration promised to improve conditions. Elections in June succeeding in unionizing only a small group of lab technicians. In the fall overseers approved raises for staff as of the beginning of 1973 and appropriations for improved medical benefits in the next fiscal year's budget.[35]

Focused Improvements in a World of Scarcity

With the achievement of a balanced budget, the college returned to a more leisurely pace of activity than it had seen for many years. During the summer of 1972 Spalding was finally able to take a three-month leave that been postponed because of the financial crisis. The leave was supported by a Danforth Foundation program aimed at giving college and university administrators a chance to reflect on broad issues in education.[36]

Franklin & Marshall had managed to achieve what one educational analyst called a "fragile stability," but its leaders recognized that the new "steady state" in higher education required rethinking mission and practices. Many feared that without regular infusions of new faculty, stability might mean intellectual stultification and institutional ossification. Having a high proportion of faculty in the upper ranks might also present financial difficulties. These concerns prompted the overseers to raise the idea of a moratorium on tenure. Already 62 percent of faculty were tenured; if promotions were offered at the present rate, in five years the proportion would rise to 85 percent. Lafayette College had recently instituted a cap on tenure, and the overseers instructed Spalding, Vanderzell, and the PSC to recommend how the college could avoid becoming overtenured — with the veiled threat that the overseers might otherwise "be unwilling to consider further recommendations" for tenure. The PSC's response was delayed for more than a year and a half to include results of several major studies — one of twelve Pennsylvania colleges (including Franklin & Marshall) by the Institute for Educational Development, and another by a joint AAUP and American Council on Education Commission on Academic Tenure in Higher Education. Both studies affirmed tenure's central role in higher education but recommended changes in practice. Likewise, the PSC argued against quotas but admitted that "institutional and departmental concerns" might occasionally warrant denying tenure when a department was close to becoming fully tenured. It recommended periodic reviews of tenured faculty. Reassured, trustees agreed to leave the matter in the hands of the dean and the PSC.[37]

Meanwhile, tenure had already become a more elusive prize. Where 94 percent of candidates coming up for tenure between 1967 and 1970 had succeeded, the proportion fell to 56 percent over the next five years, with only three of nine receiving tenure in 1973. The proportion of tenured faculty peaked at 68 percent in 1973–1974 and began to decline. In future, as supply of Ph.D.s continued to exceed demand, expectations of excellence in both scholarship and teaching mounted. Although the PSC's tenure deliberations were at times difficult and controversial, its rigor was sustained by the central role that the committee had come to play in the faculty's culture. In an increasingly litigious environment its procedures were repeatedly refined to ensure due process. Some faculty expressed concern that quantitative measures like numbers of publications and COTE scores played too large a role. Revisiting the issues several years later, the faculty amended PSC guidelines to underline the importance of scholarly publication while giving credit for curricular innovation and interdisciplinary efforts.[38]

For the rest of the decade the college worked to balance conflicting demands to control spending and enhance quality. Amid rapidly rising general inflation, leaders hesitated to undertake innovations that expanded the budget base. But they supported interdisciplinary programs, such as those in environmental studies and American and European studies, that promised to enrich the curriculum without creating new departments. By 1975 the financial situation had improved sufficiently to allow creation of a few "reserve positions." Even so, no opening was automatically filled; each position had to be justified anew.[39]

The otherwise lean 1972–1973 budget included the "Academic Innovation Fund" to support faculty development and projects to improve the learning environment. With a planning grant from the National Endowment for the Humanities, the college launched its experimental Humanities Interdisciplinary Enrichment Program in 1973. Participants were given reduced course loads to audit courses outside their disciplines and participated in a summer faculty seminar. The immediate goal was fostering new interdisciplinary courses and improving existing ones, but the broader goal was to encourage intellectual exchange across departmental lines. A $250,000 grant for humanities programs from the Andrew W. Mellon Foundation supported further interdisciplinary efforts, including formation of a long-desired program in the history and philosophy of science.[40]

The administration faced the same balancing act between fiscal restraint and quality. Faculty often complained about growth in nonacademic staff, but in many cases these staff members provided services necessary to enrich student life — and unlike most faculty, they could be let go if financial conditions required it. Spalding frequently reorganized his administration in the interest of efficiency and flexibility. Under Spalding the college continued to pay close attention to new developments in the wider world of higher education management, and he sent executive officers to Harvard Business School's Institute for Educational Management.[41]

Spalding charged a special committee of the Board of Visitors to evaluate the administration's efficiency. Headed by William Bevan, an alumnus and trustee and former provost of Johns Hopkins, the committee concluded that the college was generally well managed. The committee pointed out that much of the increase in administrative costs stemmed from federal social legislation, health and safety regulations, and overhead costs for grants. It recommended some organizational changes, particularly elevating the role of the dean of the college, and expressed concern that the governance system gave students too much power over curriculum and personnel. When Richard P. Traina succeeded Vanderzell as dean of the college in 1974, another administrative reorganization expanded his control over academic and extracurricular affairs.[42]

Spalding and the board followed conservative fiscal policies aimed at protecting the college from economic fluctuations. A series of lean budgets produced substantial surpluses, which were moved into reserves for instructional expenses and capital improvements and later transferred into unrestricted endowment as a cushion against adversity. Spalding worked closely with the senate's Committee on Budget Priorities to educate it about the need for fiscal restraint. Using computer models showing three-year outcomes of budget decisions, the committee kept a close watch on the long-term expansion of the budget. After the stock market plunged in 1974, the board added an additional layer of financial security by recycling endowment income as had been done for annual giving. The 1975–1976 budget was based on endowment income earned in the preceding calendar year.[43]

Large operating surpluses were mainly due to enrollments that exceeded estimates. Admissions officers responded to faculty complaints by explaining that fluctuating yield rates made it hard to control enrollment numbers precisely. Later budgets stressed raising faculty salaries so that levels returned to the median of the twenty-college comparison group. The overseers formally reaffirmed commitment to the parity system in 1975, in response to faculty pressure to follow the consumer price index instead.[44]

Overseers held increases in tuition and fees to the general rate of inflation. Between 1973–1974 to 1977–1978, tuition and fees grew more than 40 percent, to $3,780. Even so, the cost of attending Franklin & Marshall was significantly below most of its twenty comparison colleges: in 1977–1978 it stood sixteenth in tuition and fees and seventeenth in total costs. Its costs were also low relative to a separate list of "competitive" colleges and universities — those with whom it competed most directly for students.[45]

Applications declined slightly over the decade, as numbers of students graduating from high school began to ebb in the mid-1970s. Yet they did so less than at many other schools, and Franklin & Marshall was able to fill large classes without discernible decline in quality as reflected in SAT scores and class rankings. As a result, the college increased its relative selectivity; a 1977 study of private colleges by education researcher Alexander Astin listed Franklin & Marshall as a "very highly selective" college.[46]

Yet it was clear that the college needed substantial physical improvements to compete for students. The long-deferred College Center project was seen as especially crucial. Existing student facilities were poor — the grill in Campus House had to be closed in 1973 when it failed to meet federal OSHA safety standards, and with its brick-on-timber construction, Hartman Hall was widely acknowledged to be a firetrap. There was considerable pride that the new center had been designed by the Minoru Yamasaki firm, now gaining increased renown for New York's World Trade Center. To be built of brick — brown rather than the ubiquitous red — the building's modern lines were a marked departure from the neo-Colonial style that had dominated campus for half a century. Inside, a spacious two-story atrium provided a focal point for rooms designed for a wide range of cocurricular functions. Ground was finally broken in October 1973.[47]

Even as the college remained on a tight budget, funds were found for one-time investments to improve quality. The overseers used some of the 1972–1973 surplus for a cultural affairs endowment fund for on-campus programs. Funds were set aside to celebrate the Green Room's seventy-fifth anniversary with a gala performance of Bertolt Brecht and Kurt Weill's *The Threepenny Opera* at the Fulton Theater in downtown Lancaster. Renewed attention was paid to the condition of buildings and the appearance of the campus, both of which had suffered from years of deferred maintenance. Extensive beautification work in 1975 included restoration of the brick entry gate in front of Old Main, supported by a fund in memory of trustee Henry J. Marshall. To recognize his extensive service to the college, it was rechristened the Henry J. Marshall Gate.[48]

Plans for new buildings made in the expansive 1960s were shelved in the more constrained economic conditions of the 1970s. Instead, as the coming U.S. bicentennial spurred appreciation of the nation's heritage, Franklin & Marshall awoke to the value — economic, historic, and aesthetic — of preservation. The college's heritage was an important component of a "development strategy" that Spalding outlined in 1975. It involved limiting overhead and emphasizing the campus's "historic character" by consolidating operations in fewer and — in light of rising energy costs — more efficient buildings. The original three buildings were placed on the National Register of Historic Places and refurbished. Goethean Hall became home to the government department and was renamed the John C. Kunkel Center for the Study of Government. Old Main was extensively renovated to serve as the college's administrative center. The Green Room Theatre and older dormitories were refurbished. With completion of the College Center in mid-1976, Campus House was turned into offices and renamed Distler Hall in honor of the president emeritus. Hartman Hall, however, was not suitable for restoration, and the College Center had been sited so close to East Hall that the latter building could not be preserved. These buildings were razed and replaced by large expanses of lawn. The former site of Hartman Hall was rededicated as Hartman Green; that of East Hall was later renamed Spalding Plaza.[49]

New Challenges to Liberal Education

Nationwide it was a time of reassessment in higher education. The tightened economy of the 1970s revived questions about whether colleges should focus on general intellectual development or more specific preparation for careers or professions. Spalding told the board that students were under external pressure from a "public predisposition toward career education, and public policy which favors vocational education." The U.S. commissioner of education cajoled small private colleges to "roll with the times," and some less-selective colleges added vocationally oriented programs. As opportunities for academic careers declined, many students shifted to medicine, law, and business; enrollments in business, economics, psychology, and government rose dramatically, while those in modern languages fell by half. Two consequences were elimination of the Russian Area Studies program and merger of the German and Russian departments. The senate imposed regulations to block students attempting to use the Central Pennsylvania Consortium to take vocationally oriented courses not offered at the college.[50]

Franklin & Marshall's continued strength in the sciences produced some confusion regarding its identity as a liberal arts institution. It boasted an impressive record in placing premedical students — during the later 1960s, 86 percent of approved students were admitted to at least one medical school, while the national average was 45 percent. Even after coeducation, applicants continued to be disproportionately interested in pre–healing arts programs. In 1972, for example, more than 3,400 applied for some 550 places in the freshman class. Of these, 44 percent sought the 160 places reserved for pre–healing arts majors. Some on the faculty and the board argued that the college should build on this reputation and expand these enrollments, but Spalding opposed the idea. "To emphasize vocationalism in the Franklin and Marshall program at the expense of the contributions which the humanities, social sciences and sciences can make to the growth and maturing of an individual irrespective of professional interests," he argued, "would be to distort and ultimately destroy the unique, utilitarian legacy which the liberal arts can provide for any student."[51]

The strength of the College's pre–healing arts program was in many ways a by-product of its excellence in the pure sciences. Science faculty and students regularly received research grants at a rate equal to the most prestigious private colleges and all but the top research universities. In 1970 the National Science Foundation continued its tradition of supporting Franklin & Marshall's science programs by awarding a second COSIP grant of $240,000 — making it the first college in the nation to receive a second COSIP. The following year, chemistry professor Claude Yoder, '60, received a substantial Teacher Scholar Grant from the Dreyfus Foundation, the only one so recognized who was not teaching at a Ph.D.-granting institution. Attesting to the college's strength in the sciences, a 1975 report by the National Academy of Sciences on the undergraduate origins of Ph.D.s found Franklin & Marshall third in the nation in the number of graduates between 1920 and 1973 who earned doctorates in the physical sciences. It ranked second in earth sciences — and first in the preceding five years. When all Ph.D.s were considered, the college stood nineteenth among private undergraduate colleges.[52]

Seeking greater balance in the curriculum and student body, college leaders hoped to strengthen humanities programs while supporting continued excellence in the sciences. They received financial assistance from the new National Endowment for the Humanities (NEH), which, though modest by NSF standards, played a growing role in higher education in the 1970s. Humanities faculty regularly received NEH grants for summer and sabbatical research. A NEH planning grant sparked cooperation among humanities and social sciences faculty, which produced interdisciplinary programs in American and European studies that were launched in 1975. A new program in the history and philosophy of science was aided by a large grant from the Andrew W. Mellon Foundation.[53]

Franklin & Marshall leaders continued to speak out about the importance of liberal education, now with attention to the dangers of professionalization. In a Phi Beta Kappa address delivered soon after his appointment as dean, Richard Traina acknowledged tension between the general "formative" dimension of liberal studies and the "graduate education model" of education focused on specialized disciplines and methods. "If any generation of scholars can be said to have helped make liberal arts campuses grim places," he confessed, "it was probably mine": "We brought graduate style training to the undergraduate level, reduced questions to those answerable in 'objective' terms, and all too commonly bored our students to tears. Many of us have spent much of our energies over the past few years groping to find our way out of that dead-end street." Traina urged his colleagues to consider how to restore crucial dimensions of liberal education, such as the central role of "synthesizing, integrating, and bridge-building skills," "sensitivity to values," and recognition that students "need each other to maintain a socially and intellectually supportive environment."[54]

The college also stressed cocurricular programs to help students make the increasingly difficult postgraduation transition. A full-time placement officer was appointed to develop internship opportunities. "Project Careers" forums brought alumni in various occupations back to campus to discuss their experiences and how their education helped them in the marketplace. Statesmen and corporate leaders came for extended periods under the aegis of visiting fellow programs sponsored by the Woodrow Wilson and Metropolitan Life foundations. The January semester in 1977 experimented with an internship program in which sixty alumni and friends of the college hosted undergraduates. Spalding also hoped that noncredit programs offered at the College Center would fulfill student demands for "nonacademic" courses.[55]

To an unusual degree, Franklin & Marshall resisted a nationwide trend toward grade inflation — often to the dismay of students, who protested that they were handicapped in competition for graduate schools and fellowships. Students also complained about overcrowding caused by the college's retrenchment. Class sizes increased markedly, particularly in the most popular, career-friendly majors. Repeated "overenrollments" pushed the student body over 2,000 for the first time in the college's history — more than 2,100 in the fall of 1975. College facilities were strained beyond their capacities. The library functioned as both social hub and study center, neither entirely satisfactorily. During the later 1960s, fewer students had wanted to live in campus dormitories, but demand revived in the 1970s. Upperclassmen were dismayed to discover that they weren't guaranteed space in the dormitories. Nonetheless, Spalding repeatedly resisted calls for another dormitory because construction costs were rising uncontrollably, and he did not want to saddle the college with expensive space that changing student tastes might make unnecessary. He told the overseers that his goal was to put the college in a position in which it could "in case of economic crisis" survive with an enrollment as low as 1,200.[56]

Campus Life Revives — with Some Changes

Even so, the mood on campus improved as the decade progressed. Returning from his leave in the fall of 1972, Spalding observed that students were "more reasonable in thought and attitude." They combined "a sense of humor" and "deep earnestness about their studies" with "interests which traditionally have attracted adolescents." Two years later he enthused to his friend Graeme Smith about "the dramatic change in the nature of young people" attending Franklin & Marshall: "They have 'gone young' again. . . . They are winsome, charming, handsome children and they don't even mind admitting their childhood status. They are remarkably at ease and relaxed in our company." They were also, he continued, "of course very full of certitude" and quick to rebel. Rebellion could involve violence against property, particularly when students felt they were being "ripped off" — such as the spring evening in 1973 when three malfunctioning soda machines were sent flying over dormitory balconies.[57]

In fact, even as they expressed anxiety about careers, many students seem to rediscover the idea that college should be fun. The return of playfulness was reflected in students' creation of the First Annual F and M Spring Games in May 1973. An afternoon of such competitions as cage ball, tug-of-war, and capture the flag climaxed with a chaotic "marathon relay" involving large quantities of pie, shaving cream, balloons, and beer. With the addition of a beer-drinking contest, the games took place for several years under IFC sponsorship. But the new mood on campuses nationwide was most vividly symbolized by the "streaking" fad, which hit Franklin & Marshall in a big way on a March weeknight in 1974. The antics of more than one hundred fleet-footed nude students were reported by local television and campus radio.[58]

More traditional aspects of college life also returned to favor. Under head coach Robert Curtis, the football team excelled in the 1970s as it had not done in several decades, winning the Middle Atlantic Conference (MAC) Southern Division championship four years in a row between 1971 and 1974 and again in 1976, going undefeated in 1971, 1972, and 1974. It received the 1972 Lambert Bowl for the most outstanding performance by a small college in the East, though injuries forced the team to decline an invitation to play in the Knute Rockne Bowl. Students celebrated their teams' success in traditional ways, such as tearing down a goalpost at the end of the Muhlenberg game that clinched the title in 1971.[59]

Student athletes excelled in other sports, reviving under new academic conditions Franklin & Marshall's long winning tradition. Men's soccer garnered numerous titles in this period, including four MAC Southwest championships in a row between 1975 and 1978. In 1977 the cross-country team went undefeated and won its first MAC title; the following year runners Eric Holmboe and Brian Goss were named to the Division III All-American team. In 1975 the men's basketball team won the MAC Southern Division championship for the first time in more than twenty years, plus an invitation to the National Collegiate Athletic Association (NCAA) Division III national tournament. Continuing its winning ways, the team finished third in the national NCAA tournament in 1978. Donald Marsh capped an outstanding career by capturing numerous All-American and MVP awards. In 1978 three wrestlers won invitations to the Eastern Intercollegiate Wrestling Association tournament, and two advanced to the NCAA championship. Men's swimming, tennis, and track teams also regularly brought home conference titles.[60]

Moreover, despite a general belief at the advent of coeducation that women were not interested in athletics, Franklin & Marshall women proved avid and successful athletes. By 1976 the college had women's varsity teams in field hockey, volleyball, swimming, lacrosse, tennis, basketball, and squash. There were eight other club sports, of which several were later upgraded to varsity level. In 1975 the basketball team narrowly lost the MAC title, and the following year the field hockey team became the college's first women's team to win a league title, when it captured the Penn-Mar championship, followed by the MAC title; the team repeated the feat the following year. In 1978 women captured the MAC Southwest basketball title, and Wendy Stabolepszy was named conference most valuable player. As a freshman Trink Prinz became the college's first All-American woman swimmer. Still, female athletes had to deal with unequal facilities and equipment and the lack of full-time coaches or women trainers. Complaints met pleas of limited finances and space.[61]

At several points in the 1970s, Spalding reaffirmed the college's desire for a comprehensive intercollegiate, intramural, and recreational athletic program. He acknowledged that in an "increasingly organized and specialized" world, students came to college with substantial experience in organized sports and a desire to continue to compete at a high level. But he resented governing sports organizations that tried to impose complicated, expensive, and often irrelevant rules more suited to major university programs. NCAA had recently formed new divisions, placing most schools, like Franklin & Marshall, that did not offer athletic scholarships in Division III. The college obtained permission to continue wrestling in Division I, where most of its traditional rivals were located. But Spalding resisted Middle Atlantic Conference efforts to compel schools to participate in postseason championship competitions, because these often conflicted with academic demands and increased danger of player injury. In 1978 he established a requirement that teams petition to participate in postseason competition. When the MAC sought to realign conference football schedules to facilitate identification of a "true champion," Spalding helped initiate a movement to create a separate football conference. The Centennial Conference, composed of Franklin & Marshall, Dickinson, Gettysburg, Johns Hopkins, Muhlenberg, Swarthmore, Ursinus, and Western Maryland, was founded in 1981 and began its first season two years later. Its success in uniting schools with similar athletic philosophies led to expansion into all sports in the early 1990s. The original eight members were joined by Bryn Mawr, Haverford, and Washington colleges.[62]

After reaching a low point in the early 1970s, Franklin & Marshall's fraternities also saw a resurgence. Nearly half of freshmen men pledged in 1975, and several chapters that had become moribund were resurrected. Also experiencing a comeback were quaint customs like semiformal dances. "If a fraternity dance is a sufficient harbinger, there seems to be some return to the social graces of the 40's and 50's," Spalding told the overseers in 1973.[63]

Pi Lambda Phi experimented with admitting women, but in 1975 a group of women sought an organization of their own. They lobbied the administration to rescind the ban on sororities imposed at the introduction of coeducation. The overseers complied, recognizing that it was discriminatory to maintain the ban now that fraternities seemed likely to survive. A dozen women formed a Sigma Sigma Sigma chapter in 1977. A second sorority, Alpha Phi, followed in 1981.[64]

Even with increased student interest, Greek organizations faced considerable obstacles. Gradual increase in the proportion of female students reduced the potential pool of fraternity members. With smaller membership rolls, it was hard to maintain aging chapter houses, while stiff local zoning regulations kept fraternities and sororities from obtaining new ones. College authorities largely remained aloof from the situation, but they did help Zeta Beta Tau's attempt to re-establish itself in 1975 by agreeing to lease one of its houses on College Avenue — and fighting a lengthy legal battle with the zoning board for the right to do so.[65]

Fraternities' increased popularity seemed due less to a renewed appreciation for small-group bonding than to their reputation for partying. To aid in competition for members, once-exclusive parties were opened to the entire community and armed with ample supplies of alcohol. The loud and undisciplined affairs that often resulted further antagonized local residents and accelerated the physical deterioration of the houses. After repeated instances of "declining regard for behavioral amenities," Lambda Chi Alpha's chapter was put on probation when seven members went on a rampage on campus in May 1974. In 1975 the Student Rules Committee and the Inter-fraternity Council developed a new pledge training code as part of a never-ending quest to regulate the pledging process.[66]

Despite the resilience of old ways, the advent of coeducation changed many aspects of Franklin & Marshall student culture forever. Belatedly, the overseers in 1976 approved revision of the lyrics of the alma mater: where since 1909 the fourth line had begun "as loyal sons and true," it now read "as sons and daughters true."[67]

Although not reverting to pre-1960s levels, numbers of African American and Hispanic students did not grow as had been hoped, remaining under 4 percent of the student body for most of the period. PREP was discontinued after the end of its tenth summer session in 1973, because its leaders believed its approach had outlived its effectiveness. As for admissions, Spalding told overseers that experience had shown it unwise to admit students who were not well prepared for the college's level of academic work. In 1977 the College Senate narrowly rejected a proposal by its Committee on Minority and Women's Affairs to set a goal of 6 percent African American and Hispanic students; many disliked the idea of formal quotas. As at many other colleges, admissions added staff specifically charged with recruiting minority students, and succeeded in reaching 4.7 percent with the freshman class enrolling in 1980. But, as in other areas, schools with greater prestige and larger endowments won the competition for minority students, especially because they offered more attractive aid packages. In the absence of a substantial minority presence, administrators hoped to help rectify the "unthinking racism" of many white students by integrating racial issues into academic courses and cocurricular programs.[68]

Efforts to increase numbers of women and minorities on the faculty and staff showed limited success. In 1972 the overseers ordered that greater attention be paid to equity and equal opportunity in hiring, within constraints "peculiar to institutions of higher learning" as well as "the financial pressures operating on the College." In 1974 overseers formally adopted an equal opportunity policy. More women, African Americans, and Hispanics were hired, but many did not stay long. For example, women comprised 49 percent of administrators and 27 percent of faculty hired between 1972 and 1980, and minorities 11 percent and 2 percent respectively. But by 1980 many had left, in part because many faculty were hired for one-year positions. In 1980 only 9 percent of regular faculty were women, while four of nine visiting appointments and five of the thirteen adjunct positions were held by women. Consequently, the percentage of women among total faculty increased only from 9 to 12 percent during this period, and minority numbers declined. Moreover, Spalding noted that the college tended to hire administrators and staff at the entry level. After they gained a few years' experience, promising people often moved on to "larger, prestigious universities" that offered greater opportunity. He pointed to the example of a black alumnus who had been hired away by an "Ivy League institution" after two years in the financial aid office.[69]

As the college celebrated the nation's bicentennial in 1976 and began to look toward its own in 1987, it took pride in recent achievements. In the spring the long-awaited College Center opened; the following year it became the Steinman College Center in recognition of contributions from the James Hale Steinman Foundation and John F. Steinman Foundation. The centerpiece of bicentennial events was the world premier of *Buchanan Dying*, John Updike's play based on a biography by Franklin & Marshall alumnus and former faculty member Philip Shriver Klein. Despite its rather grim depiction of the last days of the former president in retirement at nearby Wheatland, college leaders had dreamed of a Green Room production from the moment of the work's publication as a "closet drama" in 1974. Edward S. Brubaker, '49, directed and Peter Vogt, '66, returned from New York to take the demanding leading role. Thrilled to participate in an original production, student thespians were excited but nervous when Updike attended a rehearsal. At the opening night reception at Wheatland, Updike acknowledged having gotten "quite carried up with" the production.[70]

Another Look at the Curriculum

Remaining challenges were highlighted by an extensive self-study in advance of the next Middle States Association's evaluation. The three-hundred-page report pointed to recurrent concerns: curriculum, governance, conditions in the library and classroom buildings, and inadequate endowment. After visiting in November 1977, the Middle States team complimented recent advances while affirming the need to address problems identified in the self-study, especially inadequate library and endowment. Reviewers also questioned whether the curriculum's distribution system was sufficient to ensure a liberal education.[71]

The self-study had provided an opportunity for faculty to voice concerns. Dissatisfaction with the curriculum had been mounting for some time, particularly out of a sense that students were less prepared to do college-level work. But the enduring trauma of rostering made many reluctant to tinker with the status quo. After a series of combative meetings in the fall of 1976, for example, faculty voted down most changes proposed by the Curriculum Committee. It finally acted on concern about the worsening quality of student writing — part of a nationwide decline in verbal skills in the 1970s — by establishing a requirement to "demonstrate proper command and comprehension of the English language." Students could fulfill this by passing a standardized test or college-administered essay or completing a special English course. After much debate about how to improve writing, the faculty agreed that it

was a collegewide responsibility but created a writing center to do much of the remedial work.[72]

Many faculty felt that presence of students in the College Senate confused the faculty's role in governance. But though a 1976 survey of faculty opinion by an ad hoc AAUP
committee underlined unhappiness with the senate-committee system, it also found a
majority opposed to every suggested governance structure. Responses revealed "considerable malaise, uneasiness, or alienation among members of the faculty, especially untenured ones." Seeing no mandate, the committee advised against major changes.[73]

Following Middle States recommendations, Spalding proposed faculty-
administration task forces to focus on the education program and learning facilities.
Once more, the college's examination of its curriculum (the first in more than two
decades) coincided with a national reconsideration of general education. Harvard had
recently instituted a new curriculum, which replaced divisional requirements with
required courses in seven general areas of inquiry. After a year of deliberation, Franklin
& Marshall's education task force agreed that current departmental and divisional
categories "no longer provide a defensible basis for determining the components of a
general education." In particular, the categories did not accommodate the growing
number of interdisciplinary programs. In 1980 the final report of the task force proposed replacing the current distribution system with the College Studies Program, which
required nine courses in seven areas: one each in the arts, foreign cultures, historical
studies, literature, and systems of knowledge and belief; and two courses each in scientific inquiry and social analysis. To offer students "a liberating field of vision" wider than
their area of concentration, the committee outlined criteria for each course to ensure
that it fulfilled liberal education goals rather than departmental interests. In addition,
as the "cornerstone" of the curriculum, the final report recommended that all freshmen
take a one-semester course in critical analysis aimed at developing skills in reasoning,
close reading, and writing.[74]

Once more meeting as a committee of the whole, the faculty debated the proposals during fourteen meetings stretching from February through May 1980. In the end,
the faculty adopted the nine-course requirement but rejected the first-year course on
critical analysis as too difficult to implement — largely because few faculty wanted to
teach it.[75]

Conservation and Campus Beautification

Meanwhile, the task force on learning facilities grappled with upgrading buildings
central to the college's humanities programs. Fackenthal Library and Keiper Liberal
Arts had both been largely untouched since their construction in the 1930s. Renovat-
ing them would also improve energy efficiency and meet new regulations for handicapped access. In fact, concerted conservation efforts throughout campus in this period
substantially lowered the college's energy consumption. Work on Keiper was completed in mid-1980 at a cost of about $700,000. Previous plans to build a new library
on the site of Hartman Hall were dropped in favor of expanding the present building.

In keeping with the new emphasis on preservation, priorities were given to "honor the exterior design characteristics of existing buildings" while creating interior space for a "fully modern college library," enlarging reader seating and collection storage and reducing total energy consumption. Much of the additional space was obtained by adding a new wing on the south. The Boston firm of Shepley, Bulfinch, Richardson, and Abbott, which had extensive national experience in college library renovation, was engaged to plan work budgeted at $4.25 million. Overseen by Richard Kneedler, now vice president for administration, the project was completed early in 1983.[76]

Revision of state building codes in the early 1980s made it more feasible to preserve older buildings, prompting the board to reconsider a previous decision to tear down Stahr Hall. Instead, it now planned extensive renovations to provide more faculty offices and a new audiovisual learning center. In this period the college also installed a campuswide telephone system and a new administrative computer and installed more energy-efficient windows throughout campus.[77]

Outside, the quadrangle in front of Old Main was restored to the "quiet scenic area" that it had been in the days before automobiles. Marshall Gate was narrowed to block vehicular traffic and the grounds landscaped to create a "walking campus." New trees were planted throughout campus to replace aging trees and many damaged by severe storms in 1980. "Especially distressing was a twister which destroyed a unique cucumber tree (planted in the mid-1800s) and a linden located in the court fronting Old Main," Spalding informed the overseers.[78]

New Energy on the Board

The Middle States report also stressed that Franklin & Marshall needed a larger endowment to support its aspirations to excellence. No one disagreed — the college had always been chronically underfunded — but no one had yet been able to do much to change the situation. Most of the substantial money raised in Spalding's administration had gone into new programs and physical plant, and in 1975 the endowment stood at $12,591,000 — or $5,773 per student. This per-student amount put it seventeenth on its list of comparison colleges, far below Amherst's $57,956, Swarthmore's $46,408, or Lafayette's $20,379. Seeking to reduce the college's dependence on tuition, the board resolved to add $15 million to endowment over the next twelve years and raise $10 million for physical plant and $25 million for the operating budget.[79]

As the college looked to step up its fund-raising, it was fortunate in attracting a new generation of benefactors. Arthur and Katherine Shadek, parents of students Lawrence, '72, and Katherine, '81, had taken an active interest in college affairs; Arthur joined the board in 1973. The couple first offered a challenge grant of $225,000 to match contributions to the 1975 annual fund, to be used by the president on "projects and ventures of the kind that preserve the essential vitality of the College and its programs."[80]

The following year, William M. Hackman, '39, announced his intention to donate ten thousand shares of stock over a ten-year period. The gift was a vivid illustration of the often-belated returns on an institution's investment in its students. Back in the 1930s Hackman had been the first member of his rural Pennsylvania family to attend college and had majored in chemistry. He allowed the college to use the gift at first to complete financing of the College Center but hoped that it would eventually become an endowed fund to underwrite scholarships for students from small towns or rural areas and for improvements in education, research, and faculty development.[81]

In 1978, under new board chairman L. James Huegel, '38, trustees began to plan the next capital campaign. Led by Aaron J. Martin, '50, a campaign to raise $9 million within four years was launched at the end of 1979. It began auspiciously, with the announcement of matching grants from the NEH and from the Shadeks, a portion of which was earmarked to endow the Arthur and Katherine Shadek Humanities Professorships. This gift had already pushed their contributions to the college above those of any other individual donors in its history, but in 1980 they added to the sum by establishing a fund to support the library's renovations and continuing operations. In recognition, the overseers named the new library wing in their honor; the entire building was renamed the Shadek-Fackenthal Library. By the end of 1982, with substantial grants from the Armstrong Corporation, the Kresge Foundation, Pew Memorial Trust, and the Charles A. Dana, Andrew W. Mellon, and William and Flora Hewlett foundations, the campaign exceeded its overall goal. In the meantime, a series of challenge grants helped spur giving to the annual fund, raising alumni participation from slightly more than 15 percent in 1968 to almost 32 percent in 1978.[82]

New leadership on the board also pressed for improving investment practices as another way to build the endowment, which stood near $13 million in 1979. The Finance Committee, under new chairman William Simeral, '48, decided in mid-1979 to shift responsibility for investment of most of the endowment to outside professionals. The board also agreed in 1982 to take advantage of recent state legislation permitting independent colleges and universities to issue tax-exempt bonds through local higher education authorities. The first bonds were used to refinance internal borrowing for capital improvement projects. The new approach quickly began to show results; by the end of June 1982 the market value of the endowment jumped to more than $19.5 million.[83]

Early in 1982, the overseers acted to make official the de facto separation that had existed for some time between Franklin & Marshall College and the United Church of Christ. Although the college no longer had UCC-elected representatives on the board, it had maintained membership in the UCC's Council for Higher Education. During the 1970s Spalding repeatedly resisted council efforts to develop consortial ties among member institutions; he told the board that he feared increased demands on the college's time and financial resources. Finally, the UCC's General Synod called upon council members in 1982 to participate in a new covenant relationship. Franklin & Marshall's overseers responded that it wished to retain its identity "as an independent and free-standing institution of higher learning" while continuing to acknowledge its historic relationship to the UCC and its predecessors. It hoped that Church officers would recognize a "historically related" category of colleges but "willingly" forswear any claim on UCC resources or interest in active participation in its council.[84]

With so many recent projects near completion, Spalding announced early in 1982 his intention to step down as president at the close of the 1982–1983 academic year. True to his acute sense of strategy, he explained to Huegel that he chose the moment "for reasons of strategic timeliness." A new president would be able to take advantage of the college's upcoming bicentennial to launch new programs: "Clearly the time is right for new, energetic leadership." It was an anticlimactic conclusion to an often tumultuous twenty-year administration that had frequently drawn harsh criticism from faculty members; Spalding's announcement was greeted with universal dismay. Even many erstwhile opponents could not imagine Franklin & Marshall without Spalding in the presidency. Many felt — as Sidney Wise put it at a gala dinner in his honor at Philadelphia's Franklin Institute — that Keith Spalding had always been president of Franklin & Marshall College. An earlier generation of Americans had felt much the same way about U.S. President Franklin D. Roosevelt, Wise quipped, but Spalding had actually been president longer.[85]

CHAPTER THIRTEEN

Enriching Liberal Education, 1983–2002

—⁓—

During the closing decades of the twentieth century, Franklin & Marshall College came to fulfill aspirations first set out in its midcentury emergence as a national liberal arts college, even as it reconfirmed its traditional mission to foster the development of the "whole" student. In contemporary context, this meant offering a wide range of academic subjects, a growing array of cocurricular experiences, and a high-quality residential life. Reduced class sizes and student-teacher ratios and opportunities for independent study and research partnerships worked toward closer student-faculty ties. Curricular revisions restored an emphasis on broad themes in liberal education. The student body became more geographically diverse, including a growing number of international students; women played increasingly prominent roles among students, faculty, and administration, and racial minorities were better represented in the faculty, if not the student body. Even as it enriched the quality of the student experience, the college's leaders strove to attract the quality of student suited to its mission. In the process, the college found itself enmeshed in an increasingly stratified national educational marketplace that often worked to the advantage of the most prestigious and wealthiest institutions.[1]

In Search of Greater Prominence

Among the many changes during Keith Spalding's two decades at Franklin & Marshall had been a transformation in the college's governance. Evidence of this was a joint committee of five trustees, three faculty, and two students appointed to search for a new president-though as the charter stipulated the board had the final say. After a national search, James Lawrence Powell, interim president of Oberlin College, came to campus to meet with representatives of all college constituencies; afterward he was invited to become Franklin & Marshall's twelfth president. An MIT-trained geologist, Powell had served Oberlin as faculty, associate dean, provost, and vice president before becoming its acting president in 1981. He was the first scientist elected to the Franklin & Marshall presidency in nearly half a century.[2]

Arrival of forty-six-year-old Powell in mid-1983 brought new energy to campus. The feeling of forward movement was symbolized by his early call for the college to embrace the personal computer, just emerging as the latest stage in the computer revolution. At his urging, faculty looked at how to integrate computing across the curriculum. One result was a decision to adopt the new Apple Macintosh as the campuswide standard; beginning in 1985 incoming students were "strongly encouraged" to purchase their own, obtainable from the college at a discount. Even so, the college had begun to move in this direction even before Powell's arrival. It had secured a Sloan Foundation grant to encourage development of computer literacy throughout the academic community and offered financial support to faculty wishing to acquire their own personal computers. A new mainframe administration computer freed up terminals and computer time for student use. College leaders nonetheless refused to yield to demands for computer science courses, fearing that they threatened Franklin & Marshall's identity as a liberal arts college.[3]

Powell addressed persistent concerns about the college's reputation, noting that it was less well known than its quality merited. After the turmoil of the 1960s, Spalding had kept a low profile, once confiding to a trustee his ambivalence "about the matter of our having a nationwide public image." He believed that the college was able to do "quietly and discreetly a great many things" that would be more difficult in "the glare of publicity." Yet, as the pool of potential students began to shrink in the 1980s, it was clear that the college needed to work harder to promote itself. It had a national reputation, Powell told the *College Reporter*, "because of its record in producing people who have [gone] on to get Ph.D.s and medical degrees, law degrees and so on." But he wanted to broaden its recruiting area beyond the Northeast.[4]

The principal speaker at Powell's inauguration in March 1984 was Ernest Boyer, president of the Carnegie Foundation for the Advancement of Teaching. As a nationally known expert on higher education, Boyer was well suited to the college's desire to open "an exciting new chapter" in its pursuit of distinction in liberal arts education. He emphasized the importance of "liberal learning" as a process of "seeing connections in all aspects of life." In his own address, Powell laid out plans to strengthen the college's arts programs.[5]

Powell set several new initiatives in motion in his first months in office. To prepare for a capital campaign, he created a task force on facilities planning, chaired by Richard Kneedler. As a newcomer, Powell was particularly sensitive to the "blighted" appearance of Harrisburg Pike, which marked the campus's northern boundary with a mixture of commercial and industrial sites. Kneedler approached owners of the Posey Iron Works, located directly north of the college, about buying frontage land for a buffer strip. He found them eager instead to sell their entire operation. Powell told the overseers that this offered the college "an unusual, probably unique opportunity . . . at once to improve its neighborhood, to protect it from unfriendly future developments, and to provide the site for expansion" in the future. To aid in developing the site and other possible revenue-generating projects, the board created the for-profit John Marshall Investment Corporation.[6]

As he pressed trustees for action, Powell stressed that the college was at a crucial turning point. It was "on the edge of the most elite group of institutions in the nation." But, noting the declining college-age population, he warned, "The next few years will determine whether Franklin and Marshall established itself firmly in the rank of those elite colleges or falls back to the status of a less selective local or regional institution." His first priority was to complete renovation of Stahr Hall, whose rundown condition he deemed "a real detriment" to the quality of educational programs and a threat to maintaining the college's "position among the most favored colleges in the nation." Members of the board stepped forward to ensure funds necessary to launch the project, including a gift of $500,000 from Aaron and Jean Martin. Work began the following spring, with construction on the west side of a large entrance atrium, and was completed in the spring of 1985. In 1988 the building was renamed Stager Hall in recognition of numerous contributions by Henry P. Stager, '32, and Mary B. Stager. A renovated auditorium on the first floor was christened the John Summers Stahr Auditorium, to continue to honor the memory of the former president.[7]

Managing Student Life

Noting that the "quality of student life" had been "a continual subject of discussion" since his arrival, Powell created a commission of trustees, faculty, administrators, students, and alumni to study the issue. "Obviously he has heard the rumors that there is *no* student life on campus," quipped the *College Reporter*. He also directed creation of a student "hangout" in the basement of the Benjamin Franklin dining hall. Dubbed "Ben's Underground," the student-run club opened September of 1984.[8]

The Commission on the Quality of Student Life built upon previous attempts to deal with complaints about social life at the college and the related issue of Greek organizations. As did many other colleges and universities, Franklin & Marshall saw a dramatic increase in student alcohol abuse in this period. While students in the 1960s expressed dissatisfaction with academic pressure by protesting or using drugs, many in the late 1970s and the 1980s seemed to turn to periodic binge drinking to let off steam. The popular 1978 movie *Animal House* helped transform fraternities' image from bastions of conservatism to sites of subversive hedonism. As enthusiasm for Saturday night fraternity parties grew, attendance at campus activities like the foreign film series decreased.[9]

But the dangers of binge drinking, including alcohol poisoning, accidental injury, and sexual violence, were becoming all too clear, as was an increase in lesser behavioral problems. In 1979 Spalding responded to a resurgence of complaints from the city and neighbors about fraternities by creating a new standing committee, the Fraternity-Sorority Review Board (FSRB), to evaluate each chapter annually to determine whether the college continued its recognition. Using the Inter-fraternity Council's own credo, FSRB criteria included demonstrating "understanding and support of the college's educational mission," assuming responsibility for "the intellectual and social maturation of its individual members," and exemplifying "the professed goals of brotherhood and responsibility to the community."[10]

Under the FSRB, the college entered into a frustrating cycle of reform and regression, with little lasting progress. Many students suspected FSRB to be part of a plot to eliminate fraternities one by one, but it actually sought to help Greek organizations meet college expectations. In 1980 the Committee on Student Conduct recommended withdrawing recognition from Lambda Chi Alpha after a long series of offenses, but the FSRB wanted to give it one more chance. The fraternity's national organization put it on inactive status, however, and the following year its Alumni Council sold the chapter house to the college, which converted it for use as the admissions office. Administrators, particularly assistant dean of student affairs Paul Leavenworth, worked hard to persuade fraternities to reform objectionable practices like open parties, alcohol abuse, and hazing and to improve community relations and strengthen cultural programs. Though individual chapters showed temporary improvement, the system as a whole moved in the opposite direction, as competition for pledges gave rise to more rather than less emphasis on alcohol at parties. "Many houses are now moving toward mid-week parties to help attract prospective pledges," Leavenworth admitted.[11]

As Powell assumed office, two events underlined the review system's failure to effect true reform. In spring 1983, local police investigated reports of a gang rape at Phi Sigma Kappa of an inebriated female student from another school. Although no charges were brought, the incident capped numerous previous infractions by the fraternity. Denouncing the students' behavior as "immoral, reprehensible, and intolerable within the College," Spalding withdrew recognition of the chapter. Then in August, the city's bureau of health closed Sigma Pi's house as unfit for human habitation, even though its alumni board had spent $70,000 to refurbish it only six years before. "The last time I visited the Sigma Pi house I was appalled by and ashamed of its condition, and came away broken-hearted," John Hicks, '34, later wrote the college. "During my time at F&M (in the depth of the depression) we were forced to keep things up ourselves, and we kept the place spotless." At the suggestion of the national organization, the college purchased the house and converted it into a coeducational cooperative house.[12]

The fraternity question was only one of the issues addressed by the Commission on the Quality of Student Life — there were also subcommittees on housing, leisure activities, campus collegiality, the arts and music, and the freshman year. In deciding to initiate the project, Powell noted the comments of an outside consultant that too few students participated in leisure activities at the college. Many seemed to experience the college as an academic "boot camp" and to think that social life consisted only of dating and drinking. Perhaps not coincidentally, there were three serious alcohol-related incidents on campus that year. The need to encourage students to stop and smell the roses became something of a mantra for the project.[13]

Nonetheless, the subcommittee charged with examining the Greek system, headed by biology professor Richard Fluck, attracted greatest attention and aroused anxiety in some quarters. The committee gathered information and opinions from the community; it met with Greek leaders, was inundated with statements, and held numerous open meetings. The "lively and sometimes heated" tone of a meeting with faculty and administrators attested to strong differences of opinion. Many faculty held the Greek system responsible for everything they found wrong with the campus environment, particularly anti-intellectualism and weak sense of community. The dean of faculty affairs, Bradley Dewey, wanted the Greek system "phased out as soon as possible and replaced with healthier alternatives which are more in harmony with the college's goals." He worried that the prevalence of "heavy-drinking fraternity parties" had "found its way into the college guide books and thus [might] be influencing the type of student that F and M can attract." Above all, he argued, "[the Greek system] interferes with intellectual growth, slows social maturation, distorts ethical development, dulls esthetic sensibilities." In short, it was seen as the antithesis of a true liberal education.[14]

Franklin & Marshall was not the only institution scrutinizing fraternities' role in student life. "After more than a decade of giving students as much social independence as possible," the *New York Times* wrote that spring, "colleges and universities across the nation are becoming more involved in the non-academic lives of their students." With greater sensitivity to racism and sexism, faculty and administrators sought to eliminate discriminatory aspects of traditional campus life. At Dartmouth College a detailed set of minimum standards was introduced for fraternities and sororities; trustees at Colby College abolished Greek organizations after the failure of a three-year experiment with similar guidelines, and Amherst's faculty and trustees voted to close its fraternities.[15]

At stake was not simply the existence of Greek organizations but the school's power to shape students' experience in a way consonant with its vision of quality liberal education. As dean of student affairs Peter Balcziunas put it, Franklin & Marshall's fraternities and sororities exerted greater influence over student life than did any other group. The current evaluation of all aspects of student life raised the issue of "the compatibility of the fraternities' goals and ideals with those of the College." "[Franklin & Marshall] seeks to retain its quality and reputation and any group perceived as a road block will be cut," he commented. Philosophy professor Leon Galis distributed a letter to the entire college community, stressing that "the two most distinctive marks of a liberally educated person" were "*tolerance* of values and views other than one's own and *independent judgment* informed by critical reason." Peer pressure hampered the development of these qualities, he contended, and fraternities' "enforced social conformity" compounded "the peer pressure that college-age people are already so vulnerable to." Like many on the faculty, Galis was dismayed that the commission's survey found that nearly 70 percent of current students considered college education only a means to an end. He believed the Greek system to be "a major factor in attracting to the College people who think of going to college as little more than 'doing time' between high school and a lucrative upper-middle-class career."[16]

Although it was not overtly addressed, the growing sense of alienation between faculty and Greek students may have had a political dimension. The faculty, drawn from throughout the nation and increasingly from abroad, was considerably more liberal in its political and cultural outlook than were many students, who in the 1980s were often more conservative than the previous generation. A poll by government students in 1983 found that 42 percent of students called themselves Republicans, 30 percent Democrats, and 28 percent independents. Male students, generally more conservative, gave Reagan a 66 percent approval rate, while 52 percent of females disapproved.[17]

By a 4–2 vote, the subcommittee on fraternities recommended reform rather than abolition, but only if "wide-ranging, specific reforms" occurred. These included postponing rush to the second semester and keeping it dry, ending Hell Week hazing and open parties, instituting more responsible practices regarding alcohol, creating stronger ties with college and alumni advisors, and enriching fraternity life through leadership training and community service. After debating into the early morning hours, the full Student Life Commission agreed. Asserting its independent role in policy making, the board appointed its own ad hoc Committee on Student Life and announced plans to reassess the entire situation in four years. Powell notified presidents of all Greek organizations that the new rules would take effect in the fall of 1984. "If Franklin and Marshall College is to continue to have fraternities, the only way it can happen is for the fraternities to become fully part of the college, and like all other parts, to conform to the principles, rules, and educational goals of the institution. There can be no other way."[18]

Powell's administration was especially determined to reshape the character of the student body. Obviously, admissions was important as a practical matter, but it was also seen as crucial to achieving the desired mix of students. It had long been a commonplace within higher education that a diverse and intellectually capable student body was an essential component of a quality liberal education; increasingly, the very measures of these characteristics were seen as markers of an institution's quality. Diversity was typically defined in terms of students' race, geographic origin, income level, and intellectual ability in terms of SAT scores and high school class ranking. Administrators devoted ever-greater effort and creativity in attempts to improve measures of both. Yet as competition grew in the 1980s, many schools saw yield rates decline. In 1983, for example, even though it received a record 3,712 applications, Franklin & Marshall's admission rate rose from 46 to 51 percent to make up for a decline in its yield from 34 to 33 percent. Powell suggested to the trustees that the college plan for the possibility that it would not be able to maintain both the present quantity and quality of students. "I am firmly committed to quality at all costs," he stated. "A college that has it can always regain quantity when times are better. A college that loses its quality may well have lost both its *raison d'être* and its ability to exist."[19]

Seeking a New Niche in the Academic Marketplace

In keeping with a trend among liberal arts colleges, a strategic long-range plan produced over the next two years came to a similar conclusion: to maintain or even improve the college's national reputation, Franklin & Marshall should maintain selectivity — the ratio of admissions to applications — at or below 50 percent. To do this at a time when the college student population was expected to decline, the college would gradually lower its enrollment to 1,650 by 1991. The size of the faculty would be held constant, thereby lowering the student-teacher ratio; the college would also be able to house most students on campus, strengthening its residential character. The plan also called for spending more on financial aid, to attract the most desirable students in terms of selectivity and diversity and also to make up for declining federal and state support.[20]

These changes were expensive. To make up for loss of tuition revenues caused by smaller enrollments, the plan called for gradually raising tuition, increasing the percentage taken from the endowment's total return, and ultimately adding to the endowment through fund-raising. The college had been extraordinarily conservative in these areas — in 1985 total fees stood sixteenth among the list of twenty comparison institutions and twenty-seventh among the thirty-five competitive schools. Its usual draw of under 3.5 percent on the total return was well below the national average of 5.5 percent. This careful stewardship enabled the college to take full advantage of the bullish stock market of the 1980s, which helped push its endowment from $17.5 million in 1981 to $34 million in 1985 and nearly $60 million a year later. Powell argued that it was now time to use these resources to compete with "the most prestigious liberal arts colleges." His executives pointed out that the previous policy of holding tuition below levels charged by competitors had meant foregoing substantial revenues "to the detriment of the educational program." Moreover, they noted that increased tuition at peer institutions had not deterred prospective students.[21]

In fact, the economic environment for higher education changed dramatically in the 1980s. The economic return for investing in a college degree, which had declined in the 1970s, rose significantly — in large part because of the disappearance of well-paying manufacturing jobs. This prompted a larger percentage of the college-age population to seek higher education and many older adults to return to school. Meanwhile, explosive growth in the stock market and redistribution of wealth toward higher-income brackets raised higher education's fund-raising potential. Demand rose for luxury goods — including high-quality higher education. Many schools discovered that fears of being priced out of the market were unwarranted. Indeed, increasingly price was seen as evidence of quality instead of a drawback. "All of us are beginning to realize that to some degree in this market, people judge quality by price," David W. Breneman, president of Kalamazoo College, noted in 1988. "Increasingly — rightly or wrongly — we are seeing price as a statement to the public of who we are." Tuition at private institutions skyrocketed, growing by 106 percent between 1981 and 1989. At many selective institutions, increases were offset by growth in need-based financial aid.[22]

In announcing the college's plan to get smaller, Powell argued that it was "an act of strength, of will, of discipline" and "a way to enroll a more able student body." He promoted the approach in an article for the *College Board Review*. By 1988 the plan seemed to be working admirably. Applications increased, producing a 30 percent rise in the college's "market share," or measure of applications as a percent of high school graduates. (The term itself reflected how far the admission process had gone in adopting a marketing ethos.) After declining to 3,350 in 1985, applications rose to 3,852 in 1986 and 4,133 in 1987, pushing acceptance rates down from 62 percent in 1985 to 38 percent in 1987. The number of early-decision applicants also increased, under an increasingly popular option offering consideration of students' applications several months in advance of standard deadlines in exchange for a binding promise to enroll if accepted. By making this commitment, students generally improved their odds of acceptance, while schools raised their yield rates. Meanwhile, a 50 percent increase in college-funded financial aid enabled Franklin & Marshall for the first time to meet the needs of all admitted students, even as the proportion of federal aid fell. Student scores rose, and the total number of minority students went up 11 percent. The proportion of Pennsylvania students rose over the two years to 33 percent, though there were small increases in numbers from outside the Northeast.[23]

But as usual in admissions, not everything went according to plan. An unanticipated 5 percent increase in yield in 1986 pushed the freshman class that year over projections. Moreover, as the college's increased selectivity became more widely known, applications began to decline. Powell speculated that high school — counselors were discouraging applicants who were unlikely to be admitted. And as the college sought to compete for the best students with more prominent schools — who also offered increased financial aid — its yield rates declined.[24]

Meanwhile, the college responded to Student Life Commission recommendations by redoubling attention to student programming. More concerts and lectures by better-known figures were scheduled. A dean of freshmen, coordinator of students activities, and director of residential life were added to the administration. New programs directed at improving student retention succeeded in significantly raising the percentage of students who returned after the freshman year. New special-interest residential opportunities were introduced: the French House and the Arts House (later renamed Murray House in honor of alumnus Paul G. Murray, '16) joined the Cooperative House in former fraternity houses on James Street; Meyran and Deitz Halls were restored to their original identities as student housing. Yet efforts to create a faculty fellows program in the dormitories to encourage out-of-classroom contact was dropped for lack of faculty interest. Planning went forward on a large number of new projects, including a new residence hall, a science library, venues for performing and visual arts, and enlarged athletic facilities on the newly acquired North Campus. These would be funded as part of a $51 million capital campaign to be publicly announced during the college's bicentennial. When Aaron Martin became chairman of the board in 1985, Arthur Shadek took charge of the campaign.[25]

Turnover in executive positions increased. Richard Traina left as dean in 1984 to assume the presidency of Clark University, and Powell quickly appointed associate dean Bradley Dewey to replace him. He stepped down at the end of 1986, and John

Vanderzell served as acting dean until Gordon Douglass, professor of economics at Pomona College, assumed the position in mid-1987. When John Synodinos resigned as vice president for development, Richard Kneedler took over the position and responsibility for the capital campaign.[26]

In 1986, as the college's bicentennial year began and in preparation for another Middle States evaluation, the Educational Planning Committee identified the governance system, junior faculty conditions, and out-of-class relations between students and faculty as areas most in need of improvement. Governance was the most pressing, for neither students nor faculty believed that the College Senate represented their interests. The committee recommended returning responsibility for most matters to the full faculty, with standing committees and a faculty council acting as an executive committee. Students could participate in governance by serving on committees. A committee appointed to propose a new system agreed that the senate had failed because faculty and student constituencies "bring widely different experiences, values, and interests to discussions, making progress on 'deep' issues difficult." Because sensitive topics were often hard to discuss in a public forum like the senate, the college often resorted to ad hoc task forces. The faculty approved a council-based system in the spring of 1988. In addition to the Committee on Professional Standards and the Committee on Budget Priorities, the Committee on Education Policy — consisting of four faculty, two students, and the dean of the college — was established to shape the curriculum. On their own initiative, students created a separate student congress and elected their first representatives in March of 1988.[27]

College leaders had long expressed concern about the situation of junior faculty, who faced rising expectations for excellence in research as well as teaching. Typically, one-third of those seeking tenure at Franklin & Marshall did not succeed. In a few instances those denied tenure protested, most notably in 1983, when a French professor charged discrimination because of his foreign nationality. The federal EEOC took the case and demanded records of all tenure cases going back ten years. First Spalding and then Powell resisted, arguing that opening personnel files "would have a most chilling effect on" the college's system of peer review. The resulting legal case was supported at the U.S. District Court level by eight other Pennsylvania colleges, and an appeal to the U.S. Court of Appeals was joined by the national AAUP and fifty-one other colleges and universities. These and an attempt to take the case to the U.S. Supreme Court failed, and the college was finally forced to turn over some 8,400 pages of records. In due course the EEOC announced that it could find no evidence of discrimination.[28]

The ad hoc AAUP Committee on the Concerns of the Junior Faculty reported a perception that while the college expected the best from its junior faculty, it was not itself doing its best to support them. There were complaints about lack of clarity in communicating expectations and about inaccuracy and unfairness in the evaluation process, as well as tension between departmental expectations and those of the college as a whole. Faculty at all levels were troubled by overreliance on the COTE questionnaires, whose results were most influenced by the size of classes and complexity of subject. The report included a senior faculty member's lament on the "decline in collegiality" during his twenty years at the college, resulting from the weight of heavy teaching loads and pressures to publish and participate in governance. He urged reassessing "the qualities we most value and the procedures by which we implement them":

> An important part of the Liberal Arts tradition that we represent is a concern for the quality of human life and for the value of human relationships within an ongoing community. There must be a better way to acknowledge and support these concerns than the system we now have in effect. Our current treatment and evaluation of junior faculty *may* produce a more impressive collection of individual faculty members; I am unconvinced that it produces better departments or a better College, or that it provides a better education for our students. Certainly it does little to demonstrate a concern for the humane values we profess to represent.[29]

To aid junior faculty, the faculty instituted a system of research leaves after teachers passed their third year reviews. Administration concerns about legal issues slowed attempts to introduce a more liberal maternity leave policy. In 1988 the faculty expanded the kinds of information used in evaluations, and the PSC worked to improve counseling of probationary faculty. The following year the faculty placed greater emphasis on teaching in its criteria for merit evaluations. It also approved new student questionnaires, dubbed Student Perceptions of Teaching (SPOT), intended to provide more detailed information.[30]

The Educational Planning Committee also urged reconsidering the curriculum, particularly the freshman year experience. To address the fear that freshman orientation focused too exclusively on social adjustment, a new program, A Liberal Education, was created in 1987 to acclimate freshmen to the "rigors of academic life at the College." Freshmen attended one of thirty-one minicourses taught over the three days of orientation by faculty and administrator volunteers — Powell himself offered a section, Evolution and Creationism. Interdisciplinary programs were launched in Asian studies, performance studies, and biomedical sciences. More students went abroad to study. Beginning in 1985, the Hackman Summer Fellows Program enabled dozens of students to pursue joint research projects with faculty mentors. Surveying these innovations, Dean Douglass envisioned "a new campus ethos breaking down the distinction between 'fun' and 'work,' blurring the lines between academic and non-academic, reducing the grimness that sometimes attends academic pursuits at the College and building a new sense of community."[31]

Celebrating Two Centuries of Liberal Education

The college took full advantage of the opportunity afforded by the bicentennial of the founding of Franklin College to publicize itself and its long history in education.

Observances began with "Ben's Birthday Bash" on January 17, the 281st anniversary of Benjamin Franklin's birth, with a keynote address by journalist Robert MacNeil followed in the evening by a lighter performance by political satirist Mark Russell. A large tapestry displaying symbols of the college' s history, the product of hundreds of hours of community volunteer labor, was unveiled in Steinman Center, accompanied by a historical exhibit in its Dana Gallery. Franklin & Marshall's past missionary role and its aspirations to a wider international presence were reflected in honorary degrees awarded to Tetsuo Seino and Shozo Kodama, president and chairman of the board of Japan's Tohoku Gakuin University, founded in 1886 by alumnus William Hoy. That institution had previously acknowledged Franklin & Marshall's historic ties by awarding Powell an honorary degree at its centenary celebrations. Franklin & Marshall also celebrated its long history by publishing *Hullabaloo Nevonia: An Anecdotal History of Student Life at Franklin and Marshall College* by John H. Brubaker III. During the spring of 1987, an unusually rich array of luminaries appeared, from Daniel Patrick Moynihan and E. L. Doctorow to I. Bernard Cohen and Wynton Marsalis.[32]

June 6, 1987, saw a reenactment on the streets of downtown Lancaster of the founding ceremonies with which Franklin College had been publicly launched two centuries earlier. An evening concert on Williamson Field by Ella Fitzgerald concluded with fireworks. Festivities closed in October with homecoming and public launch of the Campaign for the College. Its ambitious goal of $51 million included $25 million for endowment, $15 million for operating funds, and $11 million for a new residence hall, science library, arts center, and upgraded athletic facilities.[33]

Showdown with the Greeks

Despite manifest signs of progress, a disquieting undercurrent of unrest ran through the community. It focused on the unfinished business of Greek life, but in many ways the issue was merely a symptom of the gap between visions of the college held by the administration and faculty on the one hand and many students on the other.

In 1984–1985, the first year after the Student Life Committee's reform report went into effect, the college hired David Stameshkin as associate dean of student affairs and charged him to work with Greek organizations and develop related programs, such as alcohol awareness. During that year, sororities cooperated in implementing reforms, but most fraternities dragged their feet. Fraternity and sorority leaders did form the Greek Council, which sought to improve their collective image by organizing charity fund-raisers and joining with other campus groups to sponsor lectures by visiting notables, such as Shirley Chisholm.[34]

In response to increased incidents of alcohol abuse on campus, the administration restricted consumption in college public spaces. To fight this policy, fraternity leaders enlisted support from independent students by pointing out that their social lives would suffer the most from closed parties. This was already true for freshmen, who were barred from fraternity houses by new rush restrictions. Phi Kappa Tau members made their point by selling 450 T-shirts printed with Powell's likeness and the words "Fun Buster." The Greek Council organized a silent protest on Hartman Green to express dissatisfaction with social life at the college; about three hundred students were said to have attended, including many independents. In November the Fraternity-Sorority Review Board brokered a compromise that allowed freshmen into fraternity parties on two weekends. In fact, however, some fraternities continued to hold open parties, and a good deal of illegal rushing took place in off-campus apartments.[35]

A few improvements were made over the next two years. With support from the college's alumni office, each chapter's alumni advisory board was strengthened. But violations remained common; fraternity leaders protested that they could not control their members and that they had to break rules to compete with other chapters. After repeated faculty complaints about the adverse academic effects of midweek parties, the Interfraternity Council (IFC) finally imposed a 1:00 A.M. curfew on weeknights. In contrast, sororities adjusted to the reforms easily and were flourishing. A third, Chi Omega, was launched in 1986 and within a year had close to one hundred members. In 1987 Sigma Sigma Sigma leased its own house on West James Street and was selected as top chapter nationwide.[36]

It was not until spring semester 1987 that Greeks as a whole, led by IFC president David Coyne, '87, began to engage seriously with the reform process. Coyne was aided by the fact that all of the fraternities' presidents had entered the college since reform discussion began; they were more willing to accept change in order to preserve the system. Moreover, implications of Pennsylvania's new host liability legislation finally began to sink in for fraternity advisers and national organizations. This law held establishments and private individuals that served alcohol equally responsible for the actions of patrons or guests not only while they were on the host's premises but after they left. As a consequence, after much debate the IFC finally voted that spring to end open parties.[37]

Unfortunately, events undercut this progress. After an early Sunday morning brawl at the Pi Lambda Phi chapter house on College Avenue, the local neighborhood organization demanded that the college take greater control. Powell announced that in light of the fraternity's repeated violations, the college was withdrawing recognition from the chapter. If the group did not attempt to maintain a "shadow" fraternity and presented a plan outlining how they would ensure acceptable conduct in the future, they could apply for recognition in a year.[38]

From this point on, the entire community seemed obsessed with the Greek issue, and discussion polarized along predictable lines. The executive director of Pi Lambda Phi's national office, angered that Powell had rejected the national organization's proposal to reorganize the chapter, declined to revoke its charter. Instead the director encouraged its members to defy the college and remain open under the national organization's supervision. He had concluded that the administration was bent on getting rid of fraternities in any event. In September, Pi Lam's members voted unanimously to continue operation as an unrecognized fraternity.[39]

The national organization's defiance stunned Powell and the board. Even though Franklin & Marshall's IFC ejected Pi Lambda Phi and barred it from rush and pledging activities, board leaders were haunted by "larger questions" that the incident raised "about the longterm relationship of national fraternities with the College." In fact, perhaps in reaction to antifraternity actions at a number of colleges, the National Interfraternity Council was considering amending its rules to allow fraternities to exist without recognition of their home campuses. Powell consulted with the college's attorney but could see no course of action against the students that was sure of success. "It appears to me that for now an outlaw fraternity chapter, like Pi Lambda Phi, is effectively beyond our control," he told board chair Aaron Martin. The only recourse was to institute a policy requiring juniors to live on campus, which could not take effect for two years.[40]

For their part, many students greeted news of the Pi Lam suspension together with the new residential policy as signs that the administration was bent on controlling student life. Over one-quarter of students currently lived off campus in apartments as well as fraternities. While announcing plans for the new residence hall, college leaders stressed their goal to make Franklin & Marshall 90 percent residential. "In essence, the very character of the school is on the line," protested *College Reporter* columnist Kevin Braun. He depicted an administration intent on making "the 'Residence Halls' the focus of student social life," the dormitories to be populated by a "troop of happy hall dwellers" under the domination of "den mother" RAs. Other students took up the cry against college "paternalism," which was seen as threatening not only the fraternities but individual freedoms of all students wishing to live off campus. Suspicions were further aroused when the Committee on Academic Status restricted extracurricular activities — including Greek membership — for freshmen who failed to achieve a 2.0 GPA during their first semester. "Franklin and Marshall does not want a diverse student body committed to more intellectual pursuits," charged Ken Mehlman, '88. "It wants a one-dimensional student, an unchallenging receptacle for administration orders." As ominously, the College Senate debated measures to make rules of the Committee on Student Conduct more specific; Rita Byrne, vice president of student life, explained that revisions had been made necessary by "our more litigious society." Issues of the *Reporter* were filled with complaints that the college was out to deny students' rights and freedom of choice.[41]

Meanwhile, the Educational Planning Committee's report frankly acknowledged a wide gap between students and faculty, hastening to note that this was common at many schools. "Many students, especially, display a fragmented and compartmentalized conception of campus life," it noted, "in which what goes on inside the classroom has no connection with what goes on outside." It faulted both sides for an excessive focus on grades and course requirements and called for "re-education of the campus community about the essence of learning and about the concept of co-curricular learning." In response, one student blamed the schism on the faculty's negative attitude: "Aside from claiming that F&M students are anti-intellectual and illiterate, the faculty claimed in a meeting with the EPC last April and I quote, 'We want different kinds of kids.' Period. This hardly constitutes a basis for a warm relationship."[42]

During the fall semester the IFC finally adopted a carding system to restrict underage drinking at parties and set grade point requirements for pledging, but its leaders continued to skirmish with administrators over rushing regulations. The *College Reporter* campaigned for a large turnout to approve the new Student Congress, emphasizing the need for an organization to offset the administration. Number one among the "Top Ten Reasons for a Student Congress" was "Many students feel that administrators are pinheads." Sixty-seven percent of the student body voted for a Congress.[43]

In this environment, the board's Student Life Committee, headed by William E. Seachrist, '52, began its re-evaluation of Greek life. With their fiduciary responsibility to protect the college's financial well-being, many trustees focused on liability issues. Following a student's injury in an alcohol-related accident on campus in 1984, the college had been named as a party in a lawsuit. At first, attorneys claimed grounds of general negligence, but more recently sought to bring the college's alcohol policy into the case by alleging that Franklin & Marshall had failed to enforce it adequately. Ironically, by stepping up efforts to educate students about dangers of alcohol abuse and limit underage drinking, the college had increased its vulnerability to legal action if anything went wrong. Noting this, its legal counsel explained early in 1987 that it faced considerable financial exposure because of the possibility of assessment of punitive damages, which were not insurable. He thought it might be necessary to shift the emphasis of college policy from education to enforcement. Examining the college's relationship to fraternities, leaders realized that by becoming involved in a reform program, they had heightened the institution's legal vulnerability.[44]

As the Student Life Committee reviewed information provided by the Greek chapters, it told the overseers that it was thinking about "the legal liability that the college may experience through recognition of fraternities" and the threat to the college's ability "to control fraternities" clearly manifested by "the Pi Lambda Phi incident." When Powell spoke to the full board of his vision of the college in the future, he thought it equally possible that the fraternity system would have been reformed or that "the trustees will have decided, perhaps for legal reasons if for no other, that the college can no longer afford a Greek system."[45]

The eleven-person committee, including Powell, contained only trustees. Seven members were alumni, of whom five had been fraternity members; four others were women and not alumni. After its first meeting on December 16, the group commented that there was "room for a lot of improvement" in the fraternities' reform efforts, citing reports of continuing alcohol abuse, underage drinking, and rush/pledging infractions. Moreover, trustees and students viewed events through different time frames: fraternity leaders, who had been in office less than a year, pointed to the "amazing strides" made recently in changing behaviors, while trustees retained long memories of past transgressions. They saw fraternities' original slowness in undertaking reform as proof of a lack of "a good faith effort."[46]

Early in March, the committee asked the faculty to express its collective opinion of whether the Greek system made "a positive contribution to a F&M education." Faculty debated the issue over two meetings. Most agreed with the position expressed by philosophy professor Michael Roth, that despite recent instances of exemplary behavior, there was "an awful lot of evidence cited on the other side, the rotten things that go on: the rapes, the gang bangs, the drugs, the alcohol." Many dismissed recent reforms as "cynical" and "cosmetic." Conversely, English professor Anthony Ugolnik, who had served as faculty advisor to Zeta Beta Tau, was convinced that there had been a genuine effort to reform. He charged that many faculty acted out of prejudice rather than real knowledge of fraternities. Others chided their colleagues for unfairly branding fraternities as a whole for the misbehavior of a few individuals. Nevertheless, on March 24 the faculty voted 84 to 11, with one abstention, "that fraternities and sororities endorse values and pursue activities that too often are inimical to the goals of liberal education." The faculty recommended that trustees withdraw recognition and support from the system and "develop alternative social programs more in harmony with the goals of the college."[47]

An Abrupt Presidential Transition

Four days later, the college was rocked by James Powell's announcement that he was resigning effective July 1 to assume the presidency of Reed College. Publicly, he cited family considerations, but he acknowledged privately to Richard Kneedler a belief that a new president would be better able to deal with the aftermath of derecognition. The board would have to address the matter of finding a successor at its off-campus meeting on April 12 and 13.[48]

Although the Student Life Committee had originally planned to make its final report in June, consideration of the Greek issue was moved up to the April meeting. The Student Congress, formally organized only a few weeks before, urged trustees to postpone their decision, in order to give the congress a chance to work with the Greeks. The congress had just created its Committee on Greek Reform, and new president Peter Kastor, '89, asked that students be given "an adequate opportunity to show that they are capable of responsibly governing themselves and their interests in such a way as to contribute to the educational goals of the College." A campuswide referendum showed 98 percent of the 757 students who voted favored continuing recognition. Demonstrating that the campus was not oblivious to outside issues, the Student Congress also unanimously called on the board to divest its investments in corporations doing business in South Africa.[49]

On April 12 the board first dealt with the investment issue, approving an ad hoc committee's recommendation to invest only in companies that adhered to the Sullivan Principles and to carefully monitor the companies' behavior. It also called on the president to establish closer links with and to better inform the college community about South Africa.[50]

The rest of the day was spent in executive session discussing the presidency. Powell's departure came at an awkward time — in the midst of a major fund-raising campaign, a Middle States evaluation, and the highly divisive move against fraternities. In the weeks preceding the meeting, board chairman Aaron Martin consulted with other trustees and "leading members" of the faculty. A full national search for a new president typically takes up to a year, and board leaders feared that during that time an acting president would not be able to exert strong leadership. Hence, Martin explained, trustees had concluded that it was crucial "to elect immediately a well-respected person who knows the college well to lead it through this critical phase of its history." They decided upon a somewhat awkward compromise: the board tapped A. Richard Kneedler to be Franklin & Marshall's thirteenth president. But it promised after one year to appoint a committee on the presidential search process, to assess whether to undertake a national search. "After careful consultation with senior members of the faculty and administration," Martin announced, "it was clear to me and the board that Dick Kneedler possesses the experience, abilities and vision necessary to guide Franklin & Marshall during this period."[51]

The board took up the Student Life Committee's report on April 13. Its eighteen pages devoted less than one page to an evaluation of the reform process itself, characterizing the results as "sorely disappointing." It discounted fraternities' claims to have reformed, calling their actions "too little and too late." Most of the document was devoted to sweeping criticisms of the fraternity system as a whole, commentary that went beyond the prescribed reforms. These criticisms included charges that the fraternity system hampered academic performance and moral development, promoted anti-intellectualism, created self-selected groups that lacked diversity, and fostered an adversarial attitude toward the college. Even more fundamentally, the report argued that the single-sex character of fraternities violated the college's nondiscrimination policy (it denied that sororities wielded comparable social influence), promoted sexism, and engendered "arrogance, hypocrisy, even dishonesty." Perhaps most telling, the report concluded that alcohol abuse and hazing prevalent in fraternities "subject the college to unacceptable legal risk." Finally, it pointed out that national fraternity offices and the National Interfraternity Conference no longer required approval of college administrations: "We find unacceptable the prospect of a system that may be beyond our control and influence." It concluded "that Franklin and Marshall College should withdraw recognition from its fraternity system" and replace it with "a program of enhancements to student life." The report paid little attention to the college's sororities but stated that though "there [was] little to object to" in their behavior, they operated according to the same discriminatory principles. The report continued, "On the practical side, it would be unfair to withdraw recognition from fraternities and continue it for sororities." Hence, the entire Greek system "must go." With remarkably little discussion, the board adopted the committee's recommendations.[52]

Afterward, administrators and trustees returned to campus to inform the college's various constituencies of the board's decisions. Unsurprisingly, many students

were outraged by derecognition. The day before, students had rallied outside the College Center to show their support for the Greek system. Now a crowd of several hundred gathered at Old Main to express their anger. They watched senior Ken Mehlman,
past president of Phi Kappa Tau, burn a check made out to the college, vowing he
would never give it a cent. Hearing that there was to be a press conference, the swelling group moved on to the Huegel Alumni House nearby. Kneedler came out to meet
them, delivering his first speech as president-elect to a most unfriendly audience: "This
is a terrible night for the College," he acknowledged. He noted that over half of students were Greeks and pointed out that he himself was a member of Phi Kappa Tau:
"I feel also the sadness and pain that they feel. I intend to work for you and for
everyone on campus. From the bottom of my heart I mean this."[53]

As Kneedler spoke, many students became agitated, some shouting obscenities
and a few calling on the crowd to rush him. IFC president Jack Shilling, '89, jumped
on the porch and faced them down. "Screaming at Mr. Kneedler won't accomplish anything," he declared. "They might think we're animals but we don't have to act that
way." He succeeded in quieting the crowd. Afterward, fraternity supporter J. Gabriel
Neville admitted in the *College Reporter* that it had taken "guts" for Kneedler to "get
up before several hundred angry-as-hell students and talk to them," but he had "endeared himself" by doing so: "He showed that he cared, even if he was at that moment
one of the bad guys." Afterward, trustees and administrators met with each of the four
classes to answer questions about derecognition, in sessions that were often "emotional and fiery."[54]

In the cold light of day, Shilling and other fraternity leaders expressed hope that
Greeks would survive derecognition. "If we manage ourselves responsibly, we can
continue," he asserted. "We will be here next year, and the year after." National offices
confirmed their support for Franklin & Marshall's local chapters. In fact, unlike other
colleges that had moved against their fraternities, Franklin & Marshall had little actual control. With two exceptions it did not own Greek chapter houses: Chi Phi owned
its chapter house, while the college owned the land, and Zeta Beta Tau leased its
house from the college. Ironically, the reform period had made fraternities more capable of surviving on their own. Even Ken Mehlman acknowledged as much when he
wrote in the *Reporter* that Greeks owed the board a debt of gratitude because its mandated reforms made the Greek system physically, financially, and organizationally
able to survive without recognition. Now they also had the help of alumni angered by
the board's actions.[55]

As the Powell administration came to a rather abrupt close, Franklin & Marshall
found itself in far better shape physically and financially than it had been at the beginning of the 1980s. After dipping in the stock market correction of October 1987, the
college's endowment stood at $68.6 million. Construction began that summer on a new
residence hall, planning was well under way for a science library and computing center, and a commercial development on North Campus was under consideration. The
unsatisfactory yoking of student and faculty in the College Senate had finally been re-

placed by the Student Congress and Faculty Council. Nevertheless, the Kneedler administration would have to deal with tense relations between faculty and students and a continuing need to raise the college's endowment and its public profile.[56]

Redoubled Focus on Student Life

Perhaps no one person better represented the recent history of Franklin & Marshall College than A. Richard Kneedler, '65. A native of western Pennsylvania, he had strong family ties to the college and the Reformed Church — his father and uncles attended the college after World War I. Nevertheless, he had considered several other schools before being recruited by Franklin & Marshall in 1961. He arrived in Lancaster just as the academic revolution of the Bolman years reached its climax. One of the first students selected for the College Scholar honors program, he participated energetically in academic and extracurricular life. A rather combative columnist and co-editor of the *College Reporter*, he was selected for the *Wall Street Journal*'s summer internship program after his junior year. After graduation he embarked on advanced study in French at the University of Pennsylvania. Always something of an nonconformist, he once interviewed with a CIA recruiter at Penn largely because student protestors tried to bar him from doing so. He returned to Franklin & Marshall as an instructor in 1968, rising to assistant professor upon completion of his doctorate in 1970. A year later he moved into administration at the invitation of Dean John Vanderzell and served a rigorous apprenticeship at that time of retrenchment. Since then he had served the college in a wide range of functions, even running the library for a time when a director left on short notice. Equally adept at navigating French literary discourse and financial spreadsheets, he was well suited to assume leadership of a liberal arts college.[57]

In addition to his obvious dedication to Franklin & Marshall, Kneedler's lively sense of humor and ability to relate comfortably to students were welcome qualities at a troubled moment in the college's history. Less than a month into the new academic year, a *Reporter* columnist commented that Kneedler was "warm, personal, and most importantly, a presence on campus." His accessibility had "removed some of the boundaries that once separated the President from the student body."[58]

Recognizing that humor was an excellent way to create community and defuse tensions, Kneedler, then vice president of development, collaborated in 1985 with David Stameshkin, Chaplain Barbara Brummett, and Indira Rankin, '84, to plan a hugely successful comic revue, *High and Dry*. Written by Stameshkin and his wife, Colleen Stameshkin, and directed by Rankin, it was the first of the series of Fum Follies that allowed faculty and staff to show their lighter side while acknowledging pressing issues of the day. ("Fum," a compression of "F and M," had come into general use around 1970 to refer to students or members of the college community. Faculty and staff had put on a talent show in 1971 called Fum Follies to raise funds for PREP.) *Town and Gown* followed in 1986, and *Marshall and Franklin* offered a humorous take on the college's history during the 1987 bicentennial. There was no revue during the tense spring of

1988, but the tradition was revived during the first year of Kneedler's presidency with *Doom and Gloom (or The Phantom of the College)*. Taking aim at national debates then raging over college curricula, it had "the evil Professor Alan Gloom"—a parody of conservative critic Alan Bloom — scheming "to transform the entire College into a Great Books paradise." Kneedler appeared in a cameo appearance as frenetic car salesmen Joe Isuzu, plugging "good old F&M." (Among its many "incredible" features, he touted its wonderful new dormitory, "Tajma Hall.") "In his willingness to participate in these shows (and in some wild Orientation skits early in his presidency)," Stameshkin recalled, "Dick not only demonstrated that he was a good sport, but also acknowledged that, even at a very serious place such as F&M, there is room for some institutional laughter and good-natured fun."[59]

Kneedler's first task was to mollify student and alumni anger over derecognition while carrying out the board's mandate. Judging the Student Life Committee's report to be "not helpful," he reversed plans to distribute the full text to alumni and parents. Instead, a condensed four-page version focused on trustee concerns about "unacceptable legal risk" and the lack of cooperation from national Greek organizations. Under the new system, college administrators observed the letter of the board's derecognition decision but refrained from aggressive measures against Greek organizations. Fraternities and sororities were not allowed to use college facilities, but they were given access to alumni address lists and allowed to recruit new pledges. Sophomores were required to live on campus, but Kneedler eventually dropped plans to demand it of juniors as well. The college was nonetheless rigorous in insisting that Zeta Beta Tau and Chi Phi adhere to existing legal agreements. Citing numerous code violations, the college terminated its lease with Zeta Beta Tau and converted the house into the International Living Center. After a series of serious breaches by Chi Phi, the most significant of which were the alcohol poisoning death of a member in 1991 and a sexual assault in 1996, trustees suspended operations indefinitely in 1998.[60]

Most administrators and faculty expected Greek organizations to play a diminishing role in student life. Yet, even without college support, student interest remained strong. In January 1990, for example, more than half the freshman class pledged, 64 percent of men and 40 percent of women. Moreover, as fraternity leaders recognized that the college was "no longer there to protect us," they often assumed greater responsibility for policing themselves. Many alumni accepted the board's decision, but ongoing dissatisfaction fueled support for Greek organizations.[61]

Meanwhile, the new administration moved quickly to deal with perceived problems with residential life. Alice Drum, formerly dean of freshmen, became the new dean of students and vice president for educational services. She created a summer internship program that charged a group of students with identifying ways to improve living conditions on campus. After visiting other colleges, Bowdoin, Williams, Colby, and Amherst, that had also cut ties with fraternities, they recommended specific improvements in housing, social and study spaces, athletic facilities, and meal plans. The students also proposed new ways to handle alcohol at student parties, in response to recent state legislation imposing substantial new restrictions and penalties for serving minors. Meanwhile, more weeknight and weekend entertainments were planned.[62]

Other problems were harder to rectify. Most of the college's dormitories had been constructed in the 1950s and 1960s, when holding down costs was given priority over quality of life. It was not possible to replace them, but extensive improvements were made over the next three years, such as installing new carpeting, draperies, and furniture and reconverting some rooms into kitchens, lounges, and study areas. Planning had begun under Powell for a new hall to enclose the north end of the residential quadrangle. Franklin & Marshall parent and trustee Patricia Weis was particularly interested in improving the residential environment and was a strong supporter of the project. Upon its completion in 1989, it was named the Robert F. and Patricia Ross Weis Residence Hall. Designed by Shepley, Bulfinch, Richardson, and Abbott, Weis was one of the first dormitories to use single-loaded corridors, in which doors ran along only one side, with windows on the other. A combination of suites, single rooms, and double rooms accommodated more than 160 students, with room for socializing, study, and recreation. After its opening, Drum observed that the improved atmosphere seemed "to encourage students to behave more appropriately."[63]

During Kneedler's first year the college successfully negotiated its Middle States review and continued its capital campaign. Construction began in spring 1989 on a new science library, also designed by Shepley, Bulfinch, Richardson, and Abbott. It was completed in 1990 and dedicated in April 1991 as the Aaron and Jean Martin Library for the Sciences, in recognition of the couple's many contributions to the college. Located north of Fackenthal Laboratories, the library provided expanded study space and gathered together most holdings in the sciences. The Center for Information Services and Computing on the ground floor served as the hub of the college's rapidly developing network, which now used an optical fiber system that gradually expanded to connect all members of the campus community. A computerized circulation system connected the two libraries, and by the end of 1992 students could access the online catalogue from their rooms, as well as e-mail and file servers.[64]

Kneedler was formally inaugurated as Franklin & Marshall's president on November 20, 1988. As principal speaker, U.S. House Majority Whip William Gray III, '63, joined Kneedler in honoring the college's liberal arts tradition while noting the need to increase access and improve facilities. Franklin & Marshall's 1989 commencement honored another prominent political alumnus, Kneedler's classmate Kenneth Duberstein, '65, who had served as President Reagan's last chief of staff. As promised, the Committee on the Presidential Search Process, composed of four trustees and four faculty, was created to assess Kneedler's presidency after a year. The committee affirmed that though it was "the tradition of Franklin & Marshall College to select its president through a process of national search," Kneedler enjoyed the faith and confidence of the college community. The committee advised against opening a full search on this occasion. The board's action did not provoke open opposition like that which greeted Anthony Appel's unilateral election in 1962, but there was residual resentment within the faculty; some felt that they had not been sufficiently consulted before Kneedler's initial appointment.[65]

Kneedler's fourteen-year administration continued the pattern of enriching academic and cocurricular programs and physical facilities at Franklin & Marshall within a framework of careful planning and fiscal management. Although fluctuations in the national economy and in student populations inevitably affected finances, Franklin & Marshall's disciplined management and solid reputation enabled the college to avoid the extreme ups and downs of the past.

Planning for continuous improvement reached many levels of the college's administration and faculty. Soon after assuming office, Kneedler began to push for a new round of comprehensive long-range planning, noting, "Today we face, not a fiscal crisis, but a perplexing variety of needs, claims and priorities." To compete for students, the college needed to improve or add facilities for the arts, athletics, and recreation, and many of the buildings constructed in the previous forty years, especially laboratories, now needed major renovations. Meanwhile, higher education experts warned of an impending shortage of new Ph.D.s by the mid-1990s, suggesting that attention should be paid to faculty compensation and working conditions. There were always calls for new programs and more interdisciplinary and team-taught courses. To deal with proliferating demands, the college engaged in several rounds of planning in the 1990s. Faculty members Robert Friedrich, Alan Glazer, '69, and Joseph Voelker, '69, led a second process in 1995 and 1996; participation by much of the community was aided by new communication technologies, particularly e-mail and Internet bulletin boards. To help focus deliberation on the college's educational mission, a concise new mission statement was developed that embodied the college's understanding of liberal education at the cusp of a new century:

> Franklin and Marshall is a residential college dedicated to excellence in undergraduate liberal education. Its aims are to inspire in young people of high promise and diverse backgrounds a genuine and enduring love for learning, to teach them to read, write, and think critically, to instill in them the capacity for both independent and collaborative action, and to educate them to explore and understand the natural, social, and cultural worlds in which they live. In so doing, the College seeks to foster in its students qualities of intellect, creativity, and character, that they may live fulfilling lives and contribute meaningfully to their occupations, their communities, and their world.[66]

Continuing Fiscal Conservatism

In overseeing the administration, Kneedler sought to ensure that it functioned as efficiently as possible to channel resources toward educational programs. During his first year he quietly began cutting administrative expenses; over three years staff and administrative personnel were reduced by nearly 10 percent. Budget surpluses were reinvested or applied to new initiatives or improvements in facilities. These economies helped the college weather the economic downturn of the early 1990s more smoothly than many other institutions did. Even so, burgeoning costs for employee health care, new facilities, and student financial aid steadily eroded Franklin & Marshall's annual surpluses so that in 1992 it narrowly avoided its first deficit in twenty years. To control spending on medical care, the college formed its own coordinated care/preferred provider plan. In 1995 further cuts reduced administrative and staff positions 20 percent below 1988 levels. Kneedler was determined that no cuts be made in the faculty; it was already smaller than most of its peers, and he hoped to avoid the damage to morale done by the rostering process of the early 1970s.[67]

Following the trend in the business world in the 1990s, Kneedler took a close look at many of the college's nonacademic activities to determine whether they were consistent with its core mission. He had philosophical as well as financial reasons for being uneasy about proliferation of nonacademic personnel during the 1980s. "Institutions in the process of straying from their basic mission tend to multiply administrators as they delegate and subdivide various tasks," he later explained. He concluded that college resources could be put to better use by outsourcing some activities and spinning off others. Hence, the campus print shop was closed in 1989, and the following year the College subcontracted management of its bookstore. More controversially, Kneedler was for similar reasons reluctant to establish a day care center on campus, arguing that it "is simply not our line of work." He warned trustees that they must resist pressures to "undertake new missions and costs which are not central to a college's mission" on the one hand and to avoid "changes which will control costs or enhance revenues" on the other. In 1990 the college contracted with the Lancaster YWCA to operate a day care center in the basement of Marshall-Buchanan Hall.[68]

The divestment process for other programs was more complicated. A dedicated student of the college's history, Kneedler believed that the path of progress lay in returning to its liberal arts roots. Hence, the college turned over to Lebanon Valley College responsibility for continuing education programs that the Evening Division had long offered to the local community. Franklin & Marshall gradually relinquished control and financial responsibility for the North Museum to a nonprofit corporation. The move was first proposed in 1990 by the Museum Study Commission headed by emeritus president Keith Spalding. "It's our mission to be a College, and not a museum," Kneedler explained to the *College Reporter*. Under direction of a community-based board, the North Museum Corporation took control in 1993, while Franklin & Marshall provided an annual subsidy and support services for the next five years. With court approval in 1998 of complete separation of the institutions, the college turned over $2 million in restricted endowment and trust funds associated with the museum; it also pledged to provide free rent, utilities, maintenance, and other services until 2015.[69]

Although it meant foregoing revenues, the college stepped back from its policy of aggressive tuition increases. "Simply because the market will bear what we have chosen to charge does not mean that there are not resentments, that there will be no long-term costs to pay," Kneedler warned overseers in 1989. Pointing to negative reactions in the local community, the national press, and foundations, he feared creating a climate of opinion that might undermine higher education institutions' charitable status. With the board's agreement, tuition increases in the mid-1990s were held generally at or below the rate of inflation. In conjunction with planning exercises in the early 1990s, the board reconsidered enrollment levels; in accordance with the previous plan, they had been reduced by 1993 to around 1,675. To increase revenues and help support a wider range of programs, trustees approved increasing enrollments over four years to 1,850, while holding the student-faculty ratio below twelve to one.[70]

Meanwhile, college leaders redoubled fund-raising efforts in the 1990s. The Campaign for the College concluded one year ahead of schedule at the end of 1989, after raising more than $1 million over its initial $51 million goal. For the next few years development staff focused on strengthening annual giving, which typically reached $8 million a year in the mid-1990s. Total contributions had not been appreciably hurt by derecognition of fraternities, but alumni participation rates fell to a low of 26 percent in 1989. They gradually recovered, reaching 42 percent in 1994; though high compared to schools in the region, this rate was lower than peer institutions nationally. Inevitably, work soon began on another major campaign. Headed by trustee Stanley J. Dudrick, '57, Franklin & Marshall 2001: Leadership in the Liberal Arts began its private phase in 1993. It aimed to raise at least $125 million by the end of 2001, to implement goals of the long-range strategic plan by increasing endowment, funding physical improvements, and providing additional operating funds. By the time of the public launch in October 1997, some $70 million had been given or pledged, although much of it was in the form of deferred gifts.[71]

Contributions to endowment and a resurgent stock market pushed Franklin & Marshall's endowment ever higher. At the end of 1989 it stood at $92.6 million. As the stock market regained momentum in the mid-1990s, it reached $190 million in 1996. Overseen by trustees Dale Frey, '54, and John Bonin, '72, investments enjoyed a 31 percent return in 1997 and hit $285 million in 1998. Subsequently, the Committee on Investments moved to diversify holdings, which limited growth but cushioned the fall when the market dropped at the turn of the century. In mid-2002, the endowment was over $273 million. Meanwhile, Standard and Poor's and Moody's both recognized the college's solid financial condition by upgrading its financial ratings to A+ and A1 respectively.[72]

Although the college's growing resources made it a richer institution, they did not alter its position relative to other selective liberal arts institutions. In 1998 it ranked fifteenth among its list of twenty comparison colleges in terms of total endowment. As in so many things in higher education, the richest institutions kept getting richer, while raising the stakes for all the rest. By 2002, as endowments for three of its comparison colleges — Grinnell, Williams, and Pomona — broke the $1 billion mark, Franklin & Marshall found itself slipping to nineteenth on the list.[73]

Enriching the Whole Educational Experience

Franklin & Marshall employed its growing resources in ambitious programs designed to serve its goal to become, in Kneedler's words, "a standard of excellence for liberal arts colleges." The college added major new arts and athletic facilities, multiplied programs aimed at attracting talented students, and once more revamped its curriculum.[74]

During the 1990s the college undertook its first extensive period of construction since the 1960s. College Square, a multipurpose commercial center, opened on North Campus in 1991. It was developed by the John Marshall Investment Corporation, the college's for-profit subsidiary, with goals to create places near campus for students to eat and socialize, to provide services in a convenient location, and to move off campus commercial enterprises such as the college bookstore. College leaders hoped that the development would improve relations with the local community by enlarging the tax base and avoiding use of tax-exempt facilities to conduct commercial activities. An elevated footbridge over Harrisburg Pike connected the building to campus.[75]

A sustained effort to improve athletics facilities was capped by construction of the Alumni Sports and Fitness Center, completed in 1995. Located north of College Square, it contained a fifty-meter swimming pool (a long-needed replacement for the Fackenthal Pool) and a field house large enough to hold five full-size basketball courts, a two-hundred-meter indoor track, and an elevated jogging track, as well as a fitness center and a meeting room with catering facilities. The substantial facility was designed by RDG Bussard Dikis, David Lynch and Associates (Lynch graduated from the college in 1954), and pool consultants Counsilman/Hunsaker. The first major fruit of the new capital campaign, the Center was made possible by many donors. The Kunkel Aquatic Center honored the late Congressman John C. Kunkel; and the McGinness Pool, long-time swimming coach George McGinness. Schnader Field House acknowledged trusts established by former board chairman William Schnader.[76]

The college paid significant attention throughout the decade to upgrading facilities for its arts programs. Nevin Chapel in Old Main, for several decades used mainly for lectures and music recitals, was renovated to provide an acoustically excellent recital hall, with gifts from Harold Miller, '46, and Houghton Mifflin Publishing Company on the occasion of his retirement as its chairman and CEO. Leonard Rothman, '41, and his wife, Mildred Rothman, supported renovation of the former bookstore space in the College Center to create a permanent gallery for the college's art collections, gathered from their previous home in North Museum and from offices around campus. At the end of the decade, further renovations made possible by trustee Thomas G. Phillips, '54, and Virginia Phillips created the Phillips Museum of Art in the Steinman College Center. The museum incorporated the Dana and Rothman galleries with new galleries and storage and work areas, forming a space of twelve thousand square feet on three levels.[77]

Continuing its practice of creative reuse of its older buildings, the college built the Barshinger Center for Musical Arts, a state-of-the-art concert hall, within the shell of Hensel Hall. It was made possible by a substantial gift from Ann and Richard Barshinger, '43, and donations in memory of John Peifer, '36, founder and longtime director of the college band. Radical renovations planned by Ann Beha Architects preserved a landmark building — albeit one with notoriously bad acoustics — and gave the college a five-hundred-seat auditorium with admirable acoustics for large concerts, lectures, and films. Its dedication in the spring of 2000 was celebrated by a semester-long performance festival. In the course of the work, Meyran Hall directly to the south of Hensel was renovated to provide offices and classrooms for music and theater, dance and film departments.[78]

The college's long campaign to create appropriate spaces for the arts culminated with construction of a new performance center for theater and dance. After research by American Studies professor David Schuyler uncovered the long-forgotten fact that eminent architect Charles Klauder had designed the college's 1920s-era campus, a decision was made to preserve the Fackenthal Pool building and adapt it for dance and art studios and theater workshops. Meanwhile, by nesting the new performing arts center in the space between Fackenthal and Steinman Center, an arts quadrangle was created while preserving most open space on Spalding Plaza. Work on the Roschel Center for the Performing Arts, named in honor of Robert L. Roschel, '54, began in 2001; it was dedicated during homecoming in 2003.[79]

Meanwhile the college's physical sciences building, first constructed in the 1960s, was thoroughly renovated. Outmoded mechanical systems were replaced and new laboratories, classrooms, and offices added. At its rededication in 1998, the building was designated as the William M. Hackman Physical Sciences Laboratories in recognition of the support of Hackman and his wife, Lucille. The name is particularly appropriate because the building serves as a center of much of the college's teaching and research in the sciences, much of the collaborative work being done under the auspices of the Hackman Scholars Program.[80]

These prodigious efforts in planning, fund-raising, and construction were expended in the interests of further enriching Franklin & Marshall's learning environment. In many cases, they were also deemed essential to recruit the desired "young people of high promise and diverse backgrounds." But admissions continued to present significant challenges. After reaching a record high in 1987, numbers of applications declined substantially in the late 1980s, dropping 24 percent within three years. Measures of student quality were not greatly affected, but the acceptance rate necessarily rose above the magic 50 percent level associated with highly selective colleges. The college responded vigorously by placing admissions under Vice President Drum's purview and hiring outside consultants to examine the entire enrollment management system.[81]

Consultants noted that the decline, "one of the sharpest [they had] encountered anywhere in the country," could only partly be explained by demographic changes.

They concluded that the sharp increase in selectivity in 1987 was the primary cause. Rejection of "bread and butter" students who had typically been accepted in the past subsequently discouraged applications from similar students. "The movement toward higher selectivity and a perceived higher image of quality in the marketplace usually must occur in an evolutionary, not revolutionary, way," they advised. "Rising selectivity without strong evidence of concurrent elevation in other tangible measures of academic quality and prestige may prove counter-productive."[82]

Though the consultants commended the campus's appearance, they thought its immediate surroundings left something to be desired. They suggested recommending that visitors to campus follow a different route, noting that Harrisburg Pike's "junk piles and unattractive commercial areas" were "a definite negative for marketing purposes." The large water towers in Buchanan Park also detracted from the campus's appearance. This concern was resolved in 1996, when the City of Lancaster demolished the towers — though the nostalgic were sorry to see "George" and "Martha" go. But the unprepossessing appearance of Harrisburg Pike remained a thorny problem.[83]

Many in the community were uncomfortable about the idea of "marketing" Franklin & Marshall, but it became increasingly clear that more must be done to make the college better known. "We must make the public aware of the nature and the value of what we do," Kneedler stated. "If we do not, the entire enterprise of the liberal arts is seriously at risk." At the recommendation of the Joint Commission on Marketing, chaired by trustee Andrew Rouse, the college retained a consultant specializing in higher education market research to advise on admissions strategy, and another firm to revise its publications. Using their insights, admissions officers employed more personalized recruitment methods. To encourage early decision applications, successful students had to pay only tuition and fees in effect at the time of their application. Like many other liberal arts colleges, Franklin & Marshall began to augment need-based financial aid with merit scholarships. It introduced scholarship programs such as the Presidential Scholars and Regional Scholars from Pennsylvania. The John Marshall Scholars Program, intended to attract exceptionally promising students, supplemented tuition grants with research support, a computer, and special activities.[84]

College leaders also kept jealous watch on results of the various media exercises rating the nation's colleges and universities. Like administrators everywhere, they anxiously awaited *U.S. News and World Report*'s annual rankings, which were based on surveys of academic reputation and measures of selectivity, student scores, and financial resources. When it first began in 1983, the magazine listed only the top ten institutions in each category, followed by others in groups of twenty-five. Franklin & Marshall was typically included in the first quartile among national liberal arts institutions, allowing it to claim a place among the top thirty-five colleges. When lists were extended, the college was generally placed in the low to mid-thirties, the precise position varying as the magazine adjusted its formulas. In time the rankings engendered a backlash, as many educators noted that they measured inputs, such as SAT scores, rather than institutions' actual effects on students. As authors of a growing number of guidebooks urged prospective students and their parents to look beyond prestige "brand" names, Franklin & Marshall College frequently appeared on lists of "under-appreciated" schools. Even so, hopes within the college community of raising its standing relative to its peer institutions have generally met with frustration. Observing a general "stasis" within higher education's "positional market," economist Gordon Winston has noted that "the rich, within this hierarchy, get richer while the positional ranking itself remains remarkably stable."[85]

All these efforts gradually bore fruit in increased applications. Despite the growth in enrollments, the college's admit rate crept downward, ever closer to the desired 50 percent, finally falling to 49 percent in 1999. Reciprocally, student quality improved, with average SAT scores exceeding 1,250 in 1996 (in part, the result of inflation related to the "recentering" of scores that year). The following year, 80 percent of incoming students ranked in the top quintile of their high school classes, while 63 percent were in the top decile. But after peaking at nearly four thousand that year, application numbers again began to recede in the early years of the new century.[86]

Increased recruitment outside the Middle Atlantic region broadened the geographic range somewhat; in 1997 forty states were represented in the student body, with increased numbers from the southwestern United States. But the bulk of students continued to come from the Northeast, with Pennsylvania, New York, and New Jersey predominating. One particularly bright spot in the admissions picture was a dramatic increase in numbers of international students. In the mid-1980s the college began offering financial aid to foreign students and devoting more attention to international recruiting. Based primarily on enthusiastic word of mouth from college advisers and satisfied alumni, Franklin & Marshall quickly developed a strong reputation among the growing number of students around the world seeking to attend American schools. To aid their adjustment, the college established the Office of International Students and held a special freshman orientation program for international students and their American roommates. The number of foreign applications mushroomed, and by 1997 the college had 147 students from sixty-eight nations. They added a much desired element of cultural diversity and were typically among the college's most highly motivated and academically capable students. At commencement in 2002 their academic strengths were underlined by the fact that, of sixteen seniors receiving summa cum laude honors, four were from Bulgaria. The world financial crisis of 1998 underlined the volatility of this segment of the market, however. Changed economic conditions kept eight international freshmen from enrolling, while the college had to augment aid packages for three others. With dramatic changes in the world situation after September 11, 2001, it remained to be seen whether this strong international presence could be sustained.[87]

While international students represented 9 percent of incoming students in 1998, the level of African Americans changed little, despite continued efforts to raise it. In 1990 alumnus and trustee William H. Gray III established a scholarship fund as a memorial to his father, the Reverend William H. Gray II, which went beyond financial aid to offer a range of additional support services for minority students. Learning that black and Hispanic families were often reluctant to go into debt for college, admissions officers augmented grants in the financial aid packages it offered to financially needy racial minority applicants. Numbers of Latino and Asian American students grew more appreciably. By 1998 federal figures on U.S. minority and international enrollments placed Franklin & Marshall behind only Swarthmore and Bryn Mawr in total diversity among independent colleges in Pennsylvania.[88]

Efforts to increase women and racial minorities in faculty, staff, and administration were more successful. The college participated in a minority scholars-in-residence program sponsored by a regional consortium of liberal arts colleges. A voluntary affirmative action program developed by the collegewide Commission on Minority and Multicultural Affairs sought to ensure a diverse pool of applicants for positions, without impinging on departmental prerogatives. The percentage of women among full-time faculty grew steadily, rising from 23 to 35 percent between 1987 and 1997, while that of minorities increased from 4 to 11 percent. These demographic changes were helped by faculty turnover, much of it prompted by an early retirement program. In addition, the faculty grew in size from 129 in 1987 to 165 by the end of the century.[89]

Reinterpreting Development of the "Whole Student"

Under leadership of a series of dedicated academic deans, the enrichment process at Franklin & Marshall embraced both curricular and cocurricular life. Gordon Douglass stepped down in mid-1990, and psychology professor Charles N. Stewart served as interim until Susanne Woods arrived in January 1991. The first woman to serve as dean of the college, Woods had previously been associate dean of the faculty at Brown University. When she resigned in 1995 to assume the presidency of the College of Wooster, mathematics professor George Rosenstein became interim dean until the election in early 1996 of P. Bruce Pipes, professor of physics and deputy provost at Dartmouth College.[90]

Curricular revisions in the 1990s, like previous changes, strove to counter the dominance of departmental majors. One avenue was continued expansion of interdepartmental programs. In 1989 the faculty approved a women's studies program and minor, and subsequently minors were added in Judaic studies and public policy, and a certificate program in international studies was created. New majors were created in Africana studies, biochemistry, biological foundations of behavior (with specializations in animal behavior or neuroscience), and the scientific and philosophical studies of mind. Geology was transformed into the earth and environment department, with majors in geosciences, environmental sciences, and environmental studies, and the physics and astronomy department introduced majors in astrophysics and astronomy.[91]

Meanwhile, a review of the College Studies curriculum at the beginning of the decade restored a language requirement and expanded first-year seminars. The seminars were intended to include a strong emphasis on writing, in connection with increased focus on writing in College Studies and major courses. Departments were not required to offer seminars, however, and though their numbers increased from four in 1989 to twenty in 1993, they were still not sufficient to make them a graduation requirement.[92]

As significant as specific curricular designs in reshaping the tenor of academic life in the 1990s were efforts to encourage student-teacher interaction. The college had already increased financial support to allow individual students to participate in collaborative research projects with faculty during the summers. Now the college sought to make it possible for more students to work closely with faculty during the academic year. Most prominent of these efforts was reducing the standard teaching load from six courses per year to five, three one semester and two the next. Other liberal arts colleges, such as Grinnell and Wellesley, had recently adopted a three/two load to help faculty balance teaching and research. Franklin & Marshall leaders emphasized that they intended the change primarily to give faculty time to offer more independent studies and tutorials, conduct research with students, and develop new courses. First proposed in 1988–1989 by the Joint Commission on Faculty Professional Working Conditions, the idea met resistance. Students worried that it would reduce courses available, and some science faculty complained that the system did not recognize special conditions in laboratory teaching. Soon after her arrival at Franklin & Marshall, Susanne Woods championed the change, pointing out that the college's heavy teaching load hampered its ability to recruit and retain faculty. To facilitate the shift, the college added a dozen permanent teaching positions, some created by converting sabbatical leave replacement positions to the tenure-track level. The success of the effort was soon measured in an increase in the proportion of students taking independent study projects or tutorials during their careers, from 20 percent in 1990 to 75 percent in 1997.[93]

This period of curricular ferment climaxed with the first top-to-bottom assessment of the curriculum since the 1950s. A faculty symposium in August 1995 launched discussions that continued into 1997, through traditional debates in numerous faculty meetings and the innovative use of an electronic bulletin board. The new curriculum sought to put liberal education at the center of the student experience by focusing attention on broad areas of thought, once the core of the nineteenth-century classical curriculum but downgraded by the emergence of specialized disciplines in the twentieth century. During their first two years, students at Franklin & Marshall must take one course each in three "foundational" areas: mind, self, and spirit; community, culture, and society; and the natural world. The courses offered are specially designed to directly address "questions and ideas that are central to human thought, perception, expression and discovery," drawing upon knowledge from various disciplines while also seeking to call their assumptions into question. As George Rosenstein, then associate vice president for academic affairs, explained when foundational areas were first implemented, "Our intentions have been to introduce to students early in their career the notion that problems that are encountered here in this world don't fit into disciplinary boxes." Foundations courses aim to help students "appreciate the value of free inquiry about questions and ideas that are central to human existence," learn to employ a variety of perspectives, and develop "skills of gathering, evaluating and integrating knowledge, which are needed to confront complex issues." To enable and encourage faculty to develop new courses that the curriculum required, the college provided released time and conducted special summer seminars. Participating in the intellectual excitement inspired by the new curriculum, President Kneedler and Vice President Drum teamed up to teach a freshman seminar on autobiography.[94]

In addition to fulfilling requirements for a major, Franklin & Marshall students must also design and complete an "exploration," at least three courses in a coherent area of interest outside the major. Distribution requirements for courses in the humanities, social sciences, natural sciences, and language studies were retained, with the addition of a course in non-Western cultures. First-year seminars have been made a more central part of the freshman experience: students in most seminars are housed together, and their professors serve as academic advisers. Upperclassmen participate as preceptors, helping to advise and offer support to new students. Collaborative experiences such as preceptorships are a voluntary component of the new curriculum, which includes potential for joint faculty-student research and public service projects. Students can also earn credit for academically related internships. The new curriculum was first implemented in the fall of 1998 for the class of 2002.[95]

Taking Liberal Education Outside the Classroom

The same spirit of transcending boundaries carried over into cocurricular programs aimed at developing habits of good citizenship — again, a rediscovery of a traditional responsibility of liberal education. Sharing in increased national enthusiasm for community service in the 1990s, Franklin & Marshall multiplied opportunities for students and other members of the community. The Reverend Barbara Brummett, chaplain of the college, created the Community and Public Service Institute. Under its guidance, students designed Our Neighbors, Ourselves, or ONO, which organizes several weekend community service projects each year. The National Association of College and University Residence Halls recognized ONO in 1997 as its national Program of the Year. The Spalding Leadership Program, honoring president emeritus Spalding and his wife, Dorothy M. Spalding, provides local internships in city government and agencies. During a visit to campus for the Black Cultural Arts Weekend in 1998, the Reverend Leon Sullivan challenged the college to be the first in the country to raise $10,000 to build a school in South Africa. With the success of the drive, a delegation of students, faculty, and administrators were invited to attend the African-African American Summit in Ghana the following year.[96]

Additional support from the ongoing Leadership in the Liberal Arts capital campaign deepened opportunities for internship and research experiences. With a contribution from Paul Ware, '72, the Ware Institute for Community and Public Service expanded its programs. The Rouse Scholars Program, endowed by trustee emeritus

Andrew Rouse, seeks to attract to the college exceptionally engaged students; the Buchanan Scholars Program recognizes students' prior involvement in community service.[97]

Launched in 1999, the Center for Liberal Arts and Society (CLAS) emphasizes the role of the liberal arts in creating and maintaining an informed citizenry. As he received a variety of proposals for smaller cocurricular projects, Dean Pipes first conceived of CLAS as an umbrella organization with sufficient resources to promote problem-oriented programs that enabled students and faculty to see connections between liberal education principles and wider social needs. Its first director, government professor Stanley Michalak, explained that it allows members of the college "to do things they can't do in their departments, facilitate a wide variety of faculty projects, and work out the relationship between liberal arts and their profession." CLAS includes under its umbrella the Bonchek Institute for Rational Thought and Inquiry; the Seachrist Institute for Entrepreneurial Studies; and the Floyd Institute for Policy Analysis and Community Affairs, intended to offer students opportunities to work in small groups with faculty to apply policy analysis skills to real situations. CLAS also organizes public lecture series and annual debates focusing on major topics, such as global warming.[98]

The blurring of boundaries reflected in Franklin & Marshall's new curriculum and expansion of cocurricular learning opportunities carried into relations among faculty, students, administrators, and staff. The college's academic programs continued to be marked by rigor, as the faculty resisted the grade inflation common elsewhere. But the "boot camp" atmosphere that once prevailed was replaced by a more flexible and collaborative learning environment in which many faculty took pride in mentoring relationships with students. Persistence of Greek organizations continued to be a source of underlying concern. But many alumni once alienated by derecognition restored ties with the college; fifteen years after vowing never to give Franklin & Marshall a cent, Ken Mehlman, by then a prominent Republican politician, joined the Board of Trustees. Students continued to complain about a lack of accessible entertainment, but campus life was far richer than at any time in the college's history.

Setting the Stage for Future Change

After a period of relative stability, Franklin & Marshall College entered a transitional period in its leadership. At the board level, terms of service for chairmen had been shorter in recent years than was the case in an earlier era of dominant trustees, but there had been significant continuity. Longtime investment committee head William G. Simeral served as chairman from 1991 to 1994 and was succeeded by William E. Seachrist. Upon his resignation at the end of 1998, Doreen Boyce became the first woman to head Franklin & Marshall's board. A board member since 1982, Boyce was president of the Buhl Foundation, a Pittsburgh-based philanthropy focusing on education and social science causes.[99]

The administration underwent a new round of reorganization in 2000. Seeking greater integration of academic and cocurricular programs, Kneedler adopted the provost model, increasingly common in higher education, in which the provost serves as chief program officer, responsible for all internal programs, while the president focuses on fund-raising and other external matters. Bruce Pipes was asked to assume the office, and with it much of the work of defining the new administrative structure. In April 2001, Kneedler announced plans to retire at the end of the following academic year. His public statement explained that it seemed the right time for the move. "The college in 2001 is a vital, vibrant institution of national renown and its current status is the work of many talented people. It has been an honor to lead the college during this formative period," he said. The capital campaign closed at the end of 2001 with almost $140 million in contributions and pledges. After a national search by a joint committee of trustees, faculty, and students, the board announced selection of John Anderson Fry, executive vice president at the University of Pennsylvania.[100]

On May 7, 2002, members of the college community gathered in Barshinger Center for a special academic convocation in Kneedler's honor. A number of present and former colleagues offered often humorous memories and sincere tributes to his lifetime of effective service to Franklin & Marshall College. The event concluded with an announcement that the Richard Kneedler Sculpture Garden would be created at the entrance to the Phillips Museum of Art on the south side of Steinman College Center. Bridging the space between the center and Barshinger Center, the sculpture garden would form an appropriate keystone to the arts cluster that he had done so much to create.[101]

A Return to Historic Roots and a Point of Departure

One component of the curricular reassessments of the 1990s — the creation of the Scientific and Philosophical Studies of Mind Program in 1997 — brought Franklin & Marshall College to a point remarkably close to its historic beginnings. By the end of the twentieth century, scholars had become aware of the limitations of narrow specialization and disciplinary boundaries. With funding from the National Science Foundation, the National Endowment for the Humanities, and the Fund for the Improvement of Postsecondary Education, members of the psychology and philosophy departments envisioned a new major focused on the human mind. Through it they hoped to bridge the chasm between the sciences and the humanities and to engage large questions about the relationship between mind and nature and about the individual as a moral agent. Although few, if any, faculty were aware of it, this integrative movement and the desire to bridge physical and metaphysical inquiry had been at the heart of the work of Marshall College's first president, Frederick Rauch. In the century and a half since his death, scholarship had moved far from his dialectical vision, but it seemed that the time had come for a reappreciation of the large philosophical questions that he had engaged, now to be informed by knowledge obtained through empirical research. To underline the importance of this reintegration, planning began for a new building to serve as a center for psychology, biology, and philosophy departments.[102]

This new building would be one of the first projects undertaken by John Fry after he assumed office in 2002. He was well known for the extensive urban redevelopment projects that he had directed in the University of Pennsylvania's West Philadelphia neighborhood, and his administration at Franklin & Marshall promised ambitious new initiatives to physically transform the college and its Lancaster neighborhood. Coming at the end of a period of careful stabilization and enrichment and coinciding with the beginning of a new century, this transition seems an appropriate point to conclude an account of an institution that has faced many cycles of expansion, crisis, stability, and transformation in its long history.

For over two centuries Franklin & Marshall strove to fulfill its mission of liberal education, even as understandings of what that entails continued to evolve. For much of this time the college struggled to survive, often barely able to secure financial resources for essential buildings and programs. The college nevertheless held steadfastly for generations to its initial purpose of serving the educational needs of its German American community and the German Reformed Church. With the rise of universities in the later nineteenth century, it and many other small religiously oriented colleges faced predictions of their inevitable demise. Yet Franklin & Marshall persisted and over the course of the twentieth century flourished as it found new niches in preparing young men, and eventually young women, for the changing challenges of adult life. At times more or less oriented toward preparation for vocations or advanced professional training, the college has continually struggled to honor its fundamental commitment-to serve the developmental needs of students through the exacting but satisfying interaction between scholar and apprentice, or, as Frederick Rauch put it, the experience of "mind awakening mind."[103]

F&M Annual Enrollment Figures, 1853–2008

—⁓—

YEAR	NO. ENROLLED	YEAR	NO. ENROLLED	YEAR	NO. ENROLLED
1853	53	1876	66	1899	171
1854	60	1877	66	1900	184
1855	55	1878	87	1901	164
1856	73	1879	90	1902	163
1857	91	1880	97	1903	180
1858	88	1881	95	1904	186
1859	90	1882	96	1905	204
1860	96	1883	91	1906	220
1861	98	1884	92	1907	213
1862	101	1885	90	1908	214
1863	74	1886	83	1909	241
1864	60	1887	97	1910	263
1865	49	1888	107	1911	293
1866	46	1889	114	1912	298
1867	59	1890	126	1913	302
1868	59	1891	126	1914	326
1869	72	1892	136	1915	291
1870	75	1893	143	1916	319
1871	26	1894	171	1917	244
1872	79	1895	168	1918	224
1873	84	1896	184	1919	318
1874	71	1897	185	1920	316
1875	67	1898	165	1921	406

YEAR	NO. ENROLLED	YEAR	NO. ENROLLED	YEAR	NO. ENROLLED
1922	505	1951	1,002	1980	2,072
1923	531	1952	1,004	1981	2,054
1924	527	1953	1,077	1982	1,967
1925	656	1954	1,057	1983	1,968
1926	650	1955	1,147	1984	1,981
1927	667	1956	1,195	1985	1,963
1928	715	1957	1,151	1986	2,037
1929	752	1958	1,204	1987	1,969
1930	757	1959	1,254	1988	1,926
1931	733	1960	1,338	1989	1,875
1932	703	1961	1,332	1990	1,807
1933	695	1962	1,405	1991	1,815
1934	675	1963	1,403	1992	1,794
1935	689	1964	1,492	1993	1,808
1936	805	1965	1,601	1994	1,794
1937	848	1966	1,601	1995	1,813
1938	914	1967	1,650	1996	1,848
1939	966	1968	1,691	1997	1,859
1940	983	1969	1,816	1998	1,882
1941	879	1970	1,942	1999	1,904
1942	940	1971	1,915	2000	1,911
1943	905	1972	2,000	2001	1,893
1944	981	1973	2,051	2002	1,942
1945	861	1974	2,086	2003	1,933
1946	861	1975	2,077	2004	1,993
1947	1,302	1976	2,028	2005	2,056
1948	1,398	1977	2,044	2006	2,063
1949	1,323	1978	2,077	2007	2,141
1950	1,149	1979	2,090	2008	2,215

Presidents of Franklin & Marshall College and Its Predecessor Institutions, 1787–Present

—〰—

Franklin College (1787–1853)

1787–1815	Gotthilf Heinrich Ernst Muhlenberg
1815–1853	[College operated by Board of Trustees]

Marshall College (1836–1853)

1836–1841	Frederick Augustus Rauch
1841–1853	John Williamson Nevin

Franklin & Marshall College (1853–   )

1853–1855	Presidency vacant*
1855–1866	Emanuel Vogel Gerhart (Marshall College 1838)
1866–1876	John Williamson Nevin
1876–1877	William Marvel Nevin, acting president
1877–1889	Thomas Gilmore Apple (Marshall College 1850)
1889–1909	John Summers Stahr (F&M 1867)
1909–1935	Henry Harbaugh Apple (F&M 1889)
1935–1941	John Ahlum Schaeffer
1941	H. M. J. Klein, acting (F&M 1893)
1941–1954	Theodore August Distler
1954–1955	Interim period — College administered by a trustee committee
1955–1956	William Webster Hall
1956–1962	Frederick deWolfe Bolman Jr.
1962	Anthony Roberts Appel
1962–1963	G. Wayne Glick, acting president

1963–1983	Keith Spalding
1983–1988	James Lawrence Powell
1988–2002	A. Richard Kneedler (F&M 1965)
2002–	John Anderson Fry

*During the merger of Franklin College and Marshall College and the transition to Franklin & Marshall College in 1852 and early 1853, John Williamson Nevin, President of the former Marshall College, served as the unofficial de facto President of Franklin & Marshall College. After Nevin turned down the Board of Trustees' official offer of the presidency, Philip Schaff, Professor at the Theological Seminary in Mercersburg, Pennsylvania, was elected President in March 1853, an offer he ultimately turned down in November of that year. During the search for another candidate, William Marvel Nevin of the faculty was named President pro tem and served during the year 1854 until the election and seating of Emanuel Gerhart as Franklin & Marshall's first President.

Notes

—◠◠◠—

Unless otherwise noted, all primary sources come from the Archives and Special Collections, Shadek-Fackenthal Library, Franklin & Marshall College, which is referred to as the Archives.

Franklin & Marshall catalogues are preserved in the Archives in bound volumes, each containing a range of years. In my notes I cite the volume using this range of years. References to the catalogues cite only the specific year.

In addition, all emphases and misspellings in the quotations are reproduced exactly as in the originals.

FOREWORD

1. Joseph Henry Dubbs, *History of Franklin and Marshall College* (Lancaster: Franklin & Marshall College Alumni Association, 1903).
2. H. M. J. Klein, *History of Franklin and Marshall College, 1787–1948* (Lancaster: Franklin & Marshall College Alumni Association, 1952).

INTRODUCTION

1. Inaugural Address, Speeches Folder, Kneedler Papers, Archives (hereafter, Kneedler Papers).
2. Frederick A. Rauch, "Rauch on Education," *Mercersburg Review* 10 (July 1858): 443–545 (quotations on 444, 446, 450–51).
3. Inaugural Address, Speeches Folder, Kneedler Papers.
4. For citations of background sources, see the extended discussions of these issues in later chapters.
5. Helen Lefkowitz Horowitz, *Campus Life: Undergraduate Cultures from the End of the Eighteenth Century to the Present* (New York: Alfred A. Knopf, 1987).
6. Christopher Jencks and David Riesman, *The Academic Revolution* (New York: Doubleday, 1968), 20–27.

CHAPTER 1

1. For a discussion of the cultural messages embodied in such processions, see Robert Darnton's "A Bourgeois Puts His World in Order: The City as Text," in *The Great Cat Massacre and Other Episodes in French Cultural History* (New York: Vintage, 1984), 116–24.
2. Joseph Henry Dubbs, *History of Franklin and Marshall College* (Lancaster: Franklin & Marshall College Alumni Association, 1903), 40–47; H. M. J. Klein, *History of Franklin and*

Marshall College, 1787–1948 (Lancaster: Franklin & Marshall College Alumni Association, 1952), 16 (all quotations); Jerome Herman Wood Jr., "Conestoga Crossroads: The Rise of Lancaster, Pennsylvania, 1730–1789" (Ph.D. diss., Brown University, 1969), 1:60.

3. Klein, *History*, 14. This letter is reprinted in L. H. Butterfield, ed., *Letters of Benjamin Rush* (Princeton: Princeton University Press, 1951), 1:420–29, and *A Letter by Dr. Benjamin Rush Describing the Consecration of the German College at Lancaster in June, 1787* (Lancaster: Franklin & Marshall College, 1945).

4. Dubbs, *History*, 48.

5. On the background of colonial colleges, see Jurgen Herbst, *From Crisis to Crisis: American College Government, 1636–1819* (Cambridge, Mass.: Harvard University Press, 1982). For a discussion of education in eighteenth-century Lancaster, see Wood, "Conestoga Crossroads," 1:26–27, 233–36.

6. Herbst, *From Crisis to Crisis*, 176–83; Dubbs, *History*, 8–13. On Helmuth's educational visions, see A. G. Roeber, "J. H. C. Helmuth, Evangelical Charity, and the Public Sphere in Pennsylvania, 1793–1800," *Pennsylvania Magazine of History and Biography* 121 (Jan./Apr. 1997): 77–100.

7. Marianne S. Wokeck, *Trade in Strangers: The Beginnings of Mass Migration to North America* (University Park: Pennsylvania State University Press, 1999), 37–57; James T. Lemon, *The Best Poor Man's Country: A Geographical Study of Early Southeastern Pennsylvania* (New York: W. W. Norton, 1972), 14, 17; Aaron Spencer Fogleman, *Hopeful Journeys: German Immigration, Settlement, and Political Culture in Colonial America, 1717–1775* (Philadelphia: University of Pennsylvania Press, 1996), 81.

8. Wokeck, *Trade in Strangers*.

9. Klein, *History*, 22.

10. Wokeck, *Trade in Strangers*, 2–13, 29; Fogelman, *Hopeful Journeys*, 139–48.

11. Dubbs, *History*, 4–5; Sally Schwartz, *"A Mixed Multitude": The Struggle for Toleration in Colonial Pennsylvania* (New York: New York University Press, 1987), 185–93; Wood, "Conestoga Crossroads," 236–38.

12. Benjamin Rush to Richard Price, May 25, 1786, in Butterfield, *Letters*, 1:388; second quotation from Rush, "Address to the People of the United States," *American Museum* 1 (Jan. 1787): 8; David W. Robson, *Educating Republicans: The College in the Era of the American Revolution, 1750–1800* (Westport, Conn.: Greenwood Press, 1985), 187–218.

13. "To the Citizens of Pennsylvnia of German Birth and Extraction: Proposal of a German College," in Butterfield, *Letters*, 2:364–68.

14. Benjamin Rush to the Trustees of Dickinson College, May 23, 1785, in Butterfield, *Letters*, 1: 353; Harry Marlin Tinkcom, *The Republicans and Federalists in Pennsylvania, 1790–1801* (Harrisburg: Pennsylvania Historical and Museum Commission, 1950); Glenn Weaver, "Benjamin Franklin and the Pennsylvania Germans," *William and Mary Quarterly*, 3rd ser., 14 (Oct. 1957): 536–59.

15. Lemon, *Best Poor Man's Country*, 132; E. Digby Baltzell, *Puritan Boston and Quaker Philadelphia* (New Brunswick, N.J.: Transaction Publishers, 1996; originally published 1979 by the Free Press), 161–62.

16. Thomas R. Winpenny, *Industrial Progress and Human Welfare: The Rise of the Factory System in Nineteenth Century Lancaster* (Washington, D.C.: University Press of America, 1982), 12–13. See the broadsides "A Friend to Trade" (Philadelphia, Dec. 13, 1771), American Antiquarian Society, Worcester, Mass., and "Good Public Roads" [Philadelphia, 1773], Library Company of Philadelphia.

17. Daniel Calhoun, *The Intelligence of a People* (Princeton: Princeton University Press, 1973), 41; Wood, "Conestoga Crossroads," 177–78, 420–21; Franklin Ellis and Samuel Evans, *History of Lancaster County, Pennsylvania* (Philadelphia: Everts and Peck, 1883), 226; J. M. Opal, "Exciting Emulation: Academies and the Transformation of the Rural North, 1780s–1820s," *Journal of American History* 91 (Sept. 2004): 445–70.

18. Weaver, "Franklin and the Pennsylvania Germans," 556; Muhlenberg quotation from *The Journals of Henry Melchior Muhlenberg*, trans. Theodore G. Tappert and John W. Doberstein (Philadelphia: Evangelical Lutheran Ministerium of Pennsylvania and Adjacent States and Muhlenberg Press, 1958), 3:725; charter petition quoted in Dubbs, *History*, 18–19; Roeber, "J. H. C. Helmuth."

19. All quotations from Dubbs, *History*, 18–19; Herbst, *From Crisis to Crisis*, 200–201. In the version passed by the legislature, the size of the board was enlarged to forty-five, with fifteen each to be Lutheran and Reformed.

20. Dubbs, *History*, 25–27; Ellis and Evans, *History of Lancaster County*, 226; Charles I. Landis, "History of the Philadelphia and Lancaster Turnpike," *Pennsylvania Magazine of History and Biography* 42 (1918): 133, 236–37.

21. Benjamin Rush to John Montgomery, Dec. 20, 1786, Rush Papers, Library Company of Philadelphia (hereafter, Rush Papers).

22. James Henry Morgan, *Dickinson College, 1783–1933* (Carlisle: Dickinson College, 1933), 10–12; second quotation from Rush to John Montgomery, Jan. 21, 1787, Butterfield, *Letters*, 1:410. Rush to John Montgomery, Feb. 17, 1787, in Butterfield, *Letters*, 1:412; Benjamin Rush to Richard Price, Feb. 14, 1787, in L. H. Butterfield, "Further Letters of Benjamin Rush," *Pennsylvania Magazine of History and Biography* 78 (Jan. 1954): 27–28.

23. Franklin College Trustees Minutes, Archives (hereafter, Franklin College Trustees Minutes).

24. Tappert and Doberstein, *Journals of Henry Melchior Muhlenberg*, 3:733; Dubbs, *History*, 33–35 (quotation p. 33).

25. William Hendel to Benjamin Rush, Aug. 4, 1787, Rush Papers.

26. Dubbs, *History*, 62–66; Butterfield, *Letters*, 1:424.

27. On dissension among Pennsylvania Germans, see Franklin K. Levan, "The Beginnings of Our Literary Institutions," *Reformed Quarterly Review*, 3rd ser., 5 (1883): 529–31.

28. O. S. Ireland, "The Crux of Politics: Religion and Party in Pennsylvania, 1778–1789," *William and Mary Quarterly*, 3rd ser., 42 (Oct. 1985): 453–75.

29. Dubbs, *History*, 50–52.

30. Quoted in Joseph F. Kett, *The Pursuit of Knowledge Under Difficulties: From Self-Improvement to Adult Education in America, 1750–1990* (Stanford: Stanford University Press, 1994), 32.

31. Dubbs, *History*, 71–74, 85.

32. Ibid., 29–30, 61.

33. Franklin College Trustees Minutes, Sept. 12, 1787; John Hubley, circular letter, Sept. 20, 1787, Rush Papers.

34. Benjamin Rush to G. H. E. Muhlenberg, Feb. 15, 1788, Archives; [John Hubley] to Rush, Feb. 23, 1788, Franklin College Trustees Minutes.

35. Fogleman, *Hopeful Journeys*, 150; Kenneth W. Keller, *Rural Politics and the Collapse of Pennsylvania Federalism* (Philadelphia: Transactions of the American Philosophical Society, 1982), vol. 72, pt. 6, 17–21.

36. Paul Zantzinger to John Hubley, copy in Franklin College Trustees Minutes; Dubbs, *History*, 86–87.

37. Franklin College Trustees, Board Minutes, June 6, 1788; John Hubley to Benjamin Rush, June 8, 1788, Rush Papers.

38. Dubbs, *History*, 63, 87, 88, 91; Benjamin Rush to John Hubley, Feb. 13, 1789, Franklin College Trustees Minutes; Muhlenberg Diary, Aug. 6, 1789, quoted in H. M. J. Klein, "The Muhlenberg Family in Lancaster County" (paper for Lancaster County Historical Society, 1942), in Klein Papers, Archives; Henry Muhlenberg to Rush, Nov. 26, 1792, Rush Papers.

39. Dubbs, *History*, 96–103, 107–9 (quotation on 100); Franklin Ellis and Samuel Evans, *History of Lancaster County* (Philadelphia: Everts and Peck, 1883), 404–6; J. Hubley to S. Dale, n.d. [1810], Franklin College Trustees Minutes; summary based on Franklin College Trustees Minutes.

40. Summary based on Franklin College Trustees Minutes.

41. See, for example, Alan Taylor, *William Cooper's Town: Power and Persuasion on the Frontier of the Early American Republic* (New York: Random House, 1995); Franklin College Trustees Minutes; Dubbs, *History*, 111–13.

42. Franklin College Trustees Minutes, May 29, July 7, and Oct. 23, 1840; Dubbs, *History*, 118, 124–25, 129. It was not unusual for colleges to hold investments in banks; in 1824 almost half of Yale's endowment was invested in the Eagle Bank, whose managers had close connections to the college's leaders (Peter Dobkin Hall, *The Organization of American Culture, 1700–1900: Private Institutions, Elites, and the Origins of American Nationality* [New York: New York University Press, 1984], 164–65).

43. Franklin College Trustees Minutes, Apr. 6, 1841, Jan. 4, 1842; Dubbs, *History*, 127–28, 135.

44. Franklin College Trustees Minutes, June 7, 1844; Carl F. Kaestle, *Pillars of the Republic: Common Schools and American Society, 1780–1860* (New York: Hill and Wang, 1983); Ellis and Samuel Evans, *History of Lancaster County*, 402; James Mulhern, *A History of Secondary Education in Pennsylvania* (Philadelphia: privately published, 1933), 476, quotation on 491.

45. Franklin College Trustees Minutes, Mar. 2, 1846, June 21, 1847, June 5, 1848, Aug. 14, 1849; Dubbs, *History*, 134.

46. Franklin College Trustees Minutes, Sept. 3 and Dec. 3, 1849.

47. Franklin College Trustees Minutes, Dec. 3 and 4, 1849; Dubbs, *History*, 138–41.

CHAPTER 2

1. David Potts pointed out in 1971 that there was a pattern of local-denominational alliance in college founding before the Civil War, which yielded to greater denominational control thereafter. This view has been challenged recently, but it seems to characterize the situation of (the separate) Franklin and Marshall colleges. See Potts, "American Colleges in the Nineteenth Century: From Localism to Denominationalism," *History of Education Quarterly* 11 (Winter 1971): 363–80; James Findlay, "Agency, Denominations, and the Western Colleges, 1830–1860," in *The American College in the Nineteenth Century*, ed. Roger L. Geiger (Nashville: Vanderbilt University Press, 2000), 115–26.

2. Daniel Boorstin, *The Americans: The National Experience* (New York: Vintage, 1965), 152–61; Steven M. Nolt, "Liberty, Tyranny, and Ethnicity: The German Reformed 'Free Synod' Schism (1819–1823) and the Americanization of an Ethnic Church," *Pennsylvania Magazine of History and Biography* 125 (Jan./Apr. 2001): 35–60, quotation on 37; H. M. J. Klein, *The History of the Eastern Synod of the Reformed Church in the United States* (Lancaster: Eastern Synod, 1943), 80–81, 126.

3. Quotation from Nolt, "Liberty, Tyranny, and Ethnicity," 36; Theodore Appel, *Recollections of College Life at Marshall College* (Reading, Pa.: Daniel Miller, 1886), 67; Bruce A. Kimball, *The "True Professional Ideal" in America: A History* (Cambridge, Mass.: Blackwell Publishers, 1992), 183–86; H. M. J. Klein, *History of the Eastern Synod*, 138.

4. H. M. J. Klein, *History of the Eastern Synod*, 92–96: E. V. Gerhart, *Additional Professorships in the Theological Seminary of the Reformed Church in the United States* (Lancaster: Inquirer Printing and Publishing, 1884), 3; E. V. Gerhart, "The German Reformed Church," in *The Bibliotheca Sacra and Biblical Repository* (Jan. 1863): 1–77 (quotations on 35, 18, and 20, respectively); Bruce Kuklick, *Churchmen and Philosophers: From Jonathan Edwards to John Dewey* (New Haven: Yale University Press, 1985), 45–46; Sidney E. Ahlstrom, *A Religious History of the American People* (New Haven: Yale University Press, 1972), 439–41; Paul K. Conkin, *The Uneasy Center: Reformed Christianity in Antebellum America* (Chapel Hill: University of North Carolina Press), 169–70. See also John B. Frantz, "The Return to Tradition: An Analysis of the New Measure Movement in the German Reformed Church," *Pennsylvania History* 31 (July 1964): 311–26; and John B. Frantz, "The Religious Development of the Early German Settlers in 'Greater Pennsylvania': The Shenandoah Valley of Virginia," *Pennsylvania History* 68 (Winter 2001): 66–100.

5. Gerhart, "The German Reformed Church," quotations on 23 and 24.

6. Kuklick, *Churchmen and Philosophers*, 85–87; H. M. J. Klein, *History of the Eastern Synod*, 100–102, 104, 110–13 (quotation on 104).

7. H. M. J. Klein, *History of the Eastern Synod*, 100, 104–8; Nolt, "Liberty, Tyranny, and Ethnicity," 44–49 (quotations on 48 and 49).

8. H. M. J. Klein, *History of the Eastern Synod*, 136–37. In 1825, Reformed congregations in Ohio formed a separate synod; the original body was then referred to as the Eastern Synod of the German Reformed Church in the United States. Unless otherwise stated, all references to "synod" in the text refer to this body.

9. Ibid., all quotations on 138, 139–41, 143, 146, 152, 154, 157.

10. Ibid., 145, 148, 153–56.

11. Joseph Henry Dubbs, *History of Franklin and Marshall College* (Lancaster: Franklin & Marshall College Alumni Association, 1903), portrait between 168 and 169, 173–75; Appel, *Recollections of College Life*, 210–11.

12. Howard J. B. Ziegler, *Frederick Augustus Rauch, American Hegelian* (Lancaster: Franklin & Marshall College, 1953), 3–17; Conkin, *Uneasy Center*, 170. In the German system, the Ph.D. was a first rather than a final degree. Rauch's age at receiving his doctorate, twenty-one, was about average for the period. See Charles D. McClelland, *State, Society, and University in Germany, 1700–1914* (Cambridge: Cambridge University Press, 1980), 195.

13. John W. Nevin, *Life and Character of Frederick Augustus Rauch, First President of Marshall College* (Chambersburg, Pa., 1859), 14–15; Dubbs, *History*, 159–61; H. M. J. Klein, *History of the Eastern Synod*, 158–60; "Catalogue of the Members and Library of the Goethean Literary Society of Marshall College, Mercersburg, Pa.," Archives. For examples of such stories, see Appel, *Recollections of College Life*, 210; Dubbs, *History*, 174; Richard C. Schiedt, *A Tribute to Dr. Frederick Augustus Rauch, First President of Marshall College, Eminent Educator and Philosopher in Commemoration of the 125th Anniversary of His Birth, 1806-1931* (n.p., n.d. [ca. 1931]), 6–7.

14. H. M. J. Klein, *History of the Eastern Synod*, 160–62, 164, 171; Dubbs, *History*, 164–67 (quotation on 167); Franklin College Trustees Minutes, Sept. 23 and 27, 1835, Archives (hereafter, Franklin College Trustees Minutes).

15. The Woman's Club of Mercersburg, Pennsylvania, *Old Mercersburg* (New York: Frank Allaben Genealogical, 1912), 19, 42, 45, 50; Philip Shriver Klein, *President James Buchanan: A Biography* (University Park: Pennsylvania State University Press, 1962), 4–5; Dubbs, *History*, 177.

16. Woman's Club of Mercersburg, *Old Mercersburg*, 49, 50.

17. Quotation appears in Marshall College Trustees Minutes, July 12, 1836, Archives (hereafter, Marshall College Trustees Minutes); H. M. J. Klein, *History of the Eastern Synod*, 39–40, 42. On the rising prestige of the law in this period, see Kimball, *True Professional Ideal*.

18. Quotations from Marshall College Trustees Minutes, July 12, 1836. Beginning in the mid-1820s, a few of the more prominent colleges, such as Harvard, Columbia, and Princeton, had begun to offer instruction in German. At Middlebury College, German was briefly offered in the early 1820s but did not become a regular offering until 1847. See Richard Spuler, "American *Germanistic* and German Classicism: A Nineteenth-Century Exchange," in *Germans in America: Aspects of German-American Relations in the Nineteenth Century*, ed. E. Allen McCormick (New York: Social Science Monographs, 1983), 60; David M. Stameshkin, *The Town's College: Middlebury College, 1800–1915* (Middlebury: Middlebury College Press, 1985), 78.

19. H. M. J. Klein, *History of the Eastern Synod*, 40; quotation from Marshall College Trustees Minutes, July 13, 1836. For a description of some typical educational practices in nineteenth-century colleges, see Roger L. Geiger with Julie Ann Bubolz, "College as It Was in the Mid-Nineteenth Century," in *American College in the Nineteenth Century*, ed. Geiger (Nashville: Vanderbilt University Press, 2000), 81–82.

20. Rüdiger vom Bruch, "A Slow Farewell to Humboldt? Stages in the History of German Universities, 1810–1945," in *German Universities Past and Future*, ed. Mitchell G. Ash (Providence, R.I.: Berghahn Books, 1997), 3–27 (quotation on 14).

21. Bruch, "Slow Farewell to Humboldt?" quotation on 10; R. Steven Turner, "University Reformers and Professorial Scholarship in Germany, 1760–1806," in *The University in Society*, ed. Lawrence Stone (Princeton: Princeton University Press, 1974), 2:495–531; Peter Novick, *That Noble Dream: The "Objectivity Question" and the American Historical Profession* (New York: Cambridge University Press, 1988), 24; McClelland, *State, Society, and University in Germany*, 110–50, 171–81 (quotations on 124).

22. Konrad H. Jarausch, *Students, Society, and Politics in Imperial Germany: The Rise of Academic Illiberalism* (Princeton: Princeton University Press, 1982), 8–9; McClelland, *State, Society, and University in Germany*, 118, 172–73; Michael J. Hofstetter, *The Romantic Idea of a University: England and Germany, 1770–1850* (New York: St. Martin's Press, 2001).

23. Jarausch, *Students, Society, and Politics in Imperial Germany*, 9; Caroline Winterer, *The Culture of Classicism: Ancient Greece and Rome in American Intellectual Life, 1780–1910* (Baltimore: Johns Hopkins University Press, 2002).

24. Douglas Sloan, *The Scottish Enlightenment and the American College Ideal* (New York: Teachers College Press, 1971); Gilman M. Ostrander, *Republic of Letters: The American Intellectual Community, 1776–1865* (Madison, Wis.: Madison House Publishers, 1999), 22–28; David W. Robson, *Educating Republicans: The College in the Era of the American Revolution, 1750–1800* (Westport, Conn.: Greenwood Press, 1985), 64–66; Daniel Walker Howe, *Making the American Self: Jonathan Edwards to Abraham Lincoln* (Cambridge, Mass.: Harvard University Press), 50–57; Henry F. May, *The Enlightenment in America* (New York: Oxford University Press, 1976), 32–34.

25. May, *Enlightenment in America*, 341–50; Howe, *Making the American Self*, 5–8, 128–30; Daniel Walker Howe, *The Unitarian Conscience: Harvard Moral Philosophy, 1805–1861* (Cambridge, Mass.: Harvard University Press, 1970); Louise L. Stevenson, *Scholarly Means to Evangelical Ends: The New Haven Scholars and the Transformation of Higher Learning in America, 1830–1890* (Baltimore: Johns Hopkins University Press, 1986), 16–17; George M. Marsden, *Fundamentalism and American Culture: The Shaping of Twentieth-Century Evangelicalism* (New York: Oxford University Press, 1980).

26. Stevenson, *Scholarly Means to Evangelical Ends*, 31–37, 176; Kuklick, *Churchmen and Philosophers*, 118; James T. Kloppenberg, *Uncertain Victory: Social Democracy and Progressivism in European and American Thought, 1870–1920* (New York: Oxford University Press, 1986), 16, 18; Ziegler, *Frederick Augustus Rauch*; Jurgen Herbst, *The German Historical School in American Scholarship: A Study in the Transfer of Culture* (Ithaca: Cornell University Press, 1965), 65. Kuklick recognizes Rauch as one of the first American academic writers to challenge the prevailing Common Sense philosophy.

27. Nevin, *Life and Character of Frederick Augustus Rauch*, 19 (first quotation on 12); Ziegler, *Frederick Augustus Rauch*, 48–51; James A. Good, introduction to Frederick Augustus Rauch, *Psychology, or a View of the Human Soul* (reprint, Bristol, England: Thoemmes Press, 2002); Richard C. Schiedt, "A Tribute to Dr. Frederick Augustus Rauch, First President of Marshall College, Eminent Educator, and Philosopher in Commemoration of the 125th Anniversary of His Birth, 1806–1931, reprinted from 'The Reformed Church Messenger'" (n. loc., n. pub., n.d. [ca. 1931]), 12–13; Frederick A. Rauch, *Psychology, or a View of the Human Soul* (New York: M. W. Dodd, 1840) (subsequent Rauch quotations on 2); unsigned review, *New Englander* 1 (Apr. 1843): 297–98 (quotation on 297); Robert Clemmer, "Historical Transcendentalism in Pennsylvania," *Journal of the History of Ideas* 3 (Oct.–Dec. 1967): 579–92; Lewis Perry, *Intellectual Life in America* (Chicago: University of Chicago Press, 1989), 212–13, 249, 252; "The Promotion of Scientific Learning Through 150 Years," *Franklin and Marshall Papers*, no. 9 (1937): n.p.

28. Kloppenberg, *Uncertain Victory*, 16, 18; Rauch, *Psychology*, 48, 163–64, 180–81; Merle Curti, "The American Exploration of Dreams and Dreamers," *Journal of the History of Ideas* 27 (1966): 401.

29. Rauch, *Psychology*, 47–48, 63 (quotation), 175–79, 183–84. On Rauch's influence on Bushnell, see Ahlstrom, *Religious History*, 620.

30. Frederick A. Rauch, "Rauch on Education," *Mercersburg Review* 10 (July 1858): 443–545 (quotations on 444, 446).

31. *Reports on the Course of Instruction in Yale College* (New Haven: Yale College, 1828), quotations on 6, 7, 30; Stevenson, *Scholarly Means to Evangelical Ends*, 15. On ideas of mental discipline in this period at Middlebury College, see Stameshkin, *The Town's College*, 73–75.

32. Rauch, "Rauch on Education," 450–51.

33. Ibid., 453–54.

34. "Classical School of the German Reformed Church, York, Pa., Report of the Progress of the Classes during the Last Session," Archives; Dubbs, *History*, 169.

35. Dubbs, *History*, 175; G. William Welker, *Eulogy on the Life and Character of Frederick A. Rauch* (Chambersburg, Pa.: Office of Publication of the German Reformed Church, 1841), 16; Nevin, *Life and Character of Frederick Augustus Rauch*, 23.

36. Matriculation signatures for 1847 and 1848 in the Marshall College Trustees Minutes; penalties summarized from Marshall College Faculty Minutes, Archives.

37. Marshall College Faculty Minutes, June 3, 1837 (quotation), and July 12, 1838; Dubbs, *History*, 225.

38. Marshall College Faculty Minutes, Jan. 31, Feb. 1, Mar. 13, and Aug. 31; quotation from Rauch to B. C. Wolf[f], [March, 1839?], Rauch Papers, Archives.

39. Marshall College Faculty Minutes, Aug. 21, 1838.

40. Quoted in H. M. J. Klein, *History of the Eastern Synod*, 36–37.

41. "Recollections of O. C. Hartley, Esq." *College Days* Jan. 1873, 3.

42. *Catalogue of the Officers and Students in Marshall College, Mercersburg, PA 1840–41* (Gettysburg: H. C. Neinstedt, 1841), 16–17. On Romanticism and college campuses, see Paul Venable Turner, *Campus: An American Planning Tradition* (New York: Architectural History Foundation, 1984), 101–6.

43. *Catalogue*, 17.

44. H. M. J. Klein, *History of the Eastern Synod*, 35; Marshall College Faculty Minutes, Aug. 17, 1837.

45. Dubbs, *History*, 223–26; Appel, *Recollections of College Life*, 108–110; Woman's Club of Mercersburg, *Old Mercersburg*, 34, 46. On Blanchard, see George M. Marsden, *Fundamentalism and American Culture: The Shaping of Twentieth-Century Evangelicalism* (New York: Oxford University Press, 1980), 27–28.

46. Marshall College Faculty Minutes, July 1837, and Aug. 17, 1837.

47. H. M. J. Klein, *A Century of Education at Mercersburg, 1836–1936* (Lancaster: Mercersburg Academy, 1936), 124–25; Appel, *Recollections of College Life*, 117–18 (quotation on 117); Woman's Club of Mercersburg, *Old Mercersburg*, 39, 49; H. M. J. Klein, *History of the Eastern Synod*, 175–76; Dubbs, *History*, 178–79; Turner, *Campus*, 90–100.

48. Dubbs, *History*, 180–83; *Catalogue of the Officers and Students of Marshall College, Mercersburg, Pa., 1838–1839* (Chambersburg: Printed by Henry Ruby, 1839); Marshall College Trustees Minutes, Sept. 27, 1837, and Feb. 14, 1838.

49. Roger L. Geiger, "The Era of Multipurpose Colleges in American Higher Education, 1850–1890," in *The American College in the Nineteenth Century*, ed. Geiger (Nashville: Vanderbilt University Press, 2000), 126–52.

50. James Findlay, "Agency, Denominations, and the Western Colleges, 1830–1860," in *The American College in the Nineteenth Century*, ed. Roger L. Geiger (Nashville: Vanderbilt Uni-

versity Press, 2000), 115–26; Dubbs, *History*, 179, 184; Marshall College Trustees Minutes, Apr. 24, Sept. 26, and Sept. 27, 1837, and Sept. 24, 1839.

51. Marshall College Trustees Minutes, June 7, 1838; Dubbs, *History*, 243. On the widespread use of perpetual scholarships, see Frederick Rudolph, *The American College and University: A History* (New York: Vintage Books, 1962), 190–92.

52. Marshall College Trustees Minutes, June 23, 1838, Apr. 10, 1844; Woman's Club of Mercersburg, *Old Mercersburg*, 67.

53. Dubbs, *History*, 183–84, *Catalogue of the Officers and Students of Marshall College, Mercersburg, Pa., 1840–41*; Marshall College Trustees Minutes, 1837–1841, esp. Sept. 29, 1841.

54. Marshall College Trustees Minutes, Sept. 24 and Nov. 8, 1839, and "Protest from the Citizens of Mercersburg," Marshall College Trustees Minutes, Dec. 17, 1849.

55. Marshall College Trustees Minutes, Nov. 8, 1839, Sept. 29 and 30, 1840, Apr. 7, 1841, Sept. 27, 1842, and Sept. 9, 1845; Woman's Club of Mercersburg, *Old Mercersburg*, 38 (quotation on 49).

56. Frantz, "The Return to Tradition," 314–19. On the Second Great Awakening in general, see William G. McLoughlin, *Revivals, Awakenings, and Reform* (Chicago: University of Chicago Press, 1978), chap. 4.

57. H. M. J. Klein, *History of the Eastern Synod*, 182–84; Ziegler, *Frederick Augustus Rauch*, 32–33; John W. Nevin, *My Own Life: The Earlier Years* (Lancaster: Historical Society of the Evangelical and Reformed Church, 1964), 106–117, 152–58; Dubbs, *History*, 191–92.

58. Nevin, *My Own Life*, 6, 8–12. On the Second Great Awakening in New York State, see Whitney R. Cross, *The Burned-Over District: A Social and Intellectual History of Enthusiastic Religion in Western New York, 1800–1850* (Ithaca: Cornell University Press, 1950), and Paul E. Johnson, *A Shopkeeper's Millennium: Society and Revivals in Rochester, New York, 1815–1837* (New York: Hill and Wang, 1978).

59. Nevin, *My Own Life*, 23–25 (quotation on 23), 37–39.

60. Ibid., first quotation on 92; second quotation on 125. On efforts to define American culture in terms of New England norms, see Joseph A. Conforti, *Imagining New England: Explorations of Regional Identity from the Pilgrims to the Mid-Twentieth Century* (Chapel Hill: University of North Carolina Press, 2001).

61. Nevin, *My Own Life*, 125, 140–41; William DiPuccio, "Nevin's Idealistic Philosophy," in *Reformed Confessionalism in Nineteenth-Century America: Essays on the Thought of John Williamson Nevin*, ed. Sam Hamstra Jr. and Arie J. Griffioen (Lanham, Md.: American Theological Library Association and Scarecrow Press, 1995), 47–49.

62. Nevin, "Comments at Seventieth Birthday Tribute" [1873], Nevin Papers, Archives.

63. Dubbs, *History*, 192; Nevin, *Life and Character of Frederick Augustus Rauch*, 18.

64. Appel, *Recollections of College Life*, 292 (quotation); Ziegler, *Frederick Augustus Rauch*, 30–34, 52–53; H. M. J. Klein, *History of the Eastern Synod*, 43–44.

65. Dubbs, *History*, 188.

66. Nevin, *Life and Character of Frederick Augustus Rauch*, 28.

67. Marshall College Trustees Minutes, Mar. 4 and Apr. 7, 1841 (quotation); Dubbs, *History*, 188; H. M. J. Klein, *History of the Eastern Synod*, 44.

68. First quotation, Marshall College Trustees Minutes, Sept. 28, 1842; Marshall College Faculty Minutes, July 29, 1840, and Sept. 28, 1841; Theodore Appel, *The Life and Work of John Williamson Nevin* (Philadelphia: Reformed Church Publication House, 1889), 422–23; *College Student*, memorial issue (Apr.); Dubbs, *History*, 181 (second quotation).

69. DiPuccio, "Nevin's Idealistic Philosophy," 54–55; Frantz, "The Return to Tradition," 320–21; Gary K. Pranger, "Philip Schaff: His Role in American Evangelical Education," in *German Influences on Education in the United States to 1917*, ed. Henry Geitz, Jurgen Heidenkind, and Jurgen Herbst (Cambridge: Cambridge University Press, 1995), 213–26.

70. John W. Nevin, *The Anxious Bench, A Tract for the Times*, 2nd ed. (Chambersburg, Pa.:

Publication Office of the German Reformed Church, 1844), 14 (first quotation), 27 (second and fourth quotation), 49, 52 (third quotation), 53, 64, 119, 125, 129.

71. Kuklick, *Churchmen and Philosophers*, 161–70, 173; Stevenson, *Scholarly Means to Evangelical Ends*, 176; Frantz, "The Return to Tradition," 323–35.

72. Marshall College Trustees Minutes, Sept. 28 and 29, 1841, Sept. 28, 1842, Apr. 11, 1844; Luther J. Binkley, *The Mercersburg Theology*, Franklin and Marshall College Studies, no. 7 (Lancaster, 1953); Ahlstrom, *Religious History*, 615–32, 615n (quotation on 615, 616); Kuklick, *Churchmen and Philosophers*, 176–77. An extensive bibliography on Nevin and the Mercersburg Theology can be found in Sam Hamstra Jr. and Arie J. Griffioen, eds., *Reformed Confessionalism in Nineteenth-Century America: Essays on the Thought of John Williamson Nevin* (Lanham, Md.: American Theological Library Association and Scarecrow Press, 1995). See also James Hastings Nichols, *Romanticism in American Theology: Nevin and Schaff at Mercersburg* (Chicago: University of Chicago Press, 1961).

73. Binkley, *Mercersburg Theology*, 52–73 (all quotations on 62).

74. Gerhart, "The German Reformed Church," 51–52; Appel, *Life and Work of Nevin*, 299; Perry Miller, first quotation quoted in Robert Clemmer, "Historical Transcendentalism in Pennsylvania," *Journal of the History of Ideas* 30 (Oct.–Dec. 1967): 579–92; second quotation Kuklick, *Churchmen and Philosophers*, 183. On the role of denominational reviews, see Thomas Bender, *New York Intellect: A History of Intellectual Life in New York City, from 1750 to the Beginnings of Our Own Time* (Baltimore: Johns Hopkins University Press, 1987), 42–43.

75. Nevin, *The Church: A Sermon Preached at the Opening of the Synod of the German Reformed Church at Carlisle, October 15, 1846* (Chambersburg, Pa.: Publication Office of the German Reformed Church, 1847).

76. Marshall College Trustees Minutes, Apr. 7, 1841, and Sept. 27 and 28, 1842 (first quotation); John C. Bowman, "Facts and Lessons from Our Educational History," *Reformed Church Review* 7 (Apr. 1903): 265–68; John S. Stahr, "The Financial Development of Franklin and Marshall College," *Reformed Church Review* 7 (Apr. 1903): 164–65 (second quotation); H. M. J. Klein, *Century of Education*, 173.

77. Marshall College Trustees Minutes, Sept. 27, 1842, and Sept. 26, 1843; Dubbs, *History*, 212.

78. *Catalogue of the Officers and Students of Marshall College, Mercersburg, Pa., 1845–1846* (Philadelphia: J. B. Lippincott and Co., 1846), 17–18; *Catalogue of the Officers and Students of Marshall College, 1846–7* (Mercersburg, PA: D. J. Schnebly, 1847) 17–18 (italics in the original).

79. Faculty to J. N. Brewer and William D. McKinstry, Nov. 1, 1847, Marshall College Faculty Minutes.

80. Marshall College Faculty Minutes, Sept. 6, 1847; Dubbs, *History*, 226–27.

81. Dubbs, *History*, 213–17; quotations from *Catalogue of the Officers and Students of Marshall College, 1846–47*, 21. On college literary societies, see Louise L. Stevenson, "Preparing for Public Life: The Collegiate Students at New York University, 1832–1881," in *The University and the City: From Medieval Origins to the Present*, ed. Thomas Bender (New York: Oxford University Press, 1988), 150–77, and Leon Jackson, "The Rights of Man and the Rites of Youth: Fraternity and Riot at Eighteenth-Century Harvard," in *The American College in the Nineteenth Century*, ed. Roger L. Geiger (Nashville: Vanderbilt University Press, 2000), 46–79. On general societies, see Joseph F. Kett, *The Pursuit of Knowledge Under Difficulties: From Self-Improvement to Adult Education in America, 1750–1990* (Stanford: Stanford University Press, 1994).

82. *Catalogue of the Members and Library of the Goethean Literary Society of Marshall College* [Mercersburg: Marshall College, 1844].

83. Dubbs, *History*, 213–17, 221; Marshall College Faculty Minutes, Aug. 12, 1845; "A Visitor," clipping from *Weekly Messenger* [1848], Archives.

84. Dubbs, *History*, 217–20; Marshall College Faculty Minutes, May 10, 1847; *Catalogue of the Officers and Students of Marshall College, 1846–7*, 21; Aimee K. Kulp, "History of the Libraries of Marshall College," typescript, n.p., Archives; Frederick Augustus Rupley, "The Humorous Side of Life at Marshall College," typescript, n.d., Archives.

85. Dubbs, *History*, 214; Marshall College Trustees Minutes, Sept. 26, 1843, Apr. 8 and May 29, 1845; *Catalogue of the Officers and Students of Marshall College, 1846–7*, 22; E. V. Gerhart, "History of the D. L. Society," typescript [1841], Gerhart Papers, Archives.

86. Dubbs, *History*, 214; *Catalogue of the Officers and Students of Marshall College, 1844–45*, 24; Marshall College Faculty Minutes, Feb. 15, 1847; Marshall College Trustees Minutes, Apr. 1, 1845 (quotation) and June 15, 1853; Nevin, *A Funeral Sermon with Reference to the Death of James Edgar Moore* (Mercersburg, Pa.: Diagnothian Literary Society, 1844).

87. Appel, *Recollections of College Life*, 154–55; *Rupjonjim*, Nov. 14, 1840, and Jan. 1, 1841, Archives; Dubbs, *History*, 233–35 (quotation on 235).

88. Rupley, "The Humorous Side of Life at Marshall College."

89. *Catalogue of the Officers and Students of Marshall College, 1846–1847*, 20–21.

90. *Catalogue of the Officers and Students of Marshall College, 1844–45*, 21; John W. Nevin, *The German Language, an Address, Delivered Before the Goethean Literary Society of Marshall College, at Its Anniversary, August 29, 1842* (Chambersburg, Pa.: Goethean Literary Society, 1842), 15. On the role of particularism in the formation of German American ethnicity, see Steven Nolt, *Foreigners in Their Own Land: Pennsylvania Germans in the Early Republic* (University Park: Pennsylvania State University Press, 2002), 20 and passim.

91. *Catalogue of the Officers and Students of Marshall College, 1846–1847*, 21–22.

92. Summary of catalogues throughout the 1840s, Archives; Stevenson, *Scholarly Means to Evangelical Ends*, 87. Gilbert Allardyce reports that in 1869 Harvard had only one "dear old gentleman" who taught history, and as late as 1881, there were only eleven full-time professors of history in American colleges and universities (Allardyce, "The Rise and Fall of the Western Civilization Course," *American Historical Review* 87 [June 1982]: 699; Kett, *Pursuit of Knowledge Under Difficulties*, 165).

93. Summary of catalogues throughout the 1840s, Archives; Marshall College Faculty Minutes, Feb. 1, 3, 7, and 21 (quotation), 1848. These enrollment numbers were above the average for the 1840s, which was seventy-eight. See Colin Burke, *American Collegiate Populations: A Test of the Traditional View* (New York: New York University Press, 1982), 54.

94. Marshall College Trustees Minutes, Apr 21, 1848 (quotation). Green and Nevin had also tangled over the question of whether animals possessed minds of the same order as humans. See [J. W. Nevin], *To the Students of Marshall College: A Review of Dr. T. Green's Theory of Animal Mind* (Philadelphia: J. B. Lippincott, 1847).

95. Marshall College Trustees Minutes, Sept. 8, 1846, June 7, 1838, Mar. 29, 1839, Apr. 21, 1848; Dubbs, *History*, 197; Appel, *Life and Work of Nevin*, 437–38.

96. Appel, *Life and Work of Nevin*, 432 (quotation); John B. Payne, "Schaff and Nevin, Colleagues at Mercersburg: The Church Question," *Church History* 61 (June 1992): 169–90.

97. Reprinted in *Lancaster Examiner and Herald*, June 5, 1850.

98. Franklin College Trustees Minutes, Dec. 4, 1849; Appel, *Life and Work of Nevin*, 432; H. M. J. Klein, *History of the Eastern Synod*, 214; Dubbs, *History*, 241.

99. Marshall College Trustees Minutes, Dec. 26, 1849.

100. Correspondence regarding merger with Franklin College, Marshall College Trustees Records, Archives. Students of Marshall College to the Board of Trustees, n.d. [prob. 1849], Doc. 8, Records of Committee on Removal, Marshall College Trustees Records, Archives.

101. Protest from the Citizens of Mercersburg, [Dec. 24, 1849], Doc. 11, Records of Committee on Removal; Marshall College Trustees Minutes, Dec. 27; Daniel Zacharias to Trustees of Marshall College, Dec. 26, 1849, Marshall College Trustees Minutes.

102. Marshall College Trustees Minutes, Dec. 27 and 28, 1849; H. M. J. Klein, *History of the Eastern Synod*, 215–16.

103. Franklin College Trustees Minutes, Feb. 12, 1850, June 7, July 12, Dec. 21, 1852, and Mar. 1, 1853; Appel, *Life and Work of Nevin*, 434–37; *Lancaster Examiner and Herald*, Jan. 23 (first quotation) and Mar. 6, 1850 (second quotation).

104. *Lancaster Examiner and Herald*, Mar. 13, 1850, and Jan. 22, 1851; Appel, *Life and Work of Nevin*, 434–36.

105. Appel, *Life and Work of Nevin*, 434–37; Dubbs, *History*, 260; *Lancaster Examiner and Herald*, Dec. 11, 1850 (quotation); Stahr, "Financial Development of Franklin and Marshall College," 167.

CHAPTER 3

1. Franklin & Marshall College Trustees Minutes, Archives (hereafter, Trustees Minutes).

2. *Lancaster Examiner and Herald*, Oct. 20, 1852 (quotation); Thomas R. Winpenny, *Industrial Progress and Human Welfare: The Rise of the Factory System in Nineteenth Century Lancaster* (Washington, D.C.: University Press of America, 1982), 29–45.

3. Steven M. Nolt, *Foreigners in Their Own Land: Pennsylvania Germans in the Early Republic* (University Park: Pennsylvania State University Press, 2002).

4. Philip Shriver Klein, *President James Buchanan: A Biography* (University Park: Pennsylvania State University Press, 1962), 222–23; Trustees Minutes, Jan. 25, Mar. 2, Apr. 19, 1853; Winpenny, *Industrial Progress and Human Welfare*, 34.

5. John Nevin, "Comments at Seventieth Birthday Tribute" [1873], Nevin Papers, Archives (hereafter, Nevin Papers); John B. Payne, "Schaff and Nevin, Colleagues at Mercersburg: The Church Question," *Church History* 61 (June 1992): 169–90; Theodore Appel, *The Life and Work of John Williamson Nevin* (Philadelphia: Reformed Church Publication House, 1889), 439; H. M. J. Klein, *History of the Eastern Synod of the Reformed Church in the United States* (Lancaster: Eastern Synod, 1943), 216–17; James I. Good, *History of the Reformed Church in the U.S. in the Nineteenth Century* (New York: Reformed Church in America, 1911), 286–21.

6. Trustees Minutes, Mar. 2, Apr. 19 (Nevin quotation) and 20, and June 7, 1853; Joseph Henry Dubbs, *History of Franklin and Marshall College* (Lancaster: Franklin & Marshall College Alumni Association, 1903), 265–66; Appel, *Life and Work of Nevin*, 440–41; Good, *History of Reformed Church*, 296–97.

7. Trustees Minutes, Jan. 25, Mar. 1 and 2, Apr. 20, 1863; Dubbs, *History*, 275–76; E V. Gerhart, "Early Struggles of Our College," *Oriflamme* (Lancaster, Pa., Students of Franklin & Marshall College, 1903), 169.

8. William H. Pierson Jr., *American Buildings and Their Architects: Technology and the Picturesque, The Corporate and the Early Gothic Styles* (Garden City, N.Y.: Doubleday, 1978); Calder Loth and Julius Trousdale Sadler Jr., *The Only Proper Style: Gothic Architecture in America* (Boston: New York Graphic Society, 1975), 48, 74, 90–91; Phoebe B. Stanton, *The Gothic Revival and American Church Architecture: An Episode in Taste, 1840–1856* (Baltimore: Johns Hopkins University Press, 1968); Appel, *Life and Work of Nevin*, 482–86. Nevin often used the term "Puritan" when referring to the mistakes of current Protestantism. See Appel, *Life and Work of Nevin*, 350.

9. Trustees Minutes, June 8, 1853; *Lancaster Intelligencer*, July 5, 1853; Dubbs, *History*, 277.

10. Trustees Minutes, Apr. 20, June 7, 8, and 28 (quotation), July 27, Aug. 31, and Nov. 11, 1865; Dubbs, *History*, 276–77.

11. Trustees Minutes, Mar. 1, 2, and 3 (first quotation), and Apr. 19, 1853 (last quotation); Dubbs, *History*, 284–87; Dennis B. Downey, *"We Sing to Thee": A History of Millersville University* (Millersville, Pa.: Millersville University Press, 2004). Princeton required faculty to be Presbyterians until 1876; see P. C. Kemeny, *Princeton in the Nation's Service: Religious Ideals and Educational Practice, 1868–1928* (New York: Oxford University Press, 1998), 61–62.

12. Trustees Minutes, June 28, 1853 (first quotation); Dubbs, *History*, 255; Philip Shriver Klein, *James Buchanan*, 224; *Formal Opening of Franklin and Marshall College* (Lancaster: Franklin & Marshall College, 1853), 7–8 (second quotation).

13. *Formal Opening of Franklin and Marshall College*, 9–35 (quotations on 23, 25, 33, and 35, respectively).

14. H. M. J. Klein, *History of Franklin and Marshall College: 1787–1948* (Lancaster: Franklin and Marshall College Alumni Association, 1952), 70–71.

15. Joseph Henry Dubbs, "College Days in the Olden Time: From an Unfinished Autobiography," [Franklin & Marshall] *College Student*, Dec. 1909, 87–90 (hereafter, *College Student*).

16. Kenneth Cmiel, *Democratic Eloquence: The Fight over Popular Speech in Nineteenth-Century America* (New York: William Morrow, 1990), 24–31.

17. Dubbs, *History*, 257–58; Dubbs, "College Days," 89; Trustees Minutes, Apr. 19, 1853 (quotation).

18. Trustees Minutes, Mar. 2, 1853; Dubbs, *History*, 255 (quotation), 275; H. Y. S., "The Men Who Did Not Graduate," *College Student*, Feb. 1900, 157.

19. Statement of the Funds and Property of Marshall College, sent to Trustees of Franklin College, Dec. 31, 1849, Marshall College Trustees Minutes, Archives; Trustees Minutes, Apr. 20, Aug. 31, and Nov. 11, 1853, and July 25, 1865; E. V. Gerhart to Board, July 27, 1857, and July 23, 1860, Trustees Minutes; Gary K. Pranger, "Philip Schaff: His Role in American Evangelical Education," in *German Influences on Education in the United States to 1917* (Cambridge: Cambridge University Press, 1995), 223.

20. Faculty Minutes, May 8, 1853, July 25, 1854, Archives (hereafter, Faculty Minutes); *Catalogue of the Officers and Students of Franklin and Marshall College, 1852–1853* (Lancaster: Franklin and Marshall College Senior Class, 1853); *Catalogue of the Officers and Students of Franklin and Marshall College, 1853–1854* (hereafter, *Catalogue*).

21. Trustees Minutes, Apr. 20, June 28, Dec. 20, 1853, July 25 (quotation) and 26, 1854, and June 24, 1874; Dubbs, *History*, 270, 277–78; H. M. J. Klein, *History of the Eastern Synod*, 71; Philip Shriver Klein, *James Buchanan*, 227.

22. Marshall College Trustees Minutes, Sept. 29, 1841; James I. Good, *Rev. E. V. Gerhart, D.D. as Professor of Theology at Tiffin, Ohio* (n.p., 1920), 2–4, 11; Good, *History of the Reformed Church*, 217–19.

23. E. V. Gerhart to S. Bowman and N. A. Keyes, Aug. 3, 1854 (first quotation), and E. V. Gerhart to S. Bowman, Sept. 30, 1854 (second quotation), Gerhart Papers, Archives (hereafter, Gerhart Papers); H. M. J. Klein, *History of the Eastern Synod*, 73–74; Good, *History of Reformed Church*, 297.

24. J. H. Dubbs, "Eulogy of E. V. Gerhart," unidentified clipping, May 19, 1904, Dubbs Papers, Archives; Trustees Minutes, May 3, 1855; Faculty Minutes, May 22, 1855; K. Kulp, "History of the Libraries of Marshall College," typescript, n.p., Archives.

25. E. V. Gerhart to Board, July 24, 1855, July 21, 1856, and July 27, 1857 (quotation), Gerhart Papers; Faculty Minutes, Feb. 18, 1857, Archives; Dubbs, *History*, 353; Paul R. Deslandes, "Competitive Examinations and the Culture of Masculinity in Oxbridge Undergraduate Life, 1850–1920," *History of Education Quarterly* 42 (Winter 2002): 544–78.

26. Faculty Minutes, Mar. 19, 1856, Archives; *Dedication of Franklin and Marshall College* (Chambersburg, Pa.: Franklin & Marshall College, 1856), 7–8 (quotations); Appel, *Life and Work of Nevin*, 628.

27. Trustees Minutes, Aug. 31, 1853, July 25, 1854, Apr. 11, and May 3, 1855.

28. Faculty Minutes, Mar. 18, 1857; Dubbs, "College Days," 92.

29. Henry Kyd Douglas, *The Douglas Diary: Student Days at Franklin and Marshall College, 1856–1858*, ed. Frederic Shriver Klein and John Howard Carrill (Lancaster: Franklin & Marshall College, 1973), 101.

30. Dubbs, "College Days," 91–92 (quotation); William Rupp, "Franklin and Marshall Forty Years Ago," *College Student*, Mar. 1901, 181–85.

31. Rupp, "Forty Years Ago," 185. In terms of seriousness and maturity, Franklin & Marshall students more closely resembled those at New York University in this period than the

more rowdy students at elite New England colleges featured in Helen Horowitz's accounts of college life. See Louise L. Stevenson, "Preparing for Public Life: The Collegiate Students at New York University, 1832–1881," in *The University and the City: From Medieval Origins to the Present*, ed. Thomas Bender (New York: Oxford University Press, 1988), 150–77; Helen Lefkowitz Horowitz, *Campus Life: Undergraduate Cultures from the End of the Eighteenth Century to the Present* (New York: Alfred A. Knopf, 1987).

32. H. M. J. Klein, *History of the Eastern Synod*, 227, 231, 234, 239; Dubbs, *History*, 280; D. B. Albright, "The Moving of Marshall College," *Oriflamme* (1903), 164; Dubbs, "College Days," 95 (quotation).

33. E. Anthony Rotundo, *American Manhood: Transformations in Masculinity from the Revolution to the Modern Era* (New York: Basic Books, 1993), 63–65; Dubbs, "College Days," 94–95; J. W. Nevin, "College Fraternities," pamphlet, n.p. [1860s]; Faculty Minutes, Apr. 29 and Aug. 28, 1873; W. Bruce Leslie, *Gentlemen and Scholars: College and Community in the "Age of the University," 1865–1917* (University Park: Pennsylvania State University Press, 1992), 103–5; *College Days*, Apr. 1874, July 1875, July 1876, Oct. 1876 (quotation).

34. H. M. J. Klein, *History of the Eastern Synod*, 80, 84; Douglas, *Diary*, 19–20, and passim; Diary of Daniel N. Schaeffer, Jan. 28 and Feb. 9, 1876, Archives (hereafter, Diary of Daniel N. Schaeffer).

35. James Mulhern, *A History of Secondary Education in Pennsylvania* (Philadelphia: privately published, 1933), 347–48; Trustees Minutes, July 29, 1862; *Oriflamme* (1883), 27.

36. Douglas, *Diary*, 178–80; E. V. Gerhart diary transcript, Oct. 4, 1860, and June 2, 1861, Gerhart Papers.

37. Douglas, *Diary*, 75–76; Faculty Minutes, June 16, 1858.

38. E. V. Gerhart, *The Destruction of Man: A Discourse on the Death of Daniel F. Wommer* (Lancaster: Franklin & Marshall College Sophomore Class, 1856), 14–15; Faculty Minutes, July 8, 1856.

39. Appel, *Life and Work of Nevin*, 628; *Addresses Delivered at the Inauguration of Rev. Emanuel V. Gerhart, A.M., as President of Franklin and Marshall College, Lancaster, Pa., July 24th, 1855* (Chambersburg, Pa.: M. Kieffer, 1855), 11–13, 25; E. V. Gerhart to Board, July 27, 1857, Gerhart Papers.

40. Dubbs, *History*, 279–80; H. M. J. Klein, *History of the Eastern Synod*, 82; *Catalogue* for 1859–1860; Douglas, *Diary*, 25, 68.

41. Douglas, *Diary*, 38, 40–41.

42. Dubbs, *History*, 295–96 (quotation on 295); Dubbs, "College Days," 93; N. L. Britton, "The Progress of Systematic Botany in North America," in *Addresses in Honor of Prof. Thos. Conrad Porter* (Easton: Lafayette College, 1897), 15; Richard C. Schiedt, "The Natural Sciences Then and Now," *Reformed Church Review* (Apr. 1903): 201–21; H. M. J. Klein, *History of Franklin and Marshall College*, 80; Douglas, *Diary*, 5. Porter solicited contributions from naturalist S. F. Baird in 1853. See Baird to Louis Agassiz, Nov. 14, 1853, in *Correspondence Between Spencer Fullerton Baird and Louis Agassiz—Two Pioneer American Naturalists*, ed. Elmer Charles Herber (Washington, D.C.: Smithsonian Institution, 1963), 66–67.

43. Dubbs, *History*, 260–62; H. M. J. Klein, *History of the Eastern Synod*, 79–80; Douglas, *Diary*, 2.

44. Douglas, *Diary*, 141; Dubbs, "College Days," 92; Peter D. Wanner, "F. and M. in War Times," *Oriflamme* (1903), 182.

45. E. V. Gerhart diary quoted in H. M. J. Klein, *History of the Eastern Synod*, 79–80; Faculty Minutes, May 27 and June 3, 1857.

46. E. V. Gerhart to Board, July 21, 1856, and July 27, 1857, Gerhart Papers; Trustees Minutes, July 23, 1856, July 28 and 29, 1857, July 27 and 28, 1858.

47. Winship, *Industrial Progress and Human Welfare*, 41–47; E. V. Gerhart to Board, July 27, 1857, Gerhart Papers; Trustees Minutes, July 27 and 28, 1858, and July 25, 1865.

48. Winship, *Industrial Progress and Human Welfare*, 73–74; Leslie, *Gentlemen and Scholars*.

49. Trustees Minutes, July 22, 1856; John W. Nevin, *Life and Character of Frederick Augustus Rauch* (Chambersburg, Pa.: M. Kiefer, 1859), 3, 27.

50. E. V. Gerhart to Board, July 22, 1861, Gerhart Papers; Faculty Minutes, Feb. 18 and 27, and May 7, 1861; L. Kryder Evans to H. M. J. Klein, Apr. 18, 1921, Klein Papers, Archives (hereafter, Klein Papers); H. M. J. Klein, *History of the Eastern Synod*, 87, 88; *F&M Weekly*, Dec. 18, 1907; *Student Weekly*, Apr. 20, 1932, 4.

51. Wanner, "F. and M. in War Times," 182 (quotation); *Catalogue* for 1853–1864; E. V. Gerhart to Board, July 22, 1861, Gerhart Papers.

52. Faculty Minutes, Oct. 13 and Dec. 12, 1859, Mar. 1, 1860, Jan. 11, 1861, July 24, 1861 (quotations); W. D. Lefevre et al. to E. V. Gerhart, Mar. 18, 1861, Gerhart Papers; *College Student*, January 1901.

53. Appel, *Life and Work of Nevin*, 443–44, 590–91, 603, 605–6; Trustees Minutes, Dec. 7, 1928.

54. H. M. J. Klein, *History of the Eastern Synod*, 243.

55. E. V. Gerhart to Board, July 22, 1861, Gerhart Papers; H. M. J. Klein, *History of the Eastern Synod*, 243, 245–47; Trustees Minutes, July 25, 1865.

56. E. V. Gerhart to Board, July 27, 1863, Gerhart Papers; H. M. J. Klein, *History of the Eastern Synod*, 90–91.

57. Faculty Minutes, July 11, 1864, and Apr. 11, 1865.

58. H. M. J. Klein, *History of the Eastern Synod*, 92–93; Trustees Minutes, July 25, 1865 (quotation); Dubbs, *History*, 350–51; Frederick Augustus Rupley, "The Humorous Side of Life at Marshall College," manuscript, n.d., Archives; *College Student*, Dec. 15, 1893; "John Cessna Dead," unidentified clipping, Dec. 14, 1893, Cessna File, Archives.

59. "Committee to Examine General Condition of the College," 1865 (quotations), Trustees Minutes, Jan. 24, 1866, and E. V. Gerhart to Board, July 25, 1865, Gerhart Papers; H. M. J. Klein, *History of the Eastern Synod*, 93; Douglas, *Diary*, 85; Faculty Minutes, Feb. 8, 1866; H. M. J. Klein, *Century of Education at Mercersburg, 1836–1936* (Lancaster: Mercersburg Academy, 1936), 366, 371–72.

60. Trustees Minutes, Jan. 24, 1866.

61. Roger L. Geiger, "The Rise and Fall of Useful Knowledge" and "The Era of Multipurpose Colleges in American Higher Education, 1850–1890," in *The American College in the Nineteenth Century*, ed. Roger L. Geiger (Nashville: Vanderbilt University Press, 2000), 153–68 and 127–52; Appel, *Life and Works of Nevin*, 628–30.

62. Trustees Minutes, Jan. 24, May 24 and 25, 1866.

63. Trustees Minutes, Jan. 24, May 24 and 25, and June 28, Sept. 20, 1866, July 23, 1867; Appel, *Life and Works of Nevin*, 630–31; John S. Stahr, "The Financial Development of Franklin and Marshall College," *Reformed Church Review* 7 (Apr. 1903): 169–70.

64. Trustees Minutes, July 24, 1866 (quotation); Stahr, "Financial Development of Franklin and Marshall College," 169–70.

65. H. M. J. Klein, *History of the Eastern Synod*, 96–97; E. V. Gerhart, Diary Transcripts, Gerhart Papers.

66. Trustees Minutes, July 24, 1866, and July 23, 1867; H. M. J. Klein, *History of the Eastern Synod*, 249–50 (quotation).

67. H. M. J. Klein, *History of the Eastern Synod*, 250, 251, 359; Dubbs, *History*, 318–19; Good, *History of Reformed Church*, 426–29, 437 (quotation), 505; Trustees Minutes, July 8, 1868, and June 29, 1869.

68. Trustees Minutes, July 23 (quotations) and 24, 1867; Dubbs, *History*, 317–18; Stahr's inaugural address, reprinted in *Lancaster New Era*, Sept. 11, 1890; Nevins to Board, July 23, 1867, Trustees Minutes.

69. Trustees Minutes, July 23 and 24, 1867, and July 7 and 8, 1868.

70. J. W. Nevin, "Master and Disciple, An Address at the Opening of Fall Term of Franklin and Marshall, Sept. 12, 1866," *German Reformed Messenger*, n.d., clipping in Nevin Papers.

71. J. W. Nevin, *Address to the Graduating Class of 1867, and the Alumni of Franklin and Marshall College, Lancaster, Pa., July 25th, 1867* (Philadelphia: S. R. Fisher, 1867), 8, 13, 17.

72. Ibid., 21, 23–24.

73. Ibid., 24. Philip Scranton has brought attention to the continuing economic importance of batch and custom manufacturing in *Endless Novelty: Specialty Production and American Industrialization, 1865–1925* (Princeton: Princeton University Press, 2000).

74. Trustees Minutes, June 30, 1869; "Franklin and Marshall," nos. 1, 2 and 3, 5, and 7 (quotation, emphasis in original), newspaper clippings, n.p., n.d. [1869], Nevin Papers.

75. "Franklin and Marshall," no. 7, Nevin Papers.

76. *Catalogues* for 1867, 1868–1869, and 1871.

77. "Philosophy of History," *College Days*, Jan. 1873, 2; Apr. 1874, 2.

78. Ibid., Nov. 1874, 3.

79. Trustees Minutes, June 29 and 30, 1869; Theodore Appel, "Addressed to Future Generations," MS dated June 28, 1871, Appel Papers, Archives.

80. Trustees Minutes, June 27, 1872.

81. H. M. J. Klein, *History of the Eastern Synod*, 259; Trustees Minutes, Nov. 28, 1871, and June 25, 1872.

82. Trustees Minutes, Nov. 28, 1871, and June 25, 1872 (quotations), June 27, 1877; Nolt, *Foreigners in Their Own Land*, 141; H. M. J. Klein, *History of the Eastern Synod*, 261; Appel, *Life and World of Nevin*, 665; *College Days*, June 1876, 4. On the popularity of preparatory programs, see Colin Burke, *American Collegiate Populations: A Test of the Traditional View* (New York: New York University Press, 1982), chap. 5; Leslie, *Gentlemen and Scholars*, 91–92, 213–17; Kemeny, *Princeton in the Nation's Service*, 73–74.

83. Trustees Minutes, June 27, 1872; *College Days*, Jan. 1873, 4.

84. Trustees Minutes, June 29 and 30, 1869, Jan. 3 and June 27, 1871; H. M. J. Klein, *Century of Education*, 112–15; H. M. J. Klein, *History of the Eastern Synod*, 259.

85. Trustees Minutes, Jan. 6, 1870, and June 27 and 28, 1871; H. M. J. Klein, *History of the Eastern Synod*, 227, 258, 260.

86. Trustees Minutes, June 27, 1872, and June 25, 1873.

87. Trustees Minutes, Jan. 6, 1870, and June 27 and 28, 1871, June 25, 1873; H. M. J. Klein, *History of the Eastern Synod*, 227, 258, 263; Dubbs, *History*, 318; Good, *History of Reformed Church*, 517–24, 535–36; Thomas G. Apple, "Transitions to Rome," MS, n.d., Apple Papers, Archives (hereafter, Apple Papers); *College Days*, Jan. 1874, 4; *College Days*, May 1874, 4; *College Days*, May 1875, 4; *F&M Weekly*, Apr. 30, 1902; Stahr, "Financial Development of Franklin and Marshall College," 170.

88. *Catalogue* for 1873–1874 to 1875–1876; Dubbs, *History*, 323; Trustees Minutes, Nov. 28, 1871, and June 26, 1872; Faculty Minutes, Dec. 2 and 10, 1872; *College Student*, Jan. 1889, 62.

89. Trustees Minutes, June 26, 1872; Leslie, *Gentlemen and Scholars*, 37–40, 52–54, 125–28.

90. Appel, *Life and Work of Nevin*, 656; Dubbs, *History*, 326–27; Trustees Minutes, June 23, 1874.

91. See clippings and correspondence in Dubbs Scrapbook, vol. 1, Archives (hereafter, Dubbs Scrapbook); Horatio Gates Jones to Joseph Henry Dubbs, Nov. 20, 1872, and clipping from *Lancaster Express*, June 30, 1870, both in Dubbs Scrapbook, vol. 1; *F&M Weekly*, June 1, 1892; J. H. Dubbs, *Conditions of Success in Life: An Address Delivered Before the Alumni Association* (Philadelphia: Reformed Church Publication Board, 1870); *College Days*, Mar. 1875, 5.

92. Trustees Minutes, June 29 and 30, 1875; Faculty Minutes, Sept. 2, 1875.

93. *College Days*, Jan. and Feb. 1876 (quotations); Diary of Daniel N. Schaeffer, Jan. 19, 1876; Good, *History of Reformed Church*, 607–8.

94. *College Days*, Feb. 1876, 6; *College Days*, July 1876, 3.

95. Trustees Minutes, June 28, 1876, and June 26, 1877.

96. Trustees Minutes, June 26, 1877.

97. Nolt, *Foreigners in Their Own Land*, 141; Trustees Minutes, June 27, 1877.

98. *College Days*, Apr. (Hensel quotation), May (Reformed Missionary quotation), June, Oct., and Nov.–Dec. 1876.

99. Trustees Minutes, July 8, 1868, and June 27, 1877; Dubbs, *History*, 334–35.

100. Trustees Minutes, Aug. 3, 1877; Faculty Minutes, Sept. 3, 1872, and July 7, 1876: *Franklin and Marshall Alumnus* 1 (Nov. 1924): 18.

101. *Catalogue* for 1877–1878 and 1878–1879.

102. H. M. J. Klein, *History of the Eastern Synod*, 267; Good, *History of Reformed Church*, 578–83; *College Student*, Sept. 1878; Thomas G. Apple, "The Peace Measure," MS, n.d., in Apple Papers; H. M. J. Klein, "The Present Status of the Reformed Church in the United States—Doctrine, Cultus, Polity, and Usages" [ca. 1910], MS in Klein Papers.

103. Trustees Minutes, June 18, 1878.

104. Thomas G. Apple, "The Philosophic Course in Franklin and Marshall College," MS, n.d. (quotation), and "The True Idea of Liberal Education," MS, n.d. [1880s], both in Apple Papers.

105. Thomas G. Apple, "The Argument Against the Ancient Classics," MS, n.d., Apple Papers; Thomas G. Apple, "The Idea of a Liberal Education," *Proceedings of the College Association of Pennsylvania*, 1887–1888; Peter Dobkin Hall, "Noah Porter Writ Large? Reflections on the Modernization of American Education and Its Critics, 1866–1916," in *American College in the Nineteenth Century*, 196–220; Louise L. Stevenson, *Scholarly Means to Evangelical Ends: The New Haven Scholars and the Transformation of Higher Learning in America, 1830–1890* (Baltimore: Johns Hopkins University Press, 1986), 49–51.

106. The most influential treatment of this period, which relies heavily on the rhetoric of promoters themselves, is Laurence Veysey, *The Emergence of the American University* (Chicago: University of Chicago Press, 1965). Much recent work has served to qualify the dichotomous views of college and university, for example, Leslie, *Gentlemen and Scholars*; Stevenson, *Scholarly Means to Evangelical Ends*; Julie A. Reuben, *The Making of the Modern University: Intellectual Transformation and the Marginalization of Morality* (Chicago: University of Chicago Press, 1996).

107. George E. Peterson, *The New England College in the Age of the University* (Amherst: Amherst College Press, 1964); Leslie, *Gentlemen and Scholars*; *College Student*, Jan. 1881 (quotations).

108. Dubbs, *History*, 341–43; Trustees Minutes, June 15, 1880, and June 16, 1891; *F&M Weekly*, Apr. 8, 1891; Stahr, "Financial Development of Franklin and Marshall College," 171–72.

109. *College Student*, Jan. 1881 and Apr. 1882; *F&M Weekly*, Nov. 4, 1891; Trustees Minutes, Mar. 18, 1884; *Student Weekly*, May 17, 1916.

110. Trustees Minutes, June 15, 1880, June 19 and 20, 1883, and Mar. 18, 1884; Faculty Minutes, Mar. 15, 1880.

111. Trustees Minutes, June 17, 1884 (Kershner quotation), June 16, 1885, June 15, 1887, and June 11, 1889; *College Student*, Feb., June, July, and Oct. 1884, and June 1886.

112. Appel, *Life and Works of Nevin*, 754–55 (quotations); *Examiner*, June 1886, clipping in Nevin Papers.

113. Trustees Minutes, June 17, 1884 (quotation); *Student Weekly*, Mar. 8, 1922, 4.

114. H. M. J. Klein, *History of the Eastern Synod*, 272; Trustees Minutes, June 18, 1884, and June 15, 1886.

115. Clippings from *Lancaster Daily Examiner*, June 15 and 16, 1887, from *Lancaster Intelligencer*, June 15, 16, and 17, 1887, and from *Daily New Era*, June 17, 1887, all from Franklin & Marshall Centennial Files, Archives; *College Student*, July 1887.

116. William Pepper, *An Address on Benjamin Franklin, Delivered at Franklin and Marshall College, Lancaster, Pa., on the Centennial Anniversary of Its Foundation* (Philadelphia: Dando Printing, 1887), 17, 25–26.

117. *College Student*, Apr. 1881; *F&M Weekly*, Feb. 24, 1892; Lewis H. Steiner, *The College and the Old College Curriculum* (Philadelphia: Reformed Church Publication Board, 1887), 5, 12, 17.

118. *Lancaster Daily Examiner*, June 15 and 16, 1887.

CHAPTER 4

1. David A. Hollinger, "Inquiry and Uplift: Late Nineteenth-Century American Academics and the Moral Efficacy of Scientific Practice," in *The Authority of Experts: Studies in History and Theory*, ed. Thomas L. Haskell (Bloomington: Indiana University Press, 1984), 142–56; Julie A. Reuben, *The Making of the Modern University: Intellectual Transformation and the Marginalization of Morality* (Chicago: University of Chicago Press, 1996); T. J. Jackson Lears, *No Place of Grace: Antimodernism and the Transformation of American Culture, 1880–1920* (New York: Pantheon Books, 1981), 188–89.

2. For comparable developments at another college, see P. C. Kemeny, *Princeton in the Nation's Service: Religious Ideals and Educational Practice, 1868–1928* (New York: Oxford University Press, 1998), 87–125.

3. Franklin & Marshall College Faculty Minutes, Fall Session of 1867–1868 and Sept. 10, 1872, Archives (hereafter, Faculty Minutes); Franklin and Marshall College Trustees Minutes, July 8, 1868, June 27, 1871, June 25 and 26, 1872, June 15, 1886 (quotation), Archives (hereafter, Trustees Minutes); *The Morning Call* [biography of John S. Stahr] (Allentown, Pa.), Oct. 23, 1943, in Stahr Papers, Archives (hereafter, Stahr Papers).

4. George W. Richards, "Dr. Stahr and the Reformed Church," in *In Memoriam, John Summers Stahr* (n.p., 1915), 129, in Stahr Papers; Theodore F. Herman, "Dr. Stahr and the *Reformed Church Review*," in *In Memoriam*, 135; Richard C. Schiedt, "Reminiscences of the Halcyon Days of Yore," *Reformed Church Messenger*, Oct. 18, 1934, 7–10. On the developing view of academics as an independent vocation, see Louise L. Stevenson, *Scholarly Means to Evangelical Ends: The New Haven Scholars and the Transformation of Higher Learning in America, 1830–1890* (Baltimore: Johns Hopkins University Press, 1986). On the dominant role of theological seminaries in postgraduate education, see 73–74, 159.

5. Paul K. Conkin, *The Uneasy Center: Reformed Christianity in Antebellum America* (Chapel Hill: University of North Carolina Press, 1995), 176; Sidney E. Ahlstrom, *A Religious History of the American People* (New Haven: Yale University Press, 1972), 620; Gary K. Pranger, "Philip Schaff: His Role in American Evangelical Education," in *German Influences on Education in the United States to 1917* (Cambridge: Cambridge University Press, 1995), 220–25; Richards, "Dr. Stahr and the Reformed Church," 131; *F&M Weekly*, Apr. 15, 1891.

6. Herman, "Dr. Stahr and the *Reformed Church Review*," 137; Schiedt, "Reminiscences," 7.

7. John S. Stahr, "The Scope of Science," *College Student*, Oct. 1886; John S. Stahr, "Genesis of the Earth," *College Student*, Sept. 1882. James Turner notes that thinkers who took the idealistic view that God could not be understood through purely rational means were less threatened by the new scientific perspectives. See Turner, *Without God, Without Creed: The Origins of Unbelief in America* (Baltimore: Johns Hopkins University Press, 1985), 106–8. On debates over the relation between science and religion, see Reuben, *Making of the Modern University*, chap. 2.

8. Schiedt, "Reminiscences," 8; Steven Conn, *Museums and American Intellectual Life, 1876–1926* (Chicago: University of Chicago Press, 1998). Sophomore class histories in *Oriflamme* invariably give greatest attention to the exploits during the spring botanical expeditions.

9. Faculty Minutes, Jan. 6, 1876; Trustees Minutes, June 18, 1884, June 16, 1885; *F&M Weekly*, Oct. 21, 1896.

10. *College Student*, May 1886 (first quotation); Stahr, "Scope of Science" (second quotation); Trustees Minutes, June 15, 1886. On the shift from Baconianism to "progressivist" definitions of science, see Reuben, *Making of the Modern University*, chap. 2.

11. *College Student*, May 1886.

12. Ibid.

13. Ibid.

14. Trustees Minutes, June 16, 1885, June 15, 1886, June 15, 1887, and June 12, 1888; John S. Stahr, "The Financial Development of Franklin and Marshall College," *Reformed Church Review* 7 (Apr. 1903): 174.

15. Trustees Minutes, June 12 and 13, 1888; *College Student*, May 1886.

16. *College Student*, Dec. 1881, Dec. 1884, Oct. 1885, May 1886, Apr. 1887, Nov. 1888 (quotation), Mar., Apr., and June 1889, Jan. 1890; Trustees Minutes, June 15, 1887, June 11 and 12, 1889.

17. Schiedt, "Reminiscences," 7; "Dr. Schiedt, Noted F&M Scholar, Is Ninety Tomorrow," *Lancaster New Era*, Sept. 20, 1949, clipping in Schiedt Papers, Archives.

18. Schiedt, "Reminiscences," 7 (quotation); *College Student*, Jan. 1889; Richard C. Schiedt, "The Natural Sciences Then and Now," *Reformed Church Review* 7 (Apr. 1903): 209 (quotation).

19. *F&M Weekly*, June 3, 1891, Sept. 7 and Dec. 14, 1892, Feb. 15 and May 10, 1893, May 31, 1899.

20. "Dr. Schiedt, Noted F&M Scholar"; Faculty Minutes, June 1 and 4, 1888.

21. Turner, *Without God, Without Creed*, 122–24; George Marsden, "The Soul of the American University: An Historical Overview," in *The Secularization of the Academy*, ed. George Marsden and Bradley J. Longfield (New York: Oxford University Press, 1992), 17; Schiedt, "Reminiscences," 7; *College Student*, Jan. 1886 (quotation).

22. Schiedt, "Reminiscences," 8 (quotation); *F&M Weekly*, Sept. 7, 1892.

23. In the 1880s, the percentages of seniors affiliated with the Reformed Church ranged from 50 to 90 percent, while those planning to enter the ministry ranged from 25 to 65 percent (*Oriflamme* [Lancaster, Pa.], 1886–1891). On the proliferation of college activities and its representation in this period, see Helen Lefkowitz Horowitz, *Campus Life: Undergraduate Cultures from the End of the Eighteenth Century to the Present* (Chicago: University of Chicago Press, 1987), 41–55; Kemeny, *Princeton in the Nation's Service*, 92–93; W. Bruce Leslie, *Gentlemen and Scholars: College and Community in the "Age of the University," 1865–1917* (University Park: Pennsylvania State University Press, 1992), 109–14. *College Student*, Jan. 1881; *Oriflamme* (1883), 5.

24. *College Student*, Dec., 1881 (quotation); Feb., Mar., and Nov. 1882; Jan. and July 1884; Feb. and Nov., 1886, July 1890; *College Days*, Nov. 1875, *Oriflamme* (1883), 49; Horowitz, *Campus Life*, 54–55; David Bishop Skillman, *The Biography of A College: Being the History of the First Century of the Life of Lafayette College* (Easton: Lafayette College, 1932), 2:43–44.

25. *College Student*, Jan. 1881, Feb. 1884, July and Oct. 1888; Trustees Minutes, June 13, 1888.

26. *Oriflamme* (1883), 29, 46–47.

27. *Oriflamme* (1884), 18.

28. Klein, *History of Franklin and Marshall College*, 113–14, 125; *Oriflamme* (1883), 13, 16, 21, 26–27; *Oriflamme* (1885), 114 (first quotation); Faculty Minutes, Oct. 14 and 15, 1878 (second quotation); *College Student*, Oct. 1881, Oct. and Nov. 1885, Sept. 15, 1893.

29. *Oriflamme* (1883), 26–27 (first quotation); *College Student*, Jan. 1887, Nov. and Dec. 1889, Jan. and Oct. 1890, Dec. 1892 (second quotation); *Oriflamme* (1891), 29; "College Students Arrested," *Lancaster New Era*, Sept. 11, 1902.

30. Klein, *History of Franklin and Marshall College*, 114; *Oriflamme* (1889), 18. On other campuses, see Skillman, *Biography of a College*, 2:17–19.

31. *College Days*, Oct. 1878; *College Student*, Feb., June, and Oct. 1881 (quotation), Oct. 1882, Feb. and Nov. 1886, June 1888, June 1889; *Oriflamme* (1884), 27.

32. Trustees Minutes, June 11, 1889.

33. Michael Oriard, *Reading Football: How the Popular Press Created an American Spectacle* (Chapel Hill: University of North Carolina Press, 1993), 23–28; *College Student*, Dec. 1881, Nov. 1888 (quotation); H. H. Apple, "Reminiscences on Football in Franklin and Marshall College," Oct. 18, 1935, H. H. Apple Papers, Archives (hereafter, H. H. Apple Papers); Faculty Minutes, Oct. 12, 1888.

34. Apple, "Reminiscences"; *In Memoriam: William Mann Irvine* (Mercersburg: Mercersburg Academy, 1928); William Mann Irvine, "Reminiscences," *College Student*, Nov. 1889, Oct. 1897.

35. *College Student*, Oct. 1888, and Oct. and Nov. 1889; Apple, "Reminiscences."

36. *College Student*, Nov. 1889; Irvine, "Reminiscences"; *Lancaster New Era*, "A Famous Victory," n.p. [Nov. 29, 1889], Clippings File, Athletics Files, Archives (hereafter, Athletics Files); Banquet Program, Dec. 4, 1889, Athletics Files.

37. *College Student*, Dec. 1889; Irvine, "Reminiscences" (Gerhart quotation); Faculty Minutes, Nov. 29, 1889; Trustees Minutes, June 17, 1890.

38. *College Student*, Nov. (first quotation) and Dec. 1889 (fourth quotation); "Played to a Tie," n.p. [Oct. 13, 1889] (third quotation), Clippings File, Athletics Files; "A Famous Victory" (second quotation); Oriard, *Reading Football*, 57–133.

39. *College Student*, Dec. 1889, July 1890, Nov. 1897 (quotation); Banquet Program, Dec. 4, 1889, Athletics Files.

40. *Oriflamme* (1890), 109; *College Student*, Apr. 1890.

41. Trustees Minutes, June 17 and 18, 1890; *College Student*, Apr. and July 1890; Stahr, "Financial Development of Franklin and Marshall College," 169, 174.

42. *College Student*, July 1890.

43. *College Student*, July 1890 (quotations); Trustees Minutes, July 16, 1891.

44. *College Days*, Jan. 1873, Mar. 1874, Oct. 1878 (quotation); J. Barry Girvin, "The Life of William Uhler Hensel," *Journal of the Lancaster County Historical Society* (1966): 185–248; *F&M Weekly*, Mar. 3, 1915, 2.

45. Stahr, "The Place and Office of the College in Our Educational System," *College Student*, Oct. 1890.

46. Ibid.

47. Trustees Minutes, June 16, 1891 (quotation), and June 14 and 15, 1892; *F&M Weekly*, Apr. 8, May 27, and Nov. 18, 1891; *College Student*, Nov. 1891, Jan. 1892.

48. Trustees Minutes, June 17, 1890; *College Student*, Feb. 1889 (quotation).

49. *College Student*, June 1890, Oct. 1890 (article quotation), Jan. 1891. On the development of the library profession in this period, see Dee Garrison, *Apostles of Culture: The Public Librarian and American Society, 1876–1920* (New York: Free Press, 1979).

50. *College Student*, Oct. 1889 (first quotation), July 1890, Dec. 1890, and Feb. 1891, Oct. 1892; *F&M Weekly*, Oct. 14, 1891, Mar. 2 and 30, 1892, Jan. 16, 1895; Trustees Minutes, June 12, 1889, June 17, 1890 (quotation); Schiedt, "Sciences Then and Now," 210.

51. *College Student*, Feb. 1891; *F&M Weekly*, Sept. 7, 1892, Oct. 17, 1894; *Oriflamme* (1893).

52. Franklin & Marshall College Catalogues, 1890–1897 (hereafter, *Catalogue*); Robert L. Geiger, "The Crisis of the Old Order: The Colleges in the 1890s," in *The American College in the Nineteenth Century*, ed. Geiger (Nashville: Vanderbilt University Press, 2000), 264–276.

53. E. Anthony Rotondo, *American Manhood: Transformations in Masculinity from the Revolution to the Modern Era* (New York: Basic Books, 1993), 222–46.

54. Oriard, *Reading Football*, 189; *College Student*, Jan. 1881; *F&M Weekly*, Nov. 18, 1891, Jan. 13, 1892, Feb. 3, 1892.

55. *F&M Weekly*, Nov. 23, 1892, and Oct. 24, 1894.

56. *College Student*, Nov. 1897.

57. *F&M Weekly*, Jan. 27, 1892, Apr. 8, 1891.

58. *College Student,* Nov. and Dec. 1884, Feb., Mar., and Oct. 1886, Feb. and Oct. 1889, Nov. 1890, Dec. 1892; *F&M Weekly,* May 13, 1891, Sept. 28, 1892, *Catalogue* for 1888–1889.

59. *F&M Weekly,* June 1 and Sept. 26, 1894 (quotation), Sept. 25, 1895, Oct. 30, 1895, Sept. 22, 1897; *College Student,* Oct. 1895

60. Clifford Putney, *Muscular Christianity: Manhood and Sports in Protestant America, 1880–1920* (Cambridge, Mass.: Harvard University Press, 2001); *College Student,* Nov. 1897.

61. James I. Good, *History of the Reformed Church in the U.S. in the Nineteenth Century* (New York: Reformed Church in America, 1911), 607–8; H. M. J. Klein, *History of the Eastern Synod of the Reformed Church in the United States* (Lancaster: Eastern Synod, 1943), 268, 271, 272–73; *College Student,* Oct. 1885, June–July 1895; *F&M Weekly,* May 22, 1895.

62. *College Student,* July and Oct. 1884, Feb. 1886, Nov. and Dec. 1888, Oct. and Nov. 1889.

63. *College Student,* Nov. 1889, Dec. 1890; *F&M Weekly,* Apr. 15, 1891 (quotation).

64. *Oriflamme* (1891), 14; *F&M Weekly,* Nov. 4, 1891, Oct. 5, 1892, June 20, 1893, Sept. 23, 1896.

65. *College Student,* Jan. and Mar. 1890.

66. Faculty Minutes, Feb. 21 and Oct. 3, 1890, Dec. 5, 1891, Apr. 10, 1895.

67. *F&M Weekly,* Mar. 18, 1891, Sept. 14, 1892; *College Student,* May 1898.

68. *College Student,* Mar. 1891, May 1898.

69. *F&M Weekly,* Apr. 15, 1891, June 11, 1895 (quotation); *College Student,* May 1898.

70. *F&M Weekly,* Mar. 25, 1891, Apr. 29, 1891, May 27, 1891, Sept. 30, 1891. On the promotional role of local newspapers in this period, see Sally Foreman Griffith, *Home Town News: William Allen White and the Emporia Gazette* (New York: Oxford University Press, 1989).

71. *F&M Weekly,* May 3, 1893.

72. *F&M Weekly,* Oct. 7 and 14, 1891, Mar. 2, 1892.

73. *College Student,* Mar. and May 1892.

74. *F&M Weekly,* Apr. 8, 1891; E. Ernest Wagner, "The Teaching of English at Franklin and Marshall," *Reformed Church Review* 7 (Apr. 1903): 217; *Oriflamme* (1890), 102–3, and (1896), 168. Laurence R. Veysey refers to the divide in this period between the "fashionable," who came from established families and emphasized extracurricular life, and the "unfashionable," who sought upward mobility through higher education (Veysey, *The Emergence of the American University* [Chicago: University of Chicago Press, 1965], 270–71).

75. *College Student,* June–July 1895; Ute Frevert, "The Taming of the Noble Ruffian: Male Violence and Dueling in Early Modern and Modern Germany," in *Men and Violence: Gender, Honor, and Rituals in Modern Europe and America,* ed. Pieter Spierenburg (Columbus: Ohio State University Press, 1998), 37–63; Bonnie G. Smith, "Gender and the Practices of Scientific History: The Seminar and Archival Research in the Nineteenth Century," *American Historical Review* 100 (1995): 1150–76; Paul R. Deslandes, "Competitive Examinations and the Culture of Masculinity in Oxbridge Undergraduate Life, 1850–1920," *History of Education Quarterly* 42 (Winter 2002): 544–78.

76. *F&M Weekly,* May 20, 1891; Trustees Minutes, June 16, 1891; Faculty Minutes, Oct.–Dec. 1891.

77. Faculty Minutes, Dec. 13, 1895.

78. *Catalogue* for 1894–1895; Trustees Minutes, June 17, 1890, June 19, 1894.

79. *Catalogue* for 1894–1895; Faculty Minutes, Sept. 21 and 28, 1894; *College Student,* Nov. 1894, Feb. 1895.

80. Hugh Hawkins, *Banding Together: The Rise of National Associations in American Higher Education, 1887–1950* (Baltimore: Johns Hopkins University Press, 1992), 139, 262n1; Faculty Minutes, Jan. [16], 1894, Sept. 20, 1895, June 6, 1896, Feb. 12, 1897, June 22, 1901; Trustees Minutes, June 19, 1894 (quotation), June 11, 1895, June 9 and 10, 1896, June 8, 1897; *F&M Weekly,* Sept. 26, Oct. 10 and 31 (quotation), 1894, Feb. 26, 1896, Apr. 22, 1897, Dec. 16, 1903; *College Student,* Feb. 1, 1894, Feb. 1895, Oct. 1895; *Student Weekly,* Oct. 18, 1916, 8.

81. *Catalogue* for 1870–1871; *College Student,* July 1890, Jan. 15, Feb. 1, 1894; *F&M Weekly,*

Jan. 17, 1894; Trustees Minutes, June 19 and 20, 1894; Faculty Minutes, Nov. 5, 1897; *Student Weekly*, Jan. 15, 1936.

82. Trustees Minutes, June 19, 1894.

83. Girvin, "Life of William Uhler Hensel," 214 (first quotation); *College Student*, Feb. 1898 (second quotation).

84. Trustees Minutes, June 16, 1891, June 14, 1892, June 13, 1893, June 19, 1894; *Catalogue* for 1892–1893; *F&M Weekly*, June 19, 1891.

85. Klein, *History of the Eastern Synod*, 282–84; Trustees Minutes, June 13, 1893; Leslie, *Gentlemen and Scholars*, 125–26.

86. Trustees Minutes, June 13, 1893; *F&M Weekly*, Dec. 20, 1893; Joseph Henry Dubbs, *History of Franklin and Marshall College* (Lancaster: Franklin and Marshall College Alumni Association, 1903), 356–57; "John Cessna Dead," Dec. 14, 1893, unidentified clipping, Cessna Folder, Archives.

87. Trustees Minutes, June 19, 1894, June 10, 1914; Edward J. Davies, "Baer, George Frederick," in *American National Biography*, ed. John A. Garraty and Mark C. Carnes, published under the auspices of the American Council of Learned Societies (New York: Oxford University Press, 1999), 1:866–7; Jean Strouse, *Morgan: American Financier* (New York: Random House, 1999), 251–52, 323; Wayne E. Homan, "George Baer's Industrial Empire," *Reading Sunday Eagle Magazine*, Apr. 10, 1966, Baer Papers, Archives; *College Student*, May 1891, 151.

88. Girvin, "Life of William Ulher Hensel"; *College Student*, Apr. 1887.

89. Trustees Minutes, June 19, 1894.

90. Trustees Minutes, June 19 and 20, 1894; W. U. Hensel to H. H. Apple, Mar. 21, 1910, H. H. Apple Papers.

91. Dubbs, *History*, 363–65; *F&M Weekly*, Sept. 16, 1896, Jan. 20, 1897.

92. Dubbs, *History*, 363–65; J. E. Outwater to J. H. Dubbs, Dec. 13, 1892, Dubbs Papers, Archives (hereafter, Dubbs Papers); Trustees Minutes, June 14, 1892, June 14, 1894, June 9, 1896, June 8, 1897; *College Student*, Jan. 1897; *F&M Weekly*, June 20, 1893, Jan. 20, 1897; Klein, *History of Franklin and Marshall College*, 127; A. H. Rothermel to T. A. Distler, Feb. 8, 1947, Distler Papers, Archives.

93. *F&M Weekly*, Jan. 20 (quotation) and Nov. 3, 1897, Feb. 9 and 16, 1898; *College Student*, Nov. 1897; Trustees Minutes, June 7, 1898.

94. *College Student*, Jan. 1890, July and Dec. 1892; *F&M Weekly*, Apr. 20 and Nov. 30, 1892.

95. *F&M Weekly*, Apr. 20, 1892, Sept. 19, 1894, Apr. 3, 1895, June 3 and Sept. 16, 1896; *College Student*, Apr. 1889 (quotation), Oct. and Dec. 1896; Trustees Minutes, June 17, 1891, June 19, 1894, June 11, 1895, June 8, 1897.

96. *F&M Weekly*, Sept. 7, 1892, Sept. 13, 1893, Sept. 19 and Oct. 17, 1894, Feb. 6, 1895; Trustees Minutes, June 17 and 18, 1890, June 16, 1891, June 13, 1893, June 18, 1897.

97. *F&M Weekly*, Feb. 14, Mar. 7, Oct. 10, 1894, Apr. 29, 1896; *College Student*, Mar. 1, 1894; *Oriflamme* (1895), 112; Faculty Minutes, Oct. 6, 1899.

98. *College Student*, Nov. 1894; *F&M Weekly*, Nov. 1, Nov. 29, 1893, Dec. 5, 1894; Faculty Minutes, Jan. 18, 1895.

99. *F&M Weekly*, Jan. 23 (second quotation), May 15 (first quotation), 1895, May 6, Sept. 30 (third quotation), Nov. 25, 1896; Trustees Minutes, June 7, 1898; Faculty Minutes, Sept. 16, 1898.

100. *Oriflamme* (1896), 165–65.

101. *F&M Weekly*, Feb. 27, 1895; Trustees Minutes, June 14, 1887, June 16, 1891, June 14 and 15, 1892, June 13, 1893; *Oriflamme* (1894).

102. *F&M Weekly*, Sept. 21, 1892, Apr. 29 and Sept. 16, 1896; Trustees Minutes, June 13, 1893, June 19, 1894, June 9, 1896, June 7, 1898.

103. Thomas Bender, *New York Intellect* (Baltimore: Johns Hopkins University Press, 1987), 275–84 (quotations on 283–84); Jurgen Herbst, *The German Historical School in American Scholarship: A Study in the Transfer of Culture* (Ithaca: Cornell University Press, 1965); A. V.

Hiester, "Political Economy," *Reformed Church Review* 7 (Apr. 1903): 226–42 (quotation on 233); *Student Weekly*, Nov. 30, 1927, 1.

104. *F&M Weekly*, Sept. 18, 1895; Trustees Minutes, June 8, 1897, June 7, 1898.

105. *Oriflamme* (1896); *Catalogue* for 1896; Faculty Minutes, Jan. 8 and 15, 1897 (quotation), Sept. 25, 1902, Jan. 15 and Sept. 5, 1903.

106. Faculty Minutes, June 20, 1878 (first quotation), Dec. 22, 1889, Sept. 5, 1890 (second quotation); *Catalogue* for 1884–1885; *F&M Weekly*, Sept. 13, 1893; Trustees Minutes, June 14, 1892 (third quotation).

107. Faculty Minutes, Apr. 29, 30 and May 4, 1887 (quotation), June 28, 1890; *Catalogue* for 1892–1893. Swarthmore had previously adopted this system; see Leslie, *Gentlemen and Scholars*, 218–24.

108. Leslie, *Gentlemen and Scholars*, 221; E. H. Magill to J. H. Dubbs, Nov. 28, 1887, Dubbs Papers; *F&M Weekly*, Dec. 2, 1891, Nov. 30, 1892, Nov. 18 and Dec. 9, 1896, Dec. 1, 1897.

109. Faculty Minutes, Mar. 7 and May 16, 1901; Leslie, *Gentlemen and Scholars*, 221.

110. *F&M Weekly*, Mar. 30, 1899; Faculty Minutes, Mar. 12, 1897; *College Student*, Jan. 1898.

111. *F&M Weekly*, Feb. 22, 1893 (second quotation), Mar. 30, 1898 (first quotation); *College Student*, Jan. 1898; Faculty Minutes, Dec. 4, 1897, May 22, 1898.

112. Faculty Minutes, Oct. 28, 1898.

113. George Baer to W. U. Hensel, Nov. 28, 1898, Baer Papers, Archives (hereafter, Baer Papers).

114. Trustees Minutes, June 7, 1898.

115. E. M. Hartman to J. S. Stahr, July 21, 1897, Hartman Papers, Archives (hereafter, Hartman Papers).

116. E. M. Hartman to J. S. Stahr, July 31, 1897, and W. R. Stuckert to E. M. Hartman, July 20, 1898, Hartman Papers.

117. E. M. Hartman to J. S. Stahr, July 15 and 27, Aug. 2, 1898, Hartman Papers.

118. *Oriflamme* (1898); Leslie, *Scholars and Gentlemen*. Leslie reports that 60 percent of students enrolled between 1853 and 1903 graduated; this can be compared with a figure of 40 percent for Swarthmore College in the 1870s and 1880s (95–96).

119. Faculty Minutes, Dec. 9, 1898; Trustees Minutes, June 6, 1899 (quotation).

120. Trustees Minutes, June 6 and 7, 1899.

121. Faculty Minutes, July 13, 1899, Jan. 12, 1900.

122. *Catalogue* for 1903–1904, 14–15.

123. *Oriflamme* (1899), 179; Trustees Minutes, June 6, 1899, June 7, 1898 (quotation); [Board of Trustees], *Science Building* (Lancaster, Pa., Franklin & Marshall Board of Trustees, 1900), 1; Jefferson E. Kershner, "Mathematics, Physics, and Astronomy," *Reformed Church Review* 7 (Apr. 1903): 194.

124. [Trustees], *Science Building*, 2 (quotation); Trustees Minutes, June 6, 1899.

125. Schiedt, "Reminiscences," *Reformed Church Messenger*, 7–10; [Trustees], *Science Building*, 3–12; *College Student*, Oct. 1899, 31; Trustees Minutes, Mar. 1, June 12, 1900. Schiedt later recalled that he had drawn up the plans "in cooperation with a young architect and then had to fight for its adoption by the Committee of Board who had friends among the 12 competitors whose plans were practically worthless" (R. C. Schiedt to H. M. J. Klein, Dec. 2, 1936, Klein Papers, Archives [hereafter, Klein Papers]).

126. Trustees Minutes, June 12, 1900, June 11, 1901 (quotations).

127. Trustees Minutes, June 10, 1902.

128. Trustees Minutes, June 10 and 11, 1902; *F&M Weekly*, Dec. 11, 1901; R. C. Schiedt to H. M. J. Klein, Dec. 2, 1936, Klein Papers; J. E. Kershner to G. F. Baer, June 6, 1908, and Baer to Kershner, June 8, 1908, both in Baer Papers. On Hershey, see Joel Glenn Brenner, *The Emperors of Chocolate: Inside the Secret World of Hershey and Mars* (New York: Random House, 1999).

129. Homan, "George Baer's Industrial Empire"; *F&M Weekly*, Jan. 22, 1902 (quotation).

130. Nell Irvin Painter, *Standing at Armageddon: The United States, 1877–1919* (New York: W. W. Norton, 1987), 180–84 (quotations on 183–84); Rowland Berthoff, "Writing a History of Things Left Out," *Reviews in American History* 14 (Mar. 1986): 8.

131. "Programme for the Golden Jubilee of Franklin and Marshall College," Faculty Minutes, June 1903; Dubbs, *History* iii; Franklin and Marshall College Alumni Association, *Obituary Record* (Lancaster, 1897–1909); *Catalogue of Officers and Students 1787–1903* (Lancaster: Franklin and Marshall College Alumni Association, 1903).

132. Trustees Minutes, June 9, 1903; *Oriflamme* (1905), 155–59; Klein, *History of Franklin and Marshall College*, 135–36 (quotations); "Programme for the Golden Jubilee"; *F&M Weekly*, June 12, 1903.

133. *College Student*, Oct. 1900 (first quotation); Trustees Minutes, June 12, 1901 (second quotation). Of the nine alumni elected to the advisory board, the three ministers were the oldest; the youngest were the three lawyers and a librarian (*F&M Weekly*, Jan. 22, 1902).

134. Stahr, "Financial Development of Franklin and Marshall College," 176.

135. John B. Kieffer, "Franklin and Marshall College and the Classics," *Reformed Church Review* 7 (Apr. 1903): 180, 183, 186–87.

136. Ibid., 184–85, 187.

137. Jefferson E. Kershner, "Mathematics, Physics, and Astronomy," *Reformed Church Review* 7 (Apr. 1903): 190, 192; Schiedt, "Sciences Then and Now," 208–9, 212.

138. C. Ernest Wagner, "The Teaching of English at Franklin and Marshall," *Reformed Church Review* 7 (Apr. 1903): 220–21; A. V. Hiester, "Political Economy," *Reformed Church Review* 7 (Apr. 1903): 240–41; William Rupp and George W. Richards, "The Significance of the Establishment of Franklin and Marshall College," *Reformed Church Review* 7 (Apr. 1903): 293–312.

139. Samuel H. Ranch, "The Literary Societies—What the Students Have Done for Them and What They Have Done for the Students," *Reformed Church Review* 7 (Apr. 1903): 243–54; *F&M Weekly*, Apr. 4, 1894; Kenneth Cmiel, *Democratic Eloquence: The Fight over Popular Speech in Nineteenth-Century America* (New York: William Morrow, 1990).

140. Faculty Minutes, Nov. 23, 1892, Feb. 10, 1893, Oct. 25, and Nov. 15, 1895, Nov. 12, 1896, Nov. 24, 1897; Trustees Minutes, June 12, 1900, Stahr (quotation); *F&M Weekly*, Mar. 10, 1897.

CHAPTER 5

1. H. H. Apple to George Baer, Oct. 13, 1909, Baer Papers, Archives (hereafter, Baer Papers); *F&M Weekly*, Oct. 13, 1909, and Jan. 13, 1910; H. M. J. Klein, *History of Franklin and Marshall College, 1787–1948* (Lancaster: Franklin and Marshall College, 1952), 148–49.

2. G. F. Baer to W. U. Hensel, Dec. 16, 1909, and Hensel to Baer, Dec. 18, 1909 (quotation), Baer Papers.

3. Klein, *History of Franklin and Marshall College*, 149; *F&M Weekly*, Nov. 17, 1909.

4. "The Inaugural at Lancaster," *Reformed Church Messenger*, Jan. 13, 1910, and "College Inaugural a Brilliant Success," *Lancaster New Era*, Jan. 8, 1910, both clippings in H. H. Apple Papers, Archives (hereafter, H. H. Apple Papers).

5. Franklin & Marshall College Trustees Minutes, June 11, 1907, Archives (hereafter, Trustees Minutes). Laurence R. Veysey notes the prewar tendency to oppose the German research model with humanistic education at Cambridge and Oxford. See Veysey, *Emergence of the American University* (Chicago: University of Chicago Press, 1965), 180–82, 196–97.

6. Veysey, *Emergence of the American University*, chap. 2; Julie A. Reuben, *The Making of the Modern University: Intellectual Transformation and the Marginalization of Morality* (Chicago: University of Chicago Press, 1996), 267.

7. David W. Breneman, *Liberal Arts Colleges: Thriving, Surviving, or Endangered?* (Washington, D.C.: Brookings Institution, 1994), 20; P. C. Kemeny, *Princeton in the Nation's Service: Religious Ideals and Educational Practice, 1868–1928* (New York: Oxford University Press, 1998), 130; Reuben, *Making of the Modern University*, 230–43 (Butler quotation on 232).

8. W. Bruce Leslie, *Gentlemen and Scholars: College and Community in the "Age of the University," 1865–1917* (University Park: Pennsylvania State University Press, 1992), 178–79, 187–88, 231–36; Veysey, *Emergence of the American University*, chap. 4.

9. *Nation*, July 4, 1903, clipping in Joseph Henry Dubbs Papers, Archives; clippings in Paul Kieffer Files, Archives; *F&M Weekly*, Mar. 18 and 25, Dec. 16, 1903, Sept. 15, 1910.

10. *F&M Weekly*, Sept. 25, 1907, Nov. 2, 1911, Feb. 5, 1908.

11. Nathan C. Schaeffer, "Dr. Stahr and the Public Schools," *College Student*, Feb. 23, 1916, 8–9; James Mulhern, *A History of Secondary Education in Pennsylvania* (Philadelphia: privately printed, 1933), 487; Franklin & Marshall College Catalogue, 1898–1899, 33 (hereafter, *Catalogue*); *F&M Weekly*, Sept. 18, 1895, Sept. 18, 1901, Sept. 24, 1912.

12. Trustees Minutes, June 9, 1903.

13. Trustees Minutes, Jan. 4, 1904 (quotations), Dec. 2, 1927; *F&M Weekly*, June 12, 1903.

14. E. M. Hartman to J. S. Stahr, July 15 and 19, 1903, Hartman Papers, Archives (hereafter, Hartman Papers).

15. E. M. Hartman to J. S. Stahr, Sept. 25, 1903, Hartman Papers.

16. *F&M Weekly*, Oct. 14, 1903 and Jan. 13, 1904; Trustees Minutes, June 7, 1904.

17. E. M. Hartman to J. S. Stahr, Jan. 27, 1905, Hartman Papers; Trustees Minutes, June 13, 1905; Ellen Condliffe Lagemann, *The Politics of Knowledge: The Carnegie Corporation, Philanthropy, and Public Policy* (Middletown: Wesleyan University Press, 1989), 16–19; Joseph Frazier Wall, *Andrew Carnegie* (New York: Oxford University Press, 1970).

18. E. M. Hartman to J. S. Stahr, Mar. 23 and Apr. 1, 1905, and Hartman to Finance Committee of Franklin and Marshall College, Apr. 1, 1905, Hartman Papers; Trustees Minutes, June 13 and 14, 1905, June 12 and 13, 1906, June 11, 1907 (quotation), and June 9, 1908; W. U. Hensel to B. F. Fackenthal, June 4, 1909, Fackenthal Papers, Archives (hereafter, Fackenthal Papers).

19. *F&M Weekly*, Mar. 11 and May 27, 1908; Klein, *History of Franklin and Marshall College*, 144 (quotation).

20. Trustees Minutes, June 9, 1908 (quotation); Nathan C. Schaeffer to G. F. Baer, Apr. 22, 1908, Baer Papers; Wm. H. Hager to W. U. Hensel, May 16, 1908, J. S. Stahr to Baer, May 16, 1908, Hensel to Hager, May 18, 1908, Hensel to Baer, May 18, 1908, Hensel to Baer, May 18, 1908, Baer to Stahr, May 19, 1908, all in Baer Papers; B. F. Fackenthal Jr., "Biographical Notice of Rev. Nathan Christ Schaeffer," *Proceedings of the Pennsylvania-German Society* 30 (1924): 54.

21. W. U. Hensel to G. F. Baer, May 18, 1908 (quotation), Baer to N. C. Schaeffer, June 15, 1908 (quotation), Baer to Hensel, Aug. 25, 1908, and Schaeffer to Baer, Aug. 29, 1908, Baer to Schaeffer, Apr. 30, 1909, Petition to Baer, Hensel and B. F. Fackenthal, Apr. 12, 1909, all in Baer Papers.

22. N. C. Schaeffer to G. F. Baer, May 1, 1909, W. U. Hensel to Baer, May 21, 1909, all in Baer Papers; E. R. Eschbach to Henry Harbaugh Apple, May 30, 1908, S. R. Bridenbaugh to Apple, May 30, 1908, Bridenbaugh to Apple, June 10, 1909, J. Spangler Kieffer to Apple, June 19, 1909, J. Rauch Stein to Apple, July 19, 1909, all in H. H. Apple Papers, Archives (hereafter, H. H. Apple Papers); Baer to B. F. Fackenthal, June 4, [1909], Fackenthal Papers; *F&M Weekly*, June 2, 1909; *Reformed Church Messenger*, June 17, 1909, 4.

23. "Dr. Apple, President Emeritus of F&M, Succumbs," *Lancaster Intelligencer*, May 20, 1943, clipping in H. H. Apple Papers; "President-Elect Henry Harbaugh Apple," *Reformed Church Messenger*, June 17, 1909, 4; *F&M Weekly*, Nov. 6, 1896, 2.

24. Unidentified clippings, June 3, 1901, and May 27, 1906, in Apple Scrapbook, H. H. Apple Papers; H. H. Apple, "The Pastor in Relation to the Civic Life of the Community," *Reformed Church Review*, 4th ser., 9 (July 1905): 357; H. H. Apple, "Men for the Mill," speech to Manufacturers' Association of York, 1907, H. H. Apple Papers.

25. B. F. Fackenthal to G. F. Baer, June 11, 1909, Baer Papers; B. F. Fackenthal to H. H. Apple, June 18, 1909, H. H. Apple Papers.

26. A. Thos. G. Apple to H. H. Apple, June 14, 1909, H. H. Apple Papers; *F&M Weekly*, May 26, 1909; *Oriflamme* (Lancaster, Pa., 1910).

27. H. H. Apple to G. F. Baer, Oct. 13, 1909, H. H. Apple Papers; Faculty Minutes, Aug. 11, Oct. 11, and Dec. 13, 1909, Archives (hereafter, Faculty Minutes).

28. Ellen Condliffe Lagemann, *Private Power for the Public Good: A History of the Carnegie Foundation for the Advancement of Teaching* (Middletown: Wesleyan University Press, 1983) (quotation on 37–38); Hugh Hawkins, *Banding Together: The Rise of National Associations in American Higher Education, 1887–1950* (Baltimore: Johns Hopkins University Press, 1992), 104–10.

29. J. S. Stahr to G. F. Baer, Sept. 19, 1908, and Baer to Stahr, Sept. 21, 1908, Baer Papers.

30. Monell Sayre to H. H. Apple, Oct. 6, 1909, Apple Papers; Franklin & Marshall College Board Minutes, June 6, 1911, Archives (hereafter, Board Minutes).

31. Standardization is discussed in Leslie, *Gentlemen and Scholars*, 221; Faculty Minutes, Feb. 14, 1910 (quotation); Board Minutes, Jan. 7, 1914; *F&M Weekly*, Mar. 24, 1910.

32. H. H. Apple to G. F. Baer, Oct. 13, 1909, Feb. 7, 1911, Baer Papers; Board Minutes, June 7, 1910, June 6, 1911.

33. Faculty Minutes, Mar. 31, 1905, Apr. 12, 1907; Trustees Minutes, June 13, 1905; *Catalogue* for 1898–1899, 33 (quotation).

34. J. S. Stahr to G. F. Baer, Nov. 20, 1905, Baer Papers; F. T. Gates to J. D. Rockefeller, June 6, 1905, quoted in E. Richard Brown, *Rockefeller Medicine Men: Medicine and Capitalism in America* (Berkeley: University of California Press, 1979), 54, 56 (quotation on 54).

35. H. H. Apple to G. F. Baer, Oct. 13, 1909, and Jan. 18, 1910 (quotation), Baer to Andrew Carnegie, Jan. 19, 1910, all in Baer Papers.

36. Board Minutes, Jan. 7, 1910, June 6 and 7, 1910, June 6, 1911; W. M. Irvine to H. H. Apple, Jan. 13, 1910, H. H. Apple Papers.

37. *F&M Weekly*, Nov. 2, 1911, 6; Board Minutes, June 11, 1912 (quotation).

38. H. H. Apple to G. F. Baer, Jan. 2, 1910, Apple Papers; Board Minutes, Jan. 7, 1910 (quotation), June 6 and 7, 1911, June 11, 1912, June 10 and 11, 1913.

39. Board Minutes, June 7, 1910; *F&M Weekly*, Nov. 2, 1911; Leslie, *Gentlemen and Scholars*, 215, 248.

40. Board Minutes, June 8, 1910.

41. *F&M Weekly*, Feb. 1 and Mar. 7, 1912; S. P. Heilman to H. H. Apple, Sept. 18, 1911, Apple to G. F. Baer, Sept. 18, 1911 (quotation), H. H. Apple Papers.

42. *F&M Weekly*, Sept. 24 and Dec. 17, 1912, and Mar. 4, 1913; Board Minutes, Dec. 6, 1912, and June 11, 1913; H. H. Apple to G. F. Baer, July 2, 1913, Baer to Apple, July 7, 1913, Baer Papers.

43. W. U. Hensel to H. H. Apple, Sept. 8, 1914, H. H. Apple Papers; W. U. Hensel, "A Message to the Friends of Franklin and Marshall College in the Reformed Church," *Reformed Church Messenger* [1914]; *F&M Weekly*, Nov. 5, 1914, Feb. 17, 1915; Trustees Minutes, June 8, 1915, June 6, 1916; H. M. J. Klein, *The History of the Eastern Synod of the Reformed Church in the United States* (Lancaster: Eastern Synod, 1943), 309.

44. Board Minutes, June 9, 1914.

45. Board Minutes, June 7, 1910; *F&M Weekly*, Sept. 15, 1910.

46. Board Minutes, June 8, 1910; Fackenthal Remarks at Unveiling of Portrait, June 2, 1936, Fackenthal Papers; *F&M Weekly*, June 5, 1895, Nov. 6, 1895, Sept. 19, 1912, Apr. 30, 1913.

47. R. C. Schiedt to H. M. J. Klein, June 26, 1910, Klein Papers, Archives.

48. Geo. F. Mull to H. H. Apple, June 13, 1909, H. H. Apple Papers; Mull to Apple, July 22, 1913, and July 16, 1914, Mull Papers, Archives; Mull to B. F. Fackenthal Jr., June 12, 1910, Fackenthal Papers.

49. Geo. F. Mull to H. H. Apple, Dec. 9, 1909, H. H. Apple Papers.

50. *F&M Weekly*, Oct. 15, 1912.

51. Faculty Minutes, Feb. 12, June 6, 1902, Jan. 5, 1903; *F&M Weekly*, May 21 and Oct. 15, 1902, Feb. 26, 1908.

52. Faculty Minutes, May 20 and May 21, 1913.

53. Faculty Minutes, May 27, 1913; Board Minutes, June 11, 1913.

54. Faculty Minutes, Jan. 19, 1914, Feb. 8 and 12, 1917; *F&M Weekly*, Jan. 14, 1914.

55. *F&M Weekly*, Nov. 17, 1910; Faculty Minutes, Feb. 10 and Oct. 27, 1913, Apr. 14, 1914; Board Minutes, June 8, 1915.

56. *F&M Weekly*, May 6, 1896; *Student Weekly*, Jan. 19 and Nov. 1, 1916, May 28, 1924; Faculty Minutes, Nov. 9, 1906, Apr. 15 and Oct. 11, 1907.

57. *F&M Weekly*, Oct. 2, 1901. See Sally Foreman Griffith, *Home Town News: William Allen White and the Emporia Gazette* (New York: Oxford University Press, 1989), 138–58; Jean Quandt, *From the Small Town to the Great Society: The Social Thought of Progressive Intellectuals* (New Brunswick: Rutgers University Press, 1970).

58. Kemeny, *Princeton in the Nation's Service*, 111 (Wilson quotation); *F&M Weekly*, Sept. 16, 1903 (Hiester quotation), Sept. 17, 1902 (third quotation), Feb. 18, 1903 (fourth quotation).

59. Board Minutes, June 8, 1915.

60. *F&M Weekly*, Nov. 6, 1907, Oct. 29, 1914.

61. *Oriflamme* (1893), 41, (1900), 50; *F&M Weekly*, Sept. 18 and Sept. 25, 1901, Sept. 24, 1902, Sept. 30, 1908 (quotation), Sept. 22, 1909, Sept. 15 and Oct. 27, 1910 (quotation), Sept. 19, 1912; Alvin Kneedler, postcard, Sept. 12, 1914, MS 55, Kneedler Family Papers, Archives. For a lively discussion of cane rushes and other traditions, see John H. Brubaker III, *Hullabaloo Nevonia: An Anecdotal History of Student Life at Franklin and Marshall College* (Lancaster: Franklin and Marshall College, 1987). On the shift elsewhere, see David M. Stameshkin, *The Town's College: Middlebury College, 1800–1915* (Middlebury: Middlebury College Press, 1985), 265; David Bishop Skillman, *The Biography of a College* (Easton: Lafayette College, 1932) 2:160–61.

62. "College Students Arrested," *Lancaster New Era*, Sept. 11, 1902; Faculty Minutes, Apr. 19, 21 (quotation), 25, and 28, 1905; Brubaker, *Hullabaloo Nevonia*, 77 (quotation).

63. *F&M Weekly*, Sept. 22, 1910 (quotation), Nov. 23 and 30, 1910; *Student Weekly*, Sept. 16 and 22 (quotation), 1915.

64. Faculty Minutes, Dec. 13, 1909; *F&M Weekly*, Nov. 30, 1911, Mar. 7, 1912. Hazing seems to have been more prevalent at New England colleges in the nineteenth century, though it was increasingly common at Middle Atlantic schools like Princeton and Lafayette College in the 1880s and 1890s. Similar freshman regulations had been introduced at Gettysburg College around 1905, with the argument that "every college of note has its established traditions." See Helen Lefkowitz Horowitz, *Campus Life: Undergraduate Cultures from the End of the Eighteenth Century to the Present* (Chicago: University of Chicago Press, 1987), 42, 43; Veysey, *Emergence of the American University*, 277, 285; Skillman, *Biography of a College*, 29, 55, 84; Charles H. Glatfelter, *A Salutary Influence: Gettysburg College, 1832–1985* (Gettysburg: Gettysburg College, 1987), 670–71 (quotation).

65. *F&M Weekly*, Oct. 13, 1909, Nov. 24, 1910, Dec. 10, 1913.

66. *Student Weekly*, Oct. 6, 1915 (quotations), Jan. 19, 1916.

67. "College Inaugural a Brilliant Success," *Lancaster New Era*, Jan. 8, 1910, clipping in H. H. Apple Papers. On the study of classical languages as a rite of passage, see Walter J. Ong, *Rhetoric, Romance, and Technology* (Ithaca: Cornell University Press, 1971), 113–41, and

Fighting for Life: Contest, Sexuality, and Consciousness (Ithaca: Cornell University Press, 1981), 119–48.

68. "College Administration" (Nov. 7, 1910), in H. H. Apple Papers.

69. Board Minutes, June 11, 1912, and June 8, 1915.

70. Faculty Minutes, Nov. 16 and 30, 1908, Dec. 12, 1910, Oct. 13, 1913, Jan. 11 and Mar. 8, 1915; Board Minutes, June 8, 1915; *Catalogue* for 1915, 51; Reuben, *Making of the Modern University*, 241–42; Leslie, *Gentlemen and Scholars*, 178–80, 181–82. This same shift to alphabetical listings was occurring at the same time at universities that had long since abandoned the classical curriculum (Reuben, *Making of the Modern University*, 234, 335).

71. Board Minutes, June 8, 1915, June 6, 1916.

72. Wayne E. Homan, "George Baer's Industrial Empire," *Reading Sunday Eagle Magazine*, Apr. 10, 1966, Baer Papers.

73. Hensel quoted in Klein, *History of Franklin and Marshall College*, 168–69; Board Minutes, Wed., June 9, 1915.

74. "Fackenthal Trustee of F–M Since 1899," Oct. 10, 1941, unidentified clipping, Fackenthal Papers; Fackenthal quoted in his obituary in *Lafayette Miner*, Mar. 1942, in Fackenthal Papers.

75. Board Minutes, June 8, 1915, June 6, 1916; Trustees Minutes, June 7, 1910.

76. Edgar Fahs Smith to H. H. Apple, July 23, 1917, H. H. Apple Papers; Lecture Notes on Aesthetics and Ethics, box 6, H. H. Apple Papers.

77. See Russell A. Kazal, *Becoming Old Stock: The Paradox of German-American Identity* (Princeton: Princeton University Press, 2004).

78. *F&M Weekly*, Sept. 24, 1914, 1 (first quotation), Oct. 9, 1914, 1 (all other quotations).

79. *F&M Weekly*, Oct. 9, 1914, 1; Faculty Minutes, Oct. 12 and 26, 1914.

80. [H. H. Apple], "Case of R. C. Schiedt," in H. H. Apple Papers; for example, see R. C. Schiedt letter to the editor, *Lancaster Intelligencer*, Oct. 29, 1915, in Schiedt Papers; Richard Schiedt, "Germany and the Formative Forces of the Great War," reprint from *Reformed Church Review* (1915), in Schiedt Papers; *F&M Weekly*, Jan. 7, 1915, Feb. 10, 1915, May 13, 1915; *Student Weekly*, Mar. 15, 1916.

81. [H. H. Apple], "Case of R. C. Schiedt," in H. H. Apple Papers; John Higham, *Strangers in the Land: Patterns of American Nativism, 1860–1925* (New Brunswick: Rutgers University Press, 1955; paper reprint, 1992), 196–98.

82. "Case of R. C. Schiedt"; R. C. Schiedt letter to the editor, and "Dr. Scheidt on Vandalism and Atrocities," *Lancaster Intelligencer*, Oct. 29, 1915, in Schiedt Papers. See also "Dr. Scheidt Again on the War Path," *Lancaster Intelligencer*, Nov. 5, 1915.

83. Page proof of talk, H. H. Apple Papers.

84. Press clippings, H. H. Apple Papers; *Student Weekly*, Mar. 22, 1916, 5; Joseph H. Appel to H. H. Apple, Mar. 16, 1916, H. H. Apple Papers.

85. *Student Weekly*, March 8, 15, 22, 1916; Trustees Minutes, June 7, 1916; Klein, *History of Franklin and Marshall College*, 173; *Oriflamme* (1916), 33:8.

86. *Student Weekly*, Oct. 11, 18, Dec. 6, 13 (quotation) and 20, 1916; Klein, *History of Franklin and Marshall College*, 174; Trustees Minutes, June 5, 1917.

87. Trustees Minutes, June 6, 1916, and June 5, 1917 (quotation).

88. Faculty Minutes, Apr. 11, 16, and 18, 1917; *Student Weekly*, Mar. 28, 1918, 3, 6; Klein, *History of Franklin and Marshall College*, 174–75; Trustees Minutes, June 5, 1917.

89. Faculty Minutes, May 7 and 21, 1917; Trustees Minutes, June 5, 1917 (all quotations), May 17, 1918; Klein, *History of Franklin and Marshall College*, 175.

90. David M. Kennedy, *Over Here: The First World War and American Society* (New York: Oxford University Press, 1980), 147–50; Klein, *History of Franklin and Marshall College*, 176; Board Minutes, June 5, 1917 (quotation), May 7, 1918.

91. *Student Weekly*, Oct. 17, Nov. 28, 1917; Klein, *History of Franklin and Marshall College*, 178; Trustees Minutes, May 6, 1918; H. H. Apple to B. F. Fackenthal, Feb. 6, 1918, H. H. Apple Papers.

92. *Student Weekly*, Apr. 25, 1918, 6–7.

93. Kennedy, *Over Here*; Higham, *Strangers in the Land*, 207–9; *The Great Advance: The Story of the Forward Movement, 1919–1926* (Philadelphia: Forward Movement Commission, 1926), 18–20.

94. "Dr. R. C. Schiedt to Leave the Faculty of F. and M. College," *Lancaster New Era*, Jan. 30, 1918, clipping in H. H. Apple Papers (quotations); [H. H. Apple], "Case of R. C. Schiedt," in H. H. Apple Papers.

95. "Case of R. C. Schiedt."

96. *Reformed Church Messenger*, Oct. 11, 1917 (second Scheidt quotation); R. C. Schiedt to C. Baker, Dec. 2, 1917 (first Scheidt quotation), H. H. Apple Papers; "Dr. Schiedt Partially Vindicated-Wellesley Teacher Repudiates Disloyalty Stories Circulated by Her," *Student Weekly*, Mar. 13, 1918, 1, 8 (quotations).

97. "Dr. R. C. Schiedt to Leave"; "Case of R. C. Schiedt"; Trustees Minutes, Nov. 23, 1917.

98. Trustees Minutes, Nov. 23, 1917.

99. Scheidt quotations R. C. Schiedt to C. Baker, Dec. 2, 1917; Charles G. Baker, S. P. Heilman, and A. H. Rothermel to B. F. Fackenthal, Dec. 11, 1917, Rothermel to H. H. Apple, Dec. 4, 1917, J. W. Wetzel to Baker, Dec. 21, 1917 (final quotation), and Fackenthal to Apple, Dec. 24, 1917, all in H. H. Apple Papers.

100. "F. and M. Invaded by Propagandist in Anonymous Writing," *Lancaster New Era*, Jan. 24, 1918 (all quotations); "College is Stirred by Attack on Hillis," *North American*, Jan. 24 [1918], clippings in H. H. Apple Papers.

101. H. H. Apple to B. F. Fackenthal, Feb. 6 and Feb. 20, 1918, H. H. Apple Papers.

102. H. H. Apple to B. F. Fackenthal, Feb. 20, 1918, G. D. Robb to H. H. Apple, Feb. 1, 1918, H. H. Apple Papers.

103. William H. Hager to H. H. Apple, Feb. 16, 1918, Apple to B. F. Fackenthal, Feb. 6 and Feb. 20, 1918, Petition of Feb. 8, 1918, "Case of R. C. Schiedt," all in H. H. Apple Papers; *Student Weekly*, Jan. 31, Feb. 7, 1918.

104. Faculty Minutes, [ca. February] 1918.

105. S. K. Loy to Charles W. Levan, Mar. 14, 1918, J. Andrew Frantz to Apple, Feb. 7, 1918, Frantz to Milton F. Baringer, Feb. 14, 1918, all in H. H. Apple Papers.

106. J. W. Wetzel to H. H. Apple, Feb. 16, 1918, Wetzel to J. Andrew Frantz, Feb. 16, 1918, A. H. Rothermel to Frantz, Feb. 18, 1918, all in H. H. Apple Papers.

107. J. Andrew Frantz to A. H. Rothermel, Feb. 18, 1918, S. K. Loy to Charles W. Levan, Mar. 21, 1918, H. H. Apple Papers; "Dr. Schiedt Partially Vindicated," *Student Weekly*, Mar. 13, 1918, 1.

108. "Dr. R. C. Schiedt to Leave."

109. Trustees Minutes, May 7, 1918 (quotations); Faculty Minutes, Apr. 29, 1918; David O. Levine, *The American College and the Culture of Aspiration, 1915–1940* (Ithaca: Cornell University Press, 1986), 25–26.

110. Trustees Minutes, June 17, 1919 (quotation); H. H. Apple to B. F. Fackenthal, Feb. 20, 1918, Apple Papers.

111. Trustees Minutes, June 17, 1919; Carol S. Gruber, *Mars and Minerva: World War I and the Uses of the Higher Learning in America* (Baton Rouge: Louisiana State University Press, 1975), 214, 217; Skillman, *Biography of a College*, 244–47.

112. Faculty Minutes, Sept. 24, 1918; Leslie, *Gentlemen and Scholars*, 251–53 (Wilson quotation on 253); Skillman, *Biography of a College*, 246–47 (quotation); Gruber, *Mars and Minerva*, 213.

113. Trustees Minutes, June 17, 1919; Faculty Minutes, May 12, 1919 (quotation).

114. Trustees Minutes, June 17, 1919.

CHAPTER 6

1. Franklin & Marshall College Board Minutes, June 17, 1919, Archives (hereafter, Board Minutes).

2. On increasing standardization in this period, see John R. Thelin, *A History of American Higher Education* (Baltimore: Johns Hopkins University Press, 2004), 238–39; and Richard M. Freeland, *Academia's Golden Age: Universities in Massachusetts, 1945–1970* (New York: Oxford University Press, 1992), 50–51.

3. James Mulhern, *A History of Secondary Education in Pennsylvania* (Philadelphia: privately published, 1933), 487; Franklin & Marshall College Catalogues (1914–1915); Board Minutes, June 17, 1919; "Pennsylvania's Marvelous Transformation," *Pennsylvania School Journal* 69 (Mar. 1921): 371.

4. Board Minutes, Jan. 20 and June 8, 1920 (first quotations), June 7, 1921; *Student Weekly*, Nov. 5, 1919, 1; *Catalogue* for 1920; *Annual Reports of the President and Treasurer to the Board of Trustees of Franklin and Marshall College* (Lancaster: [Franklin & Marshall College], 1929), 10 (second quotation) (hereafter, *Report of the President*).

5. David O. Levine, *The American College and the Culture of Aspiration, 1915–1940* (Ithaca: Cornell University Press, 1986), 18–19, 38–49, 57–60; William Shand and Dean Keller, "Twentieth Century Industrial Development of Lancaster," *Journal of the Lancaster County Historical Society* 100 (1998): 445–52; Philip Scranton, *Endless Novelty: Specialty Production and American Industrialization, 1865–1925* (Princeton: Princeton University Press, 1997).

6. See discussion of curriculum in *Pennsylvania School Journal* 69 (Feb. 1921): 361; Peter Novick, *That Noble Dream: The "Objectivity Question" and the American Historical Profession* (New York: Cambridge University Press, 1988), 185–89; Board Minutes, June 8, 1920; H. M. J. Klein, *History of Franklin and Marshall College, 1787–1948* (Lancaster: Franklin & Marshall College Alumni Association, 1952), 202.

7. Franklin and Marshall College Faculty Minutes, Feb. 14 (quotation), Mar. 14, and Apr. 11, 1921, Archives (hereafter, Faculty Minutes).

8. Board Minutes, June 7, 1921.

9. Ibid.; Levine, *American College and the Culture of Aspiration*, 46–49.

10. Board Minutes, June 7, 1921.

11. Board Minutes, June 13, 1922, and throughout the decade; *Report of the President* (1928–1929), 10.

12. *Catalogue* for 1920–1921.

13. Board Minutes, June 7, 1921, June 12, 1923; Jefferson E. Kershner obituary, Board Minute Book, Archives.

14. Board Minutes, June 17, 1919, Jan. 20, June 8, and Dec. 17, 1920; B. F. Fackenthal to H. H. Apple, June 28, 1920, H. H. Apple Papers, Archives (hereafter, H. H. Apple Papers); B. F. Fackenthal Remarks at Alumni Luncheon, June 9, 1920, Fackenthal Papers; *The Great Advance: The Story of the Forward Movement, 1919–1916* (Philadelphia: Forward Movement Commission, 1926).

15. Board Minutes, Dec 17, 1920, June 7 and Oct. 28, 1921, June 13, 1922; B. F. Fackenthal to H. H. Apple, July 2, 1921, H. H. Apple Papers.

16. Board Minutes, Oct. 28, 1921; *Student Weekly*, Feb. 1, 8 (first quotation), and 15 and Nov. 1, 1922 (second quotation).

17. Faculty Minutes, Jan. 8, 1923; *Student Weekly*, Jan. 17 (quotation), Mar. 7, and June 12, 1923; Board Minutes, Jan. 26 and June 12, 1923, June 9, 1924.

18. Board Minutes, June 13, 1922 (quotation), Jan. 26, 1923; *Student Weekly*, Feb. 15, 1922, Feb. 21, Mar. 28, and May 9, 1923; David Schuyler, "The 'New' Franklin & Marshall: Charles Z. Klauder, Henry Harbaugh Apple, and Campus Design in the 1920s," http://www.fandm.edu/x6937 (accessed 1/14/2000).

19. Paul Venable Turner, *Campus: An American Planning Tradition* (Cambridge, Mass.: MIT Press, 1984), 163–235 (quotation on 186); Schuyler, "The 'New' Franklin & Marshall."

20. Turner, *Campus*, 235, 238; Carol Hoffecker, "A Brief History of the UD Green," http://www.udel.edu/TheGreen/history.html (accessed 1/14/2000).

21. Turner, *Campus*, 202; H. M. J. Klein, "Sixty Years: Milton Thomas Garvin, 1934," (quotation), pamphlet in Klein Papers, Archives. The square at the heart of Lancaster, originally called Centre Square, was renamed Penn Square in the 1870s.

22. Board Minutes, Dec. 7, 1923 (quotation); Special Committee Minutes, Dec. 28, 1923; B. F. Fackenthal Jr. to George Mull, Dec. 29, 1923, included with Board Minutes; Report of Alumni Trustees to Alumni Association, June 1924, in H. H. Apple Papers; Board Minutes, June 9, 1924.

23. Board Minutes, June 12 and Dec. 7, 1923, June 9, 1924 (quotation).

24. *Student Weekly*, Dec. 3, 1924, and Apr. 28, 1926 (quotation); Board Minutes, Dec. 12, 1924 (quotation); Schuyler, "The 'New' Franklin & Marshall"; *Franklin and Marshall Alumnus* 1 (May 1925): 3.

25. Board Minutes, June 9, 1924; *Franklin and Marshall Alumnus* 1 (Feb. 1925); *Franklin and Marshall Alumnus* 1 (Nov. 1924): 1, 3.

26. Board Minutes, Dec. 12, 1924, June 5, 1925; *Franklin and Marshall Alumnus* 1 (Feb. 1925): 1, (quotations on 5, 6), 7; *Franklin and Marshall Alumnus* 1 (May 1925): 14; *Franklin and Marshall Alumnus* 2 (Nov. 1925): 1; *Student Weekly*, Mar. 25, 1925, 1, and *Student Weekly*, Apr. 8, 1925, 1.

27. *Franklin and Marshall Alumnus* 2 (Nov. 1925): 1; *Franklin and Marshall Alumnus* 3 (June 1927): 111; *Franklin and Marshall Alumnus* 4 (Mar. 1928): 1; Board Minutes, June 3, 1927 (quotation).

28. *Student Weekly*, Dec. 15, 1926, 3; *Student Weekly*, Jan. 12, 1927, 1; *Student Weekly*, Feb. 16, 1927, 1; *Student Weekly*, Mar. 2, 1927, 1; *Student Weekly*, Mar. 23, 1927, 2; *Student Weekly*, May 11, 1927, 1; *Student Weekly*, May 18, 1927, 1; Board Minutes, June 3, 1927.

29. *Student Weekly*, Sept. 21, 1927, 2; *Student Weekly*, Oct. 12, 1927, 1; *Student Weekly*, Oct. 26, 1927 (quotation), 1; *Student Weekly*, Mar. 7, 1928, 2; *Report of the President* (1928–1929): 29–30; Board Minutes, Dec. 2, 1927.

30. Board Minutes, Dec. 2, 1927.

31. Board Minutes, June 2, 1928; *Student Weekly*, Sept. 26, 1928, 1; *Student Weekly*, Dec. 12, 1928, 3; *Franklin and Marshall Alumnus* 5 (Nov. 1928): 10; *Franklin and Marshall Alumnus* (Feb. 1929), 49; Schuyler, "The 'New' Franklin & Marshall."

32. Klein, *History of Franklin and Marshall College*, 220–21 (quotation); *Report of the President* (Dec. 1929): 6–7; Board Minutes, Dec. 7, 1928.

33. *Report of the President* (Dec. 1929): 20–22; *Student Weekly*, Sept. 25, 1929, 3.

34. *Student Weekly*, Apr. 28, 1926, 2; *Student Weekly*, Nov. 7, 1928, 2; *Student Weekly*, May 29, 1930, 1; *Student Weekly*, Sept. 24, 1930, 1; *Report of the President* (1929–1930): 48; Board Minutes, June 5, 1925, May 31, 1930, and Jan. 22, 1931; President's Newsletter, October 27, 1945, Distler Papers, Archives; Schuyler, "The 'New' Franklin & Marshall."

35. *College Reporter*, Aug. 28, 1996, 1.

36. Board Minutes, June 9, 1924, and June 5, 1925; *Report of the President* (1925–1926): 27; *Report of the President* (1928–1929): 57.

37. *Catalogue* for 1918–1919; *Report of the President* (1928–1929): 11.

38. John Higham, "Specialization in a Democracy," in *Hanging Together: Unity and Diversity in American Culture*, ed. Carl J. Guarneri (New Haven: Yale University Press, 2001), 67–82; Faculty Minutes, May 19, 1924; Board Minutes, June 9, 1924 (quotation); *Report of the President* (1928–1929): 11.

39. *Report of the President* (1928–1929): 11. On the loss of an all-inclusive vision, see Julie A. Reuben, *The Making of the Modern University: Intellectual Transformation and the Marginalization of Morality* (Chicago: University of Chicago Press, 1996), 176–88.

40. Board Minutes, Dec. 12, 1924, and June 5, 1925.

41. *Report of the President* (1928–1929): 11; *Catalogue* for 1928–1929.

42. Board Minutes, June 4, 1926, and Dec. 2, 1927, and passim.

43. Board Minutes, Dec. 2, 1927.

44. Faculty Minutes, May 19, 1924, May 11, 1925, Mar. 17, Apr. 11, and Oct. 9, 1927; Board Minutes, June 9, 1924, June 5, 1925, Dec. 3, 1926, and Dec. 2, 1927.

45. Board Minutes, June 9 (quotations) and Dec. 12, 1924; *Student Weekly*, Nov. 12, 1924; Hugh Hawkins, *Banding Together: The Rise of National Associations in American Higher Education, 1887–1950* (Baltimore: Johns Hopkins University Press, 1992), 84–88. In an early attempt to rank American institutions of higher education, the U. S. Bureau of Education placed Franklin & Marshall in its second group, along with other local schools, like Swarthmore, Bucknell, Muhlenberg, Rutgers, and Penn State. The report was never released because of political pressure from schools that were dissatisfied with their ranking. In 1921 Franklin & Marshall was placed on the "White List" of the Association of Colleges and Preparatory Schools of the Middle Atlantic States and Maryland (*Student Weekly*, Apr. 19, 1916, and Nov. 30, 1921).

46. Board Minutes, June 8, 1920; Carol S. Gruber, *Mars and Minerva: World War I and the Uses of the Higher Learning in America* (Baton Rouge: Louisiana State University Press, 1975), 242–45.

47. Faculty Minutes, Jan. 19, 1927, May 9, 1927, and Dec. 10, 1928; Board Minutes, Dec. 7, 1928 (quotation); *Student Weekly*, Mar. 13, 1929, 2.

48. Ellen Condliffe Lagemann, *Private Power for the Public Good: A History of the Carnegie Foundation for the Advancement of Teaching* (Middletown: Wesleyan University Press, 1983), 99–114; Faculty Minutes, Dec. 9, 1929 (quotation).

49. Levine, *American College and the Culture of Aspiration*, 108–9; Frederick Rudolph, *Curriculum: A History of the American Undergraduate Course of Study Since 1636* (San Francisco: Jossey-Bass Publishers, 1981), 230–31, 235–36; *Report of the President* (1929–1930) (quotation): 12–26; *Report of the President* (1931–1932): 9; Faculty Minutes, Dec. 9, 1929 (quotation), Apr. 14, 1930, and Dec. 15, 1930.

50. Lagemann, *Private Power for the Public Good*, 100 (quotation); Levine, *American College and the Culture of Aspiration*, 110–12; *Report of the President* (1929–1930): 3, 25; *Report of the President* (1930–1931): 3–5 (first quotation on 3; second, third, and fifth quotation on 4); *Report of the President* (1931–1932): 7–8 (fourth quotation).

51. *Student Weekly*, Apr. 25, 1917, 5 (first quotation); *Report of the President* (1926–1927) (second quotation); and *Report of the President* (1930–1931).

52. Sydney E. Ahlstrom, *A Religious History of the American People* (New Haven: Yale University Press, 1972), chap. 53; Robert G. Mickey, "Religion at Franklin and Marshall, 1920–1930: How the Department of Religion Originated" (paper presented to Women's Auxiliary, Franklin and Marshall Infirmary, Jan. 19, 1987), in Archives.

53. Howard R. Omwake, "The Problem of Religious Education as It Affects the College," *Reformed Church Review*, 5th ser., 2 (Apr. 1923): 128–36; H. M. J. Klein, *The History of the Eastern Synod of the Reformed Church in the United States* (Lancaster: Eastern Synod, 1943), 319; P. C. Kemeny, *Princeton in the Nation's Service: Religious Ideals and Educational Practice, 1868–1928* (New York: Oxford University Press, 1998), 173–85, 215.

54. Board Minutes, Jan. 26, June 12, 1923, June 9, 1924; Faculty Minutes, Sept. 16, 1923; *Franklin and Marshall Alumnus* 5 (May 1929): 106; quotations in Mickey, "Religion at Franklin and Marshall."

55. Quotations from Mickey, "Religion at Franklin and Marshall"; Klein, *History of the Eastern Synod*, 323.

56. *Catalogue* for 1923–1924 through 1926–1927, 90–91 (quotation); Ahlstrom, *Religious History*, 905.

57. *Student Weekly*, Oct. 11, 1916, Apr. 14, 1926, Mar. 30, 1927, Dec. 7, 1928; Board Minutes,

June 5, 1925; Faculty Minutes, Sept. 7, 1928; interview with Paul Whitely, Mar. 18, 1980, Oral History Project, Archives (hereafter, Oral History Project); interview with John B. Noss, '16, Apr. 16, 1980, Oral History Project; quotation from Mickey, "Religion at Franklin and Marshall."

58. *Student Weekly*, Mar. 7, 1917, and Apr. 21, 1920 (quotation).

59. *Student Weekly*, Mar. 3 and 10, and Apr. 7, 1920; *Student Weekly*, Nov. 1, 1922, 2; *Student Weekly*, Sept. 23, 1926, 2; Mickey, "Religion at Franklin and Marshall"; Faculty Minutes, May 3, 1926; interview with Noel P. Laird, Apr. 8, 1980, Oral History Project.

60. *Student Weekly*, Jan. 16, 1924, 2.

61. Faculty Minutes, Apr. 30, 1928.

62. Mickey, "Religion at Franklin and Marshall" (quotation); *Student Weekly*, January 23, 1924, 1; Board Minutes, June 13, 1922; Faculty Minutes, Sept. 17, 1928; Faculty Minutes, Dec. 7, 1928.

63. Frederick Rudolph, *The American College and University* (New York: Vintage Books, 1962), 434–36; Board Minutes, June 9, 1914, June 17, 1919 (quotation), June 7, 1921; Faculty Minutes, Feb. 8, 1937.

64. Faculty Minutes, Oct. 11, 1926; Board Minutes, Dec. 13, 1929; *Student Weekly*, Jan. 14, 1930, 1.

65. Faculty Minutes, May 19, 1924 (quotation); Board Minutes, June 2, 1928; *Student Weekly*, Jan. 14, 1930; *Student Weekly*, May 31, 1932, 1; interview with Herbert B. Anstaett, Apr. 22, 1980, Oral History Project.

66. Board Minutes, June 9, 1903, June 7, 1904, June 8, 1915, June 17, 1919, June 4, 1926; *Student Weekly*, Sept. 23, 1926, 1; *Student Weekly*, Mar. 2, 1932, 4; *Student Weekly*, Mar. 22, 1933, 1; *Student Weekly*, Apr. 5, 1933, 1.

67. Board Minutes, Dec. 2, 1927.

68. Board Minutes, June 11, 1913, June 8, 1915. For a comparable situation at Gettysburg College, see Charles H. Glatfelter, *A Salutary Influence: Gettysburg College, 1832–1985* (Gettysburg: Gettysburg College, 1987), 658–67.

69. "Communication of Advisory Council of Alumni in re Athletics," Dec. 12, 1924, in Dec. 12, 1924, Meeting Folder, Box 18, Trustees Files, Archives.

70. Board Minutes, June 12, 1923, June 9, 1924 (quotation), June 4, 1926, June 3, 1927; *Report of the President* (Jan. 1931): 12–13; *Student Weekly*, May 12, 1926, 2; *Student Weekly*, Mar. 23, 1927, 1; *Student Weekly*, Jan. 23, 1929, 1; *Student Weekly*, Jan. 17, 1934, 1.

71. Board Minutes, Dec. 7, 1928, May 31, 1930, Jan. 22, 1931; *Report of the President* (1929–1930): 6; *Report of the President* (Jan. 1931): 12–13 (quotation); *Report of the President* (1930–1931): 6–7; *Student Weekly*, Apr. 28, 1931.

72. Board Minutes, Dec. 13, 1929, Jan. 22 and May 30, 1931; *Report of the President* (Jan. 1931): 7–9; *Report of the President* (1930–1931): 7–10.

73. Board Minutes, May 30, 1931; Faculty Minutes, Oct. 4, 1944.

74. Paula S. Fass, *The Damned and the Beautiful: American Youth in the 1920s* (New York: Oxford University Press, 1977).

75. *Student Weekly*, Mar. 19, 1930, 1; Freeland, *Academia's Golden Age*, 35–36. A 1931 study that defined a "national institution" as one enrolling students from at least three-quarters of the states and less then 30 percent from the home state found only ten colleges and universities that met these criteria. (See Levine, *American College and the Culture of Aspiration*, 239n17.) On alumni recruitment, see Questionnaire, Darlington Papers, Archives.

76. *Student Weekly*, Nov. 14, 1923, 4; *Oriflamme* 32 (1915): 261.

77. Interview with Frederic Klein, '23, Apr. 7, 1980, Oral History Project.

78. Levine, *American College and the Culture of Aspiration*, 146–56; Thomas Bender, *New York Intellect: A History of Intellectual Life in New York City, from 1750 to the Beginnings of Our Own Time* (Baltimore: Johns Hopkins University Press, 1987), 288–92; Kemeny, *Princeton*

in the Nation's Service, 198; Morton Keller and Phyllis Keller, *Making Harvard Modern: The Rise of America's University* (New York: Oxford University Press, 2001), 47–51.

79. *Student Weekly*, Oct. 29, 1919, 1.

80. *Student Weekly*, Nov. 2, 1921, Nov. 21, 1923, Nov. 24, 1926, Oct. 24, 1928; *Student Weekly*, Oct. 1, 1930, 1; *Student Weekly*, Oct. 15, 1930, 4; Faculty Minutes, Oct. 13 and Nov. 24, 1930.

81. Robert and Jay Kneedler to Aunt, Sept. 23, 1923, and n.d. [fall 1924], Kneedler Family Papers, Archives (hereafter Kneedler Family Papers); *Student Weekly*, Oct. 3, 1923, Sept. 24, 1924, and Nov. 17, 1926; Faculty Minutes, Oct. 8, 1923; *Franklin and Marshall Alumnus* 1 (Nov. 1924): 14.

82. Faculty Minutes, Oct. 8, 1923; *Student Weekly*, Sept. 24, 1924.

83. *Student Weekly*, Dec. 10, 1913, Nov. 1, 1922 (quotations).

84. *Student Weekly*, Oct. 17 and 24 (quotations), 1923; Robert and Jay Kneedler to Folks, Oct. 17, 1923, Kneedler Family Papers.

85. *Student Weekly*, Sept. 24 and Oct. 1, 1924, Oct. 21, 1925, Oct. 6, 1926, Oct. 5, 1927, Oct. 3, 1928; Robert and Jay Kneedler to Folks [Oct. 1924], Kneedler Family Papers.

86. *Student Weekly*, Oct. 5, 1927, Oct. 3, 1928, Oct. 9, 1929; Faculty Minutes, Sept. 27, 1920.

87. *Student Weekly*, Feb. 12, 1930, 1; *Student Weekly*, Oct. 1, 1930, 1; *Student Weekly*, Oct. 15, 1930, 4; Natanya Di Bona, "Initiation into the Campus Life at Franklin & Marshall College" (independent project paper, May 12, 1995, Franklin and Marshall College) (quotations on 20, 23).

88. *Student Weekly*, Mar. 12, 1930, 2. Friedenberg was a member of Zeta Beta Tau, the Jewish fraternity. See *Oriflamme* 49 (1932).

89. Levine, *American College and the Culture of Aspiration*, 113–23; John H. Brubaker III, *Hullabaloo Nevonia: An Anecdotal History of Student Life at Franklin and Marshall College* (Lancaster: Franklin and Marshall College, 1987), 97–99.

90. Board Minutes, June 7, 1910; *F&M Weekly*, Jan. 19, 1912; Fass, *Damned and the Beautiful*, 201–3.

91. *Student Weekly*, Nov. 3, 1915, 4; *Student Weekly*, Feb. 16, 1916, 6; *Student Weekly*, Mar. 7, 1917, 7; *Student Weekly*, Jan. 22, 1930, 4; Faculty Minutes, Nov. 9, 1912, Dec. 13, 1915, Feb. 14, 1916, Apr. 11 and Dec. 10, 1917.

92. *Student Weekly*, Feb. 27, 1918, 1; *Student Weekly*, Apr. 3, 1918, 3 (quotation); *Student Weekly*, Apr. 17, 1918, 3; *Student Weekly*, Feb. 11, 1920, 2; Faculty Minutes, Jan. 14, Mar. 11 and 18, and Apr. 8, 1918, Dec. 8, 1919.

93. Faculty Minutes, Nov. 17 (quotation) and Dec. 8, 1919; *College Reporter*, Oct. 3, 1969, S4.

94. *Student Weekly*, Nov. 19, 1919; Faculty Minutes, Nov. 17, 1919.

95. Faculty Minutes, Nov. 17, 1919, Jan. 12, 1920; *Student Weekly*, Nov. 19 (quotation) and 26, 1919.

96. *Student Weekly*, Feb. 18, 1920, Nov. 16, 1921, and Nov. 7, 1923, 1; Faculty Minutes, Feb. 9, 1920, Jan. 10 and Oct. 31, 1921.

97. *Oriflamme* 40 (1923) and 43 (1926); *Student Weekly*, May 30 and Dec. 12, 1923, and Nov. 25, 1925; Board Minutes, June 12, 1923; Faculty Minutes, Nov. 10, 1924, and Nov. 8, 1926.

98. Board Minutes, June 13, 1922, Dec. 12, 1924, June 5, 1925 (quotation).

99. *Student Weekly*, Dec. 8, 1926; Board Minutes, June 4 and Dec. 3 (Klauder quotation), 1926, Dec. 2, 1927; *Franklin and Marshall Alumnus* 5 (Nov. 1928): 15; Schuyler, "The 'New' Franklin & Marshall."

100. Board Minutes, Dec. 12, 1924, Dec. 7, 1928, May 31, 1929 (quotation), Dec. 13, 1929, May 31, 1930; *Student Weekly*, Sept. 24, 1930, 1.

101. Faculty Minutes, Jan. 19 and May 14, 1927, Nov. 11 (quotation), Dec. 9, 1929, Feb. 10, 1930; Interview with Frederic Klein, '23, Apr. 7, 1980, Oral History Project; *Student Weekly*, Apr. 22, 1931, 1.

102. *Student Weekly*, Nov. 2, 1921, 1 (quotation), Mar. 14, 1923, 1, Dec. 14, 1927, 1, June 1, 1928, and May 7, 1930, 1.

103. *Student Weekly*, Jan. 11, 1922, Jan. 23, 1924, Dec. 7, 1927, Mar. 21 and May 9, 1928; *F&M Weekly*, Jan. 12, 1911 (quotation).

104. *Student Weekly*, Jan. 11, 1922, 3; *Student Weekly*, Mar. 26, 1930, 1.

105. *Student Weekly*, Jan. 23, 1929, Mar. 20, 1929, Apr. 10 and Oct. 30, 1929, and Apr. 30, 1930; Faculty Minutes, Mar. 24, 1966; Richard D. Altick, *A Little Bit of Luck: The Making of an Adventurous Scholar* ([Philadelphia]: [Xlibris], 2002), 38–39; *Student Weekly*, Feb. 1, 1957, 3.

106. Faculty Minutes, Mar. 12, 1917, Feb. 9, 1920, Nov. 2, 1925, and Oct. 13, 1930; *Student Weekly*, Jan. 21, and Feb. 18, 1925; *College Reporter*, Sept. 30, 1966, 1; Altick, *Little Bit of Luck*, 29–30.

107. Fass, *Damned and the Beautiful*, 334–35; David P. Setran, "Student Religious Life in the 'Era of Secularization': The Intercollegiate YMCA, 1877–1940," *History of Higher Education Annual* 21 (2001): 58–71; *Student Weekly*, Nov. 7, 1923, Dec. 9, 1925, Feb. 23, Mar. 2, and Nov. 30, 1927, Apr. 18 and Oct. 10, 1928.

108. *Student Weekly*, Mar. 14 (quotation) and 21, Feb. 22, May 9 and 16, 1928, and Mar. 26, 1930.

109. Interview with William Hartman, '30, Apr. 8, 1980, and Frederic Klein, '23, Apr. 7, 1980, both Oral History Project; *Student Weekly*, Mar. 9, 1932.

110. *Student Weekly*, May 12, 1920, Apr. 6, 1927, Nov. 30, 1927, Oct. 17, 1928, Feb. 20, 1929; *Student Weekly*, Dec. 18, 1929, 2; *Student Weekly*, Mar. 26, 1930, 2 (quotation); *Student Weekly*, Oct. 29, 1930, 2; Fass, *Damned and the Beautiful*, 336–37.

111. Board Minutes, Jan. 20 and June 8, 1920, June 12, 1923; *Student Weekly*, Oct. 24, 1928, 2; *Student Weekly*, Apr. 13, 1932, 2.

112. *Student Weekly*, Nov. 24, 1926; *Oriflamme* 40 (1923): 63.

113. Kneedler Family Papers.

114. Board Minutes, June 9, 1924, Dec. 4, 1925; Elwood Misier, "Mortality in Scholarship," *Franklin and Marshall Alumnus* 4 (Nov. 1927): 9 (quotation); Faculty Minutes, Oct. 5, 1925.

115. *Report of the President* (1928–1929): 6; Faculty Minutes, Oct. 21, 192[1], Oct. 5 and Nov. 2, 1925, Nov. 8, 1926, Apr. 13 and Nov. 23, 1931; quotation from interview with William Hartman, '30, Apr. 8, 1980, Oral History Project.

116. Faculty Minutes, Dec. 13, 1909, Nov. 10, 1913, Sept. 28, 1914; *Student Weekly*, Feb. 2, 1916, 10 (quotation); *Student Weekly*, Mar. 29, 1922, 4; *Student Weekly*, May 7, 1923, 1. For comparable events at Gettysburg, see Glatfelter, *Salutary Influence*, 663–64.

117. Loring Pickering to H. H. Apple, Aug. 8, 1925, Lemuel F. Parton to Apple, Aug. 28, 1925, H. H. Apple, "Shall Intercollegiate Football Be Abolished?" *Literary Digest*, Oct. 10, 1925, clipping, all in H. H. Apple Papers.

118. Board Minutes, Dec. 12, 1924, June 5, 1925, June 4, 1926, June 3, 1927, June 2, 1928; Charles Wimbert Taylor, "A History of Intercollegiate Athletics at Franklin and Marshall College" (master's thesis, University of Maryland, 1962), 25.

119. *Student Weekly*, Oct. 30, 1929, 2; *Report of the President* (1929–1930): 5–7.

120. *Report of the President* (1927–1928): 7–8. On the AAC and its criteria, see Hawkins, *Banding Together*, 88–90.

121. *Report of the President* (1927–1928), 35–37; Board Minutes, June 2, 1928; Taylor, "History of Intercollegiate Athletics," 26; interview with Herbert B. Anstaett, Apr. 22, 1980, Oral History Project; interview with James Farmer, '32, Apr. 8, 1981, Oral History Project.

122. *Report of the President* (1931–1932): 5, 12, 16; *Report of the President* (Dec. 1932): 2–4, 20; *Report of the President* (1932–1933): 2, 17 (quotation).

123. Faculty Minutes, May 8, 1933; *Report of the President* (1932–1933): 2–9; *Report of the President* (1933–1934): 18.

124. "The College, Address Delivered by President Henry Harbaugh Apple at the Opening of the 144th Year of Franklin and Marshall College, Sept. 18, 1930," pamphlet, H. H. Apple Papers; *Report of the President* (1933–1934): 15.

125. H. H. Apple, "Training for Leadership in a New Age" (Lancaster: Franklin and Marshall College, 1932); "F. & M. Head Sees Demand for New Type Leadership," *Lancaster Intelligencer Journal*, Sept. 23, 1932, clipping in H. H. Apple Papers.

126. First quotations in *Lancaster New Era*, Feb. 13, 1933, clipping in H. H. Apple Papers; *Student Weekly*, Sept. 26, 1934, final quotations on 1, 5; clippings in H. H. Apple Papers.

127. *Report of the President* (1933–1934): 30; *Report of the President* (Dec. 1934): 3–4; *Student Weekly*, Mar. 15, 1933, 2.

128. Faculty Minutes, June 7, 1926; interview with Harold R. Diffenderfer, Apr. 7, 1981, Oral History Project; Board Minutes, May 31, and Dec. 2, 1932; B. F. Fackenthal to H. H. Apple, July 25, 1934, H. H. Apple Papers.

129. H. H. Apple to B. F. Fackenthal, Aug. 3, 1934, Apple to Board, Aug. 15, 1934, Apple to Fackenthal, Aug. 20, 1934, Fackenthal to H. H. Apple, Aug. 24 and 28, 1934, H. H. Apple Papers; Board Minutes, Dec. 7, 1934.

130. *Report of the President* (Dec. 1934): 5.

CHAPTER 7

1. Quotation in Franklin & Marshall College Faculty Minutes, Apr. 1941, Archives (hereafter, Faculty Minutes); David O. Levine, *The American College and the Culture of Aspiration, 1915–1940* (Ithaca: Cornell University Press, 1986), 136–42.

2. "Dr. Apple Urges Naming of F.&M. Head at Once," *Lancaster New Era*, Mar. 1, 1935, clipping in H. H. Apple Papers, Archives (hereafter, H. H. Apple Papers); B. F. Fackenthal to H. H. Apple, Mar. 11, 1935, Fred. B. Gernerd to H. H. Apple, Jan. 23, 1935, both in H. H. Apple Papers.

3. B. F. Fackenthal to H. H. Apple, Mar. 11, 1935, H. H. Apple Papers; Lee M. Erdman to John A. Schaeffer, May 18, 1935, Erdman to Schaeffer, June 3, 1935, both in John A. Schaeffer Papers, Archives (hereafter, Schaeffer Papers); *Lancaster New Era*, June 4 and 10, 1935, clippings in Schaeffer Papers; Board Minutes, June 4 and 28, 1935, Archives (hereafter, Board Minutes); Fackenthal to H. R. Barnes, June 15 and July 3, 1935, both in Folder for June 28, 1935, Meeting, Board Records, Archives (hereafter, Board Records); Schaeffer to B. F. Fackenthal, June 15, 1935, Fackenthal Papers, Archives (hereafter, Fackenthal Papers).

4. John A. Schaeffer obituary, *New York Times*, Apr. 8, 1941, Biographical File, John A. Schaeffer Papers; B. F. Fackenthal to H. R. Barnes, June 15, 1935, Folder for June 28, 1935, Meeting, Board Records.

5. B. F. Fackenthal to H. R. Barnes, June 15, 1935, Folder for June 28, 1935, Meeting, Board Records; biography in "Wet Paint" column, *Drugs, Oils, and Paints* (August 1933): 294–95, clippings in Schaeffer Papers; *Student Weekly*, Apr. 25, 1918, 3; *Franklin and Marshall Alumnus* 11 (June 1935): 97.

6. John A. Schaeffer to B. F. Fackenthal, June 15, 1935, Fackenthal Papers; Schaeffer to H. H. Apple, July 3, 1935, H. H. Apple Papers.

7. *Report of the President of Franklin and Marshall College* (Winter 1935): 1, 8–9 (quotation) (hereafter, *Report of the President*); *Report of the President* (Winter 1936): 2.

8. Faculty Minutes, Sept. 14, 1935, and Feb. 10, 1936; *Report of the President* (Winter 1935): 1, 8–9 (all quotations); *Report of the President* (1935–1936): 1, 15–16; *Student Weekly*, Feb. 26, 1936, 2; *Alumnus Magazine* 10 (May 1934): 82.

9. *Report of the President* (Winter 1935): 3–4; Faculty Minutes, Sept. 21, 1942; Henry Lamar Crosby and John Nevin Schaeffer, *An Introduction to Greek* (Boston: Allyn and Bacon, 1928).

10. Faculty Minutes, Oct. 15, 1935 (all quotations); Morton Keller and Phyllis Keller, *Making Harvard Modern: The Rise of America's University* (New York: Oxford University Press, 2001), 24, 33, 146–47.

11. Faculty Minutes, Oct. 15, 1935; *Report of the President* (Winter 1935): 4–5.

12. Levine, *American College and the Culture of Aspiration*, 136–46; Julie A. Reuben, *The Making of the Modern University: Intellectual Transformation and the Marginalization of Morality* (Chicago: University of Chicago Press, 1996), 262–65; Faculty Minutes, Oct. 15, 1935.

13. Interview with John B. Noss, Apr. 16, 1980, Oral History Project, Archives (hereafter, Oral History Project). The *President's Report* for 1933–1934 no longer recorded the number of students "dropped from the rolls" for academic reasons. The campus American Association of University Professors (AAUP) was particularly concerned about the quality of transfers, but its study of the records of transfers in 1934 found that they performed as well as other students on average. A 1954 AAUP report stated that between 1932 and 1939 no student was asked to leave for academic reasons, "to the detriment of the academic reputation of the institution" (AAUP Minutes, Apr. 30, Nov. 19, 1934, Feb. 2, 1954, AAUP Files, Archives [hereafter, AAUP Minutes]).

14. Board Minutes, June 4, 1926, May 31, 1929, May 31, 1930; *Student Weekly*, Nov. 1, 1922, 2.

15. *Report of the President* (Nov. 1936): 3–4 (quotation); *Report of the President* (Winter 1938): 4–5; *Alumnus Magazine* 12 (Mar. 1936): 85; Board Minutes, Dec. 2, 1938.

16. *Report of the President* (1937–1938): 8–9; *Report of the President* (Winter 1938): 7–8; *Report of the President* (Winter 1939): 8–9; *Report of the President* (1938–1939): 18–22; *Report of the President* (1939–1940): 18–23; Faculty Minutes, Dec. 13, 1937; *Student Weekly*, Mar. 11, 1936.

17. Quotations in J. A. Schaeffer to F. D. Fackenthal, Sept. 30, 1939, Fackenthal Papers; *Report of the President* (Winter 1939): 9.

18. *Report of the President* (Winter 1937): 17; *Report of the President* (1937–1938): 8–9 (first quotation); *Report of the President* (1938–1939): 14 (second quotation); *Report of the President* (1939–1940): 18.

19. *Report of the President* (1937–1938): 15 (first quotation); *Report of the President* (1938–1939): 15–16; *Report of the President* (1939–1940): 15–16 (second quotation); Faculty Minutes, Sept. 14, 1936.

20. Faculty Minutes, Sept. 12, 1938, Sept. 16, 1940; *Report of the President* (Winter 1936): 3; *Report of the President* (1939–1940): 29–30; *Report of the President* (Winter 1938): 7; *Report of the President* (Winter 1940): 4 (quotation); *Student Weekly*, Sept. 24, 1931, 1.

21. *Report of the President* (Winter 1940): 5–6 (quotation); *Report of the President* (Winter 1938): 12; *Student Weekly*, Nov. 8, 1933, 1; *Franklin and Marshall Alumnus* 14 (Dec. 1937): 61.

22. Levine, *American College and the Culture of Aspiration*, 142–46 (quotation on 146), 239n17; Christopher Jencks and David Riesman, *The Academic Revolution* (New York: Doubleday, 1968), 155; Richard M. Freeland, *Academia's Golden Age: Universities in Massachusetts, 1945–1970* (New York: Oxford University Press, 1992), 55–56.

23. Levine, *American College and the Culture of Aspiration*, 146–57; *Report of the President* (1935–1936): 20; Faculty Minutes, Dec. 15, 1936, Jan. 11, 1937, and Sept. 16, 1940.

24. *Franklin and Marshall Alumnus* 12 (Dec. 1935): 35–38.

25. Ibid., 35.

26. *Student Weekly*, Feb. 14, 1928, Sept. 24, 1930, and Sept. 27, 1933 (quotation); Faculty Minutes, Sept. 16, 1929, Sept. 18, 1933, and Oct. 9, 1939; *Report of the President* (Winter 1938): 13; *Franklin and Marshall Alumnus* 13 (Dec. 1936): 50, 51.

27. Faculty Minutes, Jan. 10, Mar. 7, 1938 (quotation), Sept. 16, 1940.

28. *Report of the President* (Fall 1936): 5–6 (first, second, third quotations); *Report of the President* (1936–1937): 24–26; *Report of the President* (Winter 1937): 14; *Report of the President* (Winter 1938): 13, 22 (fourth quotation); *Alumnus Magazine* 13 (Mar. 1937): 72.

29. *Report of the President* (Winter 1937): 14–15; *Report of the President* (Winter 1938): 22–23.

30. *Student Weekly*, Feb. 7, 1917, 10; *Student Weekly*, Mar. 14, 1928, 1; *Student Weekly*, Dec. 16, 1931, 1; *Student Weekly*, Jan. 9, 1935, 1; *Student Weekly*, May 13, 1936, 1 (quotation); *Franklin and Marshall Alumnus* 1 (Feb. 1925): 27; *Franklin and Marshall Alumnus* 3 (May 1927): 85;

William F. Early, "Armstrong's Advertising and Marketing Services Department, 1911–1994," *Journal of the Lancaster County Historical Society* 98 (Summer 1996): 50–53.

31. *Franklin and Marshall Alumnus* 13 (Sept. 1936): 1 (quotations); *Student Weekly*, [Sept.] 27, 1938, 1 (final quotation).

32. John A. Schaeffer to Paul Kieffer, Feb. 13, 1936, Kieffer Papers, Archives (hereafter, Kieffer Papers); *Report of the President* (1935–1936): 13; *Report of the President* (1937–1938): 14.

33. *Report of the President* (1935–1936): 3 (quotation); *Report of the President* (Winter 1937): 4–5; *Report of the President* (Winter 1938): 15; *Report of the President* (1937–1938): 9–10.

34. *Report of the President* (Winter 1937): 5–7; *Report of the President* (Winter 1938): 9–10; *Report of the President* (Winter 1940): 11; Faculty Minutes, May 11, 1936, Apr. 17 and Sept. 18, 1939 (quotation); *Student Weekly*, Feb. 21, 1939, 1.

35. Faculty Minutes, Nov. 13, 1939, and Feb. 17, 1941; "Report of the Curriculum Committee on the Question of Making Ethics an Elective Instead of a Required Course," Dec. 6, 1940, File, Board Records.

36. *Student Weekly*, Mar. 11, 1931; *Student Weekly*, Mar. 1, 1933, 1 (quotation); *Student Weekly*, Apr. 18, 1934, 1; *Franklin and Marshall Alumnus* 10 (May 1934): 72.

37. Board Minutes, Nov. 10, 1935; *Report of the President* (1935–1936): 15.

38. *Student Weekly*, Mar. 31, 1926, 1; *Student Weekly*, Sept. 24, 1930; *Student Weekly*, Oct. 8, 1930; *Student Weekly*, Dec. 29, 1930, 1; *Student Weekly*, Apr. 22, 1931; *Student Weekly*, Mar. 2, 1932; *Franklin and Marshall Alumnus* 1 (July 1925): 10; *Franklin and Marshall Alumnus* 4 (Mar. 1928): 35.

39. *Report of the President* (1934–1935): 9; *Student Weekly*, Feb. 19, Mar. 18 and 25 (quotation), 1936; interview with John B. Rengier, '32, Apr. 14, 1981, Oral History Project.

40. Board Minutes, May 31, 1932, Apr. 3 and June 2, 1936; B. F. Fackenthal to H. Barnes, Nov. 13, 1935, Folder for June 4, 1935, Meeting, Board Files; Fackenthal to H. H. Apple, Nov. 26, 1935, Apple Papers.

41. *Franklin and Marshall Alumnus* 13 (Dec. 1936): 33.

42. Board Minutes, Mar. 19, 1937.

43. Ibid.; A. H. Rothermel to T. A. Distler, Apr. 7, 1947, H. B. Anstaett to Distler, Apr. 8, 1947, Distler Papers, Archives (hereafter, Distler Papers).

44. *Report of the President* (1936–1937): 12; *Report of the President* (1947–1948): 54; Board Minutes, June 1, 1937; *Franklin and Marshall Alumnus* 13 (Mar. 1937): 68; *Franklin and Marshall Alumnus* 14 (Sept. 1937): 21 (second quotation); H. M. J. Klein, *History of Franklin and Marshall College, 1787–1848* (Lancaster: Franklin and Marshall College, 1952), 256–57; Faculty Minutes, Mar. 17, 1955 (first quotation).

45. Board Minutes, Mar. 19, 1937; "Hunts Library Donor, Finds He's the One," *New York Times*, March 21, 1937, 36, reprinted on Postcard for Sesqui-Centennial Fund, May 1937, Fackenthal Papers; *Franklin and Marshall Alumnus* 13 (Mar. 1937): 65–66; *Franklin and Marshall Papers*, no. 7 (Apr. 1937).

46. Board Minutes, Dec. 4, 1936; *Franklin and Marshall Alumnus* 12 (June 1936): 28; *Franklin and Marshall Papers*, no. 1 (October 1936): n.p.; *Franklin and Marshall Papers*, no. 10 (August 1937): n.p.

47. "Sesqui-Centennial Celebration Addresses," *Franklin and Marshall Papers*, no. 12 (Dec. 1937): 6–23 (Fox quotations on 6, 7, 8, 10, and 11, respectively).

48. Ibid., 27 (first quotation), 31, 45 (second quotation), 58–59 (third quotation).

49. Ibid., 66–69 (quotations on 66, 69).

50. David Dunn et al., *A History of the Evangelical and Reformed Church* (Philadelphia: Christian Education Press, 1961), 279–90.

51. Board Minutes, Mar. 19 and Dec. 3, 1937, Dec. 9, 1939, and June 4, 1940; "New F.&M. Charter Before the Court," clipping in June 4, 1940, Folder, Board Files; Early, "Armstrong's Advertising and Marketing," 52.

52. Board Minutes, Mar. 19, 1937; *Report of the President* (Winter 1937): 2.

53. *Student Weekly*, Mar. 19, 1935, 1; *Student Weekly*, Nov. 19, 1935, 3 (quotation). The chapter's minutes, typed up several years later, began on Apr. 30, 1934 (AAUP Minutes).

54. *Report of the President* (Winter 1935): 9–10; *Report of the President* (1935–1936): 11; *Student Weekly*, Oct. 8, 1935, 1.

55. Richard D. Altick, *A Little Bit of Luck: The Making of an Adventurous Scholar* ([Philadelphia]: Xlibris, 2002), 26–29, 30–31; *Franklin and Marshall Alumnus* 14 (Sept. 1937): 7.

56. Interview with John Peiffer Jr., May 19, 1981, Oral History Project.

57. *Student Weekly*, Nov. 14, 1917, 9; *Student Weekly*, Feb. 20, 1924, 2; *Student Weekly*, Mar. 19, 1924, 1; *Student Weekly*, Apr. 2, 1924, 1; *Student Weekly*, Mar. 4, 1925; *Student Weekly*, Feb. 25, 1925, 3; *Student Weekly*, May 13, 1931, 3; H. H. Apple to H. M. J. Klein, Apr. 22, 1922, and Apr. 21, 1926, Klein to B. F. Fackenthal [Apr. 1926], all in Klein Papers; Michael J. Birkner, "A Conversation with Philip S. Klein," *Pennsylvania History* 56 (Oct. 1989): 243–61.

58. "Moral Education in Our Higher Institutions of Learning," Dec. 26, 1912, MS in Klein Papers; Birkner, "A Conversation with Philip S. Klein," 250.

59. *Student Weekly*, Oct. 15, 1930, 1; *Student Weekly*, Mar. 2, 1932, 1; *Student Weekly*, Oct. 26, 1932, 4 (quotation); *Student Weekly*, May 16, 1934, 1; *Student Weekly*, Oct. 18, 1938, 1; *Report of the President* (Winter 1936): 10; *Report of the President* (1936–1937): 8; *Report of the President* (1938–1939): 25; *Report of the President* (1939–1940): 28–29; H. M. J. Klein, *History of Franklin and Marshall*, 266, 303; Frederic S. Klein, "A College Research Course in Pennsylvania History," *Pennsylvania History* 1 (Oct. 1934): 232–36.

60. Birkner, "Conversation with Philip S. Klein," 257, 259; *Student Weekly*, Apr. 2, 1940, 1.

61. *Student Weekly*, Feb. 21, 1934, 2 (first quotation); *Student Weekly*, Feb. 28, 1934, 2 (second quotations); *Student Weekly*, Feb. 14, 1939, 2 (third quotation).

62. *Report of the President* (1936–1937): 6.

63. Faculty Minutes, Feb. 10, 1936, Nov. 14, 1938 (quotation), May 9, 1938.

64. *Student Weekly*, Mar. 19, 1935 (quotation), Oct. 4, 1938, 2; *Franklin and Marshall Alumnus* 13 (June 1937): 117; John H. Brubaker III, *Hullabaloo Nevonia* (Lancaster: Franklin and Marshall College, 1987), 150.

65. *Report of the President* (Winter 1941): 19; *Student Weekly*, Oct. 25, 1938, 2.

66. *Student Weekly*, Apr. 9, 1940, 2.

67. *Student Weekly*, Apr. 17, 1940, 1, 2, 4 (first quotations); *Student Weekly*, Oct. 8, 1940, 2; F. B. Gernerd to J. A. Schaeffer, Apr. 16, 1940, Schaeffer to Gernerd, Apr. 18, 1940, Schaeffer to Howard J. Benchoff, Apr. 23, 1940, Schaeffer Papers.

68. *Student Weekly*, Nov. 14, 1939, 2; *Student Weekly*, Apr. 23, 1940, 4 (quotation); *Student Weekly*, Apr. 30, 1940, 1; *Student Weekly*, Oct. 29, 1940, 1; *Student Weekly*, Oct. 15, 1940, 1.

69. *Student Weekly*, Apr. 30, 1940, 1; *Student Weekly*, Oct. 1, 1940, 1; *Report of the President* (Winter 1941): 20; *Student Weekly*, Oct. 2, 1941, 1.

70. *Student Weekly*, Mar. 7, 1934, 2; *Student Weekly*, Oct. 17, 1934, 2; *Student Weekly*, Mar. 4, 1936, 1; *Student Weekly*, Feb. 14, 1939, 1; *Report of the President* (1935–1936): 11 (quotation); *Report of the President* (1937–1938): 6–8; *Report of the President* (1938–1939): 11.

71. Board Minutes, Mar. 19 and June 1, 1937, June 3, 1941; quotation in "Plan Presented by the Music Committee and Student Senate," Mar. 19, 1937, Folder, Board Files; *Student Weekly*, Oct. 18, 1938, 1; *Student Weekly*, Nov. 1, 1938, 1 (Whiteman quotation); *Report of the President* (Winter 1938): 20; "Paul Whiteman Appeared in Lancaster in 1938," *Lancaster Intelligencer Journal*, Dec. 29, 1967, clipping in Frederic Klein Papers.

72. *Report of the President* (Winter 1935): 10–11; *Report of the President* (Winter 1940): 17–18; Faculty Minutes, Sept. 14, 1935.

73. *Student Weekly*, Nov. 7, 1934, 1, 4; *Student Weekly*, Oct. 15, 22, and 29, 1935, 1; *Student Weekly*, Oct. 25, 1938, 1; *Student Weekly*, Nov. 1, 1938, 1; *Student Weekly*, Oct. 22, 1940, 1, 2 (quotation); *Student Weekly*, Nov. 5, 1940; Faculty Minutes, Nov. 1, 1940; interview with John H. Peifer Jr., May 19, 1981, Oral History Project.

74. *Student Weekly*, Nov. 8, 1933, 2; *Student Weekly*, Oct. 24, 1939, 2 (first quotation); *Student Weekly*, Nov. 14, 1939, 2 (second quotation); *Student Weekly*, Oct. 28, 1942, 2 (third quotation); J. A. Schaeffer to John Wright, June 2, 1939, Schaeffer Papers.

75. Keller and Keller, *Making Harvard Modern*, 37; quotation in Brubaker, *Hullabaloo Nevonia*, 128.

76. *Student Weekly*, May 6, 1941, 1 (first quotation); *Student Weekly*, Oct. 28, 1941, 1 (quotations), 2; *Student Weekly*, Nov. 11, 1941, 1. Historians of the University of Pennsylvania defined "rowbottoms" as "a Pennsylvania way of blowing off steam," common there before the 1950s (David R. Goddard and Linda C. Koons, "A Profile of the University of Pennsylvania," in *Academic Transformation: Seventeen Institutions Under Pressure*, ed. David Riesman and Verne A. Stadtman [New York: McGraw-Hill, sponsored by Carnegie Commission on Higher Education], 232).

77. *Report of the President* (1935–1936): 11–12; *Report of the President* (Winter 1940): 16; *Student Weekly*, Oct. 22, 1940, 2 (quotations); interview with Myrtle Doner, Apr. 4, 1980, Oral History Project.

78. *Report of the President* (1938–1939): 22–23; *Report of the President* (1939–1940): 23–28; *Report of the President* (1940–1941): 21; *Student Weekly*, Jan. 9, 1940, 1; *Student Weekly*, Oct. 1, 1940, 1; *Student Weekly*, Nov. 13, 1946, 2.

79. *Report of the President* (Winter 1938): 3–4.

80. *Report of the President* (1936–1937): 13–14; *Report of the President* (1937–1938): 16–18. See Freeland, *Academia's Golden Age*, 66.

81. Informal notes taken at a conference of presidents of some of the men's colleges, University Club, New York City, July 8, 1940, Distler Papers; *Report of the President* (Winter 1940): 1–2; *Student Weekly*, Oct. 15, 1940, 1 (quotation); *Student Weekly*, Dec. 10, 1940, 2.

82. H. M. J. Klein, *History of Franklin and Marshall*, 303–4, *Report of the President* (1939–1940): 28–29; *Report of the President* (Winter 1940): 3; *Report of the President* (1940–1941): 9, 24; *Student Weekly*, Sept. 26, 1939, 1; *Student Weekly*, Dec. 10, 1940, 1; Faculty Minutes, Sept. 28, 1941.

83. *Student Weekly*, Feb. 11, 1941, 1; H. M. J. Klein, *History of Franklin and Marshall*, 275; Faculty Minutes, Feb. 17, 1941; *Student Weekly*, Apr. 8, 1941, 2; condensed financial report to June 1, 1941, in June 3, 1941, Folder, Board Files; quotations from B. F. Fackenthal to William Keller, Apr. 14, 1941, in Apr. 9, 1941, Folder for Meeting, Board Files.

84. Board Minutes, Apr. 9, 1941; Altick, *A Little Bit of Luck*, 79; Faculty Minutes, Apr. 21, 1941.

85. John R. Thelin, *A History of American Higher Education* (Baltimore: Johns Hopkins University Press, 2004), 257; Altick, *A Little Bit of Luck*, 79; interview with John B. Noss, '16, Apr. 16, 1980, Oral History Project.

86. *Report of the President* (Winter 1941): 8; B. F. Fackenthal to H. M. J. Klein, July 30, 1941, Acting President Folder, Klein Papers.

87. Altick, *A Little Bit of Luck*, 77–80 (first quotation on 79); B. F. Fackenthal to "My dear Friend" (copy), Aug. 1, 1941 (second quotation), and H. M. J. Klein to Fackenthal, Aug. 1, 1941 (subsequent quotations), both in Acting President Folder, Klein Papers.

88. Klein to Fackenthal, Aug. 1, 1941, and Fackenthal to "My dear Friend," Aug. 1, 1941, Acting President Folder, Klein Papers.

89. H. M. J. Klein, *History of Franklin and Marshall College*, 280; Faculty Minutes, May 31 and Sept. 29, 1941; *Report of the President* (Winter 1941): 1 (first quotation), 7–8 (second quotation).

90. Board Minutes, Oct. 10, 1941.

91. Ibid.; Theodore Distler Interview, Feb. 17, 1981, Oral History Project; *Student Weekly*, May 19, 1954, 1.

92. *Lancaster New Era*, Oct. 10, 1941, clipping in Fackenthal Papers; Board Minutes, Dec. 10, 1941; "Fackenthal Wills F&M $30,000 for Books in Library," unidentified clipping, Fackenthal Papers.

93. Brubaker, *Hullabaloo Nevonia*, 150; Distler Interview, Feb. 17, 1981, Oral History Project; *Annual Report of Franklin and Marshall College* (1941–1942), 25.

94. Frederic S. Klein, "Aviation Training During World War II," in H. M. J. Klein, *History of Franklin and Marshall*, 309.

95. T. A. Distler telegram to F. D. Roosevelt, Dec. 10, 1941, Distler Papers.

96. "Address of Paul Kieffer," Jan. 30, 1942, Kieffer Papers Archives.

97. First quotation, ibid.; second quotation, Paul Kieffer to Keith Spalding, Oct. 15, 1965, Kieffer Papers.

98. Faculty Minutes, Dec. 10, 1941, Sept. 21 and Oct. 14, 1942. Although academic departments controlled hiring at the leading universities by the 1920s, practices at smaller institutions were more traditional. See Freeland, *Academia's Golden Age*, 48–50.

99. *Annual Report of Franklin and Marshall College* (1941–1942), 11.

100. Hawkins, *Banding Together*, 148 (quotation); John Andrew, "Struggle for the Liberal Arts: Franklin and Marshall College, 1941–1982," unpublished MS, John Andrew Publications Files, Archives, chap. 1, 43–44; Distler, "Address at Fall Commencement and Opening Exercises," Sept. 24, 1942, Distler Papers.

101. H. M. J. Klein, *History of Franklin and Marshall*, 292; *Annual Report of Franklin and Marshall College* (1941–1942), 4–5, 8; Board Minutes, June 24, 1944 (first quotation); Faculty Minutes, Jan. 19, 1942 (second quotation); John Andrew, "Struggle for the Liberal Arts," chap. 1, 42.

102. Faculty Minutes, Sept. 21, 1942; Board Minutes, Feb. 19, 1943 (quotations); *Report of the President* (1942–1943): 28–29.

103. H. M. J. Klein, *History of Franklin and Marshall*, 295; *Annual Report of Franklin and Marshall College* (1941–1942), 9–10; *Report of the President* (1942–1943): 5–6; Hawkins, *Banding Together*, 148; Faculty Minutes, Mar. 16, 1942.

104. F. S. Klein, "Aviation Training During World War II," 309–311 (quotations on 310); *Report of the President* (1943–1944): 3–4; Board Minutes, June 24, 1944.

105. *Student Weekly*, Dec. 17, 1940, 1; Board Minutes, May 15 and Oct. 16, 1942; Executive Committee Minutes, Dec. 20, 1942, Archives (hereafter, Executive Committee Minutes); Faculty Minutes, Mar. 16, 1942; H. M. J. Klein, *History of Franklin and Marshall*, 296; Distler Interview, Feb. 17, 1981, Oral History Project; *Report of the President* (1942–1943): 9.

106. Hawkins, *Banding Together*, 148; *Annual Report of Franklin and Marshall College* (1941–1942), 2.

107. *Annual Report of Franklin and Marshall College* (1941–1942), 2–3.

108. H. M. J. Klein, *History of Franklin and Marshall College*, 288, 290–91; Distler's Inaugural Address, unidentified clipping, Distler Papers.

109. Hawkins, *Banding Together*, 148–49; William M. Tuttle Jr., "Higher Education and the Federal Government: The Triumph, 1942–1945," *Teachers College Record* 71 (1969–1970): 487–90; *Report of the President* (1942–1943): 1–3, 11–12, 20–21; Distler, Address at Fall Commencement and Opening Exercises, Sept. 24, 1942, Distler Papers; Brubaker, *Hullabaloo Nevonia*, 152.

110. T. A. Distler to Charles J. Turck, Sept. 15, 1942, Distler to W. H. Cowley, Oct. 2, 1942 (first quotation), H. C. Holdridge, Adjutant General's School, to Distler, Nov. 24, 1942, J. Roland Kinzer, U.S. House of Representatives, to Distler, Dec. 2, 1942, Distler to Felix Morley, Haverford College, Dec. 8, 1942 (third quotation), Distler to W. W. Behrens, Dec. 21, 1942 (second quotation), all in Distler Papers.

111. F. Morley to T. A. Distler, Dec. 9, 1942, Distler Papers, Archives; Tuttle, "Higher Education and the Federal Government," 489–90; Hawkins, *Banding Together*, 151–52.

112. Executive Committee Minutes, Dec. 20, 1942; Hartman's Report to Academy Committee, Feb. 18, 1943, Archives; Board Minutes, Feb. 19 (first quotation) and May 22, 1943 (second quotation), June 24, 1944, and June 23, 1945.

113. H. M. J. Klein, *History of Franklin and Marshall*, 297–98 (first quotation); Faculty Minutes, Feb. 8, 1943; Brubaker, *Hullabaloo Nevonia*, 152 (second quotation); Board Minutes, Feb. 19, 1943.

114. Henry Herge et al., *Wartime College Training Programs of the Armed Services* (Washington, D.C.: American Council on Education, 1948), 11; *Report of the President* (1942–1943): 2–3, 8–9; *Report of the President* (1943–1944): 7; Faculty Minutes, Apr. 12 and Aug. 9, 1943 (quotation); Randall Jacobs and William W. Behrens to T. A. Distler, Mar. 25, 1943, Distler Papers; Executive Committee Minutes, Mar. 31, 1943; President's Newsletter, Aug. 14, 1943, Distler Papers.

115. Board Minutes, June 24, 1944; *Report of the President* (1943–1944): 1–3, 9; *Report of the President* (1944–1945): 6; H. M. J. Klein, *History of Franklin and Marshall*, 297, 316; President's Newsletter, Aug. 14, 1943 (quotation), Distler Papers; Faculty Minutes, Mar. 6, 1944.

116. President's Newsletter, Aug. 14, 1943, Distler Papers; *Report of the President* (1943–1944): 9 (quotation).

117. H. M. J. Klein, *History of Franklin and Marshall*, 316–18; Distler Interview, Feb. 17, 1981, Oral History Project; Faculty Minutes, July 12, 1943.

118. Altick, *A Little Bit of Luck*, 94–95; President's Newsletter, Aug. 14, 1943, Apr. 20, 1944, Distler Papers; Board Minutes, October 16, 1942, May 22, 1943; *Report of the President* (1943–1944): 11; Faculty Minutes, Mar. 8, 1943, May 15, 1969; Charles Spotts, "Tribute to the Late Professor Frederick S. Foster," Oct. 9, 1952, in author's possession.

119. Distler Interview, Feb. 17, 1981, Oral History Project.

120. Executive Committee Minutes, Feb. 19 and June 23, 1943; Altick, *A Little Bit of Luck*, 94; Board Minutes, May 15, 1942, May 22 and Oct. 8, 1943, June 24, 1944; Distler Interview, Feb. 17, 1981, Oral History Project.

121. Andrew, "Struggle for the Liberal Arts," chap. 1, 49–50; interview with Albert L. Bell, '35, Apr. 16, 1981, Oral History Project.

122. President's Newsletter, Aug. 14 and Oct. 9, 1943, Apr. 20, 1944, Distler Papers.

123. President's Newsletter, Aug. 14 (first and second quotations), Oct. 9, 1943, Aug. 30 and Oct. 31, 1944 (third quotation), Distler Papers.

124. Board Minutes, Oct. 16, 1942 (first quotation), Feb. 19, 1943 (subsequent quotations); Faculty Minutes, Nov. 9, 1942, Jan. 11, 1943.

125. Board Minutes, Feb. 19, 1943.

126. Ibid. and Board Minutes, May 22, 1943 (Prentis quotation), Feb. 11, 1944 (quotation); *Report of the President* (1943–1944): 29; Faculty Minutes, Dec. 14, 1942.

127. *Report of the President* (1942–1943): 37 (quotations); *Report of the President* (1943–1944): 19–20; Faculty Minutes, Oct. 11, 1943.

128. *Report of the President* (1943–1944): 3–4 (first quotation), 6 (second quotation), 42–43 (third quotation); Board Minutes, Feb. 11 and June 24, 1944; Keith W. Olson, *The GI Bill, the Veterans, and the Colleges* (Lexington: University Press of Kentucky, 1974); Hawkins, *Banding Together*, 154–55.

129. Hawkins, *Banding Together*, 154–55; *Report of the President* (1943–1944): 42–43.

130. Board Minutes, June 24, 1944 (quotation); Faculty Minutes, Oct. 4, 1944.

131. Faculty Minutes, Sept. 6, 1945; *Report of the President* (1944–1945): 12, 29 (first quotation); *Report of the President* (1945–1946): 20–22 (quotations on 22).

132. *Student Weekly*, Nov. 18, 1941, 2; *Student Weekly*, Nov. 25, 1941, 1.

133. Board Minutes, Feb. 19, 1943, June 24, 1944.

134. Faculty Minutes, Oct. 4, Dec. 11, 1944; Board Minutes, Oct. 21, 1944.

135. President's Newsletter, Dec. 30, 1944, Distler Papers; Committee on Coeducation to Fellow Alumni, May 21, 1945, Henry I. Stahr to T. A. Distler, Feb. 3, 1945, Distler to Lee Erdman, Jan. 31, 1945, all in Coeducation Folder, Distler Papers; Board Minutes, Feb. 9, 1945 (quotation).

136. Faculty Minutes, Mar. 5, 1945 (quotation); "Report of the Committee... to Study the Factors Involved in Changing Franklin and Marshall College to a Fully Accredited Coeducational College," 1945, Coeducation Folder, Distler Papers; Board Minutes, June 23, 1945; Leslie Miller-Bernal and Susan L. Poulson, eds., *Going Coed: Women's Experiences in Formerly Men's Colleges and Universities, 1950–2000* (Nashville: Vanderbilt University Press, 2004), 7–9.

137. Andrew, "Struggle for the Liberal Arts," chap. 1, 80; Faculty Minutes, Dec. 11, 1944, July 23 and 30, 1945, June 3, 1946; Board Minutes, June 23, 1945; *Report of the President* (1945–1946): 15–16, 26, 45; President's Newsletter, Distler Papers, Aug. 30, 1945 (quotation).

138. President's Newsletter, Dec. 30, 1944, Distler Papers.

139. Board Minutes, June 3, 1941, June 24 and Oct. 21, 1944, Feb. 9, June 23, and Oct. 12, 1945; *Report of the President* (1942–1943): 10, 34; *Report of the President* (1943–1944): 40–41; *Report of the President* (1945–1946): 26–27, 39; Distler Interview, Feb. 17, 1981, Oral History Project.

140. Faculty Minutes, Apr. 3, 1945; *Report of the President* (1943–1944): 11; *Report of the President* (1944–1945): 2; Board Minutes, Feb. 9, 1945.

141. "An Educational Program for Veterans at Franklin and Marshall College," pamphlet, Mar. 1945, Distler Papers; *Report of the President* (1944–1945): 40 (second quotation); *Report of the President* (1945–1946): 3; Board Minutes, Oct. 12, 1945 (third quotation).

142. *Report of the President* (1945–1946): 3, 6–7; Faculty Minutes, Mar. 6, 1946.

143. President's Newsletter, Feb. 27, 1946, Distler Papers.

144. H. M. J. Klein, *History of Franklin and Marshall*, 323.

145. *Report of the President* (1944–1945): 41.

CHAPTER 8

1. Christopher Jencks and David Riesman, *The Academic Revolution* (New York: Doubleday, 1968); Richard M. Freeland, *Academia's Golden Age: Universities in Massachusetts, 1945–1970* (New York: Oxford University Press, 1992) (quotation on 44). Jencks and Riesman define a university college as "a college whose primary purpose is to prepare students for graduate work of some kind—primarily in the arts and sciences but also in professional subjects ranging from law and medicine to business and social work" (24).

2. Roger L. Geiger, "Differentiation, Hierarchy, and Diversity: An Overview of Higher Education in the United States," in *Trends in American and German Higher Education* (Cambridge, Mass.: American Academy of Arts and Sciences, 2002), 22–23; Franklin & Marshall College Board Minutes, Oct. 11, 1946, June 7, 1947, Archives (hereafter, Board Minutes); Calvin B. T. Lee, *The Campus Scene: Changing Styles in Undergraduate Life* (New York: McKay, 1970), 75–78; H. M. J. Klein, *History of Franklin and Marshall College, 1787–1948* (Lancaster: Franklin & Marshall College, 1952); John Andrew, "Struggle for the Liberal Arts: Franklin and Marshall College, 1941–1982," unpublished MS, John Andrew Publication Files, Archives, chap. 3.

3. *Report of the President of Franklin and Marshall College* (1946–1947): 50–51 (hereafter, *Report of the President*); H. M. J. Klein, *History of Franklin and Marshall*, 334; Board Minutes, Oct. 11, 1946; Board Minutes, Oct. 11, 1946.

4. Board Minutes, Feb. 8, 1946 (quotation); Distler Interview, Feb. 17, 1981, Oral History Project, Archives (hereafter, Oral History Project); *Student Weekly*, Oct. 1, 1946, 1; *Student Weekly*, Dec. 8, 1949, 2; *Report of the President* (1946–1947): 28, 33.

5. "Report of the Study of Teaching Loads," (1946), AAUP Files, Archives (hereafter, AAUP Files); *Report of the President* (1946–1947): 4–5 (first quotation).

6. "Report of the Study of Teaching Loads," AAUP Minutes, Dec. 16, 1946, Feb. 24 and May 28 (quotation), 1947, AAUP Files (hereafter, AAUP Minutes); Franklin & Marshall College Faculty Minutes, Mar. 5, 1947, Archives (hereafter, Faculty Minutes).

7. Board Minutes, Oct. 12, 1945.

8. Board Minutes, Feb. 8 (second quotation) and June 29 (first quotation), 1946, June 7, 1947.

9. Board Minutes, Feb. 8, 1946 (first quotation); Distler Interview, Feb. 17, 1981, Oral History Project.

10. Faculty Minutes, Jan. 14, and June 3, 1946; *Report of the President* (1947–1948): 2, 15–18; *Report of the President* (1948–1949): 16; *Report of the President* (1949–1950): 15, 18–20; Board Minutes, June 7, 1949; *Student Weekly*, Oct. 26, 1949, 1; "Report of Visit to Franklin and Marshall College for the Middle States Association," Mar. 8–10, 1950, Archives (hereafter, "Report of Visit").

11. Board Minutes, Oct. 12, 1945, June 29, 1946.

12. APD Committee Minutes, Mar. 14, and Apr. 22, 1947, Archives (hereafter, APD Committee Minutes), "Report of Visit."

13. APD Committee Minutes, Feb. 8, and Mar. 14, 1947.

14. *Student Weekly*, Mar. 24, 1948; Board Minutes, June 11, 1948; *Student Weekly*, Sept. 24, 1948; *Report of the President* (1947–1948): 24, 51, 31–32; *Report of the President* (1948–1949): 35; *Report of the President* (1949–1950): 26; "'First Lady' of F&M Science," *Franklin and Marshall* (Spring/Summer 2004): 27.

15. *Report of the President* (1948–1949): 5–6.

16. "Data Presented for Consideration of . . . Middle States Association of Colleges and Secondary Schools," Jan. 23, 1950, 23, Archives; Board Minutes, Feb. 9, 1945.

17. Board Minutes, Oct. 28, 1949; "Report of Visit," Mar. 1950.

18. APD Committee Minutes, Feb. 18 (quotation) and Apr. 6, 1948, Jan. 21 and 26, Feb. 1, Mar. 4 and 10, 1949; Board Minutes, Oct. 8, 1938.

19. Faculty Minutes, Dec. 12, 1947 (first quotation); APD Committee Minutes, Dec. 20, 1948 (second quotation), Jan. 4, 1949, Feb. 7, 16, and 23, Mar. 6, Apr. 4 and 8, 1950.

20. *Report of the President* (1946–1947): 47–48; *Report of the President* (1947–1948): 7; Board Minutes, Feb. 7 and June 7, 1947 (quotation), Oct. 28, 1949; Faculty Minutes, Nov. 7, 1949.

21. Faculty Minutes, Apr. 17, 1950, Mar. 11, 1952; Board Minutes, June 5, 1950; *Report of the President* (1949–1950): 4, 8; *Report of the President* (1950–1951): 8.

22. Agreement, Nov. 2, 1946, Unger-Bassler Collection Folder, Archives; Andrew, "Struggle for the Liberal Arts," chap. 3; *Report of the President* (1947–1948): 24–25; APD Committee Minutes, Mar. 14, 1948 (quotation); Board Minutes, June 6, 1952; *Student Weekly*, Apr. 13, 1949, 1.

23. *Student Weekly*, Sept. 24, 1948, 1; *Student Weekly*, Oct. 27, 1948, 2; *Student Weekly*, Mar. 23, 1949, 1 (quotation); *Report of the President* (1948–1949): 23–24; APD Committee Minutes, Apr. 19, 1949.

24. *Student Weekly*, Dec. 14, 1949, 2; Board Minutes, June 7, 1949, June 1, 1956; APD Committee Minutes, Feb. 16, 1950; *Student Weekly*, May 10, 1950, 1; *Student Weekly*, Apr. 13, 1949, 1.

25. Freeland, *Academia's Golden Age*, 75–78 (quotations on 75, 76, 77–78 respectively); Hugh Hawkins, *Banding Together: The Rise of National Associations in American Higher Education, 1887–1950* (Baltimore: Johns Hopkins University Press, 1992),169–72.

26. Freeland, *Academia's Golden Age* (quotations on 77); Fred Millett, *The Rebirth of Liberal Education* (New York: Harcourt Brace, 1945), 5, 127–29.

27. Andrew, "Struggle for the Liberal Arts," chap. 3; Gilbert Allardyce, "The Rise and Fall of the Western Civilization Course," *American Historical Review* 87 (June 1982): 716–17; Morton Keller and Phyllis Keller, *Making Harvard Modern: The Rise of America's University* (New York: Oxford University Press, 2001), 43–45 (quotations on 44).

28. Allardyce, "Western Civilization Course," 710.

29. *Franklin and Marshall College Catalogue* for 1945–1946, 18–22, 24–25; Faculty Minutes, Jan. 31, July 10, Aug. 7, and Nov. 6, 1944, Dec. 12, 1947, Oct. 4, 1948; Board Minutes, Feb. 9, 1945.

30. Faculty Minutes, Jan. 9, 1948.

31. Faculty Minutes, Jan. 16 (quotation) and Feb. 16, 1948; Board Minutes, Feb. 13, 1948. The committee included Gibson, chair; Breidenstine and Barr, ex officio; Carroll, Heller, Foose, and Murray for the natural sciences; Neprash, Toth, Pitcher, and Munson, for the social sciences; Francis, Prakken, Noss, and Jameson, for the humanities; Laird, Bell, Okuda, and Everett, for business administration.

32. *Report of the President* (1947–1948): 7–8 (first and second quotations); *Report of the President* (1948–1949): 7–8 (third quotation); *Report of the President* (1949–1950): 1–2, 9; Board Minutes, Feb. 10, 1950 (fourth quotation).

33. *Report of the President* (1949–1950): 9; *Report of the President* (1950–1951): 2; Faculty Minutes, Dec. 12, 1949 (quotations).

34. "Report of Visit."

35. Ibid.

36. Ibid.; *Student Weekly*, Sept. 20, 1950, 1; *Report of the President* (1949–1950): 7 (quotation).

37. Andrew, "Struggle for the Liberal Arts," chap. 4; *Report of the President* (1949–1950): 3.

38. "Address at Fall Commencement and Opening Exercises," Sept. 24, 1942 (second quotation), and "Remarks at 162nd Opening," Sept. 21, 1948 (first quotation), Distler Papers, Archives (hereafter, Distler Papers); *Student Weekly*, May 9, 1954, 1.

39. Faculty Minutes, Jan. 9, 16 (quotation), Mar. 9, and Apr. 18, 1948; *Student Weekly*, Apr. 28, 1948, 1.

40. Board Minutes, Feb. 9, June 23, 1945, June 29, Oct. 11, 1946, Feb. 7, 1947; David Dunn et al., *A History of the Evangelical and Reformed Church* (Philadelphia: Christian Education Press, 1961), 300–301; *Student Weekly*, May 14, 1947, 3.

41. *Report of the President* (1946–1947): 5–8.

42. Ibid., 5–6; *Report of the President* (1947–1948): 8–9; *Report of the President* (1948–1949): 9; *Report of the President* (1949–1950): 13.

43. Faculty Minutes, June 19, 1946; *Student Weekly*, Oct. 24, 1947, 1; *Student Weekly*, Sept. 24, 1948, 1; *Student Weekly*, Nov. 2, 1949, 1; *Student Weekly*, Sept. 20, 1950, 1; *Student Weekly*, Oct. 4, 1950, 4; *Franklin and Marshall Alumnus* 25 (Apr. 1949): 1.

44. Linda Whipple, "Portraits of Pioneers," *Franklin and Marshall* (Autumn 2003): 14–21; *Oriflamme* (Lancaster, Pa.: 1953, 1954, 1955).

45. *Student Weekly*, Oct. 1, 1946, 2; *Student Weekly*, Oct. 23, 1946, 1; *Student Weekly*, Nov. 6, 1946, 2.

46. *Student Weekly*, Sept. 18, 1947, 1; *Student Weekly*, Oct. 24, 1947, 1 (first quotation); *Student Weekly*, Oct. 1, 1947, 1 (second quotation); *Student Weekly*, Oct. 8, 1947, 1 (third quotation), 2 (final quotation); *Student Weekly*, Sept. 28, 1949, 1.

47. *Student Weekly*, Oct. 15, 1947, 1; *Student Weekly*, Oct. 1, 1948, 1.

48. *Student Weekly*, Oct. 29, 1947, 1 (all quoted phrases); *Student Weekly*, Dec. 10, 1947, 2; *Student Weekly*, Oct. 20, 1948, 4; *Student Weekly*, Oct. 27, 1948, 1; *Student Weekly*, Oct. 26, 1949, 1; *Student Weekly*, Oct. 25, 1950, 1; *Student Weekly*, Oct. 22, 1952, 1; *Student Weekly*, Oct. 19, 1955, 2; *Student Weekly*, Sept. 25, 1957, 1.

49. *Student Weekly*, Mar. 17, 1948, 2; *Student Weekly*, Sept. 27, 1951, 6; *Student Weekly*, Oct. 20, 1954, 2; *Student Weekly*, Sept. 28, 1955, 3 (last quotation).

50. David M. Stameshkin, "A History of Fraternities and Sororities at Franklin and Marshall College, 1854–1987," unpublished paper, Archives.

51. Stameshkin, "History of Fraternities and Sororities"; Faculty Minutes, July 23, and Nov. 12, 1945, Sept. 22 and Dec. 3, 1946, Jan. 7, Feb. 5 (first quotation), and Apr. 9, 1947 (second quotation); *Student Weekly*, Sept. 18, 1947, 1; *Student Weekly*, Oct. 1, 1948, 1; *Student Weekly*, Sept. 20, 1950, 1.

52. *Student Weekly*, Mar. 1, 24, 1948 (quotation); *Student Weekly*, Apr. 7, 1948, 2; Faculty Minutes, Mar. 9, and May 12, 1948.

53. *Student Weekly*, Mar. 23, 1949, 7 (first quotation); *Student Weekly*, Apr. 27, 1949, 1 (second

quotation); *Student Weekly*, May 4, 1949, 1; *Student Weekly*, Sept. 20, 1950, 1; Faculty Minutes, Nov. 7, 1949 (Spotts quotations).

54. Faculty Minutes, Mar. 13, May 9 (first quotation), May 22 (second quotation), and June 2, 1950 (third quotation).

55. *Student Weekly*, Feb. 10, 1949, 1, 2.

56. Board Minutes, Feb. 9, 1945; *Student Weekly*, Nov. 5, 1947; *Student Weekly*, Mar. 9, 1949, 1; *Student Weekly*, Mar. 15, 1949, 1; *Student Weekly*, Mar. 23, 1949.

57. Faculty Minutes, Oct. 11, 1943, Sept. 17, 1945; H. M. J. Klein, *History of Franklin and Marshall*, 348–50; Andrew, "Struggle for the Liberal Arts," chap. 3; Board Minutes, Feb. 8, June 28, and Oct. 11, 1946; *Report of the President* (1946–1947): 51; *Student Weekly*, Oct. 8, 1946, 1.

58. Faculty Minutes, Oct. 7 and 30, 1946; *Student Weekly*, Nov. 6, 1946, 1; Board Minutes, Oct. 11, 1946 (all quotations); H. M. J. Klein, *History of Franklin and Marshall*, 338.

59. Paul Kieffer to T. A. Distler, Mar. 7, 1947, Distler Papers; Board Minutes, Oct. 11, 1946, Oct. 8, 1948, June 7, 1949; *Report of the President* (1948–1949): 2.

60. *Report of the President* (1948–1949): 2; *Report of the President* (1949–1950): 77; *Student Weekly*, Oct. 26, 1949, 1; *Student Weekly*, Dec. 14, 1949, 1; *Student Weekly*, Sept. 27, 1950, 5; Faculty Minutes, Nov. 7, 1949.

61. *Report of the President* (1949–1950): 1; *Student Weekly*, Nov. 2, 1949, 1 (first quotation); *Student Weekly*, Mar. 8, 1950, 1 (second quotation); *Student Weekly*, Apr. 26, 1950, 4; Elizabeth Fones-Wolf, "Business Propaganda in the Schools: Labor's Struggle Against the Americans for the Competitive Enterprise System, 1949–1954," *History of Education Quarterly* 40 (Spring 2000): 255–78.

62. Board Minutes, June 7, 1949.

63. *Student Weekly*, Oct. 12, 1949, 2 (middle quotations); *Student Weekly*, Oct. 19, 1949, 2 (final quotation); Faculty Minutes, Dec. 12, 1949 (first quotation).

64. *Student Weekly*, Feb. 18, 1948, 3; *Student Weekly*, Feb. 25, 1948, 1; *Student Weekly*, Apr. 14, 1948, 2; *Student Weekly*, Nov. 17, 1948, 2; *Student Weekly*, May 4, 1949, 2; *Student Weekly*, Feb. 22, 1950, 2 (quotations); Faculty Minutes, Jan. 16, and Feb. 16, 1948.

65. Faculty Minutes, Dec. 12, 1947, Mar. 13, 1950; *Student Weekly*, Mar. 29, 1950, 2 (quotation); *Student Weekly*, May 10, 1950, 2.

66. *Student Weekly*, Dec. 10, 1947, 2 (final quotation); *Student Weekly*, Oct. 19, 1949, 1 (first quotation); *Student Weekly*, Oct. 8, 1948, 2 (second quotation).

67. *Student Weekly*, Mar. 26, 1947, 3; *Student Weekly*, May 21, 1947, 2 (all quotations); *Student Weekly*, Feb. 25, 1948, 1; *Student Weekly*, Mar. 16, 1949, 1.

68. *Lancaster Intelligencer Journal*, Jan. 16, 1950, clipping in Gibbs Murder Files, Archives (hereafter, Gibbs Murder Files). These files contain clippings of the hundreds of news stories relating to the case.

69. *Lancaster New Era*, Jan. 19, 1950, Gibbs Murder Files; Board Minutes, Feb. 10, 1950.

70. Board Minutes, Feb. 10, June 5, 1950.

71. Board Minutes, June 5, 1950; *Report of the President* (1944–1945): 32–38 (quotation on 33); Steven Conn, *Museums and American Intellectual Life, 1876–1926* (Chicago: University of Chicago Press, 1998); W. Fred Kinsey III, ed., *The North Museum and the Natural History Tradition of Lancaster County* (Ephrata, Pa.: Science Press, 1986).

72. Board Minutes, June 24, 1944, June 23, 1945, June 29, and Oct. 22, 1946, Oct. 10, 1947, Feb. 13, 1948, Feb. 10, and June 5, 1950 (second quotation); Memo of Museum Committee, Feb. 9, 1950, Board Minutes (first quotation); T. A. Distler to P. Kieffer, Feb. 16, 1950, Kieffer Papers, Archives; Kinsey, *North Museum*, 37–41.

73. Board Minutes, Oct. 20, 1950 (first quotation), Feb. 9 (second quotation), June 4, 1951, Oct. 5, 1951; Faculty Minutes, Oct. 2, 1950; APD Committee Minutes, Dec. 20, 1950; *Student Weekly*, Sept. 20, 1950, 1.

74. Board Minutes, Oct. 20, 1950 (quotation), Feb. 9, 1951.

75. Board Minutes, Feb. 9, 1951; *Student Weekly*, Feb. 14, 1951, 1; *Student Weekly*, Apr. 4, 1951, 1.

76. APD Committee Minutes, Dec. 20, 1950, Nov. 6, 1951; AAUP Minutes, Nov. 1, Dec. 13, 1950, May 19, 1951 (second quotation); To T. A. Distler from Franklin and Marshall Chapter AAUP, May 1951 (first quotation), AAUP Files; Board Minutes, Feb. 9, June 4, 1951.

77. AAUP Minutes, Mar. 3 and 30, 1949; interview with Robert Mickey, Oct. 1, 2003.

78. AAUP Minutes, Mar. 3 (quotation) and 30, 1949, Nov. 1, Dec. 13, 1950, Apr. 27 and 30, 1951; *Student Weekly*, Apr. 11, 1951, 1; *Student Weekly*, Oct. 14, 1953, 2.

79. *Student Weekly*, Apr. 4, 1951, 1 (first and second quotations); *Student Weekly*, Apr. 11, 1951, 2 (third quotation); Nicholas Lemann, *The Big Test: The Secret History of the American Meritocracy* (New York: Farrar, Straus and Giroux, 1999), 72–77.

80. *Student Weekly*, Apr. 25, 1951, 1; *Student Weekly*, Sept. 27, 1951, 1 (quotation); *Report of the President* (1950–1951): 7, 9.

81. AAUP Minutes, May 15, 1951; *Student Weekly*, Sept. 27, 1951, 1.

82. Interview with Noel P. Laird, Apr. 8, 1980, Oral History Project (first quotation); *Student Weekly*, Dec. 6, 1950, 2; *Student Weekly*, Nov. 7, 1951, 1; *Student Weekly*, Nov. 21, 1951, 1; *Student Weekly*, Dec. 12, 1951, 1; *Student Weekly*, Mar. 12, 1952, 1, 2; *Student Weekly*, Mar. 19, 1952, 2; *Student Weekly*, Oct. 22, 1952, 1 (final quotation); Faculty Minutes, Nov. 12, Dec. 10 (Distler quotation), 1951, Oct. 13, 1952; AAUP Minutes, Nov. 15, 1951, Feb. 19, 1952.

83. *Franklin and Marshall Alumnus* 28 (Feb. 1952): 1; Faculty Minutes, Feb. 11, Apr. 10, May 12, 1952.

84. AAUP Minutes, Mar. 17 and 31 (quotations), 1952; Faculty Minutes, May 8, 1950.

85. AAUP Minutes, Oct. 16, 1952 (quotations); Faculty Minutes, Feb. 13, 1950, Nov. 12, Dec. 10, 1951, Jan. 15, 1952.

86. *Student Weekly*, Sept. 27, 1951, 4; *Student Weekly*, Oct. 17, 1951, 1; Board Minutes, Oct. 5, 1951, Jan. 25, June 6, 1952.

87. AAUP Minutes, Oct. 27, Dec. 19, 1949, Mar. 27, 1950; Faculty Minutes, May 6, 1952; Board Minutes, June 6, 1952, June 2, 1961.

88. *Student Weekly*, [Sept.] 27, 1938, 2; *Student Weekly*, Nov. 8, 1939, 1; *Student Weekly*, Feb. 14, 1939, 1; *Student Weekly*, Nov. 12, 1947, 1; *Student Weekly*, May 11, 1949, 1; *Student Weekly*, May 16, 1951, 1; *Report of the President* (1951–1952): 5; Faculty Minutes, Sept. 10, 1954. On the postwar growth and professionalization of university presses, see Paul Parsons, *Getting Published: The Acquisition Process at University Presses* (Knoxville: University of Tennessee Press, 1989), 12–14.

89. Board Minutes, Feb. 13, 1953, Feb. 11, 1955; Faculty Minutes, Jan. 12, 1954; Hawkins, *Banding Together*, 177–78.

90. Board Minutes, June 7, 1949; Faculty Minutes, Oct. 8, 1951, Apr. 28, 1952; *Student Weekly*, Oct. 1, 1952, 2; AAUP Minutes, Feb. 19, 1952; "Intercollegiate Athletics at Franklin and Marshall College," Faculty Minutes, Apr. 24, 1953.

91. *Student Weekly*, May 28, 1947, 1; *Student Weekly*, Nov. 28, 1950, 1; *Student Weekly*, Mar. 12, 1952, 1; *Student Weekly*, Nov. 26, 1952; *Student Weekly*, Feb. 12, 1953, 4.

92. *Franklin and Marshall Alumnus* 28 (Dec. 1951): 1; *Student Weekly*, Sept. 27, 1951, 4; *Student Weekly*, Oct. 17, 1951, 1; *Student Weekly*, Nov. 14, 1951, 1; *Student Weekly*, Feb. 16, 1953; Ronald A. Smith, *Play-by-Play: Radio, Television, and Big-Time Sports* (Baltimore: Johns Hopkins University Press, 2001), 88 (quotation).

93. Faculty Minutes, Feb. 16, Apr. 24, 1953; Board Minutes, Oct. 17, 1952 (all quotations), June 5, 1953.

94. Faculty Minutes, Feb. 16, Oct. 22, 1953; Board Minutes, Jan. 22, 1954.

95. Faculty Minutes, Oct. 13 (quotations), Dec. 8, 1952; Board Minutes, Feb. 13, 1953; *Report of the President* (1952–1953): 3; *Student Weekly*, Mar. 25, 1953, 1; *Student Weekly*, Apr. 15, 1953, 2; *Student Weekly*, Apr. 22, 1953, 2.

96. *Student Weekly*, Mar. 25, 1953, 1; *Student Weekly*, Apr. 15, 1953, 2.

97. *Student Weekly*, Mar. 4, 1953, 1; *Student Weekly*, Mar. 18, 1953, 1 (quotation).

98. *Student Weekly*, Nov. 19, 1952, 2 (first quotation); *Student Weekly*, Apr. 22, 1953, 1, 2 (second quotation); *Student Weekly*, Apr. 29, 1953, 6; *Student Weekly*, May 6, 1953, 1.

99. AAUP Minutes, Dec. 9, 1952, Jan. 5, 1953; Faculty Minutes, Jan. 12, 1953; Board Minutes, Oct. 17, 1952, Feb. 13, June 5, 1953 (quotation); *Report of the President* (1952–1953): 4; *Student Weekly*, Feb. 25, 1953, 1.

100. Faculty Minutes, Oct. 13, 1952; "Report of Academic Standing Committee," Feb. 16, 1953; *Report of the President* (1952–1953): 5; AAUP Minutes, May 19, 1953 (quotation).

101. APD Committee Minutes, Jan. 15 and 23, 1953; Board Minutes, Jan. 22, 1954.

102. AAUP Minutes, May 28, 1947, Oct. 28, 1953; APD Committee Minutes, May 25, May 28 (first quotation), 1951, Feb. 20 (second quotation), Apr. 30, June 3, and July 18, 1953 (third quotation); Faculty Minutes, Sept. 14, 1953; Board Minutes, June 8, Aug. 17, 1953.

103. APD Committee Minutes, July 18, 1953 (first quotation); Faculty Minutes, Sept. 14, 1953 (second quotation); AAUP Minutes, Oct. 28, 1953 (fourth quotation), Apr. 22, and May 19, 1954; Board Minutes, Aug. 17, 1953.

104. *Student Weekly*, Oct. 14, 1953, 2 (first quotation); *Student Weekly*, Oct. 28, 1953, 5 (second quotation); *Student Weekly*, Nov. 11, 1953, 6 (third quotation).

105. Distler Interview, Feb. 17, 1981, Oral History Project; Richard J. Gessner, "Dr. Theodore A. Distler and Franklin and Marshall College During Dr. Distler's Tenure as President from 1941–1954," (undergraduate paper, Franklin & Marshall College, Apr. 1981); Board Minutes, Jan. 22, 1954; Hawkins, *Banding Together*, 206–8; Faculty Minutes, Jan. 7, 1954.

106. Board Minutes, Jan. 22, 1954; AAUP Minutes, Feb. 2, 1954.

107. Board Minutes, Jan. 22, 1954.

108. Faculty Minutes, Apr. 6, 1954.

109. Board Minutes, Oct. 8, 1954 (quotation); Faculty Minutes, Sept. 10, Oct. 21, 1954, and Sept. 24, 1956; *Lancaster New Era*, July 14 and 22, 1954; *Lancaster Intelligencer Journal*, July 23 and 29, 1954, all clippings in Hall Papers, Archives (hereafter, Hall Papers).

110. James M. Darlington, "Franklin and Marshall College: A Half-Century of Growth as Observed by a Sentimental Alumnus," May 11, 1979, Darlington Papers, Archives; Paul Kieffer to Miss Elizabeth C. Kieffer, Oct. 1954 (quotation), Hall Papers; *Lancaster New Era*, July 30, 1954, clipping in Hall Papers.

111. William Webster Hall, *The Small College Talks Back: An Intimate Appraisal* (New York: R. R. Smith, 1951), quoted in Andrew, "Struggle for the Liberal Arts," 224; *Lancaster Sunday News*, Aug. 29, 1954, *Lancaster New Era*, July 30, 1954, and undated *Lancaster New Era* clipping, all in Hall Papers; Board Minutes, Aug. 2, 1954.

112. Darlington, "Half-Century of Growth"; *Lancaster New Era*, Oct. 8, Oct. 9, 1954, clippings in Hall Papers; Faculty Minutes, Oct. 21, 1954.

113. Board Minutes, June 5, 1950, Oct. 16, 1953, Oct. 8, 1954.

114. AAUP Minutes, Dec. 7, 1954.

115. Board Minutes, Oct. 8, 1954; Executive Committee Minutes, July 22 and 28, 1954; Faculty Minutes, Sept. 10, 1954.

116. Chronological notes, Henry J. Marshall File, Board Records; Faculty Minutes, Oct. 21, Dec. 4, 1954 (first quotation), Jan. 17, 1955 (subsequent quotations), Mar. 24, 1994.

117. Unidentified clipping, Feb. 4, 1955, and *Lancaster New Era*, Feb. 17, 1955 (quotation), both in Hall Papers.

118. *Student Weekly*, Dec. 8, 1954, 1; *Student Weekly*, Feb. 23, 1955, 3; Board Minutes, Feb. 11, 1955 (petition quotations).

119. AAUP Minutes, Apr. 11, 1946, Apr. 30, 1953, Feb. 10, Mar. 15 (quotation), 1955; Executive Committee Minutes, May 25, 1955; Board Minutes, Oct. 14, 1955.

120. Faculty Minutes, Apr. 4, May 9 (first quotation), 1955; Andrew, "Struggle for the Liberal

Arts," chap. 5; AAUP Minutes, Apr. 7, 1955 (second and third quotations); Board Minutes, June 10, 1955.

121. Report of the President, in Board Minutes, June 10, 1955; Report of the President, in Board Minutes, Oct. 14, 1955; *Student Weekly*, Mar. 2, 1955, 1.

122. Paul Kieffer to William W. Hall, Mar. 28, 1955, Hall Papers; Board Minutes, June 10, 1955; Paul Kieffer to Keith Spalding, July 5, 1967, Marshall Folder, Board Files; Darlington, "Half-Century of Growth"; Report of the President, in Board Minutes, Feb. 10, 1956.

123. Report of the President, in Board Minutes, Oct. 14, 1955 (all quotations), Feb. 10, 1956; Andrew, "Struggle for the Liberal Arts," chap. 5.

124. Board Minutes, June 10, 1955, Feb. 10, and June 1, 1956.

125. Board Minutes, Oct. 14, 1955, Feb. 10, June 1, 1956; Executive Committee Minutes, Nov. 25, 1955; Faculty Minutes, Apr. 5, 1956; AAUP Minutes, Apr. 19, 1956; *Student Weekly*, Sept. 21, 1955, 1.

126. Board Minutes, Feb. 10, June 1, 1956, Oct. 18, 1957; Faculty Minutes, May 21, 1956 (quotation); Report of Curriculum Planning Committee, Feb. 27, 1958, Faculty Records, Archives.

127. Executive Committee Minutes, Nov. 25, 1955; *Student Weekly*, Jan. 11, 1956, 2; Freeland, *Academia's Golden Age*, 93 (quotation); Roger L. Geiger, *Research and Relevant Knowledge: American Research Universities Since World War II* (New York: Oxford University Press, 1993), chap. 4; Charles H. Glatfelter, *A Salutary Influence: Gettysburg College, 1832–1985* (Gettysburg: Gettysburg College, 1987), 764; David M. Stameshkin, *The Strength of the Hills: Middlebury College, 1915–1990* (Middlebury: Middlebury College Press, 1996), 114–15; Board Minutes, Feb. 10, 1956.

128. Faculty Minutes, Oct. 20, 1955; *Student Weekly*, Sept. 14, 1955, 1; Board Minutes, Feb. 10, 1956.

129. *Student Weekly*, Oct. 29, 1952, 1; T. A. Distler to Paul Kieffer, Sept. 26, 1944, Meyer File, Board Records; John D. Meyer to William A. Schnader, [Oct. 10, 1955], William A. Schnader to William Webster Hall, Oct. 11, 1955, Hall to Schnader, Oct. 14, 1955, all in Coeducation History Folder, Spalding Papers, Archives; Board Minutes, Oct. 14, 1955, Oct. 19, 1956.

130. Andrew, "Struggle for the Liberal Arts," chap. 5; Darlington, "Half-Century of Growth."

131. Report of the President, in Board Minutes, Feb. 10, 1956; *Student Weekly*, Jan. 11, 1956, 1, 2.

132. Board Minutes, June 1, 1956 (all quotations); W. W. Hall to William A. Schnader, May 26, 1956 (copy), Hall to Faculty, June 7, 1956, *Lancaster Intelligencer Journal*, June 2, 1956, and *Lancaster New Era*, June 2, 1956, all in Hall Papers; Hall to F. de W. Bolman, Sept. 4, 1956, Bolman Papers, Archives.

CHAPTER 9

1. *Lancaster New Era*, June 2, 1956, in Hall Papers, Archives; Franklin & Marshall College Faculty Minutes, Sept. 24, 1956 (quotation), Archives (hereafter, Faculty Minutes); Franklin & Marshall College Board Minutes, June 1, 1956, Aug. 7, 1956, Archives (hereafter, Board Minutes); "New F&M Head Lauds Liberal Arts Colleges' Role," unidentified clipping, Bolman Papers, Archives (hereafter, Bolman Papers).

2. Faculty Minutes, Sept. 24, 1956.

3. Clippings, Bolman Papers; Bolman obituary, *New York Times*, Aug. 19, 1985.

4. James M. Darlington, "Franklin and Marshall College: A Half-Century of Growth as Observed by a Sentimental Alumnus," May 11, 1979, Darlington Papers, Archives.

5. Board Minutes, Feb. 10 (quotation), June 1, Sept. 28, 1956; *Student Weekly*, Oct. 3, 1956, 1, 2.

6. Faculty Minutes, Sept. 24 (first quotation), Nov. 1, 1956, Feb. 28, 1957; *Student Weekly*, Jan. 9, 1957, 1 (second quotation); AAUP Minutes, Oct. 24, 1956, AAUP Files, Archives (hereafter, AAUP Minutes).

7. Faculty Minutes, Dec. 12, 1956; Report of Research Committee Meeting, Nov. 12, 1956, Faculty Minutes Files.

8. Report of Research Committee Meeting; Board Minutes, Feb. 8, 1957.

9. "A College Grapples Its Future," *Business Week* (May 13, 1961): 96; Board Minutes, Feb. 8, 1957.

10. Board Minutes, Oct. 19, 1956 (quotation), Feb. 8, 1957.

11. Board Minutes, June 1, 1956, Feb. 8, 1957; Faculty Minutes, Jan. 17, Feb. 28, 1957.

12. Board Minutes, Oct. 19, 1956, June 8, 1957; Faculty Minutes, May 23, June 3, 1957; J. M. Darlington to Faculty, May 28, 1957, in Faculty Minutes.

13. Board Minutes, Oct. 19, 1956, June 8, 1957; *Student Weekly*, Apr. 10, 1957, 1.

14. F. Bolman, "The Educated Free Mind," Apr. 6, 1957, MS, Bolman Papers.

15. The President's Commission on Education Beyond the High School, *Second Report to the President* (Washington, D.C., 1957); Board Minutes, Feb. 8, 1957; *Student Weekly*, May 22, 1957, 1.

16. *Student Weekly*, Apr. 3, 1957, 1; "Survey of the Administrative Management," Cresap, McCormick, and Paget, May 1957, Archives.

17. "Survey of the Administrative Management."

18. Board Minutes, June 8, 1957 (quotation), Oct. 18, 1957; Faculty Minutes, Oct. 31, 1957.

19. Board Minutes, Oct. 18, 1957 (quotations); Faculty Minutes, Oct. 31, 1957.

20. Board Minutes, Oct. 18, 1957, June 6, 1958, June 3, 1960 (quotation).

21. Board Minutes, June 8 (first quotation), Oct. 18 (second quotation), 1957; Faculty Minutes, Dec. 13, 1957.

22. Faculty Minutes, May 21, Nov. 1, 1956, Feb. 28, May 23, 1957 (first quotation); Board Minutes, June 8, 1957 (second quotation).

23. David Dunn et al., *A History of the Evangelical and Reformed Church* (Philadelphia: Christian Education Press, 1961), 331–36.

24. Darlington, "Half-Century of Growth"; interview with Noel P. Laird, Apr. 8, 1980, Oral History Project, Archives; AAUP Minutes, May 6, Nov. 27, 1957, Jan. 16, 1958; Board Minutes, Feb. 14, 1958.

25. Board Minutes, Oct. 18, 1957 (first quotation), Feb. 9, 1962 (second quotation); *Annual Report, 1958*, June 6, 1958, Bolman Papers.

26. *Annual Report, 1958.*

27. Ibid.

28. Ibid.

29. Ibid.; Board Minutes, June 8, 1957.

30. *Annual Report, 1958* (Lancaster: Franklin & Marshall College, 1958) was the last president's report to be published. Afterward, they were typescript reports distributed before each board meeting.

31. Report of Curriculum Planning Committee, Feb. 27, 1958 (quotations), Franklin & Marshall College Faculty Records, Archives (hereafter, Faculty Records); Faculty Minutes, Apr. 17, May 22, 1958.

32. Report of Curriculum Planning Committee, Feb. 27, 1958 (quotations), Faculty Records; Faculty Minutes, May 22, 1958.

33. Curriculum Planning Committee, "A New Curriculum for Franklin and Marshall College," 5–7, Archives.

34. Faculty Minutes, Mar. 5, 18, 30, Apr. 7, 16, 22, May 1, 5, 11, 18, 1959; Eddy quoted in the President's Report, in Board Minutes for Feb. 12, 1960.

35. Darlington, "Half-Century of Growth"; Faculty Minutes, June 1, 2, 3, 1959; Task Force on Educational Program Design to Faculty, May 25, 1979, Faculty Minutes.

36. Faculty Minutes, June 3, 1959.

37. Ibid.; Board Minutes, June 5, 1959.

38. Board Minutes, Oct. 17, 1958, Feb. 13, June 5, 1959 (quotations).

39. Board Minutes, Oct. 17, 1958, June 5 (quotations), Oct. 17, 1959.

40. Board Minutes, Feb. 13, June 5, 1959 (first quotation); F. Bolman to John D. Meyer, May 28 and July 25, 1958 (second quotation), Meyer Folder, Board Files, Archives (hereafter,

Board Files); Bolman to Oliver D. Marcks, Mar. 6, 1959, and Marcks to William Schnader, May 6 and 26, 1959, Marcks Folder, Board Files.

41. *Student Weekly*, Oct. 31, 1951, 1; *Student Weekly*, Dec. 5, 1956, 1; *Student Weekly*, Apr. 10, 1957, 2.

42. *Student Weekly*, Jan. 9, 1957 (first quotation); *Student Weekly*, Feb. 13, 1957, 2; *Student Weekly*, Feb. 13, 1957, 2 (subsequent quotations).

43. *Student Weekly*, Mar. 6, 1957, 1 (quotations); *Student Weekly*, Mar. 20, 1957, 1; Faculty Minutes, May 23, 1957; Board Minutes, June 8, 1957.

44. *Student Weekly*, Apr. 25, 1956, 2; *Student Weekly*, Apr. 6, 1960, 1 (quotation); AAUP Minutes, Nov. 1, 1957; Faculty Minutes, Dec. 13, 1957, Jan. 15, Mar. 5, May 14, Sept. 24, 1959, May 17, 1960; Board Minutes, June 5, 1959, June 3, 1960; "How Do You Rate a College?" [1960], Bolman Papers. In 1947 Middlebury's chapter of Alpha Sigma Phi had become the first local chapter to break with its national organization over the right to admit Jewish members. See David M. Stameshkin, *Strength of the Hills: Middlebury College, 1915–1990* (Hanover: Middlebury College Press, 1995), 220–21.

45. *Student Weekly*, Sept. 14, 1955, 2 (first quotation); *Student Weekly*, Sept. 21, 1955, 2; *Student Weekly*, Sept. 28, 1955, 3 (subsequent quotations).

46. *Student Weekly*, Sept. 25, 1957, 2 (first-fourth, Stern quotations); *Student Weekly*, Oct. 16, 1957, 2 (Wise quotations); *Student Weekly*, Nov. 20, 1957, 1; Faculty Minutes, Sept. 19, 1957, May 22, 1958; AAUP Minutes, Nov. 1, 1957; *The Blue Book: Franklin and Marshall College, 1959–1960* ([Lancaster]: Franklin & Marshall Student Council, 1959–1960), 64–66 (final quotation on 65).

47. *Student Weekly*, Jan. 8, 1958, 1; *Student Weekly*, Jan. 15, 1958, 1; *Student Weekly*, Feb. 11, 1959, 1 (second quotation); *Student Weekly*, Feb. 25, 1959, 1; Richard J. Stonesifer, "Having Guests on the Campus," *Journal of Higher Education* 31 (January 1960): 33–37 (first quotation on 36).

48. *Student Weekly*, Nov. 6, 1957, 1 (second quotation), 3 (first quotation); *Student Weekly*, Nov. 13, 1957, 2; *Student Weekly*, Nov. 20, 1957, 3.

49. *Student Weekly*, Apr. 15, 1959, 1, 2, 6 (first quotations); *Student Weekly*, Apr. 22, 1929, 2 (final quotations).

50. Board Minutes, Oct. 17, 1958 (Darlington quotations); June 5, 1959 (first quotation).

51. APD Committee Minutes, Dec. 31, 1957 (first quotation), Sept. 15, Dec. 9, 16, 22 (second quotation), 1958, Archives (hereafter, APD Committee Minutes); J. Darlington to F. Bolman, Aug. 1, 1958, in APD Files, Archives.

52. APD Committee Minutes, Feb. 11, Mar. 10, 1959; *Student Weekly*, Apr. 22, 1959, 1 (quotation); John Andrew, "Struggle for the Liberal Arts: Franklin and Marshall College, 1941–1982," unpublished MS, John Andrew Publications Files, Archives, chap. 6.

53. Academic Council Minutes, Sept. 13, 15, 1959, Archives; Faculty Minutes, Sept. 24, Oct. 12 (quotation), 1959.

54. Board Minutes, June 5, 1959 (emphasis in original); Morton A. Rauh, *College and University Trusteeship* (Yellow Springs, Ohio: Antioch Press, 1959); Beardsley Ruml, *Memo to a College Trustee: A Report on Financial and Structural Problems of the Liberal College* (New York: McGraw-Hill, 1959).

55. Frederick DeWolfe Bolman Jr., "The College Looks to the Future," *Franklin and Marshall Alumnus* 35 (January 1960): 3–6; F. Bolman to Elmer Bobst, Mar. 24, 1960, Bobst Folder, Board Files.

56. Board Minutes, Oct. 17, 1959 (quotations); Minutes of Faculty-Administration Smoker, May 6, 1960, Coeducation History Folder, Spalding Papers, Archives (hereafter, Spalding Papers).

57. "Proceedings of the Seminar of the Board of Trustees," Oct. 15–17, 1959 (quotations), Archives; Board Minutes, Oct. 17, 1959, Feb. 12, 1960.

58. Board Minutes, Oct. 17, 1959.

59. Roger L. Geiger, *Research and Relevant Knowledge: American Research Universities Since World War II* (New York: Oxford University Press, 1993) (first quotation on 165); F. Bolman to the Board of Trustees and Faculty, Nov. 24, 1959 (Bolman quotations), and Peter Seadle, AAUP Secretary, to Bolman, Dec. 8, 1959, Board Files; AAUP Minutes, Jan. 9, Feb. 20, 1959; Board Minutes, Feb. 13, 1959.

60. W. Schnader to F. Bolman, Nov. 27, 1959 (quotation), Loyalty Oath File, Archives; Board Minutes, Feb. 12, 1960.

61. Faculty Minutes, Jan. 11, 1960; Board Minutes, Feb. 12, 1960 (quotations), June 2, 1961; *Student Weekly*, Sept. 16, 1961, 1.

62. "Franklin and Marshall College Book-of-the-Semester, Spring 1960," Board Minutes, Feb. 12, 1960.

63. Board Minutes, Feb. 12, 1960; "Long Range Plans for Franklin and Marshall College, 1960–1970," Preliminary Report, Aug. 1, 1960, Archives; Sidney G. Tickton, *Financing Higher Education: 1960–70* (New York: McGraw-Hill, 1959); "A College Grapples Its Future," 96; *College Reporter*, Sept. 21, 1971, 3.

64. "Franklin and Marshall College Today and Tomorrow: A Review of the College's Purposes, Programs, and Long Range Plans, 1961–1971," Feb. 1962, 33, Archives (hereafter, "Today and Tomorrow").

65. "Long Range Plans," 5; "Today and Tomorrow," 32–33.

66. "Today and Tomorrow," 35–36. On planning under the "Tickton system," see Stanley Michalak, "Statement," Poconos Conference, Sept. 1971, Archives.

67. "Today and Tomorrow," 36, 37, 39, 41; Board Minutes, Feb. 12, 1960, Feb. 8, June 1, 1963.

68. William Schnader to G. Wayne Glick, Mar. 8, 1960, F. Bolman to John Cranford Adams, May 4, 1960, Bolman to G. W. Glick, July 9, 1960, Bolman to Margaret Habein, July 14, 1960, all in Coeducation History Folder, Spalding Papers.

69. Minutes of Faculty-Administration Smoker, May 6, 1960, Coeducation History Folder, Spalding Papers.

70. Board Minutes, Oct. 22, 1960; "A College Grapples Its Future," 95–97.

71. Board Minutes, June 3 (quotations), and Oct. 22, 1960.

72. Board Minutes, Oct. 22, 1960.

73. *Student Weekly*, Sept. 28, 1960, 1 (quotation); *Student Weekly*, Oct. 26, 1960, 1; *Student Weekly*, Nov. 2, 1960, 1; Board Minutes, Oct. 22, 1960.

74. *Student Weekly*, Feb. 20, 1957, 2; *Student Weekly*, Mar. 30, 1960, 1; *Student Weekly*, Apr. 6, 1960, 1; *Student Weekly*, Apr. 27, 1960, 1; *Student Weekly*, Sept. 28, 1960, 1.

75. Board Minutes, Feb. 12, 1960.

76. *Stupid Weakly*, Halloween Extra, Oct. 30, 1960, 1; *Student Weekly*, Nov. 2, 1960, 2; *Student Weekly*, Mar. 1, 1961, 1 (quotation), 7.

77. *Student Weekly*, Apr. 19, 1961, 1, 2; Board Minutes, June 2, 1961.

78. *Student Weekly*, Apr. 19, 1961, 1, 2; author conversation with a participant, October 2003.

79. *Student Weekly*, Apr. 19, 1961, 2.

80. Faculty Minutes, Apr. 17, 1961 (first quotation); Executive Committee Minutes, May 12, 1961; F. Bolman to the Board, May 5, 1961 (Bolman quotations); Board Minutes, June 2, 1961; Elmer Bobst to Bolman, May 9, 1961, Bobst Folder, Board Files.

81. F. Bolman to the Board, May 5, 1961 (first and second quotations); Board Minutes, June 2, 1961 (third, fourth, fifth quotations).

82. Board Minutes, June 2, 1961; John B. Meyer to William Schnader, Oct. 4, 1961, Meyer File, Board Records.

83. Board Minutes, June 2, 1961, Feb. 9, 1962. Many colleges established honors programs for gifted students in the late fifties and early sixties. See Michael Brick and Earl J. McGrath, *Innovation in Liberal Arts Colleges* (New York: Teachers College Press, 1969), 21–26.

84. Board Minutes, Feb. 10, 1961.

85. Board Minutes, Feb. 13, June 11, Oct. 8, 1948, Jan. 25, Oct. 17, 1952, Feb. 13, 1953, Oct. 8, 1954, Feb. 10, 1956, Feb. 14, 1958, June 5, 1959, Feb. 12, 1960; William A. Schnader, "History of the Negotiation and Consummation of the Contract Between Mr. A. Douglas Oliver and Franklin and Marshall College," Jan. 4, 1962, Oliver Folder, Bolman Papers.

86. W. Schnader, "History of the Negotiation"; Board Minutes, Oct. 14, 1961 (quotation); "Special Report of the President," Board Minutes, Feb. 9, 1962.

87. Board Minutes, Feb. 9, 1962 (quotation). The stenographic transcript of the meeting noted that after asking for a show of hands, Schnader announced that the vote was 8 in favor to 7 against (out of 23 in attendance); the secretary commented that she counted 8 to 8, and a marginal note by F. Bolman states that another board member said it was 9 to 8 against.

88. Board Minutes, Feb. 9, 1962; William Schnader to H. R. Reidenbaugh, Feb. 13, 1962, Bolman Papers.

89. *Student Weekly*, Feb. 21, 1962, 9, 10.

90. W. Schnader to F. Bolman, Mar. 3, 1962, Bolman to Schnader, Mar. 8, 1962, Bolman Papers.

91. Henry Marshall to F. Bolman, Nov. 24, 1958, W. Schnader to Bolman, June 25, 1959, Government Department File, Archives, cited in Andrew, "Struggle for the Liberal Arts," chap. 6, nn. 22, 24; Arthur B. Sinkler to Schnader, July 21, 1959, Sinkler Folder, Board Records.

92. *Student Weekly*, Nov. 1, 1961, 1; *Student Weekly*, Nov. 15, 1961, 1; *Student Weekly*, Feb. 7, 1962, 5.

93. *Student Weekly*, Feb. 14, 1962, 1; W. Schnader to F. Bolman, Mar. 3, 1962, Bolman to Schnader, Mar. 8, 1962 (quotation), Bolman Memo, May 4, 1962, all in Bolman Papers.

94. W. Schnader to F. Bolman, Mar. 14, 1962 (first quotation), Bolman Papers; "Schnader, Bolman Differences Get Airing at F&M," *Lancaster Sunday News*, Mar. 18, 1962, 1; "Six Local Trustees Call for F-M Unity," *Lancaster New Era*, Mar. 19, 1962, 1, 2 (second quotation); Faculty Minutes, Mar. 20, 1962; "Faculty Backs Bolman in Note to Schnader," *Lancaster New Era*, Mar. 22, 1962, 1, 2; *Student Weekly*, Mar. 21, 1962, 1.

95. "Dr. Bolman Answers Critics of F&M College," *Lancaster Intelligencer Journal*, Apr. 7, 1962, copy in Bolman Papers.

96. "Dr. Bolman Answers Critics"; Faculty Minutes, May 10, 1963; Christopher Jencks and David Riesman, *The Academic Revolution* (New York: Doubleday, 1968), 26. This pattern of decreasing local enrollment was common throughout the more selective liberal arts colleges. See Thomas D. Hamm, *Earlham College: A History, 1847–1997* (Bloomington: Indiana University Press, 1997), 239–50.

97. Report of the Chairman of the Board of Trustees," June 1962, Board Minutes; Bolman notes, May 4, 1962, Bolman Papers.

98. Paul R. Linfield to W. Schnader, July 31, 1962, Bolman Papers.

99. W. Schnader to F. Bolman, Oct. 15, 1962, Bolman Papers; Board Minutes, Oct. 27, 1962. The wording of the board's statement is nearly identical to that of a letter Schnader wrote to a faculty member. See Wm. A. Schnader to Robert G. Mickey, Oct. 8, 1962, Bolman Papers.

100. See F. Bolman to Robert A. Maes, June 15, 1962, Maes Folder, Trustees Records; Bolman to Board, Aug. 24, 1962, Bolman Papers.

101. Board Minutes, Sept. 5, 1962; articles from *Lancaster Intelligencer Journal*, Sept. 6, 1962, 1, 10, and *Philadelphia Bulletin*, Sept. 6, 1962, Bolman Papers.

102. Board Minutes, Feb. 8, 1957, Sept. 5, 1962; Faculty Minutes, Sept. 7, 1962.

103. Peter H. Binzen, "Faculty Backs Ousted President in Struggle with F&M Trustees," *Philadelphia Sunday Bulletin*, 1, 8, n.d., clipping in Bolman Papers.

104. *Lancaster Intelligencer Journal* editorial, Sept. 7, 1962, 26, *Lancaster New Era*, Sept. 7, 1962, 10, clippings in Bolman Papers.

105. *Lancaster Intelligencer Journal*, Sept. 7, 1962, clippings in Bolman papers; Faculty Minutes, Sept. 7, 1962.

106. Faculty Minutes, Sept. 7, 1962.

107. Ibid.

108. "F&M Trustees Are Polled on New President," *Lancaster Intelligencer Journal*, Sept. 25, 1962; "Schnader Answers Critics at F&M," *Lancaster Sunday News*, Sept. 16, 1962; "Questions for Mr. Schnader"; *Student Weekly*, Sept. 19, 1962; Binzen, "Faculty Backs Ousted President," *Philadelphia Bulletin*, n.d., clippings in Bolman Papers; F. Bolman to W. Schnader, Oct. 1, 1962, Schnader to Bolman, Oct. 15, 1962, Bolman Papers.

109. Conversations with John J. McDermott and Ira N. Feit, Nov. 13, 2003; "F&M Head Quits in Fight," *Philadelphia Bulletin*, Sept. 6, 1962, clipping in Bolman Papers.

110. Bolman to Faculty, Nov. 1, 1962, Bolman Papers.

CHAPTER 10

1. *Student Weekly*, Sept. 26, 1962, 1; *Student Weekly*, Oct. 17, 1962, 2; *Student Weekly*, Nov. 7, 1962, 1; Search Committee File, quoted in John Andrew, "The Struggle for the Liberal Arts: Franklin and Marshall College 1941–1982," unpublished MS, John Andrew Publications files, Archives, chap. 8, n1; author interview with Keith Spalding, Apr. 6, 2004; Franklin & Marshall College Board Minutes, Feb. 8, 1963, Board Minutes (hereafter, Board Minutes).

2. Interview with Keith Spalding, Apr. 6, 2004; *Student Weekly*, Feb. 13, 1963, 1.

3. Interview with Keith Spalding, Apr. 6, 2004; Stephen E. Ambrose and Richard H. Immerman, *Milton S. Eisenhower, Educational Statesman* (Baltimore: Johns Hopkins University Press, 1983), 194–95; Board to Alumni, Feb. 8, 1963, Spalding Papers, Archives (hereafter, Spalding Papers).

4. John Moss to K. Spalding, Nov. 22, 1962, quoted in Andrew, "Struggle for the Liberal Arts," chap. 8, n8; Board Minutes, Feb. 8, 1963; *Student Weekly*, Apr. 24, 1963, 1.

5. Board Minutes, Oct. 26, 1962; Frederick Bolman to Robert Maes, May 10, 1962, Richard Stonesifer to Maes, May 14, 1962 (second quotation), both in Maes Folder, Trustees Records, Archives (hereafter, Trustees Records); *Student Weekly*, Feb. 6, 1963, 6; *College Reporter*, Sept. 12, 1965, 1. On Ford grants in this period, see John R. Thelin, *A History of American Higher Education* (Baltimore: John Hopkins University Press, 2004), 282–84; Roger L. Geiger, *Research and Relevant Knowledge: American Research Universities Since World War II* (New York: Oxford University Press, 1993), 110–16 (first quotation on 113); Hans Jenny and G. Richard Wynn, *The Golden Years: A Study of Income and Expenditure Growth and Distribution of Forty-eight Private Four-Year Liberal Arts Colleges, 1960–1968* (Wooster: College of Wooster, 1970); Thomas D. Hamm, *Earlham College, A History, 1847–1997* (Bloomington: Indiana University Press, 1997), 241; Richard M. Freeland, *Academia's Golden Age: Universities in Massachusetts, 1945–1970* (New York: Oxford University Press, 1992), 207; David M. Stameshkin, *The Strength of the Hills: Middlebury College, 1915–1990* (Hanover: Middlebury College Press, 1995), 120–21. Gettysburg College was also turned down the following year, reportedly because it was not "thinking nor acting big enough" (Charles H. Glatfelter, *A Salutary Influence: Gettysburg College, 1832–1985* [Gettysburg, Pennsylvania: Gettysburg College, 1987], 767).

6. Middle States Association of Colleges and Secondary Schools, Commission on Institutions of Higher Education, Report of the Evolution of Franklin & Marshall College, Lancaster, Pa., Mar. 11, 12, 13, 14, 1962.

7. Ibid.

8. Ibid.

9. Board Minutes, June 8, 1962; AAUP Minutes, Nov. 16, 1962, AAUP Files, Archives (hereafter, AAUP Minutes).

10. Franklin & Marshall College Faculty Minutes, Oct. 10 (first four quotations) and 18 (last two quotations), Nov. 2, 1962, Archives (hereafter Faculty Minutes); Board Minutes, Oct. 26–27, 1962.

11. Faculty Minutes, Sept. 20, Nov. 2, 1962, Jan. 10, Feb. 14, Mar. 21, 1963; *Student Weekly*, Nov. 14, 1962, 1; Board Minutes, Feb. 8, June 1, 1963.

12. Board Minutes, Oct. 26–27, 1962, Feb. 8, 1963; *Student Weekly*, Sept. 15, 1962, 1; *Student Weekly*, Nov. 14, 1962, 2; AAUP Minutes, Nov. 16, 1962.

13. *Student Weekly*, Dec. 13, 1961, 1, 2 (quotation); *Student Weekly*, Dec. 12, 1962, 2; *Student Weekly*, Jan. 9, 1963, 1; *Student Weekly*, Apr. 17, 1963, 1, 10.

14. Franklin & Marshall College Freshman Handbooks for 1961–1962 (second quotation on 23), 1962–1963 (first quotation on 24), and 1964–1965 (third quotation on 21), Archives; author interview with Richard Kneedler, Apr. 13, 2004; Board Minutes, June 4, 1965, Archives; *College Reporter*, Sept. 22, 1967, 1.

15. Interview with Keith Spalding, Apr. 6, 2004 (quotation); *Student Weekly*, Apr. 24, 1963, 1; Board Minutes, May 31, 1963.

16. Interview with Keith Spalding, Apr. 6, 2004.

17. *Student Weekly*, Apr. 24, 1963, 12; *Student Weekly*, Sept. 25, 1963, 8; Board Minutes, May 31 (quotation), Oct. 11, 1963.

18. Board Minutes, Feb. 8 (first quotation), May 31 (subsequent quotations), Oct. 11, 1963.

19. "Text of Spalding's Address at Franklin and Marshall Inauguration," *Lancaster Intelligencer Journal*, Sept. 27, 1963, clipping in Spalding Papers.

20. Ibid.

21. *Student Weekly*, Sept. 25, 1963, 3; *Student Weekly*, Nov. 3, 1963, 10. On segregation in Lancaster, see David Schuyler, *A City Transformed: Redevelopment, Race, and Suburbanization in Lancaster, Pennsylvania, 1940–1980* (University Park: Pennsylvania State University Press, 2002), 9–10, 27–29.

22. *Student Weekly*, Nov. 6, 1963, 10 (first quotation); *College Reporter*, May 1, 1964, 6; Faculty Minutes, Oct. 18, 1963 (second quotation), Jan. 23, Mar. 19, 1964; Board Minutes, May 31, 1963, Feb. 14, 1964.

23. Board Minutes, Oct. 11, 1963; *Student Weekly*, Sept. 25, 1963, 2; *Student Weekly*, Oct. 9, 1963, 1; Faculty Minutes, Mar. 21, 1963, Feb. 20, 1964.

24. *Student Weekly*, Oct. 2, 1963, 2; Faculty Minutes, Nov. 18, 1963 (quotation); AAUP Minutes, Dec. 12, 1963, Jan. 6, 1964, Keith Spalding to R. Robert Miller, Dec. 27, 1963, all in AAUP Files, Archives (hereafter, AAUP Files).

25. *Student Weekly*, Sept. 25, 1963, 8 (quotation); *Student Weekly*, Oct. 23, 1963, 8; interview with Bernard Jacobson, Apr. 4, 1985, Oral History Project; Haynie obituary, *University at Buffalo Reporter*, July 26, 2001; Kenneth J. Heineman, *Campus Wars: The Peace Movement at American State Universities in the Vietnam Era* (New York: New York University Press, 1993), 110. On the emergence of this cohort in history, see Peter Novick, *That Noble Dream: The "Objectivity Question" and the American Historical Profession* (New York: Cambridge University Press, 1988), 415–21.

26. *Student Weekly*, Oct. 23, 1963, 8 (quotations); *Student Weekly*, Dec. 18, 1963, 5.

27. *Students Weekly*, Dec. 18, 1963, 1 (first quotation), 5 (second quotation).

28. *Student Weekly*, Dec. 11, 1963, 8 (first quotation); AAUP Minutes, Mar. 9, 1964; Faculty Minutes, Mar. 10 and 19, 1964; *College Reporter*, Mar. 17, 1964, 1; *College Reporter*, Apr. 3, 1964, 1 (second quotation).

29. Board Minutes, Feb. 14, 1964; Executive Committee Minutes, May 6, 1964, Archives (hereafter, Executive Committee Minutes); Faculty Minutes, Mar. 19, Apr. 16, May 14, Oct. 15, 1964; David Rockefeller to Spalding, Apr. 29, 1964, Faculty Files, Archives; *College Reporter*, May 5, 1964, 1 (second quotation); *College Reporter*, Sept. 29, 1964, 1.

30. Faculty Minutes, Mar. 11, 1965; *College Reporter*, Apr. 13, 1965, 1; *College Reporter*, Sept. 17, 1965, 1; *College Reporter*, Sept. 24, 1965, 1.

31. *Student Weekly*, Oct. 2, 1963, 12; *College Reporter*, Nov. 13, 1963, 6; *College Reporter*, Feb. 5, 1964, 1; interview with Keith Spalding, Apr. 5, 2004.

32. Interview with Keith Spalding, Apr. 5, 2004; interview with Keith Spalding, Apr. 14, 1987, Oral History Project.

33. Faculty Minutes, Jan. 23, Feb. 20, 1964; Board Minutes, Feb. 14, 1964; *College Reporter*, Apr. 21, 1964, 1.

34. Faculty Minutes, Apr. 1, 1963, May 14, 1964.

35. Faculty Minutes, May 14, Dec. 10, 1964, Feb. 18, May 13, 1965; Academic Council Minutes, Dec. 8, 1964, Archives (hereafter, Academic Council Minutes); *College Reporter*, Oct. 27, 1964, 2; Board Minutes, Feb. 12, June 4, 1965.

36. Faculty Minutes, Feb. 18, Apr. 8, May 13 and 17 (quotation), 1965; Report and Proposal of the Ad Hoc Committee on Area Studies, Apr. 19, 1965, Faculty Minutes; Wayne Glick to Donald Western, Feb. 6, 1965, K. Spalding to Glick, May 5, 1965, both in Academic Council File, Archives.

37. Faculty Minutes, Mar. 24, 1966 (quotations); Board Minutes, Feb. 11, 1966; Curriculum Files, Wank Papers, Archives. On the decline of the survey course in this period, see Novick, *That Noble Dream.*

38. Faculty Minutes, Apr. 16, 1964; Executive Committee Minutes, May 6, 1964; *College Reporter*, Apr. 17, 1964, 1.

39. *Student Weekly*, Mar. 11, 1964, 1; *College Reporter*, Mar. 17, 1964, 1; *College Reporter*, Apr. 17, 1964, 2, 6 (first quotation); *College Reporter*, Apr. 24, 1964, 6 (Sprey quotations).

40. Keith Spalding to R. Graeme Smith, Aug. 9, 1966, Smith Folder, Board File, Archives (hereafter, Board Files).

41. Board Minutes, Feb. 9, 1951, Feb. 8, 1963, Feb. 14 (second quotation), May 29, 1964; Professional Standards Committee Minutes, Nov. 19, 1963 (first quotation), Mar. 26, Apr. 29 and 30, 1964, Archives (hereafter, PSC Minutes); Faculty Minutes, Feb. 20, 1964; [K. Spalding] to Arthur B. Sinkler, Dec. 5, 1963 (third quotation), Sinkler Folder, Board Files.

42. Faculty Minutes, Sept. 1, 1964, and K. Spalding to Faculty, Oct. 13, 1964; Board Minutes, May 29, 1964 (first quotation); Spalding to Mrs. M. Walter Smith, May 8, 1978, Smith Folder, Board Files.

43. Faculty Minutes, Oct. 15, 1964.

44. Ibid.

45. Darlington quotations in James M. Darlington, "Franklin and Marshall College: A Half-Century of Growth as Observed by a Sentimental Alumnus," May 11, 1979, Darlington Papers, Archives; *College Reporter*, Mar. 17, 1964, 2 (Spalding quotations); *College Reporter*, Apr. 3, 1964, 1; *College Reporter*, Apr. 10, 1964, 2; *College Reporter*, Sept. 18, 1964, 1; *College Reporter*, Sept. 25, 1964, 1; AAUP Executive Committee Minutes, Oct. 21, 1963 (quotation), AAUP Files; AAUP Minutes, Jan. 10, Apr. 2, 1964; Executive Committee Minutes, July 22, 1964.

46. K. Spalding to Dear Colleague, Oct. 12, 1964 (quotation), Archives; Faculty Minutes, Oct. 15, 1964; *College Reporter*, Oct. 6, 1964, 1.

47. *College Reporter*, Sept. 18, 1964, 5; *College Reporter*, Apr. 24, 1964, 4.

48. Interview with David L. Shaw, '65, Mar. 20, 1985 (all but last quotation), Oral History Project; *College Reporter*, Sept. 22, 1964, 1; *College Reporter*, Oct. 2, 1964, 1 (last quotation); Schuyler, *A City Transformed.*

49. *College Reporter*, May 8, 1964, 2 (first quotation); *College Reporter*, Sept. 16, 1964, 2; Memo to Faculty and Administration, Feb. 24, 1964 (subsequent quotations), Faculty Minutes.

50. Interview with Larry Graham and Steven Hall, both class of 1965, Apr. 1985, Oral History Project; *College Reporter*, Nov. 13, 1964, 2.

51. *College Reporter*, Oct. 23, 1964, 1, 12; *College Reporter*, Oct. 30, 1964, 1.

52. *College Reporter*, Oct. 30, 1964, 2 (second quotation); *College Reporter*, Nov. 6, 1964, 1, 3 (third quotation); *College Reporter*, Nov. 20, 1964, 1.

53. Faculty Minutes, Sept. 1, Oct. 15, Dec. 10, 1964; Board Minutes, Oct. 9, 1964 (first quotation); AAUP Minutes, Oct. 16 (quotations), 1964; Executive Committee Minutes, Jan. 8, 1965; *College Reporter*, Sept. 12, 1965, 1. On the amateurism of development operations of most small colleges in this period, see David W. Breneman, *Liberal Arts Colleges: Thriving, Surviving, or Endangered?* (Washington, D.C.: Brookings Institution, 1994), 110.

54. Board Minutes, Feb. 12, 1965; AAUP Minutes, Oct. 16, 1964, Feb. 17, 1965; Executive Committee Minutes, Nov. 12, Dec. 15, 1964, Feb. 16, 1965; Faculty Minutes, Feb. 18, 1965.

55. Board Minutes, Feb. 12, 1965; Faculty Minutes, Feb. 18, 1965.

56. AAUP Minutes, Feb. 26 (first quotation), Mar. 29 (next four quotations), 1965; Faculty Minutes, Apr. 8, 1965; Executive Committee Minutes, Apr. 9, 1965 (final quotation); *College Reporter*, May 4, 1965, 1; *College Reporter*, May 14, 1965, 1.

57. Faculty Minutes, Apr. 8, May 17, 1965; AAUP Executive Committee, Apr. 2 and 13, 1965; Board Executive Committee, May 24, 1965, Archives (hereafter Board Executive Committee); Board Minutes, June 4, 1965.

58. Board Minutes, June 4, 1965; *College Reporter*, Sept. 12, 1965, 1; *College Reporter*, Mar. 12, 1968, 4.

59. Faculty Minutes, Mar. 11, 1965; Committee on Inter-racial Affairs to Academic Council, Mar. 8, 1965, Faculty Minutes; *College Reporter*, Mar. 12, 1965, 4; *College Reporter*, Mar. 30, 1965, 5.

60. Faculty Minutes, Mar. 11, 1965; Board Executive Committee Minutes, Sept. 15, 1965; *College Reporter*, Nov. 17, 1964, 2; *College Reporter*, Feb. 9, 1965, 1; *College Reporter*, Mar. 26, 1965, 3.

61. *College Reporter*, Feb. 16, 1965, 1; *College Reporter*, Feb. 19, 1965, 2; *College Reporter*, May 7, 1965, 1; Board Executive Committee Minutes, May 24, 1965.

62. "Spalding Explains F&M Lack of Student Revolt," *Lancaster Intelligencer Journal*, June 23, 1965, clipping in Spalding Papers.

63. *College Reporter*, Sept. 21, 1965, 1 (quotation); Glick, "Helks, Hammerskjold, and the Grand Inquisitor," Convocation Address, Sept. 16, 1965, Glick Papers, Archives (hereafter, Glick Papers).

64. Faculty Minutes, Sept. 23, 1965 (first quotation); Executive Committee Minutes, Sept. 15, 1965; Academic Council Minutes, Oct. 4, 1965 (subsequent quotations); *College Reporter*, Jan. 28, 1966, 1; PSC Minutes, July 1, Sept. 30, Oct. 12, 1965.

65. *College Reporter*, Sept. 21, 1965, 1; *College Reporter*, Sept. 28, 1965, 1; *College Reporter*, Oct. 1, 1965, 1, 2; *College Reporter*, Oct. 8, 1965, 1; quotation from unidentified handout (ca. Sept. 1965), Sinkler Folder, Board Files.

66. *College Reporter*, Oct. 8, 1965, 2 (first quotation); *College Reporter*, Oct. 12, 1965, 1 (*New Era* quotation); *College Reporter*, Oct. 15, 1965, 1; Board Minutes, Oct. 8, 1965 (subsequent quotations).

67. *College Reporter*, Oct. 19, 1965, 3 (quotations); *College Reporter*, Oct. 26, 1965, 1; Faculty Minutes, Oct. 21, 1965.

68. Faculty Minutes, Oct. 21, 1965; *College Reporter*, Oct. 26, 1965, 1; *College Reporter*, Oct. 29, 1965, 1; *College Reporter*, Nov. 2, 1965, 4.

69. *College Reporter*, Oct. 1, 1965, 1; *College Reporter*, Oct. 30, 1965, 1 (second quotation); *College Reporter*, Nov. 1, 1965, 1; *College Reporter*, Dec. 3, 1965, 2 (first quotation); "Library Celebrates Year of Quality Poetry Readings," *Claremont Courier*, Jan. 15, 2004.

70. *College Reporter*, Oct. 30, 1965, 1; *College Reporter*, Nov. 1, 1965, 1; all quotations from Statement of Robert Mezey, Oct. 30, 1965, Glick Papers; Board Minutes, Dec. 3, 1965.

71. *College Reporter*, Nov. 2, 1965, 1 (quotation); Andrew, "Struggle for the Liberal Arts," chap. 9.

72. PSC Minutes, Nov. 2–5, Nov. 8–10, Nov. 12, Nov. 16–18, and Nov. 23, 1965; Board Minutes, Dec. 3, 1965.

73. PSC Statement, Nov. 22, 1965.

74. Spalding to the Board of Trustees, Nov. 22, 1965, Glick Papers.

75. Board Minutes, Dec. 3, 1965.

76. *College Reporter*, Dec. 7, 1965, 1 (Mezey quotations), 2; Thomas J. Hopkins to W. Glick, PSC, Dec. 9, 1965 (PSC quotations), PSC Minutes.

77. W. Glick to Richard Winters, Nov. 30, 1965, Glick Papers; Faculty Minutes, Nov. 18 (Glick quotation) and 21 (Faculty quotation), 1965. In January, the board granted Glick a sabbatical for the spring semester; soon thereafter came word of Glick's appointment as president of Keuka College for Women in New York (Executive Committee Minutes, Jan. 12, 1966; *College Reporter*, Jan. 28, 1966, 1).

78. AAUP Minutes, Nov. 23, 1965 (first quotation); C. Holzinger to Executive Committee, Nov. 30, 1965 (second quotation), AAUP Files.

79. *College Reporter*, Nov. 9, 1965, 2; Everett Carl Ladd Jr. and Seymour Martin Lipset, *The Divided Academy: Professors and Politics* (New York: McGraw-Hill, 1975).

80. *College Reporter*, Nov. 16, 1965, 3; PSC Minutes, Nov. 12, 1965; quotation, Schier-Haynie File, Glick Papers; Donald W. Western to Keith Spalding, Feb. 10, 1966, Professional Standards Committee Files, Archives (hereafter, PSC Files). Haynie later helped found Tolstoy College, an alternative college within SUNY–Buffalo, and was one of the "Faculty Forty-five" arrested in 1970, when they occupied an administration building (Heineman, *Campus Wars*, 241; Haynie obituary, *University of Buffalo Reporter*, July 26, 2001).

81. Arthur B. Sinkler to William A. Schnader, Dec. 8, 1965, Sinkler Folder, Board Files; Kenneth Bates to Schnader, Jan. 5, 1966, Bates Folder, Board Files; Board Minutes, Feb. 11, 1966.

82. Board Executive Committee Minutes, Nov. 17, 1965; Faculty Minutes, Nov. 18, 1965, Archives; Speech at Highland Presbyterian Church, Nov. 22, 1965, Spalding Papers.

83. AAUP Minutes, Mar. 24, 1966; Faculty Minutes, Mar. 24 and 28, 1966.

84. *College Reporter*, Nov. 19, 1965, 1; Faculty Minutes, Mar. 29 and 31 (first quotation), Apr. 5 and 6 (second quotation), 1966; Academic Council Minutes, Feb. 3 and 8, 1965; Board Minutes, June 3, 1966 (third quotation); Task Force on Educational Program Design to Faculty, May 25, 1979, Faculty Minutes.

85. *College Reporter*, Dec. 14, 1965, 1; *College Reporter*, Apr. 1, 1966, 1; *College Reporter*, Apr. 5, 1966, 1, 5; *College Reporter*, Apr. 15, 1966, 6; *College Reporter*, Apr. 19, 1966, 1; "Haynie-Klos Assault Case Thrown Out," *Lancaster Intelligencer Journal*, Apr. 7, 1966.

86. *College Reporter*, Feb. 25, 1966, 2 (first quotation); *College Reporter*, Apr. 29, 1966, 4 (second quotation), 6.

87. *College Reporter*, May 6, 1966, 1; *College Reporter*, Sept. 20, 1966, 2; *Annual Report of Franklin and Marshall College* (1965–1966).

88. Faculty Minutes, Dec. 16, 1965; Committee to Study Student Life, "Recommendations and Report on Student Life at Franklin and Marshall College," May 1966, Archives.

89. Committee to Study Student Life, "Recommendations and Report on Student Life."

90. Ibid.; interview with Frederic Klein, Apr. 7, 1980, Oral History Project.

91. Committee to Study Student Life, "Recommendations and Report on Student Life."

92. Ibid.

93. Ibid.

94. Board Minutes, June 3, 1966 (quotation); Keith Spalding to Faculty and Students, Nov. 8, 1966, Spalding Papers; Spalding to Elmer Bobst, Apr. 26, Sept. 1, 1966, Bobst Folder, Board Files; *College Reporter*, Summer Issue, 1966, Oct. 6, 1967, 1.

95. Faculty Minutes, Sept. 22, Oct. 20, 1966, Jan. 12, 1967; Spalding to Faculty and Students, Nov. 8, 1966; *College Reporter*, Summer Issue, 1966, 2; *College Reporter*, Sept. 27, 1966, 2; *College Reporter*, Oct. 14, 1966, 1 (quotation); *College Reporter*, Nov. 4, 1966, 1; *College Reporter*, Feb. 7, 1967, 1; *College Reporter*, Feb. 24, 1967, 2; AAUP Minutes, Mar. 3, 1967.

96. *College Reporter*, Sept. 20, 1966, 1; Executive Committee Minutes, July 25, 1966; [Keith Spalding] to Graeme Smith, Aug. 6, 1966, Smith Folder, Board Files.

97. [Keith Spalding] to Graeme Smith, Aug. 6, 1966 (first quotation) Smith to Henry J. Marshall, Oct. 17, 1966, both in Smith Folder, Board Files; interview with Keith Spalding, Apr. 6, 2004.

98. Interview with Keith Spalding, Apr. 6, 2004; William Schnader to Elmer Bobst, Oct. 12, 1966, Bobst to K. Spalding [Dec. 17, 1966], Bobst Folder, Board Files; Board Minutes, Dec. 9, 1966.

99. Board Minutes, June 3, Dec. 9, 1966; Faculty Minutes, Dec. 15, 1966; Elmer Bobst to William Schnader, Apr. 11, 1966, K. Spalding to Bobst, Apr. 26, 1966, both in Bobst Folder, Board Files.

100. *College Reporter*, Summer Issue, 1966, 1; *College Reporter*, Sept. 20, 1966, 1; Faculty Minutes, Sept. 22, Oct. 20 (quotation), 1966.

101. Office of the Dean to Faculty, Oct. 31, 1966 (first quotation), AAUP Files; Faculty Minutes, Sept. 13, Nov. 17, 1966, Feb. 16, Mar. 16, 1967; *College Reporter*, Dec. 13, 1966, 1 (second quotation); *College Reporter*, Feb. 21, 1967, 1; "State of the College," June 14, 1969, Spalding Papers.

102. Faculty Minutes, Sept. 13 and 22, 1966; Board Minutes, Oct. 13, 1966; *College Reporter*, Sept. 23 and 30; *College Reporter*, Nov. 4, 1966, 1; *College Reporter*, Feb. 28, 1967, 1, 2.

103. Donald W. Western to K. Spalding, Feb. 10, 1966, PSC Files; *College Reporter*, Nov. 1, 1966, 1; *College Reporter*, Nov. 4, 1966, 3 (quotations).

104. Faculty Minutes, Nov. 17, Dec. 15, 1966, Mar. 16, 1967 (quotation); AAUP Minutes, Mar. 3, 1967; *Lancaster Intelligencer Journal*, Mar. 10, 1967, clipping in Spalding Papers.

105. Faculty Minutes, Mar. 16, 1967 (quotation); *College Reporter*, Feb. 17, 1967, 2; statement by President Keith Spalding, Mar. 16, 1967, AAUP Files.

106. Faculty Minutes, May 16, 18, 19 and 24 (quotation), 1967.

107. Board Minutes, Oct. 13, 1966; K. Spalding to E. Bobst, Apr. 26, Sept. 1, 1966, Bobst Folder, Board Files; Faculty Minutes, Nov. 17, Jan. 12, 1967, Jan. 12, 1967.

108. Keith Spalding to Arthur Sinkler, Aug. 29, 1967 (quotation), Sinkler Folder, Board Files; Board Minutes, Apr. 28, 1967 (quotation); *College Reporter*, Sept. 15, 1967, 3; *College Reporter*, Sept. 19, 1967, 1.

109. Board Minutes, Oct. 13, 1967, Apr. 26, 1968; *College Reporter*, Oct. 3, 1967, 2; *College Reporter*, Oct. 6, 1967, 1; *College Reporter*, Oct. 13, 1967, 1; *College Reporter*, Oct. 27, 1967, 1; *College Reporter*, Dec. 13, 1967, 1; *College Reporter*, Feb. 13, 1968, 1; Faculty Minutes, Jan. 18, 1968; Overseers Minutes, Sept. 17, 1975, Archives (hereafter, Overseers Minutes); [Keith Spalding] to Arthur B. Sinkler, Dec. 6, 1967, Sinkler Folder, Board Files; Spalding to Robert Sarnoff, Nov. 10, 1967, Bobst Folder, Board Files.

110. Faculty Minutes, May 16, 1968; Board Minutes, Apr. 26, Oct. 11, 1968; *College Reporter*, May 10, 1968, 4; Overseers Minutes, Feb. 8, May 9, 1968; interview with Keith Spalding, Apr. 4, 2004; Spalding to John Livingood, Sept. 10, 1968, Livingood Folder, Board Files.

CHAPTER 11

1. Franklin & Marshall College Faculty Minutes, Oct. 18, 1967, Feb. 15, Feb. 23, Mar. 28, Apr. 18, May 9, 1968, Archives (hereafter, Faculty Minutes); *College Reporter*, Mar. 1, 1968, 1; *College Reporter*, Apr. 2, 1968, 1.

2. Franklin & Marshall College Board Minutes, Apr. 26 (quotation), Oct. 11, 1968, Archives (hereafter, Board Minutes); *College Reporter*, Feb. 20, 1968, 2; *College Reporter*, Feb. 23, 1968, 1; *College Reporter*, Apr. 2, 1968, 1. On a similar movement during the previous fall at Tulane University, see Clarence L. Mohr and Joseph E. Gordon, *Tulane: The Emergence of a Modern University, 1945–1980* (Baton Rouge: Louisiana State University Press, 2001), 330–34.

3. *College Reporter*, Oct. 18, 1966, 1; *College Reporter*, Apr. 13, 1967, 1; *College Reporter*, Aug. 24, 1967, 1; *College Reporter*, Sept. 19, 1967, 1; *College Reporter*, Nov. 3, 1967, 1; *College Reporter*, Sept. 10, 1969, 3; *College Reporter*, Sept. 23, 1969, 1; Board Minutes, May 29,

1964, Oct. 13, 1967, Apr. 26, 1968, Oct. 11, 1968; Overseers Minutes, Feb. 15, 1967, Feb. 8, Mar. 14, 1968, Sept. 11, 1969, Dec. 10, 1970, Archives (hereafter, Overseers Minutes); College Senate Minutes, March 5, 1973, Archives (hereafter, College Senate Minutes).

4. Executive Committee Minutes, May 27, 1966, Archives (hereafter, Executive Committee Minutes); Board Minutes, June 3, 1966, Apr. 26, Oct. 11, 1968, Oct. 23, 1970; Overseers Minutes, Apr. 13, 1967, July 11, 1968; *College Reporter*, Oct. 6, 1967, 1; *College Reporter*, Sept. 13, 1968, 6; *College Reporter*, Sept. 27, 1968, 1.

5. Interview with Keith Spalding, Apr. 14, 1987, Oral History Project, Archives (hereafter, Oral History Project) (first quotation); Overseers Minutes, May 11, Nov. 9, 1967; Board Minutes, Oct. 13, 1967, Apr. 26, 1968 (final quotation).

6. Board Minutes, June 4, 1965, June 3, 1966, Apr. 28, 1967, Apr. 26, 1968 (quotation); Leslie Miller-Bernal and Susan L. Poulson, eds., *Going Coed: Women's Experiences in Formerly Men's Colleges and Universities, 1950–2000* (Nashville: Vanderbilt University Press, 2004), 9–13, 156, 309.

7. Faculty Minutes, Jan. 18, March 28 (first quotation), 1968; Overseers Minutes, May 9, 1968; *College Reporter*, Feb. 16, 1968, 1, 6 (second quotation); *College Reporter*, Apr. 9, 1968, 1; K. Spalding to Task Force, July 17, 1968, Coeducation Folder, Spalding Papers, Archives (hereafter, Spalding Papers).

8. *College Reporter*, Apr. 19, 1968, 1; Paul Newland to Task Force, June 10, 1968, Coeducation Files, Spalding Papers; interview with Jessica May, '70, Apr. 10, 1987, Oral History Project; College Senate Minutes, Oct. 24, 1968.

9. Interview with Jessica May, '70, Apr. 10, 1987, Oral History Project; Bradley Dewey to Task Force, June 25, 1968, Coeducation Folder, Spalding Papers; Paul Newland to Task Force, Aug. 13, 1968, Coeducation Costs Folder, Spalding Papers; Overseers Minutes, July 11, 1968; K. Spalding to Task Force, July 17, 1968, Coeducation Folder, Spalding Papers.

10. Board Minutes, Oct. 11, 1968.

11. Executive Committee Minutes, May 27, 1966; Overseers Minutes, Dec. 14, 1967, Feb. 8, 1968 (first quotation), Apr. 10, 1969, Sept. 11, 1969, Feb. 12, 1970 (second quotation); *Franklin and Marshall College Bulletin 1967–68* (August 1967) (hereafter, *Catalogue*).

12. Board Minutes, Oct. 11, 1968; *College Reporter*, Oct. 11, 1968, 1; *College Reporter*, Oct. 15, 1968, 3; Coeducation Student Petition Folder, Spalding Papers.

13. Task Force on Coeducation, "Summary Conclusions and Recommendations," Oct. 25, 1968, Coeducation Memoranda Folder, Spalding Papers; quotations from Task Force on Coeducation, "Report," Nov. 25, 1968.

14. Task Force on Coeducation, "Report," Nov. 25, 1968.

15. David M. Stameshkin, "A History of Fraternities and Sororities at Franklin and Marshall College," Archives; *College Reporter*, Feb. 28, 1969, 2; Overseers Minutes, Dec. 10, 1975.

16. Task Force on Coeducation, "Report," Nov. 25, 1968; all quotations from Ruth Van Horn to Task Force, n.d., Coeducation History Folder, Spalding Papers.

17. *College Reporter*, Oct. 25, 1968, 1, 4–5; Bradley Dewey to Task Force, Oct. 21, 1968, Coeducation History Folder, Spalding Papers; Board Minutes, Jan. 17, 1969; K. Spalding to Faculty, Oct. 29, 1968, and K. Spalding to Task Force, Dec. 3, 1968, Coeducation Memoranda Folder, Spalding Papers; College Senate Minutes, Dec. 2, 1968; Spalding to Trustees, Dec. 9, 1968, Correspondence with Trustees Folder, Spalding Papers.

18. K. Spalding to Task Force, Dec. 3, 1968, Coeducation Memoranda Folder, Spalding Papers.

19. Quotations ibid.; interview with Keith Spalding, Apr. 14, 1987; Spalding to Trustees, Jan. 7, 1969, Board Minutes.

20. K. Spalding to Faculty and Students, Dec. 9, 1968 (quotation), Coeducation Memoranda, Spalding Papers; Spalding to Trustees, Nov. 27 and Dec. 9, 1968, Correspondence with Trustees Regarding Coeducation Folder, Spalding Papers.

21. E. H. Smoker to K. Spalding, Dec. 10, 1968, Correspondence with Trustees, Spalding Papers.

22. K. Spalding to Trustees, Jan. 7, 1969, Board Minutes.

23. Interview with Nancy Honaman Rutter, Apr. 7, 1987, and interview with Keith Spalding, Apr. 14, 1987, both in Oral History Project; K. Spalding to Trustees, Jan. 7, 1969, Board Minutes.

24. Board Minutes, Jan. 17, 1969; Faculty Minutes, Feb. 6, 1969 (first quotation); Edward O. Butkofsky to Paul Newland, Feb. 6, 1969 (second quotation), Butkofsky Folder, Board Files; Nathaniel E. Hager to Trustees, Jan. 13, 1969, Paul C. Wagner to Sarnoff, Jan. 15, 1969, K. Spalding to Oliver D. Marcks, Jan. 29, 1969, and K. Spalding to Harold K. Schilling, Jan. 30, 1969, all in Correspondence with Trustees Regarding Coeducation Folder, Spalding Papers; Announcement text in Office of Public Relations, Plan to Announce Affirmative Decision on Coeducation, Dec. 20, 1968, Coeducation History Folder, Spalding Papers.

25. *College Reporter*, Oct. 18, 1966, 2; *College Reporter*, Oct. 10, 1967, 1; *College Reporter*, Oct. 24, 1967, 4; *College Reporter*, Oct. 31, 1967, 1 (first quotation); *College Reporter*, Nov. 7, 1967, 1; *College Reporter*, Nov. 17, 1967, 1 (second quotation); *College Reporter*, Dec. 8, 1967, 2; *College Reporter*, Apr. 2, 1968, 1.

26. *College Reporter*, Apr. 14, 1967, 1; *College Reporter*, Apr. 25, 1967, 1; *College Reporter*, Oct. 3, 1967, 1; *College Reporter*, Oct. 17, 1967, 1 (quotations); *College Reporter*, Nov. 17, 1967, 1; *College Reporter*, Sept. 27, 1968, 3; *College Reporter*, Nov. 5, 1968, 3; K. Spalding to Thomas W. Georges Jr., Jan. 23, 1968, in Overseers Minutes, Feb. 8, 1968.

27. *College Reporter*, March 3, 1970, 1, 4 (first quotation); Board Minutes, Apr. 23, 1970 (second quotation). Reports on campus drug use were a journalistic staple of the 1960s: the *New York Times* estimated in 1964 that up to half of Harvard students had tried pot, though the administration put it at 10 percent (Morton Keller and Phyllis Keller, *Making Harvard Modern: The Rise of America's University* [New York: Oxford University Press, 2001], 299).

28. Board Minutes, Oct. 13, 1967; *College Reporter*, Dec. 14, 1965, 6; *College Reporter*, Apr. 15, 1966, 1; *College Reporter*, Sept. 20, 1966, 1; *College Reporter*, Oct. 21, 1966, 1; *College Reporter*, Feb. 28, 1967, 1; *College Reporter*, Oct. 24, 1967, 1.

29. James Gilbert, *Another Chance: Postwar America, 1945–1968* (New York: Alfred A. Knopf, 1981), 251; *College Reporter*, Dec. 6, 1966, 1; *College Reporter*, Feb. 28, 1967, 2; *College Reporter*, Apr. 28, 1967, 3 (Jordan quotations); *College Reporter*, May 5, 1967, 1 (Bowser quotations); *College Reporter*, Oct. 6, 1967, 3; *College Reporter*, March 8, 1968, 1.

30. Richard E. Peterson and John A. Bilowsky, *May 1970: The Campus Aftermath of Cambodia and Kent State* (Washington, D.C.: Carnegie Commission on Higher Education, 1971). On the comparably mild experience at Earlham College in the 1960s, see Thomas Hamm, *Earlham College: A History, 1847–1997* (Bloomington: Indiana University Press, 1997), 255–69.

31. *College Reporter*, Apr. 9, 1968, 1; Board Minutes, Apr. 26, 1968 (quotation).

32. *College Reporter*, Apr. 26, 1968, 1; *College Reporter*, May 3, 1968, 1; *College Reporter*, May 10, 1968, 2; Overseers Minutes, May 17, 1968 (quotations); K. Spalding to Richard Schier, May 29, 1968, Memoranda Folder, Spalding Papers.

33. Overseers Minutes, May 11, 1967, May 17, 1968; *College Reporter*, May 10, 1968, 1; Senate Minutes, May 27 (first, second, and third quotations), Sept. 19, 1968 (fourth quotation).

34. O. W. Lacy to Colleague, Aug. 20, 1968, Committee to Investigate May 22 Files, Archives; *College Reporter*, Sept. 13, 1968, 1, 2; *College Reporter*, Sept, 17, 1968, 1 (quotation).

35. *College Reporter*, Sept. 20, 1968, 6.

36. *College Reporter*, Sept. 27, 1968, 1; *College Reporter*, Oct. 18, 1968, 1, 3 (Wise quotations); *College Reporter*, Oct. 22, 1968, 4 (Bowser quotations); *College Reporter*, Oct. 29, 1968, 4 (Galis quotation).

37. *College Reporter*, Dec. 11, 1964, 2; *College Reporter*, Oct. 24, 1967, 2; *College Reporter*, Apr. 5, 1968, 1; *College Reporter*, Oct. 11, 1968, 2; *College Reporter*, Oct. 25, 1968; *College Reporter*, Nov. 1, 1968, 1; *College Reporter*, Nov. 22, 1968, 1, 2; *College Reporter*, Oct. 3, 1969, PS3.

38. *College Reporter*, Jan. 17, 1969, 1; *College Reporter*, Feb. 4, 1969, 1.

39. Clipping from *Lancaster New Era,* Feb. 18, 1969, Campus Unrest: Drugs Folder, Spalding Papers; *College Reporter,* Feb. 4, 1969, 8; *College Reporter,* Feb. 14, 1969, 1; "To the Administration of Franklin and Marshall College," Feb. 9, 1969 (first, second, and third quotations), and SDS position paper, n.d. (fourth quotation), both in SDS File, Spalding Papers; K. Spalding to [G.] Hall, [R.] Lawrence, and [T.] Worthington, Feb. 10, 1969, Memorandum Folder, Spalding Papers; *Lancaster New Era* and *Lancaster Intelligencer Journal* clippings, Feb. 12, 1968, SDS Folder, Office of College Relations Records, Archives.

40. K. Spalding to Hall, Lawrence, and Worthington, Feb. 10, 1969 (quotations), Overseers Minutes, Feb. 13, 1969.

41. Overseers Minutes, Feb. 13, Mar. 13, 1969; *College Reporter,* Feb. 21, 1969, 1; *College Reporter,* Feb. 24, 1969, 1; *College Reporter,* Apr. 3, 1970, 2; Keith Spalding to College Senate, Feb. 26, 1969, College Senate Minutes.

42. K. Spalding to All Members of the College, Feb. 11, 1969, 3:00 p.m., Memorandum Folder, Spalding Papers.

43. Ibid; K. Spalding to Members of the College, Feb. 11, 1969, 5:00 p.m., Memorandum Folder, Spalding Papers.

44. Overseers Minutes, Feb. 13, 1969; College Senate Minutes, Feb. 13, 1969; *College Reporter,* Feb. 14, 1969, 1; *College Reporter,* Feb. 18, 1969, 1; *College Reporter,* Mar. 11, 1969, 1.

45. Overseers Minutes, Mar. 13, Apr. 10, 1969; *College Reporter,* Mar. 7, 1969, 1; *College Reporter,* Mar. 7, 1969, 5 (first and second quotations); *College Reporter,* Mar. 11, 1969, 1 (third, fourth, and fifth quotations).

46. *College Reporter,* Mar. 4, 1969, 1, 2; *College Reporter,* Mar. 7, 1969, 2, 4; *College Reporter,* Mar. 11, 1969, 1, 2 (all quotations).

47. *College Reporter,* May 14, 1968, 2; *College Reporter,* Sept. 24, 1968, 1; *College Reporter,* Oct. 1, 1968, 1, 6; *College Reporter,* Dec. 6, 1968, 1; *College Reporter,* Feb. 4, 1969, 3.

48. *College Reporter,* Mar. 28, 1969, 1 (first, second, and third quotations); *College Reporter,* Apr. 22, 1969, 1, 2 (fourth quotation).

49. *College Reporter,* Feb. 4, 1969, 3; *College Reporter,* Feb. 7, 1969, 1, 4; Faculty Minutes, May 22, 1969; quotation from "Report of the Committee to Investigate May 22," Nov. 24, 1969, Committee to Investigate May 22.

50. Overseers Minutes, Apr. 10, 1969; Board Minutes, Apr. 25, 1969; College Senate Minutes; Apr. 29, May 12 and 26, 1969; *College Reporter,* Apr. 15, 1969, 1 (first quotation), 2 (second quotation); *College Reporter,* Apr. 18, 1969, 1; *College Reporter,* Apr. 24, 1969, 1, 2; *College Reporter,* May 6, 1969, 2; Faculty Minutes, May 15, 1969.

51. Materials in this and succeeding paragraphs taken from the files of the Committee to Investigate May 22 and its final report. The eight faculty were Louis L. Athey, Gerald E. Enscoe, Leon Galis, Thomas L. Glenn, Adebisi O. Otudeko, Murli Sinha, Donald J. Tyrrell, and Sidney Wise. Sinha was not present during the events described. Text of the "Initial Demands" from a copy in May 21–22, 1969, Folder, Solomon Wank Papers, Archives.

52. Faculty Minutes, May 22, 1969 (quotation); "The Appropriate Context," June 14, 1969, Spalding Papers.

53. Faculty Minutes, May 22, 1969.

54. K. Spalding to Faculty, May 23, 1969 (quotations), Spalding to the College, May 25, 1969, both in Faculty Minutes; Spalding to Kenneth O. Bates, June 5, 1969, May 22, 1969, Correspondence Folder, Spalding Papers.

55. Secretary of the Senate to the Faculty, May 27, 1969, Faculty Minutes.

56. *College Reporter,* Apr. 15, 1969, 1; Faculty Minutes, June 8, 1969 (quotation).

57. "The Appropriate Context."

58. Summary of Meeting, July 17, 1969, Committee to Investigate May 22 Files; interview with Ron Potier, Apr. 7, 1987, Oral History Project; *College Reporter,* Oct. 24, 1969, 1. Robert Taylor,

formerly the Franklin & Marshall chaplain, served on the committee in the summer but resigned to assume a new position at Millersville State College.

59. The analysis in this and succeeding paragraphs is a synthesis of the final report and interviews in the May 22 Files.

60. Report of Dean John H. Vanderzell, Apr. 26, 1974, Overseers Minutes, May 10, 1974; Vanderzell Comments at Spalding Retirement, May 1983, Spalding Papers.

61. College Senate Minutes, Dec. 2, 1968; Faculty Minutes, May 15, Sept. 16, 1969; Overseers Minutes, July 17, Sept. 11, 1969, Mar. 12, 1975; *College Reporter*, Sept. 10, 1969, 1; *College Reporter*, Oct. 3, 1969, 1; interviews with Ron Potier, Apr. 8, 1987, with Nancy Honaman, Apr. 7, 1987, and with Keith Spalding, Apr. 14, 1987, all in Oral History Project.

62. Interviews with Sean Flaherty, '73, Apr. 14, 1987, with Keith Spalding, Apr. 14, 1987, with Cathy Voelker, '75, Apr. 15, 1987, all in Oral History Project; *College Reporter*, Sept. 10, 1969, 1; *College Reporter*, Dec. 9, 1969, 1; *College Reporter*, Feb. 24, 1970, 2.

63. *College Reporter*, Sept. 23, 1969, 4; *College Reporter*, Sept. 30, 1969, 1; *College Reporter*, Oct. 3, 1969, S3; K. Spalding to Graeme Smith, Sept. 29, 1969, Smith Folder, Board Files.

64. *College Reporter*, Sept. 26, 1969, 1, 2; *College Reporter*, Sept. 30, 1969, 1; *College Reporter*, Oct. 3, 1969, 1; J. Vanderzell to Faculty, Sept. 30, 1969, Campus Unrest: Vietnam Moratorium Folder, Spalding Papers; Memo to Vanderzell, Oct. 7, 1969, Professional Standards Committee Files (hereafter, PSC Files).

65. *College Reporter*, Oct. 7, 1969, 1; *College Reporter*, Oct. 10, 1969, 4 (first quotation); *College Reporter*, Oct. 14, 1969, 1 (second quotation); *College Reporter*, Oct. 17, 1969, 1, 2; Oliver Marcks to K. Spalding, Nov. 13, 1969, Spalding to Marcks, Nov. 19, 1969 (third and fourth quotations), both in Marcks Folder, Board Files.

66. *College Reporter*, Sept. 30, 1969, 1; *College Reporter*, Oct. 21, 1969, 1, 5; John H. Brubaker III, *Hullabaloo Nevonia: An Anecdotal History of Student Life at Franklin and Marshall College* (Lancaster: Franklin & Marshall College, 1987), 191.

67. K. Spalding to Senate, Sept. 11, 1969, May 22 Folder, Spalding Papers; Overseers Minutes, July 17, Dec. 11, 1969; *College Reporter*, Oct. 24, 1969, 1; *College Reporter*, Oct. 31, 1969, 3; *College Reporter*, Feb. 3, 1970, 1; *College Reporter*, Feb. 6, 1970, 1; *College Reporter*, May 1, 1970, 1; *College Reporter*, Oct. 1, 1974, 5.

68. Quotations from K. Spalding to Senate, Sept. 11, 1969, May 22 Folder, Spalding Papers; *College Reporter*, Oct. 28, 1969, 2; *College Reporter*, Mar. 17, 1970, 1; *College Reporter*, Apr. 28, 1970, 5; Faculty Minutes, Feb. 16, May 19, 1970.

69. Overseers Minutes, Jan. 10, Mar. 13, 1970 (quotation); Faculty Minutes, Feb. 6, 1969, Oct. 5, 1970; *College Reporter*, Oct. 17, 1969, 3; *College Reporter*, Dec. 9, 1969, 4.

70. *College Reporter*, Nov. 7, 1969, 1; *College Reporter*, Nov. 11, 1969, 1; *College Reporter*, Nov. 14, 1969, 1; Faculty Minutes, Dec. 11, 1969; Overseers Minutes, Nov. 13, 1969, Feb. 12, 1970; A. Sinkler to Charles Siegfried, Feb. 17, 1970, Sinkler Folder, Board Files.

71. *College Reporter*, Oct. 28, 1969, 1; *College Reporter*, Oct. 31, 1969, 1; *College Reporter*, Nov. 4, 1969, 4; *College Reporter*, Nov. 21, 1969, 5. For example, Earlham College abandoned its system of letter grades in 1970 but returned to it two years later (Hamm, *Earlham College*, 252–53).

72. Henry Mayer, "A View from the South: The Idea of a State University," in *The Free Speech Movement: Reflections on Berkeley in the 1960s*, ed. Robert Cohen and Reginald E. Zelnik (Berkeley: University of California Press, 2002), 157–69, 578; Caleb Foote, Henry Mayer et al., *The Culture of the University: Governance and Education* (San Francisco: Jossey-Bass, 1968); quotation in W. Walter Menninger, "Student Demonstrations and Confrontations," *Menninger Quarterly* (Spring 1969): 6–7, cited in John Andrew, "The Struggle for the Liberal Arts: Franklin and Marshall College, 1941–1982" unpublished MS, John Andrew Publications Files, Archives, chap. 11, n62.

73. *College Reporter*, Oct. 3, 1969, 1; *College Reporter*, Oct. 28, 1969, 1; *College Reporter*, Nov. 4, 1969, 4; Elizabeth Miller to Spalding, n.d. [received Feb. 16, 1970], Spalding Papers.

74. Russell, Brookshire, and Suydam, to Professional Standards Committee and Solomon Wank, Feb. 28, 1970, PSC Files.

75. Quotation in ibid.; *College Reporter*, Feb. 10, 1970, 1; Faculty Minutes, Feb. 16, 1970.

76. Robert H. Wiebe, "The Sixty-second Annual Meeting of the Organization of American Historians," *Journal of American History* 56 (Dec. 1969): 634 (first quotation); S. Wank to Curriculum Committee, Nov. 20, 1969 (second quotation), PSC Files; H. Mayer to Wank, Feb. 4, 1970 (third quotation), cited in Andrew, "Struggle for the Liberal Arts," chap. 11, n37; Faculty Minutes, Feb. 16, 1970.

77. Richard Schier, "The Problem of the Lumpenprofessoriat," *AAUP Bulletin* 56 (Winter 1970): 361–65; Faculty Minutes, and Feb. 16, 1970; *College Reporter*, Feb. 10, 1970, 5.

78. PSC Minutes, Jan. 2, 19 (first quotation), and Feb. 2 (second quotation), 1970, PSC Files.

79. PSC Minutes, Feb. 5, 1970, PSC Files; *College Reporter*, Feb. 10, 1970, 19 (first, second, third and fourth quotations); *College Reporter*, Feb. 13, 1970, 1 (fifth quotation).

80. K. Spalding to All Members of the College, Feb. 4, 1970, in Faculty Minutes; PSC Minutes, Feb. 10, 1970, PSC Files; "Strike Statement," [Feb. 11, 1970], Lazroe-Mayer File, Spalding Papers.

81. K. Spalding to Students and Faculty of Franklin and Marshall, Feb. 12, 1970, Faculty Minutes; "Strike Statement."

82. PSC Minutes, Feb. 10, 1970, PSC Files.

83. *Lancaster New Era*, Feb. 12, 1970, 1; *Lancaster New Era*, Feb. 13, 1970, 5; *College Reporter*, Feb. 17, 1970, 1, 2; Arthur Sinkler to Charles Siegfried, Feb. 17, 1970, Sinkler Folder, Board Files; Overseers Minutes, Feb. 12, 1970; quotations from "Resolution to the College Community" [Feb. 12, 1970], and K. Spalding to Faculty, Feb. 15, 1970, both in Lazroe-Mayer File, Spalding Papers.

84. Faculty Meeting, Feb. 16 and 17 (quotation), 1970; *Lancaster Intelligencer Journal*, Feb. 17 and 18, 1970, clippings in Unrest Folder, Spalding Papers; K. Spalding to the College Community, Feb. 18, 1970, Day of Discussion Folder, Spalding Papers; *College Reporter*, Feb. 17, 1970, 1, 2; PSC Minutes, Feb. 17, 1970, PSC Files.

85. David R. Millard to K. Spalding, Feb. 19, 1970, Spalding to the College, Feb. 23, 1970, O. W. Lacy to All Students, Feb. 24, 1970, all in Day of Discussion Folder, Spalding Papers; *College Reporter*, Feb. 20, 1970, 2; *College Reporter*, Feb. 24, 1970, 1; *College Reporter*, Mar. 3, 1970, 1.

86. "Common Sense: The Tom Paine Program," Feb. 16, 1970, Day of Discussion Folder, Spalding Papers.

87. Ibid.

88. First quotation in ibid.; Mayer, "A View from the South," 164 (second quotation).

89. Faculty Minutes, Feb. 26, 1970; K. Spalding to the College Community, Feb. 26, 1970, Memorandum Folder, Spalding Papers.

90. Faculty Minutes, Apr. 1, 1963; College Senate Minutes, Dec. 8, 1969, Apr. 14 and 27, 1970; Overseers Minutes, Sept. 11, Dec. 11, 1969, Mar. 12, June 11, 1970; Board Minutes, Oct. 24, 1969, Apr. 23, 1970; Mar. 13, 1970, 1; *College Reporter*, Apr. 10, 1970, 1 (quotation); *College Reporter*, Apr. 17, 1970, 1; *College Reporter*, Apr. 24, 1970, 1; *College Reporter*, May 8, 1970, 3; PSC Minutes, Feb. 25, 1970, PSC Files.

91. PSC Minutes, Feb. 18, 1970; R. Russell, K. Brookshire, and F. Suydam, to Professional Standards Committee and Solomon Wank, Feb. 28, 1970 (quotations), PSC Files; Russell, Brookshire, and Suydam to the College Community, Apr. 23, 1970, Lazroe-Mayer File, Spalding Papers.

92. K. Spalding to PSC, June 6, 1968, and to Richard Schier, June 6, 1968, PSC Minutes, Mar. 2 (quotation), 17 and 25, 1970; Vanderzell to Spalding, Mar. 3, 1971, PSC Files; *College Reporter*, Apr. 7, 1970, 1; *College Reporter*, Apr. 14, 1970, 1.

93. PSC Minutes, March 5, 17, and Apr. 6, 13, 17, 1970; PSC to Solomon Wank, Apr. 7, 1970, and Russell, Brookshire, and Suydam to College Community, Apr. 23, 1970, both in PSC Files; *College Reporter*, Apr. 17, 1970, 1.

94. *College Reporter*, Apr. 14, 1970, 1; *College Reporter*, Apr. 17, 1970, 1, 2, 5 (quotation); *College Reporter*, Apr. 21, 1970, 3; *College Reporter*, Apr. 24, 1970, 1.

95. *College Reporter*, Apr. 21, 1970, 1; *College Reporter*, Apr. 28, 1970, 2 (quotations); Board Minutes, Apr. 23, 1970.

96. *College Reporter*, Apr. 28, 1970, 1; Russell, Brookshire, and Suydam to College Community, Apr. 23, 1970 (quotations), PSC Files.

97. *College Reporter*, Apr. 28, 1970, 1, 3; "Students Sitting in Second Floor East Hall," to the College Community [Apr. 27, 1970], Lazroe-Mayer File, Spalding Papers; Faculty Minutes, Apr. 30, 1970.

98. J. Vanderzell to Faculty, Apr. 27, 1970, Faculty Minutes, Apr. 30, 1970 (quotation); K. Spalding to Faculty and Students of the College, Apr. 30, 1970, Lazroe-Mayer File, Spalding Papers; Memorandum, May 28, 1970, Campus Unrest: National Student Strike Folder, Spalding Papers.

99. Students did, however, examine unlocked administration files; they reported evidence of an effort to bolster the case against Mayer's candidacy (Andrew, "Struggle for the Liberal Arts," chap. 12).

100. *College Reporter*, May 1, 1970, 1; *Lancaster Intelligencer Journal*, May 1, 1970, 1; K. Spalding to Faculty, noon, May 1, 1970 (quotation), Lazroe-Mayer File, Spalding Papers; Overseers Minutes, May 14, 1970.

101. "Notice Distributed to Students," Apr. 30, 1970 (first quotation), Students Who Have Liberated East Hall, to [K.] Spalding and College Community [Apr. 30, 1970] (second and third quotations), Spalding to Faculty, noon, May 1, 1970, all in Lazroe-Mayer File, Spalding Papers; *College Reporter*, May 5, 1970, 1; Overseers Minutes, May 14, 1970.

102. *College Reporter*, May 8, 1970, 1; K. Spalding to the Faculty, midnight [May 4, 1970], "Why Strike" [May 4, 1970] (first, second, and third quotations), Campus Unrest Folder, Spalding Papers; Spalding Statement Taped for 11:00 p.m., WWFM, May 4, 1970 (fourth and fifth quotations), Public Relations Files, Archives (hereafter, Public Relations Files).

103. *College Reporter*, May 8, 1970, 1; K. Spalding to the Faculty, midnight, [May 4, 1970], Campus Unrest Folder, Spalding Papers; Telegram to Hugh Scott and Richard Schweiker, May 5, 1970, in Faculty Minutes; Statement Issued at Noon, May 5, 1970, Public Relations Files.

104. *College Reporter* [May] 6, 1970, 1; *College Reporter*, May 8, 1970, 1; Faculty Minutes, May 5, 1970 (first quotation); Office of the President to the College Community, May 5, 1970 (second quotation), Memoranda Folder, Spalding Papers.

105. Interview with John Vanderzell, Apr. 14, 1987, and with Sean Flaherty, '73, Apr. 14, 1987, Oral History Project; *College Reporter*, May 8, 1970, 1; *Lancaster Intelligencer Journal* clipping, May 8, 1970, Public Relations Files; Overseers Minutes, May 14, 1070; Nicholas P. Ciotola, "Blessed Are the Peacemakers: The F&M Reaction to Kent State," *Journal of the Lancaster County Historical Society* 99 (Fall 1997): 102–23.

106. Fearing radical violence, the administration had kept close watch over organizations such as the SDS throughout the preceding year (see SDS files in Spalding Papers). In his manuscript history of Franklin & Marshall, John Andrew reported that FBI informers on campus monitored student events during the spring, "compiling dossiers on individual students and demonstrations." He also stated that the CIA investigated student activism among a number of Pennsylvania colleges, particularly over threats to resist on-campus recruitment (Andrew, "Struggle for the Liberal Arts," chap. 11, nn.56, 67).

107. Faculty Minutes, May 4, 1970, May 19, 1970 (quotations); K. Spalding to G. Smith, May 26, 1970, Smith Folder, Board Files.

108. Faculty Minutes, May 4, 5, 19, 25, 1970; Roth and Rosenstein to John Vanderzell, Aug. 13, 1970, PSC Files; Overseers Minutes, May 14, 1970.

CHAPTER 12

1. Economists describe this condition, common to all labor-intensive activities, as Baumol's Disease. For discussions of how it affected other kinds of nonprofit organizations, see Jed I. Bergman, *Managing Change in the Nonprofit Sector: Lessons from the Evolution of Five Independent Research Libraries* (San Francisco: Jossey-Bass, 1996), 124–26.

2. Earl F. Cheit, *The New Depression in Higher Education* (New York: McGraw-Hill, 1971); Richard M. Freeland, *Academia's Golden Age: Universities in Massachusetts, 1945–1970* (New York: Oxford University Press, 1992); Earl F. Cheit, *The New Depression in Higher Education—Two Years Later* (Berkeley: Carnegie Foundation for the Advancement of Teaching, 1973); Elizabeth A. Duffy and Idana Goldberg, *Crafting a Class: College Admissions and Financial Aid, 1955–1994* (Princeton: Princeton University Press, 1998).

3. *College Reporter*, Nov. 13, 1970, 2.

4. *College Reporter*, Apr. 27, 1971, 1; Overseers Minutes, May 13, 1971, Archives (hereafter, Overseers Minutes); Franklin & Marshall College Faculty Minutes, Apr. 8, 1971, Archives (hereafter, Faculty Minutes).

5. Franklin & Marshall College Board Minutes, Apr. 23, Oct. 23, 1970, Oct. 27, 1971, Archives (hereafter, Board Minutes); Bergman, *Managing Change in the Nonprofit Sector*, 162–64.

6. Overseers Minutes, Apr. 10, 1969, Mar. 12, 1970; Board Minutes, Apr. 23, Oct. 23, 1970; Spalding to John E. Livingood, May 12, 1969, Livingood Folder, Board Files, Archives (hereafter, Board Files).

7. Overseers Minutes, Mar. 14, Sept. 24, Dec. 6, 1968, May 22, 1969; Spalding to Senate, Nov. 5, 1968, Archives; Spalding to Board, Oct. 17, 1969, LRPC File, Wank Papers, Archives (hereafter, Wank Papers); Spalding to Long-Range Planning Council, Sept. 29, 1970, Memorandum Files, Spalding Papers, Archives (hereafter, Spalding Papers).

8. Faculty Minutes, Sept. 24, Oct. 5, 1970 (quotation); Overseers Minutes, Sept. 7, Sept. 10, and Oct. 15, 1970; *College Reporter*, Nov. 10, 1970, 1, 3.

9. Faculty Minutes, Oct. 8, 1970; *College Reporter*, Dec. 4, 1970, 1; College Senate Minutes, Oct. 21, Nov. 9, 1970, College Senate Minutes, Archives (hereafter, College Senate Minutes); Overseers Minutes, Dec. 10, 1970; *College Reporter*, Dec. 1, 1970, 1; College Senate, Apr. 8, 1969, Mar. 11, 1970, and Report of the Committee on Registration Procedures and Course Enrollments, Feb. 20, 1970, Archives; Professional Standards Committee Minutes, Oct. 20, 1970, Professional Standards Committee Minutes Archives (hereafter, PSC Minutes); Solomon Wank to John H. Vanderzell [ca. Oct. 29, 1970], Vanderzell to Wank, Nov. 17, 1970, Wank to Vanderzell, Nov. 30, Dec. 22, 1970, all in Rostering Folder, Wank Papers; author interview with Richard Kneedler, Nov. 4, 2004.

10. Overseers Minutes, Dec. 10, 1970, May 10, 1972, Feb. 13, 1974; Faculty Minutes, Mar. 11, 1971; Overseers Minutes, Mar. 11, 1971; *College Reporter*, Apr. 2, 1971, 1; College Senate Minutes, Jan. 6, 1969, May 10, 1971; Committee on Curriculum to College Senate, Apr. 30, 1971, College Senate Minutes; *College Reporter*, Apr. 13, 1971, 1; *College Reporter*, May 4, 1971, 1; Duffy and Goldberg, *Crafting a Class*, 30.

11. Board Minutes, Oct. 23, 1970; Overseers Minutes, May 13, 1971, May 9, July 11, 1973.

12. Faculty Minutes, Sept. 24, Oct. 8, 1970; College Senate Minutes, Oct. 12, 1970; Vanderzell to Faculty, Apr. 23, 1971; PSC Minutes, Apr. 23, 1971.

13. Report of the Committee on Teaching Effectiveness, Apr. 16, 1971, Archives.

14. Committee on Committees to College Senate, Apr. 3, 1970, College Senate Minutes; Report of the Committee on Educational Goals, Jan. 28, 1971 (quotations), Archives; Faculty Minutes, Sept 24, 1970. The Committee on Educational Goals was composed of four faculty (Donald Western, Stanley Michalak, Gerald Enscoe, and William Ward) and four students (Frederick Goldberg, '71, Ronald Early, '71, Amy Schnetter, '73, and James Lapine, '71).

15. Report of the Committee on Educational Goals.

16. Ibid.

17. *College Reporter*, Dec. 4, 1970, 5; *College Reporter*, Dec. 11, 1970, 4; *College Reporter*, May 12, 1971, 3 (quotation); *College Reporter*, Sept. 10, 1971, 1; PSC Minutes, Mar. 9, 1971.

18. Spalding to Faculty and Administrative Officers, May 19, 1971, Memorandum Folder, Spalding Papers; Overseers Minutes, Dec. 10, 1970, May 13, 1971; Committee on Budget Priorities to College Community, Mar. 9, 1971, and Committee on Budget Priorities to Senate, Apr. 29, 1971, College Senate Minutes; *College Reporter*, Mar. 12, 1971, 1; William McCleery, "One University's Response to Today's Financial Crisis," *University* (Winter 1970–1971): 15–19, 41–46 (included in Senate Minutes); Vanderzell to the Faculty, Sept. 2, 1971, Poconos Conference File; Dean of the College Files, Archives; Cheit, *Two Years Later*.

19. Overseers Minutes, June 10, Dec. 8, 1971; *College Reporter*, Summer 1971, 1; Board Minutes, Oct. 27, 1971; Faculty Minutes, Dec. 32, 1971, Sept. 21, 1972.

20. College Senate Minutes, Sept. 7, 1971; all quotations from Vanderzell to College Community, Sept. 14, 1971, Poconos Conference File; Board Minutes, Oct. 27, 1971.

21. Spalding to College Community, Sept. 14, 1971, Poconos Files; Overseers Minutes, Oct. 14, 1971, Sept. 16, 1971; *College Reporter*, Sept. 7, 1971, 1; *College Reporter*, Sept. 28, 1971, 1, 4, 5; Spalding to Faculty, Sept. 23, 1971, Poconos Conference File; Budget Priorities Committee to College Community, Sept. 23, 1971, Senate Minutes; "Another Viewpoint on the Poconos Conference," Sept. 30, 1971, Poconos Folder, Wank Papers.

22. All quotations from Committee on Alternative Budgetary Models to Faculty, Oct. 11, 1971, College Senate Minutes; *College Reporter*, Oct. 15, 1971, 1.

23. Curriculum Committee to the Faculty, Nov. 29, 1971 (first quotation); Report of the Budget Priorities Committee, Nov. 30, 1971 (second and third quotations); College Senate Minutes, Dec. 9, 1971; "Remarks by Dr. Leon Galis," December, 1971, Senate Files, Archives (hereafter, Senate Files).

24. Faculty Minutes, Dec. 2, 1971 (first and second quotations); "Remarks by Dr. Leon Galis" (third, fourth, and fifth quotations); John Moss to Arthur Sinkler, Dec. 4, 1971 (sixth quotation), Sinkler Folder, Board Files; AAUP Minutes, Dec. 8, 1971, Archives.

25. Faculty Minutes, Dec. 16, 1971; College Senate Minutes, Dec. 9, 1971, Feb. 14, 1972; Office of the President to College Community, Apr. 26, 1972, Senate Files; Overseers Minutes, Jan. 12, May 10, 1972; Board Minutes, Mar. 17, 1972.

26. Interview with Richard Kneedler, Nov. 4, 2004.

27. Board Minutes, Oct. 27, 1971, Mar. 17, 1972; Overseers Minutes, Mar. 8, 1972; Keith Spalding to Arthur Sinkler, Apr. 29, 1971, Sinkler Folder, Board Files; Press Release, Apr. 5, 1972 (quotations), College Senate Minutes, Apr. 3, 1972.

28. Board Minutes, Mar. 17, 1972 (quotations); Overseers Minutes, Mar. 8, Oct. 20, 1972.

29. Overseers Minutes, Mar. 8, 1972.

30. *College Reporter*, Oct. 5, 1971, 1; *College Reporter*, Nov. 16, 1971, 2; *College Reporter*, Feb. 4, 1972, 1 (quotation); K. Spalding to Members of the Afro-American Society, Oct. 1, 1971, College Senate Minutes, Oct. 4, Dec. 9, 1971; Overseers Minutes, Dec. 8, 1971.

31. *College Reporter*, Mar. 7, 1972, 1; *College Reporter*, Apr. 4, 1972, 7; Overseers Minutes, Mar. 8, 1972.

32. *College Reporter*, Mar. 7, 1972, 1; interview with Sean Flaherty, '73, Apr. 14, 1987 (first quotation), Oral History Project; Sanford Pinsker to Keith Spalding, Mar. 24, 1972 (second, third, and fourth quotations), Campus Unrest Folder, Spalding Papers.

33. K. Spalding to Senate, Apr. 3, 1972, College Senate Minutes, Apr. 4, May 1, 1972; Overseers Minutes, Apr. 12, May 10, 1972.

34. *College Reporter*, Nov. 19, 1971, 1; *College Reporter*, Mar. 10, 1972, 1; Overseers Minutes, Jan. 12, Feb. 8, Mar. 8, 1972; College Senate Minutes, May 1, 1972.

35. *College Reporter*, Feb. 15, 1972, 1; Overseers Minutes, May 10, June 14, Sept. 13, Nov. 8, 1972.

36. Overseers Minutes, Mar. 11, 1972.

37. Cheit, *Two Years Later*, 15 (first quotation); Overseers Minutes, Sept. 16, Dec. 14, 1971 (sec-

ond quotation), Feb. 14, 1973; Professional Standards Committee Minutes, Sept. 7, 1971, Jan. 20, Apr. 5, 1972, Professional Standards Committee to K. Spalding, Oct. 6, 1971 and Oct. 3, 1972, Professional Standards Committee to Faculty, Apr. 20, 1973 (third quotation), all in Professional Standards Committee Files, Archives (hereafter, PSC Files); *College Reporter*, Oct. 6, 1972, 1; Faculty Minutes, Sept. 21, 1972; Board Minutes, Apr. 26, 1974.

38. PSC Minutes, June 8, 1973, and passim; Faculty Minutes, May 14 and 20, 1975; Overseers Minutes, Jan. 12, 1977.

39. Faculty Minutes, Apr. 11, 1974, Dec. 11, 1975; Overseers Minutes, June 12, Oct. 2, 1974, Mar. 12 (quotation), Oct. 23, 1975.

40. John Vanderzell to the Faculty, Sept. 22, 1972, College Senate Minutes; Overseers Minutes, Sept. 11, 1972, Jan. 10, 1973.

41. Overseers Minutes, Feb. 8, 1972, Apr. 10, May 17, 1974; Board Minutes, Nov. 9, 1973, Apr. 26, 1974.

42. *College Reporter*, Sept. 17, 1974, 3; *College Reporter*, Dec. 6, 1974, 1; Overseers Minutes, Apr. 22, 1976; Faculty Minutes, Apr. 11, Sept. 12, 1974, Mar. 30, 1976.

43. Overseers Minutes, Nov. 8, 1972, Apr. 15, June 25, 1975.

44. Overseers Minutes, May 10, Sept. 13, 1972, July 11, Sept. 12, 1973, Sept. 17, 1975; Faculty Minutes, Sept. 21, 1972; Report of the Budget Priorities Committee, Dec. 14, 1976, Overseers Minutes, Jan. 12, 1977; Report of AAUP Economic Status Committee, Sept. 1978, AAUP Files, Archives.

45. Overseers Minutes, June 12, 1974, Jan. 12, June 8, 1977. The list of competitive institutions included Allegheny, Dickinson, Gettysburg, Hamilton, Hobart, Lafayette, Muhlenberg, Trinity, Union, Ursinus, and Washington and Jefferson colleges, Bucknell, Carnegie Mellon, Colgate, Cornell, Drew, Johns Hopkins, Lehigh, and Tufts universities, and the University of Pennsylvania.

46. Board Minutes, Oct. 27, 1971, Nov. 3, 1973; Overseers Minutes, Feb. 13, 1974, Jan. 14, 1975; Alexander W. Astin et al., "New Measures of College Selectivity," *Research in Higher Education* 6 (1977) 1–9; Faculty Minutes, Sept. 13, 1973.

47. Board Minutes, Apr. 27, Sept. 12, Nov. 9, 1973; Overseers Minutes, July 11, 1973; College Senate Minutes, Sept. 10, 1973; Press release, Apr. 27, 1973, in Overseers Minutes, May 9, 1973; Faculty Minutes, May 3, 1972, Sept. 13, 1973.

48. Overseers Minutes, Sept. 12, Dec. 12, 1973, Jan. 12, 1977; Report of the Budget Priorities Committee, Dec. 14, 1976, Budget Priorities Committee Files, Archives; *College Reporter*, Sept. 16, 1975, 1; Board Minutes, Oct. 13, 1967; *College Reporter*, Oct. 1, 1974, 7; *College Reporter*, Sept. 30, 1975, 5.

49. Faculty Minutes, Nov. 4, 1975; Overseers Minutes, Apr. 24, Oct. 23, Dec. 10, 1975, Feb. 11, May 19, Sept. 15, Oct. 21, Dec. 8, 1976, Jan. 12, 1977; *College Reporter*, May 6, Sept. 16, 1975; College Senate Minutes, Mar. 3, 1975.

50. Brooks Blevins, *Lyon College, 1872–2002: The Perseverance and Promise of an Arkansas College* (Fayetteville: University of Arkansas Press, 2003), 274–80; Board Minutes, Apr. 26 (first quotation), June 12, 1974 (second quotation); *College Reporter*, Mar. 11, 1975, 1; Overseers Minutes, May 14, 1975; College Senate Minutes, Nov. 10, Dec. 8, 1975.

51. Board Minutes, Apr. 28, 1972, Apr. 27, 1973; Overseers Minutes, Sept. 12, 1973 (quotation).

52. Overseers Minutes, June 11, Oct. 15, 1970, Jan. 29, Dec. 8, 1971, June 25, 1975; Board Minutes, Apr. 28, 1972, June 12, 1974.

53. Board Minutes, Apr. 28, 1972; Faculty Minutes, Apr. 11, 1974, Apr. 15, Dec. 11, 1975; Overseers Minutes, June 12, Oct. 2, 1974, Mar. 12, Oct. 23, 1975; College Senate Minutes, May 27, 1968, Mar. 3, 1975, May 3, 1976.

54. Richard P. Traina, "A Time of Exploration: Liberal Education in Transition," June 2, 1974, Wank Papers.

55. Faculty Minutes, Apr. 15, Sept. 15, 1975; Board Minutes, Apr. 26, 1974 (first quotation); *College Reporter*, Apr. 22, 1975, 3; Overseers Minutes, Jan. 14, Mar. 12, Oct. 23, 1975 (second quotation), Apr. 21, 1977.

56. Overseers Minutes, May 17, Sept. 11, 1974, Apr. 24, 1975 (second quotation); Faculty Minutes, Apr. 15, 1975 (first quotation); College Senate Minutes, Oct. 13, Nov. 10, 1975.

57. K. Spalding to Graeme Smith, Sept. 9, 1974, Smith Folder, Board Files; Overseers Minutes, Oct. 11 (first quotation), Nov. 8, 1972; *College Reporter*, May 15, 1973, 4.

58. *College Reporter*, May 4, 1973, 1; *College Reporter*, May 8, 1973, 1; *College Reporter*, Mar. 12, 1974, 1; *College Reporter*, May 4, 1976, 1.

59. *College Reporter*, Nov. 16, 1971, 6; *College Reporter*, Nov. 14, 1972, 1; *College Reporter*, Nov. 17, 1972, 1; *College Reporter*, Mar. 12, 1974, 1; *College Reporter*, Nov. 19, 1974, 8.

60. John Andrew, "Struggle for the Liberal Arts: Franklin and Marshall College, 1941–1982," unpublished MS, John Andrew Publications Files, Archives, chap. 14.

61. Ibid.; *College Reporter*, Mar. 5, 1975, 8; *College Reporter*, Sept. 16, 1975, 8; *College Reporter*, Nov. 16, 1976; College Senate Minutes, Dec. 8, 1975.

62. Overseers Minutes, Sept. 11, Oct. 2 (first quotation), Nov. 14, 1974, Apr. 20, Sept. 27, 1978, Feb. 13, 1980 (second quotation), Apr. 14, 1981, Feb. 10, 1982; *F&M News* (June/July 1992): 18.

63. David M. Stameshkin, "A History of Fraternities and Sororities at Franklin and Marshall College," Archives; *College Reporter*, Feb. 28, 1969, 2; *College Reporter*, Feb. 9, 1971, 1; Overseers Minutes, Dec. 12, 1973.

64. *College Reporter*, Dec. 5, 1972, 1; *College Reporter*, Dec. 11, 1973, 2; *College Reporter*, Sept. 17, 1974, 1; *College Reporter*, Nov. 19, 1974, 1; *College Reporter*, Mar. 11, 1975, 3; *College Reporter*, Dec. 9, 1975, 1; *College Reporter*, Sept. 14, 1976, 1; Overseers Minutes, Dec. 11, 1974, June 10, 1981.

65. Overseers Minutes, Nov. 12, Dec. 10, 1975, Apr. 21, June 8, Sept. 14, 1977.

66. Overseers Minutes, Dec. 12, 1973, June 12 (quotation), Sept. 11, 1974; *College Reporter*, Sept. 17, 1974, 4; *College Reporter*, Apr. 22, 1975, 5.

67. Overseers Minutes, June 9, 1976.

68. Overseers Minutes, Sept. 12, 1973, Feb. 13, 1974, Apr. 22, June 9, Sept. 15, 1976, June 8, 1977, Oct. 20, 1978, Sept. 10, 1980; *College Reporter*, Apr. 16, 1974, 1; *College Reporter*, Oct. 7, 1975, 1; Faculty Minutes, May 5, 1977, Feb. 14, 1978 (quotation); College Senate Minutes, Dec. 2, 1974, Sept. 22, Nov. 10, 1975, May 10, 1977; Duffy and Goldberg, *Crafting a Class*, 140–55.

69. Overseers Minutes, Jan. 12, 1972, Feb. 13, 1974, Dec. 10, 1980 (Spalding quotation).

70. Overseers Minutes, June 12, 1974, May 19, 1976, Oct. 21, 1977; *College Reporter*, Apr. 6, 1976, 7; *College Reporter*, Apr. 13, 1976, 7; *College Reporter*, May 4, 1976, 4 (quotation).

71. Faculty Minutes, Apr. 27, Sept. 27, 1976, May 5, Oct. 11, Nov. 3, Dec. 13, 1977; Overseers Minutes, Sept. 15, 1976, Sept. 14, 1977; Keith Spalding to Faculty, Jan. 16, 1978, Spalding Memos, Spalding Papers.

72. Faculty Minutes, Oct. 12, 20, Nov. 4, 10 and 16, 1976, Apr. 14, 20, 1977 (quotation); College Senate Minutes, May 9, 10, 1977.

73. Faculty Minutes, Apr. 15, 1975, May 5, Oct. 11, 1977; AAUP Committee on College Governance Final Report, Apr. 1977, Archives.

74. College Senate Minutes, Oct. 10, 1977; Faculty Minutes, Feb. 14, May 2 and 9, 1978; College Senate Minutes, Oct. 10, 1977; Morton Keller and Phyllis Keller, *Making Harvard Modern: The Rise of America's University* (New York: Oxford University Press, 2001), 469–71; Task Force on Educational Program Design to Faculty, May 25, 1979 (first quotation), Faculty Minutes; Faculty Minutes, May 10, 1979; Report of the Educational Program Design Task Force, Feb. 11, 1980, Archives; author interview with George Rosenstein, Jan. 25, 2005.

75. Faculty Minutes, Feb. 20, 1980; interview with George Rosenstein, Jan. 25, 2005.

76. Overseers Minutes, Jan. 10, Mar. 7, Oct. 25, 1979, Feb. 13, Apr. 24, Sept. 10, Oct. 14, 1980, Apr. 14, 1981 (quotation), Feb. 10, Oct. 12, 1982, Feb. 9, 1983.

77. Overseers Minutes, Sept. 15, Oct. 12, Dec. 8, 1982, Apr. 19, 1983; author interview with Richard Kneedler, Dec. 13, 2004.

78. Overseers Minutes, Sept. 10, 1980 (quotations), Sept. 16, 1981.

79. Faculty Minutes, Sept. 27, 1976; Overseers Minutes, June 25, Sept. 17, 1975.

80. Board Minutes, September 12, 1973; Overseers Minutes, June 25, 1975 (quotation), Jan. 14, 1976.

81. Overseers Minutes, Sept. 15, 1976.

82. Overseers Minutes, May 5, 1977, Sept. 27, 1978, Jan. 10, Mar. 7, June 13, Nov. 7, 1979, Feb. 13, Sept. 10, Oct. 14, 1980, June 10, 1981, Apr. 13, 1982, Feb. 9, 1983.

83. Overseers Minutes, Jan. 10, Mar. 7, June 13, Sept. 12, 1979, Apr. 13, Sept. 15, 1982.

84. Overseers Minutes, May 14, 1975, Jan. 10, 1979, Feb. 10, 1982 (quotation).

85. *Lancaster New Era*, Feb. 11, 1982, clipping in Spalding Papers; Keith Spalding to L. James Huegel, Mar. 29, 1982, Memoranda Folder, Spalding Papers; *College Reporter*, Apr. 5, 1983, 4.

CHAPTER 13

1. Elizabeth A. Duffy and Idana Goldberg, *Crafting a Class: College Admissions and Financial Aid, 1955–1994* (Princeton: Princeton University Press, 1998); Roger L. Geiger, "Markets and History: Selective Admissions and American Higher Education Since 1950," *History of Higher Education Annual* 20 (2000): 93–108.

2. Overseers Minutes, Sept. 15, 1982, Archives (hereafter, Overseers Minutes); Franklin & Marshall College Faculty Minutes, May 6, Nov. 4, 1982, Archives (hereafter, Faculty Minutes); Professional Standards Committee Minutes, Oct. 28, 1982, Archives (hereafter, PSC Minutes); Biographical Folder, Powell Papers, Archives (hereafter, Powell Papers); Press Release, Feb. 19, 1982, Memoranda Folder, Spalding Papers, Archives (hereafter, Spalding Papers). The Search Committee was comprised from the board, Aaron Martin, '50, chair; L. James Huegel, '38, board chairman; Sally M. Gibson; Sigmund M. Hyman, '47; William G. Simeral, '48; from faculty, classics professor Robert Barnette; chemistry professor Claude Yoder, '62; government professor John Vanderzell; and from students, Ann T. Titcomb, '84, and Stephen J. Wetzel, '83.

3. Overseers Minutes, Oct.12, Dec. 8, 1982; Faculty Minutes, Apr. 23, 1984; *College Reporter*, Apr. 26, 1983, 4; *College Reporter*, Sept. 21, 1983, 6; James Powell to Prospective Students, Jan. 22, 1985, Correspondence Folder, Powell Papers; Report on Uses of the Arthur and Katherine Shadek Endowed Presidential Discretionary Fund, Jan. 27, 1986, Memoranda Folder, Powell Papers.

4. Keith Spalding to Clair R. McCollough, Jan. 29, 1969, Correspondence with Trustees about Coeducation, Spalding Papers; Overseers Minutes, Sept. 14, 1983; *College Reporter*, Jan. 25, 1983, 7. On growing concern in the 1980s with status and prestige among a comparable group of colleges in Massachusetts and Ohio, see Duffy and Goldberg, *Crafting a Class*, esp. 69–70.

5. *College Reporter*, Feb. 29, 1984, 1; *College Reporter*, Mar. 7, 1984, 1 (quotations).

6. Overseers Minutes, Sept. 14 (first quotation), Dec. 14, 1983 (second quotation); author interview with Richard Kneedler, Dec. 13, 2004.

7. Overseers Minutes, Sept. 14 (quotations), Dec. 14, 1983; Franklin & Marshall College Board Minutes, Oct. 16, 1987, June 8, 1988, Archives (hereafter, Board Minutes).

8. Overseers Minutes, Sept. 14, 1983; *College Reporter*, Feb. 1, 1984, 2.

9. *College Reporter*, Sept. 25, 1978, 3. On the prevalence of alcohol in this period, see Michael Moffatt, *Coming of Age in New Jersey: College and American Culture* (New Brunswick: Rutgers University Press, 1989).

10. Keith Spalding to [Fraternity Presidents], Nov. 8, 1979 (quotations), Memoranda Folder, Spalding Papers; Overseers Minutes, Sept. 12, 1979; David M. Stameshkin, "A History of Fraternities and Sororities at Franklin and Marshall College, 1954–1987," Powell Papers.

11. Leavenworth quoted in Stameshkin, "History of Fraternities."

12. *College Reporter*, Apr. 19, 1983, 1; *College Reporter*, Apr. 26, 1983, 2; *College Reporter*, Aug. 31, 1983, 1; Spalding to Faculty and Administrative Officers, May 10, 1983 (Spalding quotation), Memoranda Folder, Spalding Papers; Hicks quoted in Stameshkin, "History of Fraternities."

13. *College Reporter*, Sept. 21, 1983, 1 (quotation); *College Reporter*, Feb. 1, 1984, 1; *College Reporter*, Feb. 22, 1984, 1; *College Reporter*, Sept. 6, 1984, 3.

14. *College Reporter*, Feb. 22, 1984, 4; *College Reporter*, Feb. 29, 1984, 1; *College Reporter*, Mar. 14, 1984, 1; *College Reporter*, Apr. 4, 1984, 1 (first quotation); Bradley Dewey, "Position Paper on Fraternities and the Quality of Student Life," Dec. 7, 1983, Powell Papers.

15. *New York Times*, Feb. 24, 1984, quoted in *College Reporter*, Apr. 4, 1984, 5.

16. *College Reporter*, Feb. 29, 1984, 3 (first quotation); *College Reporter*, Apr. 4, 1984, 2; Leon Galis to the College Community, Apr. 11, 1984, Powell Papers.

17. *College Reporter*, Nov. 2, 1983, 3. About one-third of students in the early 1980s came from Pennsylvania, with another two-fifths from New York and New Jersey (Board Minutes, June 8, 1988).

18. *College Reporter*, Apr. 11, 1984, 1 (first quotation); *College Reporter*, Apr. 25, 1984, 1, 3; Powell quoted in Stameshkin, "History of Fraternities."

19. Faculty Minutes, Dec. 7, 1983; Overseers Minutes, Sept. 14, 1983 (quotation); Duffy and Goldberg, *Crafting a Class*, 48–50, 53, 61–68.

20. James L. Powell to Administration, Faculty, and Staff, June 2, 1986, Powell Papers; Board Minutes, June 8, 1988; Duffy and Goldberg, *Crafting a Class*, 30, 61–68, 193–216.

21. Overseers Minutes, June 13, 1984, Feb. 13, June 12, 1985, Feb. 11, 1987 (quotation), Feb. 10, 1988.

22. Kevin Phillips, *The Politics of Rich and Poor: Wealth and the American Electorate in the Reagan Aftermath* (New York: Random House, 1990), chap. 1; David W. Breneman, *Liberal Arts Colleges: Thriving, Surviving, or Endangered?* (Washington, D.C.: Brookings Institution, 1994), 30–34; Jean Evangelauf, "President Says One Hundred Private Colleges Follow Crowd: The Higher Their Prices, the More Students Apply," *Chronicle of Higher Education*, Mar. 2, 1988, A29; Charles T. Clotfelter, *Buying the Best: Cost Escalation in Elite Higher Education* (Princeton: Princeton University Press, 1996), 59–62, 254–56; Duffy and Goldberg, *Crafting a Class*, 190–203.

23. *Lancaster New Era*, Feb. 18, 1986, 1 (quotation), 4; J. L. Powell, "At Franklin and Marshall College, Smaller Is Better," *College Board Review* (Fall 1987): 26–29; Board Minutes, June 8, 1988; Overseers Minutes, June 11, 1986; Faculty Minutes, Sept. 4, 1986, Sept. 3, 1987. Applications to liberal arts colleges increased 20 percent between 1983 and 1988, which suggests that the phenomenon was not unique to Franklin & Marshall (Breneman, *Liberal Arts Colleges*, 51).

24. Faculty Minutes, Sept. 4, 1986, Apr. 23, 1987; Overseers Minutes, Feb. 10, 1988; Clotfelter, *Buying the Best*, 258.

25. Faculty Minutes, Nov. 3, Dec. 7, 1983, Feb. 8, 1984, Feb. 21, Mar. 13, June 12, Oct. 7, 1985, Sept. 4, Oct. 1, 1986; Overseers Minutes, Feb. 12, 1986; Board Minutes, June 8, 1988; *F&M Today*, Aug. 1985, 33.

26. *College Reporter*, Apr. 4, 1984, 1; *College Reporter*, Apr. 18, 1984, 1; *College Reporter*, Apr. 25, 1984, 1; Overseers Minutes, Sept. 10, 1986, Feb. 11, 1987; author interview with Richard Kneedler, Nov. 4, 2004.

27. Faculty Minutes, Sept. 4, 1986 (quotation), Apr. 20, 1988; Overseers Minutes, Dec. 9, 1987, June 8, 1988; *College Reporter*, Oct. 23, 1984, 4; *College Reporter*, Feb. 1, 1987, 5; *College Reporter*, Mar. 30, 1987, 4; *College Reporter*, Apr. 20, 1987, 1; *College Reporter*, Apr. 27, 1987, 1; *College Reporter*, Nov. 23, 1987, 1; *College Reporter*, Mar. 7, 1988, 1.

28. Overseers Minutes, Sept. 14, 1983, Sept. 14, Dec. 11, 1985, June 11, 1986, Dec. 9, 1987; James Powell to Board, July 1, 1983 (quotation), Correspondence Folder, Spalding Papers.

29. Faculty Minutes, Mar. 25, 1987.

30. Faculty Minutes, Oct. 1, Nov. 5, Dec. 2, 1986, Mar. 4, Apr. 23, 1987, Feb. 9, Nov. 3, 1988, Oct. 25, 1989.

31. Board Minutes, June 8, 1988; *College Reporter*, Aug. 31, 1987, 1, 3 (first quotation); Overseers Minutes, Sept. 9, 1987 (second quotation).

32. *College Reporter*, Apr. 20, 1987, 3; *College Reporter*, Apr. 27, 1987, 3; Overseers Minutes, Dec. 10, 1986, June 11, 1987.

33. *College Reporter*, Oct. 19, 1987, 1; Overseers Minutes, June 11, Sept. 9, 1987.

34. Stameshkin, "History of Fraternities"; *College Reporter*, Sept. 6, 1984; *College Reporter*, Oct. 9, 1984, 1; *College Reporter*, Oct. 23, 1984, 3.

35. Stameshkin, "History of Fraternities"; *College Reporter*, Sept. 19, 1984, 1; *College Reporter*, Sept. 26, 1984, 1; *College Reporter*, Oct. 23, 1984, 1; *College Reporter*, Oct. 30, 1984, 1; *College Reporter*, Nov. 13, 1984, 1.

36. Stameshkin, "History of Fraternities."

37. Ibid.; *College Reporter*, Apr. 25, 1984, 1; *College Reporter*, Mar. 30, 1987, 1, 5.

38. Stameshkin, "History of Fraternities"; *College Reporter*, Mar. 30, 1987, 1; *College Reporter*, Sept. 14, 1987, 1.

39. Stameshkin, "History of Fraternities"; *College Reporter*, Aug. 31, 1987, 6; *College Reporter*, Sept. 14, 1987, 1.

40. Overseers Minutes, Sept. 9, 1987 (first quotation); J. Powell to A. Martin, Jan. 18, 1988, Archives.

41. *College Reporter*, Sept. 14, 1987, 5 (first quotation); *College Reporter*, Sept. 28, 1987, 1, 5 (second quotation), 8; *College Reporter*, Oct. 5, 1987, 1 (third quotation); *College Reporter*, Nov. 2, 1987, 4.

42. *College Reporter*, Oct. 12, 1987, 1, 5; Moffatt, *Coming of Age in New Jersey*.

43. *College Reporter*, Nov. 1, 1987, 1; *College Reporter*, Nov. 16, 1987, 3, 4 (quotation); *College Reporter*, Nov. 23, 1987, 1, 3; *College Reporter*, Dec. 7, 1987, 1.

44. Overseers Minutes, Feb. 11, 1987; Ben Gose, "Lawsuit 'Feeding Frenzy,'" *Chronicle of Higher Education*, Aug. 17, 1994.

45. Overseers Minutes, Sept. 9, Dec. 9, 1987; Board Minutes, Oct. 16, 1987.

46. Report of the Student Life Committee, Apr. 13, 1988, Board Minutes; *College Reporter*, Jan. 25, 1988, 1; *College Reporter*, Feb. 1 [1988], 1 (all quotations), 5; *College Reporter*, Apr. 11, 1988, 4, 7.

47. Report of Student Life Committee (first quotation); Overseers Minutes, Feb. 10, 1988; Faculty Minutes, Mar. 10 (second, third, fourth quotations) and 24 (fifth and sixth quotations), 1988; *College Reporter*, Apr. 11, 1988, 6; *College Reporter*, Apr. 18, 1988, 9.

48. *Lancaster Intelligencer Journal*, Mar. 29, 1988, in Powell Papers; interview with Richard Kneedler, Dec. 13, 2004.

49. *College Reporter*, Apr. 4, 1988, 1, 9, 11; *College Reporter*, Apr. 11, 1988, 1 (quotation).

50. Board Minutes, Apr. 12, 1988.

51. Ibid.; Board Minutes, June 8–10, 1989 (first quotation); *College Reporter*, Apr. 18, 1988, 1 (second and third quotations).

52. Report of Student Life Committee, Board Minutes, Apr. 12, 1988.

53. Board Minutes, Apr. 13, 1988, Apr. 13, 1993; *College Reporter*, Apr. 18, 1988, 3, 6.

54. *College Reporter*, Apr. 18, 1988, 3, 6.

55. Ibid., 3, 4.

56. Board Minutes, June 8, 1988.

57. Author interviews with Richard Kneedler, Apr. 13, Nov. 4, and Dec. 13, 2004.

58. *College Reporter*, Sept. 19, 1988, 7.

59. *College Reporter*, May 4, 1971, 1; *College Reporter*, Mar. 5, 1985; *College Reporter*, Apr. 9, 1985; *College Reporter*, Mar. 3, 1986; *College Reporter*, Feb. 27, 1989, 5 (first and second quotations); *College Reporter*, Mar. 6, 1989, 11; *College Reporter*, Mar. 13, 1989, 14 (third, fourth, and fifth quotations); Stameshkin quotation in Kneedler Anecdotes File, Kneedler Papers, Archives (hereafter, Kneedler Papers).

60. *College Reporter*, Apr. 25, 1988, 1 (first quotation), 3 (second quotation); *College Reporter*, Aug. 29, 1988, 1, 3; *College Reporter*, Nov. 7, 1988, 1; *College Reporter*, Sept. 11, 1989, 1; *College Reporter*, Oct. 2, 1989, 1; *College Reporter*, Apr. 13, 1992, 1; *College Reporter*, Aug. 31, 1992, 1; *College Reporter*, Sept. 3, 1997, 1; *College Reporter*, Feb. 23, 1998, 1, 3; Faculty Minutes, Sept. 9,

1988, Feb. 24, 1998; Overseers Minutes, Feb. 8, Sept. 13, 1989; Board Minutes, Apr. 12, 1989; Richard Kneedler to Trustees, Sept. 8, 1988, Trustees Folder, Kneedler Papers. Zeta Beta Tau continued without a chapter house for a time, until the national organization withdrew its charter. Zeta Beta Tau survived as a local fraternity for several years before ceasing to exist.

61. Overseers Minutes, Sept. 14, 1988; *College Reporter*, Nov. 21, 1988, 3; *College Reporter*, Jan. 29, 1990, 3.

62. *College Reporter*, Aug. 29, 1988, 1, 10, 13.

63. *President's Report 1988–1998* (Office of the President, Franklin & Marshall College, 1998): 34; Executive Committee Minutes, Sept. 19, 1989 (quotation), Sept. 14, 1990, Executive Committee Minutes, Archives (hereafter, Executive Committee Minutes).

64. Overseers Minutes, Sept. 14, 1988; Faculty Minutes, Sept. 9, Nov. 3, 1988; Board Minutes, Apr. 25, 1990; *College Reporter*, Sept. 21, 1992, 2.

65. *College Reporter*, Nov. 21, 1988, 1; Overseers Minutes, Sept. 14, 1988; Faculty Minutes, Sept. 9, 1988; Board Minutes, June 8–10, 1989.

66. Kneedler quotation Draft Memo, 1988 Planning Folder, Kneedler Papers; William G. Bowen and Julie Ann Sosa, *Prospects for Faculty in the Arts and Sciences: A Study of Factors Affecting Demand and Supply, 1987 to 2012* (Princeton: Princeton University Press, 1989); Overseers Minutes, Feb. 8, Sept. 13, 1989; *President's Report 1989–1998*: 11–14.

67. Overseers Minutes, Sept. 14, 1990; Board Minutes, Oct. 11, 1991, Oct. 12, 1992; 1991; Planning Paper, Kneedler Papers; Karen Grassmuck, "Signs of Bad Times," *Chronicle of Higher Education*, Dec. 5, 1990; Richard N. Ostling, "Big Chill on Campus," *Time*, Feb. 3, 1992, 61; Faculty Minutes, Sept. 18, 1990, Jan. 22, 1991, Jan. 27, 1992, Feb. 1995; *College Reporter*, Feb. 3, 1992, 2; *College Reporter*, Apr. 6, 1992, 3; *President's Report 1988–1998*: 45–46; interview with Richard Kneedler, Dec. 13, 2004.

68. Kneedler Planning Paper 1991; *President's Report 1988–1998*: 44–45 (first quotation); Overseers Minutes, Dec. 13, 1989; Board Minutes, June 9, 1990 (second quotation); *College Reporter*, Sept. 17, 1990, 3.

69. Overseers Minutes, Dec. 12, 1990, Sept. 11, 1991; Faculty Minutes, Feb. 21, 1989; Board Minutes, June 9, 1990; *College Reporter*, Jan. 25, 1993, 3; *College Reporter*, Nov. 1, 1993, 1, 3; *College Reporter*, Mar. 23, 1998, 1 (quotation); *President's Report 1988–1998*: 12.

70. Overseers Minutes, Dec. 13, 1989; *President's Report 1988–1998*: 44; Interim Report to Middle States Association, Apr. 1, 1994, Kneedler Papers.

71. Overseers Minutes, Sept. 13, Dec. 13, 1989; Executive Committee Minutes, Sept. 11, 1991; Board Minutes, June 9, 1990, Oct. 11, 1991; Richard Kneedler to Richard Chait, Apr. 20, 1995, Kneedler Papers; Faculty Minutes, Sept. 24, 1997; Press Releases, Oct. 31, 1997, Oct. 21, 1998, College Relations Files, Archives; *President's Report 1988–1998*: 53.

72. Board Minutes, June 9, 1990; Faculty Minutes, Oct. 24, 1996; *President's Report 1988–1998*: 48, 65; *College Reporter*, Nov. 17, 1997, 2; Kim Strosnider, "Bullish Stock Market Pushes Endowments Up," *Chronicle of Higher Education*, Feb. 20, 1998; Sequel to President's Ten-Year Report [2002], Kneedler Papers; Financial Report 2001–2002, Franklin & Marshall College Office of the Vice President for Finance and Administration.

73. John L. Pulley, "The Rich Got Richer in 2000, Study of Endowments Shows," *Chronicle of Higher Education*, Apr. 13, 2001; *Chronicle of Higher Education* Database of College and University Endowments, http://chronicle.com/stats/endowments (accessed 2/10/2010).

74. Franklin & Marshall College Press Release, Oct. 31, 1997.

75. *President's Report 1988–1998*: 35; *College Reporter*, Aug. 26, 1991, 1.

76. *President's Report 1988–1998*: 35–36; President's Report to Trustees, Dec. 12, 1997, Archives (hereafter, President's Report to Trustees).

77. *President's Report 1988–1998*: 34–35; Executive Committee Minutes, Sept. 14, 1990; Remarks to the Trustees, May 1999, Trustees Folder, Kneedler Papers.

78. *President's Report 1988–1998*: 37; President's Reports to Trustees, Aug. 7, 1997, Aug. 27, 1998, Trustees Folder, Kneedler Papers.

79. President's Report to Trustees, Aug. 27, 1998, Report to the Executive Committee, Sept. 3, 2001, Trustees folder, Kneedler Papers.

80. *President's Report 1988–1998*: 37.

81. Faculty Minutes, Sept. 7, 1989, Apr. 26, 1990; Overseers Minutes, Apr. 25, 1990.

82. Board Minutes, Oct. 24, 1990.

83. First quotation in ibid.; *College Reporter*, Aug. 28, 1996, 1.

84. Interim Report to the Middle States Association, Apr. 1, 1994, Kneedler Papers; Breneman, *Liberal Arts Colleges*, 15–16; Duffy and Goldberg, *Crafting a Class*, 61–68.

85. Loren Pope, *Looking Beyond the Ivy League: Finding the College That's Right for You* (New York: Penguin Books, 1990; repr. 1995); Winston quoted in Roger L. Geiger, "Markets and History: Selective Admissions and U.S. Higher Education Since 1950," Review Essay, *History of Higher Education Annual* 20 (2000): 97–98.

86. Faculty Minutes, Feb. 11, 1993, Sept. 24, 1997; President's Report to the Trustees, Sept. 30, 1996, Mar. 19, May 6, 1997, Mar. 28, 2002, Trustee Folder, Kneedler Papers; 1999 Admission Data File, Kneedler Papers; *President's Report 1988–1998*: 6.

87. Executive Committee Minutes, Sept. 14, 1990; *President's Report 1988–1998*: 7, 65; Sequel to President's Ten-Year Report; Richard Kneedler, "American Colleges Should Become More Accessible to Foreign Students," *Chronicle of Higher Education*, Mar. 27, 1991; *College Reporter*, Sept. 5, 1989, Aug. 26, 1991; President's Report to the Trustees, Oct. 6, 1998, and to Executive Committee, Oct. 26, 2001, Kneedler Papers.

88. Overseers Minutes, Dec. 12, 1990; *College Reporter*, Feb. 25, 1991, 7; Scott Jaschik, "Green Light for Minority Scholarships," *Chronicle of Higher Education*, Mar. 2, 1994; *President's Report 1988–1998*: 7–8.

89. Faculty Minutes, Sept. 9, 1988, Jan. 24, Feb. 8, 1989, Apr. 26, 1990, Apr. 12, 1991; *President's Report 1988–1998*.

90. Faculty Minutes, Mar. 14, 1990, Feb. 15, 1996.

91. Faculty Minutes, Apr. 13, 1989; *President's Report 1988–1998*; Sequel to President's Ten-Year Report.

92. Faculty Minutes, Mar. 3, 5, 1992, Feb. 11, 1993; Overseers Minutes, Sept. 14, 1990.

93. Robin Wilson, "Undergraduates Offered a Summer to Discover Research," *Chronicle of Higher Education*, July 31, 1991; Scott Heller, "Stronger Push for Research at Liberal-Arts Colleges Brings Fears That Their Culture Is Threatened," *Chronicle of Higher Education*, July 5, 1990; "A Short History of 3/2," Faculty Minutes, Nov. 1, 1992, Kneedler Papers; Faculty Minutes, Mar. 12, Sept. 19, 1991, Dec. 1, 1992, Feb. 11, 1993; *President's Report 1988–1998*: 3, 22; *College Reporter*, Mar. 30, 1998, 3.

94. *College Reporter*, Aug. 29, 1995, 2; *President's Report 1988–1998*: 16–19, 59; quotations from "Foundations User's Guide 2004."

95. *President's Report 1988–1998*: 59.

96. *President's Report 1988–1998*: 25–28; *College Reporter*, Apr. 14, 1998, 1; *College Reporter*, Sept. 13, 1999, 10.

97. *College Reporter*, Oct. 30, 2000, 7; Sequel to President's Ten-Year Report.

98. *College Reporter*, Feb. 8, 1999, 2, Oct. 18, 1999, 2; Sequel to President's Ten-Year Report; Proposal for the Center for the Liberal Arts and Society, 1998, Pipes Papers, Archives; author interview with Bruce Pipes, Apr. 19, 2005.

99. *College Reporter*, Sept. 10, 1991, 3; *College Reporter*, Apr. 18, 1994, 3; *College Reporter*, Dec. 7, 1998, 1.

100. R. Kneedler and D. Boyce to Board, Apr. 14, 2000, Trustee Folder, Kneedler Papers; Faculty Council Minutes, Apr. 11, 2000, Archives; Press Release, Apr. 13, 2001, Public Relations Files.

101. *Intelligencer Journal*, May 8, 2002, B1.

102. *President's Report 1988–1998*, 38.

103. Frederick A. Rauch, "Rauch on Education," *Mercersburg Review* 10 (July 1858): 444.

Index